Lecture Notes in Compute

Commenced Publication in 1973
Founding and Former Series Editors:
Gerhard Goos, Juris Hartmanis, and Jan van L   ...

Judi Romijn   Graeme Smith
Jaco van de Pol (Eds.)

Integrated
Formal Methods

5th International Conference, IFM 2005
Eindhoven, The Netherlands
November 29 – December 2, 2005
Proceedings

 Springer

Volume Editors

J.M.T. Romijn
Eindhoven University of Technology, Computing Science Department
P.O. Box 513, 5600 MB Eindhoven, The Netherlands
E-mail: jromijn@win.tue.nl

G.P. Smith
The University of Queensland
School of Information Technology and Electrical Engineering
4072 Australia
E-mail: smith@itee.uq.edu.au

J.C. van de Pol
Centre for Mathematics and Computer Science (CWI)
P.O. Box 94079, 1090 GB Amsterdam, The Netherlands
E-mail: Jaco.van.de.Pol@cwi.nl

Library of Congress Control Number: 2005935883

CR Subject Classification (1998): F.3, D.3, D.2, D.1

ISSN   0302-9743
ISBN-10   3-540-30492-4 Springer Berlin Heidelberg New York
ISBN-13   978-3-540-30492-0 Springer Berlin Heidelberg New York

Springer is a part of Springer Science+Business Media

springeronline.com

© Springer-Verlag Berlin Heidelberg 2005
Printed in Germany

Typesetting: Camera-ready by author, data conversion by Scientific Publishing Services, Chennai, India
Printed on acid-free paper   SPIN: 11589976   06/3142   5 4 3 2 1 0

Preface

This is the 5th edition of the International Conference on Integrated Formal Methods (IFM). Previous IFM conferences were held in York (June 1999), Dagstuhl (November 2000), Turku (May 2002) and Canterbury (April 2004). This year's IFM was held in December 2005 on the campus of the Technische Universiteit Eindhoven in The Netherlands.

This year IFM received 40 submissions, from which 19 high-quality papers were selected by the Program Committee. Besides these, the proceedings contain invited contributions by Patrice Godefroid, David Parnas and Doron Peled.

It was 10 years ago that Jonathan P. Bowen and Michael G. Hinchey published their famous *Ten Commandments of Formal Methods* in IEEE Computer 28(4). Their very first commandment — *Thou shalt choose an appropriate notation* — touches the heart of the IFM theme: Complex systems have different aspects, and each aspect requires its own appropriate notation.

Classical examples of models for various aspects are: state based notations and algebraic data types for data, process algebras and temporal logics for behavior, duration calculus and timed automata for timing aspects, etc. The central question is how the models of different notations relate. Recently, Bowen and Hinchey presented their *Ten Commandments Revisited* (in: ACM proceedings of the 10th International Workshop on Formal Methods for Industrial Critical Systems). They distinghuish variations in combining notations, ranging from *loosely coupled viewpoints* to *integrated methods*.

The loosely coupled viewpoints are quite popular (cf. the success of UML) and are easy to adopt in a leightweight process. They could be useful for specifying and analyzing isolated system aspects. However, the main advantage of formal methods — being able to specify and verify the correctness of complete systems — is lost.

In order to specify and verify complete systems, an integrated approach is inescapable. Integrated methods provide an underlying concept, a semantic integration of models, an integrated methodology and integrated verification algorithms. The added value is that questions regarding inter-model consistency, completeness and correctness of implementations become meaningful and can be answered effectively. Bowen and Hinchey acknowledge this as the central theme of the series of IFM conferences.

These proceedings contain new insights in the field of integrated formal methods. The various papers contribute to integration at notational, semantic and tool level. We hope that the reader will find inspiring material and useful knowledge. Ultimately, we hope that the field contributes to more reliable software and hardware systems, constructed with less effort.

We would like to thank all PC members and all anonymous referees for their excellent and timely job in assessing the quality of the submitted papers. We also thank the invited speakers for their contributions. We are grateful to Holger Hermanns for his invited tutorial on QoS modelling and analysis for embedded systems. Finally, we thank our home institutes Technische Universiteit Eindhoven, University of Queensland and CWI for their support.

September 2005   Judi Romijn, Graeme Smith, Jaco van de Pol

Program Committee

Didier Bert (France)
Eerke Boiten (UK)
Jonathan Bowen (UK)
Michael Butler (UK)
Paul Curzon (UK)
Jim Davies (UK)
John Derrick (UK)
Steve Dunne (UK)
Jin Song Dong (Singapore)
Andy Galloway (UK)
Chris George (Macau, SAR China)
Wolfgang Grieskamp (USA)
Henri Habrias (France)
Maritta Heisel (Germany)
Soon-Kyeong Kim (Australia)
Michel Lemoine (France)
Shaoying Liu (Japan)
Dominique Mery (France)
Stephan Merz (France)

Richard Paige (UK)
Luigia Petre (Finland)
Jaco van de Pol
    (Co-chair, The Netherlands)
Judi Romijn
    (Co-chair, The Netherlands)
Thomas Santen (Germany)
Steve Schneider (UK)
Wolfram Schulte (USA)
Kaisa Sere (Finland)
Jane Sinclair (UK)
Graeme Smith
    (Co-chair, Australia)
Bill Stoddart (UK)
Kenji Taguchi (Japan)
Helen Treharne (UK)
Heike Wehrheim (Germany)
Kirsten Winter (Australia)
Jim Woodcock (UK)

Sponsors

We thank NWO and FME for sponsoring the invited lectures, IPA for sponsoring the welcome reception, and BCS-FACS for sponsoring the best paper awards.

External Referees

Besides the Program Committee members, several external anonymous referees read the submitted papers. Without their help, the conference would have been of a lesser quality. The following is a list, to the best of our knowledge, of external referees.

Bernhard Aichernig
Pascal André
Victor Bos
Chunqing Chen
Neil Evans
David Faitelson
Lars Grunske
Ping Hao

Bart Jacobs
Hironobu Kuruma
Alistair McEwan
Sotiris Moschoyiannis
Stephane Lo Presti
Ivan Porres Paltor
Jean-Claude Reynaud
Rimvydas Ruksenas

Colin Snook
Yasuyuki Tahara
Nikolai Tillmann
Leonidas Tsiopoulos
G. Vidal-Naquet
James Welch
Hirokazu Yatsu

Table of Contents

Invited Papers

Session: Components

Session: State/Event-Based Verification

Session: System Development

Session: Applications of B

Session: Tool Support

Session: Non-software Domains

Session: Semantics

Session: UML and Statecharts

A Family of Mathematical Methods for Professional Software Documentation

David Lorge Parnas

Software Quality Research Laboratory (SQRL),
Department of Computer Science and Information Systems,
Faculty of Informatics and Electronics,
University of Limerick, Limerick, Ireland

1 Introduction

The movement to integrate mathematically based software development methods is a predictable response to the fact that none of the many methods available seems sufficient to do the whole job (whatever that may be) on its own. This talk argues that integrating separately developed methods is not the most fruitful possible approach. Instead we propose a family of methods, based on a common model, designed to be complementary and mutually supportive.

The method family being developed at the Software Quality Research Lab at the University of Limerick is characterised by two major decisions:

- Software developers must prepare and maintain a set of documents whose content (not format) is specified by the relational model presented in [3].
- The relations are represented using mathematical expressions in tabular form. [5].

This talk will motivate these decisions, describe the model, illustrate the concept of tabular expressions, and discuss the uses of such documents in software development.

2 Why We Need Better Software Development Documentation

Software has its, well earned, bad reputation in large part because developers do not provide an appropriate set of design documentation. When developers are trying to extend, correct, or interface with a piece of software, they need detailed information that is both precise and correct. This information is usually hard to find, missing, imprecisely expressed, or simply wrong. Some developers estimate that they spend 80% of their time seeking information about existing software. When they don't have an interface description, they often use implementation information that is subject to change. The result is software in which small changes have surprising effects.

Engineers who design physical products are taught how to use mathematics to specify properties of their products and analyse their designs. Software developers simply do not know how to do that and their managers do not expect them to do it. In fact, the profession doesn't know how to do it. Finding ways to use mathematics to produce precise, well-organized development documentation should be a major research effort.

J. Romijn, G. Smith, and J. van de Pol (Eds.): IFM 2005, LNCS 3771, pp. 1–4, 2005.

3 Why Models are not Generally Descriptions

It has become fashionable to propose the use of "model based development" (MBT) to solve some of these problems. Formal looking[1] models are prepared to express design decisions. Unfortunately, these models do not constitute documentation; to understand why, it is important to distinguish between descriptions, specifications, and models.

- A *description* of a product provides accurate information about that product.
- A *specification* is a description that states all of the requirements but contains no other information.
- A *model* has some of the properties of the product-of-interest but may also have properties that differ from those of the product. Some models are themselves products, but here we are concerned primarily with mathematical models.

We use the word "*document*" to mean either a specification or another description.

It is important to note that the above are statements of intent, most attempts at descriptions are not completely accurate and it is very difficult to write a complete specification (using any method).

- A description of a product provides information about that product. A single description need not be complete; we can use a collection of descriptions. However, everything that the description states must be true of the product, else the description is wrong. A description is only useful if it is easier to derive information from the description than to derive it from the product itself.
- If a specification is correct but not an accurate description of a product, it is the product that is wrong. If the specification is true of a product, but the product is not satisfactory, the specification must be wrong (either inaccurate or just incomplete). If the specification is not true of a product, but the product is satisfactory, the specification is deficient (either an overspecification or incorrect).
- A model is something with some of the properties of a product; however, not all of the model's properties need be true of the product itself. A model may not be a specification or a description. Models are potentially dangerous because one can derive information from a model that is not true of the product. All information that is based on a model must be taken "with a grain of salt".

4 No New Mathematics

For the work described in the remainder of the talk, there is no new mathematics; we have merely found new ways to apply classical mathematical concepts. This is common in Engineering research.

The logic used is very close to the classical logic presented in textbooks. Our only deviation from the most basic logic is that the meaning of predicates involving partial functions is fully defined (predicates are total). [2]

We make heavy use of the concepts of function (including functions of time) and relation. We represent functions in the traditional way, using mathematical expressions.

---

[1] The meaning of these models is often not precisely defined.

Relations that are not functions are represented by giving the characteristic predicate of the set of ordered pairs, again using a mathematical expression. The use of the relational model in [3] is the most basic innovation in our work.

The only mathematics that may appear new is our use of a multi-dimensional format for expression, which we call tabular expressions. These are no more "powerful" than traditional expressions; in fact, we define their meaning by telling how to construct an equivalent traditional expression. The advantage is purely notational; For the class of functions/relations of interest to us, the tabular form of the expression is usually easier to construct, check and read. The talk provides numerous illustrations of this notation.

5   Need for Document Definitions

When industrial developers take the time to write a basic document such as a requirements document, there are often debates about what should be in it. While, there is a plethora of standards in the software field, those standards detail format and structure but not contents. As a result, even documents that satisfy standards, usually lack essential information. The standards provide no way of saying that a document is complete. When we had produced the first such [1], there was widespread agreement that it was an unusually useful document, but strong disagreement about which standard it satisfied. In contrast, many documents that fully satisfied the standards that were in place were not found useful because they did not contain essential information.

In [1] we have proposed definitions of the following documents:

1. "System Requirements Document"- Treats computer systems as "black-box".
2. "System Design Document"- Describes computers and communication.
3. "Software Requirements Document" - Describes required software behaviour
4. "Software Function Specification": Describes actual software behaviour.
5. "Software Module Guide": How to find your module. (informal document).
6. "Module Interface Specifications": Treats each module as black-box.
7. "Uses Relation Document": Range and domain comprise module programs.
8. "Module Internal Design Documents": Describe data structure and programs.

For each of the above except 5, which is informal, we have stated what variables should be defined in the document and what relations must be represented/defined by the document. These definitions provide an unambiguous basis for deciding what should be contained in a document. Documents may still be incomplete, but we can identify the missing information and check for important properties.

6   Tabular Notation

Although conventional mathematical notation is capable of describing the functions and relations called for by our definitions, many find those expressions very hard to parse. Documents written using conventional notation are precise but difficult to review and not very useful as reference documents. This is because the nature of the functions that we encounter in software. Traditional engineering mathematics stresses functions that are continuous and differentiable. With digital computers we implement functions that approximate piecewise-continuous functions. Through experience we have discovered that multi-dimensional forms of expressions are well suited to this class of functions. Many practical applications have shown that tabular expressions are better accepted, more easily prepared, more easily checked, and more useful than the conventional expressions that they replace. Of course, conventional expressions are still essential: (1) the innermost cells of a tabular expression always contain conventional expressions and (2) our new approach to defining the meaning of these expressions shows how to transform it to an equivalent conventional expression.

The last point is important. Many who see these expressions find them simpler and easier to read than "formal method" examples and assume that they are somehow less formal than other methods. Formality need not mean "hard to read". Tabular expressions are just as formal as the conventional expressions that they replace.

7 Practical Advantages of Mathematics

The fact that our documents are based on conventional mathematics has a great many practical advantages. It allows us to use existing theorem proving programs to check tables for consistency and completeness, to use computer algebra systems to transform and simplify documents, to evaluate expressions when simulating something that we have specified, to generate test oracles from specifications, and to generate test cases based on black box documents. We have also found these documents extremely valuable for inspecting critical software. [4]

8 Future Work

Based on our new, much more general (yet simpler) definition of tabular expressions, we are building a new generation of tools to support the use of this approach.

References

[1] Heninger, K., Kallander, J., Parnas, D.L., Shore, J., "Software Requirements for the A-7E Aircraft", NRL Report 3876, November 1978, 523 pgs.
[2] Parnas, D.L., "Predicate Logic for Software Engineering", *IEEE Transactions on Software Engineering*, Vol. 19, No. 9, September 1993, pp. 856 - 862 Reprinted as Chapter 3 in [6]
[3] Parnas, D.L., Madey, J., "Functional Documentation for Computer Systems Engineering" *Science of Computer Programming* (Elsevier) vol. 25, no. 1, Oct. 1995, pp 41-61
[4] Parnas, D.L. "Inspection of Safety Critical Software using Function Tables", *Proceedings of IFIP World Congress 1994, Volume III*" August 1994, pp. 270 - 277. Also Ch. 19 in [6]
[5] Janicki, R., Parnas, D.L., Zucker, J., "Tabular Representations in Relational Documents", Chapter 12 in *"Relational Methods in Computer Science"*, Ed. C. Brink and G. Schmidt. Springer Verlag, pp. 184 - 196, 1997, ISBN 3-211-82971-7. Reprinted as Chapter 4 in [6].
[6] Hoffman, D.M., Weiss, D.M. (eds.), *"Software Fundamentals: Collected Papers by David L. Parnas"*, Addison-Wesley, 2001, 664 pgs., ISBN 0-201-70369-6.

Generating Path Conditions for Timed Systems

Saddek Bensalem[1], Doron Peled[2,*], Hongyang Qu[2], and Stavros Tripakis[1]

[1] Verimag, 2 Avenue de Vignate, 38610 Gieres, France
[2] Department of Computer Science, University of Warwick,
Coventry, CV4 7AL United Kingdom

Abstract. We provide an automatic method for calculating the path condition for programs with real time constraints. This method can be used for the semiautomatic verification of a unit of code in isolation, i.e., without providing the exact values of parameters with which it is called. Our method can also be used for the automatic generation of test cases for unit testing. The current generalization of the calculation of path condition for the timed case turns out to be quite tricky, since not only the selected path contributes to the path condition, but also the timing constraints of alternative choices in the code.

1 Introduction

Software testing often involves the use of informal intuition and reasoning. But it is possible to employ some formal methods techniques and provide tools to support it. Such tools can help in translating the informal ideas and intuition into formal specification, assist in searching the code, support the process of inspecting it and help analyzing the results. A tester may have a vague idea where problems in the code may occur. The generation of a condition for a generated suspicious sequence may help the tester to confirm or refute such a suspicion. Such a condition relates the variables at the beginning of the sequence. Starting the execution with values satisfying this condition is necessary to recreate the execution.

We generalize the calculation of a path condition, taking into account only the essential conditions to follow a particular path in the execution. We start with a given path merely from practical consideration; it is simpler to choose a sequence of program statements to execute. However, we look at the essential partial order, which is consistent with the real-time constraints, rather than at the total order. We cannot assume that transitions must follow each other, unless this order stems from some sequentiality constraints such as transitions belonging to the same process or using the same variable or from timing constraints.

For untimed systems, there is no difference between the condition for the partial order execution and the condition to execute any of the sequences (linearizations) consistent with it. Because of commutativity between concurrently

---

* This research was partially supported by Subcontract UTA03-031 to The University of Warwick under University of Texas at Austin's prime National Science Foundation Grant #CCR-0205483.

J. Romijn, G. Smith, and J. van de Pol (Eds.): IFM 2005, LNCS 3771, pp. 5–19, 2005.

executed transitions, we obtain the same path condition either way. However, when taking the time constraints into account, the actual time and order between occurrences of transitions does affect the path condition (which now includes time information).

After the introduction of the untimed path condition in [3], weakest precondition for timed system was studied in [2, 8, 9]. The paper [2] extended the guarded-command language in [3] to involve time. But it only investigated sequential programs with time constraints. The paper [9] gave a definition of the weakest precondition for concurrent program with time constraints, based on discrete time, rather than dense time. The weakest precondition in [8] is defined for timed guarded-command programs or, alternatively, timed safety automata.

We model concurrent systems using timed transition systems. Our model is quite detailed in the sense that it separates the decision to take a transition (the enabling condition) from performing the transformation associated with it. We allow separate timing constraints (lower and upper bounds) for both parts. Thus, we do not find the model proposed in [7], which assigns a lower and upper time constraints for a transition that includes both enabling transition and a transformation, detailed enough. Alternative choices in the code may compete with each other, and their time constraints may affect each other in quite an intricate way. Although we do not suggest that our model provides the only way for describing a particular real-time system, it is detailed enough to demonstrate how to automatically generate test cases for realistic concurrent real-time systems.

In our solution, we translate the timed transition system into a collection of extended timed automata, which is then synchronized with constraints stemming from the given execution sequence. We then obtain a directed acyclic graph of executed transitions. We apply to it a weakest precondition construction, enriched with time analysis based on time zone analysis (using difference bound matrices).

2   Modeling Concurrent Timed Systems

As mentioned in the introduction, we describe concurrent real-time systems using timed transition systems (TTS). The latter model is given a semantics in terms of extended timed automata (ETA). This is done by defining a modular translation where each process in the TTS model is translated into an ETA. Thus the entire TTS model is translated into a network of synchronizing ETA. This section defines the two models and the translation.

2.1   Timed Transition Systems

We consider *timed transition systems* over a finite set of processes $P_1 \ldots P_n$. Each process consists of a finite number of transitions. The transitions involve checking and updating control variables and program variables (over the integers). An enabling condition is an assertion over the program variables. Although the processes are not mentioned explicitly in the transitions, each process P_i has its own location counter loc_i. It is possible that a transition is jointly performed by two processes, e.g., a synchronous communication transition. We leave out the details for various modes of concurrency, and use as an example a model that has only shared variables.

A transition t includes (1) an enabling condition c, (2) an assertion over the current process P_j location, of the form $loc_j = \hat{l}$, (3) a transformation f of the variables, and (4) a new value $\hat{l}'$ for the location of process P_j. For example, a test (e.g., `while` loop or `if` condition) from a control value $\hat{l}$ of process P_j to a control value $\hat{l}'$, can be executed when $(loc_j = \hat{l}) \wedge c$, and result in the transformation f being performed on the variables, and $loc_j = \hat{l}'$.

We equip each transition with two pairs of time constraints $[l, u], [L, U]$ such that:

l is a lower bound on the time a transition needs to be *continuously* enabled until it is selected.

u is an upper bound on the time the transition can be *continuously* enabled without being selected.

L is a lower bound on the time it takes to perform the transformation of a transition, after it was selected.

U is the upper bound on the time it takes to perform the transformation of a transition, after it was selected.

We allow shared variables, but make the restriction that each transition may change or use at most a single shared variable.

Every process can be illustrated as a directed graph G. A location is represented by a node and a transition is represented by an edge. Figure 1 shows the graphic representation of a transition.

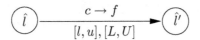

Fig. 1. The edge

2.2   Extended Timed Automata

An *extended timed automaton* is a tuple $\langle V, X, B, F, S, S^0, \Sigma, Cl, E \rangle$ where

- V is a set of variables.
- X is a finite set of assertions over the set of variables V.
- B is a set of Boolean combinations of assertions over clocks of the form $x \# \hat{c}$, where x is a clock, $\#$ is a relation from $\{<, >, \geq, \leq, =\}$ and $\hat{c}$ is a constant (not necessarily a value, as our timed automaton can be parameterized).
- F is a set of transformations for the variables. Each component of F can be represented e.g., as a multiple assignment to some of the variables in V.

- S is a finite set of states.[1] A state $s \in S$ is labeled with an assertion s^X from X and an assertion s^B on B that need to hold invariantly when we are at the state.
- $S^0 \subseteq S$ are the initial states.
- Σ is a finite set of labels.
- Cl is a finite set of clocks.
- E the set of edges over $S \times 2^{Cl} \times \Sigma \times X \times B \times F \times S$. The first component of an edge $e \in E$ is the source state. The second component e^{Cl} is the set of clocks that reset to 0 upon firing this edge. A label e^Σ from Σ allows synchronizing edges from different automata, when defining the product. We allow multiple labels on edges, as a terse way of denoting multiple edges. An edge e also includes an assertion e^X over the variables, an assertion e^B over the time variables that has to hold for the edge to fire, a transformation e^F over the variables and a target state.

The above definition extends timed automata [1] by allowing conditions over variables to be associated with the edges and states, and transformations on the variables on the edges (similar to the difference between finite state machines and extended finite state machines).

Semantics. The semantics of extended timed automata is defined as a set of executions. An *execution* is a (finite or infinite) sequence of triples of the form $\langle s_i, V_i, T_i \rangle$, where

1. s_i is a state from S,
2. V_i is an assignment for the variables V over some given domain(s), such that $V_i \models s_i^X$ and
3. T_i is an assignment of (real) time values to the clocks in Cl such that $T_i \models s_i^B$.

In addition, for each adjacent pair $\langle s_i, V_i, T_i \rangle \langle s_{i+1}, V_{i+1}, T_{i+1} \rangle$ one of the following holds:

An edge is fired. There is an edge e from source s_i to target s_{i+1}, where $T_i \models e^B$, $V_i \models e^X$, T_{i+1} agrees with T_i except for the clocks in e^{Cl}, which are set to zero, and $V_{i+1} = e^F(V_i)$, where $e^F(V_i)$ represents performing the transformation over V_i.

Passage of time. $T_{i+1} = T_i + \delta$, i.e., each clock in Cl is incremented by some real value δ. Then $V_{i+1} = V_i$.

An infinite execution must have an infinite progress of time. An initialized execution must start with $s \in S^0$ and with all clocks set to zero. However for generation of test cases we deal here with finite consecutive segments of executions, which do not have to be initialized.

---

[1] We use the term "state" for extended timed automata to distinguish from "location" for timed transition systems.

The Product of ETA. Let $ETA_1 = \langle V_1, X_1, Cl_1, B_1, F_1, S_1, S_1^0, \Sigma_1, E_1 \rangle$ and $ETA_2 = \langle V_2, X_2, Cl_2, B_2, F_2, S_2, S_2^0, \Sigma_2, E_2 \rangle$ be two ETAs. Assume the clock sets Cl_1 and Cl_2 are disjoint. Then the product, denoted $ETA_1 \parallel ETA_2$, is the ETA $\langle V_1 \cup V_2, X_1 \cup X_2, Cl_1 \cup Cl_2, B_1 \cup B_2, F_1 \cup F_2, S_1 \times S_2, S_1^0 \times S_2^0, \Sigma_1 \cup \Sigma_2, E \rangle$. For a compound state $s = (s_1, s_2)$ where $s_1 \in S_1$ with $s_1^{X_1} \in X_1$ and $s_1^{B_1} \in B_1$ and $s_2 \in S_2$ with $s_2^{X_2} \in X_2$ and $s_2^{B_2} \in B_2$, $s^{X_1 \cup X_2} = s_1^{X_1} \wedge s_2^{X_2}$ and $s^{B_1 \cup B_2} = s_1^{B_1} \wedge s_2^{B_2}$. The set E of edges are defined as follows. For every edge $e_1 = \langle s_1, e_1^{Cl_1}, e_1^{\Sigma_1}, e_1^{X_1}, e_1^{B_1}, e_1^{F_1}, s_1' \rangle$ in E_1 and $e_2 = \langle s_2, e_2^{Cl_2}, e_2^{\Sigma_2}, e_2^{X_2}, e_2^{B_2}, e_2^{F_2}, s_2' \rangle$ in E_2,

- joint edges: if $e_1^{\Sigma_1} \cap e_2^{\Sigma_2} \neq \emptyset$, E contains
  $\langle (s_1, s_2), e_1^{Cl_1} \cup e_2^{Cl_2}, e_1^{\Sigma_1} \cup e_2^{\Sigma_2}, e_1^{X_1} \wedge e_2^{X_2}, e_1^{B_1} \wedge e_2^{B_2}, e_1^{F_1} \cup e_2^{F_2}, (s_1', s_2') \rangle$.
  Any variable is allowed to be assigned to a new value by either e_1 or e_2, not both.
- edges only in ETA_1 or ETA_2: if $e_1^{\Sigma_1} \cap e_2^{\Sigma_2} = \emptyset$, E contains
  $\langle (s_1, s''), e_1^{Cl_1}, e_1^{\Sigma_1}, e_1^{X_1}, e_1^{B_1}, e_1^{F_1}, (s_1', s'') \rangle$ for every state $s'' \in S_2$ and
  $\langle (s', s_2), e_2^{Cl_2}, e_2^{\Sigma_2}, e_2^{X_2}, e_2^{B_2}, e_2^{F_2}, (s', s_2') \rangle$ for every state $s' \in S_1$.

2.3   Translating a TTS into ETAs

We describe the construction of a set of extended timed automata from a timed transition system. We should emphasize that this construction *defines* the semantics of a timed transition system as the semantics of the corresponding set of extended timed automata.

We first show how to construct states and edges for one particular location. An ETA is generated after all locations in a TTS process are translated. Any location in a process is said to be the *neighborhood* of the transitions that must start at that location. The enabledness of each transition depends on the location counter, as well as an enabling condition over the variables. Location counters are translated in an implicit way such that each different location is translated into a different set of states. For a neighborhood with n transitions $t_1, \ldots, t_n$, let $c_1, \ldots, c_n$ be the enabling conditions of n transitions respectively. The combination of these conditions has the form of

$$C_1 \wedge \ldots \wedge C_n,$$

where C_i is c_i or $\neg c_i$. Each transition t_j in the neighborhood has its own local clock x_j. Different transitions may have the same local clocks, if they do not participate in the same process or the same neighborhood.

1. we construct 2^n *enabledness* states, one for each Bool-ean combination of enabling condition truth values. For any enabledness states s_i and s_k (note that s_i and s_k can be the same state), there is an *internal* edge starting at s_i and pointing to s_k. Let $\mathcal{C}_i$ and $\mathcal{C}_k$ be the combinations for s_i and s_k, respectively. The edge is associated with $\mathcal{C}_k$ as the assertion over the variables. For any condition C_j which is $\neg c_j$ in $\mathcal{C}_i$ and c_j in $\mathcal{C}_k$, the clock x_j is reset ($x_j := 0$) upon the edge, for measuring the amount of time that the corresponding transition is enabled. We do not reset x_j in other cases.

2. We also have an additional *intermediate* state per each transition in the neighborhood, from which the transformation associated with the selected transition is performed. For any enabledness state s with the combination C in which the condition C_j corresponding to the transition t_j is c_j, let s'_j be the intermediate state for t_j and do the following:

    (a) We have the conjunct $x_j < u_j$ as part of s^X, the assertion over the variable of s, disallowing t_j to be enabled in s more than its upper limit u_j.

    (b) We add a *decision* edge with the assertion $x_j \geq l_j$ from s, allowing the selection of t_j only after t_j has been enabled at least l_j time continuously since it became enabled. On the decision edge, we also reset the clock x_j to measure now the time it takes to execute the transformation.

    (c) We put the assertion $x_j < U_j$ into s'_j, not allowing the transformation to be delayed more than U_j time.

    (d) We add an additional *transformation* edge labeled with $x_j \geq L_j$ and the transformation of t_j to from s' any of the enabledness states representing the target location of t_j. Again, this is done according to the above construction. There can be multiple such states, for the successor neighborhood, and we need to reset the appropriate clocks. We add an assertion over variables to the transformation edge. The assertion is the combination of enabling conditions which is associated to the target state of the transformation edge.

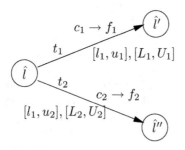

Fig. 2. A neighborhood of two TTS transitions

Figure 2 illustrates a neighborhood with two transitions and Figure 3 provides the ETA construction for this neighborhood. The states s_1, s_2, s_3 and s_4 are enabledness states, corresponding to the subset of enabling conditions of t_1 and t_2 that hold in the current location $\hat{l}$. The edges to s_5 correspond to t_1 being selected, and the edges to s_6 correspond to t_2 being selected. The edges into s_5 also reset the local clock x_1 that times the duration of the transformation f_1 of t_1, while the edges into s_6 zero the clock x_2 that times the duration of f_2. The state s_5 (s_6, respectively) allows us to wait no longer than U_1 (U_2, resp.) before we perform t_1 (t_2). The edge from s_5 (s_6) to s_8 (s_8) allows delay of no less than L_1 (L_2) before completing t_1 (t_2). Note that s_7 (as well as s_8) actually represents

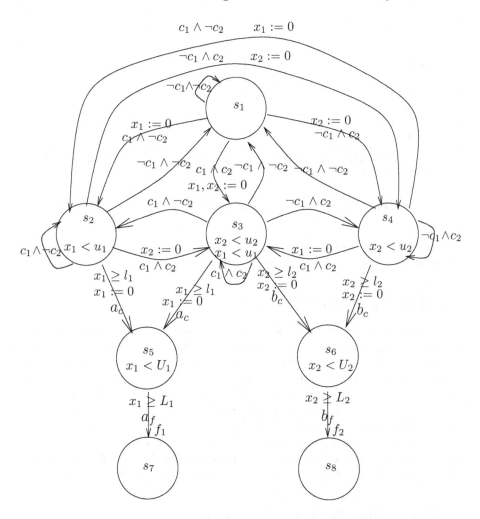

Fig. 3. The ETA for the neighborhood of two TTS transitions

Fig. 4. Two sequential TTS transitions

one of a set of enabledness states, in the pattern of s_1 to s_4, for the location $\hat{l}'$ ($\hat{l}''$, resp), according to the enabledness of transitions in it (depending on the enabledness of the various transitions in the new neighborhood and including the corresponding reset of enabledness measuring clocks).

Figure 4 shows two consecutive transitions and Figure 5 provides the ETA construction for these transitions. For simplicity, the self loops are omitted. Lo-

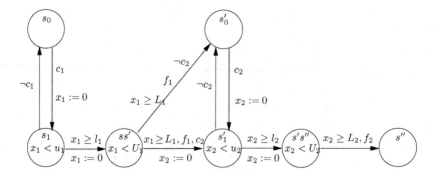

Fig. 5. The ETA for the two sequential TTS transitions

cation $\hat{l}$ is translated into states s_0 and s_1, location $\hat{l}'$ into s_0' and s_1', and location $\hat{l}''$ into s''. States ss' and $s's''$ are intermediate states.

2.4   Modeling Shared Variables

We present the procedure of modeling shared variables in a mutual exclusion manner. A shared variable needs to be protected by mutual exclusion when two or more transformations attempt to write it concurrently. For each shared variable v we provide a two state automaton, {$used$, $unused$}. We synchronize the decision edge of each transition that references such a variable with an edge from $unused$ to $used$, and each transformation edge of such a transition with an edge from $used$ to $unused$. When a decision edge acquires v, all other processes accessing v are forced to move to corresponding states by synchronizing the decision edge with proper internal edges in those processes. For the same reason, a transformation releasing v is synchronized with relative edges to enable accessing v.

3   Calculating the Path Conditions

In order to compute the path condition, the first step of our method involves generating an acyclic ETA (which we will call a DAG, or *directed acyclic graph*). Then the path condition is computed by propagating constraints backwards in this DAG. The DAG is generated using, on one hand, the set of ETAs corresponding to the TTS in question, and on the other hand, the TTS path (i.e., program transition sequence) provided by the user.

3.1   The Partial Order in a TTS Path

Given a selected sequence σ of occurrences of transitions, we calculate the *essential* partial order, i.e., a transitive, reflexive and asymmetric order between the execution of the transitions, as described below. This essential partial order is represented as a formula over a finite set of *actions* $Act = A_c \cup A_f$, where the actions A_c represent the selections of transitions, i.e., waiting for their enabledness, and the actions A_f represent the transformations. Thus, a transition a is split into two components, $a_c \in A_c$ and $a_f \in A_f$. The essential partial order imposes sequencing all the actions in the same process, and pairs of actions that use or set a mutual variable. In the latter case, the enabledness part b_c of the latter transition succeed the transformation part a_f of the earlier transition. However, other transitions can interleave in various ways (e.g., $d_c \prec e_c \prec e_f \prec d_f$). This order relation $\prec$ corresponds to a partial order over Act. The formula is satisfied by all the sequences that satisfy the constraints in $\prec$, i.e., the linearizations (complementation to total orders) over Act. In particular, σ is one (but not necessarily the only) sequence satisfying the constraints in φ.

The partial order can be illustrated as a directed graph, where a node represents an action and an edge represents a $\prec$ relation. For example, we assume that transitions a and b belong to a process and a transition d belongs to another process. A partial order requires $a_c \prec a_f$, $a_f \prec b_c$, $b_c \prec b_f$, $d_c \prec d_f$ and $a_f \prec d_c$. The partial order is shown in Figure 6.

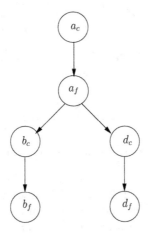

Fig. 6. A partial order

3.2 Generation of an Acyclic ETA from a Partial Order

After we generate the set of the ETAs for the different processes, we label each transition in the ETAs with respect to Act. For example in Figure 3, the edges $s_2 \to s_5$ and $s_3 \to s_5$ can be labeled with a_c, the edges $s_3 \to s_6$ and $s_4 \to s_6$ can be labeled with b_c. The edge $s_5 \to s_7$ can be marked by a_f and s_6 to s_8 by b_f.

Let $\mathcal{A}_\prec$ be a finite partial order among occurrences of Act (note that an action from Act can occur multiple times.). We generate an automaton $Lin_\prec$ with edges labeled with actions of Act. The automaton $Lin_\prec$ accepts all the linearizations of $\mathcal{A}_\prec$. Hence, it also necessary accepts the original sequence from which we generated $\mathcal{A}_\prec$.

The algorithm for generating $Lin_{\prec}$ is as follows. The sets of states of $Lin_{\prec}$ are subsets $\mathcal{S} \subseteq St$, the set of occurrences of $\mathcal{A}_{\prec}$, such that for each such subset $\mathcal{S}$, it holds that if $\alpha \prec \beta$ and $\beta \in \mathcal{S}$ then also $\alpha \in \mathcal{S}$. They are the *history closed* subsets of St. A transition is of the form $\mathcal{S} \xrightarrow{\alpha} \mathcal{S} \cup \{\alpha\}$ where α is an occurrence of an action. The empty set is the initial state and the set St is the accepting state. Figure 7 shows the automaton for the partial order in Figure 6.

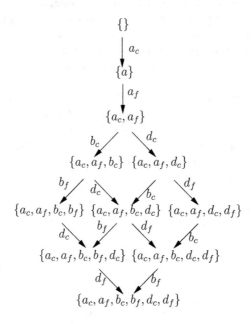

Fig. 7. A partial order automaton

We generate now the acyclic ETA $ETA_{\prec}$, whose executions are linearizations of $Lin_{\prec}$, with a collection of extended timed automata $T_1, \ldots, T_n$. At first, we describe the synchronization of a transition $\bar{\alpha}$ marked with an action $\bar{a} \in Act$ on $Lin_{\prec}$ with the edges in a component T_i:

1. Synchronization of $\bar{\alpha}$ with an edge labeled as $\bar{a}$. This corresponds to the selection or the transformation of a transition in the TTS being taken.
2. Synchronization of $\bar{\alpha}$ with an internal edge τ which references a shared variable v if $\bar{a}$ acquires or releases v. This corresponds to an enabledness condition being changed. If there exists an edge which has the same source state as τ has and is labeled as $\bar{a}$, τ is not allowed to be synchronzed with $\bar{\alpha}$.

Now we generate the initial states of $ETA_{\prec}$. For every participant process T_j, we find the set $\hat{S}_j$ of enabledness states for the first transition occurring in $\mathcal{A}_{\prec}$. At any initial states of $ETA_{\prec}$, T_j stays at one of the states in $\hat{S}_j$. If a process T_k does not have any transitions occurring in $\mathcal{A}_{\prec}$, we asssume it stays at one of its initial states and thus we use the set of initial states as $\hat{S}_k$. An initial state of $ETA_\prec$ is composed of such states that each state belongs to a different set $\hat{S}_j$. Each initial state of $ETA_\prec$ is matched to the initial state of $Lin_\prec$.

The successive states of $ETA_\prec$ is generated in a deductive way from the initial states. For clarity, a state $g = \langle g^1, \ldots, g^n \rangle$ of $ETA_\prec$ is denoted by a *global state* and the states $g^1, \ldots, g^n$ composing g are denoted by *component* states. Any global state g has a matched state on $Lin_\prec$ as this is guaranteed by the deductive generation method. Let g be a global state whose successive global states have not be generated and $\bar{g}$ be the matched state of g on $Lin_\prec$. The successive global states of g are generated in the following way:

We synchronize each transition $\bar{\beta}$ starting at $\bar{g}$ on $Lin_\prec$ with ETA edges whose source states are component states of g. For any T_j, let w_j be the set of edges that are synchronized with $\bar{\beta}$ and $|w_j|$ be the number of edges in w_j. A component state g^j in g is the source state of the edges in w_j. A successive state g' with respect to $\bar{\beta}$ is generated by replacing each g^j by the target state of an edge in w_j. If $|w_j| = 0$, T_j does not change its state in g'. If $|w_j| > 1$, the number of successive global states with respect to $\bar{\beta}$ is increased $|w_j|$ times. These successive global states are matched to the target state of $\bar{\beta}$ on $Lin_\prec$.

Note that we remove any global states from which there is no path leading to the global states matched to the accepting state on $Lin_\prec$. Since there is often a nondeterministic choice for taking such labeled edges, this choice increases the branching degree on top of the branching already allowed by $\mathcal{A}_\prec$. The synchronous execution forms a DAG structure, which will be used later calculating the path precondition.

3.3   Data Structure for Backward Reachability Analysis

Time constraints are a set of relations among lock clocks. These contraints can be obtained from reachability analysis of clock zones. Difference-Bound Matrix (DBM) [4] is a data structure for representing clock zones.

A DBM is a $(m + 1) \times (m + 1)$ matrix where m is the number of local clocks of all processes. Each element $D_{i,j}$ of a DBM D is an upper bound of the difference of two clocks x_i and x_j, i.e., $x_i - x_j \leq D_{i,j}$. We $x_1, \cdots, x_m$ to represent local clocks. The clock x_0 is a special clock whose value is always 0. Therefore, $D_{i,0}$ ($i > 0$), the upper bound of $x_i - x_0$, is the upper bound of clock x_i; $D_{0,j}$ ($j > 0$), the lower bound of $x_0 - x_j$, is the negative form of the lower bound of clock x_j. To distinguish non-strict inequality $\leq$ with strict inequality $<$, each element $D_{i,j}$ has the form of (r, F) where $r \in \mathbb{R} \cup \{\infty\}$ and $F \in \{\leq, <\}$ with an exception that F cannot be $\leq$ when r is ∞. Addition $+$ is defined over $F, F' \in \{\leq, <\}$ as follows:

$$F + F' = \begin{cases} F, & \text{if } F = F' \text{ and} \\ <, & \text{if } F \neq F' \end{cases}$$

Now we define addition $+$ and comparison $<$ for two elements (r_1, F_1) and (r_2, F_2).

$$(r_1, F_1) + (r_2, F_2) = (r_1 + r_2, F_1 + F_2).$$

$$(r_1, F_1) < (r_2, F_2) \text{ iff } r_1 < r_2 \text{ or } (r_1 = r_2) \wedge (F_1 = <) \wedge (F_2 = \leq).$$

The minimum of (r_1, F_1) and (r_2, F_2) is defined below:

$$min((r_1, F_1), (r_2, F_2)) = \begin{cases} (r_1, F_1) & \text{if } (r_1, F_1) < (r_2, F_2) \\ (r_2, F_2) & \text{otherwise} \end{cases}$$

A DBM D is *canonical* iff for any $0 \leq i, j, k \leq m$, $D_{i,k} \leq D_{i,j} + D_{j,k}$. A DBM D is *satisfiable* iff there is no such a sequence of indices $0 \leq i_1, \cdots, i_k \leq m$ that $D_{i_1,i_2} + D_{i_2,i_3} + \cdots + D_{i_k,i_1} < (0, \leq)$. An unsatisfiable DBM D represents an empty clock zone.

Calculating time constraints following an edge τ backwards from its target state s to its source state s' has been explained in [11]. Let $I(s')^c$ be the assertion on clocks in state invariant of s', and ψ^c be the assertion on clocks within the edge τ. The DBM D represents the time constraints at s. Assertions $I(s')^c$ and ψ^c are represented by DBMs too. The time constraints D' at s' is defined as follows:

$$D' = (((([\lambda := 0]D) \wedge I(s')^c \wedge \psi^c) \Downarrow) \wedge I(s')^c \quad (1)$$

"$\wedge$" is conjunction of two clock zones. Calculating $D' = D^1 \wedge D^2$ is to set each element $D'_{i,j}$ in D' to be the minimum value of the element $D^1_{i,j}$ in D^1 and the element $D^2_{i,j}$ in D^2, i.e.,

$$D'_{i,j} = min(D^1_{i,j}, D^2_{i,j}).$$

"$\Downarrow$" is time predecessor. Calculating $D' = D \Downarrow$ is to set lower bound of each clock to 0, i.e.,

$$D'_{i,j} = \begin{cases} (0, \leq) & \text{if } i = 0 \\ D_{i,j} & \text{if } i \neq 0 \end{cases}$$

"$[\lambda := 0]D$" is reset predecessor. Calculating $D' = [\lambda := 0]D$ is as follows:

1. Resetting a clock x to 0 can be seen as substituting x by x_0. Let x' be a clock which is not reset. Before resetting, we have constraints $x' - x_0 \leq c_1$ and $x' - x \leq c_2$. After resetting, we obtain constraints $x' - x_0 \leq c_1$ and $x' - x_0 \leq c_2$ by replacing x with x_0. Then these constrains are conjunct into $x' - x_0 \leq min(c_1, c_2)$. Therefore, when we calculate time constraints from after resetting back to before resetting, we substitute $x' - x_0$ by $min(x' - x_0, x' - x)$ and $x_0 - x'$ by $min(x_0 - x', x - x')$. Therefore, for a clock x_i which is not reset, update its upper and lower bounds as follows:
   (a) $D'_{i,0} = min\{D_{i,k} | x_k \in \lambda \cup \{x_0\} \text{ for every } k\}$.
   (b) $D'_{0,i} = min\{D_{k,i} | x_k \in \lambda \cup \{x_0\} \text{ for every } k\}$.
2. On the other hand, for a clock x_k which is reset, its value before resetting can be any non-negative real number. Thus its lower bound is 0 and upper bound is ∞, i.e., $D'_{0,k} = (0, \leq)$ and $D'_{k,0} = (\infty, <)$. Furthermore, for any other clock x_j $(j \neq k \wedge j > 0)$, $D'_{k,j} = (\infty, <)$.
3. For a clock x_i which is not reset and a clock x_k which is reset, update $x_i - x_k$ as $D'_{i,k} = D'_{i,0}$. (Note that this step must be done after the upper bound of x_i is updated.)
4. For two clocks x_i and x_j that are not reset, $D'_{i,j} = D_{i,j}$.

Note that D' needs to be changed to canonical form after each operation. This is done using Floyd-Warshall algorithm [5, 10] to find the all-pairs shortest paths.

3.4   Path Condition for a DAG

We can now calculate the condition for that DAG from the leaf states backwards. The condition would use the usual *weakest* precondition for variables, and a similar update for time variables that involve local clocks and time parameters. When a state has several successors, we disjoin the conditions obtained on the different edges.

At first, we give a brief description of updating a condition over variables backwards from a given state to another state over an edge with condition c and transformation of the form $v := expr$, where v is a variable and $expr$ is an expression. Let φ be the condition over variables at the given state. The new condition φ^R is defined as follows:

$$\varphi^R = \varphi[expr/v] \wedge c, \tag{2}$$

where $\varphi[expr/v]$ denotes substituting $expr$ for each free occurrence of v in φ.

The backward calculation of the precondition for a DAG is described as follows:

1. Mark each leaf state as *old* and all other states as *new*. Attach the assertion on variables $\varphi = true$ and the assertion on clocks represented by DBM D_0 to each leaf, noted by $\varphi \wedge D_0$. The DBM D_0 is defined below:

$$\varphi_0 = \begin{pmatrix} (0, \leq) & (0, \leq) & \cdots & (0, \leq) \\ (\infty, <) & (0, \leq) & \cdots & (\infty, <) \\ \vdots & \vdots & \vdots & \vdots \\ (\infty, <) & (\infty, <) & \cdots & (0, \leq) \end{pmatrix} \tag{3}$$

When we start at a leaf state to calculate time constraints backwards, we do not know the exact value of any local clock when the system enters the leaf state. Thus their values ranges from 0 to ∞. Their exact value scopes can be computed during backward calculation.

2. While there are states marked with *new* do
    (a) Pick up a state z that is marked *new* such that all its successors $Y = \{y_1, \ldots, y_k\}$ are marked *old*.
    (b) Assume each $y_i \in Y$ is attached an assertion over variables and clocks. The assertion has the form of

$$\bigvee_{1 \leq j \leq m_i} (\varphi_{i,j} \wedge \mathcal{D}_{i,j}).$$

(note that $m_i = 1$ if y_i is a leaf state.) We obtain $\varphi_{i,j}^R$ from $\varphi_{i,j}$ according to the formula (2) and $\mathcal{D}_{i,j}^R$ from $\mathcal{D}_{i,j}$ according to the formula (1).

(c) Attach

$$\bigvee_{\substack{y_i \in Y \\ 1 \leq j \leq m_i}} (\varphi_{i,j}^R \wedge \mathcal{D}_{i,j}^R) \tag{4}$$

to the state z. Mark z as *old*.

Note: when $\varphi_{i,j}^R = false$ or $\mathcal{D}_{i,j}^R$ is not satisfiable, $\varphi_{i,j}^R \wedge \mathcal{D}_{i,j}^R$ is removed from formula (4).

3. When an initial node is reached backwards, the combination of conditions over variables that it represents (refer to Section 2.3 for detail) must be conjuncted with the condition calculated at this state in order to get the initial precondition for this state, because this combination is not processed during the backward calculation. The combinations represented by non-initial nodes are processed through the edges pointing to them. All initial preconditions of initial states are disjuncted together to form the initial precondition of the DAG.

4   Discussion

We described here a method for calculating the path condition for a timed system. The condition is calculated automatically, then simplified using various heuristics. Of course we do not assume that the time constraints are given. The actual time for lower and upper bounds on transitions is given symbolically. Then we can make various assumptions about these values, e.g., the relative magnitude of various time constants. Given that we need to guarantee some particular execution and not the other, we may obtain the time constraints as path conditions, including e.g., some equations, whose solutions provide the appropriate required time constants.

We believe that the constructed theory is helpful in the automatic generation of test cases. The test case construction can also be used to synthesize real time system time. Another way to use this theory is to extend it to encapsulate temporal specification. This allows verifying a unit of code in isolation. Instead of verifying each state in separation, one may verify the code according to the program execution paths. This was done for the untimed case in [6], and we are working on extending this framework for the timed case. Such a verification method allows us to handle infinite state systems (although the problem is inherently undecidable, and hence we are not guaranteed to terminate), and parametric systems e.g., we may verify a procedure with respect to arbitrary allowed input. This is done symbolically, rather than state by state.

References

1. R. Alur, D.L. Dill, A Theory of Timed Automata, *Theoretical Computer Science* 126, 1994, 183–235.
2. N. Budhiraja, K. Marzullo, F. B. Schneider, Derivation of sequential, real-time process-control programs, *Foundations of Real-Time Computing: Formal Specifications and Methods*, 1991, 39-54

3. E. W. Dijkstra, Guarded commands, nondeterminacy and formal derivation of programs, *Communications of the ACM* 18, 1975, 453–457
4. D. L. Dill, Timing assumptions and verification of finite-state concurrent systems, *Automatic Verification Methods for Finite State Systems*, LNCS 407, 1989, 197–212
5. R. W. Floyd, Algorithm 97: Shortest Path, *Communications of the ACM*, 5(6), 1962, 345
6. E. Gunter, D. Peled, Unit Checking: Symbolic Model Checking for a Unit of Code, *Verification: Theory and Practice 2003*, LNCS 2772, 548–567.
7. T. A. Henzinger, Z. Manna, A. Pnueli, Temporal proof methodologies for timed transition systems, *Information and Computation* 112, 1994, 273–337
8. T. A. Henzinger, X. Nicollin, J. Sifakis, S. Yovine, Symbolic model checking for real-time systems, *Information and Computation* 111, 1994, 193–244
9. D. J. Scholefield, H. S. M. Zedan, Weakest Precondition Semantics for Time and Concurrency, *Information Processing Letters* 43, 1992, 301-308
10. S. Warshall, A theorem on boolean matrices, *Journal of the ACM*, 9(1), 1962, 11–12
11. S.Yovine, Model checking timed automata, *Lectures on Embedded Systems*, LNCS 1494, 1998, 114–152

Software Model Checking: Searching for Computations in the Abstract or the Concrete

Patrice Godefroid[1] and Nils Klarlund[2,⋆]

[1] Bell Laboratories, Lucent Technologies
[2] Google

Abstract. We review and discuss the current approaches to software model checking, including the complementary views of validation versus falsification and those of static versus dynamic analysis. For falsification, also known as bug finding, we advocate the need for blended approaches that combine the strengths of both static and dynamic analysis. We outline possible directions of research in this area.

1 Introduction

Software model checking is a family of analyses that involve the automatic exploration of the state space of a program. The *state space* is at worst all the possible memory configurations that the program can read and write (such as RAM and disk space). With the combinatorial explosion that follows from this view—state spaces are often so big that "astronomical" is a powerless word to describe their sizes—the challenge is to search intelligently the state spaces of programs.

Model checking when applied to software has become a somewhat confusing concept, so we start by explaining its origin and the two complementary meanings it has come to take on. Model checking originally meant to pursue a goal complementary to testing, namely to *verify*—to assert with certainty—that the program satisfies some property. In particular, model checking in its original meaning rests on an assumption that a finite graph of manageable size, representing the behavior of the program, can be constructed so that properties of it can be checked by exhaustive search. The term model checking comes from mathematical logic, where a *model*, let us call it M, represents a set of states that are connected. A program P generates—mathematically speaking—a model M, when all possible inputs to it are considered. The states are connected by transitions, each representing a program step, either in its mathematical semantics or at the machine level. Thus, the word "model" does not refer to a desired, abstract specification of the behavior, but to a representation of the behavior of the program. The model, in turn, describes the set of executions of the program. Each execution α is a path in the model.

⋆ The work of this author was done partly at Bell Laboratories.

J. Romijn, G. Smith, and J. van de Pol (Eds.): IFM 2005, LNCS 3771, pp. 20–32, 2005.

2 The Main Approaches to Software Model Checking

We survey the landscape of model checking, static and dynamic analysis techniques.

2.1 The Validation View

For a property ϕ about models (programs), such as "an error state is never encountered", and an execution α of a model M, we say that α of M satisfies ϕ, and we write $\alpha, M \vDash \phi$, if ϕ is true of α. We are interested in knowing whether ϕ holds for all α of M. If that is the case, then we say that M satisfies ϕ, or in symbols, $M \vDash \phi$.

In practice, it is of course impossible to directly check whether $M \vDash \phi$ because M is anything but manageable, and can even be infinite. Instead, an approach to model checking attempts to reduce the problem to one that involves a smaller representation M' of M, for example through the technique of *predicate abstraction* [17]. Whatever the algorithm is for model checking, the outcome is either "yes","don't know", or "no". If the algorithm does not provide a "yes" or "no" in reasonable time, we will treat this as a "don't know" outcome.

If our emphasis is to validate a program, then it is crucial of course that an answer of "yes" implies $M \vDash \phi$. This criterion is *soundness* with respect to validation. It is also desirable but not mandatory—under this view—that if $M \vDash \phi$ holds then the answer delivered by the algorithm is "yes". This criterion is *completeness* with respect to validation.

Note that a model checking algorithm that is both sound and complete never returns the answer "don't know".

2.2 Static Analysis

Model checking under the validation view requires generating a conservative, "may" abstraction M' of the intractable model M, which includes at least all the behaviors of M and typically many more, and is therefore essentially a method of *static analysis*, that is, an automated analysis of the program that does not involve running the executable code. For instance, *type checking* can be seen as a sound, but incomplete, method of verifying that values of program variables always take their declared types. Type checking is typically incomplete since it is possible for a program to always assign at runtime values to variables according to their declared types even though the program does not pass muster with the limited reasoning powers of a type checker.

In theory, methods of static analysis tend to be sound, but not complete. In practice however, most software model checking tools based on static analysis (e.g., [22, 7, 1, 21, 6]) are actually unsound (in addition to being incomplete). Indeed, it is not always possible to guarantee that an invalidating path found in the abstracted model M' corresponds to a real execution in M, just as type checking is unsound as a bug finding method.

The weakness of predicate abstraction techniques—and other software model checking tools based on static analysis—is that a reported error often lacks an explanation that can be readily understood by a human. In contrast, the validation engine of a type checker is usually able to pinpoint the exact place and circumstances of a typing error. From this information, the programmer may take corrective action, such as inserting a type coercion. The best explanation in the context of static software model checking may be a program execution path fragment that may or may not be feasible under the concrete semantics. Infeasibility is often a result of the limited understanding that a typical abstract interpretation framework has about pointers. The existence of such spurious bugs imposes an extra workload on the programmer that may lead to frustration and disuse of the tool.

Spurious error reports can be reduced if the tool itself makes assumptions that seem reasonable. For example, a tool based on local analysis will report many uses of null pointers for input parameters of functions unless the programmer has been careful to always test input parameters before they are dereferenced. To avoid inundating the programmer with error messages, the tool may choose to not report errors that stem from the dereferencing of input parameters. In this way, the tool is no longer complete, but is still useful for finding bugs. Most static-analysis tools sacrifice soundness to reduce the number of false alarms, and static software model checkers are no exception.

2.3   The Falsification View

Somewhat surreptitiously, model checking in software has evolved to also denote the complementary goal of validation, namely that of *falsification*, where success is exhibiting a path that does not satisfy the property. In this sense, falsification shares goals with program testing. This change of emphasis is precipitated by the difficulty of verifying a universally quantified statement, as in the original model checking problem "does $M \vDash \phi$ hold?". It is sometimes easier to find an invalidating computation, that is, to solve the negation of $M \vDash \phi$. So, we may use "bug finding" as a synonym for "falsification".

The meaning of soundness and completeness for a program analysis algorithm become interchanged under the bug-finding view. *Soundness* with respect to falsification means that reported invalidating paths are indeed real bug traces in the sense that some set of input values does drive the program according to the path; we call the resulting bugs *sound*. *Completeness* now means that if the program is invalid then an invalidating path is indeed reported, that is, all bugs are found.

With model checking of software, we claim that most researchers have adopted (consciously or not) the falsification point of view [15]: the main practical goal of software model checking is to find bugs that would be hard to find using other techniques, and not to prove the absence of errors. So perhaps the effort would be better known as *model testing*.

2.4   Static Analysis for Falsification

One of the earliest proposals for using static analysis as a kind of program testing method was proposed by King almost 30 years ago [24]. The idea is to symbolically explore the tree of all computations a program unit (such as a function) exhibits when all possible value assignments to input parameters are considered. For each *control path* ρ, that is, a sequence of control locations of the program, a *path constraint* ϕ_ρ is constructed that characterizes the input assignments for which the program executes along ρ. For (small) programs, all the paths can be enumerated by a search algorithm that explores all possible branches at conditional statements. The paths ρ for which ϕ_ρ is satisfiable are *feasible* and are the only ones that can be executed by the actual program. The solutions to ϕ_ρ exactly characterize the inputs that drive the program through ρ.

A prototype of this system allowed the programmer to be presented with feasible paths and to experiment with assertions in order to force new and perhaps unexpected paths. Assuming that the theorem prover used to check the satisfiability of all formulas ϕ_ρ is sound and complete, this use of static analysis amounts to a kind of symbolic testing.

King noticed that assumptions, now called preconditions, also formulated in the logic could be joined to the analysis forming, at least in principle, an automated theorem prover for Floyd's verification method, included the inductive invariants need for programs that contain loops. Such a general tool for program verification has proven elusive, even after 30 years.

However, this work was followed by a rich literature on test-vector generation using static analysis and symbolic execution (e.g., see [29, 10]) and has received a renewed interest recently (e.g., [4, 3, 39, 40, 8]).

2.5   Dynamic Analysis for Falsification

Dynamic analysis operates by executing a program and observing its executions. Testing and profiling are standard dynamic analyses.

In the rest of the paper, we discuss a class of software model checkers where repeated executions, perhaps thousands or millions, are *directed* using runtime information collected dynamically through program instrumentation techniques. The program being analyzed may be a single functional unit whose input values or formal parameters are open or may be multithreaded and governed by a nondeterministic scheduler. In any case, the program can execute only if choices are made along the way by supplying input values and decisions about which thread to execute next. In this way, the instrumented program runs by itself, systematically or randomly making choices but—crucially—with built-in awareness that many choices lead to equivalent behaviors and only one such choice from each equivalence class needs to be considered. We mention two orthogonal equivalence concepts that have been investigated:

- *symbolic execution* that characterizes executions paths: equivalent input vectors produce computations that take the same program path (e.g., [25, 16, 5]; and
- *partial order reduction* that characterizes interleavings of a concurrent software system: equivalent interleavings produce the same significant state changes (e.g., [14, 12]).

We might classify such analyses as *directed execution*, because the analysis is execution-based but directed by analysis. Obviously, tools for directed execution (e.g., [14, 38, 28, 9, 16, 32]) are complementary to and should be used in conjunction with tools for detecting runtime errors, such as Purify [20] among many others (e.g., [30, 26, 37]).

Most software model checking methods based on dynamic analysis are sound with respect to bug finding, simply by virtue of anchoring the analysis in concrete executions of the program itself. Since an execution is a real execution, not an abstraction of an execution as in static analysis, errors encountered will usually be interesting. These analyses do not produce spurious error reports, for example suggesting impossible execution paths that are really due to a lack of computational reasoning power on behalf of the analyzer.

However, with these dynamic analyses, there is no conservative approximation or warranty typical of static analysis. In fact, the usual goal of static analysis, to consider all computations, will almost certainly not be attained. Programs are not verified, they are only tested.

We refer the reader to [11] for a general discussion on the duality and synergies between traditional static and dynamic analysis.

3   Recent Work on Directed Execution

Recently [16], we have proposed a new approach to directed execution for falsification that addresses the main limitation hampering unit testing, namely the need to write test driver and harness code to simulate the external environment of a software application. This approach combines three main techniques:

- *automated* extraction of the interface of a program with its external environment using static source-code parsing;
- automatic generation of a test driver for this interface that performs *random* testing to simulate the most general environment the program can operate in; and
- dynamic analysis of how the program behaves under random testing with automatic generation of new test inputs that *direct* the execution along alternative program paths.

Together, these three techniques constitute *Directed Automated Random Testing*, or *DART* for short. Thus, the main strength of DART is that testing can be performed *completely automatically* on any program that compiles – there is no need to write any test driver or harness code. During testing, DART can detect standard errors such as program crashes, assertion violations, and non-termination.

DART's integration of random testing and dynamic test generation using symbolic reasoning is best explained with an example, taken from [16].

Consider the function h shown in Figure 1. The function h is defective because it may lead to an abort statement for some value of its input vector, which consists of the input parameters x and y. Running the program with random

```
int f(int x) { return 2 * x; }
int h(int x, int y) {
  if (x != y)
    if (f(x) == x + 10)
      abort();        /* error */
  return 0;
}
```

Fig. 1. Example of program

values of x and y is unlikely to discover the bug. The problem is typical of random testing: it is difficult to generate input values that will drive the program through *all* its different execution paths, which implies that random testing usually provides low code coverage (e.g., [31]).

In contrast, DART is able to dynamically gather knowledge about the execution of the program in what we call a *directed search*. Starting with a random input, a DART-instrumented program calculates during each execution an input vector for the next execution. This vector contains values that are the solution of symbolic constraints gathered from predicates in branch statements during the previous execution. The new input vector attempts to force the execution of the program through a new path. By repeating this process, a directed search attempts to force the program to sweep through all its feasible execution paths.

For the example above, the DART-instrumented h initially guesses the value 269167349 for x and 889801541 for y. As a result, h executes the then-branch of the first if-statement, but fails to execute the then-branch of the second if-statement; thus, no error is encountered. The execution defines a path ρ through the program. Intertwined with the normal execution, the predicates $x_0 \neq y_0$ and $2 \cdot x_0 \neq x_0 + 10$ are formed on-the-fly according to how the conditionals evaluate; x_0 and y_0 are *symbolic variables* that represent the values of the memory locations of variables x and y. Note the expression $2 \cdot x_0$, representing f(x): it is defined through an interprocedural, dynamic tracing of symbolic expressions.

The path constraint $\phi_\rho = \langle x_0 \neq y_0, 2 \cdot x_0 \neq x_0 + 10 \rangle$ represents an equivalence class of input vectors, namely all the input vectors that drive the program through the path that was just executed. To force the program through a different equivalence class, the DART-instrumented h calculates a solution to the path constraint $\langle x_0 \neq y_0, 2 \cdot x_0 = x_0 + 10 \rangle$ obtained by negating, say, the last predicate of the current path constraint. A solution to this path constraint is $(x_0 = 10, y_0 = 889801541)$ and it is recorded. When the instrumented h runs again, it reads the values of the symbolic variables that have been previously recorded. In this case, the second execution then reveals the error by driving the program into the abort() statement as expected.

DART is thus a general framework parameterized by the kinds of constraints that can be collected and by their solvers. We refer the reader to [16] for a detailed presentation of the DART approach, including its formalization, several examples, the description of a simple DART implementation for the C programming language, and preliminary results of experiments. For instance, DART was able to find automatically attacks in various C implementations of a well-known flawed security protocol (Needham-Schroeder's), as well as hundreds of ways to crash the about 600 externally visible functions provided in the oSIP library, an open-source implementation of the SIP protocol.

The directed search outlined above is closely related to prior work on dynamic test generation (e.g., [25, 19]). The main difference is that the DART approach attempts to cover *all* executable program paths in a style similar to model checking, while prior work on dynamic test generation was mostly focused on generating test inputs to exercise a *specific* program path or branch using branch/predicate classification techniques. DART is also related to test-vector generation using static analysis and symbolic execution (e.g., see [24, 29, 10, 18, 4, 3, 39, 40, 8]). Symbolic execution is limited in practice by the imprecision of static analysis and of theorem provers. As discussed in [16], DART is able to alleviate some of the limitations of symbolic execution by exploiting dynamic information obtained from a concrete execution matching the symbolic constraints, by using dynamic test generation, and by using randomization when automated reasoning is impossible or difficult. Thus symbolic execution degrades gracefully in the sense that randomization takes over, by suggesting concrete values, when automated reasoning fails to suggest how to proceed.

Independently, Cadar and Engler [5] have recently proposed a testing technique very similar to the directed search used in DART. They also describe encouraging experimental results with their implementation. CUTE [34] is a DART implementation that extends the one described in [16] by handling simple types of constraints on pointers (namely equalities and inequalities).

4   Future Work

We believe the next few years will see much research combining the static and dynamic approaches to software model checking. In this section, we outline several possible directions for future work in this area. We start this discussion with some short-term extensions to prior work on directed execution and on DART in particular. We then discuss several more open-ended problems and present specific ideas to tackle these.

4.1   Short Term

Faster Constraint Solvers. The efficiency of DART implementations critically depends on the availability of efficient constraint solvers. This point is illustrated by the following experiment. Figure 1 compares the efficiency of two DART implementations on the Needham-Schroeder protocol benchmark (with a Dolev-Yao intruder model) discussed in [16].[1] The first implementation uses

---

[1] All experiments were performed on a Pentium III 800Mhz processor running Linux; runtime is user+system time as reported by the Unix `time` command and is always roughly equal to elapsed time. The depth parameter limits the number of messages received by protocol entities.

Table 1. Impact of constraint solver on DART efficiency

depth	error?	Implementation 1	Implementation 2
1	no	5 runs (<1 second)	4 runs (<1 second)
2	no	85 runs (<1 second)	30 runs (<1 second)
3	no	6,260 runs (22 seconds)	554 runs (<1 second)
4	yes	328,459 runs (18 minutes)	9,926 runs (57 seconds)

a simple constraint solver that supports only conjunctions and handles disjunctions, such as those arising from inequalities (example: $x \neq 1$ corresponds to $x < 1 \lor x > 1$), by considering in isolation each possible way of satisfying them. The second implementation uses a smarter constraint solver allowing the disjunctions that result from inequalities to be handled directly. The different approaches to inequalities reflect a seemingly innocuous choice: are two different computations that execute the same sequence of program statements to be considered distinct, in different equivalence classes, if they satisfy some disjunction in different ways? Table 1 shows the difference between a "yes" (Implementation 1) and a "no" (Implementation 2) answer to this question: for each implementation we have stated the number of executions needed to explore all equivalence classes (in order to reach an error). Table 1 shows that directly dealing with disjuncts dramatically reduces the search space. We anticipate that even faster results could be obtained for this benchmark by using general constraint solvers for handling directly all disjunctions appearing in the program's conditional statements.

Out of curiosity, we also ran (on the same machine) the static software model checker BLAST [21] (version 2.0) on this benchmark. BLAST reports "no error found" after 20 seconds for depth=1, and after 51 seconds for depth=2, but stops after reporting a spurious error after 6 minutes of search for depth=3. This spurious error is likely due to the presence of pointers in this benchmark and the limitations of the current alias analysis in BLAST.

More Constraint Types and Decision Procedures. DART reduces to random testing when no symbolic constraints on inputs can be generated. But code coverage is usually low with random testing alone, so we know that the more kinds of constraint are supported, the more effective the search for errors will be. This is true at least so long as the constraint solving itself does not become the bottleneck.

The DART framework and tool architecture are not dependent on specific constraint solvers. For instance, the first DART implementation described in [16] supported essentially integer linear constraints only, and the corresponding constraint solver used was lp_solve [27], which can solve efficiently any linear constraint using real and integer programming techniques. But we also expect to see directed execution tools that use symbolic constraints on other popular data types such as pointers, arrays, strings, or bit-vectors, in combination with more sophisticated constraint solvers, such as CVC Lite [2], ICS [23], or Simplify [35], among others. Borrowing again from static program analysis, we may use theories for uninterpreted functions and algebraic data types to reason about frequently-used functions in specific application domains such as cryptographic libraries in security protocols.

Concurrency. We have already pointed out that directed execution encompasses separate techniques for dealing with the nondeterminism of concurrency (whom to schedule) and for the mostly orthogonal issue of nondeterminism of input data (what values to provide). Indeed, concurrent programs can be sequentialized using an interleaving semantics (e.g., [14, 33]). Therefore, DART can easily be extended to multi-threaded programs and take advantage of partial-order reductions (e.g., [13, 12]). This is conceptually easy since all the threads share the same memory address space, and the formalization of [16] can be used as is. The case of multi-process programs is more complicated since a good solution requires tracking symbolic variables across processes boundaries and through operating systems objects such as message queues.

4.2   Longer Term

Combining Static and Dynamic Software Model Checking. Directed execution, where the search attempts to systematically sweep all possible execution paths, may be infeasible due to combinatorial explosion. This is a particular problem if the property of interest is a localized one, such as a specific assertion in a program.

In that case, a static analysis can be used to restrict the search space to program paths that may lead to the assertion, hence eliminating irrelevant paths. This reduction can be performed using static program slicing (e.g., [36]), possibly combined with dynamic slicing, in order to prove a priori that some inputs are irrelevant.

Conversely, the precision (and hence practicality) of current static software model checker is seriously limited by the presence of calls to unknown library functions or code fragments that are beyond the capability of current symbolic execution technology such as hash functions or cryptographic functions. Because calls to libraries are frequent in systems code, this is a serious practical limitation for these model checkers, which require models for external libraries. The limitation can be alleviated by using directed execution to test the feasibility of program paths involving calls to libraries or any code that symbolic execution cannot handle easily (such as pointer-intensive code, loops, etc.). In this way, directed execution can be used by static analysis tools as a subroutine to test the feasibility of specific program paths.

Specifying Preconditions. In order to effectively analyze *open* programs, an analysis tool must rely on realistic *environment assumptions*, which represent constraints on program inputs that are believed to hold.

Such constraints are also known as *preconditions*. Two broad approaches exist for specifying preconditions. The first approach consists in program annotations, usually specified directly in some fragment of mathematical logic that is understood by the analysis tool. The second approach consists of adding code in the program itself to filter out unrealistic inputs, for instance using assertions that can be turned on for testing purposes or optionally for runtime monitoring. Ideally, one would like to combine the best of both approaches:

- specify preconditions in the host programming language (say C or Java), which is already familiar to the programmer and includes constructs for expressing sophisticated constraints on input data structures,
- yet have those preconditions interpreted without any loss of precision by the analysis tool as if they had been specified directly in logic.

We call *constraint inference* the latter problem of interpreting code as precisely as if specified directly in logic.

Note that many applications already contain input filtering code: for instance, a protocol implementation will typically first analyze the format of any incoming packet and discard it if it is not well formed. Analysis of such applications thus subsumes analysis of input filtering code; in other words, we need constraint inference capabilities.

Similarly, postconditions could be exploited, not only to check correctness of outputs, but also to direct executions towards potential postcondition violations. Moreover, the postcondition of a component is often the precondition of another one, so specifying pre- and postconditions are closely related problems.

Scalability. As in traditional model checking, *state explosion* is a significant practical limitation of software model checking. Systematically exercising all executable program paths can be prohibitively expensive when the number of such paths is large (or infinite). This problem can be mitigated by *compositional testing* for large programs. For instance, consider a program P that consists of a main function f that calls exactly once another function g. If the set of inputs to f is disjoint from the set of inputs to g, the number $paths(P)$ of execution paths in P is $paths(f) * paths(g)$; but since the inputs to f are independent of those of g, both functions could instead be tested in isolation for a cost of $paths(f) + paths(g)$ while providing the same code and state-space coverage. When the inputs of f and g are not independent, compositional testing amounts of summarizing the results of g when analyzing f. The analysis of g could be summarized using pre- and postconditions constraints, in a manner similar to what is currently done in interprocedural static analysis. This form of *component summarization* extended with temporal behaviors (i.e., information about sequences of inputs/outputs at the component interface) is also similar to *assume/guarantee reasoning* in verification.

5   Conclusions

Over the last ten years, we have seen the birth of the first *software model checkers* for programming languages such as C, C++ and Java. Roughly speaking, two broad approaches have emerged so far. The first approach consists of automatically extracting a model out of a software application by statically analyzing its code and abstracting away details, applying traditional model checking to analyze this abstract model, and then mapping abstract counter-examples back to the code or refining the abstraction (e.g., [1, 21, 7]). The second approach consists of systematically exploring the state space of a software system by driving its executions at run-time via a scheduler and specific inputs (e.g., [14, 38, 28, 9, 16]). As discussed earlier in this paper, both of these approaches to software model checking have their advantages and limitations.

We strongly believe that, over the next ten years, an important topic of research will be combining the static and dynamic approaches to software model checking for falsification purposes. On one hand, there is a real need to improve the effectiveness of current bug finding tools, which are almost all based on imprecise, "may" static analysis and therefore prone to report (too) many false alarms, which in turn has hindered a wider adoption of these tools. On the other hand, there is a large number of static analysis techniques that have not yet been adopted to direct execution.

In this paper, we outlined several possible directions for future work in this area. We also presented specific ideas to tackle some of the key problems faced in this endeavor.

Acknowledgements

We thank Dennis Dams, Cormac Flanagan, Alan Jeffrey, Rupak Majumdar, Kedar Namjoshi, Koushik Sen, Howard Trickey, and Vic Zandy for stimulating discussions on this work. Glenn Bruns provided helpful comments on a draft of this paper. This work was funded in part by NSF CCR-0341658.

References

1. T. Ball and S. Rajamani. The SLAM Toolkit. In *Proceedings of CAV'2001 (13th Conference on Computer Aided Verification)*, volume 2102 of *Lecture Notes in Computer Science*, pages 260–264, Paris, July 2001. Springer-Verlag.
2. C. Barrett and S. Berezin. CVC Lite: A New Implementation of the Cooperating Validity Checker. In *Proceedings of CAV'2004 (16th Conference on Computer Aided Verification)*, Boston, July 2004.
3. D. Beyer, A. J. Chlipala, T. A. Henzinger, R. Jhala, and R. Majumdar. Generating Test from Counterexamples. In *Proceedings of ICSE'2004 (26th International Conference on Software Engineering)*. ACM, May 2004.
4. C. Boyapati, S. Khurshid, and D. Marinov. Korat: Automated testing based on Java predicates. In *Proceedings of ISSTA'2002 (International Symposium on Software Testing and Analysis)*, pages 123–133, 2002.
5. C. Cadar and D. Engler. Execution Generated Test Cases: How to Make Systems Code Crash Itself. In *Proceedings of SPIN'2005 (12th International SPIN Workshop on Model Checking of Software)*, volume 3639 of *Lecture Notes in Computer Science*, San Francisco, August 2005. Springer-Verlag.
6. E. Clarke, D. Kroening, and F. Lerda. A Tool for Checking ANSI-C Programs . In *Tools and Algorithms for the Construction and Analysis of Systems (TACAS 2004)* , volume 2988 of *Lecture Notes in Computer Science*, pages 168–176. Springer, 2004.

7. J. C. Corbett, M. B. Dwyer, J. Hatcliff, S. Laubach, C. S. Pasareanu, Robby, and H. Zheng. Bandera: Extracting Finite-State Models from Java Source Code. In *Proceedings of the 22nd International Conference on Software Engineering*, 2000.
8. C. Csallner and Y. Smaragdakis. Check'n Crash: Combining Static Checking and Testing. In *Proceedings of ICSE'2005 (27th International Conference on Software Engineering)*. ACM, May 2005.
9. M. B. Dwyer, J. Hatcliff, V. R. Prasad, and Robby. Exploiting Object Escape and Locking Information in Partial Order Reduction for Concurrent Object-Oriented Programs. *To appear in Formal Methods in System Design*, 2004.
10. J. Edvardsson. A Survey on Automatic Test Data Generation. In *Proceedings of the 2nd Conference on Computer Science and Engineering*, pages 21–28, Linkoping, October 1999.
11. M. D. Ernst. Static and dynamic analysis: synergy and duality. In *Proceedings of WODA'2003 (ICSE Workshop on Dynamic Analysis)*, Portland, May 2003.
12. C. Flanagan and P. Godefroid. Dynamic Partial-Order Reduction for Model Checking Software. In *Proceedings of POPL'2005 (32nd ACM Symposium on Principles of Programming Languages)*, pages 110–121, Long beach, January 2005.
13. P. Godefroid. *Partial-Order Methods for the Verification of Concurrent Systems – An Approach to the State-Explosion Problem*, volume 1032 of *Lecture Notes in Computer Science*. Springer-Verlag, January 1996.
14. P. Godefroid. Model Checking for Programming Languages using VeriSoft. In *Proceedings of POPL'97 (24th ACM Symposium on Principles of Programming Languages)*, pages 174–186, Paris, January 1997.
15. P. Godefroid. The Soundness of Bugs is What Matters (Position Paper). In *Proceedings of BUGS'2005 (PLDI'2005 Workshop on the Evaluation of Software Defect Detection Tools)*, Chicago, June 2005.
16. P. Godefroid, N. Klarlund, and K. Sen. DART: Directed Automated Random Testing. In *Proceedings of PLDI'2005 (ACM SIGPLAN 2005 Conference on Programming Language Design and Implementation)*, pages 213–223, Chicago, June 2005.
17. S. Graf and H. Saidi. Construction of Abstract State Graphs with PVS. In *Proceedings of the 9th International Conference on Computer Aided Verification*, volume 1254 of *Lecture Notes in Computer Science*, pages 72–83, Haifa, June 1997. Springer-Verlag.
18. E. Gunter and D. Peled. Path Exploration Tool. In *Proceedings of TACAS'1999 (5th Conference on Tools and Algorithms for the Construction and Analysis of Systems)*, volume 1579 of *Lecture Notes in Computer Science*, Amsterdam, March 1999. Springer.
19. N. Gupta, A. P. Mathur, and M. L. Soffa. Generating test data for branch coverage. In *Proceedings of the 15th IEEE International Conference on Automated Software Engineering*, pages 219–227, September 2000.
20. R. Hastings and B. Joyce. Purify: Fast Detection of Memory Leaks and Access Errors. In *Proceedings of the Usenix Winter 1992 Technical Conference*, pages 125–138, Berkeley, January 1992.
21. T. Henzinger, R. Jhala, R. Majumdar, and G. Sutre. Lazy Abstraction. In *Proceedings of the 29th ACM Symposium on Principles of Programming Languages*, pages 58–70, Portland, January 2002.
22. G. J. Holzmann and M. H. Smith. A Practical Method for Verifying Event-Driven Software. In *Proceedings of the 21st International Conference on Software Engineering*, pages 597–607, 1999.

23. Ics. web page: http://www.icansolve.com/.
24. J. C. King. Symbolic Execution and Program Testing. *Journal of the ACM*, 19(7):385–394, 1976.
25. B. Korel. A dynamic Approach of Test Data Generation. In *IEEE Conference on Software Maintenance*, pages 311–317, San Diego, November 1990.
26. E. Larson and T. Austin. High Coverage Detection of Input-Related Security Faults. In *Proceedings of 12th USENIX Security Symposium*, Washington D.C., August 2003.
27. lp_solve. web page: http://groups.yahoo.com/group/lp_solve/.
28. M. Musuvathi, D. Park, A. Chou, D. Engler, and D. Dill. CMC: A pragmatic approach to model checking real code. In *Proceedings of OSDI'2002*, 2002.
29. G. J. Myers. *The Art of Software Testing*. Wiley, 1979.
30. G. C. Necula, S. McPeak, and W. Weimer. CCured: Type-Safe Retrofitting of Legacy Code. In *Proceedings of POPL'02 (29th ACM Symposium on Principles of Programming Languages)*, pages 128–139, Portland, January 2002.
31. J. Offutt and J. Hayes. A Semantic Model of Program Faults. In *Proceedings of ISSTA'96 (International Symposium on Software Testing and Analysis)*, pages 195–200, San Diego, January 1996.
32. C. Pasareanu, R. Pelanek, and W. Visser. Concrete Model Checking with Abstract Matching and Refinement. In *Proceedings of CAV'2005 (17th Conference on Computer Aided Verification)*, Edinburgh, July 2005.
33. S. Qadeer and D. Wu. KISS: Keep It Simple and Sequential. In *Proceedings of PLDI'2004 (ACM SIGPLAN 2004 Conference on Programming Language Design and Implementation)*, Washington D.C., June 2004.
34. K. Sen, D. Marinov, and G. Agha. CUTE: A Concolic Unit testing Engine for C. In *Proceedings of FSE'2005 (13th International Symposium on the Foundations of Software Engineering)*, Lisbon, September 2005.
35. Simplify. web page: http://research.compaq.com/SRC/esc/Simplify.html.
36. F. Tip. A survey of program slicing techniques. *Journal of Programming Languages*, 3(3):121–189, 1995.
37. Valgrind. web page: http://valgrind.org/.
38. W. Visser, K. Havelund, G. Brat, and S. Park. Model Checking Programs. In *Proceedings of ASE'2000 (15th International Conference on Automated Software Engineering)*, Grenoble, September 2000.
39. W. Visser, C. Pasareanu, and S. Khurshid. Test Input Generation with Java PathFinder. In *Proceedings of ACM SIGSOFT ISSTA'04 (International Symposium on Software Testing and Analysis)*, Boston, July 2004.
40. T. Xie, D. Marinov, W. Schulte, and D. Notkin. Symstra: A Framework for Generating Object-Oriented Unit Tests Using Symbolic Execution. In *Proceedings of TACAS'05 (11th Conference on Tools and Algorithms for the Construction and Analysis of Systems)*, volume 3440 of *LNCS*, pages 365–381. Springer, 2005.

Adaptive Techniques for Specification Matching in Embedded Systems: A Comparative Study

Robi Malik[1] and Partha S. Roop[2]

[1] Department of Computer Science,
The University of Waikato, Hamilton, New Zealand
robi@cs.waikato.ac.nz
[2] Department of Electrical and Computer Engineering,
The University of Auckland, Auckland, New Zealand
p.roop@auckland.ac.nz

Abstract. The specification matching problem in embedded systems is to determine whether an existing component may be adapted suitably to match the requirements of a new *specification*. Recently, a refinement called *forced simulation* has been introduced to formally address this problem. It has been established that when a forced similarity relation exists between a component and its specification, an *adapter process* can be constructed so that the composition of the adapter and the component fulfil the specification. This looks very similar to synthesis methods in supervisory control theory, where a controller is constructed to make a plant satisfy a desired specification. However, due to the need for *state-based hiding* in specification matching, supervisory control theory is not directly applicable. This paper develops a supervisory control based solution to the specification matching problem by modifying the problem representation. Subsequently, a comparison of the forced simulation and supervisory control based specification matching methods is made.

KeyWords: Formal verification, specification matching, embedded systems, supervisory control, finite-state machines, bisimulation.

1 Introduction

Reuse techniques for hardware [4, 13] and software [16] have been the focus of research fuelled by increasing system complexity, shorter design cycles, and the obvious need for productivity improvement. Some of the common problems that need to tackled in both domains to facilitate reuse include:

1. *Developmental issues*: how to identify and develop generic components that are easily reusable.
2. *Database issues*: how to store, index and retrieve reusable components; also, whether generic, domain specific and open databases can be created.

J. Romijn, G. Smith, and J. van de Pol (Eds.): IFM 2005, LNCS 3771, pp. 33–52, 2005.

3. *Matching issues*: how to decide whether an existing, pre-verified component matches given requirements.
4. *Compositional issues*: how to compose a set of matched components to create a large system.

This paper addresses the third issue of matching in the context of *reactive* and *embedded systems*, hereafter referred to as the *specification matching* problem. The specification matching problem addresses the following question: given an existing component, or *device*, and a new *specification*, can the device be used to implement the specification. Specification matching is a key to automated retrieval and reuse.

Many researchers have investigated specification matching to facilitate reuse of *transformational software* [10, 26, 19, 11]. In this context, the problem is to check whether a *program* can be used for a given specification either directly or with some modification. Some of these techniques [19] rely on heuristics, while others [10, 26, 11] use pre- and post-condition matching. Matching of state-based modular components using Z-like formal notation is addressed in [8], and a graph transformation-based approach for service discovery in Web services is proposed in [5]. The problem of adaptation for software components is developed in [7]. These techniques are not directly applicable for the reuse of reactive components in embedded systems since such components are *control-dominated*, in contrast to data-dominated transformational programs.

Similar to specification matching for software, many attempts for matching hardware components have been made. In [18], an informal mapping algorithm to automatically map a design function to a system level component is proposed. Methods for specification matching and verification of circuits using polynomials are proposed in [24]. Also, low-level components such as ALUs have been successfully reused [12]. These techniques, though suitable for low-level components, are unsuitable for matching system-level components for embedded applications, which require matching of reactive behaviours (which is control-dominated and dynamic). Hence, techniques for specification matching of software or low-level hardware are not directly applicable to embedded applications.

The general problem of specification matching can be described as follows.

"Given a device D and a specification F, does there exist an adapter A that can make the device D satisfy the new specification F?"

Recently, a tailored solution to solve this problem for embedded systems has been proposed [22]. This approach uses the new concept of *forced simulation*, which provides a necessary and sufficient condition for the existence of an adapter.

At the same time, supervisory control theory of discrete event systems [20, 3] provides a general framework to solve similar problems—namely to determine whether a controller exists to make a given environment satisfy a given specification. However, due to the specific requirements of specification matching, this framework is not directly applicable. This paper shows how the specification matching problem can be reformulated for supervisory control theory to become applicable, proposes a solution to the specification matching based on supervisory control, and compares it to the tailored solution using forced simulation.

In Sect. 2, the specification matching problem is introduced by means of an example. Next, Sect. 3 provides the formal notation used in the paper. Then two solutions to specification matching are discussed, first using forced simulation in Sect. 4 and second using supervisory control in Sect. 5. Finally, Sect. 6 compares the two approaches, and Sect. 7 makes some concluding remarks.

2 Coffee Brewer Example

This section introduces the problem of component matching for embedded systems using the specification of a simple coffee brewer, which is used as a running example throughout this paper. Finite-state machines are used to present the example, as they are a common means to describe the dynamics of reactive and embedded system behaviour [3].

Figure 1 shows a finite-state machine model of the coffee brewer. This device allows the brewing of four or eight cups of coffee. Initially, the user sets the

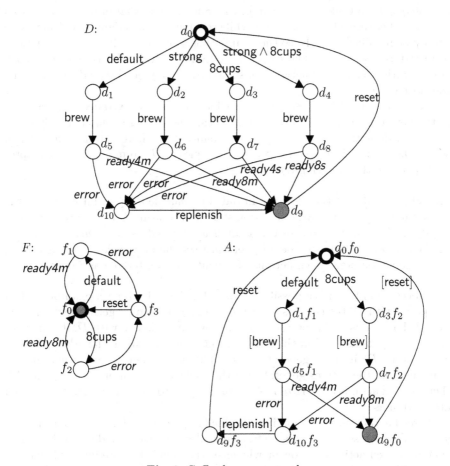

Fig. 1. Coffee brewer example

switches strong to determine the desired coffee strength, medium or strong, and 8cups to choose four or eight cups of coffee. It is possible that no switch is set (action default), exactly one switch is set (actions strong or 8cups), or that both switches are set (action strong ∧ 8cups). Then brewing is started by activating the brewcycle switch (brew). After completion, the device produces the desired amount of coffee (*ready4m*, *ready8m*, *ready4s*, or *ready8s*), or reports an *error*, indicating that the coffee powder has run out. In this case, the brewer has to be replenished with powder (replenish). Finally, there is a reset switch to return the brewer to its initial state and start another operation.

Suppose that such a brewer device has been built and is available. Let D be its finite-state machine description as shown in Fig. 1. Also suppose that an altered specification F, also shown in Fig. 1, demands a brewer that provides either four or eight cups of coffee of medium strength, and the existing device D should be used to implement it, if possible.

The central idea behind reusing an existing device to implement a new specification F is to construct an external process which moves in lock-step with D and *adapts* D so that D then matches F. Such an external process is called an *adapter*. There are a few constraints while constructing an adapter. The device D cannot be modified directly, so the adapter has to interact with it via the actions of its external interface. Therefore, the internal states of D are not accessible. However, the sequence of actions consumed by D may be observed to determine the state of D.

To achieve its objectives, an adapter has to *suppress* extraneous behaviours of the device in certain states (since D is capable of more behaviours than F), and *generate* extra inputs to the device (since D is more detailed than F) in some other states. In the coffee brewer example, for D to match F, the adapter must perform the following tasks:

1. When the device (D) is in the initial state d_0, the adapter must disable the strength switch, i.e., disable action strong, preventing D from entering states d_2 and d_4. Such actions of the adapter are termed as *disabling*.
2. When D is in state d_1, the adapter must set the brewcycle switch to on, i.e, cause action brew. Such actions of the adapter are termed as *forcing*.

Process A in Fig. 1 is a possible adapter for the coffee brewer example. When composed with D, the composite system (D and A acting together) exhibits the same behaviour as F. When the adapter moves in lock-step with D, it consumes the same inputs as D from the environment. However, when the adapter *forces* an input to D, it must generate that input itself. Hence, forced actions are different from the actions generated in the environment. In order to distinguish them, forced actions are written as $[\sigma]$, in contrast to environment actions which are written as σ.

Forced actions are common in embedded applications, for example to trigger an initialisation sequence to select a particular operation mode of a device. In general, forced actions can occur whenever the device is more detailed than its specification, so the adapter needs to trigger actions that do not appear in the specification. Sometimes, it can depend on the state of the device whether an action is forced or not. In the coffee brewer example, this occurs in state d_9 of the device, which has two matching states $d_9 f_0$ and $d_9 f_3$ in the adapter. In state $d_9 f_3$, reset occurs as an external action from the environment, while it is forced by the adapter in state $d_9 f_0$. Thus, a given signal may be hidden in one state (due to forcing) and be visible in another state (if that signal is obtained from the environment and not forced by the adapter).

This *state-based hiding* is characteristic for specification matching in embedded systems. In the coffee brewer example, the specification F is not in any way directly equivalent to the device D, nor is there an obvious *refinement relation* [2, 15] between the two. The correspondence between D and F can only be established by treating the reset action differently in states f_0 and f_3 of F.

3   Notation and Preliminaries

3.1   Languages

Traces and languages are a simple means to describe process behaviours. Their basic building blocks are *actions*, which are taken from a finite *alphabet* Σ. In addition, the *hidden* action τ does not belong to Σ. To include it explicitly, the alphabet $\Sigma_\tau = \Sigma \cup \{\tau\}$ is used.

Σ^* denotes the set of all finite *strings* or *traces* of the form $\sigma_1 \sigma_2 \cdots \sigma_k$ of actions from Σ, including the *empty trace* ε. A *language* over Σ is any subset $L \subseteq \Sigma^*$. The *concatenation* of two traces $s, t \in \Sigma^*$ is written as st. Languages and alphabets can also be catenated: $L\Sigma = \{ s\sigma \in \Sigma^* \mid s \in L, \sigma \in \Sigma \}$. The *prefix-closure* $\overline{L}$ of a language $L \subseteq \Sigma^*$ is the set of all prefixes of traces in L, i.e., $\overline{L} = \{ s \in \Sigma^* \mid st \in L \text{ for some } t \in \Sigma^* \}$.

3.2   Processes

Processes are used to describe the components of embedded systems, so the functions and devices used in specification matching are modelled as processes. Processes are represented as *labelled transition systems*

$$P = \langle \Sigma, Q, \rightarrow, q^\circ, Q^m \rangle , \tag{1}$$

where Σ is the alphabet of actions, Q is the set of *states*, $\rightarrow \subseteq Q \times \Sigma_\tau \times Q$ is the *transition relation*, $q^\circ \in Q$ is the *initial state*, and Q^m is the set of *marked* or *terminal* states. If the state set Q is finite, then P is also called a *finite-state machine*. The transition relation is also written as

$$q \xrightarrow{\sigma} q' \quad \text{if and only if} \quad (q, \sigma, q') \in \rightarrow . \tag{2}$$

Finite-state machines can be represented graphically as shown in Fig. 1. States are represented as nodes, with the initial state highlighted by a thick border and terminal states coloured grey. The transition relation is represented by labelled edges.

A process is said to be *deterministic* if it does not contain any transitions labelled τ, and $q \xrightarrow{\sigma} q'$ and $q \xrightarrow{\sigma} q''$ implies $q' = q''$. In this paper, specifications, devices, and adapters are assumed to be deterministic. Nondeterministic processes may result from abstraction and hiding.

The transition relation $\rightarrow$ is extended to a relation $\rightarrow \subseteq Q \times \Sigma_\tau^* \times Q$ by letting $q \xrightarrow{\varepsilon} q$ for all $q \in Q$, and $q \xrightarrow{s\sigma} q''$ if there exists $q' \in Q$ such that $q \xrightarrow{s} q'$ and $q' \xrightarrow{\sigma} q''$. To handle the hidden action τ, another transition relation $\Rightarrow \subseteq Q \times \Sigma^* \times Q$ describes the *visible* evolutions of a process. It is defined as

$$q \xRightarrow{\varepsilon} q' \quad \text{if} \quad q = q_1 \xrightarrow{\tau} \cdots \xrightarrow{\tau} q_n = q' \text{ for some } q_1, \ldots, q_n \in Q \ ; \tag{3}$$

$$q \xRightarrow{s\sigma} q' \quad \text{if} \quad q \xRightarrow{s} q_s \xrightarrow{\sigma} q_{s\sigma} \xRightarrow{\varepsilon} q' \text{ for some } q_s, q_{s\sigma} \in Q \ . \tag{4}$$

The *possible behaviour* of a process $P = \langle \Sigma, Q, \rightarrow, q^\circ, Q^m \rangle$ is described by the language

$$L(P) \stackrel{\text{def}}{=} \{ s \in \Sigma^* \mid q^\circ \xRightarrow{s} q \text{ for some } q \in Q \} \ . \tag{5}$$

When several processes are running in parallel, lock-step synchronisation in the style of CSP [9] is used. A shared action can only be performed if all interacting processes can perform that action. This is different from CCS style synchronisation [17], which allows a process to evolve autonomously ignoring the other processes.

Definition 1. Let $P_1 = \langle \Sigma, Q_1, \rightarrow_1, q_1^\circ, Q_1^m \rangle$ and $P_2 = \langle \Sigma, Q_2, \rightarrow_2, q_2^\circ, Q_2^m \rangle$ be two processes, both using the alphabet Σ. The *synchronous product* $P_1 \parallel P_2$ of P_1 and P_2 is defined as

$$P_1 \parallel P_2 \stackrel{\text{def}}{=} \langle \Sigma, Q_1 \times Q_2, \rightarrow, (q_1^\circ, q_2^\circ), Q_1^m \times Q_2^m \rangle \ , \tag{6}$$

where $(q_1, q_2) \xrightarrow{\sigma} (q_1', q_2')$ if and only if $q_1 \xrightarrow{\sigma}_1 q_1'$ and $q_2 \xrightarrow{\sigma}_2 q_2'$.

Furthermore, process-algebraic *hiding* is introduced in the standard way [23]. Given a process P, the result of hiding actions $\Sigma' \subseteq \Sigma$ is denoted by $P \setminus \Sigma'$. This process has action alphabet $\Sigma \setminus \Sigma'$ and is constructed from P by replacing every occurrence of an action in Σ' by the hidden action τ.

3.3 Equivalence

To address questions of specification matching and adaptation, concepts of equivalence are needed to determine whether two processes are to be considered as equal. As long as only deterministic processes are involved, it is common to use *trace equivalence*, which considers processes as equivalent if their languages are equal. This equivalence is used in supervisory control theory [20].

For nondeterministic processes, various ways of considering two processes as equivalent exist [25]. The forced simulation approach [22] uses *weak bisimulation* or *observation equivalence* [17] as the underlying equivalence. Two processes P_1 and P_2 are weakly bisimilar if every action of P_1 is matched by an identical action in P_2, possibly preceded and/or succeeded by hidden actions. The definition is recursive so that the resultant states must also be weakly bisimilar.

Definition 2. Let $P_1 = \langle \Sigma, Q_1, \rightarrow_1, q_1^\circ, Q_1^m \rangle$ and $P_2 = \langle \Sigma, Q_2, \rightarrow_2, q_2^\circ, Q_2^m \rangle$ be two processes. A relation $R \subseteq Q_1 \times Q_2$ is a *weak bisimulation* if, whenever $(q_1, q_2) \in R$, the following hold for all $\sigma \in \Sigma$.

1. If $q_1 \xrightarrow{\sigma} q_1'$ then $q_2 \xRightarrow{\sigma} q_2'$ for some $q_2' \in Q_2$ such that $(q_1', q_2') \in R$;
2. If $q_2 \xrightarrow{\sigma} q_2'$ then $q_1 \xRightarrow{\sigma} q_1'$ for some $q_1' \in Q_1$ such that $(q_1', q_2') \in R$.

P_1 and P_2 are called *weakly bisimilar*, written $P_1 \approx P_2$, if there exists a weak bisimulation $R \subseteq Q_1 \times Q_2$ such that $(q_1^\circ, q_2^\circ) \in R$.

3.4 Adapter Processes

Adapters are special processes that interact with a device by performing two types of actions—*disabling* and *forcing*. Disabling is modelled in the standard way using lock-step synchronisation between the adapter and device. To model forcing, a special kind of actions is used.

Every action in Σ can be forced by the adapter, and this is written as a separate *forced* action $[\sigma] \notin \Sigma$. For a subset $\Sigma' \subseteq \Sigma$, it is convenient to write $[\Sigma'] = \{ [\sigma] \mid \sigma \in \Sigma' \}$. Actions that are not forced, i.e., actions in Σ are called *external* as they can be observed by the environment when executed. An adapter is a process that uses forced and external actions.

Definition 3. An *adapter* is a process whose set of actions is

$$\Sigma_{\text{fsim}} = \Sigma \cup [\Sigma] . \tag{7}$$

This general definition allows adapter processes that can execute both forced and external actions in the same state, which is not desired in practice.

Definition 4. An adapter $A = \langle \Sigma_{\text{fsim}}, Q, \rightarrow, q^\circ, Q^m \rangle$ is said to be *well-formed*, if for all $q, q' \in Q$ and $\alpha \in \Sigma$ such that $q \xrightarrow{[\alpha]} q'$ the following holds:

$$\text{if} \quad q \xrightarrow{\sigma} q'' \quad \text{for some } \sigma \in \Sigma_{\text{fsim}} \quad \text{then} \quad \sigma = [\alpha] . \tag{8}$$

A well-formed and deterministic adapter has only one successor for states where forcing is performed. Other states may have more than one successor. Thus, a well-formed adapter either forces a single action, or enables some of the external actions of the device and lets the environment execute one of them.

The interaction between an adapter and a device depends on whether an action is forced or external. To describe it formally, a new *forced composition* operator is introduced in [22].

Definition 5. Let $A = \langle \Sigma_{\text{fsim}}, Q_A, \rightarrow_A, q_A^\circ, Q_A^m \rangle$ be an adapter, and let $D = \langle \Sigma, Q_D, \rightarrow_D, q_D^\circ, Q_D^m \rangle$ be a device. The *forced composition* $A \mathbin{/\!\!/} D$ of A and D is

$$A \mathbin{/\!\!/} D \stackrel{\text{def}}{=} \langle \Sigma, Q_A \times Q_D, \rightarrow, (q_A^\circ, q_D^\circ), Q_A^m \times Q_D^m \rangle , \tag{9}$$

where

$$(q_A, q_D) \xrightarrow{\tau} (q_A', q_D') \text{ if } q_A \xrightarrow{[\alpha]}_A q_A' \text{ and } q_D \xrightarrow{\alpha}_D q_D', \text{ for some } \alpha \in \Sigma; \tag{10}$$

$$(q_A, q_D) \xrightarrow{\sigma} (q_A', q_D') \text{ if } q_A \xrightarrow{\sigma}_A q_A' \text{ and } q_D \xrightarrow{\sigma}_D q_D', \text{ for } \sigma \in \Sigma. \tag{11}$$

When A forces an action, the forced composition $A \parallel D$ performs an unobservable τ transition (10)—this is called a *forced move*. Otherwise, $A \parallel D$ can perform an observable or *external move*, with both D and A simultaneously responding to the same signal (11). The forced composition $A \parallel D$ is deterministic if both A and D are deterministic and the adapter A is well-formed.

3.5   Supervisory Control

Supervisory control theory for *discrete event systems* [20, 3] is a general theory to describe under which circumstances a system can be controlled in such a way that it satisfies a given specification. The system to be controlled is called the *environment* or *plant*, and the *specification* describes a desired behaviour of this plant. In the context of specification matching, the plant corresponds to the device, and the specification corresponds to the desired function.

The plant and specification are both represented as languages. The language L of the plant, or device, describes the physically possible behaviour of the device. The specification language K characterises a largest acceptable behaviour, or a *safety property*. The objective is to control the device in such a way that it never can perform a trace that is not in K.

Supervisory control theory supports *uncontrollable* actions. These are actions performed by the plant, i.e., the device that cannot be forced or disabled by an adapter. Typical examples of uncontrollable actions are the outputs or interrupts generated by a device, which cannot be stopped by any adapter—the adapter can only observe them. Therefore, the set Σ of actions is partitioned into two disjoint subsets: the set Σ_c of *controllable actions* and the set Σ_u of *uncontrollable actions*.

Supervisory control theory is concerned about whether a given specification language K can be achieved by controlling a given device with behaviour L, with the possibility of uncontrollable actions in mind. This is defined by the fundamental concept of *controllability* [20].

Definition 6. Let K and L be two prefix-closed languages. K is said to be *controllable* with respect to L if

$$K\Sigma_u \cap L \subseteq K . \tag{12}$$

Thus, a language K is controllable with respect to L if there is no trace in K that can be followed by an uncontrollable action possible in L but not possible in K. This means that, given a device behaviour L, the behaviour given by K can be achieved by disabling controllable actions only. Note that the languages $\emptyset$, L, and Σ^* are all trivially controllable with respect to L.

If a language K is controllable with respect to a device, then it is possible to construct a *supervisor* which, when running together with the device, produces exactly the behaviour K. A supervisor is a process running in lock-step with the device, which can observe all actions of the device, but only disable controllable actions in order to achieve its objective. It is used in similar ways as an adapter in specification matching.

Not every language is controllable. If a language K is not controllable, then it is not possible to construct a supervisor, or adapter, that achieves the behaviour K, because this would lead to a critical situation where the device can execute an *uncontrollable* action not allowed by the specification K. In order to avoid such problems, the supervisor needs to disable *controllable* actions earlier to prevent the critical situation from being reached. In other words, the behaviour K needs to be restricted to some sub-behaviour K'.

Therefore, it is of interest to find a sublanguage K' of K that is controllable with respect to L. This leads to the definition of the set $\mathcal{C}(K, L)$, which contains all sublanguages of a language K that are controllable with respect to L:

$$\mathcal{C}(K, L) \stackrel{\text{def}}{=} \{ K' \subseteq K \mid K' \text{ is controllable with respect to } L \} . \tag{13}$$

It is easy to show that the union of any number of controllable languages is again controllable [20]. Therefore, the set $\mathcal{C}(K, L)$ contains a unique supremal element

$$\sup \mathcal{C}(K, L) \stackrel{\text{def}}{=} \bigcup_{K' \in \mathcal{C}(K,L)} K'. \tag{14}$$

This supremal element is known as the *supremal controllable sublanguage* of K with respect to L. It characterises the largest possible sub-behaviour within K that can be achieved by controlling L. Various algorithms to compute it are discussed in the literature [14, 1].

The existence of the supremal controllable sublanguage leads to the following result [20], which is central in supervisory control theory. It answers the fundamental question under which conditions there exists an adapter that can control a given device in such a way that its behaviour never exceeds a given specification.

Theorem 1. Let K and L be two prefix-closed languages. There exists a supervisor S which, when running together with a plant with behaviour L, can guarantee that its behaviour never exceeds K, if and only if

$$\sup \mathcal{C}(K, L) \neq \emptyset . \tag{15}$$

Thus, the nonemptiness of the supremal controllable sublanguage is a necessary and sufficient condition for the existence of a supervisor, or adapter, for a given device and specification. Furthermore, $\sup \mathcal{C}(K, L)$ characterises the maximally permissive behaviour that can be achieved by an adapter controlling the device without violating the specification.

3.6   Nonblocking

In addition to controllability, supervisors are required to perform some minimum functionality. In supervisory control theory, this is achieved by imposing a weak liveness condition, called *nonblocking* [20]. It is required that the system is always able to complete its tasks. The completion of a task is traditionally modelled using a second language, the so-called *marked* language, which is defined using the marked states of a process.

Definition 7. Let $P = \langle \Sigma, Q, \rightarrow, q^\circ, Q^m \rangle$ be a process. The *marked language* of P is defined as

$$M(P) \stackrel{\text{def}}{=} \{ s \in \Sigma^* \mid q^\circ \stackrel{s}{\Rightarrow} q^m \text{ for some } q^m \in Q^m \} . \tag{16}$$

The marked language of a process represents the set of its completed tasks. Clearly, every prefix of such a completed task is a possible behaviour of a process, i.e., $\overline{M(P)} \subseteq L(P)$. The converse inclusion, while certainly desirable, is not always satisfied. If it is, the process is called *nonblocking*.

Definition 8. A deterministic process $P = \langle \Sigma, Q, \rightarrow, q^\circ, Q^m \rangle$ is said to be *nonblocking* if $L(P) = \overline{M(P)}$.

To be nonblocking is the weak liveness requirement underlying supervisory control theory. It means that every trace can somehow be extended to form a completed task, or, in the terminology of labelled transition systems, a marked state can be reached from every reachable state. All the processes shown in Fig. 1 are nonblocking, because a grey marked state is reachable from every other state.

If a process does not have this property, it is called *blocking*. A blocking process contains states from where no terminal state can be reached anymore. This is usually not desired, as it indicates the possibility of deadlock or livelock in the system.

The property to be nonblocking is not always easy to establish. When two nonblocking processes are composed, this may result in a blocking process. Supervisory control synthesis as described by equation (14) removes transitions from processes and therefore may produce a blocking behaviour. To solve this problem, supervisory control synthesis has been extended to eliminate blocking states from the synthesis result and produce a least restrictive sub-behaviour of the specification that is both controllable and nonblocking [20, 3].

4   Specification Matching Using Forced Simulation

This section introduces the specification matching problem formally and proposes a first solution. Given a specification F and a device D, the task is to determine whether there exists an adapter A such that $A \mathbin{/\!/} D$ has equivalent behaviour to F. For specification matching, weak bisimulation is the appropriate equivalence. Therefore, the following definition is introduced in [22].

Definition 9. Let F and D be two processes. D can implement function F, or D *matches* F, if there exists a well-formed and deterministic adapter A such that $A \mathbin{/\!/} D \approx F$.

The main task in specification matching is to determine whether there exists an adapter for arbitrary pairs of devices and specifications. In [22], the following simulation relation called *forced simulation* is introduced, which provides a necessary and sufficient condition for adapter existence.

Definition 10. Let $F = \langle \Sigma, Q_F, \rightarrow_F, q_F^\circ, Q_F^m \rangle$ and $D = \langle \Sigma, Q_D, \rightarrow_D, q_D^\circ, Q_D^m \rangle$ be two processes. A relation $R \subseteq Q_F \times Q_D \times \Sigma^*$ is called a *forced simulation* between F and D, if the three conditions below hold. The notation $q_F \ R^s \ q_D$ is used as a shorthand for $(q_F, q_D, s) \in R$.

1. If $q_F \ R^\varepsilon \ q_D$, then for all $\sigma \in \Sigma$ and all $q_F' \in Q_F$ such that $q_F \xrightarrow{\sigma} q_F'$, there exist $q_D' \in Q_D$ and $s \in \Sigma^*$ such that $q_D \xrightarrow{\sigma} q_D'$ and $q_F' \ R^s \ q_D'$;
2. If $q_F \ R^{\sigma s} \ q_D$ for $\sigma \in \Sigma$ and $s \in \Sigma^*$, then there exists $q_D' \in Q_D$ such that $q_D \xrightarrow{\sigma} q_D'$ and $q_F \ R^s \ q_D'$;
3. $q_F^\circ \ R^s \ q_D^\circ$ for some $s \in \Sigma^*$.

In the above definition, there are two ways how states $q_F \in Q_F$ and $q_D \in Q_D$ can be related via a forced simulation R.

1. q_F and q_D are *directly related* if for every transition $q_F \xrightarrow{\sigma} q_F'$ in F, there is a matching transition $q_D \xrightarrow{\sigma} q_D'$ in D where q_F' and q_D' are also related. In this case, $q_F \ R^\varepsilon \ q_D$. For example, states f_1 and d_5 in Fig. 1 are directly related.
2. q_F and q_D are *related via forcing sequence* s if there exists a successor state q_D' in D such that q_D' is reachable from q_D via trace s where q_F and q_D' are related via R. In this case, $q_F \ R^s \ q_D$. For example, states f_1 and d_1 in Fig. 1 are related via forcing sequence brew.

These possibilities are formalised in the first two conditions of definition 10. In addition, the start states are required to be related via some forcing sequence s.

Definition 11. Let F and D be two processes. F is *forced similar* to D, written $F \lesssim_{\text{fsim}} D$, if there exists a forced simulation between F and D.

Example 1. In the coffee brewer example, specification F and device D in Fig. 1 are forced similar because of the following forced simulation relation.

$$R = \{ (f_0, d_0, \varepsilon), (f_0, d_9, \text{reset}), (f_1, d_1, \text{brew}), (f_1, d_5, \varepsilon), \qquad (17)$$
$$(f_2, d_3, \text{brew}), (f_2, d_7, \varepsilon), (f_3, d_9, \varepsilon), (f_3, d_{10}, \text{replenish}) \} .$$

In this example, R is unique. In general, however, there may be many forced simulation relations between a specification and a device.

The main result of [22] states that the existence of a forced simulation relation between specification and device is a necessary and sufficient condition for the existence of an adapter.

Theorem 2. Let F and D be two deterministic processes. There exists a well-formed and deterministic adapter A such that $A//D \approx F$ if and only if $F \lesssim_{\text{fsim}} D$.

Forced simulation can be computed either using a modification of simulation algorithms [22], or using tabled logic programming engines such as XSB [21]. These methods can be used to determine whether an adapter exists for a given device and specification, and if so, to compute it.

5   Specification Matching Using Supervisory Control

Supervisory control theory provides an alternative way to determine whether a given specification can be achieved by controlling a plant. At a first glance, this looks very similar to the specification matching problem, with the additional possibility to handle uncontrollable actions.

Unfortunately, it is not possible to apply supervisory control synthesis directly to component matching of a device D and specification F. The reason for this is the need for *state-based hiding* in combination with forcing. To illustrate the problem, consider the coffee brewer example in Fig. 1 once more. In the setting of supervisory control, the specification F for the coffee brewer is treated such that action reset is disallowed in state f_0, both as a forced and as an external action. However, the implemented brewer being reused (D) allows reset to occur in state d_9. Moreover, state d_9 in D needs to be matched to state f_0 in F. Since this matching cannot happen directly, reset needs to be forced, as it is done by the correct adapter A on its transition from $d_9 f_0$ to $d_0 f_0$. Such a solution is not acceptable as a supervisor, because it allows reset to occur in state f_0 of a specification, which requires that action to be disabled.

Hence, there is a need to alter the models of F and D, so that forced and external actions can be treated separately by supervisory control synthesis. First, the device D is modelled as a plant $[D]$ using different actions for the external and forced steps.

Definition 12. Let $D = \langle \Sigma, Q, \rightarrow, q^\circ, Q^m \rangle$ be a process, and $\Sigma_c \subseteq \Sigma$ be the set of controllable actions. Define the plant process $[D] = \langle \Sigma_{\text{fsim}}, Q, \rightarrow_{[D]}, q^\circ, Q^m \rangle$ where

- $q \xrightarrow{\sigma}_{[D]} q'$ if $\sigma \in \Sigma$ and $q \xrightarrow{\sigma} q'$;
- $q \xrightarrow{[\sigma]}_{[D]} q'$ if $\sigma \in \Sigma_c$ and $q \xrightarrow{\sigma} q'$.

The plant model $[D]$ is obtained from D by adding forced transitions to all transitions labelled with a controllable action. This assumes that exactly the controllable actions can be forced by the adapter. Other ways of constructing $[D]$ are conceivable, where forced transitions are included selectively only for particular actions, or only from particular states.

Example 2. Figure 2 shows the plant model $[D]$ obtained from the device D in Fig. 1, under the assumption that actions *ready4m*, *ready8m*, *ready4s*, *ready8s*, and *error* are uncontrollable.

The construction of $[D]$ captures the way how an adapter interacts with a device via the composition operator $\|$ developed for forced simulation. Given an adapter A and a device D, the following relationship is easy to see.

$$A \mathbin{/\!/} D = (A \| [D]) \setminus [\Sigma] \tag{18}$$

Having constructed the plant model $[D]$ using the extended alphabet Σ_{fsim}, the specification also needs to be modified to use the same alphabet. This is done in the standard way of supervisory control theory, by adding *selfloops*.

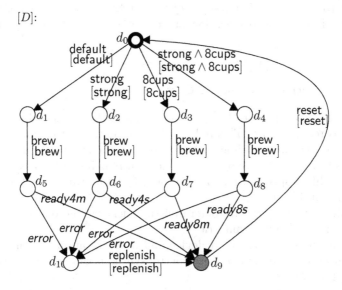

Fig. 2. Modified plant for coffee brewer

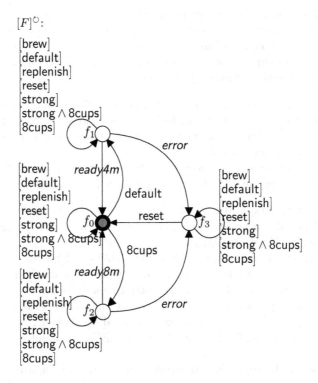

Fig. 3. Modified specification for coffee brewer

Definition 13. Let $F = \langle \Sigma, Q, \rightarrow, q°, Q^m \rangle$, and $\Sigma_c \subseteq \Sigma$ be the set of controllable actions. Define the specification process $[F]^\circlearrowleft = \langle \Sigma_{\text{fsim}}, Q, \rightarrow_{[\circlearrowleft]}, q°, Q^m \rangle$ where

- $q \xrightarrow{\sigma}_{[\circlearrowleft]} q'$ if $\sigma \in \Sigma$ and $q \xrightarrow{\sigma} q'$;
- $q \xrightarrow{[\sigma]}_{[\circlearrowleft]} q$ for each $\sigma \in \Sigma_c$ and $q \in Q$.

The modified specification $[F]^\circlearrowleft$ is obtained from F by adding selfloops for all forced actions to each state. This reflects the interpretation that forced actions are allowed to occur at any time without violating the specification, and when the device is forced, the state of the specification remains unchanged. Figure 3 shows the modified specification $[F]^\circlearrowleft$ obtained in this way from the original specification F in Fig. 1.

Obviously, $[D]$ and $[F]^\circlearrowleft$ are deterministic whenever the original device D and specification F are deterministic.

Given a plant model $[D]$ for a device and a specification automaton $[F]^\circlearrowleft$ augmented with selfloops, supervisory control synthesis can be used to compute an adapter A such that

$$L(A) = \sup \mathcal{C}(L([F]^\circlearrowleft), L([D])) . \tag{19}$$

When applied to the coffee brewer plant $[D]$ and specification $[F]^\circlearrowleft$ in Fig. 2, this leads to an adapter A as shown in Fig. 1. In this case, supervisory control synthesis produces exactly the same result as the forced simulation method.

By the results of supervisory control theory [20], the adapter process A obtained from (19) has the following properties.

1. $L(A \mathbin{/\!/} D) \subseteq L(F)$, i.e., the possible behaviours of the adapter running together with the device are all included in the allowed behaviour of F. In other words, the adapter will never allow any traces to occur that are not permitted by the specification.
2. $L(A)$ is controllable with respect to $L([D])$, i.e., the adapter will always be able to react to uncontrollable actions generated by the device.

Within these constraints, $L(A)$ describes the *least restrictive* possible behaviour. It includes all possible adapter implementations that can satisfy the specification F while still being controllable.

The supervisory control solution A in Fig. 1 obtained for the coffee brewer can directly be used as a well-formed adapter to implement the specification. This is not always the case. Being a least restrictive solution, the behaviour of A may include several possibilities of forced or external actions in some state. If this happens, the result A can simply be restricted by choosing just one of the possibilities in each state. Each choice leads to a different adapter implementation.

This is possible because the two properties 1 and 2 above are not affected when the behaviour is restricted by disabling controllable actions. This observation immediately leads to the following result.

Theorem 3. Let F and D be two deterministic processes. There exists a well-formed and deterministic adapter A, such that $L(A)$ is controllable with respect to $L([D])$ and $L(A /\!/ D) \subseteq L(F)$, if and only if $\sup \mathcal{C}(L([F]^{\circlearrowleft}), L([D])) \neq \emptyset$.

Proof (sketch). By theorem 1, $\sup \mathcal{C}(L([F]^{\circlearrowleft}), L([D])) \neq \emptyset$ if and only if there exists a supervisor process S such that $L(S)$ is controllable with respect to $L([D])$, and $L(S \parallel [D]) \subseteq L([F]^{\circlearrowleft})$. Then S can be restricted to a well-formed, deterministic, and controllable adapter A such that $L(A \parallel [D]) \subseteq L([F]^{\circlearrowleft})$. Therefore, the claim follows from (18). $\qquad\qquad\square$

Thus, it is a necessary and sufficient condition for adapter existence that the behaviour obtained from (19) is nonempty. If this test is successful, the resultant behaviour can be used to implement a well-formed, deterministic, and controllable adapter satisfying the specification.

Supervisory control synthesis produces the largest sub-behaviour of the specification that is achievable by control. This result is not guaranteed to be equivalent to the specification and may even contain incomplete traces that lead to deadlock. To avoid this problem, the synthesis result from (19) needs to be checked whether it is nonblocking; if it is not, it should not be considered as a solution to the specification matching problem.

Supervisory control synthesis has been extended to produce a least restrictive solution that is both controllable and nonblocking [20]. This solves the problem of incomplete behaviours in the synthesis result while still providing an optimal solution, but makes it more difficult to construct an adapter implementation. The result of theorem 3 is lost, because a nonblocking process may become blocking by removing transitions. This problem has also been studied: ways of synthesising nonblocking behaviours that can be implemented are shown in [6].

6 Comparison

Forced simulation and supervisory control offer two different solutions to the specification matching problem. Although both methods produce the same result in the example discussed so far, there are important differences in the way how specifications are interpreted and which solutions are obtained. Table 1 summarises the commonalities and differences.

The most important point is that the two approaches use different notions of process equivalence, and strive to find solutions with different properties. Specifications have different meanings to the two approaches. The forced simulation method tries to find behaviours that are observation *equivalent* to the specification. A supervisory control specification is interpreted as a *maximally permissible* behaviour, and the method searches its implementable *sub-behaviours*.

Since forced simulation does not support uncontrollable actions, the two methods are first compared under the assumption that all actions are controllable. In this case, it can be shown that supervisory control more often finds solutions than forced simulation does. Obviously, there are more likely to be implementable sub-behaviours than equivalent behaviours.

Table 1. Comparison of specification matching approaches

Feature	Forced simulation	Supervisory control
Relationship between A and F	$A \mathbin{/\mkern-4mu/} D \approx F$	$L(A \mathbin{/\mkern-4mu/} D) \subseteq L(F)$
Well-formedness	guaranteed	requires additional steps
Forced cycles	not possible	may occur
Nonblocking	guaranteed	can be guaranteed
Uniqueness	solutions weakly bisimilar	unique least restrictive solution
Controllability	not considered	handled
Complexity	$O(|Q_F||Q_D|^2|\Sigma|)$	$O(|Q_F||Q_D||\Sigma|)$ without nonblocking, $O(|Q_F|^2|Q_D|^2|\Sigma|)$ with nonblocking

Theorem 4. Assume $\Sigma = \Sigma_c$. Let F and D be two processes. If there exists an adapter A such that $A \mathbin{/\mkern-4mu/} D \approx F$, then $L(A \mathbin{/\mkern-4mu/} D) \subseteq \sup \mathcal{C}(L([F]^{\circlearrowleft}), L([D]))$.

Proof (sketch). $A \mathbin{/\mkern-4mu/} D \approx F$ implies $L(A \mathbin{/\mkern-4mu/} D) = L(F)$, which in turn implies $L(A\|[D]) \subseteq L([F]^{\circlearrowleft})$ by (18). Furthermore, $L(A \mathbin{/\mkern-4mu/} D)$ is controllable with respect to $L([D])$ because $\Sigma = \Sigma_c$. Therefore, $L(A \mathbin{/\mkern-4mu/} D) \in \mathcal{C}(L([F]^{\circlearrowleft}), L([D]))$, and the claim follows by definition of $\sup \mathcal{C}$.   □

If there exists an adapter that can be computed by the forced simulation method, then its behaviour is contained in the least restrictive solution from supervisory control. Moreover, the results from forced simulation and supervisory control synthesis have the same possible behaviours when hiding all forced actions. More specifically, the behaviour obtained using the adapter from forced simulation can be shown to be observation equivalent to behaviour given by the supremal controllable sublanguage. They are all equivalent to the specification F. This follows because

$$L(F) = L(A \mathbin{/\mkern-4mu/} D) \subseteq \sup \mathcal{C}(L([F]^{\circlearrowleft}), L([D])) \subseteq L([F]^{\circlearrowleft}) . \qquad (20)$$

Nevertheless, the results obtained from the two methods are not necessarily equal. They may differ when the forced actions are taken into account.

Example 3. Consider the device $D^{\dagger}$ and specification $F^{\dagger}$ in Fig. 4. Obviously, there are two ways to achieve the specified behaviour: an adapter may first force $[\alpha]$ and then enable α, or the other way round. Consequently, there are two different adapters $A^{\dagger}_{\mathrm{fsim}}$ and $A^{\ddagger}_{\mathrm{fsim}}$ obtained from two different forced simulation relations. The least restrictive solution $A^{\dagger}_{\sup \mathcal{C}}$ includes both possibilities.

This example shows that supervisory control does not aim at producing a well-formed (implementable) adapter. It produces the least restrictive possible behaviour, which contains all possible adapters. Additional steps are needed to obtain an implementation.

The least restrictive solution may also include *forced cycles*. For example, $A^{\dagger}_{\sup \mathcal{C}}$ in Fig. 4 permits an infinite loop of forcing $[\alpha][\alpha][\beta]$ in state $d_0 f_0$. Such

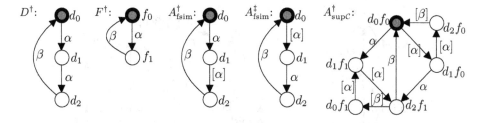

Fig. 4. Least restrictive versus well-formed adapters

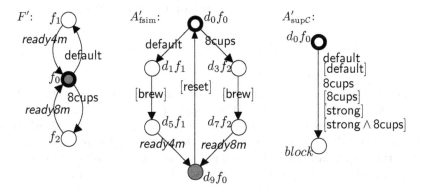

Fig. 5. Modified specification of coffee brewer and resulting adapters

loops are ruled out by the definition of forced simulation, which requires a finite string of forced actions for two states to match (definition 10).

If there is no forced simulation solution, supervisory control theory still tries to find a solution, which may not achieve the full behaviour of the specification, but the largest possible part of it.

Such sub-behaviours may include blocking states, i.e., there may be dead-locks. Therefore, most applications of supervisory control synthesis include additional steps to remove blocking states and compute a least restrictive behaviour that is both controllable and nonblocking. The forced simulation method does not require such additional effort. Since the result of the forced simulation method is observation equivalent to the specification, it is guaranteed to be nonblocking provided that the specification is nonblocking.

The result of theorem 4 is lost when uncontrollable actions are taken into account. Since forced simulation treats all actions as controllable (and enforcible), the method may find solutions for some problems to which supervisory control does not. This is illustrated in the following example.

Example 4. F' in Fig. 5 is an alternative specification for the coffee brewer D in Fig. 1, which represents an attempt to mask the *error* actions. It is understood that F' disallows *error* in all states. In this case, the forced simulation method yields the adapter A'_{fsim} in Fig. 5, which simply disables *error* in states $d_5 f_1$ and $d_7 f_2$. Supervisory control rejects this solution as uncontrollable, because

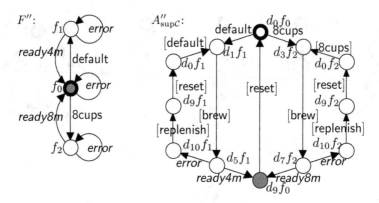

Fig. 6. Yet another specification of the coffee brewer

the adapter is trying to disable the uncontrollable action *error* in a state where it can be generated by the device. When applied to this example, supervisory control synthesis yields the least restrictive behaviour A'_{supC} in Fig. 5, which is blocking. Alternatively, when trying to synthesise a nonblocking solution, the result is the empty language. This indicates that there is no controllable and nonblocking sub-behaviour of F' that can be achieved by an adapter.

Example 5. Specification F'' in Fig. 6 is a slightly modified version of the specification F' from the previous example. This time, *error* actions are allowed in all states. Now, no adapter can achieve a behaviour observation equivalent to F'', because the device cannot produce an *error* when the specification is in state f_0. Therefore, the forced simulation method finds no solution. But when supervisory control synthesis is applied to $[F'']^\circlearrowleft$ and $[D]$ in Fig. 2, the least restrictive solution A''_{supC} in Fig. 6 is found. This shows that errors can indeed be masked using forcing—it suffices to replenish and reset the brewer, and then to restart the operation that caused the error. However, this solution is not observation equivalent to the original specification F''.

These examples show that the two approaches are completely different when uncontrollable actions are present. There are specification matching tasks that can be solved using forced simulation but not supervisory control, and vice versa.

The complexity of the forced simulation based matching algorithm is shown to be $O(|Q_F||Q_D|^2|\Sigma|)$ in [22]. The complexity of supervisory control synthesis is discussed in [14]. The synthesis of the supremal controllable sublanguage, i.e., the computation of (19) can be accomplished in $O(|Q_F||Q_D||\Sigma|)$. This complexity increases to $O(|Q_F|^2|Q_D|^2|\Sigma|)$ if nonblocking is required in addition. The preprocessing step to construct $[D]$ from D does not affect this complexity. It can be done in a single pass over the transitions of D, i.e., in $O(|Q_D||\Sigma|)$. Similarly, $[F]^\circlearrowleft$ can be constructed from F in $O(|Q_F||\Sigma|)$. These automata do not need to be constructed explicitly: their transitions can be introduced on the fly while running the synthesis algorithm.

7   Conclusions

Two different approaches for solving the specification matching problem in embedded systems have been presented and compared, namely the forced simulation method [22] and an adaptation of supervisory control theory [20]. Important differences have been found in the way how these approaches interpret specifications and accept solutions.

The forced simulation approach is a specially tailored method for component matching. It computes an adapter with observation equivalent behaviour to the original specification that can be implemented straight away. Supervisory control theory is a more general framework, which can be adapted to the specification matching problem. It then yields the most general sub-behaviour of the specification that can possibly be implemented. This result is not as easy to implement as the result from the tailored approach, but the method makes it possible to use uncontrollable actions in the model. The results obtained by the two approaches can be completely different, so it depends on the application which approach is more appropriate.

This paper opens several perspectives for future research. It would be very interesting to see how the two approaches to specification matching can be improved using features of the other. Forced simulation may be extended to support uncontrollable actions, and supervisory control theory may be extended by new methods that suit the specific needs of specification matching.

References

1. K. Åkesson, H. Flordal, and M. Fabian. Exploiting modularity for synthesis and verification of supervisors. In *Proc. 15th IFAC World Congress on Automatic Control*, Barcelona, Spain, 2002.
2. M. Abadi and L. Lamport. The existence of refinement mappings. *Theoretical Computer science*, 82(2):253–284, 1991.
3. C. G. Cassandras and S. Lafortune. *Introduction to Discrete Event Systems*. Kluwer, September 1999.
4. H. Chang, L. Cooke, M. Hunt, G. Martin, A. McNelly, and L. Todd. *Surviving the SOC revolution: a guide to platform based design*. Kluwer, 1999.
5. A. Cherchago and R. Heckel. Specification matching of web services using conditional graph transformation rules. In *Proc. 2nd International Conference on Graph Transformations*, volume 3256 of *LNCS*, pages 304–318. Springer, 2004.
6. P. Dietrich, R. Malik, W. M. Wonham, and B. A. Brandin. Implementation considerations in supervisory control. In B. Caillaud, P. Darondeau, L. Lavagno, and X. Xie, editors, *Synthesis and Control of Discrete Event Systems*, pages 185–201. Kluwer, 2002.
7. J. Guo. Software components adaptive integration. In *Proc. 8th International Conference and Workshop on the Engineering of Computer Based Systems*, pages 315–321. IEEE Computer Society, 2001.
8. D. Hemer. Specification matching of state based modular components. In *Proc. 10th Asia-Pacific Software Engineering Conference*. IEEE, 2003.
9. C. A. R. Hoare. *Communicating Sequential Processes*. Prentice-Hall, 1985.

10. C. A. R. Hoare and Jifeng He. The weakest prespecification. *Information Processing Letters*, 24(2):127–132, 1987.
11. Jun-Jang Jeng and Betty H. C. Cheng. Specification matching for software reuse: A foundation. In *Proc. ACM SIGSOFT Symposium on Software Reusability (SSR '95)*, pages 97–105, 1995.
12. P. K. Jha and N. D. Dutt. High-level library mapping for arithmetic components. *IEEE Transactions on Very Large Scale Integration (VLSI) Systems*, 4(2):1–13, 1996.
13. M. Keating and P. Bricaud. *Reuse methodology manual for System-on-a-chip design*. Kluwer, 1999.
14. Ratnesh Kumar and Vijay K. Garg. *Modeling and Control of Logical Discrete Event Systems*. Kluwer, 1995.
15. N. Lynch and F. Vaandrager. Forward and backward simulations part I: Untimed systems. *Information and Computation*, 121(2):214–233, September 1995.
16. Hafedh Mili, Fatma Mili, and Ali Mili. Reusing software: Issues and research directions. *IEEE Transactions on Software Engineering*, 21(6):528–562, 1995.
17. R. Milner. *Communication and Concurrency*. Prentice-Hall, 1989.
18. R. S. Mitra, P. S. Roop, and A. Basu. A new algorithm for implementation of design functions by available devices. *IEEE Transactions on Very Large Scale Integration (VLSI) Systems*, 4(2):170–180, June 1996.
19. J. Phenix and P. Alexander. Toward automated component adaptation. In *Proc. 9th International Conference on Software Engineering and Knowledge Engineering (SEKE)*, 1997.
20. Peter J. G. Ramadge and W. Murray Wonham. The control of discrete event systems. *Proceedings of the IEEE*, 77(1):81–98, January 1989.
21. P. S. Roop, A. Sowmya, S. Ramesh, and H. F. Guo. Tabled logic programming based IP matching tool using forced simulation. *IEE Proc. Computer and Digital Techniques*, 151(3):199–208, May 2004.
22. Partha S. Roop, Arcot Sowmya, and S. Ramesh. Forced simulation: A technique for automating component reuse in embedded systems. *ACM Transactions on Design Automation of Electronic Systems*, 6(4):602–628, October 2001.
23. A. W. Roscoe. *The Theory and Practice of Concurrency*. Prentice-Hall, 1997.
24. J. Smith and G. de Micheli. Polynomial methods for component matching and verification. In *Proc. IEEE/ACM International Conference on Computer Aided Design*, pages 678–685. ACM, 1998.
25. R. J. van Glabbeek. The linear time — branching time spectrum I: The semantics of concrete, sequential processes. In J. A. Bergstra, A. Ponse, and S. A. Smolka, editors, *Handbook of Process Algebra*, pages 3–99. Elsevier, 2001.
26. Amy Moormann Zaremski and Jeannette M. Wing. Specification matching of software components. *ACM Transactions on Software Engineering and Methodology*, 6(4):333–360, 1997.

State/Event Software Verification for Branching-Time Specifications[*]

Sagar Chaki[1], Edmund Clarke[2], Orna Grumberg[3], Joël Ouaknine[4],
Natasha Sharygina[2,5], Tayssir Touili[6], and Helmut Veith[7]

[1] Carnegie Mellon University, Software Engineering Institute, Pittsburgh, USA
[2] Carnegie Mellon University, School of Computer Science, Pittsburgh, USA
[3] The Technion, Haifa, Israel
[4] Oxford University Computing Laboratory, Oxford, UK
[5] USI (Università della Svizzera Italiana), Lugano, Switzerland
[6] LIAFA, CNRS & University of Paris7, Paris, France
[7] Technische Universität München, Munich, Germany

Abstract. In the domain of concurrent software verification, there is an evident need for specification formalisms and efficient algorithms to verify branching-time properties that involve both data and communication. We address this problem by defining a new branching-time temporal logic SE-AΩ which integrates both state-based and action-based properties. SE-AΩ is universal, i.e., preserved by the simulation relation, and thus amenable to counterexample-guided abstraction refinement. We provide a model-checking algorithm for this logic, based upon a compositional abstraction-refinement loop which exploits the natural decomposition of the concurrent system into its components. The abstraction and refinement steps are performed over each component separately, and only the model checking step requires an explicit composition of the abstracted components. For experimental evaluation, we have integrated our algorithm within the COMFORT reasoning framework and used it to verify a piece of industrial robot control software.

Keywords: Concurrent Software Model Checking, State/Event-based Verification, Branching-time Temporal Logic, Automated Abstraction Refinement.

[*] This research was sponsored by the National Science Foundation (NSF) under grants no. CCR-9803774 and CCR-0121547, the Office of Naval Research (ONR) and the Naval Research Laboratory (NRL) under contract no. N00014-01-1-0796, the Army Research Office (ARO) under contract no. DAAD19-01-1-0485, the Austrian Science Fund Project N-Z29 N04, the EU Networks GAMES and ECRYPT, and was conducted as part of the PACC project at the Software Engineering Institute (SEI). The views and conclusions contained in this document are those of the authors and should not be interpreted as representing the official policies, either expressed or implied, of NSF, ONR, NRL, ARO, SEI, the U.S. Government or any other entity.

J. Romijn, G. Smith, and J. van de Pol (Eds.): IFM 2005, LNCS 3771, pp. 53–69, 2005.
© Springer-Verlag Berlin Heidelberg 2005

1   Introduction

The practical effectiveness of model checking is characterized by a trade-off between the expressive power of the specification formalism and the complexity of the corresponding model checking algorithm. For software verification, this problem is even more acute, since software is harder to specify, and state explosion is exacerbated by the concurrent execution of multiple components. The expressive power of temporal logics such as CTL or LTL is quite limited when it comes to specifying, e.g., the periodicity of events. The last decade has seen several attempts at extending the expressiveness of temporal logics [7, 31, 29, 30, 28, 11]. Recently, Clarke et al. [9] have investigated a family of universal branching logics, called $A\Omega$, which are extensions of ACTL[1] by sets Ω of ω-regular path operators. A subtle property of $A\Omega$ is the *monotonicity* of the path operators: the semantics guarantees that the extended path operators cannot be used to implicitly define negation. While this property comes for free with the standard temporal path operators, its presence is crucial for obtaining extended *universal* branching logics. Such logics are preserved by simulation, and are therefore amenable to existential abstraction [8, 9].

Another shortcoming of standard temporal logics stems from the fact that for the verification of concurrent software conducted at the source code level, one needs to specify both *state* information (program counter location, memory contents) and *communication* among components. For example, the Bluetooth L2CAP specification [13] asserts that "when an L2CAP_ConnectRsp event is received in a W4_L2CAP_CONNECT_RSP state, within one time unit, an L2CAP process may send out an L2CA_ConnectInd event, disable the RTX timer, and move to state CONFIG." As this example shows, both states (W4_L2CAP_CONNECT_RSP and CONFIG) and events (L2CAP_ConnectRsp and L2CA_ConnectInd) are required to properly capture the desired L2CAP behavior.

Generally, in concurrent programs, communication among modules proceeds via actions (events) which can represent function calls, requests and acknowledgments, etc. These communications can be data-dependent and carry data on its channels. Existing model checking techniques typically use either *state-based* or *event-based* formalisms to represent finite-state models of programs. In principle, both frameworks are interchangeable: an action can be encoded as a change in state variables, and likewise one can equip a state with different actions to reflect different values of its internal variables. Neither approach on its own is practical, however, when it comes to the specification of data-dependent communication claims: considerable domain expertise is then required to annotate the program and to specify proper specifications in temporal logic.

In this paper, we define the specification logic SE-$A\Omega$ which combines the high expressive power of $A\Omega$ with the ability to refer to states and events simultaneously. The hybrid state/event-based semantics of SE-$A\Omega$ allows us to

---

[1] ACTL denotes the universal fragment of CTL, in which the formulas range over all possible execution paths.

represent software specifications directly without program annotations or privileged insights into program execution.

Extending branching-time logics with event modalities presents some interesting challenges. For example, there is no natural generic extension of standard CTL operators such as **U** (*until*) to a state/event-based framework (see, e.g., [18]); SE-AΩ, however, enables us to employ different variants of CTL operators for actions and data valuations simultaneously.

Notwithstanding its high expressive power and versatility, SE-AΩ lends itself naturally to an efficient verification strategy which combines counterexample-guided abstraction refinement (CEGAR [20, 6]) and compositional reasoning: starting with a coarse initial abstraction, our CEGAR scheme computes increasingly precise abstractions of the target system by analyzing spurious counterexamples until either a real counterexample is obtained or the system is found to be correct. More precisely, given a system M composed of n concurrent components $M_1, \ldots, M_n$, and a SE-AΩ specification φ, the verification of $M \models \varphi$ proceeds as follows:

1. **Abstract.** Create an abstraction $\widehat{M}$ such that all behaviors of $\widehat{M}$ are preserved by M. This is done component-wise without constructing the full state space of M.
2. **Verify.** Verify whether $\widehat{M} \models \varphi$. If so, report success and exit. Otherwise, extract an abstract counterexample $\widehat{C}$ that indicates in which way φ fails in $\widehat{M}$.
3. **Refine.** Check whether $\widehat{C}$ gives rise to a real counterexample over M. If $\widehat{C}$ corresponds to a genuine behavior of M then report a failure along with a fragment of each M_i that illustrates why $M \nvDash \varphi$. If $\widehat{C}$ is spurious, on the other hand, refine $\widehat{M}$ using $\widehat{C}$ to obtain a more precise abstraction and repeat from Step 1. This refinement step, like the initial abstraction, is performed component-wise.

Of the three steps in this abstract-verify-refine process only the verification stage of our technique requires the explicit composition of a system. The other stages can be performed one component at a time. Since verification is performed only on abstractions (which are usually much smaller than the corresponding concrete systems), our approach is able to significantly alleviate the state space explosion problem.

Another key characteristic of our algorithm is that the verification step handles both states and events *directly*, i.e., without conversion into either a pure state-based or a pure event-based framework. The model checking is therefore significantly more efficient than alternative conversion-based approaches, since it has been observed that such conversions can lead to a quadratic blowup in both time and space even for reachability properties [3, 4]. The core of the model checking algorithm relies on automata-theoretic methods to evaluate the ω-regular path operators. Note that the universality of SE-AΩ is crucial to our approach, in that it enables violations to be concisely represented as (tree-like) counterexamples.

Previously proposed state/event-based formalisms [25, 18, 16, 3, 4] have been limited to either *linear-time* specifications or *finite-state* systems. The novelty of our approach is the application of *branching-time* state/event-based reasoning to *infinite-state* concurrent systems using powerful state space reduction techniques, namely CEGAR and compositional reasoning. In this respect, not only do we substantially extend the expressiveness of the state/event linear temporal logic SE-LTL presented in [3, 4], but we also show how to validate *branching-time* counterexamples in a *compositional* manner, based on new results relating simulation and weak simulation relations for parallel processes (see Theorem 4 in Section 5).

We have implemented our approach in the CMU SEI ComFoRT [17] reasoning framework, based on the C model checker MAGIC [22]. MAGIC extracts state/event finite-state models from C programs automatically via predicate abstraction [12, 2]. We evaluated the applicability of our framework in experiments with a piece of robot controller software. In our experiments SE-AΩ has been extremely useful for both specifying the branching structure of the protocol executions, and in order to make assertions on both actions and data valuations.

The rest of this article is organized as follows. In Section 2 we summarize related work. This is followed by some preliminary definitions in Section 3. In Section 4 we present the SE-AΩ logic, followed by model-checking, counterexample-validation and abstraction-refinement procedures described in Section 5. Finally, we discuss the applications of our techniques to an industrial system in Section 6 and conclude by outlining some future work in Section 7.

2   Related Work

Extensions of temporal logics to increase the expressiveness of temporal operators have been proposed by various authors [7, 31, 29, 30, 28, 11]. Wolper [31] and Vardi and Wolper [30] extended LTL by regular expressions and Büchi automata respectively. Vardi and Wolper [29] and Thomas [28] have proposed extended branching-time logics, but have not addressed model checking. Clarke et al. [7] describe the logic ECTL that similarly to our work considers ω-regular automata in the context of branching-time logic. However, this work does not deal with abstraction refinement or compositional methods. Clarke et al. [9] define a class $A\Omega$ of universal branching logics (cf. Section 1) for a systematic study of the complexity and completeness of counterexamples in model checking. SE-AΩ extends $A\Omega$ essentially in that it incorporates events in addition to states. Note moreover that [9] does not offer a model checking algorithm for $A\Omega$. Naturally, the algorithm for SE-AΩ that we present in this paper also applies to $A\Omega$.

The formalization of a general notion of abstraction first appeared in [10]. The abstractions used in our approach are *conservative* in that whenever the abstract system meets a given specification, then so does the concrete system, but not necessarily vice-versa (see [19, 8]). Conservative abstractions usually lead to significant reductions in the state space but in general require an iterated abstraction refinement mechanism (such as CEGAR) in order to establish specification satisfaction. CEGAR has been used, among others, in [24] (in non-automated form), and [1, 26, 21, 14]. In particular, CEGAR-based schemes have been used for the verification of safety properties [1, 6, 14, 2] as well as liveness [3, 4] properties.

Compositionality and abstraction have been extensively studied in process algebra (e.g., [15, 23, 27]). However, there mainly actions (as opposed to states) have been considered. Abstraction and compositional reasoning have been combined [5] within a single CEGAR scheme to verify safety properties of concurrent C programs. Our work, on the other hand, deals with a significantly more expressive specification language.

3 Preliminaries

Definition 1 (Labeled Kripke Structure). *A labeled Kripke structure (LKS) is a 6-tuple* $(S, init, AP, \mathcal{L}, \Sigma, T)$ *where (i)* S *is a finite non-empty set of states, (ii)* $init \in S$ *is an initial state, (iii)* AP *is a finite set of atomic state propositions, (iv)* $\mathcal{L} : S \rightarrow 2^{AP}$ *is a state-labeling function, (v)* Σ *is a finite set of actions (alphabet) and (vi)* $T \subseteq S \times \Sigma \times S$ *is a transition relation.*

Note that Labeled Kripke Structures are similar to "doubly-labeled transition systems" introduced in [25].

Given an LKS $M = (S, init, AP, \mathcal{L}, \Sigma, T)$, we write $S(M)$, $init(M)$, $AP(M)$, $\mathcal{L}(M)$, $\Sigma(M)$ and $T(M)$ to mean S, $init$, AP, $\mathcal{L}$, Σ and T respectively. Given $s, s' \in S$ and $a \in \Sigma$ we write $s \xrightarrow{a} s'$ to mean $(s, a, s') \in T$. Also, let $Succ(s, a) = \{s' \in S \mid s \xrightarrow{a} s'\}$ and $Enabled(s) = \{a \in \Sigma \mid Succ(s, a) \neq \emptyset\}$. Finally, a *path* of M is an infinite sequence of consecutive transitions $s_0 \xrightarrow{a_0} s_1 \xrightarrow{a_1} s_2 \xrightarrow{a_2} \dots$. Note that we do not require paths to begin with $init$.

Definition 2 (Parallel Composition). *Let* M_1 *and* M_2 *be two LKSs such that* $AP(M_1) \cap AP(M_2) = \emptyset$. *Then the parallel composition of* M_1 *and* M_2, *denoted by* $M_1 \| M_2$, *is an LKS obeying the following conditions: (i)* $S(M_1 \| M_2) = S(M_1) \times S(M_2)$, *(ii)* $init(M_1 \| M_2) = (init(M_1), init(M_2))$, *(iii)* $AP(M_1 \| M_2) = AP(M_1) \cup AP(M_2)$, *and (iv)* $\Sigma(M_1 \| M_2) = \Sigma(M_1) \cup \Sigma(M_2)$. *Moreover, for all* $s_1, s_1' \in S(M_1)$, $s_2, s_2' \in S(M_2)$, *and* $a \in \Sigma(M_1 \| M_2)$, *the labeling function* $\mathcal{L}(M_1 \| M_2)$ *and the transition relation* $T(M_1 \| M_2)$ *are defined as follows:*

- $\mathcal{L}(M_1 \| M_2)((s_1, s_2)) = \mathcal{L}(M_1)(s_1) \cup \mathcal{L}(M_2)(s_2)$.
- *If* $s_1 \xrightarrow{a} s_1'$ *and* $s_2 \xrightarrow{a} s_2'$ *then* $(s_1, s_2) \xrightarrow{a} (s_1', s_2')$.
- *If* $s_1 \xrightarrow{a} s_1'$ *and* $a \notin \Sigma(M_2)$ *then* $(s_1, s_2) \xrightarrow{a} (s_1', s_2)$.
- *If* $s_2 \xrightarrow{a} s_2'$ *and* $a \notin \Sigma(M_1)$ *then* $(s_1, s_2) \xrightarrow{a} (s_1, s_2')$.

This notion of parallel composition is derived from CSP [15, 27]; it is commutative and associative, so that no parentheses are needed when composing more than two LKSs together.

Definition 3 (Simulation). *Let* M_1 *and* M_2 *be LKSs with* $\Sigma(M_1) = \Sigma(M_2) = \Sigma$, *and* $AP(M_2) = AP(M_1)$. *A relation* $R \subseteq S(M_1) \times S(M_2)$ *is said to be a simulation relation iff it satisfies the following conditions:*

1. If $(s_1, s_2) \in R$ then $\mathcal{L}(M_1)(s_1) = \mathcal{L}(M_2)(s_2)$.
2. For any $s_1, s_1' \in S(M_1)$, $s_2 \in S(M_2)$, and $a \in \Sigma$, if $(s_1, s_2) \in R$ and $s_1 \xrightarrow{a} s_1'$ then there exists $s_2' \in S(M_2)$ such that $s_2 \xrightarrow{a} s_2'$ and $(s_1', s_2') \in R$.

For two LKSs M_1 and M_2, if there exists a simulation relation R such that $(init(M_1), init(M_2)) \in R$ then we say that M_1 is simulated by M_2 and denote this by $M_1 \leqslant M_2$. The following is well-known [23]:

Theorem 1. *Let* $M_1, \ldots, M_n$, $N_1, \ldots, N_n$ *be LKSs such that* $N_i \leqslant M_i$ *for* $1 \leq i \leq n$. *Then* $(N_1 \| \ldots \| N_n) \leqslant (M_1 \| \ldots \| M_n)$.

In our framework, (existential) abstractions are obtained by 'lumping' together states of a concrete LKSs: abstract states are disjoint sets of concrete states; cf. [8]. In the remainder of this paper, we often use the letter M to denote a concrete LKS and its hatted counterpart $\widehat{M}$ to denote an abstract LKS. Note that an abstraction $\widehat{M}$ of M is entirely determined by an equivalence relation $R \subseteq S(M) \times S(M)$. We only consider *admissible* equivalence relations, i.e., we require that for all $s, s' \in S(M)$, whenever $(s, s') \in R$ then $\mathcal{L}(M)(s) = \mathcal{L}(M)(s')$. Given a state $s \in S(M)$, we denote its corresponding equivalence class by $[s]^R$ (or simply $[s]$ when R is clear from context.)

Definition 4 (Abstraction). *Let* M *be an LKS and* R *be an admissible equivalence relation on* $S(M)$. *Then* M^R *is the abstract quotient LKS induced by* R *such that (i)* $S(M^R) = \{[s] \mid s \in S(M)\}$, *(ii)* $init(M^R) = [init(M)]$, *(iii)* $AP(M^R) = AP(M)$, *(iv) for all* $[s] \in S(M^R)$, $\mathcal{L}(M^R)([s]) = \mathcal{L}(M)(s)$ *(well-defined since* R *is admissible), (v)* $\Sigma(M^R) = \Sigma(M)$, *and (vi)* $T(M^R) = \{([s], a, [s']) \mid (s, a, s') \in T(M)\}$.

For $s \in S(M)$ and $a \in \Sigma(M)$, the set of *abstract successors* of s along a is defined to be $AbsSucc(s, a) = \{[s'] \in M^R \mid (s, a, s') \in T(M)\}$.

It is easy to see that for any M and R, $M \leqslant M^R$. Combining this with Theorem 1 we get the following result.

Lemma 1. *Let* $M_1, \ldots, M_n$ *be LKSs and* $R_1, \ldots, R_n$ *be equivalence relations. Then* $(M_1 \| \ldots \| M_n) \leqslant (M_1^{R_1} \| \ldots \| M_n^{R_n})$.

4   The Logic SE-AΩ

Following [9], we define a universal branching-time logic called *State-Event Universal Logic* (SE-AΩ). The logic is interpreted over LKSs and can be used to specify properties involving both data and actions in a natural manner. SE-AΩ is defined in negation normal form, i.e., negations are only applied to atomic propositions. Unlike ACTL or ACTL*, it does not have a fixed set of operators. Rather, any ω-regular language can serve as a temporal operator. Since the logic is universal, every such operator is preceded by a universal path quantifier **A**.

Similarly to usual temporal operators, the new operators are applied to other formulas in the logic. Syntactically, this is done by defining an ω-regular language

O over a set of markers that serve as placeholders for the formulas to which O is applied. Since SE-AΩ is aimed at specifying both actions and data, its operators can be applied to subsets of actions as well as formulas over atomic propositions.

Formally, let $Mark = \{m_1, m_2, \ldots\}$ be a denumerable set of *markers* and let $\overline{m} = \{m_1, \ldots, m_n\}$ be a finite subset of $Mark$. Let O be an ω-regular language over the alphabet $2^{\overline{m}}$. The corresponding n-ary temporal operator will be denoted by $\mathbf{O}$. Let AP be a set of atomic propositions and Σ be a set of actions. Then the syntax of SE-AΩ is defined inductively as follows.

- If $p \in AP$ then p and $\neg p$ are formulas.
- If φ_1 and φ_2 are formulas then so are $\varphi_1 \vee \varphi_2$ and $\varphi_1 \wedge \varphi_2$.
- Let $\mathbf{O}$ be an n-ary temporal operator and for $1 \leq i \leq n$, φ_i be either a formula or a subset of Σ. Then $\mathbf{AO}(\varphi_1, \ldots, \varphi_n)$ is a formula.

The semantics of SE-AΩ is defined over LKSs. More precisely, given an SE-AΩ formula φ, an LKS M, and $s \in S(M)$ we write $M, s \models \varphi$ to mean that s satisfies φ, defined inductively as follows:

- For $p \in AP$, $M, s \models p$ iff $p \in \mathcal{L}(s)$ and $M, s \models \neg p$ iff $p \notin \mathcal{L}(s)$.
- $M, s \models \varphi_1 \vee \varphi_2$ iff $M, s \models \varphi_1$ or $M, s \models \varphi_2$.
- $M, s \models \varphi_1 \wedge \varphi_2$ iff $M, s \models \varphi_1$ and $M, s \models \varphi_2$.
- $M, s \models \mathbf{AO}(\varphi_1, \ldots, \varphi_n)$ iff for every path π starting from s, we have $M, \pi \models \mathbf{O}(\varphi_1, \ldots, \varphi_n)$ [as defined below].

Let $\pi = s_0 \xrightarrow{a_0} s_1 \xrightarrow{a_1} s_2 \ldots$ be a path of M and π^i be its suffix starting from s_i. We first define when π satisfies an argument φ_k of the operator $\mathbf{O}$. $M, \pi \models \varphi_k$ iff either $\varphi_k \subseteq \Sigma$ and $a_0 \in \varphi_k$, or φ_k is a formula and $M, s_0 \models \varphi_k$.

Let $\mathbf{O}(\varphi_1, \ldots, \varphi_n)$ be as above, and O be the ω-regular language corresponding to $\mathbf{O}$. Recall that the alphabet of O is $2^{\overline{m}}$ where $\overline{m} = \{m_1, \ldots, m_n\}$. Then $M, \pi \models \mathbf{O}(\varphi_1, \ldots, \varphi_k)$ iff there is a word $o = o_1 o_2 \cdots \in O$ such that for all $i \geq 0$ and for all $m_k \in o_i$, $M, \pi^i \models \varphi_k$. Note that this requires that for every $m_k \in o_i$, φ_k must hold. However, other φ_j may, or may not, hold as well. We will need to take this fact into account in the model checking algorithm, presented in the next section.

Lastly, we write $M \models \varphi$ to mean $M, init(M) \models \varphi$.

As an example, let $O = \{m_1, m_2\}^* \{m_1, m_3\}\{m_4\}\{\}^\omega$ be an ω-regular expression. Then $\mathbf{O}(\varphi, \{a\}, \{b\}, \psi)$ represents an 'until' operator that captures paths in which $\varphi \mathbf{U} \psi$ holds along a sequence of a actions ending with the action b. This example demonstrates that in addition to formulas φ_k that should hold, the logic SE-AΩ allows us to restrict the actions that can be performed, by using $\varphi_k \subseteq \Sigma$.

As a second example, let $O = (\{m_1\}\{\})^\omega$ be another ω-regular expression. Then $\mathbf{O}(p)$ is an operator which requires that the atomic proposition p hold at all even positions (starting at 0) along every path. Note that this formula does not constrain states that occur in odd positions. It is well-known that this formula cannot be captured in LTL.

These two examples illustrate that SE-AΩ formulas are used to describe ω-regular 'constraint patterns' along the paths of LKSs. For a much more principled and detailed account of the underlying ideas and workings of this logic, we refer the reader to [9].

An important property of the logic SE-AΩ is that it is preserved by the simulation relation. This is formalized by the following lemma.

Lemma 2. *Given two LKSs M_1 and M_2 and an SE-AΩ formula φ, if $M_2 \models \varphi$ and $M_1 \leqslant M_2$, then $M_1 \models \varphi$.*

5 Compositional CEGAR Verification for SE-AΩ

Let $M_1, \ldots, M_n$ be LKSs and let φ be an SE-AΩ formula. In seeking to determine whether $M = M_1 \| \ldots \| M_n \models \varphi$, we wish to avoid constructing the full LKS M, since the size of its state space increases exponentially with the number of its components. We therefore first compute a (typically much smaller) abstraction $\widehat{M_i}$ of each component M_i, and only then check whether $\widehat{M} = \widehat{M_1} \| \ldots \| \widehat{M_n} \models \varphi$. If this holds, we conclude that $M \models \varphi$ as well. Otherwise, we extract from $\widehat{M}$ a counterexample $\widehat{C}$ violating φ, and check whether this counterexample is valid, i.e., whether it corresponds to a real execution of M. In the affirmative, we conclude that $M \not\models \varphi$. Otherwise, we use this spurious counterexample to refine our abstractions, and repeat the process until either a real counterexample is found or the property is shown to hold. The main strength of our approach is the fact that the abstraction, counterexample-validation, and refinement steps are all carried out one component at a time, so that it is never necessary to construct the full state space of the concrete system M.[2]

5.1 Model Checking

Let $\widehat{M}$ be an LKS[3], $s \in S(\widehat{M})$, and φ be an SE-AΩ formula. We give a model-checking algorithm to determine whether $\widehat{M}, s \models \varphi$. We proceed by structural induction on φ, starting with the case in which φ is of the form $\mathbf{AO}(\varphi_1, \ldots, \varphi_n)$. Let O be the ω-regular language over $\overline{m} = \{m_1, \ldots, m_n\}$ corresponding to $\mathbf{O}$. The algorithm consists of the following steps: (i) compute from $\widehat{M}$ and s the 'smallest' ω-regular language O_s over the alphabet $2^{\overline{m}}$ such that $\widehat{M}, s \models \mathbf{AO}_s(\varphi_1, \ldots, \varphi_n)$, and (ii) check whether O_s is 'subsumed' by O.

Intuitively, the idea is to interpret each path π in $\widehat{M}$ as a sequence of maximal subsets of formulas (among $\varphi_1, \ldots, \varphi_n$ that hold along π). We then check whether replacing each φ_j with the corresponding marker m_j results in a sequence belonging to O.

In order to do so we build an automaton B_s obtained from $\widehat{M}$ by replacing every action a, in transitions of the form (q, a, q'), with the subset of markers

---

[2] Except, of course, in the worst case in which no proper abstraction of the system leads to a definite answer.

[3] In the interests of consistency and clarity, we present our approach in both this section and the next in terms of the abstract LKS $\widehat{M}$, although it naturally applies to concrete systems as well.

corresponding to the formulas that hold for the transition. More precisely, if φ_j is an SE-AΩ formula, we include the corresponding marker m_j provided that $\widehat{M}, q \models \varphi_j$, and if $\varphi_j \subseteq \Sigma(\widehat{M})$, we include m_j if $a \in \varphi_j$.

To make this more rigorous, we first recall the notion of *Büchi automata*:

Definition 5 (Büchi Automaton). *A Büchi automaton is a 5-tuple $B = (S, I, \Sigma, T, Acc)$ where (i) S is a finite non-empty set of states, (ii) $I \subseteq S$ is a set of initial states, (iii) Σ is a finite alphabet, (iv) $T \subseteq S \times \Sigma \times S$ is a transition relation, and (v) $Acc \subseteq S$ is a set of accepting states.*

A path of B is an infinite sequence $\pi = q_0 \xrightarrow{a_0} q_1 \xrightarrow{a_1} \ldots$ such that $q_0 \in I$, and for every i, $(q_i, a_i, q_{i+1}) \in T$. π is accepting if it visits the set Acc infinitely often.

The language O_s is represented by a Büchi automaton B_s, which is derived from $\widehat{M}$ as follows: $B_s = (S_s, I_s, \Sigma_s, T_s, Acc_s)$, where (i) $S_s = S(\widehat{M})$, (ii) $I_s = \{s\}$, (iii) $\Sigma_s = 2^{\overline{m}}$, (iv) $Acc_s = S(\widehat{M})$, and (v) T_s is the set of transitions such that for each $(q, a, q') \in T(\widehat{M})$, T_s includes a transition $(q, \overline{m}', q')$ such that $\overline{m}' \subseteq \overline{m}$ and the following condition holds: for $0 \leq j \leq n$, $m_j \in \overline{m}'$ iff either $\varphi_j \subseteq \Sigma(\widehat{M})$ and $a \in \varphi_j$ or φ_j is a formula and $\widehat{M}, q \models \varphi_j$.

Note that in order to construct B_s we need to know whether $\widehat{M}, q \models \varphi_i$ for every $q \in S(\widehat{M})$ and every $i \in \{1, \ldots, n\}$. This is achieved by invoking the model checking algorithm recursively.

In the second step, we must check whether O_s is *subsumed* by O. Observe first that it is not enough to simply check whether $O_s \subseteq O$. This is because the definition of $M, \pi \models \mathbf{O}(\varphi_1, \ldots, \varphi_n)$ determines which of the φ_j must be true at a certain point on π, but allows additional φ_j to be true as well.

We solve this difficulty by introducing the notion of *monotonicity* (cf. [9]). In order to define monotonicity of SE-AΩ consider two ω-regular languages O and O' over $\overline{m}$ that satisfy: for every $w = w_1 w_2 \cdots \in O$ there exists $w' = w'_1 w'_2 \cdots \in O'$ such that for every $i \geq 1$, $w_i \subseteq w'_i$. Then for every model $\widehat{M}$, if $\widehat{M} \models \mathbf{A}O'(\varphi_1, \ldots, \varphi_k)$ then $\widehat{M} \models \mathbf{A}O(\varphi_1, \ldots, \varphi_k)$. For example, let $\overline{m} = \{m_1, m_2, m_3\}$, and suppose that $O = \{m_2\}^\omega$ and that $O_s = \{m_1, m_2\}^\omega$. Then $\widehat{M}, s \models \mathbf{A}O_s(\varphi_1, \varphi_2, \varphi_3)$ and, thanks to monotonicity, $\widehat{M}, s \models \mathbf{A}O(\varphi_1, \varphi_2, \varphi_3)$ as well, even though $O_s \not\subseteq O$. It is clear that what is in fact required is to check whether $O_s \subseteq \uparrow O$, where $\uparrow O = (\{m_2\} + \{m_1, m_2\} + \{m_2, m_3\} + \{m_1, m_2, m_3\})^\omega$. The language $\uparrow O$ is called the *monotonic closure* of O and, intuitively, is obtained by replacing in O every occurrence of a set of markers $\overline{m}' \subseteq \overline{m}$ by the sum of all the sets of markers $\overline{m}''$ such that $\overline{m}' \subseteq \overline{m}'' \subseteq \overline{m}$. Formally:

Definition 6 (Monotonic Closure). *Let $B = (S_B, I_B, 2^{\overline{m}}, T_B, Acc_B)$ be a Büchi automaton accepting some ω-regular language O. The monotonic closure of O is the ω-regular language $\uparrow O$ accepted by the Büchi automaton $\uparrow B = (S_{\uparrow B}, I_{\uparrow B}, 2^{\overline{m}}, T_{\uparrow B}, Acc_{\uparrow B})$ constructed from B as follows: $S_{\uparrow B} = S_B$, $I_{\uparrow B} = I_B$, $Acc_{\uparrow B} = Acc_B$, and $T_{\uparrow B} = \{(q, \overline{m}'', q') \mid \exists \overline{m}' \subseteq \overline{m}'' \,.\, (q, \overline{m}', q') \in T_B\}$.*

The correctness of our two-step procedure is encapsulated by the following:

Theorem 2. $\widehat{M}, s \models \mathbf{AO}(\varphi_1, \ldots, \varphi_n)$ *iff* $O_s \subseteq \uparrow O$.

The other cases (in which φ is not an ω-regular operator) are straightforward. To summarize, $\widehat{M}, s \models \varphi$ iff:

- $p \in \widehat{\mathcal{L}(s)}$ if $\varphi = p$ and $p \notin \widehat{\mathcal{L}(s)}$ if $\varphi = \neg p$, where $p \in AP$.
- $\widehat{M}, s \models \varphi_1$ and $\widehat{M}, s \models \varphi_2$ if $\varphi = \varphi_1 \wedge \varphi_2$.
- $\widehat{M}, s \models \varphi_1$ or $\widehat{M}, s \models \varphi_2$ if $\varphi = \varphi_1 \vee \varphi_2$.
- $O_s \subseteq \uparrow O$ if $\varphi = \mathbf{AO}(\varphi_1, \ldots, \varphi_n)$, where O_s and $\uparrow O$ are defined as above.

5.2   Counterexample Generation

Let $\widehat{M}$ be an LKS, $s \in S(\widehat{M})$, and φ be an SE-AΩ formula. Suppose that $\widehat{M}, s \not\models \varphi$. In this section, we show how to compute a counterexample to φ, i.e., a fragment of $\widehat{M}$ beginning at state s that violates φ. As for the model-checking algorithm of SE-AΩ, we give a recursive procedure:

- If $\varphi = \varphi_1 \vee \varphi_2$, then compute counterexamples $\widehat{C}_1$ and $\widehat{C}_2$ to φ_1 and φ_2 respectively, and glue $\widehat{C}_1$ and $\widehat{C}_2$ at their initial states. Indeed, $\widehat{M}, s \not\models \varphi_1 \vee \varphi_2$ iff $\widehat{M}, s \not\models \varphi_1$ *and* $\widehat{M}, s \not\models \varphi_2$.
- If $\varphi = \varphi_1 \wedge \varphi_2$, then compute a counterexample either to φ_1 or to φ_2. Indeed, $\widehat{M}, s \not\models \varphi_1 \wedge \varphi_2$ iff $\widehat{M}, s \not\models \varphi_1$ *or* $\widehat{M}, s \not\models \varphi_2$.
- If $\varphi = \mathbf{AO}(\varphi_1, \ldots, \varphi_n)$, proceed as follows. Since $\widehat{M}, s \not\models \varphi$, there exists a pattern in O_s that is not in $\uparrow O$. Let $\pi = s_0 \xrightarrow{\overline{m}_0} s_1 \xrightarrow{\overline{m}_1} \ldots$ (where $s_0 = s$) be an accepting path of B_s such that the ω-word $\overline{m}_0 \overline{m}_1 \ldots$ does not belong to $\uparrow O$. From the theory of Büchi automata we know in fact that such a path can be chosen to be lasso-like, i.e., end in an infinite loop. Recall now that by the definition of the automaton B_s, each transition $s_i \xrightarrow{\overline{m}_i} s_i'$ in T_{B_s} corresponds to a transition $s_i \xrightarrow{a_i} s_i'$ in $T(\widehat{M})$. Let therefore $s_0 \xrightarrow{a_0} s_1 \xrightarrow{a_1} \ldots$ be the corresponding path of π in $\widehat{M}$, itself also a lasso. This path then clearly violates $\mathbf{O}(\varphi_1, \ldots, \varphi_n)$. To compute a counterexample to φ, it suffices to take this path and to glue to each state s_i counterexamples to all formulas φ_j such that $\widehat{M}, s_i \not\models \varphi_j$. (Note that, while the path is infinite, it comprises only a finite prefix followed by an infinitely-repeating finite loop.)

Observe that the counterexample $\widehat{C}$ thus obtained is an LKS that can be viewed as a fragment of $\widehat{M}$. If one desires a *tree-like*[4] counterexample, one needs simply duplicate states of $\widehat{M}$ during the construction of the counterexample to avoid inadvertently creating strongly connected components that are not cycles. In that case $\widehat{C}$ will not technically be a fragment of $\widehat{M}$ but it will still be simulated by it ($\widehat{C} \leqslant \widehat{M}$).

---

[4] Intuitively, a tree-like counterexample is an LKS whose underlying directed graph only has cycles as strongly connected components. We refer the reader to [9] for an extensive discussion of the subject.

Owing to the direct manner in which the counterexample $\widehat{C}$ is extracted from the LKS $\widehat{M}$, there is a canonical mapping $\rho : S(\widehat{C}) \to S(\widehat{M})$ which satisfies the following conditions: (i) $\rho(init(\widehat{C})) = init(\widehat{M})$, (ii) for all $q \in S(\widehat{C})$, $\mathcal{L}(\widehat{C})(q) = \mathcal{L}(\widehat{M})(\rho(q))$, and (iii) if $(q, a, q') \in T(\widehat{C})$, then $(\rho(q), a, \rho(q')) \in T(\widehat{M})$. We shall make use of ρ later on in the refinement step.

Example 1. Figure 1 (a) shows an LKS M with $AP(M) = \{p, q\}$, $\Sigma(M) = \{a, b\}$, and initial state $S1$. (b) shows the abstract quotient LKS M^R induced by the equivalence relation R having equivalence classes $\{S1, S2\}$ and $\{S3, S4\}$. Let φ be the formula (in CTL^*-like notation) $\mathbf{AG}(\{a\} \Rightarrow \mathbf{A}(p \vee \mathbf{X}p \vee \mathbf{XX}p))$. φ asserts that on all paths, whenever the action a occurs from a state s, then the atomic proposition p either holds at s or, along any path starting at s, in one of the next two states. It is not hard to see that $M^R \not\models \varphi$, and indeed (c) shows a counterexample $\widehat{C}$ illustrating this. The dotted arrows from $\widehat{C}$ to M^R represent the canonical mapping ρ.

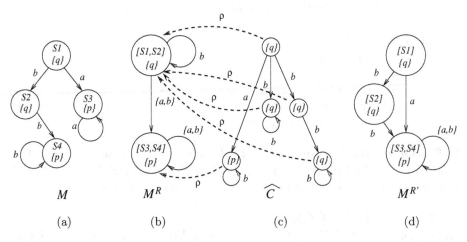

Fig. 1. (a) concrete LKS M; (b) Abstract LKS M^R; (c) counterexample $\widehat{C}$; (d) refined abstract LKS $M^{R'}$

Observe, however, that the counterexample is in fact spurious. Indeed, the abstract LKS $M^{R'}$ pictured in (d) is a refinement of M^R induced by the equivalence relation R' having equivalence classes $\{S1\}$, $\{S2\}$, and $\{S3, S4\}$. Since $M^{R'} \models \varphi$, we conclude that $M \models \varphi$ as well.

5.3   Counterexample Validation

Suppose that $\widehat{M}, s \not\models \varphi$ for some SE-AΩ formula φ, and let $\widehat{C}$ be a counterexample to φ. Recall that $\widehat{M}$ is an abstraction of a concrete LKS M. We say that $\widehat{C}$ is a *valid* counterexample iff $\widehat{C} \leqslant M$. Indeed, from Lemma 2 we get:

Theorem 3. *Let φ be an SE-AΩ formula. If $\widehat{C} \leqslant M$ and $\widehat{C} \not\models \varphi$, then $M \not\models \varphi$.*

Intuitively, this holds because SE-AΩ formulas describe properties that are quantified over all possible paths of the structure.

This result suggests a way to formally check whether a counterexample $\widehat{C}$ is valid for a concrete system M or not. However, as mentioned earlier, when M is a concurrent C program built of components $M_1, \ldots, M_n$, we are faced with the problem that even if each component M_i has a finite state space, constructing the state space of M might be prohibitive in practice due to exponential blowup. To overcome this problem, we propose to check if the concrete system M simulates the counterexample $\widehat{C}$ in a compositional way by checking whether for every $i \in \{1, \ldots, n\}$, M_i weakly simulates the ith projection of $\widehat{C}$.

Definition 7 (i^{th} Projection). *Let $M = M_1 \| \ldots \| M_n$ be a parallel composition of LKSs, and let $\widehat{C}$ be a further LKS. For any $i \in \{1, \ldots, n\}$, $\widehat{C}\!\restriction_i$ is the LKS defined by: (i) $S(\widehat{C}\!\restriction_i) = S(\widehat{C})$, (ii) $init(\widehat{C}\!\restriction_i) = init(\widehat{C})$, (iii) $AP(\widehat{C}\!\restriction_i) = AP(M_i)$, (iv) for any $s \in S(\widehat{C}\!\restriction_i)$, $\mathcal{L}(\widehat{C}\!\restriction_i)(s) = \mathcal{L}(\widehat{C})(s) \cap \mathcal{L}(M_i)$, (v) $\Sigma(\widehat{C}\!\restriction_i) = \Sigma(M_i) \cup \{\tau\}$[5], and (vi) $T(\widehat{C}\!\restriction_i)$ is defined as follows:*

- *If $(s, a, s') \in T(\widehat{C})$ and $a \in \Sigma(M_i)$ then $(s, a, s') \in T(\widehat{C}\!\restriction_i)$.*
- *If $(s, a, s') \in T(\widehat{C})$ and $a \notin \Sigma(M_i)$ then $(s, \tau, s') \in T(\widehat{C}\!\restriction_i)$.*

The introduction of τ actions also naturally leads to a *weak* version of simulation, which we define next specialized to the case in which only the system being simulated is capable of performing τ's.

Definition 8 (Weak Simulation). *Let $\widehat{C}$ and M be LKSs such that $\Sigma(\widehat{C}) = \Sigma(M) \cup \{\tau\}$ and $AP(\widehat{C}) = AP(M)$. A relation $R \subseteq S(\widehat{C}) \times S(M)$ is said to be a weak simulation relation iff R satisfies the following conditions:*

1. *If $(s_1, s_2) \in R$ then $\mathcal{L}(\widehat{C})(s_1) = \mathcal{L}(M)(s_2)$.*
2. *For any $s_1, s_1' \in S(\widehat{C})$, $s_2 \in S(M)$, and $a \in \Sigma(\widehat{C}) \setminus \{\tau\}$, if $(s_1, s_2) \in R$ and $s_1 \xrightarrow{a} s_1'$ then there exists $s_2' \in S(M)$ such that $s_2 \xrightarrow{a} s_2'$ and $(s_1', s_2') \in R$.*
3. *For any $s_1, s_1' \in S(\widehat{C})$ and $s_2 \in S(M)$, if $(s_1, s_2) \in R$ and $s_1 \xrightarrow{\tau} s_1'$ then $(s_1', s_2) \in R$.*

For two LKSs $\widehat{C}$ and M, if there exists a weak simulation relation R such that $(init(\widehat{C}), init(M)) \in R$ then we say that $\widehat{C}$ is weakly simulated by M and denote this by $\widehat{C} \preccurlyeq M$.

The following key result forms the basis of our compositional approach to counterexample validation.

Theorem 4 (Compositionality). *Let $M_1, \ldots, M_n$ be LKSs and let $\widehat{C}$ be a further LKS. Then $\widehat{C} \preccurlyeq (M_1 \| \ldots \| M_n)$ iff $\widehat{C}\!\restriction_i \preccurlyeq M_i$ for $1 \leq i \leq n$.*

---

[5] We assume that τ is a fresh action not otherwise present in the alphabet of LKSs.

Proof. (Sketch.) Consider the case $n = 2$; the general case is handled in a similar manner. Suppose first that $\widehat{C} \leqslant M_1 \| M_2$. Let $R \subseteq S(\widehat{C}) \times S(M_1 \| M_2)$ be a corresponding simulation relation. Define $R_1 = \{(s, s_1) \mid \exists s_2 \cdot \big(s, (s_1, s_2)\big) \in R\}$, and $R_2 = \{(s, s_2) \mid \exists s_1 \cdot \big(s, (s_1, s_2)\big) \in R\}$. It is readily verified that R_1 (resp. R_2) is a weak simulation relation between $\widehat{C}\!\restriction_1$ and M_1 (resp. $\widehat{C}\!\restriction_2$ and M_2). Therefore $\widehat{C}\!\restriction_1 \preccurlyeq M_1$ and $\widehat{C}\!\restriction_2 \preccurlyeq M_2$.

In the other direction, let R_1 and R_2 be two weak simulation relations witnessing $\widehat{C}\!\restriction_1 \preccurlyeq M_1$ and $\widehat{C}\!\restriction_2 \preccurlyeq M_2$ respectively. Let $R = \{(s, (s_1, s_2)) \mid (s, s_1) \in R_1 \wedge (s, s_2) \in R_2\}$. It is easy to check that R is a simulation relation between $\widehat{C}$ and $M_1 \| M_2$, as required.   □

Putting everything together, we get:

Corollary 1. *Let $M_1, \ldots, M_n$ be LKSs, φ an SE-$A\Omega$ formula, and $\widehat{C}$ an abstract counterexample to $M_1 \| \ldots \| M_n \models \varphi$. Then $\widehat{C}$ is a valid counterexample iff $\widehat{C}\!\restriction_i \preccurlyeq M_i$ for every $i \in \{1, \ldots, n\}$.*

Checking whether $\widehat{C}\!\restriction_i \preccurlyeq M_i$ is done in a standard manner by a fixpoint computation of the maximal weak simulation relation between $\widehat{C}\!\restriction_i$ and M_i.

5.4 Abstraction Refinement

We now describe our counterexample-guided refinement procedure. Suppose that $\widehat{C} \not\preccurlyeq M$; then the counterexample $\widehat{C}$ is spurious, and we need to refine our abstraction $\widehat{M} = \widehat{M_1} \| \ldots \| \widehat{M_n}$. We achieve this by examining each of the abstractions $\widehat{M_i}$ individually: for $i \in \{1, \ldots, n\}$, we refine $\widehat{M_i}$ if $\widehat{C}\!\restriction_i \not\preccurlyeq M_i$. To this end, fix j an index in $\{1, \ldots, n\}$ such that $\widehat{C}\!\restriction_j \not\preccurlyeq M_j$. Recall that $\widehat{M_j}$ is a quotient LKS of the form $M_j^{R_j}$, where R_j is an equivalence relation on $S(M_j)$. Our refinement step consists in producing a strictly finer equivalence relation than R_j.

Recall the canonical mapping $\rho : S(\widehat{C}) \to S(\widehat{M})$ defined in Section 5.2, and let $\rho_j : S(\widehat{C}) \to S(\widehat{M_j})$ be its corresponding j^{th} projection. We have:

Lemma 3. *Suppose that for any $s \in S(\widehat{C})$, any $a \in Enabled(s)$, and any $s_1, s_2 \in \rho_j(s)$, we have that $AbsSucc(s_1, a) = AbsSucc(s_2, a)$. Then $\widehat{C}\!\restriction_j \preccurlyeq M_j$.*

Since, by assumption, $\widehat{C}\!\restriction_j \not\preccurlyeq M_j$, it follows from Lemma 3 that there exist a state $s \in S(\widehat{C})$, an action $a \in Enabled(s)$, and two states $s_1, s_2 \in \rho_j(s)$ such that $AbsSucc(s_1, a) \neq AbsSucc(s_2, a)$. Let R'_j be a new equivalence relation derived from R_j by sub-partitioning the equivalence class $\rho_j(s)$ as follows: q, q' belong to the same sub-partition iff $AbsSucc(q, a) = AbsSucc(q', a)$. R'_j is clearly a *proper* refinement of R_j, and is moreover admissible since R_j was admissible. It should be noted that the refined abstract LKS $M_j^{R'_j}$ is however *not* guaranteed to refute the (projected) counterexample $\widehat{C}\!\restriction_j$.

As an example, Figure 1 shows the abstract LKS M^R and its refinement $M^{R'}$ which, in this case, refutes the spurious counterexample $\widehat{C}$.

Since the refinement procedure always yields a proper refinement and since each LKS is finite, the CEGAR-based SE-AΩ verification algorithm always terminates. In particular, spurious counterexamples are always eventually refuted.

6 Experimental Evaluation

We implemented our compositional approach for verification of branching-time logics as part of the COMFORT reasoning framework, which is based on the C model checker MAGIC developed at Carnegie Mellon [2, 22]. MAGIC extracts finite LKS models from C programs. We applied our model checking algorithm to verify a set of benchmarks whose abstract models were automatically extracted by MAGIC.

Here, we report on the verification of a piece of code provided by our industrial partner, one of the market leading robot manufacturers worldwide. We analyzed the IPC (InterProcess Communication) protocol used to mediate communication in a multi-threaded robot controller program. We model checked the synchronous communication portion of the IPC protocol which was implemented in terms of messages passed between queues owned by different threads. In the synchronous communication protocol, a sender sends a message to a receiver and blocks until an answer is received or it times out. A receiver asks for its next message and blocks until a message is available or it times out. Whenever the receiver gets a synchronous message, it is then expected to send a response to the message's sender. The target of our verification was to validate this communication scheduling.

We specified a set of more than twenty SE-AΩ properties most of which were expressed using both states and events. That was required to make proper assertions on the communication actions carrying data. Sample properties that were verified are summarized in Table 1.

The first property expresses the fact that whenever the message queue receives a request to queue a new message ($p1$) when the queue is full ($p2$) or receives a request to retrieve a message ($p3$) when the queue is empty ($p4$), then it enters an error state ($p5$). In this property propositions $p1$, $p3$ are

Table 1. Verification properties

N	Property	IPC Domain Description	Informal Description
1	AG((($p1 \wedge p2$) $\vee$ ($p3 \wedge p4$)) $\rightarrow$ AG $p5$)	Whenever the message queue receives a request to queue a new message ($p1$) when the queue is full ($p2$) or receives a request to retrieve a message ($p3$) when the queue is empty ($p4$), then along all paths it enters an error state ($p5$)	If a condition (($p1 \wedge p2$) $\vee$ ($p3 \wedge p4$)) holds, then assertion ($p5$) holds globally for each execution path.
2	AG($p1 \rightarrow$ AF $p2$)	If a condition ($p1$) true, then action ($p2$) will eventually occur	For each execution path if a condition ($p1$) is true, then it will eventually result in action ($p2$).

events *addMessage*, *takeMessage* respectively, *p2*: *numMessages* == *queue_size* and *p4*: *numMessages* == *0* are the guards of events *p1*, *p2*, and *p5*: *error* == *1* is a condition of the queue error state. The second property in Table 1 is a general description of a claim that states that if some condition (*p1*) is true, then an action (*p2*) will eventually occur. We checked the following instances of this property: *p1* was set to define a condition consisting of the event *begin_ReadMessageQueue* and the state assertion *numMessages* == *0* (*begin_ReadMessageQueue* ∧ *numMessages* == *0*); *p2* was defined for the following choices: an event *ReadMessageQueue* (i) retrieves a message from the queue; (ii) calls *PulseEvent*; (iii) does not timeout.

In our experiments SE-AΩ has been extremely useful for both (i) specifying the branching structure of the protocol executions and (ii) for to making assertions on both communications and data valuations. For example, Property 1 from Table 1 both makes use of branching and combines states and actions.

7 Conclusions and Future Work

In this paper we presented a framework for verifying branching-time temporal logic specifications on concurrent software systems. We defined a powerful universal branching-time logic, SE-AΩ, that incorporates the ability to make assertions about both states (data) and events (communication). This logic provides flexibility in specifying properties of complex distributed software systems.

We also presented a compositional abstraction-based model checking algorithm for SE-AΩ. This algorithm increasingly refines abstractions of the system under consideration based on an analysis of branching counterexamples to the specification that it generates. In this way the state explosion problem is delayed for significantly longer than if the entire system were model-checked up front. To the best of our knowledge, this is the first counterexample-guided, compositional abstraction refinement scheme to perform verification of branching-time specifications. The key ingredient enabling our compositional approach is a new result relating simulation and weak simulation relations for parallel processes.

For future work, we would like to evaluate the expressiveness of the SE-AΩ logic in comparison to other universal logics, and estimate the complexity of our algorithm.

Acknowledgements. We thank the anonymous referees for their careful reading and many insightful suggestions.

References

1. T. Ball and S. K. Rajamani. Automatically validating temporal safety properties of interfaces. In *Proceedings of the 8th International SPIN Workshop*, volume 2057 of *Lecture Notes in Computer Science*, pages 103–122. Springer, 2001.
2. S. Chaki, E. M. Clarke, A. Groce, S. Jha, and H. Veith. Modular verification of software components in C. In *Proceedings of the 25th International Conference on Software Engineering (ICSE)*, pages 385–395. IEEE Press, 2003.

3. S. Chaki, E. M. Clarke, J. Ouaknine, N. Sharygina, and N. Sinha. State/event-based software model checking. In *Proceedings of the 4th International Conference on Integrated Formal Methods (IFM)*, volume 2999 of *Lecture Notes in Computer Science*, pages 128–147. Springer, 2004.

4. S. Chaki, E. M. Clarke, J. Ouaknine, N. Sharygina, and N. Sinha. Concurrent software verification with states, events, and deadlocks. *Formal Aspects of Computing Journal (to appear)*, 2005.

5. S. Chaki, J. Ouaknine, K. Yorav, and E. M. Clarke. Automated compositional abstraction refinement for concurrent C programs: A two-level approach. In *Proceedings of the Workshop on Software Model Checking (SoftMC)*. ENTCS 89(3), 2003.

6. E. M. Clarke, O. Grumberg, S. Jha, Y. Lu, and H. Veith. Counterexample-guided abstraction refinement. In *Proceedings of the 12th International Conference on Computer Aided Verification (CAV)*, volume 1855 of *Lecture Notes in Computer Science*, pages 154–169. Springer, 2000.

7. E. M. Clarke, O. Grumberg, and R. P. Kurshan. A synthesis of two approaches for verifying finite state concurrent systems. *Journal of Logic and Computation*, 2(5):606–618, 1992.

8. E. M. Clarke, O. Grumberg, and D. E. Long. Model checking and abstraction. *ACM Transactions on Programming Languages and Systems*, 16(5):1512–1542, 1994.

9. E. M. Clarke, S. Jha, Y. Lu, and H. Veith. Tree-like counterexamples in model checking. In *Proceedings of the 17th Symposium on Logic in Computer Science (LICS)*, pages 19–29. IEEE Press, 2002.

10. P. Cousot and R. Cousot. Abstract interpretation: A unified lattice model for static analysis of programs by construction or approximation of fixpoints. In *Proceedings of the SIGPLAN Conference on Programming Languages*, 1977.

11. M. Dam. CTL* and ECTL* as fragments of the modal μ-calculus. *Theoretical Computer Science*, 126:77–96, 1994.

12. S. Graf and H. Saïdi. Construction of abstract state graphs with PVS. In *Proceedings of the 9th International Conference on Computer Aided Verification (CAV)*, volume 1254 of *Lecture Notes in Computer Science*, pages 72–83. Springer, 1997.

13. J. Haartsen, Bluetooth Baseband Specification, version 1.0.

14. T. A. Henzinger, R. Jhala, R. Majumdar, and G. Sutre. Lazy abstraction. In *Proceedings of the 29th Annual ACM Symposium on Principles of Programming Languages (POPL)*, pages 58–70. ACM Press, 2002.

15. C. A. R. Hoare. *Communicating Sequential Processes*. Prentice Hall, 1985.

16. M. Huth, R. Jagadeesan, and D. Schmidt. Modal transition systems: A foundation for three-valued program analysis. In *Proceedings of the 10th European Symposium on Programming (ESOP)*, volume 2028 of *Lecture Notes in computer Science*, pages 137–154. Springer, 2001.

17. J. Ivers and N. Sharygina. Overview of ComFoRT: A model checking reasoning framework. *CMU/SEI-2004-TN-018*, 2004.

18. E. Kindler and T. Vesper. ESTL: A temporal logic for events and states. *Lecture Notes in Computer Science*, 1420:365–383, 1998.

19. R. P. Kurshan. Analysis of discrete event coordination. In *Proceedings of the REX Workshop*, volume 430 of *Lecture Notes in Computer Science*, pages 414–453. Springer, 1989.

20. R. P. Kurshan. *Computer-aided verification of coordinating processes: the automata-theoretic approach*. Princeton University Press, 1994.

21. Y. Lakhnech, S. Bensalem, S. Berezin, and S. Owre. Incremental verification by abstraction. In *Proceedings of the 7th International Conference on Tools and Algorithms for the Construction and Analysis of Systems (TACAS)*, volume 2031 of *Lecture Notes in Computer Science*, pages 98–112. Springer, 2001.
22. MAGIC website. `http://www.cs.cmu.edu/~chaki/magic`.
23. R. Milner. *Communication and Concurrency*. Prentice-Hall, 1989.
24. G. Naumovich, L. A. Clarke, L. J. Osterweil, and M. B. Dwyer. Verification of concurrent software with FLAVERS. In *Proceedings of the 19th International Conference on Software Engineering (ICSE)*, pages 594–595. IEEE Press, 1997.
25. R. De Nicola and F. Vaandrager. Three logics for branching bisimulation. *Journal of the ACM*, 42(2):458–487, 1995.
26. C. S. Păsăreanu, M. B. Dwyer, and W. Visser. Finding feasible counter-examples when model checking abstracted Java programs. In *Proceedings of the 7th International Conference on Tools and Algorithms for the Construction and Analysis of Systems (TACAS)*, volume 2031 of *Lecture Notes in Computer Science*, pages 284–298. Springer, 2001.
27. A. W. Roscoe. *The Theory and Practice of Concurrency*. Prentice-Hall, 1997.
28. W. Thomas. Computation tree logic and regular ω-languages. In *Proceedings of REX Workshop*, Lecture Notes in Computer Science, pages 690–713. Springer, 1988.
29. M. Y. Vardi and P. Wolper. Yet another process logic. In *Proceedings of Logic of Programs*, Lecture Notes in Computer Science, pages 501–512. Springer, 1983.
30. M. Y. Vardi and P. Wolper. Reasoning about infinite computations. *Information and Computation*, 115(1):1–37, 1994.
31. P. Wolper. Temporal logic can be more expressive. *Information and Control*, 56:72–99, 1983.

Exp.Open 2.0: A Flexible Tool Integrating Partial Order, Compositional, and On-The-Fly Verification Methods

Frédéric Lang

INRIA Rhône-Alpes / VASY,
655, avenue de l'Europe, 38334 Saint-Ismier Cedex, France
Phone: +33 (0)4 76 61 55 11, Fax: +33 (0)4 76 61 52 52
Frederic.Lang@inria.fr
http://www.inrialpes.fr/vasy/people/Frederic.Lang

Abstract. It is desirable to integrate formal verification techniques applicable to different languages. We present EXP.OPEN 2.0, a new tool of the CADP verification toolbox which combines several features. First, EXP.OPEN 2.0 allows to describe concurrent systems as a composition of finite state machines, using either synchronization vectors, or parallel composition, hiding, renaming, and cut operators from several process algebras (CCS, CSP, LOTOS, E-LOTOS, μCRL). Second, together with other tools of CADP, EXP.OPEN 2.0 allows state space generation and on-the-fly exploration. Third, EXP.OPEN 2.0 implements on-the-fly partial order reductions to avoid the generation of irrelevant interleavings of independent transitions. Fourth, EXP.OPEN 2.0 allows to export models towards other tools using interchange formats such as automata networks and Petri nets. Finally, we show some practical applications and measure the efficiency of EXP.OPEN 2.0 on several benchmarks.

1 Introduction

Enumerative (or *explicit state*) *verification* is a method to check the proper behaviour of safety-critical finite-state systems. It consists in generating the state space systematically (if possible, exhaustively), and in verifying properties by *model checking, visual checking,* or *equivalence checking.* For systems involving asynchronous concurrency, the state space is often represented as a *Labelled Transition System* (LTS for short) [47].

A well-known problem with enumerative verification is the combinatorial state explosion, which often occurs as the number of concurrent processes increases. To fight state explosion, several effective techniques have been proposed:

- *Partial order reductions* (e.g., [26, 57, 50, 32, 52, 30, 48]) try to avoid the generation of irrelevant interleavings of independent transitions.
- *On-the-fly verification* (e.g., [16, 15, 38, 33, 46, 45]) consists in performing LTS generation and verification at the same time. This avoids to generate the entire LTS when the verification only requires a part of it.

J. Romijn, G. Smith, and J. van de Pol (Eds.): IFM 2005, LNCS 3771, pp. 70–88, 2005.
© Springer-Verlag Berlin Heidelberg 2005

- *Compositional verification* (e.g., [14, 44, 55, 28, 56, 60, 63, 10, 27, 42, 54, 25, 18]) consists in generating the LTS of each concurrent process first (possibly restricted using constraints derived from its environment [28, 10, 63, 27, 42, 25, 18]), then simplifying these LTSs using abstraction criteria (for instance, label hiding and reductions modulo bisimulations) that preserve the properties under verification, and finally recomposing the reduced LTSs to generate the LTS corresponding to the whole system.

In practice, many software tools have been developed to implement these ideas. Nevertheless, these tools often suffer from several limitations:

- Most tools are often dedicated to one specific input formalism, e.g., Petri nets, communicating automata, or a particular process algebra. On the opposite, a unified tool accepting several input formalisms would be more flexible by combining the expressiveness of different input languages and by having its verification algorithms accessible by a wider community of users.
- Although there exist tools combining two among the three aforementioned verification techniques, such as SPIN [37] (partial order and on-the-fly verification) and ARA [59] (partial order and compositional verification), to our knowledge, combining the three techniques has never been done.

In this article, we present EXP.OPEN 2.0, a new tool that addresses these issues. EXP.OPEN 2.0 is part of CADP [19] (*Construction and Analysis of Distributed Processes*)[1], a toolbox for protocol engineering that offers functionalities ranging from mere interactive simulation up to the most recent verification techniques. EXP.OPEN 2.0 builds upon the existing software components of CADP, especially for handling LTSs.

Earlier versions of CADP contained a tool named EXP.OPEN 1.0, developed in 1995 by L. Mounier (Université Joseph Fourier, Grenoble, France), that combined on-the-fly verification and compositional verification for LOTOS [39]. To develop EXP.OPEN 2.0, we deeply revisited the principles of EXP.OPEN 1.0 and rewrote the tool entirely from scratch to extend its input language, to provide new functionalities, and to support partial order reductions.

This article is organized as follows. Section 2 describes inputs of EXP.OPEN 2.0. Section 3 presents its functionalities. Section 4 presents practical applications and gives experimental results for several applications. Section 5 finally concludes the article.

2   The Exp.Open 2.0 Language

2.1   Labelled Transition Systems and Composition Expressions

The basic concept used by EXP.OPEN 2.0 is the standard LTS model [47], which consists of a set of *states*, an *initial state*, and a set of *transitions* between states, each transition being labelled by an event of the system. A particular

---

[1] http://www.inrialpes.fr/vasy/cadp

label written τ represents an invisible (or internal) event. The contents of states are not observable.

In practice, a label is represented by a character string. EXP.OPEN 2.0 does not impose a particular syntax and thus accepts labels from different source languages, such as CCS [47], CSP [54], LOTOS [39], E-LOTOS [40], and μCRL [31].

As regards the semantic structure of labels, most languages assume that a label consists of a *gate* (i.e., a port name, a channel name) and a (possibly empty) list of typed values, here called *offers*. For instance, if G is a gate, both labels "G !1 !2" (LOTOS notation) and "$G(1,2)$" (μCRL notation) are accepted by EXP.OPEN 2.0. Labels obtained from CCS may also start with a *co-action* symbol, generally written '.

LTSs are stored in computer files, using one of the four formats available in CADP: BCG (*Binary Coded Graph*), ALDÉBARAN (textual), sequential FC2, and SEQ for transition sequences [20]. Other file formats can be converted into BCG using the BCG_IO tool of CADP.

The input language of EXP.OPEN 2.0 allows to define compositions of LTSs, named *composition expressions*. Figure 1 presents an extended BNF describing the abstract syntax of composition expressions. The concrete syntax can be found in [43]. The symbols in italic are the non-terminal and generic terminal symbols. Subscripts are used for the sake of readability, e.g., $B_0, B_1, \ldots$ are occurrences of the same non-terminal B. The symbols "::=", "|", "[", "]", "(", ")", and "..." are meta-symbols: "::=" introduces the definition of a non-terminal symbol, "|" separates alternative clauses, "[ ]" delimit optional clauses, "( )" are used for bracketing as usual, and the infix "..." meta-symbol denotes repetition, e.g., "$L_1, \ldots, L_n$" denotes the repetition of $n \geq 0$ symbols separated by commas and "$B_1 ||\ldots|| B_n$" denotes the repetition of $n \geq 0$ symbols separated by ||. All remaining symbols are the terminal symbols, i.e., the keywords (written in bold font, such as **gate, all**) and key symbols (written in teletype font, such as "{", "→"). In particular, "[", "]", and "|" are terminal symbols distinct from the meta-symbols "[", "]", and "|".

The generic terminal symbols $L, L', L_0, L_1, \ldots$ represent arbitrary character strings, $n, n_1, n_2, \ldots$ represent arbitrary natural numbers, $S, S_0, S_1, \ldots$ represent LTSs, and $P, P_0, P_1, \ldots$ represent patterns (which will be defined below). The non-terminal symbols $B, B_0, B_1, \ldots$ represent composition expressions, *op* represents binary infix parallel composition operators, and $V, V_0, V_1, \ldots$ represent synchronization vectors.

The semantics of a composition expression is itself an LTS that we define in the following sections.

2.2 Renaming, Hiding, and Cut Operators

Renaming (replacing occurrences of a visible label), hiding (renaming a visible label into τ), and cut[2] (eliminating all transitions with a particular visible label,

---

[2] Cut is also called *restriction* in CCS and *encapsulation* in μCRL.

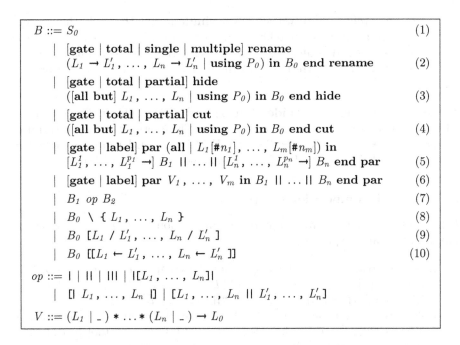

$$B ::= S_0 \hspace{11cm} (1)$$
$$\quad | \;\; [\text{gate} \mid \text{total} \mid \text{single} \mid \text{multiple}] \; \text{rename}$$
$$\quad\quad (L_1 \to L_1', \; \ldots, \; L_n \to L_n' \mid \text{using } P_0) \; \text{in } B_0 \; \text{end rename} \hspace{1.5cm} (2)$$
$$\quad | \;\; [\text{gate} \mid \text{total} \mid \text{partial}] \; \text{hide}$$
$$\quad\quad ([\text{all but}] \; L_1, \; \ldots, \; L_n \mid \text{using } P_0) \; \text{in } B_0 \; \text{end hide} \hspace{2.2cm} (3)$$
$$\quad | \;\; [\text{gate} \mid \text{total} \mid \text{partial}] \; \text{cut}$$
$$\quad\quad ([\text{all but}] \; L_1, \; \ldots, \; L_n \mid \text{using } P_0) \; \text{in } B_0 \; \text{end cut} \hspace{2.3cm} (4)$$
$$\quad | \;\; [\text{gate} \mid \text{label}] \; \text{par (all} \mid L_1[\#n_1], \; \ldots, \; L_m[\#n_m]) \; \text{in}$$
$$\quad\quad [L_1^1, \; \ldots, \; L_1^{p_1} \to] \; B_1 \; \| \; \ldots \; \| \; [L_n^1, \; \ldots, \; L_n^{p_n} \to] \; B_n \; \text{end par} \hspace{1cm} (5)$$
$$\quad | \;\; [\text{gate} \mid \text{label}] \; \text{par } V_1, \; \ldots, \; V_m \; \text{in } B_1 \; \| \; \ldots \; \| \; B_n \; \text{end par} \hspace{1.3cm} (6)$$
$$\quad | \;\; B_1 \; op \; B_2 \hspace{8.3cm} (7)$$
$$\quad | \;\; B_0 \setminus \{ \, L_1, \; \ldots, \; L_n \, \} \hspace{7.2cm} (8)$$
$$\quad | \;\; B_0 \; [L_1 \, / \, L_1', \; \ldots, \; L_n \, / \, L_n' \,] \hspace{6.4cm} (9)$$
$$\quad | \;\; B_0 \; [[L_1 \leftarrow L_1', \; \ldots, \; L_n \leftarrow L_n' \,]] \hspace{6cm} (10)$$
$$op ::= \; | \; \| \; \| \; \| \| \; \| \; |[L_1, \; \ldots, \; L_n]|$$
$$\quad | \;\; [| \; L_1, \; \ldots, \; L_n \; |] \; \mid \; [L_1, \; \ldots, \; L_n \; \| \; L_1', \; \ldots, \; L_n']$$
$$V ::= (L_1 \mid \_) \, * \ldots * \, (L_n \mid \_) \to L_0$$

Fig. 1. Abstract syntax of the Exp.Open 2.0 input language

possibly at the expense of creating unreachable states), are classical notions in process algebras.

For convenience, Exp.Open 2.0 supports the usual notations for these operators found in Ccs and Csp (Rules 8, 9, and 10). Rule 8 represents either Ccs restriction or Csp hiding, which have same syntax but different semantics. Rules 9 and 10 represent Ccs and Csp renaming, respectively. In these three rules, $L_1, L_1', \ldots, L_n, L_n'$ are simple gates.

Exp.Open 2.0 also supports more expressive operators for renaming, hiding, and cut (Rules 2, 3, and 4), which generalize classical operators in several ways:

- The labels to rename, hide, or cut can be specified either as a list $(L_1, \ldots, L_n)$, or as a *pattern* (**"using** P_0**"**), which consists of a reusable list of labels or renaming rules, stored in a separate file for convenience. The latter allows to factor rules used several times, or to isolate complex rules.
- For hiding and cut, the "**all but** $L_1, \ldots, L_n$" construct allows to define a set containing all labels but $L_1, \ldots, L_n$.
- $L_1, \ldots, L_n$ can be strings, or regular expressions (following the syntax of the Posix "regexp" library) that labels may match using three different semantics: **gate** means that a label matches only if its gate matches a regular expression; **total** means that a label matches if it matches a regular expression entirely; and **partial** means that a label matches if it contains a substring that matches a regular expression. As regards renaming, partial

matching is refined into two sub-cases: **single** means that only the first occurrence of a substring matching a regular expression is replaced, whereas **multiple** means that all such occurrences are replaced. The **gate** matching is the default, as it corresponds to the semantics found in classical process algebras.

Example 1. The expression "**hide** G **in** B_0 **end hide**" hides in B_0 every label whose gate is G, such as "G !1 !2" or "$G(1,2)$". The expression "**single rename** "\(.*\) !\(.*\) !\(.*\)" → "\1 !\3 !\2" **in** B_0 **end rename**" permutes two offers in labels, e.g., "G !A !B !C" is renamed into "G !B !A !C"[3].

2.3 Parallel Composition Operators

EXP.OPEN 2.0 contains various parallel composition operators, which can be mixed in the same expression:

- Rule 7 represents the usual binary parallel composition operators of CCS ("|"), CSP ("[| L_1, ..., L_n |]" and "[L_1, ..., L_n || L'_1, ... L'_n]"), μCRL[4] ("||"), and LOTOS ("||", "|||", and "|[L_1, ..., L_n]|").
- Rule 5 represents the n-ary "graphical" parallel composition operator of E-LOTOS [40, 23]. To our knowledge, the EXP.OPEN 2.0 tool provides the first implementation of this operator in a software tool.
- Rule 6 represents parallel composition using synchronization vectors, inspired from MEC [1] and FC2 networks [8].

We do not recall in details the semantics of these operators, which are given elsewhere. However, we present an overview of the semantics of the operators of Rules 5 and 6, which are the most general and least known of the EXP.OPEN 2.0 parallel composition operators.

For these **par** operators, unlike renaming, hiding, and cut, the L_i's and L_i^j's cannot be regular expressions. Nevertheless, EXP.OPEN 2.0 also extends these operators with a *matching mode*, as follows: **gate** means that the L_i's denote gates and that a label A matches L_i if and only if L_i is the gate of A; **label** means that the L_i's denote full labels and that a label A *matches* L_i if and only if A equals L_i (both gate and offers). The **gate** matching is the default, as it corresponds to the semantics found in classical process algebras.

A *global* state (i.e., a state of the resulting LTS) is a tuple $(s_1, \ldots, s_n)$, where s_i $(i \in 1..n)$ is a local state of the corresponding B_i. A global transition is obtained either by synchronization of several local transitions $\{s_i \xrightarrow{A_i} t_i \mid i \in I \subseteq 1..n\}$, or by asynchronous execution of a single local transition $s_i \xrightarrow{A_i} t_i$, where

---

[3] The symbols "\(" and "\)" are used to delimit sub-expressions. In the right-hand side, the symbol "\n", where n is a number (\1, \2, ...), is substituted by the string matched by the nth delimited sub-expression of the left-hand side.

[4] μCRL parallel composition depends on user-given synchronization rules, whose scope is the whole composition expression. For simplicity, we do not reproduce here the syntax of these rules.

$i \in 1..n$. The destination state of the global transition is obtained by replacing every s_i involved in a local transition by the corresponding t_i, whereas the other local states are not modified.

As regards Rule 5, we briefly recall the main features of the "graphical" parallel composition operator (see [23] for a formal description and examples):

- The simplest form, "**par** $L_1, \ldots, L_m$ **in** $B_1 \ \| \ \ldots \ \| \ B_n$ **end par**", is a generalization to n operators of the classical binary parallel composition operators of CSP and LOTOS with forced synchronization on $L_1, \ldots, L_m$. Either one single component evolves asynchronously by executing a transition whose label A does not match any L_i (in such a case, the other components remain in their current state), or all components evolve synchronously by executing transitions whose label A (the same for all components) matches some L_i. In both cases, the resulting global transition is also labelled A. The **all** keyword denotes the set of all gates or labels (depending on the matching mode) but the invisible label τ.
- If some L_i is followed by "#n_i" ($2 \leq n_i \leq n$), then only n_i (instead of n) of the components have to synchronize on L_i. This implements a relaxed form of synchronization named "m among n" synchronization, which is useful to express communication between a subgroup of components, as will be illustrated later.
- If some B_i is preceded by a list, as in "$L_i^1, \ldots, L_i^{p_i} \rightarrow B_i$", then B_i must synchronize on labels matching one of the L_i^j's with all other components also preceded by a list containing L_i^j. This is another form of relaxed synchronization.

Example 2. In "**par in** $G_{13}, G_{12} \rightarrow B_1 \ \| \ G_{12}, G_{23} \rightarrow B_2 \ \| \ G_{23}, G_{13} \rightarrow B_3$ **end par**", components B_i and B_j ($1 \leq i < j \leq 3$) communicate on gate G_{ij}. In "**par** G_0#2 **in** $B_1 \ \| \ B_2 \ \| \ B_3$ **end par**", components communicate pairwise on gate G_0.

Rule 6 implements parallel composition using synchronization vectors of the form "$(L_1 \mid \_) * \ldots * (L_n \mid \_) \rightarrow L_0$", whose elements at positions $1..n$ may be either an L_i (i.e., a gate or a label, depending on the matching mode) or the symbol "$\_$". We define the application of a synchronization vector to the current global state as follows: All components B_i such that the ith element in the vector is an L_i must execute synchronously transitions, such that the label of each transition matches the corresponding L_i (the labels of all transitions must also have the same offers in **gate** matching); the label of the resulting global transition is L_0 (followed by the offers of the synchronizing transitions in **gate** matching). τ-transitions execute asynchronously.

Example 3. In the expression "**gate par** $Snd * Rcv \rightarrow Com$ **in** $B_1 \ \| \ B_2$ **end par**", transitions of B_1 whose gate is Snd synchronize with transitions of B_2 whose gate is Rcv, provided those transitions have the same offers. The label of the resulting transition consists of the Com gate followed by these offers. In **label** matching instead of **gate**, transitions of B_1 whose label is Snd (gate without offers) would synchronize with transitions of B_2 whose label is Rcv. The label of the resulting transition would be Com, without offers.

In principle, EXP.OPEN 2.0 allows to freely combine operators originating from different languages, except in case of overloaded symbols that may have different semantics, such as " \ " (CCS restriction or CSP hiding) and "||" (LOTOS or μCRL parallel composition). In such cases, a command-line option ("-ccs", "-csp", etc.) or a specific keyword is needed to indicate to EXP.OPEN 2.0 which language is considered. Command-line options also allow to change syntactic conventions, such as the concrete notation of the invisible label τ (e.g., tau, i, t) or case-sensitivity (whether or not labels in lower and upper cases are to be considered equal).

The static semantics of EXP.OPEN 2.0 ensure that synchronization vectors have appropriate length. They also forbid synchronizing, renaming, and cutting τ-transitions, which ensures that bisimulation equivalences (strong, observational, branching, tau*.a, etc.) are congruences for all EXP.OPEN 2.0 operators [61]. Thus, arbitrary composition expressions of EXP.OPEN 2.0 can be verified compositionally, for instance by reducing component LTSs separately.

3   State Space Exploration Using Exp.Open 2.0

3.1   Translation into a Flat Network Model

To allow an homogeneous treatment of composition expressions, EXP.OPEN 2.0 first translates them into a general model, which we call *flat network of* LTSs (or simply, flat network).

Flat networks are similar to the **par** operator with synchronization vectors presented in Rule 6 of Figure 1. A flat network is a couple $((S_1, \ldots, S_n), Sync)$ consisting of a vector $(S_1, \ldots, S_n)$ of LTSs, and a set $Sync$ of synchronization vectors whose left-hand side (the part to the left of the arrow) have size n. The differences between flat networks and the **par** operator are that synchronization vectors contain "full" labels (instead of gates), including τ, and that flat networks have no nested subterms except LTSs.

Our flat network model is more general than the model used in EXP.OPEN 1.0, in which synchronization was represented only by vectors of gates (instead of labels), and a global predicate indicating whether a given gate was visible or hidden. This former model allowed to model composition expressions in which a gate was either visible everywhere or hidden everywhere, but not partially visible and partially hidden at the same time, such as in "B || (**hide** G **in** B)" (B containing an occurrence of G), which is legal LOTOS code. This problem imposed that **hide** operators occur at the top-level of expressions only. On the opposite, the whole EXP.OPEN 2.0 input language can be translated into flat networks without limitations.

A composition expression B is translated into a flat network $(s(B), v(B))$, where $s(B)$ is the vector of all LTSs used in B, in the order of their occurrence (thus LTSs occurring several times in the composition expression also occur several time in the vector), and $v(B)$ is defined recursively as follows:

- For an LTS S (Rule 1 of Figure 1), $v(S) = \{A \to A \mid A \in \text{labels}(S)\}$.
- For **rename**, **hide**, and **cut** (Rules 2, 3, 4, 8, 9, 10), $v(B_0)$ is computed first. Then, $v(B)$ is obtained by transforming each synchronization vector whose right-hand side matches a renaming, hiding, or cut rule, as follows: For renaming (respectively hiding), the right-hand side of the rule is renamed (respectively hidden) accordingly. For cut, the rule is removed.
- For parallel composition of n sub-expressions $B_1, \ldots, B_n$ (Rules 5, 6, 7), the sets $v(B_1), \ldots, v(B_n)$ are generated first. Their rules are then joined (i.e., their left-hand sides are concatenated and/or extended with an appropriate number of "$\_$" symbols) whenever their respective right-hand sides are synchronizing labels.

Note that the complexity for computing $v(B)$ depends on the number of labels in each of the LTSs in $s(B)$, but not on their number of states and transitions. Therefore, the translation from composition expressions into flat networks is not subject to state explosion.

Example 4. For the LOTOS composition expression "$B = (S_1 \mid\mid\mid S_2) \mid [G] \mid S_3$", where S_1, S_2, and S_3 are LTSs and G a list of gates, $s(B) = (S_1, S_2, S_3)$ and

$$
\begin{aligned}
v(B) = \{\ & A * \_ * \_ \to A \mid A \in \text{labels}(S_1),\ \text{gate}(A) \notin G\ \} && \cup \\
\{\ & \_ * A * \_ \to A \mid A \in \text{labels}(S_2),\ \text{gate}(A) \notin G\ \} && \cup \\
\{\ & \_ * \_ * A \to A \mid A \in \text{labels}(S_3),\ \text{gate}(A) \notin G\ \} && \cup \\
\{\ & A * \_ * A \to A \mid A \in \text{labels}(S_1) \cap \text{labels}(S_3),\ \text{gate}(A) \in G\ \} \cup \\
\{\ & \_ * A * A \to A \mid A \in \text{labels}(S_2) \cap \text{labels}(S_3),\ \text{gate}(A) \in G\ \}
\end{aligned}
$$

EXP.OPEN 2.0 allows to export flat networks into models suitable for various verification tools:

- Petri nets in the "low-level" PEP format, which can be verified using the PEP tool [6] and exported to other Petri net formats.
- Networks of communicating automata in the FC2 format, which can be verified using FC2TOOLS [8] and Jack [2].

3.2   Integration Within the OPEN/CAESAR Environment

CADP devotes a great importance to modular programming, using well-thought intermediate formats and programming interfaces. EXP.OPEN 2.0 is connected to OPEN/CÆSAR [17], a modular environment for developing on-the-fly exploration algorithms on LTSs.

The OPEN/CÆSAR architecture (see Figure 2) is based on a central language-independent API (*Application Programming Interface*), which allows to explore the states and transitions of an LTS on-the-fly. It describes types that represent labels and states, a function that computes the initial state of the system, and an ITERATE_STATE() function that enumerates the successor transitions of a given state.

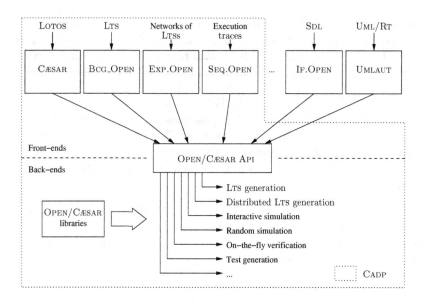

Fig. 2. Architecture of OPEN/CÆSAR

This architecture allows an orthogonal separation between the language-dependent compilers (*front-ends*) that translate a particular formalism into a C program implementing the OPEN/CÆSAR API, and the language-independent verification tools (*back-ends*) that operate on the representation of an LTS using the API. Each fromt-end can be combined with any back-end.

CADP includes four front-ends, namely EXP.OPEN 2.0, BCG_OPEN for LTSs in the BCG (*Binary Coded Graphs*) format, CÆSAR [22] for LOTOS [39], and SEQ.OPEN for traces [20]. It also includes several back-ends that provide various functionalities, such as LTS generation, possibly distributed to use the CPU and memory of a set of computers [21], on-the-fly model-checking of regular alternation-free μ-calculus [46], interactive simulation with X-window interface, generation of conformance test suites based on verification technology [41], on-the-fly behavioural comparison of systems modulo various equivalence and preorder relations [5], random execution, deadlock detection, reachability analysis, sequence searching, abstraction of an LTS w.r.t. an interface [42], etc.

EXP.OPEN 2.0 first translates the composition expression given as input into a flat network, and then generates a C program implementing the OPEN/CÆSAR API, which computes the reachable states and transitions of the composition expression. The translation performs careful analysis to reduce the number of bits allocated to represent states, and to optimize speed for the transition function.

3.3 Partial Order Reductions

Partial order reductions aim at avoiding transition interleavings that are irrelevant for a given class of properties. EXP.OPEN 2.0 implements three partial order reductions, preserving respectively the existence or absence of deadlocks, branching bisimulation [62], and stochastic branching bisimulation [36].

Partial order reduction preserving stochastic branching bisimulation operates on LTSs containing special transitions, called *stochastic*, of the form "**rate** λ", where λ is a positive real. The stochastic transitions express an internal delay in the source state, while the other transitions are immediate if their environment allows their execution. EXP.OPEN 2.0 implements the technique proposed by H. Hermanns [35], which consists in eliminating the stochastic transitions in choice with τ-transitions, the latter being always executable without delay.

To present deadlock and branching preserving partial order reductions, we define the following standard notions derived from the theory of *persistent sets* [26] (of which *stubborn sets* [57] and *ample sets* [50] are variations, see [51] for a survey on persistent set based partial order reductions), and applied to our context:

- A synchronization vector V is *enabled* in a state s if s has a successor obtained by application of V. It is *deterministic* in s if s has exactly one such successor.
- Two synchronization vectors V_1 and V_2 enabled in a state s are *commutative* if the set of states reachable by applying first V_1 then V_2 is the same as that obtained by applying first V_2 then V_1.
- Two synchronization vectors V_1 and V_2 are *independent* in a given state s if 1) V_1 and V_2 are commutative if they are both enabled in s and 2) V_1 (respectively V_2) is enabled in a successor state of s obtained by applying V_2 (respectively V_1) if and only if V_1 (respectively V_2) is enabled in s.
- A set *Sync* of synchronization vectors enabled in a state s is *persistent* in s if, in every state reachable from s by applying only synchronization vectors that do not belong to *Sync*, every synchronization vector that is enabled and does not belong to *Sync* is independent of the synchronization vectors that belong to *Sync*.

Persistent set computation is done by a careful analysis of the synchronization vectors, which we do not detail in this paper. Partial order reduction preserving the presence or absence of deadlocks is done in each reachable state of the system, by applying only the synchronization vectors that belong to the persistent set computed in the current state.

For branching bisimulation, the results of [58, 49, 24] state that, applied to our context, the persistent sets preserving branching bisimulation are those consisting of a single, deterministic synchronization vector, whose right-hand side is the label τ. In the algorithm below, we will only consider persistent sets that have this particular form. Unfortunately, finding such a persistent set is not enough to preserve branching bisimulation — and even weaker relations such as trace equivalence — because one may enter a circuit that prevents enabled synchronization vectors from ever being executed. This problem is known as the *ignoring problem* [51].

Most tools implementing partial order reductions (e.g., SPIN [37], ARA [59], etc.) solve the ignoring problem by detecting circuits in the back-end. A distinctive feature of EXP.OPEN 2.0 is to solve the ignoring problem in the front-end, thus avoiding any modification of verification back-ends, which can thus benefit from partial order reduction for free, independently of the strategy that they use to explore the LTS.

More precisely, the ignoring problem is dealt with in the ITERATE_STATE() function of the OPEN/CÆSAR API. When the ITERATE_STATE() function is called to enumerate the successors of a state s, a persistent set (which contains a single synchronization vector) is searched for. If it exists, this synchronization vector is executed, leading to a new state s'. The algorithm is then repeated, starting in s' instead of s, until reaching a state s'' that either does not have a persistent set or was already visited. In the former case, a single τ-transition from s to s'' is generated. In the latter case, the explored circuit of τ-transitions starting in s'' is just discarded (indeed, all states in a circuit of τ-transitions are branching equivalent) and the algorithm is continued by searching another persistent set in s''.

Note that the intermediate states reachable from s following persistent sets are only stored in memory temporarily by the front-end and never visible by the back-end. They are removed once ITERATE_STATE() returns, to optimize memory consumption. These states may possibly be revisited during subsequent calls to ITERATE_STATE(), but such revisits are not penalizing in practice, mostly due to the fact that persistent set computation is fast in the case of branching bisimulation. This confirms known results [4] about the fine tuning between storing or revisiting states, which were made on the basis of various storage heuristics leading to the conclusion that better verification performance can often be obtained by storing only a little amount of states.

There exist alternative partial order methods preserving branching bisimulation, which are based on τ-confluence reduction [32, 7, 48]. Persistent set methods operate a less general form of τ-confluence reduction than the algorithms presented in [32, 7, 48], but are cheaper in time and memory. In [48], persistent set methods and τ-confluence reduction are combined to reduce LTSs compositionally modulo branching bisimulation, using EXP.OPEN 2.0.

3.4   Refined Interface Constraints Generation

A potential limitation of compositional verification is that, given a system of concurrent processes, generating the LTS of each process separately may lead to state explosion, even though the LTS of the whole system has a tractable size. Indeed, generating the LTS of a process out of its context (i.e., separately from the neighbour processes with which it synchronizes) may lead to explore states that would be unreachable in the global system.

To address this problem, refined compositional verification approaches have been proposed [28, 10, 63, 11, 12, 27, 42, 9, 25], which allow to generate the LTS of a process by taking into account *interface constraints* (also known as *environment constraints* or *context constraints*). These constraints express the behavioural restrictions imposed on each process by the synchronization with its neighbour processes, thus avoiding globally unreachable states and transitions. As regards the choice of appropriate interface constraints, two approaches are possible.

In the first approach, the articles [28, 42] propose that interface constraints may be provided by the user (personal insight of the context). The risk is that these constraints are wrong and thus eliminate states and transitions that would be reachable in the global system. EXP.OPEN 2.0 (together with PROJECTOR 2.0) supports this approach. It checks automatically during the recomposition of the constrained LTS with its environment whether the eliminated states and transitions are indeed unreachable. Otherwise, it reports an error so that the user relaxes its constraints.

The second approach [10, 42] consists in building constraints automatically from the composition expression, for instance by considering a particular LTS in the environment and computing its interactions with the process to restrict. EXP.OPEN 2.0 also implements this approach. Given a flat network, in which are identified an LTS S whose labels are those of a process P to restrict and a set of LTSs $S_1, \ldots, S_n$ corresponding to processes in the environment of P, EXP.OPEN 2.0 computes refined interface constraints consisting of both an LTS S' and a set of labels L representing the potential interactions between $S_1, \ldots, S_n$ and P. S' and L are then used to restrict the LTS corresponding to P using the PROJECTOR 2.0 tool of CADP.

The precise algorithm used by EXP.OPEN 2.0 to generate interface constraints automatically will be detailed in another paper. However, we can briefly indicate the advantages of the proposed approach:

- By operating on flat networks obtained after translation of composition expressions, it can be applied to any of the languages supported by EXP.OPEN 2.0. By constrast, other methods are specific to one single language (e.g., LOTOS [42] or CSP [10]).
- It makes possible to build interface constraints obtained from several processes in the environment of S, even if these processes are distant in the composition expression, because flattening reduces the distance between algebraic terms. Other methods allow to build interface constraints only obtained from one single process.
- In the particular (but frequent) case of nondeterministic synchronization (which is a characteristic of client-server communications), it produces more accurate interface constraints, leading to better state space reductions. For instance, in the LOTOS expression "$(B_1 \;|||\; B_2) \;|[G]|\; B_3$", a G-transition of B_3 can synchronize either with a G-transition of B_1 or with a G-transition of B_2. The same also applies for more complex situations, such as nondeterministic multiway synchronization involving more than two processes, and "m among n" synchronization. Other techniques either forbid such situations using an input language that does not allow nondeterministic synchronization [10] or under-approximate the interactions between B_1 and B_3, and B_2 and B_3, by ignoring the possible synchronizations on G [42]. Instead, EXP.OPEN 2.0 generates interfaces in which every G-transition is duplicated by a τ-transition with same source and target states, which models nondeterministic synchronization.

4   Practical Applications and Experimental Results

As part of CADP, EXP.OPEN 2.0 is widely disseminated and has already been used for significant applications. We can mention for instance a few ones:

– At Eindhoven University of Technology, J. Romijn and S. Vorstenboch used it to verify the *Net Update Protocol* of the draft standard IEEE P1394.1. By combining the compositional techniques of EXP.OPEN 2.0 and the distributed state space construction tool of CADP [21], they managed to generate models of tractable size (up to 28 million states and 487 million transitions).
– At Saarland University, H. Hermanns and S. Johr used the EXP.OPEN 2.0 tool to analyze the performance of a distributed mutual exclusion algorithm. By combining EXP.OPEN 2.0 with the distributed state space construction tool of CADP, they generated a stochastic model with 224 million states and 1, 300 million transitions, which was unfortunately too big to fit on a standard 32-bit file system. Using the partial order reduction that preserves stochastic branching reduction, the state space was reduced to 44 million states and 80 million transitions and could be stored in a file on a single machine.
– At INRIA Sophia-Antipolis, E. Madelaine, T. Barros, and L. Henrio used EXP.OPEN 2.0 to compute large synchronization products corresponding to compositions of hierarchical object components [3]. Their work covers dynamic component updates, such as the dynamic replacement of a sub-component.

At least four additional examples of EXP.OPEN 2.0 are available as part of CADP:

– A **distributed summation algorithm**[5] inspired from [29]: The use of *"m among n"* synchronization allows a nice modeling of the interprocess communications, based on topological constraints encoded using data structures.
– The **ODP trader**[6] inspired from [23]: The use of *"m among n"* synchronization allows to model communications between arbitrary service providers and service users, which obtain their respective addresses using a separate process, called trader.
– The classical **distributed Erathostenes sieve**[7]: It consists of a pipeline of units, each unit blocking every input number that is a multiple of a given number. Figure 3 shows experimental data for LTS generation using EXP.OPEN 2.0 from 1 to 20 units, and confirms the effectiveness of partial order reductions.
– The **HAVi leader election protocol for home audio-video networks**[8] [53]: EXP.OPEN 2.0 is used to generate interface constraints automatically. Compared to [53], the LTS corresponding to the largest process

---

[5] http://www.inrialpes.fr/vasy/cadp/demos/demo_35
[6] http://www.inrialpes.fr/vasy/cadp/demos/demo_37
[7] http://www.inrialpes.fr/vasy/cadp/demos/demo_36
[8] http://www.inrialpes.fr/vasy/cadp/demos/demo_27

units	without partial order reduction				with partial order reduction			
	states	trans.	time (s)	mem. (MB)	states	trans.	time (s)	mem. (MB)
1	43	59	3.7	2.4	10	9	4.0	2.4
2	159	291	5.1	2.5	10	9	4.9	2.5
3	542	1 233	6.1	2.6	10	9	6.7	2.6
4	1 151	2 909	7.6	2.7	10	9	7.5	2.7
5	3 368	9 831	10.1	2.9	10	9	8.9	2.8
6	12 451	42 423	16.0	3.4	10	9	10.8	3.1
10	166 743	685 951	249.0	11.5	10	9	20.0	5.3
15	—	—	>2h	>113.0	10	9	46.5	17.3
20	—	—	—	—	10	9	99.5	45.8

Fig. 3. Generation of configurations of the Erathostenes sieve with and without partial order reduction

was reduced from $400,000$ states and 3 million transitions downto 700 states and $2,000$ transitions; the memory needed for the whole verification was reduced from 56 MB downto 8.5 MB; the verification time was divided by 10 (from 100 s downto 10 s).

At last, Figure 4 shows that EXP.OPEN 2.0 runs from 2 to 10 times faster and uses 2 times less memory than EXP.OPEN 1.0 on a benchmark consisting of the case studies available in the CADP verification toolbox[9].

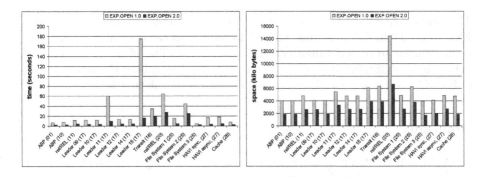

Fig. 4. Performance comparisons between EXP.OPEN 1.0 and EXP.OPEN 2.0

5 Conclusion

In this article, we presented the new EXP.OPEN 2.0 tool, which has been available in CADP since August 2004.

While other tools allowing to compute synchronization products are either specific to one language (e.g., ARA-LOTOS [59] or EXP.OPEN 1.0) or implement

---

[9] http://www.inrialpes.fr/vasy/cadp/demos

a single low-level parallel composition operator (e.g., MEC synchronization vectors [1], FC2 networks [8], TVT [34], modular Petri nets [13]), EXP.OPEN 2.0 combines both synchronization vectors [1, 8] and operators taken from several languages, namely CCS [47], CSP [54], LOTOS [39], μCRL [31], and E-LOTOS [40]. To our knowledge, EXP.OPEN 2.0 provides the first implementation of the "graphical" parallel composition operator [23] of E-LOTOS, which supports "m among n" synchronization in particular.

EXP.OPEN 2.0 combines several verification techniques in order to fight combinatorial state explosion effectively. Together with other tools of CADP, EXP.OPEN 2.0 allows to generate (possibly using the memory and CPU of several computers) and explore on-the-fly (for interactive simulation, verification of temporal logics, behavioural equivalence checking, etc.) the LTS of a composition expression. Generation and exploration can be combined with several partial order reductions preserving deadlocks, branching bisimulation, or stochastic branching bisimulation. In addition, EXP.OPEN 2.0 implements an algorithm to generate interface constraints for compositional verification automatically.

EXP.OPEN 2.0 has been used for various applications with LOTOS and CADP, which allowed to show its effectiveness. As regards future work, EXP.OPEN 2.0 could be combined with other languages and tools. Experiments with the μCRL toolset are under way in the framework of the SENVA collaboration between INRIA and CWI.

Acknowledgements

The author thanks J. van de Pol for his constructive feedback about the EXP.OPEN 2.0 tool, for the time he took to proof read the manual page [43], and for helping us to correct minor errors about the handling of μCRL labels. The author is also grateful to H. Garavel for many advices during the development of EXP.OPEN 2.0 and for his constructive remarks on this article.

References

1. A. Arnold. MEC: A System for Constructing and Analysing Transition Systems. In *Proceedings of the 1st Workshop on Automatic Verification Methods for Finite State Systems (Grenoble, France)*, volume 407 of *Lecture Notes in Computer Science*, pages 117–132. Springer Verlag, 1989.
2. A bird's eye view of JACK. Web page of the JACK project at CNR Pisa, http://fmt.isti.cnr.it/jack/OLD_JACK_PAGES/JACK/structure.html
3. T. Barros, L. Henrio, and E. Madelaine. Behavioural Models for Hierarchical Components, 2005. Submitted to the 12th International SPIN Workshop on Model Checking of Software.
4. G. Behrmann, K.G. Larsen, and R. Pelánek. To Store or Not to Store. In *Proceedings of the 15th International Conference on Computer Aided Verification CAV'2003 (Boulder, Colorado, USA)*, volume 2275 of *Lecture Notes in Computer Science*, 2003.

5. D. Bergamini, N. Descoubes, C. Joubert, and R. Mateescu. BISIMULATOR: A Modular Tool for On-the-Fly Equivalence Checking. In *Proceedings of the 11th International Conference on Tools and Algorithms for the Construction and Analysis of Systems TACAS'2005 (Edinburgh, Scotland, UK)*, volume 3440 of *Lecture Notes in Computer Science*, pages 581–585. Springer Verlag, 2005.

6. E. Best, J. Esparza, B. Grahlmann, S. Melzer, S. Römer, and F. Wallner. The PEP verification system. In *Proceedings of FEmSys'97*, 1997.

7. S. Blom and J. van de Pol. State Space Reduction by Proving Confluence. In *Computer Aided Verification 2002*, volume 2404 of *Lecture Notes in Computer Science*, 2002.

8. A. Bouali, A. Ressouche, V. Roy, and R. de Simone. The Fc2Tools set: a Toolset for the Verification of Concurrent Systems. In *Proceedings of the 8th Conference on Computer-Aided Verification (New Brunswick, New Jersey, USA)*, volume 1102 of *Lecture Notes in Computer Science*. Springer Verlag, 1996.

9. K. H. Cheung. *Compositional Analysis of Complex Distributed Systems*. PhD thesis, Department of Computer Science, Hong Kong University of Science and Technology, Hong Kong, 1998.

10. S. C. Cheung and J. Kramer. Enhancing Compositional Reachability Analysis with Context Constraints. In *Proceedings of the 1st ACM SIGSOFT International Symposium on the Foundations of Software Engineering (Los Angeles, CA, USA)*, pages 115–125. ACM Press, 1993.

11. S. C. Cheung and J. Kramer. Compositional Reachability Analysis of Finite-State Distributed Systems with User-Specified Constraints. In *Proceedings of the 3rd ACM SIGSOFT International Symposium on the Foundations of Software Engineering (Washington, DC, USA)*, pages 140–150. ACM Press, 1995.

12. S. C. Cheung and J. Kramer. Context Constraints for Compositional Reachability. *ACM Transactions on Software Engineering Methodology TOSEM*, 5(4):334–377, 1996.

13. S. Christensen and L. Petrucci. Modular State Space Analysis of Coloured Petri Nets. In *Proceedings of the 16th International Conference on Application and Theory of Petri Nets*, volume 935 of *Lecture Notes in Computer Science*, 1995.

14. J.-C. Fernandez. *ALDEBARAN : un système de vérification par réduction de processus communicants*. Thèse de Doctorat, Université Joseph Fourier (Grenoble), 1988.

15. J.-C. Fernandez, C. Jard, T. Jéron, and L. Mounier. "On the Fly" Verification of Finite Transition Systems. *Formal Methods in System Design*, 1992.

16. J.-C. Fernandez and L. Mounier. Verifying Bisimulations "On the Fly". In *Proceedings of the 3rd International Conference on Formal Description Techniques FORTE'90 (Madrid, Spain)*. North-Holland, 1990.

17. H. Garavel. OPEN/CÆSAR: An Open Software Architecture for Verification, Simulation, and Testing. In *Proceedings of the First International Conference on Tools and Algorithms for the Construction and Analysis of Systems TACAS'98 (Lisbon, Portugal)*, volume 1384 of *Lecture Notes in Computer Science*, pages 68–84, Berlin, 1998. Springer Verlag. Full version available as INRIA Research Report RR-3352.

18. H. Garavel and F. Lang. SVL: a Scripting Language for Compositional Verification. In *Proceedings of the 21st IFIP WG 6.1 International Conference on Formal Techniques for Networked and Distributed Systems FORTE'2001 (Cheju Island, Korea)*, pages 377–392. IFIP, Kluwer Academic Publishers, 2001. Full version available as INRIA Research Report RR-4223.

19. H. Garavel, F. Lang, and R. Mateescu. An Overview of CADP 2001. *European Association for Software Science and Technology (EASST) Newsletter*, 4:13–24, 2002. Also available as INRIA Technical Report RT-0254 (2001).

20. H. Garavel and R. Mateescu. SEQ.OPEN: A Tool for Efficient Trace-Based Verification. In *Proceedings of the 11th International SPIN Workshop on Model Checking of Software SPIN'2004 (Barcelona, Spain)*, volume 2989 of *Lecture Notes in Computer Science*, pages 150–155. Springer Verlag, 2004.

21. H. Garavel, R. Mateescu, and I. Smarandache. Parallel State Space Construction for Model-Checking. In *Proceedings of the 8th International SPIN Workshop on Model Checking of Software SPIN'2001 (Toronto, Canada)*, volume 2057 of *Lecture Notes in Computer Science*, pages 217–234, Berlin, 2001. Springer Verlag. Revised version available as INRIA Research Report RR-4341 (2001).

22. H. Garavel and J. Sifakis. Compilation and Verification of LOTOS Specifications. In *Proceedings of the 10th International Symposium on Protocol Specification, Testing and Verification (Ottawa, Canada)*, pages 379–394. IFIP, North-Holland, 1990.

23. H. Garavel and M. Sighireanu. A Graphical Parallel Composition Operator for Process Algebras. In *Proceedings of the Joint International Conference on Formal Description Techniques for Distributed Systems and Communication Protocols, and Protocol Specification, Testing, and Verification FORTE/PSTV'99 (Beijing, China)*, pages 185–202. IFIP, Kluwer Academic Publishers, 1999.

24. R. Gerth, R. Kuiper, W. Penczek, and D. Peled. A Partial Order Approach to Branching Time Logic Model Checking. *Information and Computation*, 150(2):132–152, 1999. A short version of this paper was previously published at the Third Israel Symposium on Theory of Computing and Systems ISTCS 1995.

25. D. Giannakopoulou. *Model Checking for Concurrent Software Architectures*. PhD thesis, Imperial College of Science, Technology and Medicine — University of London — Department of Computer Science, 1999.

26. P. Godefroid. Using Partial Orders to Improve Automatic Verification Methods. In *Proceedings of the 2nd Workshop on Computer-Aided Verification (Rutgers, New Jersey, USA)*, volume 3 of *DIMACS Series in Discrete Mathematics and Theoretical Computer Science*, pages 321–340. AMS-ACM, 1990.

27. S. Graf, B. Steffen, and G. Lüttgen. Compositional Minimisation of Finite State Systems using Interface Specifications. *Formal Aspects of Computation*, 8(5):607–616, 1996.

28. S. Graf and B. Steffen. Compositional Minimization of Finite State Systems. In *Proceedings of the 2nd Workshop on Computer-Aided Verification (Rutgers, New Jersey, USA)*, volume 531 of *Lecture Notes in Computer Science*, pages 186–196. Springer Verlag, 1990.

29. J.F. Groote, F. Monin, and J. Springintveld. A Computer Checked Algebraic Verification of a Distributed Summation Algorithm. Computer Science Report 97/14, Department of Mathematics and Computer Science, Eindhoven University of Technology, 1997.

30. J.F. Groote and J. van de Pol. State Space Reduction using Partial τ-Confluence. In *Proceedings of the 25th International Symposium on Mathematical Foundations of Computer Science MFCS'2000 (Bratislava, Slovakia)*, volume 1893 of *Lecture Notes in Computer Science*, pages 383–393, Berlin, 2000. Springer Verlag. Also available as CWI Technical Report SEN-R0008, Amsterdam, 2000.

31. J.F. Groote and A. Ponse. Syntax and semantics of μ-CRL. In *Algebra of Communicating Processes, Workshops in Computing*, pages 26–62, 1995.

32. J.F. Groote and M.P.A. Sellink. Confluence for process verification. *Theoretical Computer Science*, 170(1–2):47–81, 1996.

33. H. Hansen, W. Penczek, and A. Valmari. Stuttering-Insensitive Automata for On-the-fly Detection of Livelock Properties. In *7th International ERCIM Workshop in Formal Methods for Industrial Critical Systems*, volume 66 of *Electronic Notes in Theoretical Computer Science*, 2002.

34. H. Hansen, H. Virtanen, and A. Valmari. Merging State-Based and Action-Based Verification. In *Proceedings of the Third International Conference on Application of Concurrency to System Design*. IEEE Computer Society, 2003.

35. H. Hermanns. *Interactive Markov Chains and the Quest for Quantified Quality*, volume 2428 of *LNCS*. Springer Verlag, 2002.

36. H. Hermanns and M. Siegle. Bisimulation Algorithms for Stochastic Process Algebras and their BDD-based Implementation. In *Proceedings of the 5th International AMAST Workshop ARTS'99 (Bamberg, Germany)*, volume 1601 of *Lecture Notes in Computer Science*, pages 244–265. Springer Verlag, 1999.

37. G. Holzmann. The Model Checker SPIN. *IEEE Transactions on Software Engineering*, 23(5):279–295, 1997.

38. G.J. Holzmann. On-The-Fly Model Checking. *ACM Computing Surveys*, 28(4), 1996.

39. ISO/IEC. LOTOS — A Formal Description Technique Based on the Temporal Ordering of Observational Behaviour. International Standard 8807, International Organization for Standardization — Information Processing Systems — Open Systems Interconnection, Genève, 1989.

40. ISO/IEC. Enhancements to LOTOS (E-LOTOS). International Standard 15437:2001, International Organization for Standardization — Information Technology, Genève, 2001.

41. T. Jéron and P. Morel. Test generation derived from model-checking. In *Proceedings of the Conference on Computer-Aided Verification CAV'99 (Trento, Italy)*, volume 1633 of *Lecture Notes in Computer Science*, pages 108–122. Springer Verlag, 1999.

42. J.-P. Krimm and L. Mounier. Compositional State Space Generation from LOTOS Programs. In *Proceedings of TACAS'97 Tools and Algorithms for the Construction and Analysis of Systems (University of Twente, Enschede, The Netherlands)*, volume 1217 of *Lecture Notes in Computer Science*, Berlin, 1997. Springer Verlag. Extended version with proofs available as Research Report VERIMAG RR97-01.

43. F. Lang. The Exp.Open 2.0 manual page, 2004. Available online at http://www.inrialpes.fr/vasy/cadp/man/exp.open.html.

44. J. Malhotra, S. A. Smolka, A. Giacalone, and R. Shapiro. A Tool for Hierarchical Design and Simulation of Concurrent Systems. In *Proceedings of the BCS-FACS Workshop on Specification and Verification of Concurrent Systems (Stirling, Scotland)*, pages 140–152, Swinton, UK, 1988. British Computer Society.

45. R. Mateescu. A Generic On-the-Fly Solver for Alternation-Free Boolean Equation Systems. In *Proceedings of the 9th International Conference on Tools and Algorithms for the Construction and Analysis of Systems TACAS'2003 (Warsaw, Poland)*, volume 2619 of *Lecture Notes in Computer Science*, pages 81–96. Springer Verlag, 2003. Full version available as INRIA Research Report RR-4711.

46. R. Mateescu and M. Sighireanu. Efficient On-the-Fly Model-Checking for Regular Alternation-Free Mu-Calculus. *Science of Computer Programming*, 46(3):255–281, 2003.

47. R. Milner. *Communication and Concurrency*. Prentice-Hall, 1989.

48. G. Pace, F. Lang, and R. Mateescu. Calculating τ-Confluence Compositionally. In *Proceedings of the 15th International Conference on Computer Aided Verification CAV'2003 (Boulder, Colorado, USA)*, volume 2725 of *Lecture Notes in Computer Science*, pages 446–459. Springer Verlag, 2003. Full version available as INRIA Research Report RR-4918.

49. D. Peled. Partial Order Reduction: Linear and Branching Temporal Logics and Process Algebras. In Peled et al. [51].

50. D.A. Peled. Combining partial order reduction with on-the-fly model-checking. In *Computer Aided Verification 1994*, volume 818 of *Lecture Notes in Computer Science*. Springer-Verlag, 1994.

51. D.A. Peled, V.R. Pratt, and G.J. Holzmann, editors. *Proceedings of the Workshop on Partial Order Methods in Verification*, volume 29 of *Dimacs Series in Discrete Mathematics*, 1997.

52. Y.S. Ramakrishna and S.A. Smolka. Partial-Order Reduction in the Weak Modal Mu-Calculus. In *Proceedings of the 8th International Conference on Concurrency Theory CONCUR'97*, volume 1243 of *Lecture Notes in Computer Science*, pages 5–24. Springer Verlag, 1997.

53. J. Romijn. Model Checking the HAVi Leader Election Protocol. Technical Report SEN-R9915, CWI, Amsterdam, The Netherlands, 1999. submitted to Formal Methods in System Design.

54. A.W. Roscoe. *The Theory and Practice of Concurrency*. Prentice Hall, 1998.

55. K. K. Sabnani, A. M. Lapone, and M. U. Uyar. An Algorithmic Procedure for Checking Safety Properties of Protocols. *IEEE Transactions on Communications*, 37(9):940–948, 1989.

56. K. C. Tai and V. Koppol. Hierarchy-Based Incremental Reachability Analysis of Communication Protocols. In *Proceedings of the IEEE International Conference on Network Protocols (San Francisco, CA)*, pages 318–325, Piscataway, NJ, 1993. IEEE Press.

57. A. Valmari. A Stubborn Attack on State Explosion. In *Proceedings of the 2nd Workshop on Computer-Aided Verification (Rutgers, New Jersey, USA)*, volume 3 of *DIMACS Series in Discrete Mathematics and Theoretical Computer Science*, pages 25–42. AMS-ACM, 1990.

58. A. Valmari. Stubborn Set Methods for Process Algebras. In Peled et al. [51].

59. A. Valmari, J. Kemppainen, M. Clegg, and M. Levanto. Putting Advanced Reachability Analysis Techniques Together: the "ARA" Tool. In *Proceedings of the First International Symposium of Formal Methods Europe FME '93*, volume 670 of *Lecture Notes in Computer Science*, pages 597–616. Springer-Verlag, 1993.

60. A. Valmari. Compositional State Space Generation. In *Proceedings of Advances in Petri Nets*, volume 674 of *Lecture Notes in Computer Science*, pages 427–457. Springer Verlag, 1993.

61. J. van de Pol. Proof using the PVS theorem prover that bisimulations are congruences for synchronization vectors that do not rename, cut, nor synchronize τ-transitions. Personal communication, 2003.

62. R. J. van Glabbeek and W. P. Weijland. Branching-Time and Abstraction in Bisimulation Semantics (extended abstract). CS R8911, Centrum voor Wiskunde en Informatica, Amsterdam, 1989. Also in proc. IFIP 11th World Computer Congress, San Francisco, 1989.

63. W. J. Yeh. *Controlling State Explosion in Reachability Analysis*. PhD thesis, Software Engineering Research Center (SERC) Laboratory, Purdue University, 1993. Technical Report SERC-TR-147-P.

Chunks: Component Verification in CSP‖B

Steve Schneider[1], Helen Treharne[1], and Neil Evans[2]

[1] Department of Computing, University of Surrey,
S.Schneider@surrey.ac.uk
H.Treharne@surrey.ac.uk
[2] School of Electronics and Computer Science, University of Southampton
ne01@ecs.soton.ac.uk

Abstract. CSP‖B is an approach to combining the process algebra CSP with the formal development method B, enabling the formal description of systems involving both event-oriented and state-oriented aspects of behaviour. The approach provides architectures which enable the application of CSP verification tools and B verification tools to the appropriate parts of the overall description. Previous work has considered how large descriptions can be verified using coarse grained component parts. This paper presents a generalisation of that work so that CSP‖B descriptions can be decomposed into finer grained components, *chunks*, which focus on demonstrating the absence of particular divergent behaviour separately. The theory underpinning *chunks* is applicable not only to CSP‖B specification but to CSP specifications. This makes it an attractive technique to decomposing large systems for analysing with FDR.

Keywords: Component based verification, B-Method, CSP, decomposition.

1 Introduction

We begin with a synopsis of the CSP‖B approach which has been under development for a number of years. The main feature of the approach is the separation of event and state based descriptions using the process algebra CSP [9] and the formal development method B [1]. One primary goal of the approach is to show that a combined specification is divergence-free [12, 13, 14]. This property is at the core of the approach, and once it has been established other safety and liveness properties of the system can be described and shown to be valid [6, 7, 15].

In [14] we discussed how a B machine can have a CSP failures-divergences semantics. We also established that a component, i.e., a parallel combination of a controller/machine pair, can be shown to be divergence-free. This means that the B operations are always called within their preconditions. In this work the CSP processes (*controllers*) themselves were divergent-free because we restricted the language to a sequential non-divergent subset of CSP.

In [12] we began to refer to collections of components as a family of processes P_i indexed by some indexing set I. Using the fact that both CSP processes and B machines have a process semantics we presented results which established the

J. Romijn, G. Smith, and J. van de Pol (Eds.): IFM 2005, LNCS 3771, pp. 89–108, 2005.

divergence freedom of a parallel combination $\big\|_{i \in I} P_i$. While this might be true if the whole combination $\big\|_{i \in I} P_i$ is considered at once, large systems will make the application of tool support to demonstrate this property impractical. Thus, we needed ways of considering parts of the system at a time, and combining the results.

In [13] we introduced a rely-guarantee style of specification which enabled us to capture *assertions*, which are predicates on values being passed on channels. We made clear that divergence freedom of the whole system depended on the divergent behaviour of individual components being prevented by the rest of the system. We discussed how to break up the system into component parts and augment each part with assertions to establish its divergence freedom. This was sufficient to deduce divergence freedom of the whole system. In that work our terminology was different. Since [6] we have settled on referring to assertions in two ways. *Blocking assertions*, previously known as guards, capture the notion of what must be true when communicating values along channels. If a blocking assertion is false communication is not permitted. With *diverging assertions*, previously known as assumptions, communication is always permitted. However, if the assertion does not hold diverging behaviour is exhibited.

The results in [13] were restrictive because the components were broken down into controller/machine pairs and one large component comprising of all the CSP processes. Furthermore, that approach does not easily scale up, since the CSP part of the system has to be checked in its entirety, and this will be subject to the limitations of CSP model-checkers.

The results presented in this paper aim to further extend our ability to perform component verification. We have coined the term *chunks* because it captures the notion of splitting the combined specification into constituent parts, i.e. a small collection of processes. A chunk can comprise of a CSP process and a B machine, or a collection of CSP processes (not necessarily all of them). We will see that a chunk gives us a much more flexible component part to deal with when aiming to establish divergence freedom.

In addition to being an extension to our integrated CSP∥B approach the results presented in this paper are applicable more generally too. They could be of potential benefit to CSP specifications that cannot be shown to be divergence-free due to tool limitations. We prove that if all the identified chunks individually do not give rise to particular divergences, then we can deduce that the whole system is divergence-free. In fact the paper is structured in two main parts and we first focus on describing how to split a collection of CSP processes into constituent parts and establishing divergence freedom to give us general results. Then the contribution to CSP∥B is presented when we demonstrate the applicability of the general theory to CSP∥B. A smaller and a larger example are used to motivate the work and illustrate the results being presented.

1.1 Notation

Before presenting the first example we identify some preliminary notation. For a detailed introduction to CSP operators and the failures-divergences semantic model used in this paper the reader is referred to [11]. Similarly, the reader is referred to [1] for an overview of the B Method. The most important aspect of B to understand for this paper is that B operations are associated with preconditions, and if called outside their preconditions then they diverge. Furthermore, we do not re-iterate all the details of the syntax of CSP and B used in our approach, these can be found in [13]. Instead we discuss various points of interest when presenting the second example in Section 4.

The following introduces the key notation used in this paper, including some newly coined definitions.

The universal set of events is denoted Σ. Traces are finite sequences of events. We write $tr' \leqslant tr$ to denote that tr' is a prefix of tr.

Given a trace tr, its projection to a set A is denoted $tr \upharpoonright A$—this is the sequence of events from tr which are in the set A. For example,

$$\langle coin, choc, refill, coin \rangle \upharpoonright \{coin, choc\} = \langle coin, choc, coin \rangle$$

Given a set of traces D, its projection to a set A of events is defined as follows:

$$D \upharpoonright A = \{tr \upharpoonright A \mid tr \in D\}$$

CSP semantics associates with a process P a set of traces $\mathcal{T}[\![P]\!]$, a set of failures $\mathcal{F}[\![P]\!]$, and a set of divergences $\mathcal{D}[\![P]\!]$. This paper will be most concerned with the divergences.

The form of parallel combination we use is *alphabet* parallel (both in binary and in indexed form), in which processes are associated with an *alphabet* which is a set of events. The occurrence of an event in the combination requires the participation of all processes whose alphabet contains that event.

The following lemma allows us to identify the point on a divergent trace where the process diverges.

Lemma 1. *Given a process P such that $\langle \rangle \notin \mathcal{D}[\![P]\!]$, for any non-empty divergence $tr \in \mathcal{D}[\![P]\!]$ there is a unique event a such that $\exists tr_0 \leqslant tr.tr_0 \notin \mathcal{D}[\![P]\!] \wedge tr_0 \frown \langle a \rangle \in \mathcal{D}[\![P]\!]$. In other words, there is a unique event a on which divergence was introduced in this trace.*

Proof. Let tr_0 be the maximal prefix $tr_0 \leqslant tr$ such that $tr_0 \notin \mathcal{D}[\![P]\!]$. There is such a tr_0, since $\langle \rangle \notin \mathcal{D}[\![P]\!]$. $tr_0 \neq tr$, since $tr \in \mathcal{D}[\![P]\!]$. Thus there is some unique a such that $tr_0 \frown \langle a \rangle \leqslant tr \wedge tr_0 \frown \langle a \rangle \in \mathcal{D}[\![P]\!] \wedge tr_0 \notin \mathcal{D}[\![P]\!]$.

The above lemma means that the following is well-defined:

Definition 1. *Given a process P such that $\langle \rangle \notin \mathcal{D}[\![P]\!]$, and a divergence $tr \neq \langle \rangle$, $tr \in \mathcal{D}[\![P]\!]$, the diverging event $de(tr, P)$ is the unique event on which divergence is introduced in tr.*

Definition 2. *The set of diverging events $de(P)$ of a process P for which $\langle \rangle \notin \mathcal{D}[\![P]\!]$ is the set $\{de(tr, P) \mid tr \in \mathcal{D}[\![P]\!] \wedge tr \neq \langle \rangle\}$.*

The *minimal divergences* $\mathcal{MD}[\![P]\!]$ of a process P is the set of divergences of P that are minimal in the prefix order.

Definition 3.

$$\mathcal{MD}[\![P]\!] = \{tr \in \mathcal{D}[\![P]\!] \mid \forall\, tr' \in \mathcal{D}[\![P]\!].tr' \leqslant tr \Rightarrow tr' = tr\}$$

Various properties can be established concerning minimal divergences. One that we will use frequently is the following:

Lemma 2. *If* $tr \in \mathcal{MD}[\![P \parallel Q]\!]$ *then* $tr \restriction \alpha P \in \mathcal{MD}[\![P]\!] \vee tr \restriction \alpha Q \in \mathcal{MD}[\![Q]\!]$.

A minimal divergence of $P \parallel Q$ arises from a minimal divergence of one of its components.

2   Establishing Divergence-Freedom

Our primary aim is to establish that a system is divergence-free. So we will consider the collection of components as a family of processes P_i indexed by some indexing set I. Thus, we aim to establish that the parallel combination $\parallel_{i \in I} P_i$ is divergence-free. While this might be true if the whole combination $\parallel_{i \in I} P_i$ is considered at once it may not be possible to check the entire system using FDR in one go. Thus, we need ways of considering parts of the system at a time, and combining the results. In general, the divergence-free operation of one part of the system might be dependent on the particular behaviour of another part.

2.1   Toy Example

To illustrate the above point, we consider a small toy example in the CSP tradition: a vending machine, based on the coursework examples associated with [9]. The machine consists of a number of components, which are concerned with dispensing chocolates in return for accepting coins, refilling the machine with chocolates, and ensuring that the machine does not try to dispense chocolates when it is empty. This gives us several processes that we can group into chunks and demonstrate that they are individually divergence-free. The combination of components is illustrated in Figure 1.

The machine can diverge if too many coins are inserted without the removal of a chocolate:

$$\alpha(VM) = \{coin, choc\}$$
$$VM = coin \rightarrow ((choc \rightarrow VM) \,\square\, (coin \rightarrow \bot))$$

Each component has the natural alphabet: those events that are mentioned in its definition.

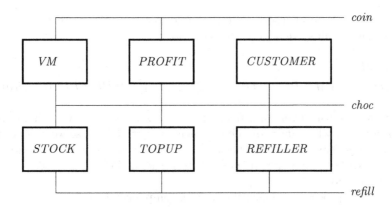

Fig. 1. Components of a vending machine

The profit counter can diverge if more chocolates are dispensed than have been paid for:

$$\alpha(PROFIT(i)) = \{coin, choc\}$$
$$PROFIT(0) = (coin \rightarrow PROFIT(1)) \,\square\, (choc \rightarrow \perp)$$
$$PROFIT(n+1) = (coin \rightarrow PROFIT(n+2)) \,\square\, (choc \rightarrow PROFIT(n))$$

Refilling the machine tops it up to 17 chocolates. The stock control tracks the remaining chocolates, and can diverge if it runs out of stock:

$$\alpha(STOCK(i)) = \{refill, choc\}$$
$$STOCK(0) = (refill \rightarrow STOCK(17)) \,\square\, (choc \rightarrow \perp)$$
$$STOCK(n+1) = (refill \rightarrow STOCK(17)) \,\square\, (choc \rightarrow STOCK(n))$$

The machine should not be refilled when it is full:

$$\alpha(TOPUP) = \{refill, choc\}$$
$$TOPUP = (refill \rightarrow FULL) \,\square\, (choc \rightarrow TOPUP)$$
$$FULL = (refill \rightarrow \perp) \,\square\, (choc \rightarrow TOPUP)$$

Finally, a counter is in control of refilling the machine:

$$\alpha(REFILLER(i)) = \{refill, choc\}$$
$$REFILLER(0) = refill \rightarrow REFILLER(17)$$
$$REFILLER(n+1) = choc \rightarrow REFILLER(n)$$

Finally, we include a description of the customer, who behaves well with respect to the insertion of coins:

$$\alpha(CUSTOMER) = \{coin, choc\}$$
$$CUSTOMER = coin \rightarrow choc \rightarrow CUSTOMER$$

The customer will never insert more than one coin for a chocolate.

Then the overall system we wish to consider is:

$SYSTEM =$

$CUSTOMER \parallel VM \parallel PROFIT(0) \parallel STOCK(0) \parallel TOPUP \parallel REFILLER(0)$

We aim to establish divergence-freedom of this system. However, there are a number of points where individual components might diverge, so we will need to check that these cannot arise in the context of the overall system. Furthermore, for a larger system it may not be possible to model and check the entire system in FDR in one go.

The way we proceed is to identify for each component P the set of events that it can diverge on. We then find appropriate associated processes $Q_1 \ldots Q_n$ which ensure that such divergences cannot occur. We call the subset of components $P, Q_1, \ldots, Q_n$ a *chunk*, which is adequate to establish that P does not diverge on events in $de(P)$.

There are four processes which contain diverging behaviour:

- *VM* can diverge on some occurrences of the event *coin*. In other words, using Definition 3, any minimal divergence of *VM* has *coin* as its last event. If we consider $VM \parallel CUSTOMER$ we find that the resulting combination $VM \parallel CUSTOMER$ cannot diverge on *coin*. Thus $\{VM, CUSTOMER\}$ is a divergence-free chunk.
- $PROFIT(0)$ can diverge on the event *choc*. However, the parallel combination $PROFIT(0) \parallel VM$ cannot diverge on *choc*. Thus $\{PROFIT(0), VM\}$ is the appropriate chunk for this case. Note it can diverge on *coin* but this is handled by the chunk which focuses on *VM* with *coin* as its diverging event.
- $STOCK(0)$ can diverge on the event *choc*. However, the parallel combination $STOCK(0) \parallel REFILLER(0)$ cannot diverge on *choc*.
- *TOPUP* can diverge on the event *refill*. However, $TOPUP \parallel REFILLER(0)$ cannot diverge on *refill*.

These are all of the cases of processes diverging on particular events. In the example all the sets of diverging events are singleton sets. However, this need not be the case in general. In each case above, there are some other processes of the system which ensure that such divergences do not occur in the system overall.

Each chunk only needs to include the process containing the diverging events and the processes which provide the control to remove those possible divergences. A chunk dealing with P need not contain all the processes that are involved in the synchronisation of the events in $de(P)$—only those that prevent the divergence from occurring are necessary. Otherwise a chunk may end up being the whole system, which is clearly not what we want because we would not have achieved any decomposition.

Furthermore, any particular diverging event can be in the set of diverging events of more than one process. In the example above, $PROFIT(0)$ and

$STOCK(0)$ can both diverge on *choc*. They are dealt with separately, each with a different chunk.

As we shall see, this is enough to guarantee that the combination of all the components, $SYSTEM$, is divergence-free.

3 Underlying Theory for Chunks

In a parallel system of processes, we aim to establish the property of divergence-freedom for the whole system by considering each of the processes in turn. The principal idea is to establish, for each process P, that it cannot diverge in the context of the rest of the system. Compositionality arises from the fact that we will only need to consider the relevant context, and do not need to include the parts of the system that are irrelevant to the analysis of P.

3.1 Divergences of a Process

The first theorems are very general, and are concerned with the way parallel composition treats divergence. Notationally in these theorems we are thinking of P as the process which is the focus of the analysis, Q as the part of the system which ensures that P does not diverge, and R as the rest of the system. Thus we are ultimately concerned with deducing properties of the system $P \parallel Q \parallel R$ simply by considering $P \parallel Q$.

Our first lemma is concerned with the special case where $P \parallel Q$ is divergence-free. We begin with this special case because it motivates the use of minimal divergences, and gives a broad idea of the approach, which is reflected in the more general theorems.

This special case is subsumed by Lemma 4, which is itself a special case of Lemma 5. Lemma 5 supports the main theorem of this section, Theorem 1, which states when divergence-freedom of a concurrent system can be deduced from particular properties of chunks. The lemmas subsequent to Theorem 1 provide different ways of establishing those properties. In general, a variety of ways of checking chunks are possible, and an analysis will make use of different approaches for different chunks.

In Lemma 3, we can deduce that any minimal divergence of the whole system is not a minimal divergence of P. In other words, the divergence was not a result of P diverging.

Lemma 3. *If $P \parallel Q$ is divergence-free, then*

$$\mathcal{MD} \, [\![P \parallel Q \parallel R]\!] \upharpoonright \alpha P \cap \mathcal{MD} \, [\![P]\!] = \varnothing$$

Proof. Assume for a contradiction that $tr \in \mathcal{MD} \, [\![P \parallel Q \parallel R]\!] \upharpoonright \alpha P \cap \mathcal{MD} \, [\![P]\!]$. Then there is some tr_0 such that $tr = tr_0 \upharpoonright \alpha P$. Then $tr_0 \upharpoonright \alpha Q \in \mathcal{T} \, [\![Q]\!]$, and we already have that $tr_0 \upharpoonright \alpha P \in \mathcal{D} \, [\![P]\!]$. Thus $tr_0 \upharpoonright (\alpha P \cup \alpha Q) \in \mathcal{D} \, [\![P \parallel Q]\!]$, contradicting the fact that $P \parallel Q$ is divergence-free.

Interestingly, the theorem applies even in the case where R can diverge on events in the alphabet of P. Informally, this is because Q prevents P's divergences from occurring, and R cannot reintroduce them because of the blocking nature of the parallel operator. Of course R can introduce other divergences with the same diverging event, but it cannot introduce any divergence of P.

For example, consider the vending machine from Section 2.1 again, with VM for P, $CUSTOMER$ for Q, and define a process $BROKEN = coin \rightarrow \perp$ for R. In this case the minimal divergence of the parallel combination $P \parallel Q \parallel R$ would be $\langle coin \rangle$ but this is not be a minimal divergence of P, so the intersection would indeed be empty. The fact that $BROKEN$ diverges on $coin$ does not affect the argument that VM's divergence on $coin$ cannot occur.

Of course, in checking the whole system there would be the separate problem of finding a chunk for $BROKEN$. In fact, this will not be possible, since there is no process that prevents $coin$ from occurring. But what we have established with the chunk for VM is that if a divergence of the system does occur, it is not the fault of VM.

Observe also that Lemma 3 must be stated in terms of minimal divergences: it is not true for general divergence sets. The example above has $\langle coin, coin \rangle$ as a divergence of both VM and $VM \parallel CUSTOMER \parallel BROKEN$, even though we have that $VM \parallel CUSTOMER$ is divergence-free. The point is that the divergence $\langle coin, coin \rangle$ is not the first point at which the system diverges, so divergence of the system is the fault of $BROKEN$, on the divergence $\langle coin \rangle$. The intention of the lemma is to allow us to deduce that VM is not responsible for any divergences of $VM \parallel CUSTOMER \parallel BROKEN$, and to establish this we need to consider the minimal divergences.

The next theorem considers a more general situation, when $P \parallel Q$ possibly contains some divergences, but not as a result of P.

Lemma 4. If $\mathcal{MD}\,[\![P \parallel Q]\!] \restriction \alpha P \cap \mathcal{MD}\,[\![P]\!] = \varnothing$, then

$$\mathcal{MD}\,[\![P \parallel Q \parallel R]\!] \restriction \alpha P \cap \mathcal{MD}\,[\![P]\!] = \varnothing$$

Proof. Assume for a contradiction that $tr \in \mathcal{MD}\,[\![P \parallel Q \parallel R]\!] \restriction \alpha P \cap \mathcal{MD}\,[\![P]\!]$. Then there is some $tr_0 \in \mathcal{MD}\,[\![P \parallel Q \parallel R]\!]$ such that $tr = tr_0 \restriction \alpha P$. Then $tr_1 = tr_0 \restriction (\alpha P \cup \alpha Q) \in \mathcal{D}\,[\![P \parallel Q]\!]$, since $tr \in \mathcal{MD}\,[\![P]\!]$. Furthermore, no prefix of tr_1 is a divergence of $P \parallel Q$, since tr_0 is a minimal divergence, so $tr_1 \in \mathcal{MD}\,[\![P \parallel Q]\!]$. Thus $tr_1 \restriction \alpha P \in \mathcal{MD}\,[\![P \parallel Q]\!] \restriction \alpha P$, i.e. $tr \in \mathcal{MD}\,[\![P \parallel Q]\!] \restriction \alpha P$, contradicting the fact that $tr \in \mathcal{MD}\,[\![P]\!]$.

This lemma would be applicable in the case of the $VM \parallel PROFIT(0)$ chunk from the previous section.

We now obtain a generalisation of Lemma 4, which is concerned only with divergence of a process P on a particular set of events A. We define $\mathcal{MD}\,[\![P]\!]_A$ to be those minimal divergences ending in some event in A:

$$\mathcal{MD}\,[\![P]\!]_A = \{tr \in \mathcal{MD}\,[\![P]\!] \mid last(tr) \in A\}$$

Lemma 5. *If* $\mathcal{MD}[\![P \parallel Q]\!] \restriction \alpha P \cap \mathcal{MD}[\![P]\!]_A = \varnothing$, *then*

$$\mathcal{MD}[\![P \parallel Q \parallel R]\!] \restriction \alpha P \cap \mathcal{MD}[\![P]\!]_A = \varnothing$$

Proof. Similar to the proof of Lemma 4.

This lemma is useful because in practice we may need to consider different diverging events independently of each other, and using different chunks. This will particularly arise when considering diverging assertions in process descriptions: we may wish to consider them separately. We will see an example of this in Section 4.

The main theorem, concerning the use of chunks to establish divergence freedom of a concurrent system, is the following:

Theorem 1. *Given a family of processes* $\{P_i\}_{i \in I}$: *if for each* P_i *and each* $a \in de(P_i)$ *there is some subset of processes* $\{P_j\}_{j \in J}$ *such that*

1. *$P_i \notin \{P_j\}_{j \in J}$ (i.e. $i \notin J$)*
2. *$a \notin de(P_i \parallel \big\|_{j \in J} P_j)$*

then $\big\|_{i \in I} P_i$ *is divergence-free.*

Proof. Assume for a contradiction that $tr \in \mathcal{MD}[\![\,\big\|_{i \in I} P_i]\!]$. Then there is some i such that $tr \restriction \alpha P_i \in \mathcal{MD}[\![P_i]\!]$. Let $a = last(tr \restriction \alpha P_i) \in de(P_i)$. Then we have a set of processes P_j for $j \in J$ meeting the two conditions above. Set

$$P = P_i$$
$$Q = \big\|_{j \in J} P_j$$
$$R = \big\|_{k \neq i, k \notin J} P_k$$

Then $\mathcal{MD}[\![P \parallel Q]\!] \restriction \alpha P \cap \mathcal{MD}[\![P]\!]_{\{a\}} = \varnothing$, since $a \notin de(P \parallel Q)$. Then by Lemma 5 we obtain $\mathcal{MD}[\![P \parallel Q \parallel R]\!] \restriction \alpha P \cap \mathcal{MD}[\![P]\!]_{\{a\}} = \varnothing$. But $tr \restriction \alpha P$ is in this intersection, yielding a contradiction. Hence $\big\|_{i \in I} P_i$ has no divergences.

3.2 Blocking Divergences

We now give some results which use blocking on some divergences, and divergence-freedom of the result, to establish the conditions required to apply Lemmas 4 and 5 above. These results will enable us to use divergence-freedom checks in FDR to obtain the results we require about the minimal divergences of processes.

We firstly define the process $BLOCK_A(T)$ for a set of traces $T \subseteq A^*$. This process has alphabet A, and is able to perform any possible traces apart from those in the set T. It is useful to introduce when reasoning about processes.

Definition 4. *The process* $BLOCK_A(T)$ *is defined, for* $T \subseteq A^*$, *as follows:*

$$\mathcal{D}[\![BLOCK_A(T)]\!] = \varnothing$$
$$\mathcal{F}[\![BLOCK_A(T)]\!] = \{(tr, X) \mid (\forall\, t \in T.t \text{ prefix } tr) \wedge \forall\, a \in X.tr \,^\frown \langle a \rangle \in T\}$$

We use Lemma 6 below to pinpoint minimal divergences, and thus the point where a combination diverges. If a parallel combination $P \parallel Q$, when blocked on particular minimal divergences D_P and D_Q of P and Q respectively, is divergence-free, then any minimal divergence of $P \parallel Q$ must be from one of the blocked divergences, D_P or D_Q.

Lemma 6. *If*

- $D_P \subseteq \mathcal{MD}[\![P]\!]$
- $D_Q \subseteq \mathcal{MD}[\![Q]\!]$
- $P \parallel BLOCK_{\alpha P}(D_P) \parallel Q \parallel BLOCK_{\alpha Q}(D_Q)$ *is divergence-free*

then if $tr \in \mathcal{MD}[\![P \parallel Q]\!]$*, then* $tr \restriction \alpha P \in D_P$ *or* $tr \restriction \alpha Q \in D_Q$.

Proof. Consider $tr \in \mathcal{MD}[\![P \parallel Q]\!]$. Assume that $tr \restriction \alpha P \notin D_P$, and that $tr \restriction \alpha Q \notin D_Q$. Wej aim to establish a contradiction.

Now from Lemma 2 either $tr \restriction \alpha P \in \mathcal{MD}[\![P]\!]$ or $tr \restriction \alpha Q \in \mathcal{MD}[\![Q]\!]$. Assume without loss of generality that $tr \restriction \alpha P \in \mathcal{MD}[\![P]\!]$.

No strict prefix of $tr \restriction \alpha P$ is in D_P, since otherwise tr is not a minimal divergence of $P \parallel Q$. Thus $tr \restriction \alpha P \in \mathcal{MD}[\![(P \parallel BLOCK_{\alpha P}(D_P))]\!]$, since $BLOCK_{\alpha P}(D_P)$ does not restrict $tr \restriction \alpha P$.

Similarly, no strict prefix of $tr \restriction \alpha Q$ is in D_Q, since otherwise tr is not a minimal divergence. Thus $tr \restriction \alpha Q \in \mathcal{T}[\![(Q \parallel BLOCK_{\alpha Q}(D_Q))]\!]$. Hence we obtain that $tr \in \mathcal{MD}[\![P \parallel BLOCK_{\alpha P}(D_P) \parallel Q \parallel BLOCK_{\alpha Q}(D_Q)]\!]$, yielding a contradiction.

The following corollary of Lemma 6 will be useful in establishing condition (2) for Theorem 1, since it provides a way of establishing the antecedent in particular cases. It is concerned with divergence on particular events from the set A. It states that if divergence-freedom can be obtained by blocking some minimal divergences not ending in A, then no minimal divergence of $P \parallel Q$ arises from a divergence of P ending in A.

Corollary 1. *If*

1. $D_P \subseteq \mathcal{MD}[\![P]\!] \setminus \mathcal{MD}[\![P]\!]_A$
2. $D_Q \subseteq \mathcal{MD}[\![Q]\!] \setminus \mathcal{MD}[\![Q]\!]_A$
3. $P \parallel BLOCK_{\alpha P}(D_P) \parallel Q \parallel BLOCK_{\alpha Q}(D_Q)$ *is divergence-free*

then $\mathcal{MD}[\![P \parallel Q]\!] \restriction \alpha P \cap \mathcal{MD}[\![P]\!]_A = \varnothing$

The first condition means that D_P cannot contain any traces ending in events from A; and the second condition means that D_Q cannot contain any traces ending in events from A. Lemma 6 yields that any $tr \in \mathcal{MD}[\![P \parallel Q]\!]$ either has $tr \restriction \alpha P \in D_P$, or else $tr \restriction \alpha Q \in D_Q$, and in both cases $last(tr) \notin A$, so we obtain $tr \restriction \alpha P \notin \mathcal{MD}[\![P]\!]_A$.

3.3   Assertions

When we are working with CSP descriptions, we will often aim to decompose them by introducing assertions onto the channels. This is especially true for CSP∥B, the driving motivation for this work. We will aim to establish that the assertions are always true within system executions. This will be achieved by considering them as diverging assertions (i.e. the process diverges if the assertion is false), and establishing divergence-freedom of the resulting system.

This is exactly the kind of situation that Theorem 1 is intended to apply to. That theorem allows consideration of divergences separately, so we can consider diverging assertions on different channels separately. In order to do this, we can convert other assertions (those that are not the focus of interest) to blocking assertions. The following theorems give the justification for this, and relate this syntactic transformation to the results of the preceding section.

Lemma 7. *If Q' is Q with diverging assertions on channels in a set C replaced by blocking assertions, then $Q' = Q \parallel BLOCK_{\alpha Q}(D)$ for some set of divergences $D \subseteq \mathcal{MD}[\![Q]\!]_{\{|C|\}}$.*

Proof. By structural induction over Q. This includes the case for parallel, thus Q can be a parallel combination of processes.

The following corollary shows how we can use a divergence-freedom check of $P' \parallel Q'$, which is $P \parallel Q$ with suitable diverging assertions replaced by blocking assertions, to show that certain divergences of P are not divergences of $P \parallel Q$.

Corollary 2. *If c is a channel of the process P such that*

1. *P' is the process P with some diverging assertions replaced by blocking assertions, but with no assertions on c replaced*
2. *$\{| c |\} \cap de(Q) = \varnothing$*
3. *Q' is the process Q with some diverging assertions replaced by blocking assertions.*
4. *$P' \parallel Q'$ is divergence-free*

then $\mathcal{MD}[\![P \parallel Q]\!] \upharpoonright \alpha P \cap \mathcal{MD}[\![P]\!]_{\{|c|\}} = \varnothing$

This is a restatement of Corollary 1 in the light of Lemma 7.

It can also be written in a form which more directly corresponds to condition (2) of Theorem 1, showing how that condition can be established for particular process channels.

Corollary 3. *Given a family of processes $\{P_i\}_{i \in I}$, and a particular P_i and subset of processes $\{P_j\}_{j \in J}$, if c is a channel of the process P_i such that*

1. *P'_i is the process P_i with some diverging assertions replaced by blocking assertions, but with no assertions on c replaced*
2. *For each $j \in J$, $\{| c |\} \cap de(P_j) = \varnothing$*
3. *For each $j \in J$, P'_j is the process P_j with some diverging assertions replaced by blocking assertions.*
4. *$P_i \parallel \big\|_{j \in J} P'_j$ is divergence-free*

then for any $a \in \{| c |\}$ we have $a \notin de(P_i \parallel \big\|_{j \in J} P_j)$.

3.4   Chunks with B Machines

The motivation for this work arises from the need to consider CSP processes in parallel with B machines. B machines have a CSP failures-divergences semantics, so the theorems from Section 3.3 are applicable, and B machines are considered as CSP processes from the point of view of Theorem 1. However, they are not written using CSP syntax, so the syntax-oriented approach from Section 3.3 of manipulating assertions is not applicable. However, some chunks may require the consideration of some B machines in a system description, since it may be the constraints imposed by the B machine that prevent divergence in some other component. In order to make use of B machines in chunks within Theorem 1, we need another approach.

There is already a theory for establishing divergence-freedom of $P \parallel M$, where M is a B machine and P is a CSP controller whose alphabet contains that of M. M interacts with P via its *machine channels*, where channel inputs and outputs correspond to parameters of operation calls of the B machine. Divergence-freedom is established by identifying a *control loop invariant* (CLI) which is true in every recursive call of P, and which ensures that divergence does not arise on an individual traversal of the control. Further details of this approach can be found in [14].

The following lemma will be useful in establishing condition (2) of Theorem 1 in cases where the chunk contains a B machine. This will be necessary in cases where the process under consideration (i.e. the P_i) is the B machine.

Lemma 8. *If C is the set of machine channels of machine M, and P is the controller for M, and P' is the process P except that non-machine channels block in P' where they diverge in P, and $P' \parallel M$ is divergence-free, then no event in $\{\mid C \mid\}$ is a diverging event for $P \parallel M$.*

Proof. This is justified by Corollary 1. If D is P's set of non-machine channels, then we are blocking P on $\mathcal{MD}\,[\![P]\!]_{\{\mid D \mid\}}$. We are also blocking M on $\varnothing$. Thus we have the following conditions (where $D_M = \varnothing$):

1. $D_M \subseteq \mathcal{MD}\,[\![M]\!] \setminus \mathcal{MD}\,[\![M]\!]_{\{\mid C \mid\}}$
2. $D_P \subseteq \mathcal{MD}\,[\![P]\!] \setminus \mathcal{MD}\,[\![P]\!]_{\{\mid C \mid\}}$
3. $M \parallel BLOCK_{\alpha M}(D_M) \parallel P \parallel BLOCK_{\alpha P}(D_P)$ is divergence-free

The first follows because $D_M = \varnothing$; the second follows because only minimal divergences on channels in D are blocked; and the third we have from the fact that $M \parallel P'$ is divergence-free. Thus we can deduce from Corollary 1 that $\mathcal{MD}\,[\![M \parallel P]\!] \upharpoonright \alpha M \cap \mathcal{MD}\,[\![M]\!] = \varnothing$.

This lemma is useful, since we can use CLI techniques to show that $P' \parallel M$ is divergence-free.

3.5   Pulling it all Together

The overall aim is to provide support for establishing that a CSP∥B system description is divergence-free. Divergences can arise when B operations are called outside their preconditions, and it is the responsibility of the designers of the CSP controllers to ensure that this does not occur.

The B machines must be considered as chunks with their controllers providing their environment. In many situations, it may be the case that a CSP controller cannot guarantee this in isolation for the machine under its control, and that constraints imposed by the rest of the system also need to be factored in. Existing results allow divergence-freedom to be established for a machine in parallel with a single sequential process, and so information from other parallel components needs to be introduced into the controller as assertions on the channels.

Having introduced diverging assertions onto some of the channels within the CSP parts of the system, we then need to identify chunks to verify that these diverging assertions do not introduce new divergences. For chunks consisting purely of CSP processes, the divergence-freedom check can be carried out using FDR. The next section will illustrate this process.

4   Example

We will begin by describing the structure of the system and its components. Then we will show how to verify that the system is divergence-free using the *chunks* technique. Consider the following system:

$$PortSystem = ShipsCtrl \parallel WaitingCtrl \parallel QuayCtrl \parallel Waiting \parallel Quays$$

It comprises of three controllers and two machines as shown in Figure 2. It tracks the entering of ships and their docking at quays. A ship can enter a port and proceed to a waiting queue. A ship can be transferred from the waiting

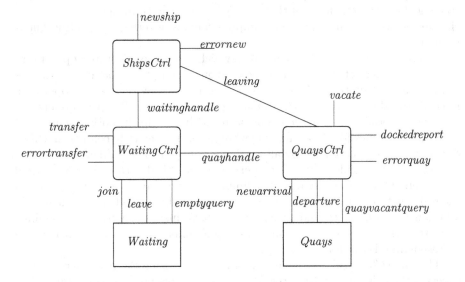

Fig. 2. Port system architecture

MACHINE *Waiting*
SEES *Bool_TYPE* , *Context*
VARIABLES *waiting*
INVARIANT *waiting* $\in$ iseq (*SHIP*)
INITIALISATION *waiting* := [ ]
OPERATIONS
  join (*ss*) $\widehat{=}$ **PRE** *ss* $\in$ *SHIP* $\wedge$ *ss* $\notin$ ran (*waiting*)
  THEN *waiting* := *waiting* $\leftarrow$ *ss*
  END ;
  ss $\longleftarrow$ **leave** $\widehat{=}$ **PRE** *waiting* $\neq$ [ ]
  THEN *ss* := first (*waiting*) $\parallel$ *waiting* := tail (*waiting*)
  END ;
  bb $\longleftarrow$ **emptyquery** $\widehat{=}$ *bb* := *bool* (*waiting* = [ ])
END

Fig. 3. *Waiting* machine

queue to a quay. A ship can also leave a quay so that it is no longer tracked by the system. Only one ship is allowed to be docked at a particular quay. A ship cannot be both waiting and docked at a quay at the same time.

The main state associated with this example is the waiting queue, and the quays at which ships can dock. This information is captured as an injective sequence of ships, *waiting*, and a partial injective function, *docked*. We would naturally use B to hold this data in separate machines and provide a rich set of operations to manipulate it. Figure 3 defines the *Waiting* machine which contains three operations: `join`, `leave` and `emptyquery`. The first operation appends a new ship to the waiting queue. The second operation extracts a ship from the head of the waiting queue. The third operation does not change the state of the queue and simply examines whether the waiting queue is empty.

Figure 4 defines the `Quay` machine which also contains three operations: `newarrival`, `departure` and `queryvacantquay`. The first operation allocates a ship to a non-deterministically chosen unoccupied quay. The second operation removes the ship which is docked at a particular quay *qq*. The third operation examines whether the quay *qq* is not occupied by a ship. In both machines we note that the types for ships and quays are given in a separate context machine, `Context`, which is accessible by all machines (but not provided here).

Let us now consider how these operations are called within their associated controllers. Our initial attempt at defining controllers is given in Figure 5 and their aim is to co-ordinate the main behaviour of ships we identified earlier. In addition to *WaitingCtrl* and *QuaysCtrl* we have included a *ShipsCtrl* to illustrate that the CSP∥B architecture can accommodate processes which have no corresponding B machines.

The *ShipsCtrl* regulates the arrival of new ships using the *newship* event and observes their departure using the *leaving* event. This process keeps track of all the ships being monitored in the port system using the set *ss*.

MACHINE *Quays*
SEES *Bool_TYPE* , *Context*
VARIABLES *docked*
INVARIANT *docked* $\in$ *QUAY* $\rightarrowtail$ *SHIP*
INITIALISATION *docked* := $\varnothing$
OPERATIONS
  quay, bb $\longleftarrow$ **newarrival** (*ss*) $\widehat{=}$
    PRE *ss* $\in$ *SHIP* $\wedge$ dom (*docked*) $\neq$ *QUAY* $\wedge$ *ss* $\notin$ ran (*docked*) **THEN**
      ANY *qq*
      WHERE *qq* $\in$ *QUAY* $-$ dom (*docked*)
      THEN *docked* (*qq*) := *ss* $\parallel$ *quay* := *qq*
            $\parallel$ *bb* := *bool(card(docked) = card(QUAY) -1)*
      END
    END ;
  ss $\longleftarrow$ **departure** (*qq*) $\widehat{=}$ **PRE** *qq* $\in$ dom (*docked*)
    THEN *docked* := { *qq* } $\unlhd$ *docked* $\parallel$ *ss* := *docked* (*qq*)
    END ;
  bb $\longleftarrow$ **quayvacantquery** (*qq*) $\widehat{=}$ **PRE** *qq* $\in$ *QUAY*
    THEN *bb* := *bool* (*qq* $\in$ dom (*docked*))
    END
END

Fig. 4. *Quays* machine

Once a new ship has arrived along channel *waitinghandle* the *WaitingCtrl* aims to place it appropriately in the waiting queue by interacting with the B machine along channel *join*. The *WaitingCtrl* also transfers a ship from the waiting queue so that the *QuaysCtrl* can record its docking at a quay. To achieve this transfer the *WaitingCtrl* queries the B machine, using *queryemptyquay*, to check that the waiting queue is non-empty, then a communication along *leave* extracts an appropriate ship which is passed to *QuaysCtrl* along *quayhandle*, which in turn records the docking using the operation *newarrival*. This operation provides the chosen quay as output, and also reports on whether the quays are now full: if they are, then no further ships will be accepted to add to the quays until some ship has left, as described by *FullQuaysCtrl*.

QuayCtrl also can deal with ships vacating a particular quay. A similar pattern of behaviour is followed where the B machine is queried to check that the quay is occupied, and if it is, the appropriate ship is extracted and *QuayCtrl* communicates with the *ShipsCtrl* to record its removal from the system using the *leaving* event.

4.1 Adding Assertions to the Controllers

In the previous section our informal description of the various patterns of behaviour that port can undertake glossed over the fact that the four modifying operations of B have nontrivial preconditions. It is the responsibility of the controllers

$SC(ss) = newship?s \rightarrow$**if** $(s \in ss)$
$$\textbf{then } errornew \rightarrow SC(ss)$$
$$\textbf{else } waitinghandle!s \rightarrow SC(ss \cup \{s\}))$$
$$\square \ leaving?s \rightarrow SC(ss - \{s\})$$
$ShipsCtrl = SC(\{\})$

$WaitingCtrl = waitinghandle?s \rightarrow join!s \rightarrow WaitingCtrl$
$$\square \ transfer \rightarrow emptyquery?b \rightarrow$$
$$\textbf{if } (b = TRUE)$$
$$\textbf{then } errortransfer \rightarrow WaitingCtrl$$
$$\textbf{else } leave?s \rightarrow quayhandle!s \rightarrow WaitingCtrl$$

$QuaysCtrl = quayhandle?s \rightarrow newarrival!s?q?b \rightarrow dockedreport!s!q \rightarrow$
$$\textbf{if } (b = TRUE)$$
$$\textbf{then } FullQuaysCtrl$$
$$\textbf{else } QuaysCtrl$$
$$\square \ vacate?q \rightarrow quayvacantquery!q?b \rightarrow$$
$$\textbf{if } (b = TRUE)$$
$$\textbf{then } errorquay \rightarrow QuaysCtrl$$
$$\textbf{else } departure!q?s \rightarrow leaving!s \rightarrow QuaysCtrl$$

$FullQuaysCtrl = vacate?q \rightarrow departure!q?s \rightarrow leaving!s \rightarrow QuaysCtrl$

Fig. 5. Initial CSP Controllers

to make sure that the operations are called within their preconditions so that they do not contribute any divergent behaviour. Let us re-examine the *WaitingCtrl* and the *QuaysCtrl* controllers. The *ShipsCtrl* can remain as in Figure 5.

Consider the `join` and `leave` operations called by *WaitingCtrl*. The precondition of the `join` operation signifies that only a ship that is not already waiting should be considered. The control flow of the processes gives us this, and so a synchronisation with *waitinghandle* ensures that the ship is a valid one. However, our aim is to prove divergence freedom by considering controller/machine pairs as single chunks in the following section. Consequently, any assumptions we need to make about ships in order to ensure that the precondition of `join` holds have to be recorded in *WaitingCtrl*. We have two ways of doing this: first we can call a query operation to see whether the ship is in the waiting queue before calling `join`, second we can annotate the appropriate channel with an assertion as is shown in Figure 6. The assertion needs to capture the fact that the ship s is not already in the queue. Therefore, the CSP needs to contain some state so that this can be expressed. It need not capture all the details of the order of the queue, it only needs to record the set of ships in the queue, represented by *wss*. This is an abstraction of the B state and is duplicated in the CSP for the purposes of proof, after which it can be dropped again. The assertion is placed at the point in the process where the value of the ship is bound, i.e., on *waitinghandle*. We choose the second option because we know that when the whole system is composed

$WC(wss) = (waitinghandle?s\{s \notin wss\} \rightarrow join!s \rightarrow WC(wss \cup \{s\}))$
$\qquad \Box\ (transfer \rightarrow emptyquery?b \rightarrow$
$\qquad\qquad\qquad \textbf{if}\ (b = TRUE)$
$\qquad\qquad\qquad \textbf{then}\ errortransfer \rightarrow WC(wss)$
$\qquad\qquad\qquad \textbf{else}\ leave?s\{s \in wss\} \rightarrow quayhandle!s \rightarrow WC(wss - \{s\}))$
$WaitingCtrl = WC(\{\})$

$QC(dss) = (quayhandle?s\{s \notin dss\} \rightarrow newarrival!s?q?b \rightarrow dockedreport!s!q \rightarrow$
$\qquad\qquad\qquad\qquad \textbf{if}\ b = TRUE$
$\qquad\qquad\qquad\qquad \textbf{then}\ FQC(dss \cup \{s\}$
$\qquad\qquad\qquad\qquad \textbf{else}\ QC(dss \cup \{s\}))$
$\qquad \Box\ (vacate?q \rightarrow quayvacantquery!q?b \rightarrow$
$\qquad\qquad\qquad \textbf{if}\ (b = true)$
$\qquad\qquad\qquad \textbf{then}\ errorquay \rightarrow QC(dss)$
$\qquad\qquad\qquad \textbf{else}\ departure!q?s\{s \in dss\} \rightarrow leaving!s \rightarrow QC(dss - \{s\}))$
$QuaysCtrl = QC(\{\})$

$FQC(dss) = vacate?q \rightarrow departure!q?s\{s \in dss\} \rightarrow leaving!s \rightarrow QC(dss - \{s\}))$

Fig. 6. Augmented CSP controllers

together the control flow ensures that the precondition is true and therefore we don't need the extra overhead of calling a query operation. We only need these annotations when breaking down the proof into chunks.

The **leave** operation should only be called when the queue is non-empty. Here, we use a query operation to check whether the queue is empty. We cannot add a diverging assertion because they are checked after communication has occurred. What we require is a way of blocking the call to the operation when wss is empty. We cannot use a blocking assertion on the machine channel because this would violate our non-discriminating property discussed in [13]. Therefore, a query operation is the only way to provide the required level of control here.

Second, the way in which we augment the $QuaysCtrl$, so that we will be in a position to prove the chunk $QuaysCtrl \parallel Quays$, is similar to the way we augmented $WaitingCtrl$. We annotate the $quayhandle$ channel with a diverging assertion to check that the ship to be docked is not already docked. Thus, when we call **newarrival** the precondition will hold. The assertion is expressed using the set dss in $QuaysCtrl$. The set is an abstraction of the docked ships. Here again, the CSP description does not need to be concerned about where the ships are docked, it simply needs to track whether they are or not. We also provide a query operation to provide the required level of control prior to calling the **departure** operation.

Notice that there are two further assertions in Figure 6, and both of these are as a result of a factoring in the constraints imposed by the rest of the system. We need to know that the ship being passed to the $QuaysCtrl$ is in fact in the waiting queue, and the diverging assertion $\{s \in wss\}$ will enable us to check this. Then we will be sure that the ships in the waiting queue and the quays do not overlap. Similarly, we need to know that when a ship is leaving that it was indeed one of the ships in a quay, and the diverging assertion $\{s \in dss\}$ will enable us to check this. Then when the state of ss in $ShipCtrl$ is updated we can be sure that the ship removed from the quay will also be removed from the whole system.

4.2   Splitting the Port System into Chunks

The resulting system from the above discussion is a port system comprising of two machines, and three controllers, two of which contain diverging assertions. We will now demonstrate the application of Theorem 1 on each of the processes to show that the overall $PortSystem$ is divergence-free.

Consider the $Waiting$ machine. An appropriate chunk is $WaitingCtrl \parallel Waiting$. in order to demonstrate that this is divergence-free we would need to show that none of the machine channels are diverging events of $WaitingCtrl \parallel Waiting$. First we transform the diverging assertion on $waitinghandle$ to a blocking assertion but leave the diverging assertion on $leave$, then we can show using the CLI technique that the transformed controller $WaitingCtrl' \parallel Waiting$ is divergence-free. Applying Lemma 8 enables us to conclude that $WaitingCtrl \parallel Waiting$ is divergence free.

Consider the $Quays$ machine. An appropriate chunk is $QuaysCtrl \parallel Quays$. In order to demonstrate that this is divergence-free we need to show that none of the machine channels are diverging events of $QuaysCtrl \parallel Quays$. First we transform the diverging assertion on $quayhandle$ to a blocking assertion but leave the diverging assertion on $departure$, then we can show using the CLI technique that the transformed controller $QuaysCtrl' \parallel Quays$ is divergence-free. Applying Lemma 8 enables us to conclude that $QuaysCtrl \parallel Quays$ is divergence free.

Now we can turn our focus to the controllers and consider the application of Theorem 1 for each of them. There is nothing to prove for $ShipsCtrl$ because it does not contain any diverging events.

Consider $WaitingCtrl$. It can diverge on two channels $waitinghandle$ and $leave$. We need not identify a chunk to show the absence of divergence on $leave$ because we have already done that as part of the first chunk above. Consider diverging on $waitinghandle$. We require the co-operation of $ShipsCtrl$ to discharge this. We transform the $leave$ assertion into a blocking assertions in line with condition 1 in Corollary 3. Then we can establish that $ShipsCtrl \parallel WaitingCtrl$ is divergence-free using FDR and this meets condition 4 of Corollary 3. Applying Lemma 8 enables us to conclude that $waitinghandle$ is not a diverging event of $WaitingCtrl \parallel Waiting$.

Consider $QuaysCtrl$. It can diverge on two channels $quayhandle$ and $departure$. We need not identify a chunk to show the absence of the divergence on $departure$ because we have already done that as part of the second chunk above. Consider diverging on $quayhandle$. We require the co-operation of $WaitingCtrl$ to discharge this diverging assertion. First we transform the diverging assertions on $leave$ from $WaitingCtrl$ and $departure$ from $QuayCtrl$ and this is in line with conditions 1 and 3 in Corollary 3. Then we can show using FDR that

QuaysCtrl ∥ *WaitingCtrl* is divergence-free and this meets condition 4 of Corollary 3. *ShipsCtrl* is a simple P_j since it is itself divergence-free and therefore condition 2 and 3 hold. This allows us to conclude that *quayhandle* does not contribute any divergent behaviour.

The above has shown that we can show that all chunks are divergence-free. Using results from [13] we can then remove any of the assertion annotations and this allows us to conclude that the original port system is divergence-free.

In the above example, it would have been possible to group all the controllers together and prove divergence freedom of the controllers on their own, and then prove the individual controller/machine pairs and deduce that the combination is divergence-free. This was the necessary approach in [13]. What we have shown above is that we can systematically go through each process in a combined system, and show that it is divergence free either by using the CLI technique or in FDR once we have transformed the chunk into an appropriate form. We have had some concerns over the scalability of the previous approach because it may not always be possible to group all the controllers together. This work gives us a much finer grained way of proving divergence-freedom which we feel will potentially be more scalable than the previous technique presented in [13].

5 Conclusion

Our principle of composing components and describing their interactions resonates in the *Reo* coordination model [2]. The main difference is that Reo does not concentrate on the entities that are connected to the interacting components, rather the method is concerned with governing the flow of data between components and developing support for dynamic reconfiguration of its connectors. The work that is most closely related to ours is csp2B [3] and the recent extensions to proB [4]. The former is a purely syntactic transformation of a CSP description into B. The CSP descriptions can be very expressive, allowing interleaving, but the work does not address any compositional verification issues. Very promising new work is emerging which has the same semantic foundations as our approach. The authors of [4] also consider a B machine as a process that can engage in events in the same way that a CSP process can and so an operation call is a synchronisation of a CSP event with its corresponding operation. To the best of our knowledge they have not yet examined the issues related to the scalability of their approach. Their work currently focuses on automating consistency checking of a combined CSP and B specification. One future avenue worth pursuing would be to investigate whether the ProB form of consistency checking could be tailored to automating the CLI proof that we carry out to show that a P ∥ M is divergence-free.

Acknowledgements

Thanks are due to the anonymous referees for their comments on an earlier draft of this paper. We are also grateful to the EPSRC for the provision of funding towards this research, both under GR/R96859 and under the TUNA project.

References

1. Abrial, J.-R.: *The B-Book*. Cambridge University Press, 1996.
2. Arbab, F.: *Reo: A channel-based coordination model for component composition*. Mathematical Structures in Computer Science (14), 329–366, 2004.
3. Butler M. J.: *csp2B: A Practical Approach to Combining CSP and B*, Formal Aspects of Computing, Volume 12 (2000).
4. Butler, M. and Leuschel, M.:*Combining CSP and B for Specification and Property Verification*. In Proceedings of Formal Methods 2005, Newcastle upon Tyne, Fitzgerald, J., Hayes, I. and Tarlecki, A., Eds. LNCS 3582, Springer, 2005.
5. Cavalcanti A., Sampaio A., and Woodcock J.: *Refinement of Actions in Circus*, In REFINE'02, FME Workshop, Copenhagen (2002).
6. Evans, N., Treharne, H.: *Investigating a File Transfer Protocol Using CSP and B*. SoSym Journal (accepted for publication 2005).
7. Evans N., Treharne H., Laleau R., Frappier M.: *How to Verify Dynamic Properties of Information Systems*. 2nd International Conference on Software Engineering and Formal Methods, IEEE, China, 2004.
8. Formal Systems (Europe) Ltd.: Failures-Divergences Refinement: FDR2 User Manual 1997.
9. Hoare, C. A. R.: *Communicating Sequential Processes*. Prentice Hall, Englewood Cliffs, 1985.
10. Leuschel M., Butler M.: *ProB: A Model Checker for B*. Proceedings FME 2003, Pisa, Italy, LNCS 2805, pages 855-874. Springer, 2003.
11. Schneider, S. A.: *Concurrent and Real-Time Systems: the CSP Approach*, John Wiley 1999.
12. Schneider S.,Treharne H.: *Communicating B Machines*. ZB2002, Grenoble, LNCS 2272, Springer, January (2002).
13. Schneider, S., Treharne, H.: *CSP Theorems for Communicating B Machines*. In Proceedings of IFM 2004, LNCS 2999, Springer-Verlag, University of Kent, 2004.
14. Treharne H., Schneider S.: *Using a Process Algebra to control B OPERATIONS*. In K. Araki, A. Galloway and K. Taguchi, editors, IFM'99, York (1999), pp437–456.
15. Treharne H., Schneider S., Bramble M.: *Composing Specifications using Communication*. In ZB2003, LNCS 2651, Springer-Verlag, Finland, 2003.

Agile Formal Method Engineering

Richard F. Paige[1] and Phillip J. Brooke[2]

[1] Department of Computer Science, University of York, UK
paige@cs.york.ac.uk
[2] School of Computing, Communications, and Electronics, University of Plymouth, UK
phil.brooke@plymouth.ac.uk

Abstract. Software development methods are software products, in the sense that they should be engineered by following a methodology to meet the behavioural and non-behavioural requirements of the intended users of the method. We argue that *agile approaches* are the most appropriate means for engineering new methods, and particularly for integrating formal methods. We show how agile principles and practices apply to engineering methods, and demonstrate their application by integrating parts of the Eiffel development method with CSP.

1 Introduction

There are substantial benefits to treating a software development method (such as the Rational Unified Process combined with UML [16], the B-Method [3], SSADM [12], etc) as a software product. A method is like any other product that must be engineered in a rigorous, disciplined, repeatable way. The process of developing a new method – either from scratch, or by integrating a number of existing methods – should be subjected to the technical and management practices that are critical in modern software projects. Given that most software projects end up tailoring the methods they use – and, in fact, some approaches strongly recommend or require tailoring, e.g., EUP [15] – being able to do so in a disciplined, managed way, following well-understood principles and practices, is of substantial importance.

Modern software development methods can broadly be classified into two groups: the *model-based* methods, and the *agile* methods, though there is not a precise division between the two. The former are characterized by their emphasis on specification and documentation; models (or specifications) are constructed at all stages of the development process, and a successive refinement or transformation process is followed in mapping these models into an executable format. Along the way, documentation can be produced to capture the transformations made, the design decisions that have been clarified, the traceability relationships between models, and the consistency arguments that need to be made. Approaches such as the Model-Driven Architecture (MDA) [19], the B-Method, various refinement calculi [13], and SSADM generally fit into this category.

The second category of methods are described as agile. These methods tend to de-emphasize models (and documentation) and are defined in terms of conformance to a small set of technical and management practices which are generally oriented towards delivering executable code quickly. These practices, in turn, are implementations of a small set of agile principles, which are meant to provide guidance when carrying out technical development and layering management cycles atop the technical process.

J. Romijn, G. Smith, and J. van de Pol (Eds.): IFM 2005, LNCS 3771, pp. 109–128, 2005.

Some well-known examples of agile methods include Extreme Programming (XP) [6], Test-Driven Development [7], Agile Modelling [5], and Feature-Driven Development [24], but there are many others as well.

Much of the previous work on formal method engineering, language integration, and formal method integration, has not treated the method to be constructed as a (software) product. Instead, the focus has been on language integration or definition (e.g., integrations of Object-Z and Timed CSP [17], and formal profiles of UML [2]). There is some work in the semiformal method community that has treated methods as engineering products, but for the most part this work has focused on heavyweight solutions: models of methods (e.g., process models [27]), process metamodels such as SPEM [20], process patterns (e.g., as in Catalysis [11] or those due to Ambler [4]), or the meta-modelling approaches used to define the concept of an MDA component [25].

In this paper, we argue for the use of agile development methods for integrating (particularly, but not exclusively) formal methods. Agile principles and practices – particularly those from the Agile Manifesto, and those from Extreme Programming – are, for the most part, applicable and helpful in rapidly and flexibly integrating methods. The result of applying agile techniques to method integration should be to produce simpler, more flexible methods that are specifically tailored to the functional and non-functional requirements for a development project.

We emphasise that we are interested in the development of *methods*, which generally encompass both modelling languages and technical (and possibly management) processes. The technical process associated with a method may be loosely and informally described, or even left implicit. We claim that agile methods are applicable to the development of software development methods that have explicit or implicit processes. The case study we present in Section 6 has an implicit process.

The paper starts with an overview of the Agile Manifesto and the principles and practices of XP, which will be used to carry out the integration of formal methods later in the paper. We then sketch how XP and the guiding principles of the Manifesto can be applied in integrating formal methods; in this sense, we are re-configuring the agile principles and practices specifically to integrating and engineering methods. We then apply these re-configured practices in a case study in integrating the Eiffel method [18] and CSP [14]; justifications for why the integration is useful and appropriate in a specific context will also be provided. We also provide a brief introduction to Eiffel – and a justification as to why it is a formal method – in Section 2.

2   Background

2.1   The Agile Manifesto

The Agile Manifesto [1] is a set of guiding principles to be observed during an agile development project. The principles are generally straightforward, and do not in themselves lead to technical processes or process phases. Usually, they are implemented using a set of agile development *practices* (examples of which are discussed in the next subsection) which provide technical and management guidance during development. One can consider agile principles as the meta-rules to which most, if not all agile methodologies, conform. The principles of the Agile Manifesto are as follows:

- Our highest priority is to satisfy the customer through early and continuous delivery of valuable software.
- Welcome changing requirements, even late in development. Agile processes harness change for the customer's competitive advantage.
- Deliver working software frequently, from a couple of weeks to a couple of months, with a preference to the shorter timescale.
- Business people and developers must work together daily throughout the project.
- Build projects around motivated individuals. Give them the environment and support they need, and trust them to get the job done.
- The most efficient and effective method of conveying information to and within a development team is face-to-face conversation.
- Working software is the primary measure of progress.
- Agile processes promote sustainable development. The sponsors, developers, and users should be able to maintain a constant pace indefinitely.
- Continuous attention to technical excellence and good design enhances agility.
- Simplicity – the art of maximizing the amount of work not done – is essential.
- The best architectures, requirements, and designs emerge from self-organizing teams.
- At regular intervals, the team reflects on how to become more effective, then tunes and adjusts its behavior accordingly.

Note the emphases on the customer and teamwork, the requirement to deal with change, and the focus on simplicity. We will argue that most of these principles apply directly to method engineering and integration in the next section.

2.2   Extreme Programming Principles and Practices

XP, due to Beck [6], is one of many agile development methods that targets the following development problems: the requirements are not met by the system that has been constructed; the resulting system is out-of-date by deployment; and system quality is so poor that the system is unusable. All agile development methods rely on two core practices: the short "inspect and adapt" cycle, and the short feedback loop, where concerns are relayed to and from customers; XP is no different. Each agile method provides principles and practices that implement these techniques.

The guiding principles of XP provide a concrete description of the method, and it is important to judge the approach against the complete set of practices and principles, rather than those that seem to be appropriate in a given context. XP principles are accomplished via a number of technical XP practices, which are employed by developers, coaches, and managers:

- *Planning game:* quickly determine the scope of the next release using business priorities and technical estimates.
- *Small releases:* put a simple system into production quickly, then release new versions on a very short cycle.
- *Metaphor:* guide development with a simple shared story of how the system works.
- *Simple design:* the system is designed as simply as possible; extra complexity is removed on discovery.

- *Testing:* programmers write unit tests, which must run flawlessly for development to continue. Customers write tests demonstrating that features are finished.
- *Refactoring:* programmers restructure the system without changing its behaviour to reduce duplication, improve communication, simplify, or add flexibility.
- *Pair programming:* all code is written with two programmers at one machine.
- *Collective ownership:* anyone can change any code in the system at any time.
- *Continuous integration:* integrate and build the system many times a day, every time a task is completed.
- *40-hour week:* work no more than 40 hours a week as a rule, without working overtime a second week in a row.
- *On-site customer:* include users on the team available full-time to answer questions.
- *Coding standards:* programmers write code in accordance with rules emphasising communication through the code.

2.3   The Eiffel Formal Method

Eiffel is an object-oriented development method [18]; its specification language provides constructs typical of the object-oriented paradigm, including classes, objects, routines (methods) and inheritance. Eiffel supports contracts, via pre- and postconditions on methods, as well as invariant properties on classes. The full details of Eiffel's syntax are not directly relevant to this paper; we introduce syntax where we need it. Computations in an Eiffel program are constructed via *feature calls*, i.e., invoking attributes or routines. These all have the form $o.f$, where o is an *entity* (i.e., a local variable, an attribute, or a parameter), and f a feature. The technical process in the Eiffel method is generally called *seamless development* [18]: classes are identified, added to, refined, and removed in the process from analysis through design and implementation.

   A subset of Eiffel can be identified and used as a formal specification language. An *Eiffel formal specification* is written using only the following constructs.

- Classes and class interfaces (containing routine signatures and attributes).
- Local variables of routines.
- Boolean expressions, including contracts.
- Routine calls of the form $o.f$.
- Assignment statements in routine bodies.
- Sequential composition of routine calls and assignment statements.

All other Eiffel constructs are excluded. This subset is roughly similar to the subset identified in the Eiffel Refinement Calculus [22], which allows Eiffel formal specifications to be refined to programs. A formal semantics for these constructs can be found in [22], excepting **separate** classes (discussed in the sequel).

2.4   SCOOP: Concurrency in Eiffel

SCOOP – Simple Concurrent Object-Oriented Programming – introduces concurrency to Eiffel by addition of the keyword **separate**; it is the responsibility of the underlying run-time system and compiler to deal with the subtle (and, in some cases, complicated) semantic problems introduced by the addition.

The **separate** keyword may be attached to the definition of a class, or the declaration of an entity, or formal routine argument. A separate class (e.g., *ROOT*) executes in its own thread (not necessarily an operating system thread). Thus, feature calls to instances of a separate class may need to block or wait until the underlying processing resource is available to execute the request.

An entity or argument declared as **separate** (*e.g.*, the second and third examples above, respectively) indicates that the data attached to the entity or argument may be shared between threads. Synchronisation facilities must be provided so that, *e.g.*, mutually exclusive writes to shared data take place.

SCOOP is based upon the notion of a *subsystem*, which defines a unit of execution in an OO system. When a **separate** object (defined in the sequel) is created, a new subsystem is also created to *handle* its processing. This subsystem is also called the object's *handler*. Thus, a processor is an autonomous thread of control capable of supporting *sequential* instruction execution [18]. A system in general may have many processors associated with it.

There are a number of complications with feature calls in SCOOP. Suppose that x is attached to a **separate** object, or the type of x is separate. For the command $x.c(a)$, execution on the current object and x synchronise; x registers the fact that c was called and either starts execution of c immediately, or when the next opportunity arises (implying that each **separate** object is associated with a queue). Then both the current call and $x.c(a)$ can proceed concurrently. If there are multiple pending requests for calls on x, they are queued and served in first-in-first-out (FIFO) order.

For a query where a result is needed from a **separate** call, a restricted version of *wait-by-necessity* is used, because the result of a call to $x.f(a)$ may not be available when the assignment $y := x.f(a)$ can take place. In SCOOP, further client calls on x will wait until the query call $x.f(a)$ has terminated.

Changes are made to the treatment of **require** clauses, to make it a *wait* condition: a call to a routine with a *false* precondition will wait and only proceed when the precondition evaluates to *true*. SCOOP also alters the semantics of argument passing in order to prevent arbitrary interleaving of concurrent calls; this is explained further in [18].

3   Agile Development of Methods

Agile principles and practices focus on delivering working software to a customer. A development method can also be treated as a software product, in the sense that *engineering practices* can be applied to build it. This is not to say that there is a clear analogy between the process of developing a software product and building a method, but there are many obvious similarities:

- Like software products, a method has behaviour, can be tailored and modified by its users, and should operate successfully on its domain.
- A method has a description, which may be text-based or diagrammatic.
- A method requires experts in order to build it and customize it.
- A method has static characteristics (i.e., its process and the languages it employs) and dynamic characteristics (i.e., the effects and deliverables it produces when it is used, the steps actually taken during its application).

At this point, we should remind the reader that we are referring to a software *product*, not just a piece of software; this term means to include deliverables beyond code, e.g., documentation such as user manuals.

There are as well obvious differences between methods and software products:

- Software generally has a single formal description, e.g., in a set of files, or a collection of diagrams. This description can be read and translated, interpreted or executed by a machine. By contrast, the description of a method is a predominantly natural language document that cannot completely be executed (though see [25] for attempts to describe parts of methods using models).
- There are engineering techniques that can be applied to determine if a software product is well-formed, e.g., using compilers, safety and security standards. There is little in the way of assessment criteria as to what constitutes a well-formed method. Iterative criteria-based assessment could be of value here [26].
- Software has dimensions: size (e.g., in KLOC), complexity, and correctness. A method *may* have dimensions (e.g., the size of the development team required to apply it) but these are more difficult to characterize and measure.

Despite the differences, the process modelling, meta-modelling, and pattern communities are arguing that treating a method like a software product for the purposes of its development can produce better methods: methods that are simpler, easier to explain and understand, more closely meet the needs of their users, and easier to tailor. While we agree with this argument, we take a different view in terms of *how* to engineer methods. Instead of using so-called heavyweight techniques, like meta-modelling, we instead apply agile principles and practices to build methods.

When we say 'build methods', we mean to include both new methods and also methods that are constructed via integration of ideas, techniques, and notations from existing methods. There is no conceptual difference between these from the perspective of applying agile principles to this task. We also include building notations or languages as part of this: invariably, languages either come with a recommended process, a full methodology, or a set of well-known practices that guide how to use it. This is particularly the case with formal languages, e.g., Z, B, and CSP. In these cases, the process may be implicit, or tailored for a specific problem domain.

In order to explain how the agile approach can be used to build methods, we do three things. First, we explain precisely how each principle from the Agile Manifesto applies to building methods. To make this more concrete and practical, we then discuss how the technical practices of XP apply to method engineering. Then, we present an agile method for engineering methods. The method, like most agile approaches, consists of a set of agile practices. This agile method is intended to work *in parallel* with actual software development. This is an essential characteristic of realistic and agile method engineering and integration: it is essential to obtain feedback from users of the method – *while they are using the method* – in order to incrementally improve the method until it is fit-for-purpose. A method should not be viewed as a static entity: it must be iteratively improved in response to feedback from real-world projects, otherwise it is always out-of-date and in need of substantial tuning.

The last part of our presentation is to illustrate the approach by integrating the Eiffel method with CSP. In this case study we show how to build an integrated method, realize that the method does not fulfill all requirements, and then refactor the method to better meet its requirements. This type of approach is important in those cases where we do not know or understand all requirements – particularly methodological requirements – up front. Of course, some refactorings and changes to a method – e.g., large-scale modelling language changes, expensive changes in supporting tools – will be difficult to carry out, but by having technical principles and practices to guide the process of change, we can hope to make difficult changes easier.

4   The Agile Manifesto of Method Engineering

We now summarize how each principle of the Agile Manifesto applies to engineering methods. We then summarize how XP practices apply (or fail to apply) to method engineering. From this, we will build up an agile method for method engineering.

We write the principles of the Agile Manifesto in *italics*, and describe its application to method engineering in Roman font. There are several re-interpretations of terminology that must be made to do this; Table 1 summarises these.

Table 1. Translation of Manifesto terminology to Method Engineering context

Original Terminology in Manifesto	Interpretation in Method Engineering
Software	Method
Customer	Developer
"Our"/"We"	Method Engineer

- *Our highest priority is to satisfy the customer through early and continuous delivery of valuable software.*
  In a realistic environment in which a method must be engineered, the first version of the method (i.e., a "method prototype" which may not satisfy all customer requirements) must be available quickly, and revisions to it must be made quickly in response to customer (i.e., developer) requests. We must engage with the customer and convince them that we can deliver what they want. We can do this by delivering a method that works (even if it is incomplete) quickly, as well as prompt revisions.
- *Welcome changing requirements, even late in development. Agile processes harness change for the customer's competitive advantage.*
  Changing requirements here mean changing requirements for the method to be built. Thus, if during the use of a method, the customer realizes that something is missing or doesn't work, they have every right to request the method engineer to change the method. Moreover, the user of the method has every right to expect these changes to be made quickly and efficiently; even further, the method engineer should anticipate that the developer will come requesting changes to the method. An implication of this is that methods should be designed to change; the other principles of agile method engineering in fact help (but do not guarantee) this.

It is unlikely that there will be massive refactorings of a method in response to customer requests; moreover, some refactorings may simply be very difficult and therefore undesirable (a fact that is acknowledged in methods like XP). An example of a large refactoring of a method might be to introduce certification or risk assessment, or a substantial change to a modelling or specification language (e.g., adding a process algebra to Object-Z). This would disrupt all phases of a method. Small refactorings might be to add a new phase to the process (e.g., "build a prototype") or to add a new proof technique (e.g., "do satisfiability checking before carrying out a refinement"). There are more likely to be small changes to requirements for the modelling languages used, since this is what the customer sees and uses on a day-to-day basis. For example, there may be a requirement to do autocode generation of test data late in the process, which may require the specification language to be strengthened with pre- and postconditions of methods. Changes to the process may be initiated by responses to standards organizations (e.g., to obtain ISO 9000 certification).

- *Deliver working software frequently, from a couple of weeks to a couple of months, with a preference to the shorter timescale.*

  The immediate implication of this is that versions of methods should be delivered frequently. The first, simplest version of the method must be available almost immediately for use, and revisions must be available quickly as well. A release plan may be useful here to help determine what can be done in the time available. For example, if the method designers have two weeks to produce Version 1, they can then take requirement requests (e.g., in the form of user stories – see Section 6) and say "we can deliver a specification language with these five features, with an integrated syntax and semantics, plus tool support for static analysis". Such an approach is useful for users of methods as well, as they can obtain rapid feedback on feasibility of requirements.

- *Business people and developers must work together daily throughout the project.*

  The method designers and the developers who will use the method work together. The developers are the customers of the method designers, and they must provide user stories. A good example of a user story might be "I model the protocol using finite state machines, and then automatically transform it into a machine-readable implementation that I can import into a CTL-based model checker."

  The emphasis on working together daily is important, from both perspectives: the developer has someone at hand who can guide them in the use of the method; and the method engineer has someone at hand who can reveal the flaws, omissions, and errors in their method based on practical experience.

- *Build projects around motivated individuals. Give them the environment and support they need, and trust them to get the job done.*

  A method engineer must be motivated to do their job. Part of this motivation will come from the ability to get frequent feedback from the people who are using the method in real projects. Additional motivation will come by providing method engineers with the facilities they need to build methods, such as access to standards documents, development tools, requirements from customers, research documents on method integration, unifying theories, etc.

- *The most efficient and effective method of conveying information to and within a development team is face-to-face conversation.*

  In the traditional agile development world, this principle suggests that developers work in teams. For example, if a project requires a method that integrates Z and Timed CSP for modelling and reasoning about concurrent real-time systems, this principle says that most efficient and effective way to build the new method would be by a team, most likely with suitable language experts.

  The other implication of this principle, as discussed earlier, is that it is necessary to have regular meetings between method engineers and the users of the methods. A complication is that the developers will likely be very busy, particularly early on, and this is where problems with the early method release may be determined. So strong coaching and tight interaction loops between method engineers and developers are needed early on, and this can be loosened later.

- *Working software is the primary measure of progress.*

  A method that works is the primary measure of progress, where 'works' means that it satisfies the functional and non-functional requirements of the developers (e.g., it's correct, robust, usable, changes are made in a timely manner). How to best capture and explain requirements for a method is an interesting and under-developed area of software engineering research. As well, demonstrating whether method requirements have been met by a particular method is also challenging.

- *Agile processes promote sustainable development. The sponsors, developers, and users should be able to maintain a constant pace indefinitely.*

  The emphasis here is on building small methods and frequent refactoring in response to new requirements from the developers; it also argues for building methods up, rather than constructing large methods from scratch. In essence, this principle provides an argument for method integration. It also argues that it is desirable to avoid large-scale (or whole-scale) changes to a method, since this is expensive and disruptive. The other agile principles in combination help to avoid this.

- *Continuous attention to technical excellence and good design enhances agility.*

  This principle suggests that we should have criteria for identifying and constructing well-designed, technically excellent methods. But what is a well-designed method? There are principles for the design of a good modelling language [23, 10], but what about a good process? This is difficult but one idea is that if we treat a method as just another piece of software, then we can use quality attributes for software as a measure of 'good design'.

- *Simplicity–the art of maximizing the amount of work not done–is essential.*

  This is absolutely fundamental. When engineering a method, we do so using the simplest specification language (e.g., the smallest syntax and semantics) and simplest process that meets the requirements of the developers that have been revealed so far. Simplicity is impossible to quantify since it depends on the functional and non-functional requirements that are obtained from user stories.

- *The best architectures, requirements, and designs emerge from self-organizing teams.*

  It is not immediately obvious how critical this is for method engineering, since building a method requires much expertise and it may not require multiple people. One interpretation of this principle seems to argue against top-down approaches to method engineering, e.g., as imposed by a standards body. This principle also seems to support many existing examples of method integration, performed by stakeholders from different communities (e.g., the Z and Timed CSP example earlier).

– *At regular intervals, the team reflects on how to become more effective, then tunes and adjusts its behavior accordingly.*

This principle is entirely compatible with method engineering: the method engineers need feedback from developers in order to evaluate how successful the method is, and this in turn will influence future changes to the method. Moreover, method engineers should self-reflect on their work. This is simply good engineering practice, to always focus on process improvement, and as such it should play a key role in method engineering as well.

4.1 XP Practices and Method Engineering

We now briefly summarize how XP practices apply to method engineering and integration. For several of the principles, their applicability is immediately obvious and the arguments for these can be traced back to the arguments given for the agile principles discussed previously. In particular, the following XP practices are immediately applicable to method engineering: The Planning Game, Small Releases, Simple Design, Refactoring, Continuous Integration, 40-Hour Week, On-Site Customer. The other practices are more complex, and require some discussion.

– *Metaphor.* This practice suggests guiding method development with a simple shared story of how the whole system (method) works. It is not clear what constitutes a simple story for a method; it is likely to be an example scenario of how a developer or a development team intends to work. We suggest some stories in the case study in Section 6, but this area of research is underdeveloped.

– *Testing.* This practice requires programmers to write unit tests that must run flawlessly in order for development to continue. There is no direct equivalent to unit tests for methods, and as such this practice does not directly apply. However, we suggest in the next section that one way to mitigate this is to have a continuous feedback loop between method engineers and developers in order to rapidly obtain feedback about progress. We do not argue, though, that this is a direct substitution for testing. An alternative approach is to define acceptance tests for methods; these could be derived from user stories, and checked via a customer-developer meeting. This is more heavyweight than the typical XP testing practice.

– *Pair Programming.* This practice could be valuable in a method engineering context, in order to catch mistakes and omissions. It is questionable whether necessary expertise exists in order to implement this (it is not easy to find method engineers). Moreover, it is not clear what constitutes a mistake in method engineering.

– *Collective Ownership*, i.e., any method engineer can change the method at any time. This may be difficult to accomplish, given the diverse skills required for method engineering (e.g., a Z expert changing the CSP parts of an integration of Z and CSP). The intent behind this practice is, in part, to help ensure that all stakeholders believe that their requirements have been met by the method – and as such it may be useful to try to apply this practice.

– *Coding Standards*. There are as of yet no coding standards for methods, but we suggest that process patterns as in Catalysis may be a key first step towards development of a standardize way to capture methods.

5 An Agile Method for Method Engineering

Based on the Manifesto for method engineering in Section 4, and the discussion on XP practices, we now present an agile method for method engineering. The method will satisfy – as much as is practicable – the principles of the Manifesto, while providing guidance on how to engineer lightweight, flexible, extensible methods using the agile principles and practices mentioned in the previous sections.

The basic approach is summarised in Fig. 1; the summary is intentionally simple, and attempts to draw parallels to process descriptions like Test-Driven Development [6], which in part will help in presenting a convincing argument that the approach is agile. The steps in Fig. 1 are intended to be iterated repeatedly (as we discuss below).

1. Construct user stories for how developers would like to apply the new method.
2. Prioritize the stories (i.e., release planning).
3. Deliver a *method increment* that satisfies the current highest-priority stories.

Fig. 1. Agile method engineering

A small set of *user stories* is developed, expressing how users of the method under development (i.e., software engineers) would like to use the method. These stories are written using the vocabulary of the engineer, and will be in terms of engineering artifacts like models, code, hardware, etc. Completeness is not specifically an issue at this stage; rather, it is identifying key stories, and then *prioritizing* the stories (Step 2) to determine what is critical to support in the method from the start, and what is currently of less importance. Step 2 is thus also called *release planning*, since it is decided, in consultation with the users, what will be released and when.

The result of release planning is a priority-ordered list of method features. Method features include modelling or specification concepts to include in the method's modelling language and process steps (e.g., risk analysis, integration testing). These are then used to drive the delivery of a *method increment*, i.e., a method that may go some way towards meeting the engineers' requirements. For example, the first increment of a method might support only a subset of the modelling languages that the engineers require (e.g., Simulink models, but not Stateflow models), or it might support only the design phases of the development process, but not autocode generation or verification. This method increment is then shown and described to the engineers.

Note that we do not prescribe (a) how to specify a method increment, nor (b) what is a *high-quality* method increment. This is in keeping with agile principles and practices: XP and TDD do not prescribe how to describe software products, nor when an increment is finished, nor when a high-quality increment has been delivered. These questions can only be answered in-context, by the method (or software) engineer. For example, a method description may take the form of a small manual for the method, or a tool supporting the method, or an instantiation of a meta-tool (e.g., XMF [29]) for the method increment. The exact form of delivery of the method will depend on non-behavioural requirements specified by the users, captured in the user stories, though it is likely that a method manual, written in natural language, will be a desirable deliverable.

The engineers can now start using the method increment in their project. Conceptually, the method increment should be immediately useful – since it captures the highest-priority user stories – and easier to understand than a full method, since it only captures a few user stories. That said, the engineers may not be fully satisfied by the method increment, but they will likely only realize this when they start to apply it. For example, they may find that elements are missing from the specification language delivered with the method increment; while work-arounds may be possible, they may not be convenient to use. By using the method increment, the engineers will improve their understanding of what they *need* from the method, what is *currently missing* from the method, and what their *current priorities* are in terms of improving the method. Priorities in terms of user stories – and hence, method requirements – may change from increment to increment. Thus, the engineers will likely come up with new requirements, or *changed* requirements, which must be fed back to the method engineers in the form of changed user stories, specific technical requirements for the method (e.g., "add a message-passing formalism to the modelling language"), and new non-behavioural requirements (e.g., "the next method increment must be delivered in two weeks"). These requirements will lead to new method increments, which in turn feed back into the engineering process.

There are several plausible outcomes of this approach.

- The method engineering process and the development process applying the method arrive at fix-points: a method is developed that satisfies all engineer requirements, and this method is applied to complete the development of the product of interest. These fix-points need not be arrived at simultaneously.
- A method fix-point is not reached (i.e., not all engineer requirements are satisfied) but the incomplete method that is delivered is usefully applied to complete the development of the product of interest. It is interesting in this situation to examine the requirements that have not been met in order to better understand why the engineers thought they would be useful, and why they were not actually needed in practice. This type of information is critical in understanding why methods are fit for specific purposes, and can also help de-clutter methods and method descriptions.
- Fix-points are not reached in both the method development and the product development. This might occur because the project is cancelled, or because the method engineers are assigned elsewhere. We suggest that this is not likely to occur for technical reasons, i.e., because the method engineers made a mistake. This is because of the iterative and incremental feedback loops between method development and system development: catastrophic failures in either process are likely to be detected as early as possible, and mitigation can thereafter be implemented.

The approach is illustrated in Fig. 2. There are two spiral development processes running in parallel: method engineering, and system engineering, with feedback from the latter to the former, and with technology insertions from the former to the latter.

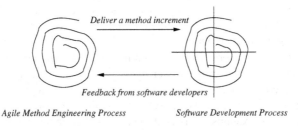

Agile Method Engineering Process   *Software Development Process*

Fig. 2. The agile method engineering and development process

Many development projects can occur in parallel with the development of a method, i.e., the method increments that are delivered can be applied in as many projects as needed. There is a complexity issue here, since the method engineers will have to respond to feedback from each project, and thereby could potentially produce specifically tailored methods – perhaps with a common core – for each development project.

6 Case Study: Agile Integration of Eiffel and CSP

We now summarise several iterations of an agile integration of the Eiffel method and CSP. The focus from the perspective of Eiffel is on its concurrency mechanism (described earlier), called SCOOP. A full specification of the features of SCOOP is presented in [18]. We assume some familiarity with CSP. Thus, the integration is of SCOOP and CSP; the nature of the integration will become clear shortly.

The initial motivation for integrating SCOOP and CSP was to be able to determine whether or not the semantics of SCOOP in Eiffel was sound. The specification of SCOOP in [18] is predominantly informal. Moreover, the nature of SCOOP – which places limited complexity on the programmer, and substantial complexity on the compiler writer – means that it is critical to ensure that its semantics is well understood and sound. In particular, it is important to be able to check that the informal understanding of SCOOP behaviour – from the programmer's perspective – is consistent with what the (informal) semantics says. The pragmatic motivation for understanding the semantics of SCOOP is that there is currently substantial, industrially sponsored effort underway in developing tools for SCOOP [21]. Finally, it is desired to provide a mechanism for reasoning about SCOOP programs, and an integration between SCOOP and CSP is reasonable approach, given CSP's tool support.

6.1 User Stories

Our initial set of user stories is very simple (as is typical of many agile developments), and is produced by starting to follow the Planning Game. It consists of one story, as follows.

We desire to be able to reason about the semantics of SCOOP programs.

Note the imprecision in this story: what sort of reasoning does the customer want to carry out? Does it encompass fully the semantics of SCOOP, or SCOOP as implemented in one of its current (incomplete) prototypes? What sort of tools would the customer like to use, if any? Are there non-functional requirements, e.g., supporting particular personnel with particular skill sets?

It is at this stage that interactions between the method engineer and developer are critical: the method engineer must answer questions like the ones above, in order to know how to proceed. It is dangerous to make assumptions, e.g., about the formalism to use for capturing the semantics. Given the expense in applying formal techniques – particularly for concurrent systems – it is vital to have a better understanding of developer requirements, and thereafter a *refined* user story, before proceeding. The agile practice of *On-Site Customer* is the one to apply to do this.

After discussion with the developers, the story is refined. The point is to not come up with a complete list of ways in which the developers would like to use the integrated method, but to provide the method engineer with *enough* understanding to get started. The refined user story follows.

> We desire to be able to reason, formally, about the semantics of SCOOP programs. For any SCOOP program we would like to be able to extract its concurrent behaviour in isolation, and reason – ideally with tool support – about the behaviour of routine calls and object reservations.

Our interpretation of this story is that a formalization of SCOOP's concurrent semantics (omitting details of object-oriented program semantics, formalized elsewhere [22]) using a suitable process algebraic framework, CSP, would be suitable for satisfying the story. We propose CSP to the developer, who accepts the argument that it is a more appropriate formalism than, say, a Hoare logic. One could argue for alternative formalisms, e.g., Circus, but the method engineers are familiar with CSP.

The user story does not express which features of SCOOP are of the most importance: SCOOP possesses a number of features that may be of interest to the user, and some of these have been mentioned in the story. In a traditional development, we might attempt to formalize the entirety of SCOOP immediately; in an agile development – which emphasizes customer/developer interactions – we will talk to the user and find out what features of SCOOP to prioritize. Here, we continue with the Planning Game and On-Site Customer, but now we move to iterations and focus on Small Releases, Simple Design, and Continuous Integration.

6.2 First Iteration: A Subsystem Model

In the Planning Game, The user suggests that the most important feature to understand is the *subsystem mechanism* of SCOOP, since this is the underlying architecture that supports threading and message passing. The method engineers thus focus on this for their first iteration, and deliver the following method increment/release. In this case, the release is described using a mixture of informal natural language (explaining the intent of the formulae) and CSP. The subsystem model can be explained as follows.

A subsystem contains objects. It also contains a 'controller', which accepts additions to a queue of calls for handled objects and engages in the processing of queued calls. This is expressed by the process $SUBSYSTEM_P(j)$, which performs the processing of a queued call, and the process $SUBSYSTEM_Q j$, which manages the queue of jobs: calls can be added and then removed when they are to be serviced.

$$SUBSYSTEM_P(j) \triangleq front.j?t \to DOCALL(t); SUBSYSTEM_P(j) \qquad (1)$$

In order to specify management of the queue of jobs, we discover that the semantics of SCOOP is ambiguous with respect to the notion of locking an object: it is not clear when a lock is released. The method engineers have to make a decision, and choose to release a lock as soon as possible.

The method engineers now need to record how and when each object is reserved, including this 'handing-on' or 'subsequent' reservation. It is complicated by the asynchronous nature of the reservations: a might call b, which itself calls c, with each reserving d, but then a finishes before b or c.

So the engineers associate a sequence of indices, R_i, with an object i:

- An index m^d is in R_i if m has a reservation on i, even if it has handed-on the reservation. The superscript d indicates which instance of the call we refer to; this is a unique number in this semantics.
- The last index in R_i is the 'active' reservation: all objects with earlier reservations have 'handed-on' the reservation to a subsequent object.

So a call d of an object m has exclusive access to i if and only if m^d is the last index in sequence R_i. m^d can remove itself from the list of reservations at any time: this represents the d-th call of m indicating its completion, thus releasing its interest in i.

$$
\begin{aligned}
SUBSYSTEM_Q(j,q) \triangleq \ &\square_{i \in handledObjects(j)} last(R_i) = m^d \Rightarrow \\
&add.(m^d, i, r, \langle \mathbf{s} \rangle) \\
&\quad \to SUBSYSTEM_Q(j, q^\frown \langle m^d, i, r, \langle \mathbf{s} \rangle \rangle) \\
&\square\, q = \langle t \rangle^\frown q' \Rightarrow \\
&front.j!t \to SUBSYSTEM_Q(j, q') \qquad (2)
\end{aligned}
$$

This completes the semantics for the subsystem, but it does not yet describe how the subsystem interacts with objects *on* the subsystem. Following our agile principles and practices (Simple Design), we do the simplest thing that satisfies the customer requirement, and will concern ourselves with refactoring (Refactoring practice) our method to include object-subsystem interactions in a future increment, when it is of more interest to the customer. At this stage, we confine ourselves to indicating that there is a set of objects to be handled by a subsystem, and we place the processes defining subsystems in parallel with their handled objects.

$$
\begin{aligned}
SUBSYSTEM(j) \triangleq \ &\|_{i \in handledObjects(j)} OBJECT(i) \\
&\| SUBSYSTEM_Q(j, \langle \rangle) \\
&\| SUBSYSTEM_P(j) \qquad (3)
\end{aligned}
$$

6.3 Second Iteration: Reservations

While the developer finds the CSP formalization of subsystems useful in improving their understanding, it does not particularly help in understanding dynamic behaviour in SCOOP. The customer thus requests the next iteration to deliver a formalization of reservations. This is substantially more difficult. The method engineers retreat to consider the problem. They realise that formalising reservations actually involves two sub-steps: formalising the process of *being reserved*, and collecting and releasing reservations. It is suggested to the customer that focusing this increment on the process of being reserved will be more profitable[1] since (a) this feature is at the heart of SCOOP's semantics; and (b) it will allow the developer to carry out deep semantic reasoning about many SCOOP programs immediately. The customer is convinced by the argument.

The method engineers retreat again to focus on the process of being reserved, and apply the practice of Simple Design. They quickly draw a rough-sketch illustrating what they believe to be one of the key challenges. Consider Fig. 3, which illustrates a (separate) object i being reserved by a second (separate) object m. Additionally, i might be reserved by n when n itself is called by m during the call that reserved i. Such a rough sketch can conveniently be shown to the customer to improve their understanding of the problem, and also to ensure that the method engineer's intuition is sensible.

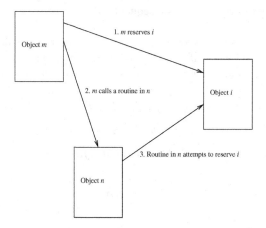

Fig. 3. Repeated reservations on an object

The method engineers assume for now that m passed on information to n indicating that it holds the lock on i. This means that n can make a 'subsequent' reservation on i. (Note that if m is the first to reserve i, then it must make both a 'global' reservation, and if it actually wishes to use i, it must also make a 'local' reservation.)

The engineers now see the need for a test of the form $isCaller(c,m)$ which is true if and only if c called m directly or via intermediate calls. This will be useful for checking whether an object is available for reservation.

---

[1] It is probably better to make a recommendation to the customer than to give them free choice amongst options. At the very least it focuses the debate on concrete issues.

The engineers can now write down a process representing i's reservation behaviour:

$$RESERVATION(i, R_i) \triangleq$$
$$R_i = \langle\rangle \vee isCaller(last(R_i), m^d) \Rightarrow$$
$$reserve.(i, m^d) \to RESERVATION(i, R_i {}^\frown \langle m^d \rangle)$$
$$\square\, R_i \neq \langle\rangle \wedge \neg isCaller(last(R_i), m^d) \Rightarrow$$
$$blocked.(i, m^d) \to RESERVATION(i, R_i)$$
$$\square\, m^d \in \sigma(R_i) \Rightarrow free.(i, m^d) \to RESERVATION(i, R_i \downarrow \{m^d\})$$
$$\square\, m^d \notin \sigma(R_i) \Rightarrow unreserved.(i, m^d) \to RESERVATION(i, R_i) \qquad (4)$$

where $s \downarrow \{A\}$ means the sequence s with the last occurrence of a member of the set A removed, and $\sigma(s)$ returns the set of elements contained in that sequence s.

Taking the clauses in the equation above one-by-one, they say:

- the d-th instance of m can reserve i if i is totally unreserved, *i.e.*, $R_i = \langle\rangle$; or, if the last reservation on i was made by c, where c is itself a caller of m.
- If m cannot reserve i, then the model only offers the '*blocked*' event.
- m can free i (for itself) at any time, provided that m had previously reserved i.
- The last clause handles m attempting to free i when it did not have a reservation.

The new functionality is integrated (Continuous Integration practice) with the previously developed model of subsystems and can be delivered to the customer for use.

6.4   Third Iteration: Completing the Formalization of Reservations

The user complains that they are unable to reason about releasing reservations: they wanted to prove that a particular SCOOP object was guaranteed to always be able to obtain a reservation at a specific time; they could only do this by ensuring that the reservation had been released. The user had tried to express a SCOOP program in the machine-readable dialect of CSP supported by FDR2, and discovered that releasing reservations was ignored. The method engineer admits that this has not been covered so far, and focuses on this for the third iteration. This is a simple iteration that results in the following CSP addition to the formalization.

$$RELEASING(i, \langle s \rangle) \triangleq (free(s_1, i) \to Skip \,\square\, unreserved(s_1, i) \to Skip)$$
$$|||\, (free(s_2, i) \to Skip \,\square\, unreserved(s_2, i) \to Skip)$$
$$\vdots$$
$$|||\, (free(s_p, i) \to Skip \,\square\, unreserved(s_p, i) \to Skip) \qquad (5)$$

This is straightforward CSP: either an object has a reservation, in which case it can be released (event *free*) or it was never held, and it is skipped (event *unreserved*). The integration of this CSP with previous releases is straightforward.

6.5 Fourth Iteration: A Refactoring

The user is now happy about being able to reason about subsystems, reservations, and calls, which make up the essence of SCOOP programs. However, while they accept the flexible formalization of locking captured in equation (6) (i.e., a lock is released as soon as possible), they find this difficult to reason about. Moreover, it has been suggested to the user by their programming team that implementing this semantics in a SCOOP compiler may be quite difficult. Since the user is interested in prototyping an implementation of SCOOP quickly, they request an alternative formalization – expected (though not proven) to be easier to implement – that does not release until all work queued by the caller on the callee has been completed. This requires the method engineers to apply the Refactoring practice to the CSP model. The engineers change equation (6) by adding an extra clause which restricts the availability of the *free* event.

$$
\begin{aligned}
SUBSYSTEM_Q(j,q) \triangleq\ &\square_{i \in handledObjects(j)} last(R_i) = m^d \Rightarrow \\
&add.(m^d, i, r, \langle \mathbf{s} \rangle) \\
&\rightarrow SUBSYSTEM_Q(j, q^\frown \langle m^d, i, r, \langle \mathbf{s} \rangle \rangle) \\
\square\ &q = \langle t \rangle^\frown q' \Rightarrow \\
&front.j!t \rightarrow SUBSYSTEM_Q(j, q') \\
\square_{i \in handledObjects(j)}\ &m^d \in \sigma(R_i) \\
&\wedge (m^d \notin \sigma(q \downarrow_1) \Rightarrow \\
&free.(i, m^d) \\
&\rightarrow SUBSYSTEM_Q(j, q') \qquad\qquad (6)
\end{aligned}
$$

By sometimes engaging in the event *free*, the subsystem queue scheduler now refuses to allow releasing of an active reservation if there is still queued work for that instance of the caller. (Here, $q \downarrow_1$ is means 'the first element of each tuple in q'.)

   Space prevents us from showing additional iterations in the integration, which will include producing an object model and executing a separate call. One point of interest occurs when producing the object model. Object behaviour needs to be linked with the subsystem model. Thus, the subsystem model is *architecturally refactored* to include this. This should be contrasted with the refactoring in Section 6.5, which was a behavioural refactoring that did not introduce new processes.

6.6 Final Iteration: A Backwards Mapping

The user is now satisfied, since they have a complete formalisation of SCOOP's semantics to work with. They spend some time using it, working with FDR2 to verify properties of SCOOP programs, e.g., deadlock freedom, liveness. Their understanding of the SCOOP semantics improves and they grow more confident that it is sound. After a while, they reach a point where the SCOOP programs they are analyzing are sufficiently complex and too large to process in reasonable time using FDR2. They generate a new user story which is passed to the method engineer: "provide tool support capable of reasoning (in reasonable time) about large SCOOP programs". The method engineer, who is a CSP expert, analyses this requirement and provides two alternatives: re-expressing the SCOOP semantics using a theorem prover like PVS; or simulation. The method engineer points out the complexity of formalising semantics of concurrent systems in PVS (e.g., referring to the thesis of Brooke [8], which shows that even simple CSP programs become intractable in PVS), and the complexity of using PVS for verification. The user decides on a simulation scheme.

After considering alternatives, the method engineer suggests an interesting approach to simulation: encoding CSP in Eiffel directly. In this way, the user can simulate a SCOOP program by interpreting the CSP semantics in Eiffel. This may provide more convincing evidence that the CSP semantics is in fact correct, and may also promote usability: the user is familiar with Eiffel and as such should find it relatively straightforward to encode simulations, interpret the results, and tailor simulations to their specific needs.

A presentation of the full encoding of CSP in Eiffel is beyond the space limitations of this paper; see [9] for details. It has some similarities to JCSP [28].

The method engineer has now delivered a lightweight method integrating SCOOP and CSP, and has been able to meet user requirements that have developed while applying early increments of the method. The user is satisfied with what has been delivered, and is able to carry out their work. Should additional requirements arise, these would be dealt with in the same way as illustrated above.

7   Conclusions

Software engineering methods are products that should be subject to engineering practices. But unlike many engineering products, methods – which are less tangible than software – must be tailored for specific development projects. The specific requirements for tailoring may not all be known up-front; thus, method engineers and integrators should be prepared to respond to requests for tailoring even as the method is being applied. Thus, method engineers should be prepared to be agile, should expect changing requirements, and should anticipate needing to talk to the users of the methods, even while the methods are being applied.

This paper has mainly focused on presenting an argument and evidence for applying agile practices and principles to building methods. There are clearly arguments for applying heavyweight approaches to method engineering, e.g., for building safety critical standards or certification standards. In all cases, several key points emerge: methods should be engineered; method engineers must expect that their methods will have to be changed; and the tailoring process should be done hand-in-hand with the users of the method, ideally while the method is being applied. The reality of using methods in software engineering is that they are always tailored; the successful methods are the ones that are flexible enough to support easy tailoring, while being prescriptive enough to prevent dangerous or wholesale changes. Agile development techniques all emphasize responding to new requirements, and building systems that can be modified easily. Some changes and refactorings will be hard, but a set of agile practices can help to manage and carry out this process. Thus, the compatibility between the needs of method users, and the facilities offered by agile development, is clear.

References

1. The Agile Manifesto, 2003. www.agilemanifesto.org.
2. M.S. Abdullah, C. Kimble, R.F. Paige, I.D. Benest, and A.S. Evans. Developing a UML profile for modelling knowledge-based systems. In *Proc. MDA: Foundations and Applications 2004, LNCS*. Springer-Verlag, 2005.
3. J.-R. Abrial. *The B-Book*. Cambridge, 1996.
4. S. Ambler. *Process Patterns*. Cambridge, 1998.
5. S. Ambler. *Agile Modeling*. John Wiley, 2002.
6. K. Beck. *Extreme Programming Explained*. Addison-Wesley, 2000.
7. K. Beck. *Test-Driven Development*. Addison-Wesley, 2002.
8. P.J. Brooke. A timed semantics for a hierarchical design notation, 1999. DPhil Thesis, University of York.
9. P.J. Brooke and R.F. Paige. Simulating CSP in Eiffel. 2005. In preparation.
10. T. Clark, A. Evans, P. Sammut, and J. Willans. *Applied Metamodelling*. Available at www.xactium.com, 2004.
11. D. D'Souza and A.C. Wills. *Objects, Components and Frameworks with UML*. AWL, 1998.
12. M. Goodland and C. Slater. *SSADM Version 4: an Introduction*. McGraw-Hill, 1995.
13. E.C.R. Hehner. *A Practical Theory of Programming (Second Edition)*. Springer-Verlag, 2003.
14. C.A.R. Hoare. *Communicating Sequential Processes*. Prentice-Hall, 1986.
15. Ronin International. Enterprise unified process. www.enterpriseunifiedprocess.com.
16. P. Kruchten. *The Rational Unified Process: an Introduction, Third Edition*. AWL, 2003.
17. B. Mahony and J.S. Dong. Deep semantic links of Timed CSP and Object-Z. *Formal Aspects of Computing*, 13(2), 2002.
18. B. Meyer. *Object Oriented Software Construction, Second Edition*. Prentice Hall, 1997.
19. Object Modelling Group. Model Driven Architecture, 2004. http://www.omg.org/mda/.
20. Object Modelling Group. Software Process Engineering Metamodel (SPEM), 2005. www.omg.org/technology/documents/formal/spem.htm.
21. Chair of Software Engineering. SCOOP web pages, 2005. http://se.inf.ethz.ch/scoop.
22. R.F. Paige and J.S. Ostroff. ERC: an object-oriented refinement calculus for Eiffel. *Formal Aspects of Computing*, 16(1), 2004.
23. R.F. Paige, J.S. Ostroff, and P.J. Brooke. Principles of modelling language design. *Information and Software Technology*, 42(10), 2000.
24. S. Palmer and M. Felsing. *A Practical Guide to Feature-Driven Development*. Prentice-Hall, 2002.
25. ModelWare EC Integrated Project. www.modelware-ist.org.
26. R. Ramsin and R.F. Paige. Criteria-based analysis of object-oriented software development methodologies, 2005. Technical Report, University of York, UK.
27. W. Scacchi. Process models in software engineering. In *Encyclopedia of Software Engineering (Second Edition)*. Wiley, 2001.
28. P. Welch, J. Aldous, and J. Foster. CSP networking for Java (CSP.net). In *Proc. ICCS 2002, LNCS*. Springer-Verlag, 2002.
29. Xactium. XMF user guide prerelease version 0.1, 2004. www.xactium.com.

An Automated Failure Mode and Effect Analysis Based on High-Level Design Specification with Behavior Trees

Lars Grunske[1], Peter Lindsay[1], Nisansala Yatapanage[1,2], and Kirsten Winter[1]

[1] University of Queensland, School of ITEE/ARC Centre for Complex Systems,
4072 Brisbane (St.Lucia), Australia
[2] Griffith University, Software Quality Institute,
4111 Brisbane (Nathan), Australia
{grunske, pal, nisansala, kirsten}@itee.uq.edu.au
http://www.accs.edu.au

Abstract. Formal methods have significant benefits for developing safety critical systems, in that they allow for correctness proofs, model checking safety and liveness properties, deadlock checking, etc. However, formal methods do not scale very well and demand specialist skills, when developing real-world systems. For these reasons, development and analysis of large-scale safety critical systems will require effective integration of formal and informal methods. In this paper, we use such an integrative approach to automate Failure Modes and Effects Analysis (FMEA), a widely used system safety analysis technique, using a high-level graphical modelling notation (Behavior Trees) and model checking. We inject component failure modes into the Behavior Trees and translate the resulting Behavior Trees to SAL code. This enables us to model check if the system in the presence of these faults satisfies its safety properties, specified by temporal logic formulas. The benefit of this process is tool support that automates the tedious and error-prone aspects of FMEA.

Keywords: Automated Hazard Analysis, FMEA, High-Level Design Specification, Model Checking, Behavior Trees, SAL.

1 Introduction

Safety critical systems are increasingly making use of embedded software for critical components [1, 2]. The rising complexity of such systems makes it important to be able to model and analyze their behaviors early in the development lifecycle, to ensure that safety is being designed into the system [3].

Failure Modes and Effects Analysis (FMEA) [4] is a widely used "what if" system-safety analysis technique that systematically considers feasible failure modes of system components and identifies the circumstances under which a component fault might lead to a hazardous system failure. With systems of even moderate complexity, however, the process of considering all possible consequences of all possible component failures, in all possible combinations of circumstances, is tedious and error-prone; hence FMEA is an ideal candidate for automation.

J. Romijn, G. Smith, and J. van de Pol (Eds.): IFM 2005, LNCS 3771, pp. 129–149, 2005.
© Springer-Verlag Berlin Heidelberg 2005

Model checking [5, 6, 7] has often been applied to system models to check that hazardous states cannot be reached during normal operation of the system: i.e., when the system behaves in accordance with its specification, as represented by the model. A number of research groups have proposed ways of injecting faults into models as a way of automating FMEA and other system safety analysis techniques (see Section 7 for a survey). However, the modelling notations involved are often difficult for system safety specialists to use, since they require good formal methods and modelling skills.

This paper proposes using model checking with the Behavior Tree (BT) system modelling notation, in order to provide automated support for FMEA. BTs provide a high-level graphical notation for system design specifications that capture functional requirements of a system given as a description in natural language. BTs thus provide a bridge from informal natural language descriptions to formal methods. The approach can be applied with system models at arbitrary levels of abstraction, including high-level system descriptions early in design, before detailed design decisions have been made. Ultimately we aim to make the formal method aspects of our approach invisible to non-expert users [8], but this part of our research is still work in progress.

Our integrated method requires users to consider the ways in which system components can be faulty (i.e., behave in ways other than those intended in the system specification): we claim that BTs offer a convenient way of doing this and of capturing the results. The user also needs to consider what are the hazard conditions of the system: i.e., the system states or conditions that might lead to harm. Often such system hazards can be expressed simply as combinations of system states and environment states, but for more complex cases we use Linear Temporal Logic [9] to formalize such conditions as temporal relationships between system states and states of the environment.

We describe a way of automatically translating BTs into the input language of the SAL model checker [10] which is similar to Action Systems [11]. The SAL model checker can then be used to discover which component faults might lead to which system hazards, which is the essence of FMEA. Where such a relationship exists, SAL provides a trace of the system behavior that illustrates how the component fault leads to the hazard, which can be very helpful for "debugging" designs. Overall our aim is for a method that enables safety analysts to work with high level models in a notation that is close to natural language, while automating the tedious aspects of FMEA.

The remainder of this paper is organized as follows: Section 2 introduces the notations used (Behavior Trees, SAL). Section 3 overviews the proposed approach to automating FMEA over high-level design specification. Section 4 presents a procedure for translating Behavior Trees to SAL code in detail. To illustrate the process and translation, the introduced techniques are applied in Section 5 to the well known industrial metal press example. Finally, Section 6 discusses related work and Section 7 contains concluding remarks and points out the directions for future work.

2 Preliminaries

2.1 Behavior Trees

The Behavior Tree notation [12] is a graphical notation to capture the functional requirements of a system given as a description in natural language. The tree-like form of Behavior Trees (BTs) allows the user to represent sequential and concurrent behavior, the impact of external events on the system, conditions on behavior, and data flow between components.

The strength of the BT notation is two-fold. Firstly, the graphical nature of the notation provides the user with an intuitive understanding of a BT model; an important factor especially for use in industry. Secondly, the process of capturing requirements is done in a stepwise fashion. That is, single requirements are modelled as single BTs, called *individual requirements trees*. In a second step these individual requirement trees are composed into one large BT, called the *integrated requirements tree*. Composition of requirements trees is done on the graphical level: an individual requirements tree is merged with a second tree (which can be another individual requirements tree or an already integrated tree) if its root node matches one of the nodes of the second tree. This stepwise approach provides a successful solution for handling very large requirements specifications [12, 13].

The syntax of the BT notation supports a number of basic constructs, of which Figure 1 presents the core that is used throughout this paper (a complete reference to the syntax can be found in [14]). Each box or node refers to a *component* of the system and its *node type* marks (a) a state realization of a component, (b) a state realization of one of the component's subcomponents, (c) a condition on the component's state, or (d) an event associated with the component. In

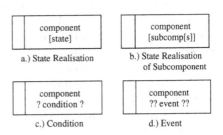

Fig. 1. Basic Syntax of Behavior Trees

the paper the following textual representation of these constructs is also used: `comp[state]`, `comp[subcomp[s]]`, `comp?condition?`, and `comp??event??`, respectively. References to a subcomponent's state can also be used as conditions (e.g., `comp?subcomp[s]?` is true if the subcomponent is in state s) or as events (e.g., `comp??subcomp[s]??` occurs when the subcomponent realizes the state s). Any leaf node can be annotated with the symbol ^ indicating that the control flow loops back to the matching node (with the same component and state/event/condition name) further up the tree. Analogously, a leaf node can be equipped with the symbol = indicating that the flow continues from the matching node (also containing an =) at any other point in the tree. A box annotated with the symbol -- models a *kill-event* which kills the thread that starts with the matching node (i.e., with same component name and node type).

We have three different versions of control flow: sequential, concurrent and selective flow. Sequential flow of control is simply modelled as a sequence of boxes which are linked by an arrow (Figure 2a). Flow of control can also branch into two or more subtrees. The meaning of a branching depends on the succeeding boxes: If both branches start with a state realization box then both branches proceed concurrently, i.e., as *threads* (Figure 2b). If a branching point is followed by condition boxes the flow follows one of the branches whose condition is satisfied (Figure 2c). In the case where more than one condition is satisfied one branch is chosen non-deterministically. If none of the conditions is true, the flow of control terminates. If the branching leads to event

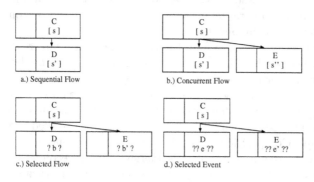

Fig. 2. Control Flow in Behavior Trees

boxes then we distinguish two cases: Without additional syntax the flow continues with the branch whose event occurs first (Figure 2d). If the event boxes additionally carry a ‖ symbol (see e.g., Figures 3a and 3c) then the branches are executed concurrently (quite similarly to Figure 2b). Hence, ‖ also marks concurrent flow of control, i.e., the beginning of a thread. Note that in the case of concurrent flow the components D and E have to be different.

As a textual representation for the different versions of control flow we use the following shorthands: `C[s]->D[s']` for sequential flow, `C[s]->(D[s']->...)‖(E[s"]->...)` for concurrent flow, `C[s]->(D?b?->...)|(E?b'?->...)` for selected flow, and `C[s]->(D??e??->...)|(E??e'??->...)` for selected event.

Concurrent and selected flow arise from a branching structure within the tree. For branching structures the BT notation allows for more variety than given in Figure 2. Whereas in the figure only two branches are depicted for each case, the tree can branch into an arbitrary (but finite) number m of threads or selections. We represent this textually as `C[s]->(...)‖`$_1$`...‖`$_m$`(...)` and `C[s]->(...)|`$_1$`...|`$_m$`(...)`, respectively. Moreover, a branching may consist of branches with different node types, so called *mixed branches*. In our work here, we only allow for three different types of mixed branches as shown in Fig-

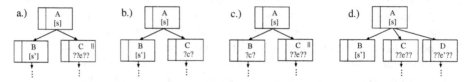

Fig. 3. Four allowed cases for mixed branches in a Behavior Tree

ures 3a, 3b and 3c. Note that in all three cases each of the branches consist of more than a single box (indicated by ... in the figure). Case a. of the figure is interpreted as concurrent flow of two independent threads, one starting with a state realization and one with an event. We represent this case textually as A[s]->(B[s']->...)∥(C??e??->...). Case b. also models concurrent flow, where one flow starts with a state realization and the other is guarded by a condition. If the condition is not satisfied at the time the control flow reaches the branching point then the guarded thread does not proceed. Textually, we get A[s]->(B[s']->...)∥(C?c?->...). Case c. of the figure models two concurrent threads, one guarded by the condition and one guarded by the occurrence of an event. The left thread can proceed if the condition is satisfied, and the right thread as soon as the event occurs. In textual form we write A[s]->(B?c?->...)∥(C??e??->...). Note that we assume for all these cases that component B is different from component C to exclude race conditions on the behavior of the threads.

All other cases in which concurrent and selected flow are mixed are ruled out in order to keep the semantics clear. However, we do allow one special case as depicted in Figure 3d: If a branch consists only of a single state realization box (and the branch does not continue after that) then it can be paired with branches of selected events. This construct is interpreted as follows: after component A realizes state s the flow of control continues with the branch whose event occurs first (i.e., as selected flow) and independently, component B also realizes state s'.

2.2   Model Checking Using the SAL Tool

SAL [10] is an open suite of tools for the analysis of state machines, including model checkers for branching and linear time temporal logic (CTL and LTL, respectively, [9]), and a deadlock checker. From this suite we use a symbolic model checker for LTL. This tool checks if a system, modelled in the SAL language, satisfies a given property, specified in LTL. If the property is violated the tool outputs a *counter-example*, i.e., a sequence of states that leads to a state which shows the violation.

For our approach this tool provides several benefits: The reachability of hazardous states can easily be modelled in LTL (using operators for next state **X**, always **G**, until **U**, and eventually **F**). Moreover, the SAL language resembles in its core the basic notion of Action Systems [11]: The transition relation is given as a set of guarded actions. In each step the system non-deterministically chooses one of those actions whose guard is satisfied in the current state and applies its updates in the next state. As will be shown in Section 4, Behavior Trees can be readily translated into a simple form of Action Systems, i.e., into SAL code.

We show a simple example of SAL code in the framed box below. Within a SAL context, *types* and *modules* can be defined, of which the latter defines the behavior, i.e., the transitions. Within a module, *local*, *global*, *input* and *output* variables can be declared. They comprise the state variables of the system. Local and output variables can be changed by the module whereas input variables cannot and global variables can change only in a limited way. The value of input variables is non-deterministically chosen from their type at each step. The *actions* comprise in their simplest form a *guard* and a set of *updates*. For instance, action A1 in the simple example on the right is guarded by light=red and contains a single update car'=stop. The updates of one action happen atomically and will be apparent in the next state of the system (SAL uses primed variables to refer to variables in the next state). At each step, the SAL system non-deterministically chooses from the list of actions (e.g., A1 to A4) one whose guard is satisfied in the current state.

```
traffic: CONTEXT =
 BEGIN Colour:TYPE={red,yellow,green};
        Move:TYPE={stop,go};
 behavior: MODULE =
 BEGIN
 LOCAL light: Color, car: Move
 INPUT pressButton: BOOLEAN
 INITIALIZATION light=yellow;car=stop
 TRANSITION
 [ A1: light=red --> car'=stop
 [] A2: pressButton --> light'=yellow
 [] A3: light=yellow --> light'=green
 [] A4: light=green --> car'=go
 [] ... ]
 END; % of module
 END % of context
```

3 Automated Hazard Analysis

The process of hazard analysis is an essential step in the development of safety critical systems. A given design of the system is investigated with regard to its behavior in the case of failures of system components. Two main questions that determine the acceptability of a design from a safety viewpoint are: what are the circumstances under which a system behaves hazardously, and what is the likelihood that these circumstances will arise.

Traditionally, hazard analysis is done on an informal level. The aim of our work is to support process automation through an integration of formal techniques. Specifically, we advocate the integration of model checking into the process. A model checker allows us to (automatically) check if a design shows hazardous behavior under the presence of faulty components. In the case where a hazardous state can be reached the tool outputs a counter-example that presents a possible behavior that leads up to the hazard. This general idea leads us to the procedure as shown in Figure 4 on the facing page.

Generation of Design Behavior Tree. The first step in this process is the construction of a *design BT* from the system requirements. Initially, an *integrated requirements BT* is created from the system requirements as described in Section 2.1 and [12, 13]. The integrated requirements BT is then decomposed into *component BTs*. We introduce this step to make component fault injection easier. Following the usual architecture of reactive systems we identify controller, sensor, and actuator components and the environment (including equipment under control and the operator). The behavior of each of these is captured in a component BT. These component BTs are then composed so that each component

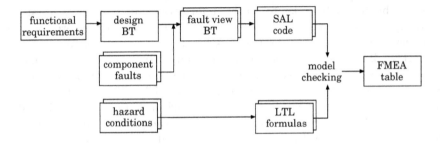

Fig. 4. Procedure for an automated hazard analysis

forms a thread of the overall system. Interactions between component threads are modelled by message-passing realized using BT events. The resulting parallel composition of components and environment and the communication between them is called the *design BT*.

We found in practice that it was necessary to extend the usual system description with an indication of the effect on the environment of all actuator states, not just the expected actuator states. (For example, what happens if the motor turns off while the plunger is rising in the case study below.) Such considerations would not always be noted in a system description which considers only the "all components function as specified" case, but are needed for hazard analysis.

Generation of Fault View BTs. A *fault view BT* describes the behavior of a system when it is affected by one or more component faults. In this paper, we consider faults where a component is no longer able to reach one or more of its normal states, but the general approach is not restricted to these kind of faults. To inject a fault into a BT, the behavior specification must be changed. The tree is pruned at nodes that involve state changes, or events, where one of the failed components is attempting to realize an unreachable state. Condition nodes describing a test of whether a failed component is in an unreachable state are also removed, as the test will never succeed. The sequential flow in a BT indicates that a node will only pass control to subsequent nodes if it has completed its action, such as a state or event realization or a condition test succeeding. Thus, if a node describing unreachable behavior is found, all of its child nodes must also be removed, as subsequent behavior will no longer occur.

In summary, we assume a component C is restricted to the set of states S. All nodes describing C realizing a state which is not an element of S are removed, including the sub-tree starting at that node. The resulting Behavior Tree will represent the system behavior in response to the component faults.

Identification and Specification of Hazard Conditions. We identify the hazards of the system with traditional risk analysis techniques [3]. To enable the later model checking, these hazard conditions are specified as temporal logic formulas. This process can be supported by the use of safety patterns [15], which are natural language constructs that can be transformed into CTL or LTL formulas.

Model Checking. In order to receive information about possible hazardous behavior of a system in the case of a faulty component, we use the corresponding fault view BT and a safety property as inputs to the LTL model checker of the SAL toolkit. The safety properties are simply the negations of the hazard conditions. The fault view BT is translated into SAL code as will be described in Section 4. The hazard condition is formalized using LTL. The tool then checks if the model of the fault view BT is able to reach a state in which the safety property is false. If yes, we receive a counter-example that presents a trace through the BT illustrating how the hazardous state can be reached.

Generation of FMEA-Tables. Finally, based on the results of the model-checking process we can compile an FMEA table, which summarizes which component failures lead to which violations of which safety properties. Where such a relationship exists, we produce a description of the identified counter-example.

4   Transformation from Behavior Trees to SAL Code

We translate a BT into a single SAL module which comprises the choice between a number of actions. To do so we have to *split* the BT into atomic transitions, each of which is then translated into a SAL action. Event and condition boxes determine the action's guard, and all state realization and data flow boxes are captured as updates. The resulting set of actions is conjoined using the SAL choice operator ([]) into the behavior of the SAL module.

Generating Variable Names. For each component in the BT that changes its state at some point (see Figure 1a) , we introduce a state variable using the component name as identifier. Its type is the enumeration of possible states of that component. The state realization component[state] can thus be captured as update component':=state. If a state realization refers to one of the component's subcomponents (see Figure 1b) then the subcomponent name, e.g., subcomp, becomes part of the variable name, i.e., component_subcomp. Condition boxes (see Figure 1c) are translated into boolean queries, e.g., component?condition? becomes component=condition. We distinguish *external* and *internal* events whereas the latter refers to a component that is controlled by the modelled system. Each external event box in the BT (see Figure 1d) is translated into a boolean input variable. An external event component??event?? is modelled by boolean input variable componentEvent. Each internal event box is translated similar to condition boxes.

Splitting BTs into Transitions. Updates within a single SAL action happen atomically in one step. Consequently, we have to identify transitions of a BT in such a way that the order (and with it also the causal dependencies) between the state realization boxes within a transition is not relevant and the transition can be considered as being *atomic*. If the order between all state realizations has to be preserved, we simply choose a fine grained splitting so that each state box becomes an update of a single transition.

If the order within a sequence of state realizations is not relevant to the problem at hand, we can combine several state realizations into one atomic transition. However, we have to ensure that within one transition the state of one component is not changed more than once. A simple algorithm which traverses the tree can provide a suitable automatic splitting of the BT: at each condition or event box and at each branching point a new transition begins. As an alternative to automatic splitting of the BT, we also allow the user to choose a splitting which supports a particular view of the system through a particular granularity of actions. Note that the validity of the chosen granularity becomes an assumption for the correctness of the results of our approach.

Sequence of Actions. The sequence in which transitions occur has to correspond to the sequence of transitions as given in the BT. We enforce this through the use of *program-counters*: At each step the value of an array of program counters determines a precise point in the BT, which essentially shows the progress of the system so far. We introduce more than one program counter if the BT includes concurrent threads. For each thread we use a separate program-counter to ensure independent progress of different threads. Evaluation of the program-counter(s) becomes part of the guard of each transition so that a transition is only "enabled" if the system has progressed to the right point in the BT.

Program-counters also provide a very simple means to regulate the flow of control at loop-back points: the program-counter is simply set to the value that corresponds to the place in the BT from which to proceed. Moreover, termination of threads (either through an explicit kill-event or a loop-back point above the branching point of threads, see [14]) is simply modelled by setting the program-counter of the terminated thread to zero.

Translation Scheme. Given the fact that for the BT notation no formal semantics is defined at present we cannot provide a formal definition of our translation from BTs into the SAL language. To illustrate our approach, however, we give a schematic template for translating the BT primitives that have to be considered.

Atomic transitions that consist only of a sequence of boxes in a BT (as shown in Figure 2a) are translated according to the cases 1 to 5 in the table below. If the transition contains no (leading) event or condition, then the resulting SAL action is only guarded by the evaluation of the program-counter pc_i (which we assume is the program-counter for this thread). Its value has to correspond to the location in the BT where the sequence occurs. The update of the action comprises all state realizations of the BT sequence (indicated by ... in the table) as well as the increment of the program-counter to

1.	`A[s1] ->...-> B[s2]`
	$pc_i=v$ `--> a'=s1;...;b'=s2;`pc_i`'=v+1`
2.	`A?c? ->...-> B[s2]`
	$pc_i=v$ `AND a=c --> ...;b'=s2;`pc_i`'=v+1`
3.	`A??e?? ->...-> B[s2]`
	$pc_i=v$ `AND ae --> ...;b'=s2;`pc_i`'=v+1`
4.	`A??e?? -> B?c? ->...-> C[s2]`
	$pc_i=v$ `AND ae AND b=c--> ...;c'=s2;`pc_i`'=v+1`
5.	`B?c? -> A??e?? ->...-> C[s2]`
	$pc_i=v$ `AND b=c AND ae --> ...;c'=s2;`pc_i`'=v+1`

the value v+1. If the sequence contains a leading event or condition (or any combination of both) then those become part of the guard of the SAL action in addition to the program-counter evaluation (cases 2-5; note that if the leading event is internal then the resulting SAL code corresponds to case 2.) Similarly to case 1, the set of updates of the action contains all state realizations and the increment of the program-counter.

The possible cases for concurrent flow (as in Figure 2b and Figure 3a-c) can be subsumed in the translation scheme given in case 6 of our table: For m concurrent branches, i.e., threads, we introduce m new program-counters (pc_{i+1} to pc_{i+m+1}) which are initially 0. Within the action

```
6. ...-> C[s] -> (...)‖1 ... ‖m(...)
   pci=v ...        -->...;c'=s; pci+1'=v+1;pci+1'=1;...;pci+m+1'=1
   pci+1=1...       -->...;  pci+1'=2
   ...
   pci+m+1=1...-->...;  pci+m+1'=2
```

leading up to the branching node C[s], we set the new program-counters to 1. That is, a program-counter of value 1 indicates that the corresponding thread is *enabled*. Apart from introducing and setting new program-counters, the translation of the transitions of each single thread follows the templates given in the cases 1 to 5 of the table above.

If the branching in the BT is interpreted as selected flow or selected event with m cases (as in Figure 2c and d), we can generalize the translation of the transitions in the following rule: Within the action of the transition that leads up to the branching, we set the program-counter of our current thread, pc_i, to the value that corresponds to the branching point in the BT, v+1. Each branch is then translated according to the cases 1 to 5 given above so that we keep the current program-counter pc_i for each branch. Each of the branching actions is now guarded by the evaluation of pc_i at the branching point, i.e., $pc_i=v+1$ (additionally to other conjuncts of the guard that arise from the transition in the branch). That is, all branching actions are enabled at the branching point. Within the branching actions, we increase pc_i in such a way that at each point within the whole branching structure it has a unique value. That is, we have to avoid

```
7. ...-> C[s] -> (...)|1...|m(...)
   pci=v ...     --> ...; c'=s; pci'=v+1
   pci=v+1 ... --> pci'=v+2;...
   pci=v+1 ... --> pci'=v+n1+1;...
   ...
   pci=v+1 ... --> pci'=v+nm-1 + 1;...
```

overlaps in the program-counter values.

Finally, we consider the special case of branching as given in Figure 3d, which is not subsumed by one of the rules above. According to the given interpretation, that in this branching structure the single state realization happens independently of the selected flow, we translate this according to case 8 in our table: The update b'=s' happens in

```
8. pci=v...              --> ...; a'=s; b'=s'; pci'=v+1
   pci=v+1 AND ce --> ...; pci'=v+2
   ...
   pci=v+1 AND de' --> ...; pci'=v+nm-1+1
```

the same step as update a'=s. Hence, this translation chooses one possible interleaving of the state realization B[s'] with the selected events C??e1?? and D??e2?? in the BT.

5   Case Study: Industrial Metal Press

We apply the hazard analysis process to the case-study of an industrial press [16], which is similar to the one described by [17]. The press is used for compressing sheets of metal into body parts for vehicles. A motor is used for raising the plunger, and is controlled by an operator pushing a button. A software controller is responsible for the press operation, and operates according to inputs from sensors. The system has the following requirements:

1. A plunger rises and is held at the top of the press with the aid of a motor, and falls to the bottom of the press when the motor is turned off.
2. Sensors are used to indicate when the plunger is at the top, the bottom or at the point-of-no-return (PONR). When the plunger is falling below the PONR, it is pointless to turn on the motor; in fact, it is dangerous to do so.
3. The plunger is initially resting on the bottom. When the power is turned on, the motor turns on and the plunger starts rising.
4. When the plunger is at the top, the operator can push and hold a button which turns the motor off, allowing the plunger to fall.
5. The operator may abort this operation by releasing the button, but only if the plunger is above the PONR. Releasing the button when the plunger is below the PONR will have no effect.
6. When the plunger reaches the bottom, the motor turns on automatically, causing the plunger to rise. The cycle then repeats. Pushing the button while the plunger is rising has no effect.

Failure of the various components of this system can lead to hazards. For example, turning on the motor after the press is below the PONR can lead to the motor exploding, exposing the operator to the danger of being hit by flying parts. Other sensor failures can lead to loss of the abort function, which has safety implications. Therefore, analysis of the consequences of each component failure is essential.

The six requirements are captured by six individual requirements BTs which are then composed into the integrated requirements BT. We identify a plunger as the environment of the system and six components: a controller, a motor as the actuator, and four sensors, a top-sensor, a bottom-sensor, a PONR-sensor, and a button. For each of these components we generate the component BT from the integrated requirements BT and extend them with the necessary communication between each other. For instance, the controller has to communicate with the sensors and the motor but it does not interact with the plunger directly since the plunger is only influenced by the behavior of the motor. The extended component BTs are then used as threads in a combined design BT as shown in Figure 5 on the next page.

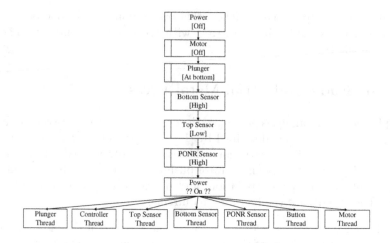

Fig. 5. Design BT of the press system

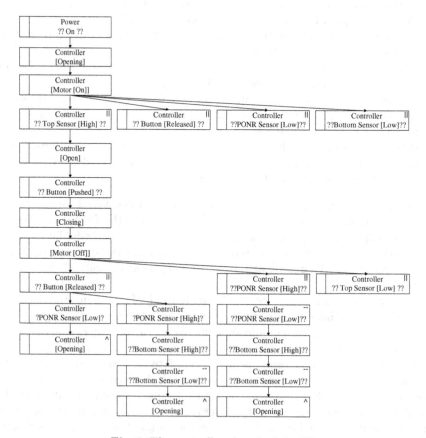

Fig. 6. The controller thread of the BT

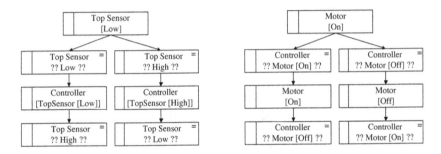

Fig. 7. The top sensor and motor threads of the BT

Figure 6 on the facing page shows the thread of the controller component in the design BT. The controller receives input from the sensor via events. For example, as soon as the top sensor (as modelled in the left tree in Figure 7 on the next page) causes the **Top sensor** subcomponent of the controller to change its state to **High** the corresponding event `Controller??TopSensor[High]??` in the controller thread will be activated and trigger the controller to respond.

The sensor and button components all follow a similar structure. The top sensor example can be seen in Figure 7. The sensors all toggle between two states: high and low (and pushed and released for the button). A change in state of the sensors leads to a message passed to the controller. The button changes state based on the external influence of the operator, but it also informs the controller of the state change in a similar fashion. The motor operates in an opposite way to the sensors: while the sensors inform the controller of a change in state, the motor changes state based on input from the controller.

The plunger is modelled by the environment thread shown in Figure 8 on the following page. This component is only influenced by the motor, and operates in a cyclic fashion between rising, reaching the top, falling and reaching the bottom. Changes in plunger state lead directly to changes in relevant sensor states.

The fault views for each possible component failure are generated, according to the rules described in Section 3. Each of these new BTs is then translated into the SAL language for model checking, to determine which failures can cause hazardous situations. There are four significant hazard conditions concerning the operation of the press, which lead to hazardous behavior if violated [16]. These hazard conditions are formalized in LTL as follows (note that **G** is the temporal operator for generally (i.e., in every state on the path), and **U** is the temporal operator for until):

1. If the plunger is at the top and the operator is not pushing the button, the motor should remain on.

   $\mathbf{G}\;((plunger = attop \wedge operator = releasebutton) \rightarrow (motor = on))$

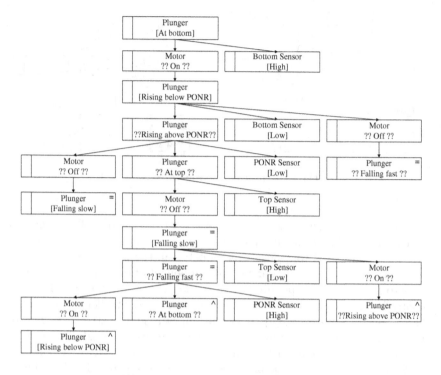

Fig. 8. The plunger thread of the BT

2. If the plunger is falling below the PONR, known as falling fast, the motor should remain off.

   G $((plunger = fallingfast) \rightarrow (motor = off))$

3. If the plunger is falling above the PONR, known as falling slow, and the operator releases the button, the motor should eventually turn on, before the plunger changes state.

   G $((plunger = fallingslow \land operator = releasebutton)$
   $\rightarrow (plunger = fallingSlow \ \mathbf{U} \ motor = on))$

4. The motor should never turn off while the plunger is rising.

   G $(\neg((plunger = risingbelowPONR \ \lor \ plunger = risingabovePONR)$
   $\land (motor = off)))$

When model checking the translated design BT with these hazard conditions we find a major problem that arises for most model checking tools: the user is only provided with a single counter-example. If this counter-example is not useful then it obstructs the overall process of automated hazard analysis. For our case study, some of the output counter-examples concern only a very small time-frame, involving an external event occurring after a sensor has changed state, but before the controller has time to receive a message about this change.

That is, the chain of internal events, that represent communication between system components, is interrupted by an external event. This is due to the fact that in the SAL tool input variables are uncontrolled and can change the value arbitrarily at each step. Although these counter-examples are correct they do not transport useful information since the probability of such an event occurring is minimal. It is desirable to ignore these cases.

Usually, undesirable counter-examples are excluded by refining the hazard conditions correspondingly. In our case, however, hazard conditions that limit the sequence in which events can occur would also exclude some of the interesting cases to be checked for. Therefore, we suggest a different solution in which we prioritize the actions in the SAL code.

Generally, our model contains both *internal* and *external* events. External events are events that are instantiated by something outside the system, such as an input from the operator. Internal events are those associated with another internal component, and provide the communication between components. An example of this is a sensor changing state and the controller waiting for this change of state. We call actions *external* if they are triggered by external events. All other actions in our model are called *internal actions*. The undesirable counter-examples all involve external actions interrupting the chain of internal actions as is possible due to the non-deterministic choice between all enabled actions within the SAL tool. We exclude these interrupts by allowing external actions only if no other internal action can occur. We extend the guard for each external action with the negative conjunction of the guards for each of the internal actions.

This process achieves our desired goal and all unlikely counter-examples are filtered out. The results of the model-checking are in agreement with the expected behavior of the press determined manually. They are presented in Table 1. It should be noted that each of these cases describe a fault which is present from the start of operation. Thus, the motor faults do not lead to any hazard violations, as the plunger remains suspended either at the top or bottom, causing no danger.

Table 1. Results of model-checking each component failure mode against the four hazard conditions

Component Failure	HC1	HC2	HC3	HC4
No failures	√	√	√	√
Top Sensor stuck Low	√	√	√	√
Top Sensor stuck High	√	√	√	X
Bottom Sensor stuck Low	√	√	√	√
Bottom Sensor stuck High	√	X	√	√
PONR Sensor stuck Low	√	X	√	√
PONR Sensor stuck High	√	√	X	√
Button stuck released	√	√	√	√
Button stuck pushed	X	√	X	√
Motor stuck on	√	√	√	√
Motor stuck off	√	√	√	√

Key: √ = hazard condition does not arise, X = hazard condition can occur

As an example of a component failure that can cause a hazard, consider the case of the failure of the bottom sensor, where the bottom sensor permanently indicates that the plunger is at bottom (Component Failure: Bottom Sensor stuck High) and consider the hazard condition **HC2**. This hazard condition states that the motor should not turn on when the plunger is falling below the point-of-no-return. The counter-example produced is as follows: The system operates normally until the plunger reaches the falling fast state, i.e. it is falling below the point-of-no-return. At this time, the controller is waiting for the event of the bottom sensor reaching the high state. Since the sensor has failed, the controller will immediately receive this event, long before the plunger has a chance to reach the bottom. The controller will then turn on the motor, thus creating the hazard.

The results demonstrate that the automated hazard analysis process described in this paper is successful for the analysis of the Industrial Press case study. All violations of the hazard conditions are correctly revealed, and the results are identical to those produced through manual analysis [16].

6   Tool Support

Complex systems may consist of numerous components and states, leading to a large increase in possible failures. Thus, to manually transform a BT into each

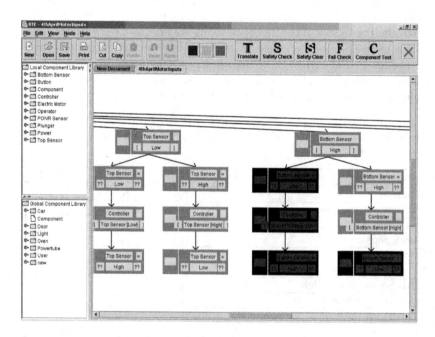

Fig. 9. Screenshot of the tool with a BT analyzed by BTFail for the Bottom Sensor stuck High failure. The blackened sections indicate blocked behavior.

failure view and the failure views into SAL modules would be an arduous task. For this reason, the hazard analysis process described in this paper has been fully automated. A software package, BTE, has been developed for designing and editing Behavior Tree specifications [18]. Add-in packages for BTE have been created for the aspects relevant to the FMEA process. They consist of two primary functions: the modification of BT's to reflect the behavior in the presence of failures and the translation of Behavior Trees into the SAL language.

The first function was implemented as the BTFail package. The purpose of this module is to convert an existing BT designed using the BT-Editor into a fault view. The fault may be comprised of a single or multiple failed components and each component may be unable to reach one or several of its states. The failure may be selected to start at the root node of the tree, representing the start of the system behavior, or at some later point. The BTFail package creates the fault views by highlighting and removing affected branches of the Behavior Tree, according to the rules specified in Section 3. Figure 9 shows a screenshot of the Behavior Tree editor with a BT which has been modified by BTFail.

The next step in the process is the translation of Behavior Trees into the SAL language. This was implemented as an export function of the BTE tool. After a BT has been modified to describe failure behavior, it can then be exported to a SAL file for use in the SAL tool. The translation operates according to the rules specified in Section 4.

Together, these modules provide a complete environment for preparing a BT specification for model-checking with the SAL suite of tools.

7 Related Work

As noted in Section 1, model checking has often been used to check safety conditions for system models of varying degrees of abstraction. We briefly survey here the use of formal methods, and model checking in particular, for automating system-safety analysis techniques such as FMEA.

A recent approach for the generation of FMEA tables [19] uses the Scade framework. In this approach, both the system model and the safety requirements must be described formally in Lustre. Faults are injected into the system model and proved by Scade Design Verifier. A similar approach has been applied using the FSAP/ NuSMV-SA tool [20], using the NuSMV model checker to identify violations of safety conditions specified in LTL. An additional feature of FSAP/NuSMV-SA tool is the ability to generate fault trees based on counter examples. This is useful since fault trees are well suited for visualizing how different combinations of component failure modes give rise to system hazards. Both of these approaches use specialized formal system modelling notations; by contrast, our approach works from a graphical specification (using the BT notation), which we believe will improve acceptance in industrial projects [12].

Papadopoulos et al. [21] describes an FMEA approach based on the fault tree generation algorithms introduced by the HiPHOPS methodology [22]. This approach generates fault trees for system-level hazards, which is more general than FMEA. Hazardous component-level failure modes can be extracted from fault tress by generating minimal cut-sets. However, in contrast to the technique presented here, the approach allows only semi-automatic FMEA construction, since local failure behavior annotations must be added to the system model by hand. Such annotations specify in tabular form, as sets of failure expressions, how deviations of component outputs can be caused by internal malfunctions and deviations of component inputs. In other words, the fault propagation logic must be supplied by hand, by contrast with our approach whereby the component fault simply needs to be modelled.

Rae and Lindsay [23] describes an approach to generating fault trees in which faults are treated as behaviors rather than simply as events or conditions. Their technique has been automated using CSP [24] and the CWB-NC model checker [25]. Their approach is similar to the approach reported here in as much as component faults are modelled as behaviors and are injected into system models. In contrast to our approach, however, modelling of system and faults is not supported by a graphical notation. The user has to provide both in CSP.

Atchison et al. [16] describes the use of Z and the Possum specification animation tool for FMEA, and the use of Spark to formally verify Ada code against the Z specification for a fault-tolerant version of the Press control logic. The animator had to be programmed by hand to do an exhaustive search of the state space, and it is doubtful if such an approach would scale very well; the approach presented here has the advantage that model checking is fully automated.

8   Conclusion and Future Work

The paper described the use of model checking with the Behavior Tree (BT) notation [12], in order to provide automated support for Failure Modes and Effects Analysis (FMEA) [4], a widely used system safety analysis technique. BTs have been successfully applied to several large systems [14]. The main benefit of BTs is that they can be smoothly translated, generated and integrated from natural language requirements. The resulting specification is an integrated requirements BT, which specifies the behavior of the complete system. This specification has to be decomposed into several component specifications, to allow a distributed and systematic construction of complex systems. The system decomposition into components provides also the foundation for component fault injection and our FMEA approach. In order to perform the FMEA, an integrated requirements BT must be transformed into a design BT. In the high-level design, each component operates independently and concurrently, achieved by modelling each component's behavior in a separate thread. Each thread describes only the component's independent behavior and its direct interactions with others. Our method requires users to consider the ways in which these system components can be faulty (i.e., behave in ways other than those intended in the system specification) and the immediate (local) effect of such failure modes; BTs offer a convenient way of doing this and capturing the results.

The component faults considered here are those cases where a component cannot reach one or more of its normal set of states. Because of the nature of BTs this covers a wide range of component failure modes. The user also needs to consider what are the hazard conditions of the system: i.e., the system states or conditions that might lead to harm. Linear Temporal Logic is used to formalize such conditions as temporal formulas which specify the relationships between system states and states of the environment. The SAL model checker is used to discover which component faults might lead to which system hazards, which is the essence of FMEA. Where such a relationship exists, SAL also provides a counter-example in the form of a system behavior trace that illustrates how the component fault leads to the hazard.

The benefit of our approach is tool support that automates the tedious and error-prone aspects of FMEA, namely, tracing through all possible consequences of component faults, through all possible environmental conditions and system states. The approach can be applied to high-level system descriptions early in design, before detailed design decisions have been made. The method requires the user to imagine what kind of functional failures could occur at component level, what would be their local effect, and what are the hazardous system conditions.

The presented method is the subject of current research and has potential for new research directions. A fundamental improvement will be to allow the occurrence of the failure at any time during system operation, rather than simply *ab initio* as done in this paper. We are currently working on this extension by creating the SAL code for all failure views and merging the resulting SAL modules with the original behavior, so that a transition from the correct system to a system which contains a failure mode is possible at any time. If we have this extension, the next step it to use probabilistic model-checking and to determine the probability of a safety critical situation if the probabilities of all failure modes are known. This will improve the process and enable the usage of this approach in the generation of safety cases.

Another suitable extension to our approach is to add more powerful failure modes to the existing set, in particular commission or protocol failures that occur if the correct ordering of events at interfaces is violated. This requires a complex fault injection mechanism and appropriate tool support.

Acknowledgements. This work was produced with the assistance of funding from the Australian Research Council (ARC) under the ARC Centres of Excellence program. The authors wish to thank their colleagues in the Dependable Complex Computer-based Systems project for their constructive suggestions, and Geoff Dromey in particular for his suggestions regarding factoring of Integrated BTs into Design BTs.

References

1. Lutz, R.R.: Software engineering for safety: a roadmap. In: ICSE - Future of SE Track. (2000) 213–226
2. Neumann, P.G.: Computer-Related Risks. ACM Press / Addison Wesley (1995)

3. Leveson, N.G.: Safeware: System Safety and Computers. Addison-Wesley (1995)
4. Department of Defence: MIL-STD-1629A, Procedures for Performing a Failure Mode, Effects and Criticality Analysis. Washington (1980)
5. Clarke, E., Grumberg, O., Peled, D.A.: Model Checking. MIT Press (1999)
6. Heitmeyer, C., Kirby, J., Labaw, B., Archer, M., Bharadwaj, R.: Using abstraction and model checking to detect safety violations in requirements specifications. IEEE Transactions on Software Engineering **24** (1998) 927–947
7. Atlee, J., Gannon, J.: State-based model checking of event-driven system requirements. IEEE Transactions on Software Engineering **19** (1993) 24–40
8. Tiwari, A., Shankar, N., Rushby, J.: Invisible formal methods for embedded control systems. Proceedings of the IEEE **91** (2003) 29–39
9. Emerson, E.A.: Temporal and modal logic. In van Leeuwen, J., ed.: Handbook of Theoretical Coomputer Science. Volume B. Elsevier Science Publishers (1990)
10. de Moura, L., Owre, S., Rueß, H., Rushby, J., Shankar, N., Sorea, M., Tiwari, A.: SAL 2. In Alur, R., Peled, D., eds.: Int. Conference on Computer-Aided Verification, (CAV 2004). Volume 3114 of LNCS., Springer-Verlag (2004) 496–500
11. Back, R.J., von Wright, J.: Trace refinement of action systems. In Jonsson, B., Parrow, J., eds.: Int. Conference on Concurrency Theory (CONCUR'94). Volume 836 of LNCS., Springer-Verlag (1994) 367–384
12. Dromey, R.G.: From requirements to design: Formalizing the key steps. In: Int. Conference on Software Engineering and Formal Methods (SEFM 2003), IEEE Computer Society (2003) 2–13
13. Wen, L., Dromey, R.G.: From requirements change to design change: A formal path. In: Int. Conference on Software Engineering and Formal Methods (SEFM 2004), IEEE Computer Society (2004) 104–113
14. GSE: Genetic Software Engineering: http://www.sqi.gu.edu.au/gse (2005)
15. Bitsch, F.: Safety patterns - the key to formal specification of safety requirements. In: Int. Conference on Computer Safety, Reliability and Security (SAFECOMP 2001). Volume 2187 of LNCS., Springer-Verlag (2001) 176–189
16. Atchison, B., Lindsay, P., Tombs, D.: A case study in software safety assurance using formal methods. Technical report, University of Queensland, SVRC 99-31, www.itee.uq.edu.au/~pal/SVRC/tr99-31.pdf (1999)
17. McDermid, J., Kelly, T.: Industrial press: Safety case. Technical report, High Integrity Systems Engineering Group, University of York (1996)
18. Smith, C., Winter, K., Hayes, I., Dromey, G., Lindsay, P., Carrington, D.: An environment for building a system out of its requirements. In: Int. Conference on Automated Software Engineering (ASE 2004), IEEE Computer Society (2004) 398–399
19. Abdulla, P.A., Deneux, J., Akerlund, O.: Designing safe, reliable systems using Scade. In: Int. Symposium on Leveraging Applications of Formal Methods (ISoLA'04). (2004)
20. Bozzano, M., Villafiorita, A.: Improving system reliability via model checking: The FSAP/NuSMV-SA safety analysis platform. In: Int. Conference on Computer Safety, Reliability, and Security (SAFECOMP 2003). Volume 2788 of LNCS., Springer-Verlag (2003)
21. Papadopoulos, Y., Parker, D., Grante, C.: Automating the failure modes and effects analysis of safety critical systems. In: Int. Symposium on High-Assurance Systems Engineering (HASE 2004), IEEE Computer Society (2004) 310–311
22. Papadopoulos, Y., McDermid, J.A., Sasse, R., Heiner, G.: Analysis and synthesis of the behaviour of complex programmable electronic systems in conditions of failure. Int. Journal of Reliability Engineering and System Safety **71** (2001) 229–247

23. Rae, A., Lindsay, P.: A behaviour-based method for fault tree generation. In: Int. System Safety Conference, System Safety Society (2004) 289–298
24. Hoare, C.: Communicating Sequential Processes. Series in Computer Science. Prentice Hall (1985)
25. Cleaveland, R., Sims, S.: The NCSU Concurrency Workbench. In Alur, R., Henzinger, T., eds.: Int. Conference on Computer-Aided Verification (CAV'96). Volume 1102 of LNCS., Springer-Verlag (1996) 394–397

Enabling Security Testing from Specification to Code

Shane Bracher* and Padmanabhan Krishnan

Centre for Software Assurance, School of Information Technology,
Bond University, Gold Coast, Queensland 4229, Australia
sbracher@student.bond.edu.au, pkrishna@staff.bond.edu.au

Abstract. In this paper, we present the idea of creating an intermediary model which is capable of being derived directly from the high-level, abstract model, but more closely resembles the actual implementation. The focus of our work is on the security properties of protocols. Not only do we show how an intermediary model can be constructed, but also how it can be used to automatically generate test sequences based on the security goals of the protocol being tested. Our aim is to show that by using this approach, we can derive test sequences suitable for a tester to use on a working implementation of the protocol.

Keywords: protocol descriptions, security modelling, model-based testing, concrete test sequences.

1 Introduction

Exhaustive testing of a software system is one way to guarantee that the system under test is secure. However, it is not practical to test all possible inputs and all possible paths through the programs. In practice, key properties are identified and sequences to test these key properties are generated. Specification or model-based techniques [1, 2, 3, 4] are approaches to reduce the testing effort. The tests are derived from a model (or a formal specification) of the system. There are two main advantages of this approach. The first is that the models provide precise knowledge of what each test actually achieves. As each test sequence is derived from the model, it corresponds directly to some expected behaviour of the system. The second advantage is that model-based testing increases the ability to reuse the tests. In many cases, there are small changes to implementations which do not affect the model of behaviour. Hence the tests generated can be reused.

While there are many approaches to testing for security properties [5, 6], there are only a few reported results on using model-based testing for security [7, 8]. This is because writing formal specifications is not prevalent as constructing the formal model incurs additional cost. However, given the complexity of security properties, developing a formal model for analysis is definitely worthwhile. Vulnerability testing by fault injection [5] is an approach to increase the robustness of a system. In this approach, the system is tested under a variety of faulty environments. This effectively checks if a system can continue to operate securely without failing. The efficacy of

---

* Currently Visiting Siemens Research.

J. Romijn, G. Smith, and J. van de Pol (Eds.): IFM 2005, LNCS 3771, pp. 150–166, 2005.

this approach depends on the design of appropriate faulty environments. This is not yet well understood and is very system specific. Hence a model for describing the desired properties and the associated environments (including potential attacks) will be useful.

Testing of firewalls [7] based on specifications expressed as finite automata is feasible. Resilience against common attacks such as intrusions, spoofing, Trojan horses etc. can be tested. However, the test sequences are not directly usable for implementations. Another approach to model-based testing of security properties [9] is to mutate the specification to detect vulnerabilities. These tests are closer to the implementation.

Bounded exhaustive checking [8] is another approach to identifying faults in the system. This is based on a fault tree analysis and testing all possible behaviours up to a certain depth in the state space. The technique is derived from bounded model checking where all states up to a certain bound are systematically explored. Although this technique is not specific to security, it can be used to specify security properties.

Usually a formal model is created to verify the key properties. The more abstract the formal model, the easier it is to verify. However, for the purposes of testing, it is too far removed from the implementation.

One of the issues related to testing security is the ability to express the desired properties. Meca [10] describes a technique for specifying annotations in programs which can then be verified by static analysis. We use a similar approach. However, the annotations used in the implementation are derived from the verification process.

The aim of our research is to use the model-based techniques idea to generate test sequences in the context of security protocols. But rather than translate the high-level test sequences into a sequence relevant for implementations, we translate a high-level model to a model closer to an implementation. The low-level model is then used to generate the test sequences. In our approach the required security goals are already specified in the high-level specification and we generate tests after translating these goals to assertions in the lower-level specification. This way, the gap between the high-level test sequences generated from the model and the implementation is narrowed. This is the main difference between our work and other works on model-based testing. The models are developed in High Level Protocol Specification Language (HLPSL) but the test sequences generated are expressed in a Java like language which reduces the effort required to translate the test sequences for an implementation.

To determine whether this idea is viable, we have conducted case studies based on the Internet Open Trading Protocol (IOTP) [11] and smaller protocols from the Open Mobile Alliance (OMA). In this paper we focus on the IOTP case study as it is representative of the other protocols. The specific techniques used in this case study are the HLPSL, Bandera Intermediate Representation (BIR) and the Bogor Model Checking Framework.

The remainder of this paper is organised as follows: Section 2 provides background information on technical information necessary for our case study and includes HLPSL, BIR and Bogor; Section 3 develops the details of the proposed idea; Section 4 reports on the characteristics of the case study and its results; and finally, Section 5 concludes the paper.

2 Preliminaries

2.1 HLPSL

HLPSL [12] is an abstract, high-level language designed for specifying and verifying a variety of protocol descriptions. In particular the focus is on large scale protocols and their security aspects. HLPSL was formulated under the AVISPA project [13], which is funded by the European Commission and involves academic, research and industrial organisations from France, Germany, Italy and Switzerland. The language aims to support the project's wider aim of providing a "push-button industrial-strength technology for the analysis of large-scale Internet security-sensitive protocols". While the semantics of HLPSL are based on Lamport's Temporal Logic of Actions (TLA) [14] one of the key design goals of this language was that it was to be easy to use and human readable and yet be amenable to automatic verification.

An advantage of using HLPSL to model security protocols is that it contains a number of built-in components common to such protocols including intruder models (e.g., Dolev-Yao) and encryption primitives. It also provides an explicit separation between roles and agents. That is, a protocol in HLPSL is constructed using a collection of roles. The two types of roles which exist are basic roles and composed roles. Basic roles represent the actions performed by a single participant (or agent) of the protocol whereas composed roles are used to instantiate a group of basic roles (such as a session consisting of multiple agents). It is also possible to specify that a single agent plays multiple roles. HLPSL permits the definition of separate channels used to communicate between agents playing different roles. Other aspects such as nonces, keys, inverse keys can also be defined.

Another feature of HLPSL is that it incorporates a notion of state, and as such, all actions performed by basic roles are described as state transitions. Some of the base types supported in this language include *agent* (representing an identity participating in the protocol), *public_key*, *text* and *channel*. By convention, if the agent is an intruder, it is denoted using the special identifier i. To model an agent's private key, the inverse of the public key is used e.g., inv(pubkey). To model nonces, this is commonly done using *text (fresh)*. This states that subsequent values of this variable should be unique and consequently, unguessable by the intruder. When modeling communication channels, an optional parameter can be declared with the data type to state the built-in intruder model to be used for the channel.

A HLPSL model also lists the security goals (such as secrecy of certain tokens, or authentication of agents) which need to be satisfied and then these goals are used as the criteria for when the model is verified. This is done in the context of an environment where a finite number of agents (along with the roles that they play) is instantiated. To verify a protocol specification modelled in HLPSL, it is translated into a lower-level language recognised by model checking tools. Intermediate Format (IF) is one such language and translation from HLPSL to IF can be automatically achieved using the tool *hlpsl2if* which accepts the HLPSL model and outputs it formatted into IF. This IF model can now be passed into a variety of model checking tools such as On-the-Fly Model Checker (OFMC) [15] for verification that the protocol's stated security goals are not violated. Should an occurrence of a violation be found, a trace showing the path of events leading to the attack (as well as details of the type of attack e.g., man-of-the-middle attack) are displayed. While such counter-examples can be used for model-based testing, they are too abstract to be directly useful for implementations.

In the context of our work, model checking of HLPSL (which can be performed using a variety of tools) is useful only to verify that a HLPSL specification meets the security goals. These tools cannot be used for generating test sequences that are concrete. In other words, a number of tools are supported; but all of them are at a similar level of abstraction and hence all the counter examples are at a very high level of abstraction. Thus all the tools are unsuitable for the purpose of generating concrete sequences for testing. Although we also use model checking technology, we translate the HLSPL specification into a more concrete description for the purposes of test generation via model checking.

2.2   BIR/Bogor

Bandera Intermediate Representation (BIR) is an intermediate language aimed to facilitate the translation of Java programs to different analysis tools. The Bandera [16] project aims to provide automated support to generate finite state abstractions from Java code, which can then be verified using model checking. In particular, BIR is used by the Bogor model checking framework [17] which is the core aspect of the Bandera project. Development on BIR and Bogor is presently being conducted by the SAnToS Laboratory at Kansas State University and ESQuaReD Group at the University of Nebraska. BIR has become a human-writable, richer and extensible input language and aims to support the object-oriented paradigm. For this reason, the constructs used in BIR are very closely aligned to features found in Java such as objects, inheritance, threads, exceptions monitor locks and references. Hence it is closer to an implementation, but still retains a level of abstractness.

In this paper we use BIR in a different fashion. We use BIR as a more concrete intermediate language with the BIR specification derived from an abstract specification. That is, we do not translate a language like Java into BIR to be converted to specifications that can be used by verification tools. We are translating a high-level specification to BIR with a view of obtaining concrete test sequences. As the source is already a high-level specification the Bogor framework can be used effectively. We could have translated HLPSL to real programming languages like Java or C and used tools such as Bandera [16], Magic [18] or Blast [19] to generate real test sequences. However, the sequences generated by the tools available for such languages were not as clear as the ones generated from an intermediate language like BIR.

In contrast to HLPSL, the design goals of both BIR and Bogor are in fact more focused towards verifying software applications than protocols. However, both BIR and HLPSL support the specification of transition systems. Each thread and function in BIR comprises of a series of locations containing guarded transformations which hence enable a BIR model to possess a notion of state. In terms of guarded transformations, these can exist as either a block transformation (a series of actions performed atomically) or as an invocation transformation (a function call). The data types and expressions supported in BIR are very similar to primitive Java. They include types such as boolean, int, float and double and expressions such as arithmetic, relational and logical. This lowers the abstraction of BIR specifications in comparison to HLPSL.

Bogor [17] is a model checking tool designed for verifying event-driven component-based software designs. This tool differentiates itself from other model checkers by

1. supporting an extensible input language (in which custom, domain-specific constructs can be designed) and
2. by possessing a modular interface design.

Rather than existing as a stand-alone program, Bogor is actually implemented as an Eclipse plug-in. This plug-in comes equipped with an integrated editor and counter example display for use within the Eclipse development environment. It is this combination of the program and counter example displays that is useful in generating the test sequences.

3   Problem Description

For security modelling and verification, using a high-level model representation of a protocol specification has the advantage of hiding many of the protocol's complexities to expose only the relevant components of interest. Such high-level models can be suitably used for verification and for detecting security vulnerabilities, but they pose the risk of being too abstract from an implementor's perspective in regards to testing. As a result, these models become less beneficial to the implementors and testers of the protocol implementation as they are unable to provide thorough test sequences which can be directly applied to a working prototype.

To address this issue, we propose adding an *intermediary* model to the equation which bridges the gap between the high-level model and the actual implementation. An appropriate intermediary language must align the construction of models with the working protocol implementation but yet, can be directly derived from the high-level specification. From this new model, it is anticipated that testers of the protocol implementation will be capable of not only comprehending the model, but also be able to manipulate it to create test sequences detailed enough to be directly applied to the working implementation. In the previous scenario where we only had a high-level model too abstract, and perhaps too difficult, for an implementor to understand, we now have an additional model, derived from the high-level model, which better suits the needs of the testers working on the actual protocol implementation. Figure 1 illustrates our proposal.

To create the intermediary model, we face the constraint of requiring a modelling language which can (i) be easily identified with by the implementors/testers and (ii) be able to translate constructs used in the high-level modelling language. For this research, we have decided to trial BIR as a potential intermediary modelling language. Our reasons for this decision are based on the fact the BIR is already used and has proven itself as a suitable language for modelling software applications. Furthermore, using a BIR model, we can feed it into the Bogor Model Checking Framework to automatically generate test sequences for testing following the standard techniques [20, 21]. For our high-level model, although development of the intermediary model should not be constrained to a single high-level modelling language, we have decided to concentrate our experiments on HLPSL as it is an abstract, easily readable and writable specification language focusing on communication and security protocols.

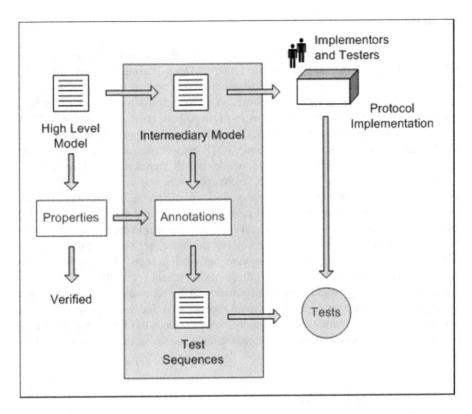

Fig. 1. Bridging the gap - how an intermediary model can be used to make model-based testing techniques more user friendly and beneficial from the implementors' and testers' perspectives

4   Case Study Using IOTP

Our aim for this case study was two-fold. Firstly, we wanted to verify that it was indeed possible to translate a high-level model into an intermediary model specified in HLPSL and BIR respectively. The focus is not just on the transition system (which can be handled by standard techniques) but on issues related to security such as knowledge, properties of encryption etc. The other aim of the case study was to determine, using this approach, whether or not it was possible to derive test sequences from the intermediary model for use on an actual implementation.

To conduct this experiment, we used a HLPSL specification of the Internet Open Trading Protocol (IOTP) and a song down load protocol from the OMA. In this paper only the relevant parts of the IOTP protocol are discussed and the results for the song down load protocol are similar. Our first task involved converting this specification into a BIR intermediary model to satisfy the first aim of the study. Following this, to create test sequences from the intermediary model, we experimented with using Bogor for this task.

4.1 IOTP

IOTP is an Internet commerce framework designed with interoperability in mind. Developed by the IETF working group titled Internet Open Trading Protocol (trade), the protocol aims to provide both a system for online trading that is independent of the payment system as well as support the situation where the customer and merchant have not previously traded. In general it aims to promote both business to business (B2B) commerce and business to consumer (B2C) commerce and supports online transactions which span over various sites. For example, IOTP supports the case where the catalog, payment handling and product delivery functions are all executed over different sites.

A relevant subset of IOTP message exchanges expressed in the basic notation is shown in the first part of Figure 2. The four entities participating in the protocol are the customer (C), the merchant (M), the payment processor (P) and the delivery agent (D). The protocol commences with an offer sent from the customer to the merchant detailing the customer's desired purchase. On receiving this message, the merchant responds with a `BrandList` listing all of the payment options it accepts. The customer selects their desired payment method and sends this to the merchant before the merchant sends the customer signed payment amount information. After receiving the signed payment message, the customer sends to the payment processor (i) details on the merchant, (ii) desired purchase information and (iii) payment details. Once this has been received and the transaction has been processed, the payment processor issues the customer with a

```
C -> M: Offer
M -> C: BrandList, Offer
C -> M: Select, Offer
M -> C: Pay, Offer, Sig_M(Pay)
C -> P: Offer, Pay, M, Sig_C(Pay)
P -> C: Receipt, Sig_P(Pay, Receipt, Offer)
C -> D: Sig_P(Pay, Receipt, Offer), Pay, Receipt, Offer
D -> C: Data, Sig_D(Data)

role Environment() def=
  knowledge(i) = {c,m,p,d,i,kc,km,kd,kp,ki,inv(ki)}
  composition
    Session(c,m,p,d,kc,km,kd,kp,scm,scp,scd,rc,rcm,rcp,rcd) /\
    Session(c,i,p,d,kc,ki,kd,kp,sci,scp,scd,rc,rci,rcp,rcd) /\
    Session(i,m,p,d,ki,km,kd,kp,sim,sip,sid,ri,rim,rip,rid)
end role

goal
Customer authenticates Merchant on Pay
end goal
```

Fig. 2. From top: the sequence of events represented in the general notation; the HLPSL code specifying the intruder's initial knowledge and the concurrent sessions; the security related goal of the HLPSL model

receipt plus a receipt signature validating the payment, receipt and offer. The final step of this model is the delivery request whereby the customer sends the delivery agent the receipt signature, payment details, receipt and offer. The delivery agent verifies this information, schedules a time for the purchased goods to be delivered to the customer and issues the customer with a signed delivery note.

The entities C, M, P and D (called roles in HLPSL) along with the corresponding data items are variables and can be instantiated with any concrete values. The simple protocol description specifies one abstract session which can be instantiated in many ways.

The HLPSL specification uses agents to act out these roles and also specifies how many concurrent sessions of the protocol are running. The agents declared in the model were 'c' (an authentic customer), 'm' (an authentic merchant), 'p' (the payment processor), 'd' (the delivery agent) and 'i' (an intruder capable of acting as either a customer or a merchant). We assume that the payment processor and the identity and behaviour of the delivery agents cannot be forged. Overall, three sessions of the protocol were modelled and checked concurrently to ensure that the goal of customer authenticates merchant on Pay was satisfied.

The HLPSL code specifying the composition of the sessions is also shown in Figure 2. The intruder (i) participates in two of the sessions playing separate roles in each. In one session, the intruder acts as a merchant (with c) and in the other session, it acts as a customer (with m). In another session, the genuine customer agent (c) plays the customer role with the genuine merchant (m). Each session in the environment specifies the parameters for the behaviour including the keys used by the agents (e.g., kc is the public key of the agent c), the initial knowledge of the intruder (i) and also defines various channels used in the communication. For instance, 'scm' is the channel used by the customer to send a message to the merchant while 'rcm' is the channel used by the customer to receive a message from the merchant. These channels are assumed to be open in that the intruder can learn about all the tokens that are exchanged using these channels. The last section is the actual authentication requirement which is specified as a goal for the verification process.

4.2   Conversion from High Level Model to Intermediary Model

Devising a plan on how to translate the HLPSL specifications into BIR was a major challenge we faced during this study. This problem was mostly due to the differing methodologies the two languages possess. On one hand, we have HLPSL which is particularly focused on protocols and security controls for that matter. On the other hand, we have BIR which is closer aligned to a programming language containing constructs such as threads, functions and records. The critical issue is that verification of a security property is related to the operational model. As we wish to be as close to an implementation as possible, we have to make certain HLPSL entities (which are abstract) more concrete in BIR. Therefore, translating some of the built-in functions of HLPSL, such as message passing and encryption, into BIR played a key role in our efforts of accomplishing this task. The full transition system is also too complex at the code level – especially given the ability of the intruder. Thus we simplify the transition system to focus on the basic behaviour and encode the requirements for security properties as suitable annotations. This enables the automatic translation of HLPSL into BIR.

Channels

The first issue was modelling the various channels that can potentially be used in a HLPSL specification. To simulate message passing in our BIR model, we created a shared object to represent the communications channel and made this object visible to the two roles using the channel. The shared object contained the channel's payload representing the data in transit along the channel. To send a message using this scheme, the sender simply sets the payload variable with the data to transmit and the receiver later reads this variable.

The question, however, is when does the receiver know when there is data waiting in the channel to be read? To resolve this, an additional variable within the shared object in the form of a boolean was added to alert the receiver when a message had been sent. Essentially, this variable functioned much like a switch between the sender and the receiver to indicate who had possession of the channel at any given time. Once the sender assigns a value to the payload variable, it then sets the switch variable. In the meantime, the receiver is in a waiting state waiting for the switch variable to be set so that it can read the channel and continue its execution. This is just a simple coding of a one place buffer without queuing. While a more elaborate data structure to hold more than one value is possible, the above encoding for HLPSL channels suffices for typical security protocols that we have considered.

Agents

The next issue we faced relates to implementing each of the agents and roles defined in the HLPSL model. It was not possible to combine, for example, a customer agent and the Customer role into the one object due to the possibility that an agent could play a different role in a different session. A situation where this occurs in our model is when in one session, the intruder agent plays a customer role and in another session, it plays a merchant role. As a result, we chose to model each agent and role as a separate object. The agent object basically contained just instance variables representing the knowledge of the agent. On the other hand, we chose to model roles as a hierarchy of classes (or records as known in BIR) with each specific role (such as Customer) extending class Role. Furthermore, each role was also implemented as a thread so that each could run as a separate lightweight process. Defined within each thread function were the sequence of state transition statements describing the actions performed by the role. As for the role's knowledge, all existing information known to it prior to its execution was declared as instance variables whereas all data either created by the role or received from other roles during its execution was stored as local variables within its thread function. By using this particular approach for implementing agents and roles, we were able to successfully model concurrent session executions of the protocol.

Data

Modelling data types is straight forward in BIR. The only data type that required special attention was message encryption. This is because encryption plays an important role in the security aspects of the behaviour. To achieve this, a special type which captures the

```
record (|Customer|) extends (|Role|) {

  /* All agents will be specified here*/
  (|Agent|) /|Customer.M|\;
  (|PublicKey|) /|Customer.Kc|\; /* All keys */
  (|Channel|) /|Customer.SND_CM|\; /* All Channels */

/* Snipped */

loc loc1: live { [|brandlist|], [|offer|], [|select|] }
  when [|this|]./|Customer.RCV_CM|\.read do invisible {
      [|brandlist|] := ((|BrandList|)) [|this|]./|Customer.RCV_CM|\.
                              /|Channel.payload|\[0];
      [|offer|] := ((|Offer|)) [|this|]./|Customer.RCV_CM|\.
                              /|Channel.payload|\[1];
      [|this|]./|Customer.RCV_CM|\.read := false;
      [|select|] := new (|Select|);
      [|this|]./|Customer.SND_CM|\./|Channel.payload|\[0] := [|select|];
      [|this|]./|Customer.SND_CM|\./|Channel.payload|\[1] := [|offer|];
      [|this|]./|Customer.SND_CM|\.read := true;
  }
  goto loc2;
```

Fig. 3. BIR Fragments

symbolic representation of encrypted items (as specified in HLPSL and other protocol description languages) was defined. Objects of this type contain both the value to be encrypted and the key used in the encryption. From this key information, the necessary decryption key required for the messages to be extracted from the encapsulation object could then be derived. This method is used for both symmetric and asymmetric key encryption.

A snippet of the BIR code which corresponds to the HLPSL encoding of the IOTP protocol is shown in Figure 3. The first part of the code shows a subset of the declaration of the customer role. Within it are the necessary data items such as the other agents (playing a role) (the corresponding merchant is shown), keys (the customer's public key is shown) and channels (the channel used to send a message to the merchant is shown). The second part shows one transition which is taken after the receipt of a message from the channel used by the merchant and the corresponding message being sent to the merchant. This is just extracting the relevant fields from the message received, creating a new Select object and sending it along with the Offer. Another BIR fragment is produced along with a test case in Figure 4 where it is associated with the HLPSL specification.

The security goals in HLPSL are not explicitly translated as part of the transition system. They are mainly used to generate the test sequences which is discussed in the next section. This is similar to their use at the high-level where the verifier determines if the protocol satisfies the property.

4.3 Deriving Test Sequences Using Bogor

For part two of this case study, once we were able to successfully convert the HLPSL specifications into BIR, we applied our BIR model to Bogor to check it for errors and to derive a series of test sequences. Although only an authentication related goal is stated in Figure 2, Bogor is also capable of providing test sequences for secrecy related goals. The secrecy related goals can be specified in HLPSL using the `secrecy_of` keyword in the goals section. To demonstrate this we created an additional hypothetical goal solely for this purpose. This goal, which will be discussed later, states that Pay is to remain secret from the Delivery Agent. This can be easily specified in the HLPSL specification as a secrecy requirement.

Whilst performing a model check, should Bogor detect any errors (e.g., in the form of a goal not being satisfied), counter examples are returned showing the traces leading to the error hence producing test sequences. Although this is fine for producing test sequences leading to an invalid end state, it does not provide us with successfully completed test sequences. Therefore, to derive such sequences, we negate the goal conditions stated in our BIR model and then recheck it.

For deriving test sequences relating to our authentication goal, we negated the assertion condition representing the request statement in our HLPSL model. To explain how the authentication related requirements were stated in our HLPSL model, first, a witness statement was made when Pay was sent from the Merchant to the Customer before later on, the request statement was made by the Customer to verify that Pay had indeed, been sent from the Merchant and had not been received previously from a separate agent. The witness statement was simply modelled as a boolean in BIR and was assigned the value of true to indicate that this predicate had been declared. So that this predicate, made by the Merchant, could be later verified by the Customer, the boolean variable was sent to the Customer in the same transition as the Pay was sent to the Customer. To simulate the request statement, we simply asserted that the value of the boolean would be true to show that the predicate had been set. Therefore, by negating this assertion statement, it reads as though the predicate has not been set and consequently, the Merchant cannot be authenticated by the Customer based on Pay. This corresponds to the HLPSL semantics of authentication.

Simplification

When we performed the model check, it found 480 test sequences - too many for the Bogor Counter Example Environment to display. Hence it is not possible to directly use these counter examples to generate test sequences. A reason for the large number is the violation is found in a variety of interleavings of the threads. Hence it is necessary to identify a sufficiently simple interleaving. To derive a basic set of test sequences from the Bogor tool, we limited the model check to a single session instance only. An example test sequence returned from this model check is shown in Figure 4. For brevity, the details of this trace have been reduced to only the send actions and the associated Bogor outputs. The transitions in Figure 4 are labelled with HLPSL code showing the channel used for that particular transition as well as the messages passed along the channel during the transition.

In general the BIR state values can be interpreted in two ways. One is as a requirement on the received value and usually follows a receive action. The other is the assignment performed by the program and will usually precede a send action. If the values received or set are different, the test oracle can signal an error. The actual variables

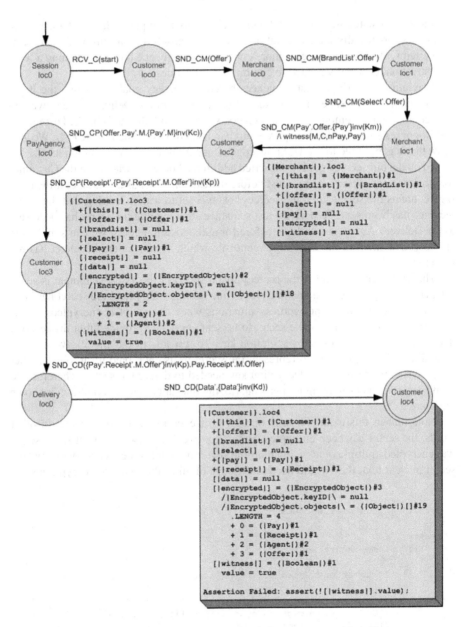

Fig. 4. A generated test sequence represented as a state transition diagram

used in the implementation could be quite different from our simple model in BIR. A mapping of BIR variables to real variables is needed before these test sequences can be applied to real implementations.

Sequences generated by this process are more concrete than the corresponding sequence generated from model checking the HLPSL specification. Such sequences also

need to be translated to actual send and receive calls for a particular implementation.
While these are usually socket operations, they could also be operations on shared memory systems. We have achieved a more concrete test sequence but still retaining a level
of abstraction, especially related to communication values.

In relation to deriving test sequences based on secrecy goals, although the IOTP
specifications do not state that Pay should be secret from the Delivery Agent, we add
this requirement to demonstrate that such goals can be modelled and checked using BIR
and Bogor respectively. Such requirements can indeed be specified in HLPSL. We also
show that it is possible to model knowledge of agents at the implementation level.

To model our secrecy goal, we inserted additional boolean variables in the Customer
role to represent secrecy tokens. Just before the Customer sends a message, if the message contains the secret, then the secrecy token is set to true indicating that the secret
message has been sent. To derive a test sequence showing that the secret has been sent
to the Delivery Agent, similarly as before for authentication goals, we can simply add
an assert statement in the Delivery Agent role which assumes that the secret has not
been sent.

This statement will fail if the secrecy token stated in the assert statement is set to
true. However, although this method works fine in situations where the secret has been
sent in clear text, it does not address situations when the secret is encrypted. In this
scenario, it is acceptable for the secret to be sent encrypted provided that the receiver
does not possess the required decryption key. To test this in our model, we inserted
an additional secrecy token to represent the secret in its encrypted form, plus another
variable stating the required decryption key needed to derive the secret. Therefore, to
derive test sequences relating to this scenario, the relevant assertion condition is shown
in Figure 5.

Note that in this example, only one level of encryption has been used. In other
words, the secret has been encrypted using only one key. However, what if the secret
was encrypted multiple times using multiple keys? In order for the receiver to extract the
secret in clear text, they would need knowledge of all of the required decryption keys.

```
assert (!/|Customer.secretSent|\.value)

assert (
    !/|Customer.secretSent|\.value ||
    (
        !/|Customer.encryptedSecretSent|\.value &&
        (
            /|Customer.decryptionKeyReqd|\ != [|this|]./|Delivery.Kc|\ ||
            /|Customer.decryptionKeyReqd|\ != [|this|]./|Delivery.Km|\ ||
            /|Customer.decryptionKeyReqd|\ != [|this|]./|Delivery.Kp|\ ||
            /|Customer.decryptionKeyReqd|\ != [|this|]./|Delivery.Kd|\
        )
    )
);
```

Fig. 5. Secrecy assert statements used in the BIR model. The first assert statement detects the
secret being received in clear text only. The second assert statement extends on the first statement
to also detect the case where an encrypted secret can be decrypted.

As our model only contains single level encryption, we did not test for secrets being encrypted with multiple keys. This keeps the knowledge that needs to be associated with the intruder to a manageable level. However, the above scheme can be expanded to include multiple levels of encryption. While the translation scheme can be altered to accommodate this, it is also possible for the tester to modify the BIR model before performing the test generation. Our approach has been to adopt a simple (e.g., in the underlying data structures) automatable translation system. The generated BIR can be altered by the tester to achieve cases not covered directly by the translator.

4.4 Lessons Learned

From our experiences with this case study, we found that the approaches we used succeeded in constructing a number of test sequences viable for a protocol implementor to apply to a working prototype. During the course of this experiment, several reasons emerged as to why this work is beneficial and of particular interest to protocol implementors and testers.

When comparing BIR models to high-level, formally specified models, it is clear that BIR models are closer to protocol implementations. Consequently, protocol testers and implementors can identify with such models more easily as they are less abstract than the high-level formal models. By using this approach, testers and implementors attain both (i) an increased understanding of the abstract model and (ii) an intermediary model that they can directly use and refer to during the implementation and testing phases of the protocol deployment. That is, the benefits of verification and testing are leveraged and a strong link between specifications and implementations is established.

In relation to the BIR language itself, due to its nature of being object-oriented as well as its close resemblance to the Java programming language, this greatly assists in lowering the learning curve for protocol implementors and testers familiar with Java or other object-oriented programming languages. As a result, this can lead to a reduction in the development time of the BIR model. While the basic BIR model can be automatically translated from HLSPL, using BIR allows the developer to refine or modify the BIR specification. This is particularly useful when generating tests from requirements not present in the HLPSL specifications. The basic translation scheme described here is sound in that, if the BIR model produces a test sequence, the test sequence can be abstracted to represent a valid run in the HLPSL specification.

To verify that the protocol's goal was satisfied in the model, we found that we were able to achieve this by simply using a combination of boolean variables (to represent predicates/claims) and assertion statements (to verify that the claims had been met). To see if this method was capable of detecting scenarios where the goal was not satisfied, we tried negating the predicates and found that this resulted in "Assertion Failed" counter examples. While model checking of the HLPSL can also produce counter examples, these sequences are at the HLPSL level. Hence to enable the generation of more concrete sequences, we could have translated the high-level counter example to a lower level. However, it is easier to translate HLPSL to a lower-level specification and use it for generating sequences. This is possible as the BIR/Bogor framework permits the model checking of code like specifications.

One aspect of Bogor we found useful was that it provided a facility for a tester to define their own, user-defined, test sequence by performing a user-guided simulation of the model. Using this facility, the user can interactively decide on the path of execution for the protocol to take and at the same time, examine current variable values and role states. In conjunction with this, the Bogor environment also provides a random simulation function which may prove beneficial to other testers trying this approach. This function randomly selects an execution pathway (test sequence) of the model during run-time and returns the outcome of the chosen sequence to the user. It is possible to add extra annotations to the BIR model to check for properties that are not really relevant at the specification level. For instance, the IOTP specifications we used did not contain any constraint on bounds on values at the HLPSL level. However, we can test variables to see if it was possible for Bogor to identify test sequences containing illegal (or out of range) values. To do this, we simply inserted relational expressions within the assertion statements and performed the model check again. As before, for the test sequences which did not satisfy the assertion condition, "Assertion Failed" counter examples were returned, hence identifying protocol traces which produced illegal values. Additionally, we could also initialise the variables with different starting values and re-perform the model check and see the results.

The ability to modify the BIR code is a definite pragmatic advantage. As programmers are more comfortable with BIR than HLPSL, they can alter the BIR code to generate tests not directly covered by the high-level specification of security properties. For instance, situations where messages are dropped, replicated or modified can be added in the BIR model. Also the effect of different message passing mechanisms can be tested. This simplifies the translation scheme as otherwise we need to define a general translator that is parametrised to produce different output.

In summary we have enabled the generation of test sequences for security properties which are closer to the implementation from a high-level specification. By translating a high-level language (HLPSL can be viewed as a sugared form of TLA for security protocols) into an object-oriented language (BIR), the tester is given a model that resembles an implementation. By using a model checker for BIR the advantages of counter examples as testing sequences is maintained.

5   Conclusion

We have demonstrated the practicability of constructing an intermediary model to use for automatically deriving test sequences specifically based on predefined security goals. To show this, we used BIR as the modelling language for our intermediary model and Bogor [17] as our model checking tool for producing test cases. As a result, we were successfully able to construct an intermediary model which was produced from a higher-level, more abstract specification, but appeared more closely aligned to an actual implementation. Furthermore, we found this approach feasible in regards to automatically generating test sequences both suitable and reusable for testers to apply to a working protocol implementation. We have combined the advantages of two specification frameworks (HLPSL [13] and BIR) in a non-standard way (at least for BIR) to generate more realistic test sequences.

The work reported here can be viewed as a specific example of providing descriptions at different levels of abstraction (one for specifications and the other for model-based test generation). The need for such an approach has been argued by Prenninger and Pretschner [22]. They make a distinction between test models and specification models as they argue for appropriate levels of abstraction for all aspects including data, communication and the functional behaviour. We have shown how HLPSL and BIR provide different but related features with the HLPSL specifications useful for high-level specification and BIR useful for lower-level test generation. It will be interesting to adapt the ideas in this paper with the notion of mutating specifications [9] to generate other types of test sequences. This can be done at both the HLPSL and the BIR level.

Acknowledgements

The authors thank Jorge Cuellar from Siemens Research for his assistance in explaining HLPSL and its use in protocol specification.

References

1. Bowen, J.P., Bogdanov, K., Clark, J., Harman, M., Hierons, R., Krause, P.: FORTEST: Formal methods and testing. In: Proc. COMPSAC 02: 26th IEEE Annual International Computer Software and Applications Conference, Oxford, UK, IEEE Computer Society Press (2002) 91–101
2. Dick, J., Faivre, A.: Automating the Generation and Sequencing of Test Cases from Model-Based Specifications. In: Formal Methods Europe. Number 670 in LNCS (1993) 268–284
3. Grieskamp, W., Gurevich, Y., Schulte, W., Veanes, M.: Generating finite state machines from abstract state machines. In: Proceedings of the International symposium on Software testing and analysis, ACM Press (2002)
4. Hartman, A., Nagin, K.: The agedis tools for model based testing. In: Proceedings of the 2004 ACM SIGSOFT international symposium on Software testing and analysis, ACM Press (2004) 129–132
5. Thompson, H.H., Whittaker, J.A., Mottay, F.E.: Software security vulnerability testing in hostile environments. In: Proceedings of the 2002 ACM symposium on Applied computing, Madrid, Spain (2002) 260–264
6. Whittaker, J.A., Thompson, H.H.: How to Break Software Security. Addison Wesley (2004)
7. Jürjens, J., Wimmel, G.: Specification-based testing of firewalls. In Bjørner, D., Broy, M., Zamulin, A., eds.: Andrei Ershov 4th International Conference "Perspectives of System Informatics" (PSI'01). Number 2244 in LNCS, Springer Verlag (2002) 308–316
8. Sullivan, K., Yang, J., Coppit, D., Khurshid, S., Jackson, D.: Software assurance by bounded exhaustive testing. In: Proceedings of the 2004 ACM SIGSOFT international symposium on Software testing and analysis, ACM Press (2004) 133–142
9. Wimmel, G., Jürjens, J.: Specification-based test generation for security-critical systems using mutations. In: Proceedings of $4^t h$ International Conference on Formal Engineering Methods (ICFEM). Number 2495 in LNCS, Shanghai, China, Springer-Verlag (2002) 471–482
10. Yang, J., Kremenek, T., Xie, Y., Engler, D.: Meca: an extensible, expressive system and language for statically checking security properties. In: Proceedings of the 10th ACM conference on Computer and communication security, ACM Press (2003) 321–334

11. IOTP: Version 1.0-RFC 2801 (Informational). http://www.ietf.org/rfc/rfc2801.txt (2000)
12. Chevalier, Y., Compagna, L., Cuellar, J., Drieslma, P.H., Mantovani, J., Mödersheim, S., Vigneron, L.: A high level protocol specification language for industrial security-sensitive protocols. Automated Software Engineering **180** (2004) 193–205
13. Armando, A., Basin, D., Boichut, Y., Chevalier, Y., Compagna, L., Cuellar, J., Drielsma, P.H., He+m, P., Mantovani, J., Moedersheim, S., von Oheimb, D., Rusinowitch, M., Santiago, J., Turuani, M., Vigan+, L., Vigneron, L.: The avispa tool for the automated validation of internet security protocols and applications. In: Computer Aided Verification (CAV) Tool presentation. (To appear 2005)
14. Lamport, L.: Specifying Systems: The TLA+ Language and Tools for Hardware and Software Engineers. Addison-Wesley (2002)
15. Basin, D., Mödersheim, S., Vigano, L.: An on-the-fly model-checker for security protocol analysis. In Snekkenes, E., Gollmann, D., eds.: Proceedings of ESORICS 03. Number 2808 in LNCS (2003) 253–270
16. Corbett, J., Dwyer, M., Hatcliff, J., Pasareanu, C., Robby, Zheng, H.: Bandera : Extracting Finite-state Models from Java Source Code. In: Proceedings of the 22nd International Conference on Software Engineering. (2000) 439–448
17. Robby, Dwyer, M.B., Hatcliff, J.: BOGOR: An Extensible and Highly-Modular Software Model Checking Framework. In: Proceedings of the 11th ACM SIGSOFT Symposium on Foundations of Software Engineering jointly held with 9th European Sofware Engineering Conference, ACM Press (2003) 267–276
18. Chaki, S., Clarke, E., Groce, A., Jha, S., Veith, H.: Modular Verification of Software Components in C. In: Proceedings of the 25th International Conference on Software engineering, IEEE Computer Society (2003) 385–395
19. Henzinger, T., Jhala, R., Majumdar, R., Sutre, G.: Software Verification with BLAST. In: Proceedings of the Tenth International Workshop on Model Checking of Software (SPIN), Lecture Notes in Computer Science 2648, Springer-Verlag (2003) 235–239
20. Gargantini, A., Heitmeyer, C.: Using Model Checking to Generate Tests from Requirements Specifications. In Nierstrasz, O., Lemoine, M., eds.: Software Engineering–ESEC/FSE. Number 1687 in LNCS, Toulouse, France, Springer Verlag (1999) 146–162
21. Jéron, T., Morel, P.: Test generation derived from model-checking. In Halbwachs, N., Peled, D., eds.: Computer Aided Verification, CAV '99. Number 1633 in LNCS, Trento, Italy, Springer-Verlag (1999) 108–121
22. Prenninger, W., Pretschner, A.: Abstractions for Model-Based Testing. In Pezze, M., ed.: Proceedings Test and Analysis of Component-based Systems (TACoS04). (2004)

Development of Fault Tolerant Grid Applications Using Distributed B

Pontus Boström and Marina Waldén

Åbo Akademi University, Department of Computer Science,
Turku Centre for Computer Science (TUCS),
Lemminkäisenkatu 14 A, 20520 Turku, Finland
{Pontus.Bostrom, Marina.Walden}@abo.fi

Abstract. Computational grids have become popular for constructing large scale distributed systems. Grid applications typically run in a very heterogeneous environment and fault tolerance is therefore very important for their correctness. Since the construction of correct distributed systems is difficult with traditional development methods we propose the use of formal methods. We use Event B as our formal framework, which we extend with new constructs such as remote procedures and notifications for reasoning about grid systems. The extended language, called Distributed B, ensures that the application can handle both node and network failures. Furthermore, the new constructs in Distributed B enable straightforward implementation of the specifications, as well as automatic generation of the needed proof obligations.

Keywords: Event B, Grid computing, Fault tolerance, Domain specific languages, Language extensions, Stepwise development.

1 Introduction

Computational grids have become a popular approach to handle vast amounts of available information and to manage computational resources. Examples of areas where grids have been successfully used for solving problems include biology, nuclear physics and engineering. Grid computing [8] is a distributed computing paradigm that differs from traditional distributed computing in that it is aimed toward large scale systems that even span organizational boundaries. Since grid applications run in a very heterogeneous computing environment fault tolerance is important in order to ensure their correct behaviour.

The development of correct grid applications is difficult with traditional software development methods. Hence, formal methods can be beneficial in order to ensure their correctness and structure their development from specification to implementation. The Action Systems formalism [4] is a formal method that is well suited for developing large distributed and concurrent systems, since it supports stepwise development. However, it lacks good tool support. The B Method [1], on the other hand, is a formal method provided with good tool support, but originally developed for construction of sequential programs. The B Method can

J. Romijn, G. Smith, and J. van de Pol (Eds.): IFM 2005, LNCS 3771, pp. 167–186, 2005.

be combined with Action Systems in order to formally reason about distributed systems as in the related methods B Action Systems [16] and Event B [2, 3]. B Action Systems models Action Systems in the B Method, while Event B also extends original B with new constructs. In this paper we use Event B as the basis for our work.

With generic formal languages like Event B, specifications are often unintentionally constructed in such a way that they cannot be implemented or are very difficult to implement efficiently. This can be due to synchronisation issues or the maintenance of atomicity of events. We have previously added extensions [5] to Event B to remedy this problem and to enable reasoning about grid applications using grid communication primitives. However, the extended Event B, referred to as Distributed B, did not consider fault tolerance. Here we will modify Distributed B to enable us to develop also fault tolerant grid applications.

The language Distributed B was designed for developing Grid applications using the Globus Toolkit [11] middleware. We here further develop this language to enable us to construct fault tolerant grid applications using only the fault tolerance mechanisms present in Globus toolkit. We add new constructs for handling exceptions raised during remote procedure calls and timeouts to handle lost notifications. These new features introduced to Event B force the developer to consider the grid environment and fault tolerance throughout the development. Furthermore, the constructs are introduced in such a manner that all needed proof obligations can be automatically generated and the system can be directly implemented.

In Section 2 we give an overview of the grid technology. Event B and the Distributed B extensions are presented in Section 3. In Section 4 we discuss the failure modes and the fault tolerance mechanisms used. Section 5 presents the extensions for developing fault tolerant grid applications. Implementation issues are discussed in Section 6 and in Section 7 we conclude.

2   Grid Systems

The purpose of grid systems is to share information and computing resources even over organizational boundaries. This requires security, scalability and protocols that are suited for Internet wide communication. The Open Grid Service Architecture (OGSA) [9] aims at providing a common standard to develop grid based applications. This standard defines what services a grid system should provide. A technical infrastructure specification defined by Open Grid Service Infrastructure (OGSI) [6] gives a precise definition of what a grid service is. The Globus Toolkit 3.x [11] is an implementation of the OGSI specification that has become de facto standard toolkit for implementing grid systems. We have chosen this toolkit as grid middleware for our extensions to Event B.

Grid systems usually have a client-server architecture, where the client initiates communication with the server that only responds to the client's request. A client may access several servers concurrently. In our grid applications a server is referred to as a grid service. Grid services as implemented in Globus Toolkit

provide features such as remote procedures, notifications, services that contain
state, transient services and service data. The main communication mechanism
of grid services is remote procedure calls from client to grid service. If a call is
unsuccessful the Globus toolkit will raise an exception for the programmer to
handle. By using notifications a grid service can asynchronously notify clients
about changes in its state. The state of grid services is preserved between calls
and grid service instances can be dynamically created. Service data adds structured data to any grid service interface. This way not only remote procedures,
but also variables are available to clients. Furthermore, Globus Toolkit contains
an index service for managing information and keeping track of different types
of services in the grid.

A grid application developed with Globus toolkit can be viewed as a collection
of remote objects. A class defining a grid service can be used by first creating an
instance of it with a specified grid service handle. These instances correspond to
remote objects in Java RMI [14] or CORBA [14] and they can be used almost
like normal local objects.

3   The Distributed B Extensions

Since constructing correct distributed applications is difficult with traditional
development methods we here propose the use of formal methods to ensure their
correctness. We have chosen to use Event B [2, 3], since it is a well supported formalism for modelling distributed systems. Event B is based on the B Method by
Abrial [1] and Action Systems by Back and Kurki-Suonio [4]. Grid applications
can be specified in Event B. However, it is not straightforward to construct these
specifications in such a manner that they can be efficiently implemented. Earlier
we proposed extensions to Event B [5] for specifying and implementing grid applications. These extensions introduced grid features such as remote procedure
calls and notifications to Event B. The semantics of the extensions is given by
their translation to B. Note that we translate to B and not Event B, since the
current tools for Event B also translate the specifications to B for verification.

We will here present the Distributed B extensions to Event B by a schematic
example of a grid application. Furthermore, we show how these extensions are
translated to B for verification. The abstract specification of an application is
first written in Event B. Using a special grid refinement grid features are then
introduced into the system in a stepwise manner. For a more formal treatment
of the extensions the reader is referred to our previous paper [5].

3.1   Event B

The abstract specification of a grid application is given in a *system*-model written
in Event B. A *system*-model contains constructs for defining sets, variables, an
invariant, as well as events defining the behaviour of the component. The events
consists of guarded substitutions. The semantics of the substitutions are given
by the weakest precondition calculus introduced by Dijkstra [7]. When the guard

of the event evaluates to *true* the event is said to be enabled. Enabled events are chosen non-deterministically for execution. When there are no enabled events left the event system terminates.

> **SYSTEM**
> $\mathcal{C}$
> **VARIABLES**
> v
> **INVARIANT**
> $I(v)$
> **INITIALISATION**
> $Init(v)$
> **EVENTS**
> $E_1 \triangleq$
>   **ANY** y **WHERE** $G_1(v,y)$ **THEN** $S_1(v,y)$ **END** ;
> $E_2 \triangleq$
>   **WHEN** $G_2(v)$ **THEN** $S_2(v)$ **END**
> **END**

The *variables*-clause defines a set of variables, v. The invariant $I(v)$ defines the type of these variables as well as additional properties that should be preserved during the execution of the system. The initialisation $Init(v)$ assign initial values to the variables. The *events*-clause contains the events, here E_1 and E_2, that describe the behaviour of the system. In event E_1 the values of the local variables y are non-deterministically chosen. When the predicate $G_1(v,y)$ evaluates to *true* the event is enabled and the substitution $S_1(v,y)$ can be executed. The event E_2 has no local variables and when $G_2(v)$ evaluates to *true*, $S_2(v)$ can be executed. When both guards $G_1(v,y)$ and $G_2(v)$ evaluates to *false* the event system terminates.

3.2 The Grid Service Machine

The *grid service machine* [5] has been introduced for giving the abstract specification of grid services. It extends the *system* model of Event B with constructs for specifying remote procedures and notifications to send. The grid service machine can be viewed as a class of which clients can obtain remote objects.

The example grid service machine presented below has a set of variables x, the remote procedures $Proc_1$ and $Proc_2$, as well as the event E_A. Moreover, it can send notifications N_1 and N_2. A client can call the remote procedures and thereby enable the event. The event is then executed concurrently with the events of the client. When all the events in the grid service has become disabled a notification is sent to the client. The client can obtain the result of the computation, x_i, by a remote procedure call to the remote procedure $Proc_2$.

In order to give our new constructs meaning and to use the tool support of B the grid service machine is translated to an ordinary B machine. Throughout this subsection the grid service machine is presented in the left column and its translation in the right one.

The B translation of the grid service machine generates an additional set, a constant and a variable. These are needed to model the instance management in B.

GRID_SERVICE
$\mathcal{A}$
VARIABLES
x
INVARIANT
$x_i \in T \wedge I_A(x)$
INITIALISATION
$Init_A(x)$

MACHINE
$\mathcal{A}_V$
SETS
A_INSTS
CONSTANTS
A_null
PROPERTIES
$A\_null \in A\_INSTS$
VARIABLES
x, A_Insts
INVARIANT
$A\_Insts \subseteq A\_INSTS \wedge$
$A\_null \notin A\_Insts \wedge$
$x_i \in A\_Insts \rightarrow T \wedge$
$I_{AV}(x, A\_Insts)$
INITIALISATION
$x_i := \emptyset \ \|$
$\ldots$
$A\_Insts := \emptyset$

The deferred set A_INSTS models all possible instances of grid service machine $\mathcal{A}$. The constant A_null models the empty instance, while the variable A_Insts models the set of instances that are currently in use by the client. Note that a grid service machine instance can only be accessed from one client. The variables are translated to take into consideration the instances. Each variable becomes a function from instance to the type defined in the grid service machine. The variables in the translation are initialised to empty sets. The instance will be initialised to $Init_A(x(inst))$ according to the initialisation clause of the grid service machine in the constructor of the instance.

The remote procedures are translated to take the instance as an additional parameter. This is needed since a remote procedure call is always made to an instance of a grid service machine. The events are also translated to take into account every possible instance via an *any*-statement.

REMOTE_PROCEDURES
$Proc_1(p) \triangleq$
  PRE $P(p)$
  THEN $S_p(x, p)$
  END ;
$r \leftarrow Proc_2 \triangleq$
  BEGIN $r := x_i$
  END

EVENTS
$E_A \triangleq$
  WHEN $G_A(x)$
  THEN $S_A(x)$
  END ;

OPERATIONS
$Proc_1(inst, p) \triangleq$
  PRE $inst \in A\_Insts \wedge P(p)$
  THEN $S_p(x(inst), p)$
  END ;
$\ldots$

$E_A \triangleq$
  ANY $inst$ **WHERE**
    $inst \in A\_Insts$
  THEN
    WHEN $G_A(x(inst))$
    THEN $S_A(x(inst))$
  END
  END

Notifications to be sent are defined in the *notifications*-clause.

NOTIFICATIONS
$N_1 \triangleq$
  GUARANTEES $Q_1(x)$
  END ;
$N_2 \triangleq$
  GUARANTEES $Q_2(x)$
  END ;
END

Each notification consists of a *guarantees*-statement. The *guarantees*-statement means that a certain condition $Q_i(x)$ holds in this grid service when the corresponding notification is sent. The notification handling is performed in the client. However, an invariant is added in the grid service machine to ensure that when the event system terminates the *guarantees*-statement of at least one notification evaluates to *true*, $\forall inst.(inst \in A\_Insts \wedge \neg G_A(x(inst)) \Rightarrow (Q_1(x(inst)) \vee Q_2(x(inst))))$.

The translated B machine contains two automatically generated operations. These are the constructor and destructor of instances.

$$
\begin{aligned}
&r \leftarrow A\_GetNew \;\hat{=}\; \\
&\textbf{ANY } inst \textbf{ WHERE} \\
&\quad A\_Insts \neq A\_INSTS - \{A\_null\} \wedge \\
&\quad inst \in A\_INSTS - A\_Insts \wedge \\
&\quad inst \neq A\_null \\
&\textbf{THEN} \\
&\quad A\_Insts := A\_Insts \cup \{inst\} \;\|\; \\
&\quad Init_A(x(inst)) \;\| \\
&\quad r := inst \\
&\textbf{END } ; \\
\\
&A\_Destroy(inst) \;\hat{=}\; \\
&\textbf{PRE } inst \in A\_Insts \\
&\textbf{THEN} \\
&\quad A\_Insts := A\_Insts - \{inst\} \\
&\quad x_i := \{inst\} \lessdot\mkern-8mu\lessdot |x_i \;\| \\
&\quad \dots \\
&\textbf{END} \\
&\textbf{END}
\end{aligned}
$$

The constructor adds the instance to the set of used instances and initialises it. In order to find instances to use, the addresses of all the instances are stored in the index service of Globus toolkit. The client can then locate a new instance by asking the index service to return the address to new free ones. The destructor of instances removes the instance from the set of used instances and modifies the variables x to reflect this change.

3.3   The Grid Refinement Machine

One of the benefits of Event B is that it supports refinement and thereby it enables stepwise development of systems. Refinement of a component preserves the behaviour of the abstract component while making it more concrete by adding variables and additional behaviour (events). An event is said to refine another event if the guard is strengthened and the behaviour of the substitutions is preserved.

In order to refine grid service machines and for introducing grid features to ordinary Event B specifications we introduce a *grid refinement machine*. The grid refinement machine extends the ordinary refinement of Event B with constructs for accessing grid service machine instances, refining remote procedures and handling notifications. The instances of grid service machines are modelled as ordinary variables. Remote procedure calls are modelled by ordinary operation calls. When all events in a grid service machine instance have become disabled a notification is received from it. The notification handlers in the grid refinement are then executed once for each notification. In order to verify that a grid refinement machine is a refinement of a more abstract specification it is translated to a refinement machine in B.

Grid refinement machines are here presented with the example C_1 that uses instances of grid service machine $\mathcal{A}$ presented in Subsection 3.2. This grid refinement is a refinement of the abstract system C presented in Subsection 3.1. The grid refinement C_1 contains the old variables v from C, new variables w and a set of instances $a_1, \ldots, a_n$ of grid service machine $\mathcal{A}$. The events E_1 and E_2 in the abstract specification are refined by more concrete events. The grid refinement machine also contains a new event F that only modifies the new variables w and a notification handler $N_1 Handler$ for handling notifications of type N_1 from instances of $\mathcal{A}$. A notification handler is also considered to be a new event and, hence, it can only assign to new variables. The grid refinement machine C_1 is given below in the left column and its translation to B in the right.

In Distributed B a new structuring mechanism [5], *references*, is used in the grid refinement to handle instances of grid service machines. This construct is translated into an *includes* statement in B. The concurrent execution of the events in the grid service machine instances and grid refinement is modelled by promoting all the events in the grid service machine into the refinement in the B model.

GRID_REFINEMENT	REFINEMENT
C_1	C_{1V}
REFINES	REFINES
C	C
REFERENCES	INCLUDES
$\mathcal{A}$	$\mathcal{A}_V$
VARIABLES	PROMOTES
$v, w, a_1, \ldots, a_n$	E_A
INVARIANT	VARIABLES
$a_1 \in \mathcal{A} \wedge$	$v, w, a_1, \ldots, a_n, A\_notif$
$\ldots$	INVARIANT
$a_n \in \mathcal{A} \wedge$	$a_1 \in A\_INSTS \wedge$
$J(v, w, a_1, \ldots, a_n)$	$a_1 \in A\_Insts \cup \{A\_null\} \wedge$
	$\ldots$
	$J_V(v, w, a_1, \ldots, a_n) \wedge$
	$A\_notif \in A\_Insts \rightarrow BOOL$

We introduce variables modelling instances of $\mathcal{A}$, a_i. The type of the variables a_i are given in the grid refinement as $\mathcal{A}$ which is then translated to the corresponding representation of instances in the traditional B model. The invariant J is also modified by the translation to take into account the changed representation of instances.

The notification handler can only be executed once for each notification from $\mathcal{A}$. Hence, we introduce variable A_notif of type function from the instances in use to boolean values. If the value is *true* for an instance, notifications can be received from it. If the value is *false* the notification has already been handled.

The initialisation of the grid refinement is similar to its B translation. The automatically generated variable A_notif is initialised to the empty set, which corresponds to the value of A_Insts.

INITIALISATION
$a_i := A\_null$ ||
. . .
$a_n := A\_null$ ||
$Init'(v, w)$

INITIALISATION
$a_1 := A\_null$ ||
. . .
$Init'(v, w)$ ||
$A\_notif := \emptyset$

Events of the grid refinement and the B translation are again similar.

EVENTS
$E_1 \triangleq$
    ANY y WHERE
        $G'_1(v, y)$
    THEN
        $S'_1(v, y)$;
        $a_i \leftarrow A\_GetNew$
    END ;
$E_2 \triangleq$
    WHEN $G'_2(v, w)$
    THEN $S'_2(v, w)$
    END ;

$F \triangleq$
    WHEN $H(v, w, a_i)$
    THEN
        $S_n(w)$ ||
        $a_i.Proc(f(v, w))$
    END ;

OPERATIONS
$E_1 \triangleq$
    ANY y WHERE
        $G'_1(v, y)$
    THEN
        $S'_1(v, y)$;
        $a_i \leftarrow A\_GetNew$;
        $A\_notif(a_i) := TRUE$
    END ;
$E_2 \triangleq$
    WHEN $G'_2(v, w)$
    THEN $S'_2(v, w)$
    END ;

$F \triangleq$
    WHEN $H(v, w, a_i)$
    THEN
        $S_n(w)$ ||
        $Proc(a_i, f(v, w))$;
        $A\_notif(a_i) := TRUE$
    END ;

The remote procedure calls are translated in such a way that the instance is given as the first parameter to the procedure. Furthermore, the assignment $A\_notif(inst) := TRUE$ is added after each remote procedure call and after the call to A_GetNew. This is done to enable the correct handling of notification originating from that instance. Note that event above E_2 does perform any remote procedure calls and hence it does not contain assignment $A\_notif(inst) := TRUE$.

Finally we study the notification handlers.

NOTIFICATION_HANDLERS
$N_1 Handler \triangleq$
    NOTIFICATION N_1
    SOURCE $inst \in \mathcal{A}$
    THEN $T_{N1}(inst, w, a_i, a_j)$
    END
END

$N_1 Handler \triangleq$
    ANY $inst$ WHERE
        $inst \in A\_Insts \wedge$
        $A\_notif(inst) = TRUE \wedge$
        $\neg \overline{G}_A(x(inst)) \wedge Q_1(x(inst))$
    THEN
        $T_{N1}(inst, w, a_i, a_j)$;
        $A\_notif(inst) := FALSE$
    END
END

Notifications of type N_1 from instance $inst$ of $\mathcal{A}$ are handled when all the events in the instance have become disabled, $\neg G_A(x(inst))$, and the condition in the *guarantees*-statement for that notification holds, $Q_1(x(inst))$. The variable A_notif is assigned *false* for this instance to denote that the notification has been handled.

Proof Obligations. Since we develop grid applications in a stepwise manner, we need to show that each new specification is a refinement of the specification developed in the previous step. In order to show that an Event B or a Distributed

B component is a refinement of another component the following properties must hold [2, 16]:

1. The initialisation of the concrete specification has to be a refinement of the initialisation of the abstract specification.
2. All events in the abstract specification have to be refined by corresponding events in the concrete specification.
3. New events that refine *skip* can be introduced in the concrete specification.
4. The new events have to terminate when executed in isolation.
5. The concrete system is not allowed to terminate more often than the abstract system.
6. The guard of a remote procedure cannot be strengthened.

The proof obligations for rules 1-5 [2, 16] can be automatically generated by the tools of Event B. The proof obligation for rule 6 [16] needs some additional constructs. Alternatively, the developer can be restricted to only use non-guarded statements in the remote procedures. The proof obligations can then be discharged by the automatic and interactive provers for B.

4   Fault Tolerance Using Globus Toolkit

Grid applications run in a very heterogeneous computing environment. This means that fault tolerance is highly important for the correct behaviour of the application. In this paper we develop extensions to Event B for developing fault tolerant grid applications using the fault tolerance mechanisms in Globus toolkit. Currently the only fault tolerance mechanism in Globus toolkit is exceptions due to failed remote procedure calls. More advanced fault tolerance mechanism such as Replication [14] and Check pointing [14] are not yet supported by the toolkit. Even with support for advanced fault tolerance mechanisms in the middleware the application needs to consider faults, since these mechanisms in the middleware might not be sufficient to handle the faults transparently.

It is not feasible to construct a system that can tolerate all types of faults [14]. We will limit the fault tolerance of Distributed B to handle two types of faults, which we consider to be most important: Firstly, a grid service instance can stop (crash) and be restarted. Secondly, network connections can fail to deliver messages to desired destinations. We do not consider situations where grid services does not satisfy its specification or where an attacker can deliberately force a grid service instance to produce erroneous results since we have proved our application correct and Globus toolkit has a very comprehensive security infrastructure. Furthermore, the grid middleware can use TLS or other secure protocols for communication and therefore we can assume that data has not been corrupted during transmission.

4.1   Faults and Fault Detection

We can identify five distinct faults that can occur in remote procedure calls from a client to a server grid service instance [14]:

1. The server grid service instance has crashed before the call.
2. The network connection fails when calling a remote procedure.
3. The server instance fails during the call.
4. The network connection fails when returning the result.
5. The client crashes during the remote procedure call.

In the client the faults 1-4 are not easily separated from each other and they are handled by not using the failed server grid service instance anymore. These faults are directly detected in the client by the Globus toolkit middleware that then raises an exception. However, the server grid service instance can crash and be restarted and it needs to detect the crash in order to respond correctly to the client. A restart can be detected if the instance creates a file on startup using its address as the filename. If the file creation fails due to the fact that the file already exists, it can be assumed that the grid service has been restarted. This holds, since file creation is atomic if the correct method is used.

In order to handle the fifth fault above the called instance needs to be able to identify when the calling client has failed, i.e., the instance has become an *orphan* [14]. To discover this we introduce an *is-alive check* in the client and an *is-alive timeout* in the server grid service instance. We first introduce a new remote procedure in every grid service instance called *isAlive*. This remote procedure returns *true*, if the instance is accessible. In the client the *is-alive check* for a given grid service instance consists of calling remote procedure *isAlive* of the instance periodically with a specified time interval. If the call fails, an exception is raised by the Globus toolkit and the client knows that there is a problem with the instance or with the network connection. The client then stops using the instance. If the *isAlive* procedure was not called with the specified time interval in the server grid service instance, an *is-alive timeout* is triggered. This means that the client has either failed or stopped using the instance. The server grid service instance is then reset in order to enable other clients to use it. It is important to note that the times for the timeout mechanism should be chosen so that the client will get the exception for a failed call to *isAlive* before the server resets itself. This can be accomplished by choosing the timeout in the server grid service instance to be greater than the time period that the client calls *isAlive* with an appropriate amount of buffer time. This check for orphans is implemented in a layer on top of Globus toolkit that then provides an easy to use interface to Distributed B.

There is an additional fault, not directly related to remote procedure calls, that needs to be considered when allocating new grid service instances. There might not be any available grid service machine instances of the correct type when the client tries to obtain new instances to use. The problem can be due to broken network connections, a broken index service or exhaustion of the pool of available services. Note that the index service is here a single point of failure for the grid application. Hence, if it fails, the application might not function correctly. The index service could, however, be transformed into a replicated index service on several computers or we could use a peer-to-peer index service.

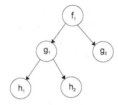

Fig. 1. The tree formed by the grid service instances

The instance allocation is also implemented in a layer on top of Globus toolkit to present a more easy to use interface to Distributed B.

4.2   Use Cases Describing the Fault Tolerance Mechanisms

In order to clarify the behaviour of the system in the presence of faults we here present the use cases for the two most complicated failure modes. We consider a tree of grid service instances as shown in Figure 1. The grid service instance f_1 references instances g_1 and g_2, where g_1 then references h_1 and h_2.

The Middle Node Crashes. The first use case describes the actions taken when the grid service instance g_1 crashes. The instance g_1 is here a middle node that has client f_1 and has references to grid service instances h_1 and h_2.

1. Instance g_1 crashes. There are now two cases to consider, steps 2 and 3.
2. If the instance g_1 is unreachable from its client, instance f_1:
    (a) An exception is raised in f_1, due to a failed remote procedure call or *is-alive check*. (A notification timeout can also be triggered by this condition).
    (b) The instance g_1 is removed from the set of used instances in f_1.
3. If the instance g_1 is reachable from f_1 but it has recovered from a failure and is in a restarted state:
    (a) The instance g_1 waits for an *is-alive timeout*. It raises exceptions for the clients remote procedure calls and *is-alive checks*. That way g_1 can make sure that the client f_1 knows that g_1 has failed.
    (b) Instance f_1 detects that instance g_1 has failed and it removes it from the set of used instances.
    (c) The instance g_1 receives an *is-alive timeout* and resets itself.
4. The instances h_i notice that g_1 has failed when they receive *is-alive timeouts* and they are then reset.

The Network Connection Fails. The second use case describes the behaviour of the system when a network connection failure between, the client f_1 and the middle node g_1 is noticed.

1. The network connection between f_1 and g_1 fails.
2. An exception is raised in f_1 due to failed remote procedure call or *is-alive check*.

3. The instance f_1 removes g_1 from its set of used instances.
4. The instance g_1 receives an *is-alive timeout*, since its services are not requested anymore. It then resets itself.
5. The instances h_i reset themselves when they receive *is-alive timeouts* due to the reset of g_1.

Final Notes. What applies to a middle node g_i also applies to a leaf node h_i. The only difference is that we do not have to consider any child nodes. If the root node f_1 crashes the program terminates and no result is obtained.

5   Fault Tolerance in Distributed B

Previously we have developed a language called Distributed B [5] based on Event B for constructing fault free grid applications. In this section we modify the language to also incorporate fault tolerance mechanisms as described in the previous section, Section 4. Distributed B provided a way to implement grid applications and the fault tolerance mechanisms will also be introduced in a manner that ensures that they can be implemented.

5.1   Specification of Instance Management

A challenging problem when introducing fault tolerance is the management of instances. In order to correctly reason about instances we need to have a model of the instance management. The model in the original version of Distributed B is described in Subsection 3.2. During the translation of grid service machine $\mathcal{A}$ to original B we there added features such as a set A_INSTS modelling all instances of $\mathcal{A}$, a constant A_null modelling the empty instance, a variable A_Insts modelling the instances in use, as well as a constructor and destructor of instances. This model of the instance management is not changed when we introduce fault tolerance into Distributed B. However, we did not specify how an instance should be treated if a fault was encountered during a remote procedure call to it or if notification was never received from it. In order to also handle faults, an instance a_i of $\mathcal{A}$ is immediately removed from the set of instances in use, A_Insts, if a problem with it is encountered.

The model of instance management described above serves as an abstract specification that need to be implemented. To increase the confidence in the system it can be developed in a stepwise manner using, e.g., Event B. The model is refined to consider the behaviour of grid service instances, the communication between them, as well as the faults described in Section 4.

We here give an overview of a refined, more concrete model of the behaviour of an instance of $\mathcal{A}$ using the statechart diagram shown in figure 2. The users of fault tolerant Distributed B will not have to consider this refined model of instance management, since it is built into the language. It only serves as an illustration on how the instance management is implemented using Globus toolkit. The instance can be in three different states: *idle* when the instance is not reserved

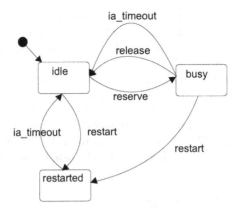

Fig. 2. The behaviour of a grid service instance

by a client; *busy* when a client has reserved the instance and *restarted* when the instance has detected that it has been restarted. The event *reserve* is generated when a client reserves the instance by a call to the operation $A\_ GetNew$. The reservation is modelled by the transition from state *idle* to state *busy*. When the event *reserve* occurs the instance is initialised, modelled in Dsitributed B by executing the *initialisation*-clause of the grid service machine. The transition *release* from state *busy* to state *idle* models that the client releases the instance by a call to operation $A\_Destroy$. The event *ia_ timeout* denotes that an *is-alive timeout* occurred and the instance is reset, i.e., it enters the state *idle*. The *restart* event models restart of the grid service instance by taking the instance to state *restarted*. When a grid service instance belongs to the set of instances in use, A_Insts, it is in either state *busy* or *restarted,* since it has then been reserved by a client. Note that the instance will raise an exception when its remote procedures are called in state *restarted*.

5.2   Extensions to Distributed B

In order to handle faults as described in Section 4 and to handle instances as described in the previous subsection we add new constructs to the original version Distributed B. New constructs are needed for handling exceptions raised from remote procedures and timeouts for notifications. We also add constructs for handling orphans with the *is-alive check*. The mechanism for handling faults only affects the grid refinement machine and hence, the constructs in the grid service machine remains the same. For simplicity we will here consider only grid applications that do not have middle nodes. Hence, a refinement of a grid service machine cannot here reference other grid service machines.

As an example of a fault tolerant grid refinement machine we modify grid refinement C_1 in Subsection 3.3 to handle faults. The fault tolerant grid refinement C_{FT} has the same variables (v, w) and instances $(a_1, \ldots, a_n)$ as C_1. The remote procedure calls to instance a_i are modified to consider faults. The notification

handling mechanism is also modified to consider timeouts due to lost notifications. Furthermore, we need an additional event to handle exceptions raised by
is-alive checks. The fault tolerant Distributed B models are again translated to
B for verification purposes. Below the fault tolerant Distributed B constructs
are given in the left column and their translation to B is given to the right. The
complete example can be found in Appendix A.

Remote Procedures. Remote procedure calls can fail in several ways as outlined in Subsection 4.1. We add a *call*-substitution for calling remote procedure
in order to model the exception handling mechanism present in Java and Globus
toolkit.

```
call_subst::=''CALL'' operation_call
               ''EXCEPTION'' NG_Substitution
               ''END''
```

The *call*-part of this construct contains a remote procedure call. The *exception*-
part then gives the non-guarded substitution that is executed if an exception is
raised during the call. The *call*-substitution is used whenever a remote procedure
in a grid service instance is called as shown in event F. The *call*-substitution
also needs to be used when calling A_GetNew to allocate a new instance since
it can fail as described in Subsection 4.1.

$F \triangleq$
   WHEN $H(v, w, a_i)$
   THEN
    $S_n(w)$ ||
    CALL $a_i.Proc(f(v, w))$
    EXCEPTION $T_f(w, a_i)$
   END
   END

$FOk \triangleq$
   WHEN $H(v, w, a_i)$
   THEN
    $S_n(w)$ ||
    $Proc(a_i, f(v, w))$;
    $A\_notif(a_i) := TRUE$
   END ;
$FFail \triangleq$
   WHEN $H(v, w, a_i)$
   THEN
    $S_n(w)$ ||
    $A\_Destroy(a_i)$;
    $A\_notif := \{a_i\} << |A\_notif$;
    $T_f(w, a_i)$
   END ;

The event F is translated to two separate operations in B, FOk and $FFail$,
which both refine the abstract specification of F. One operation, FOk, models
the successful execution of the remote procedure and the other, $FFail$, models
the failed execution [2]. The operation FOk is translated as F previously in
Distributed B, i.e., without the exception handler. In $FFail$ the instance a_i is
removed from the set of instances in use and the exception handler is executed.
The guard is identical in both events modelling that any remote procedure call
can fail.

Notifications. Failure of grid service instances can cause notifications to never
be sent or a failure of network connections can cause notification messages to
get lost. In order to detect this we introduce a timeout exception that occurs
when a notification has not arrived within the desired time. We do not specify

the time explicitly in B but we model the timeout with an event that is chosen non-deterministically for execution. The exact time is a detail that is considered later during the implementation phase.

The grammar of the notification handler substitution is modified in order to incorporate the timeout mechanism.

```
Notif_handler::='"NOTIFICATION"' Name
                 "SOURCE" Name ":" Name
                 "THEN" NG_Substitution
                 "TIMEOUT" NG_Substitution
                 "END"
```

The *notification*-part gives the name of the notification and the *source*-part gives the source of the notification as $<instance>:<grid\ service\ machine>$. When a notification is received the non-guarded substitution in the *then*-part is executed. The *timeout*-handler denotes the substitution that is executed when a notification does not arrive within the desired time.

A notification handler for notification N_1 from instance $inst$ of $\mathcal{A}$ can be defined as follows.

NOTIFICATION_HANDLERS
$N_1 Handler \triangleq$
  NOTIFICATION N_1
  SOURCE $inst \in A$
  THEN $T_{N1}(inst, w, a_i, a_j)$
  TIMEOUT $T_t(inst, w, a_i, a_j)$
  END

$N_1 HandlerOk \triangleq$
  ANY $inst$ **WHERE**
    $inst \in A\_Insts \wedge$
    $A\_notif(inst) = TRUE \wedge$
    $\neg \overline{G}_A(x(inst)) \wedge Q_1(x(inst))$
  THEN
    $T_{N1}(inst, w, a_i, a_j) \parallel$
    $A\_notif(inst) := FALSE$
  END ;
$N_1 HandlerFail \triangleq$
  ANY $inst$ **WHERE**
    $inst \in A\_Insts \wedge$
    $A\_notif(inst) = TRUE \wedge$
  THEN
    $A\_Destroy(inst);$
    $A\_notif := \{inst\} \lessdot \mid A\_notif;$
    $T_t(inst, w, a_i, a_j)$
  END

As for remote procedure calls, the notification handler $N_1 Handler$ is translated to two different operations in B, $N_1 HandlerOk$ and $N_1 HandlerFail$. The notification handler is a new event and hence, both translated operations have to refine *skip*. The operation, $N_1 HandlerOk$, modelling successful notification handling is translated as in previous version of Distributed B presented in Subsection 3.3. Failed delivery of a notification is modelled by the execution of the timeout handler, $N_1 HandlerFail$. Since it is not known if all events in the grid service machine instance $inst$ of $\mathcal{A}$ have become disabled before the failure, only $A\_notif(inst) = TRUE$ is present in the guard. The instance $inst$ is also here removed from the set of instances in use.

Checking if an Instance Is Alive. In order to handle orphans we introduce an *is-alive check* in the grid refinement machine. This check is performed in the grid refinement machine for all instances of all referenced grid service machines. If an instance is unavailable an exception is then raised. To handle these exceptions we introduce a new clause *is_alive_handlers*

```
is_alive_handlers ::="IS_ALIVE_HANDLERS" is_alive_handler+;
is_alive_handler ::= Name "="
                     "SOURCE" Name ":" Name
                     "THEN" NG_Substitution
                     "END"
```

The handler substitutions for *is-alive check* exceptions consists of two parts; a source given as $<instance>:<grid\ service\ machine>$ and a non-guarded substitution describing the behaviour of the system when an exception is raised. The handler for grid service machine $\mathcal{A}$ is given below with its translation.

$$
\begin{array}{ll}
\textbf{IS\_ALIVE\_HANDLERS} & IAHandler \triangleq \\
IAHandler \triangleq & \quad \textbf{ANY}\ inst\ \textbf{WHERE} \\
\quad \textbf{SOURCE}\ inst \in \mathcal{A} & \quad\quad inst \in A\_Insts \\
\quad \textbf{THEN}\ T_{ia}(inst, w, a_i, a_j) & \quad \textbf{THEN} \\
\quad \textbf{END} & \quad\quad A\_Destroy(inst); \\
\textbf{END} & \quad\quad A\_notif := \{inst\} << |A\_notif; \\
& \quad\quad T_{ia}(inst, w, a_i, a_j) \\
& \quad \textbf{END} \\
& \textbf{END}
\end{array}
$$

The handler is translated to an *any*-substitution in B. The *any*-substitution models that an exception can be raised at any time for all instances in use. The handler for failed *is-alive checks* is, like the handlers for notifications, a new event that refines *skip*. As for the failed remote procedure calls and notifications we remove the failed instance from the set of used instances and remove all the variables of the instance.

6   Implementation in Java

The grid application development in fault tolerant Distributed B continues until all the non-determinism has been removed and all the used constructs can be implemented, i.e., they belong to the implementable subset of the B language, B0. When all substitutions of the system belong to the B0 language, they can be automatically translated to Java [15]. The event system composed of all events in the *events*-clause can be automatically translated to a *while*-loop in Java, if all the guards Gi and the substitutions Si belong to the B0 language.

$$
\begin{array}{l}
E1 \triangleq \\
\textbf{WHEN}\ G1 \\
\textbf{THEN}\ S1\ \textbf{END} \\
\quad \ldots \\
En \triangleq \\
\textbf{WHEN}\ Gn \\
\textbf{THEN}\ Sn\ \textbf{END}
\end{array}
$$

```
while (true) {
    if(G1) S1;
    ...
    else if(Gn) Sn;
    else <stop loop>;
}
```

The place holder *<stop loop>* consists of statements that terminate the loop in the main program and statements for sending notifications and pausing the execution in implementations of grid service machines.

In the client the grid service instances are translated to objects encapsulating the grid specific features. These features include instance allocation, remote procedure calls, notification handling, notification timeouts and management of *is-alive checks*. In the implementation of grid service machines an additional layer encapsulating grid features such as state management and *is-alive timeouts* is inserted between the Globus toolkit and the translated grid service machine. The code for the objects and the additional layer need to be manually created once, but can then be reused in all Distributed B applications.

Java code is generated for each concrete grid refinement machine that is a refinement of a grid service machine and for the root grid refinement machine that is a refinement of an Event B model. When the code has been generated we have implemented the grid application in a formal manner, where we can show that the implementation is a correct refinement of the abstract specification.

7   Conclusions

We have earlier developed a language Distributed B [5] that extends Event B for designing and implementing correct grid applications. In that paper we introduced two new types of machines, *grid service machine* and *grid refinement machine,* for handling grid specific issues in Event B. In this paper we have modified Distributed B for developing fault tolerant and robust grid applications. We introduced exception handling to take care of exceptions raised due to failed remote procedure calls, as well as timeouts to discover lost notifications. In order to handle orphan grid service instances we introduced a special checking mechanism and facilities to handle exceptions raised by it. These new features force the developer to consider the fault tolerance of grid applications throughout the development and enables formal proofs of correctness. Hence, we have proposed a method for implementing fault tolerant grid applications where the implementation can be proved correct with respect to its specification.

There are several middlewares comparable to Globus toolkit that support advanced fault tolerance mechanisms. For example, fault tolerance in CORBA [10, 14] is based on replication. In CORBA replicas of an object form an object group. Object groups then provide replication transparency and failure transparency. Replication is complementary to the mechanisms presented here and both can be used together for developing very reliable grid applications. Fault detection is an important part of a fault tolerant application. A service for detecting faulty components in a grid environment using *unreliable fault detectors* is presented in a paper by Stelling et al. [13]. However, the service is no longer part of the Globus toolkit due to a number of deficiencies, such as excessive resource usage and difficulties in supporting it.

From a performance perspective our fault tolerant language for developing grid applications could be improved. One of the most challenging problems when constructing fault tolerant grid systems is to handle the orphan grid service instances. Our approach uses timers and extra remote procedure calls, which might not be optimal. The handling of orphans could be improved as discussed in detail by Panzieri and Shrivastava [12] and by Tanenbaum and Steen [14]. Furthermore, the fault tolerance mechanism will immediately delete references to grid service instances that experiences problems. This can lead to the deletion of an entire subtree of instances for one failure. Hence, more efficient mechanisms that would maintain the partial results should be investigated.

The language we proposed in this paper provides a convenient formal development process for fault tolerant grid applications. The applications will by construction have an architecture that is fault tolerant and implementable. Furthermore, the applications are modelled in terms of grid primitives with a precise meaning and the specifications of them will therefore be clear to understand. Our approach to adapt Event B to the Globus Toolkit middleware is not limited to that specific middleware, but it can be applied to other middlewares for distributed systems as well.

References

1. J. R. Abrial. *The B-Book: Assigning Programs to Meanings.* Cambridge University Press, 1996.
2. J. R. Abrial, D. Cansell and D. Méry. Refinement and Reachability in Event B. In H. Treharne et al, editors, *proceedings of the 4th international conference of Z and B users: ZB2005.* LNCS 3455, Guildford, UK, pp. 144-163, Springer-Verlag, 2005.
3. J. R. Abrial and L. Mussat. Event B Reference Manual, 2001. http://www.atelierb.societe.com/ressources/evt2b/eventb_reference_manual.pdf. (accessed 10.08.2005)
4. R. J. R. Back and R. Kurki-Suonio. Decentralization of process nets with centralized control. In *Proceedings of the 2nd ACM SIGACT-SIGOPS Symposium of Principles of Distributed Computing*, pp. 131-142, 1983.
5. P. Boström and M. Walden. An extension of Event B for developing grid systems. In H. Treharne et al, editors, *proceedings of the 4th international conference of Z and B users: ZB2005.* LNCS 3455, Guildford, UK, pp. 144-163, Springer-Verlag, 2005.
6. K. Czajkowski, et. al. Open Grid Services Infrastructure, 2003. http://www-unix.globus.org/toolkit/draft-ggf-ogsi-gridservice-33_2003-06-27.pdf. (accessed 10.08.2005)
7. E. W. Dijkstra. *A Discipline of Programming.* Prentice-Hall International, 1976.
8. I. Foster, C. Kesselman and S. Tuecke. The Anatomy of the Grid: Enabling Scalable Virtual Organizations. *The International Journal of Supercomputer Applications,* 15(3), 2001.
9. I. Foster, C. Kesselman, J. Nick and S. Tuecke. The Physiology of the Grid: An Open Grid Services Architecture for Distributed Systems Integration. Open Grid Service Infrastructure WG, Global Grid Forum, 2002. http://www.globus.org/alliance/publications/papers/ogsa.pdf. (accessed 10.08.2005)
10. Object Management Group. Fault tolerant CORBA, 2001, http://www.omg.org/docs/formal/01-09-29.pdf. (accessed 10.08.2005)

11. The Globus Alliance. Globus Toolkit. 2005. `http://www.globus.org/`. (accessed 10.08.2005)
12. F. Panzieri and S. K. Shrivastava. Rajdoot: A Remote Procedure Call Mechanism Supporting Orphan Detection and Killing. *IEEE Transactions on Software Engineering*, 14(1), pp 30-37, 1988.
13. P. Stelling, C. DeMatteis, I. Foster, C. Kesselman, C. Lee, G. von Laszewski. A Fault Detection Service for Wide Area Distributed Computations, *Cluster Computing*, 2, pp. 117-128, 1999
14. A. S. Tanenbaum and M. Van Steen. *Distributed systems principles and paradigms.* Prentice Hall. 2002
15. J. C. Voisinet, B. Tatibouet and A. Hammand. JBTools: An experimental platform for the formal B method. In *Proceedings of the inaugural conference on the Principles and Practice of programming and Proceedings of the second workshop on Intermediate representation engineering for virtual machines.* National University of Ireland, 2002
16. M. Waldén and K. Sere. Reasoning About Action Systems Using the B-Method. *Formal Methods in Systems Design*, 13:5-35, 1998.

A   A Fault Tolerant Grid Refinement Machine

GRID_REFINEMENT
$\mathcal{C}_{FT}$
REFINES
$\mathcal{C}$
REFERENCES
$\mathcal{A}$
VARIABLES
$v, w, a_1, \ldots, a_n$
INVARIANT
$a_1 \in \mathcal{A} \wedge$
$\ldots a_n \in \mathcal{A} \wedge$
$J(v, w, a_1, \ldots, a_n)$
INITIALISATION
$a_1 := A\_null \parallel$
$\ldots$
$Init'(v, w)$
EVENTS
$E_1 \hat{=}$
  ANY y **WHERE**
    $G'_1(v, y)$
  THEN
    $S'_1(v, y);$
    CALL $a_i \leftarrow A\_GetNew$
    EXCEPTION T_e
    END
  END ;
$E_2 \hat{=}$
  WHEN $G'_2(v, w)$
  THEN $S'_2(v, w)$
  END ;
$F \hat{=}$
  WHEN $H(v, w, a_i)$
  THEN
    $S_n(w) \parallel$
    CALL $a_i.Proc(f(v, w))$
    EXCEPTION $T_f(w, a_i)$
    END
  END
NOTIFICATION_HANDLERS
$N_1 Handler \hat{=}$
  NOTIFICATION N_1
  SOURCE $inst \in A$
  THEN $T_{N1}(inst, w, a_i, a_j)$
  TIMEOUT $T_t(inst, w, a_i, a_j)$
  END
IS_ALIVE_HANDLERS
$IAHandler \hat{=}$
  SOURCE $inst \in \mathcal{A}$
  THEN $T_{ia}(inst, w, a_i, a_j)$
  END

END

REFINEMENT
$\mathcal{C}_{FTV}$
REFINES
$\mathcal{C}$
INCLUDES
$\mathcal{A}_V$
PROMOTES
E_A
VARIABLES
$v, w, a_1, \ldots, a_n, A\_notif$
INVARIANT
$a_1 \in A\_INSTS \wedge$
$a_1 \in A\_Insts \cup \{A\_null\} \wedge$
$\ldots$
$J_V(v, w, a_1, \ldots, a_n) \wedge$
$A\_notif \in A\_Insts \to BOOL$
INITIALISATION
$a_1 := A\_null \parallel$
$\ldots$
$Init'(v, w) \parallel$
$A\_notif := \emptyset$
OPERATIONS
$E_1 Ok \hat{=}$
  ANY y **WHERE**
    $G'_1(v, y)$
  THEN
    $S'_1(v, y);$
    $a_i \leftarrow A\_GetNew;$
    $A\_notif(a_i) := TRUE$
  END ;
$E_1 Fail \hat{=} \ldots$
$E_2 \hat{=} \ldots$
$FOk \hat{=}$
  WHEN $H(v, w, a_i)$
  THEN
    $S_n(w) \parallel$
    $Proc(a_i, f(v, w));$
    $A\_notif(a_i) := TRUE$
  END ;
$FFail \hat{=} \ldots$
$N_1 HandlerOk \hat{=}$
  ANY $inst$ **WHERE**
    $inst \in A\_Insts \wedge$
    $A\_notif(inst) = TRUE \wedge$
    $\neg \overline{G}_A(x(inst)) \wedge Q_1(x(inst))$
  THEN
    $T_{N1}(inst, w, a_i, a_j) \parallel$
    $A\_notif(inst) := FALSE$
  END ;
$N_1 HandlerFail \hat{=} \ldots$
$IAHandler \hat{=}$
  ANY $inst$ **WHERE**
    $inst \in A\_Insts$
  THEN
    $A\_Destroy(inst);$
    $A\_notif := \{inst\} \ll |A\_notif;$
    $T_{ia}(inst, w, a_i, a_j)$
  END
END

Formal Methods Meet Domain Specific Languages

Jean-Paul Bodeveix[1], Mamoun Filali[1], Julia Lawall[2], and Gilles Muller[3]

[1] IRIT Université Paul Sabatier,
118 route de Narbonne, F-31062 Toulouse Cedex, France
{bodeveix, filali}@irit.fr
[2] DIKU University of Copenhagen, 2100 Copenhagen, Denmark
julia@diku.dk
[3] Ecole des Mines de Nantes INRIA, LINA, 44307 Nantes cedex 3, France
Gilles.Muller@emn.fr

Abstract. In this paper, we relate an experiment whose aim is to study how to combine two existing approaches for ensuring software correctness: Domain Specific Languages (DSLs) and formal methods. As examples, we consider the Bossa DSL and the B formal method. Bossa is dedicated to the development of process schedulers and has been used in the context of Linux and Chorus. B is a refinement based formal method which has especially been used in the domain of railway systems. In this paper, we use B to express the correctness of a Bossa specification. Furthermore, we show how B can be used as an alternative to the existing Bossa tools for the production of certified schedulers.

Keywords: DSL, scheduling, formal methods, refinements, decision procedure.

1   Introduction

During the last decade, the correctness of software has been a major issue. Several approaches have been proposed and tools supporting them have been implemented, some of which have been used in industry. One approach is the use of Domain Specific Languages (DSLs). A DSL contains domain-specific abstractions as well as domain-specific restrictions that enable verification of domain-specific properties. Another approach is the use of formal methods. Such methods associate mathematically rigorous proofs with each step in software design and development. In this paper, we consider how to combine these approaches, by showing how a general purpose proof environment based on the B formal method [1] can be used to express and verify some of the properties relevant to the DSL Bossa [9].

The Bossa DSL is dedicated to the development of kernel-level process schedulers and has been used in the context of Linux and the Chorus real-time operating system. Process scheduling is at the heart of all operating system (OS)

J. Romijn, G. Smith, and J. van de Pol (Eds.): IFM 2005, LNCS 3771, pp. 187–206, 2005.

behavior, making verification critical in this domain. Bossa has thus been designed with both programmability and verification in mind. It has a formal semantics and provides high-level scheduling-specific abstractions that simplify the programming of scheduling policies and make explicit information that is useful in scheduler verification. These features have, for example, enabled undergraduate students with no previous kernel programming experience to implement scheduling policies in the Linux kernel without crashing the machine.

B is a refinement-based formal method that has been used for the development of safety critical software, especially in the domain of railway systems [2, 4]. The main feature of a B development process is that it proves that the final code implements its formal specification. In this paper, we use B to express the correctness of a Bossa specification. Furthermore, we show how B can be used as an alternative to the existing Bossa tools for the production of certified schedulers.

The rest of this paper is organized as follows. Section 2 provides a review of Bossa with respect to its language and the verifications performed by its compiler. Section 3 gives a brief overview of the B method. Section 4 elaborates the B development of a Bossa specification. Section 5 describes how some of the proof obligations generated by the B development can be discharged automatically. Section 6 presents some related work. Section 7 draws some conclusions.

2   Bossa

This section introduces the Bossa DSL and the verifications performed by the Bossa compiler.

2.1   Bossa in a Nutshell

We introduce the Bossa DSL using excerpts of an implementation of a Rate Monotonic (RM) scheduling policy [5], shown in Figure 1. This policy manages a set of periodic processes, each of which is associated with a period attribute. Process election chooses the process that is ready to run and that has the shortest period. RM scheduling is useful in the context of general-purpose operating systems such as Linux for controlling multimedia applications and in the context of real-time operating systems such as Chorus [7] for managing periodic processes. The complete RM policy is implemented as 110 lines of Bossa code and is available at the Bossa web site, http://www.emn.fr/x-info/bossa. A grammar of the Bossa DSL is also available at this web site. Here, we focus on the main features of the language: declarations and event handlers.

Declarations. The declarations of a scheduling policy define the process attributes, process states, and processes ordering used by the policy.

The **process** declaration (line 2) lists the policy-specific attributes associated with each process. For the RM policy, each process is associated with its period.

The **states** declaration (lines 4-11) lists the set of process states that are distinguished by the policy. Each state is associated with a state class (RUNNING,

```
1    scheduler RM = {
       process = { time period; ... }

       states = {
5        RUNNING running : process;
         READY ready : select queue;
         READY yield : process;
         BLOCKED blocked : queue;
         BLOCKED computation_ended : queue;
10       TERMINATED terminated;
       }

       ordering_criteria = { lowest period }

15     handler(event e) {
         On process.end { e.target => terminated; }

         On unblock.preemptive {
           if (e.target in blocked) {
20           if ((!empty(running)) && (e.target > running)) {
               running => ready;
             }
             e.target => ready;
           }
25       }

         ...
       }
     }
```

Fig. 1. Excerpts of the Bossa Rate Monotonic policy

READY, BLOCKED, or TERMINATED) describing the schedulability of processes in the state and an implementation as either a process variable (process) or a queue (queue). The names of the states of the RM policy are mostly intuitive. The ready state is designated as select, indicating that processes are elected from this state. The computation_ended state stores processes that have completed their computation within the current period.

The ordering_criteria (line 14) describes how to compare two processes in terms of a sequence of criteria based on the values of their attributes. The RM policy favors the process with the lowest period.

Event Handlers. Event handlers describe how a policy reacts to scheduling-related events that occur in the kernel. Examples of such events include process blocking and unblocking and the need to elect a new process. We show only the definitions of the handlers process.end and unblock.preemptive, which are used as examples in the B development.

Event handlers are parameterized by an event structure, e, that includes the *target process*, e.target, affected by the event. The event-handler syntax is based on that of a subset of C and provides specific constructs and primitives for manipulating processes and their attributes. These include constructs for testing the state of a process (*exp* in *state*), testing whether there is any process in a given state (empty(*state*)), testing the relative priority of two processes (*exp₁* > *exp₂*), and changing the state of a process (*exp* => *state*).

A process.end event occurs when a process ends its execution. The corresponding handler (line 16) simply sets the state of the process to terminated. Because the terminated state is not associated with any data structure, this state change has the effect of removing the process from further consideration by the scheduler. An unblock.preemptive event occurs when a process unblocks. The corresponding handler (lines 18-25) checks whether the process is actually blocked, and if so sets the state of the target process to ready making it eligible for election. The handler also checks whether there is a running process (!empty(running)) and if so whether the target process has a higher priority than this running process (e.target > running). If both tests are satisfied, the state of the running process is set to ready, thus causing the process to be preempted.

2.2   Bossa Verification

The Bossa compiler verifies that a Bossa scheduling policy satisfies both standard safety properties, such as the absence of null-pointer dereferences, and safety properties derived from the scheduling requirements of the target OS. The latter properties are OS-specific and are described by a collection of *event types*. Event types are defined in terms of the state classes and specify the possible preconditions and corresponding required postconditions on process states at the time of invoking the various event handlers.

We present the event type notation using the types of the process.end and unblock.preemptive events when used with Linux 2.4. That of process.end is as follows:

```
[tgt in BLOCKED] -> [tgt in TERMINATED]
```

This type rule indicates that the target process of the event is initially in a state of the BLOCKED state class and that the handler must change the state of this process to a state of the TERMINATED state class. Because no other state classes are mentioned in the type, a process.end handler cannot perform any other state changes. The type for unblock.preemptive is as follows:

```
[tgt in BLOCKED] -> [tgt in READY]
[p in RUNNING, tgt in BLOCKED] -> [[p,tgt] in READY]
[tgt in BLOCKED] -> [tgt in BLOCKED]
[tgt in RUNNING] -> []
[tgt in READY] -> []
```

The first three type rules treat the case where the target process is in a state of the BLOCKED state class. Of these, the first two allow the handler to move the target process to a state of the READY state class, making the process eligible for election. The second rule additionally moves the running process to the READY state class, which causes it to be preempted. In the third rule, the target process remains in the BLOCKED state class, but is allowed to change state, *e.g.* to one representing a different kind of blocking. The remaining rules consider the cases where the target process is not actually blocked. In these cases, the event handler may not perform any state changes.

It is straightforward to show that the process.end and unblock.preemptive handlers presented above satisfy these types. The Bossa compiler includes a verifier that checks that a scheduling policy satisfies the event types. This verifier is based on abstract interpretation and uses the various high-level abstractions found in the Bossa language to infer the source and destination of state change operations [9].

3   A Brief Overview of the B Method

B is a state-oriented formalism that covers the complete life cycle of software development. It provides a uniform language, the Abstract Machine Notation, to specify, design, and implement systems. A typical development in B consists of an abstract specification, followed by some refinement steps. The final refinement corresponds to an implementation. The correctness of the construction is enforced by the verification of proof obligations associated with each step of the development.

A specification in B is composed of a set of modules called *(abstract) machines*. Each machine has an internal state, and provides services allowing an external user to access or modify its state. Syntactically, a machine consists of several clauses which determine the static and dynamic properties of the state.

Consider the following abstract machine, which specifies a simple system that stores a set with at most one element and provides various set operations:

MACHINE Singleton(ELEM)
VARIABLES elem, elems
INVARIANT
    elem $\in$ ELEM
$\wedge$ elems $\subseteq$ {elem}
INITIALISATION
    elem $:\in$ ELEM || elems := $\emptyset$
OPERATIONS
suppress $\triangleq$
  PRE elems $\neq \emptyset$ **THEN** /* *the precondition ensures that suppress*
                                will be called with a nonempty set */
    elems := $\emptyset$
  END;
el $\longleftarrow$ extract $\triangleq$ /* *extract returns el* */
  PRE elems $\neq \emptyset$ **THEN**

```
    el := elem || elems := ∅
  END;

add(el)  ≜ /* the precondition specifies the type of el
                 and ensures that no elements will be overridden */
  PRE el ∈ ELEM ∧ elems = ∅ THEN
    elem := el || elems := {el}  /* B multi assignment */
  END;
bb ⟵ empty  ≜
  IF elems = ∅ THEN bb := TRUE ELSE bb := FALSE END;
bb ⟵ nonempty  ≜
  IF elems ≠ ∅ THEN bb := TRUE ELSE bb := FALSE END;
bb ⟵ contains(el)  ≜
  PRE el ∈ ELEM THEN
    IF el ∈ elems THEN bb := TRUE ELSE bb := FALSE END
  END
END
```

This machine specifies a family of systems all having the same abstract properties with respect to the parameter ELEM. By convention, a parameter starting with an uppercase letter is an abstract set. Otherwise, it must be given a type within the CONSTRAINTS clause. The clause VARIABLES defines the representation of the state of the machine. In this case, we only use the variables elem and elems. The clause INVARIANT constrains the domain of these variables. It states that elem is a member of ELEM and that elems is a subset of the singleton {elem}. Note that at this stage of the development the domain ELEM is abstract. We just assume that it is nonempty.[1] The initial state of the machine, which must satisfy the invariant, is specified in the INITIALISATION clause. In this example, the variable elem is initialized with any element of ELEM and elems is initialized to the empty set.

The services provided by a machine are specified in the clause OPERA-TIONS. In this case, we specify some standard set operations. To specify operations, B uses a mechanism of *generalized substitutions*. B defines six basic generalized substitutions: skip, multi-assignment (also called parallel-assignment), selection, bounded choice, unbounded choice, and preconditioned substitution. A generalized substitution acts as a predicate transformer. For example, the generalized substitution

$$\textbf{PRE } elems \neq \emptyset \textbf{ THEN } elems := \emptyset \textbf{ END}$$

corresponds to the predicate transformer

$$[elems \neq \emptyset \,|\, elems := \emptyset \,]$$

which is defined for any predicate P as follows:

$$[elems \neq \emptyset \,|\, elems := \emptyset \,]P \quad \Leftrightarrow \quad elems \neq \emptyset \wedge [elems := \emptyset]P$$

The soundness of a machine in B is given by *proof obligations* which verify that

---

[1] In B, abstract sets are nonempty and finite.

- The initial state satisfies the invariant.
- The invariant is preserved by the operations.
- The call of an operation must satisfy its precondition.

Some other clauses allow the introduction of constants (CONSTANTS) constrained by PROPERTIES.

An abstract specification can be materialized as an implementation by a mechanism of refinement. The abstract machine acts as the interface of the implementation: although the machine will be implemented by low level concrete variables, the user of a machine is always concerned by the variables and the operations defined at the abstract level. For example, in a real implementation of our system, we can implement the preceding singleton using a boolean variable, full, indicating whether the set is empty and a variable storing the singleton element managed by an instance of the BASIC_ARRAY_VAR machine. We refine the previous Singleton machine by the following IMPLEMENTATION machine:

IMPLEMENTATION Singleton_r(ELEM)
REFINES Singleton
CONCRETE_VARIABLES full
  IMPORTS BASIC_ARRAY_VAR(0..0,ELEM) /* *generic array memory* */
INVARIANT
       full ∈ BOOL
∧ (full = TRUE ⇒ (elems ≠ ∅ ∧ elem = arr_vrb(0)))
∧ (elems ≠ ∅ ⇒ full = TRUE)
INITIALISATION
  full := FALSE
OPERATIONS
add(el) ≜
  BEGIN
    STR_ARRAY(0,el); /* *store el at index 0* */
    full := TRUE
  END;
suppress ≜ **BEGIN** full := FALSE **END**;
el ⟵ extract ≜ **BEGIN** el ⟵ VAL_ARRAY(0); full := FALSE **END**;
bb ⟵ empty ≜ **IF** full = TRUE **THEN** bb := FALSE **ELSE** bb := TRUE **END**;
bb ⟵ nonempty ≜ **BEGIN** bb := full **END**;
bb ⟵ contains(el) ≜
  VAR vv **IN**
    vv ⟵ VAL_ARRAY(0);
    IF full = TRUE ∧ el = vv **THEN** bb := TRUE **ELSE** bb := FALSE **END**
  END
END

The invariant of a refinement relates the abstract variables to the concrete ones and is called the "coupling invariant". From a user's point of view, operations provided by Singleton are also provided by Singleton_r; we cannot distinguish a call to a refined operation from a call to the abstract one.

The validity of a refinement is guaranteed by proof obligations: each concrete operation must be simulated by its abstract operation such that coupling invariant is preserved. Each abstract operation must be refined.

4   Expressing Bossa Specifications in B

This section describes how event types and scheduling policies specified in Bossa can be translated into B machines. The event types are translated into a B machine that models the abstract behavior of a scheduler. A Bossa specification is then translated into a refinement of this abstract scheduler. Thus, verifying the correctness of a Bossa specification amounts to verifying a refinement, which requires discharging a set of automatically generated proof obligations. We use the Rate Monotonic policy [5] presented in Section 2.1 to illustrate this approach.

In our approach, the information given by a Bossa scheduling policy is gradually taken into account at several levels of refinement. Figure 2 represents the architecture of the B project used in the conformance verification of the RM scheduling policy.

- The **scheduler** machine describes an abstract scheduler specified by Bossa event types.
- The **Classes** machine included by the **scheduler** machine defines classes of states and their transitions.
- The **rm** machine describes the rate monotonic policy as a refinement of the machine **scheduler**.
- The **RmTrans** machine and its refinements **RmTrans_r1** and **RmTrans_r2** describe transitions between rate monotonic policy states.
- The machines **Singleton**, **Queue**, **SelectQueue** and **VoidSet** describe the various collections of processes that can be used by a Bossa policy.

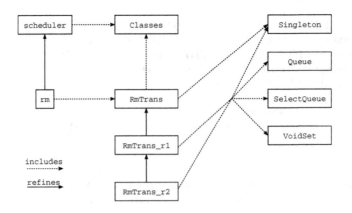

Fig. 2. Architecture of the B project

Remarks

- The preceding architecture does not depend on the scheduling policy. The machine `Classes` specifies state classes that are generic to the Bossa language. This machine can be used unchanged for all scheduling policies. The machines `Singleton`, `Queue`, `SelectQueue` and `VoidSet` specify various kinds of collections of processes that are similarly generic. The machine `scheduler` is specific to the event types for a given OS, but can be used with any policy designed for that OS. The remaining machines have generic roles, but policy-specific definitions. Of these, the machine `rm` specifies the considered policy (rate monotonic here), while the machine `RmTrans` and its refinements `RmTrans_r1` and `RmTrans_r2` specify the various states defined by the policy and the elementary transitions between them.
- The B source code of these machines could be generated automatically from the Bossa event types and from the Bossa specification of a policy.

4.1   Encoding the Event Types

The event types are defined in terms of a collection of abstract state classes. The B machine `Classes` associates each state class with the collection of processes that it contains. These collections are defined in terms of an abstract set of processes (Process), so that conformance proofs will not depend on the actual set of processes. Each state class is associated with a disjoint subset of Process. Because Bossa assumes that the target architecture has only one processor, the RUNNING state class can contain at most one process. This constraint is represented by creating a variable `running` to record the process in this state class and specifying that `Running` is either the empty set or a singleton set containing the value of this variable. The `Classes` machine also defines state transition operations. These operations either move a process from one class to another, e.g. the `CBlockedToTerminated` operation or allow an unbounded number of state changes between two given state classes, e.g. the `CReadyBlocked` operation.

MACHINE Classes
SETS
    Process
VARIABLES
    Running, Ready, Blocked, Terminated, running
INVARIANT
    Running $\subseteq$ Process
&   Ready $\subseteq$ Process
&   Blocked $\subseteq$ Process
&   Terminated $\subseteq$ Process
&   running $\in$ Process
&   Running $\cap$ Ready $= \emptyset$
&   Running $\cap$ Terminated $= \emptyset$
&   Running $\cap$ Blocked $= \emptyset$

```
&          Ready ∩ Terminated = ∅
&          Ready ∩ Blocked = ∅
&          Terminated ∩ Blocked = ∅
&          (Running ≠ ∅ ⇒ Running = {running})
```

INITIALISATION
```
        Running, Ready, Blocked, Terminated := ∅,∅,∅,∅
||      running :∈ Process /* running becomes an element of Process
```
OPERATIONS
```
  CBlockedToTerminated(tgt) ≙
   PRE tgt ∈ Blocked THEN
      Blocked :=Blocked - {tgt} || Terminated := Terminated ∪ {tgt}
   END;
  CReadyBlocked ≙
   ANY rr WHERE rr ⊆ Ready THEN
      Ready := Ready - rr || Blocked := Blocked ∪ rr
   END
   . . .
END
```

The event types describe the state changes allowed between the state classes. They are expressed by the scheduler abstract machine, which includes the Classes machine defined above and an operation for each event. The system to be built is supposed open and preconditions of the events specify call conditions.

We illustrate the translation of a set of event types to a B machine using the rules for process.end and unblock.preemptive presented in Section 2.1. The event type for process.end is below. This rule indicates that when the event occurs, the targeted process (tgt) is blocked and the event handler must cause the process to become terminated.

MACHINE scheduler
INCLUDES Classes
OPERATIONS
```
. . .
/*
[tgt in BLOCKED] -> [tgt in TERMINATED]
*/
Process_end(tgt) ≙
  PRE tgt : Process & tgt ∈ Blocked THEN
    CBlockedToTerminated(tgt)
  END
. . .
END
```

Event types can also be non-deterministic. For example, the type for unblock.-preemptive, reproduced below, allows three different behaviors if the target process is blocked, and specifies additional behaviors if the target process is

running or ready. In the B translation, SELECT is used to identify the current
state classes of relevant processes and CHOICE expresses the non-determinism.

```
/*
[tgt in BLOCKED] -> [tgt in READY]
[p in RUNNING, tgt in BLOCKED] -> [[p,tgt] in READY]
[tgt in BLOCKED] -> [tgt in BLOCKED]
[tgt in RUNNING] -> []
[tgt in READY] -> []
*/
```
Unblock_preemptive(tgt) $\triangleq$
  PRE tgt : Process $\land$ tgt $\in$ (Running $\cup$ Ready $\cup$ Blocked) **THEN**
    SELECT tgt $\in$ Blocked $\land$ Running $\neq \emptyset$ **THEN**
      CHOICE CRunningBlockedToReadyReady(tgt)
        OR CBlockedToReady(tgt)
      END
    WHEN tgt $\in$ Blocked $\land$ Running $= \emptyset$ **THEN** CBlockedToReady(tgt)
    WHEN PTRUE **THEN** skip
    END
  END

Remark. In the scheduler machine, we have only specified the transitions that
can be performed between state classes. The Bossa event types also specify when
transitions are allowed within a state class as is represented by the rule [tgt
in BLOCKED] -> [tgt in BLOCKED] of the unblock.preemptive event type.
While this transition could be expressed in B by refining the specification of the
state classes, we have not done so to maintain readability. It follows that in our
B model, state changes within a class are always allowed.

4.2 Encoding a Scheduling Policy

A scheduling policy is introduced as a refinement of the abstract scheduler. It
redefines the scheduling events using its own states, which refine the previously
introduced state classes. The management of policy-specific states is introduced
gradually in order to factorize some of the proof obligations.

- The first refinement level introduces the representation of states in terms of
  collections of processes. In order to establish the link between policy states
  and state classes, the machine Classes is included. Elementary state transitions are defined and apply both to policy states and state classes.
- The next refinement level drops the state classes, which are not used in the
  implementation. However, this machine inherits the link between states and
  state classes established by the first level.
- The last refinement level introduces the implementation of state membership.

Data Representation. The data structures used at the abstract level ensure the correctness of state changes while preserving some properties, e.g. a process cannot be lost, cardinality constraints are enforced. The preservation of these properties is established by verifying proof obligations. At the abstract level, states are represented by sets and checking the state of a process amounts to testing set membership. In order to simplify the proof of the conformity of scheduling policies, abstract machines defining sets of processes are provided. Generally, they provide insertion and extraction operations. We have developed a library of such machines with their efficient implementations.

- The `Singleton` machine (see Section 3) is used when there is at most one process in a given state. Its insertion operation is preconditioned so that processes cannot be overridden and its invariant ensures the cardinality constraint. This machine supports Bossa states declared as `process` (`running` and `yield` for RM).
- The `Queue` machine can contain any number of processes. This machine supports Bossa states declared as `queue` (`blocked` and `computation_ended` for RM).
- The `SelectQueue` machine is used when a state can contain any number of processes and processes in this state can be accessed in sorted order using the Bossa operator `select`. This machine support Bossa states declared as `select queue` (`ready` for RM).
- The `VoidSet` is used when a state does not record any processes. This machine supports Bossa states for which no implementation is specified (`terminated` for RM). The machine does not provide observation operations so that its implementation does not store any process.

State Transitions. The machine `RmTrans` establishes the link between policy states and states classes. Once established, this invariant is reused by machines including or refining `RmTrans`. To establish the link, `RmTrans` includes both the `Classes` machine and machines for each kind of state.[2] The invariant of `RmTrans` specifies how states classes are split into disjoint concrete states. In order to preserve this invariant, operations are defined as acting both on concrete states and on state classes. For example, `RMRunning2Yield` applies if running is non empty and yield is empty. The running process is deleted from the running state and added to the yield state. This operation is in parallel performed on state classes: `CRunning2Ready` is also called, as `Ready` is the state class of `yield`.

MACHINE `RmTrans`
INCLUDES
  `Classes,`
  `ru.Singleton(Process),`   /* *running state* */
  `rd.SelectQueue(Process,period),` /* *ready state* */

---

[2] The notation INCLUDES `pr.m` includes the machine `m` and adds the prefix `pr` to the identifiers of `m` in order to avoid any conflict.

```
yl.Singleton(Process),      /* yield state */
bl.Queue(Process),          /* blocked state */
ce.Queue(Process),          /* computation_ended state */
tm.VoidSet(Process)         /* terminated state */
```
INVARIANT
$$\text{bl.elems} \cap \text{ce.elems} = \emptyset$$
$$\land\ \text{rd.elems} \cap \text{yl.elems} = \emptyset$$
$$\land\ \text{Running} = \text{ru.elems}$$
$$\land\ \text{Ready} = \text{rd.elems} \cup \text{yl.elems}$$
$$\land\ \text{Blocked} = \text{bl.elems} \cup \text{ce.elems}$$
$$\land\ \text{Terminated} = \text{tm.elems}$$
OPERATIONS
RMRunning2Yield $\triangleq$
    PRE ru.elems $\neq \emptyset \land$ yl.elems $= \emptyset$ **THEN**
      yl.add(ru.elem) || ru.suppress || CRunning2Ready
    END;
  . . .
END

Elimination of Abstract Data. The refinement step RmTrans_r1 is used to redefine operations without managing state classes. The Classes machine is no longer included and operations only act on policy states.

REFINEMENT RmTrans_r1 **REFINES** RmTrans
INCLUDES
    ru.Singleton(Process), rd.SelectQueue(Process,period),
    yl.Singleton(Process), bl.Queue(Process),
    ce.Queue(Process), tm.VoidSet(Process)
OPERATIONS
RMRunning2Yield $\triangleq$
    BEGIN yl.add(ru.elem) || ru.suppress **END**;
  . . .
END

State Membership. The data-representation machines provide an abstract variable (elems) containing the set of processes in the corresponding state. In Bossa, the implementation of state membership relies on an attribute attached to each process. It is represented in B by the variable state: Process $\rightarrow$ State which is introduced in a new refinement. Its declaration is split into INVARIANT and ASSERTIONS. The ASSERTIONS clause is proved once as being implied by the invariant. Then, the preservation of the assertion predicates is ensured provided the invariant is preserved.

REFINEMENT RmTrans_r2 **REFINES** RmTrans_r1
SETS

```
State = {RmNowhere, RmRunning, RmReady, RmBlocked, RmCompEnded,
         RmYield, RmTerminated}
```
INCLUDES
```
bl.Queue,
  ...
```
VARIABLES
```
state
```
INVARIANT
```
/* state is a relation between Process and State */
state : Process ↔ State
∧ state = Process × {RmNowhere} <+ /* definition of the state */
   (rd.elems × {RmReady} ∪        /* relation */
    bl.elems × {RmBlocked} ∪
    ce.elems × {RmCompEnded} ∪
    yl.elems × {RmYield} ∪
    ru.elems × {RmRunning} ∪
    tm.elems × {RmTerminated})
```
ASSERTIONS
```
state :  Process → State /* the relation is functional */
```

The introduction of the `state` variable avoids referencing abstract sets of states for testing state membership. The refinement `RmTrans_r2` thus uses the operations of the data-collection abstract machines instead of their abstract variables.

The Algorithm. The scheduling policy is defined as a refinement of the abstract scheduler. Its B code is translated from the Bossa specification. As compared to the abstract scheduler, some tests are added in order to get the current concrete state of a process and to call the correct state transition operation.

For example, the handler for the `unblock.preemptive` event is specified in Bossa as follows:

```
On unblock.preemptive {
  if (e.target in blocked) {
    if ((!empty(running)) && (e.target > running)) {
      running => ready;
    }
    e.target => ready;
  }
}
```

The translation of this handler to B is immediate. Note that the process comparison `p1 > p2` is translated into `period(p1) < period(p2)`, thus inlining the ordering criteria defined in Section 2.1. Furthermore, policy specific variables are introduced. The Rate Monotonic policy described in Bossa defines a counter (`missed_deadlines`) and a timer variable.

```
REFINEMENT rm REFINES scheduler
INCLUDES RmTrans  /* state transition machine */
VARIABLES
  missed_deadlines, timer  /* policy specific variables */
INVARIANT
  missed_deadlines : Process --> NATURAL
& timer : Process --> INTEGER
INITIALISATION
  missed_deadlines := Process * {0} || timer := Process * {0}
OPERATIONS
  Unblock_preemptive(tgt) ≜
    VAR isbk IN
      isbk <-- RMisBlocked(tgt);
      IF isbk = TRUE THEN
        VAR hru IN
          hru <-- RMhasRunning;
          IF hru = TRUE ∧ period(tgt) < period(running) THEN
            RMRunning2Ready
          END;
          RMBlocked2Ready(tgt)
        END
      END
    END
END
```

Proof obligations generated for this machine express that it is a refinement of the abstract scheduler. They are the main properties that must be checked in order to ensure that the scheduling policy complies with the event types associated with the underlying kernel.

5   Proof Automation

The proof obligations generated for the preceding Bossa/B development are not automatically proved by the provers available with Atelier B. Although, it should be possible to add some tactics for discharging some of the remaining proofs, this section instead introduces a decidable logic fragment that supports the expression of proof obligations. It follows that their verification is automatic. We believe that identifying logic fragments for automating the proof process is essential for the scalability of a proof based approach.

5.1   An Overview of Monadic Second Order Logic and Mona

Definition 1 (S1S and WS1S logics). *Let* $\{x_1, \ldots, x_n\}$ *be a set of first order variables and* $\{X_1, \ldots, X_n\}$ *a set of monadic second order variables. A minimal grammar for these logics is defined as follows:*

- *A term t is inductively defined by:*

$$t ::= 0 \mid x_i \mid s(t)s \text{ is the successor symbol}$$

- *A formula f is inductively defined by:*

$$
\begin{aligned}
f ::= & t \in X_i \quad \text{set membership} \\
& \mid \neg f \mid f \wedge f \\
& \mid \exists_1 x_i.\ f \quad \text{first order quantification} \\
& \mid \exists_2 X_i.\ f \quad \text{second order (set) quantification}
\end{aligned}
$$

This syntax is extended as usual by first order operators and quantifiers $(\vee, \Rightarrow, \forall \ldots)$ and some arithmetic relations. For example, $a \leq b$ is defined by $\forall_2 X.\ X(a) \wedge (\forall_1 x.\ X(x) \Rightarrow X(s(x))) \Rightarrow X(b)$.

Validity of a formula. A closed formula is valid in S1S or WS1S if it is valid in the interpretation on the set $\mathbb{N}$ of natural numbers, where s is the successor function, first order variables relate to the natural numbers and second order variables to the subsets (finite in the case of WS1S) of $\mathbb{N}$. These two logics are decidable [11]. WS1S is concerned with finite sets only while S1S is also concerned with infinite sets. The Mona tool [6] implements a decision procedure for WS1S.

With respect to our study, we can use Mona to decide some of our proof obligations, specifically those that concern individual processes and sets of processes (regardless of the effective number of processes).

5.2   A Translation Example

As an example of the use of Mona in discharging proof obligations, we consider the proof obligations associated with the refinement of the `ReadyToRunning` operation. According to the B method, the proof obligation for a refinement of an abstract preconditioned operation op_a by a concrete operation op_r is:

$$
\begin{aligned}
& \text{Inv}_a(st_a) \\
& \wedge \ \text{Inv}_r(st_a, st_r) \wedge \text{Pre\_op}(st_a) \wedge op_r(st_r, st'_r) \\
& \Rightarrow \exists st'_a : \quad op_a(st_a, st'_a) \\
& \qquad\qquad\quad \wedge \text{Inv}_r(st'_a, st'_r)
\end{aligned}
$$

where:

- $\text{Inv}_a(st_a)$(resp. Inv_r) is the invariant of the abstract (resp. of the concrete) machine,[3]
- Pre_op is the precondition of the abstract operation,
- $op_a(st_a, st'_a)$(resp. $op_r(st_r, st'_r)$) is the before-after predicate of the abstract (resp. concrete) operation.

---

[3] The invariant of the refinement is expressed over the product of the abstract and concrete states in order to express the so called "coupling" invariant between the abstraction and the concretization.

Informally, the preceding formula says that each concrete step op_r can be simulated by an abstract step op_a so that the coupling invariant Inv_r is preserved.

Given the abstract and refined states introduced in Section 4.2, we can express the preceding proof obligation within Mona as follows (the complete Mona text is given in the appendix A):

```
all2 Ready, Running, Terminated, Blocked:
all1 running,running':
all2 rdelems, ruelems, ylelems,
      rdelems', ruelems', ylelems':
all1 rdelem, ruelem, ylelem,
      rdelem', ruelem', ylelem':
        Inv_a(Ready, Running, Terminated, Blocked, running)
    &   Inv_r(Ready, Running, Terminated, Blocked, running,
            rdelems,rdelem,ruelems,ruelem,ylelems,ylelem)
    &   pre_RunningToReady_a(Ready, Running, Terminated, Blocked, running)
    &   RunningToReady_r(rdelems,rdelem,ruelems,ruelem,ylelems,ylelem,
            rdelems',rdelem',ruelems',ruelem',ylelems',ylelem')
   => ex2  Ready',Running',Terminated',Blocked': ex1 running':
        RunningToReady_a(Ready, Running, Terminated, Blocked, running,
                         Ready',Running',Terminated',Blocked',running')
    &  Inv_r(Ready', Running', Terminated', Blocked',running',
            rdelems',rdelem',ruelems',ruelem',ylelems',ylelem');
```

Thanks to its decision procedure, the Mona tool establishes that the preceding predicate is valid. It outputs the following result:

```
AUTOMATON CONSTRUCTION
100% completed
Time: 00:00:00.01

Automaton has 1 state and 1 BDD-node

ANALYSIS
Formula is valid
```

6   Related Work

A large number of DSLs have been developed for a wide range of domains [12]. Many of these DSLs provide no verification, and those that do typically either rely on verification provided by a general-purpose host language [10] or use ad hoc analyzers, as was originally done for Bossa. The former approach is, however, limited to the facilities of the host language, which are rarely adequate for expressing and checking domain-specific properties, while the latter puts a huge burden on the DSL developer.

The DSLs Promela++ [3] and ESP [8] both provide both standard code generators and translators to code suitable for use with the SPIN model checker.

While these approaches are in the spirit of the work presented here, the state explosion problem implies that these languages use model checking for bug finding, but not complete verification. Furthermore, these approaches require specifying properties in the general-purpose specification language of SPIN, while the Bossa event types are domain-specific. Indeed, the high-level of the event type specification is crucial to enable our refinement-based approach.

7   Conclusion

DSLs provide a high-level means of implementing solutions to complex problems within a given domain. When the domain has critical safety or security requirements, verification of these implementations is essential. In this paper, we have shown a systematic means of using the B formal method to verify a process scheduling policy implemented using the Bossa DSL. This verification covers within a single framework both verification of the scheduler structure, as also provided by existing Bossa verification tools, and verification of part of the implementation strategy (i.e., the use of the `state` function to optimize state membership tests), which is not covered by the Bossa verifier. In the development presented here, most of the work can be reused directly for verification of other scheduling policies, except for the proofs related to the event handler definitions themselves (i.e., the second part of Section 4.2). However, using a dedicated decision procedure such as Mona should help in automating the verification of most of the proof obligations. In future work, we plan to generalize this part of the development as well, to produce an executable code and hence a certified Bossa compiler. We will also consider how this approach can be applied to other DSLs.

Acknowledgement

This work was supported in part by the CORSS:"Composition et raffinement de systèmes sûrs" project of program "ACI: Sécurité Informatique" supported by the French Ministry of Research and New Technologies.

References

1. J.-R. Abrial. *The B-Book: Assigning programs to meanings.* Cambridge University Press, 1996.
2. F. Badeau and A. Amelot. Using B as a high level programming language in an industrial project: Roissy VAL. In H. Treharne, S. King, M. Henson, and S. Schneider, editors, *ZB 2005: Formal Specification and Development in Z and B*, volume 2215 of *Lecture Notes in Computer Science*, pages 298–315. Springer-Verlag, Guildford, UK, april 2005.
3. A. Basu, M. Hayden, G. Morrisett, and T. von Eicken. A language-based approach to protocol construction. In *Proceedings of the ACM SIGPLAN Workshop on Domain Specific Languages*, Paris, France, Jan. 1997.

4. P. Behm, P. Desforges, and J.-M. Meynadier. Météor : An industrial success in formal development. In D. Bert, editor, *B'98: Recent Advances in the Development and Use of the B Method, Second International B Conference, Montpellier*, volume 1393 of *Lecture Notes in Computer Science*, page 26. Springer-Verlag, 1998.

5. F. Cottet, J. Delacroix, C. Kaiser, and Z. Mammeri. *Scheduling in Real-Time Systems*. Wiley, West Sussex, England, 2002.

6. J. Henriksen, J. Jensen, M. Jorgensen, N. Klarlund, R. Paige, T. Rauhe, and A. Sandholm. Mona: Monadic second-order logic in practice. In *Workshop on Tools and Algorithms for the Construction and Analysis of Systems*, http://www.brics.dk/~mona, pages 58–73, Aarhus, May 1995.

7. Jaluna. Jaluna Osware. http://www.jaluna.com.

8. S. Kumar, Y. Mandelbaum, X. Yu, and K. Li. ESP: a language for programmable devices. In *Proceedings of the ACM SIGPLAN'01 conference on Programming Language Design and Implementation*, pages 309–320, Snowbird, UT, June 2001.

9. J. Lawall, A.-F. Le Meur, and G. Muller. On designing a target-independent DSL for safe OS process-scheduling components. In *Third International Conference on Generative Programming and Component Engineering (GPCE'04)*, volume 3286 of *Lecture Notes in Computer Science*, pages 436–455, Vancouver, October 2004. Springer-Verlag.

10. D. Leijen and E. Meijer. Domain specific embedded compilers. In *Proceedings of the Second Conference on Domain-Specific Languages (DSL '99)*, pages 109–122, Austin, TX, Oct. 1999.

11. W. Thomas. Automata on infinite objects. In J. Leeuwen, editor, *Handbook of Theoretical Computer Science*, pages 133–192. MIT Press, 1990.

12. A. van Deursen, P. Klint, and J. Visser. Domain-specific languages: An annotated bibliography. *ACM SIGPLAN Notices*, 35(6):26–36, June 2000.

A   Mona Expression of a Proof Obligation

```
1    pred ajouter(var2 elems, var1 el, var2 elems') =
         elems' = elems union {el}
     ;
     pred atmostSingleton(var2 S, var1 e) =
     /* S1S expression that a set contaits at most 1 element */
         S sub {e}
     ;
     pred Inv_a(var2 Ready, Running, Terminated, Blocked, var1 running) =
         Running inter Ready = {} & Running inter Terminated = {}
10   & Running inter Blocked = {} & Terminated inter Blocked = {}
     & Ready inter Terminated = {} & Ready inter Blocked = {}
     & atmostSingleton(Running,running)
     ;
     pred pre_RunningToReady_a(var2 Ready, Running, Terminated, Blocked,
                               var1 running) =
     Running ~= {}
     ;
     /* Running2Ready =
         PRE HasRunning THEN Ready := Ready \/ Running || Running := {} END;
20   */
```

```
pred RunningToReady_a(
  var2 Ready, Running, Terminated, Blocked, var1 running,
  var2 Ready', Running', Terminated', Blocked', var1 running') =
  Ready' = Ready union Running & Running' = {}
& Terminated' = Terminated & Blocked' = Blocked & running' = running
;
/* Running2Ready = BEGIN rd.ajouter(ru.elem) || ru.supprimer END; */

pred RunningToReady_r(
  var2 rdelems, var1 rdelem, var2 ruelems,
    var1 ruelem, var2 ylelems, var1 ylelem,
  var2 rdelems', var1 rdelem', var2 ruelems',
    var1 ruelem', var2 ylelems', var1 ylelem') =
  ajouter(rdelems,ruelem,rdelems')
& ruelems' = {} & ylelems' = ylelems & ylelem' = ylelem
;
pred Inv_r(
  var2 Ready, Running, Terminated, Blocked, var1 running,
  var2 rdelems, var1 rdelem, var2 ruelems,
  var1 ruelem, var2 ylelems, var1 ylelem) =
  rdelems = Ready \ ylelems
& Running = ruelems & ylelems sub Ready
& atmostSingleton(ylelems,ylelem) & atmostSingleton(ruelems,ruelem)
;
/* refinement proof obligation */

all2  Ready, Running, Terminated, Blocked: all1 running,running':
all2 rdelems, ruelems, ylelems, rdelems', ruelems', ylelems':
all1 rdelem, ruelem, ylelem, rdelem', ruelem', ylelem':
    Inv_a(Ready, Running, Terminated, Blocked, running)
  & Inv_r(Ready, Running, Terminated, Blocked,running,
            rdelems,rdelem,ruelems,ruelem,ylelems,ylelem)
  & pre_RunningToReady_a(Ready, Running, Terminated, Blocked, running)
  & RunningToReady_r(rdelems,rdelem,ruelems,ruelem,ylelems,ylelem,
          rdelems',rdelem',ruelems',ruelem',ylelems',ylelem')
 => ex2 Ready',Running',Terminated',Blocked': ex1 running':
  RunningToReady_a(Ready, Running, Terminated, Blocked, running,
                  Ready',Running',Terminated',Blocked',running')
  & Inv_r(Ready', Running', Terminated', Blocked',running',
            rdelems',rdelem',ruelems',ruelem',ylelems',ylelem');
```

Synthesizing B Specifications from EB³ Attribute Definitions

Frédéric Gervais[1,2], Marc Frappier[2], and Régine Laleau[3]

[1] Laboratoire CEDRIC, Institut d'Informatique d'Entreprise,
Conservatoire National des Arts et Métiers,
18 Allée Jean Rostand, 91025 Évry Cedex, France, +33 1 69 36 73 73
`frederic.gervais@usherbrooke.ca`
[2] GRIL, Département d'informatique, Université de Sherbrooke,
Sherbrooke, Québec, Canada J1K 2R1, +1 819 821-8000x2096
`marc.frappier@usherbrooke.ca`
[3] Laboratoire LACL, Université de Paris 12,
IUT Fontainebleau, Département informatique,
Route Forestière Hurtault, 77300 Fontainebleau, France, +33 1 60 74 68 40
`laleau@univ-paris12.fr`

Abstract. EB³ is a trace-based formal language created for the specification of information systems (IS). Attributes, linked to entities and associations of an IS, are computed in EB³ by recursive functions on the valid traces of the system. On the other hand, B is a state-based formal language also well adapted for the specification of IS. In this paper, we deal with the synthesis of B specifications that correspond to EB³ attribute definitions, in order to specify and verify safety properties like data integrity constraints. Each action in the EB³ specification is translated into a B operation. The substitutions are obtained by an analysis of the CAML-like patterns used in the recursive functions that define the attributes in EB³. Our technique is illustrated by an example of a simple library management system.

Keywords: Information systems, data integrity constraints, attributes, B, EB³, recursive functions, pattern matching.

1 Introduction

The framework of our project is the formal specification of information systems (IS). Broadly speaking, an IS is a system that helps an organization to collect and manipulate all its relevant data.

1.1 Motivation

There exist several paradigms to specify IS, but we are mainly interested by two specific formal languages. On one hand, EB³ [14] is a trace-based formal language specially created for the specification of IS. EB³ provides process expressions that represent the valid traces of the system and recursive functions that compute

J. Romijn, G. Smith, and J. van de Pol (Eds.): IFM 2005, LNCS 3771, pp. 207–226, 2005.

attribute values from the valid traces. On the other hand, B [1] is a state-based formal language that is well adapted to specify IS data models [10, 22, 23]. In B, state variables represent the state space of the system and invariant properties must be preserved by each operation.

We aim at defining an integrated approach that combines both EB^3 and B in order to consider not only more viewpoints, but also better mechanisms to prove or verify properties. EB^3 and B are complementary to take the main properties of IS into account [12]. In EB^3, liveness properties, especially event ordering properties, are easier to express than in a state-based language like B. On the other hand, safety properties like static data integrity constraints, which are numerous in IS, are very difficult to check in EB^3. For instance, in a library management system, a data integrity constraint requires that the number of loans of a member is always less than some maximal number. Such a property is hard to prove for an EB^3 specification. It can be verified by model checking [9], but combinatorial explosion severely limits the applicability of model checking for IS. In B, attributes are represented by state variables and updates are specified by operations. Consequently, static data integrity constraints are represented by invariant properties on the state variables. Each B operation specifies which, when and how state variables are changed by its execution. In particular, preconditions are defined and the B method provides techniques and tools to prove that invariant properties are preserved when operations are executed within their precondition.

There exist many integrated methods that combine state-based specifications with event-based specifications, like csp2B [5], CSP-OZ [11] or Circus [24]. However, none of them is well adapted for the specification of IS [15], although a first attempt with CSP || B has been proposed in [9]. An approach like Event B [3], that is a state-based language using guarded operations to represent action systems, is not appropriate, because in IS, each action of the system requires an answer, possibly an error message. Guarded operations cannot be invoked if their guards are not satisfied, whereas operations with preconditions as in B can be implemented with the relevant error messages.

1.2   Outline of the Paper

Considering the complementarity between B and EB^3 for IS specification, we are working on a development process that consists in using EB^3 to specify the functional behaviour of IS, and then to use B invariants to specify and prove safety properties about this specification. To do so, the EB^3 specification must be translated into an equivalent B specification. In [13], Frappier and Laleau have shown how to prove this equivalence using the B refinement relation. This paper proposes an algorithm to partly automate the translation from EB^3 to B. This algorithm generates: i) the state space of the B specification; ii) the substitution of each operation body that updates the state variables; iii) the weakest precondition of each operation so that the invariant of the B specification is satisfied. The only part that is missing for a complete translation is the generation of the exact operation preconditions that represent the behaviour of the EB^3 specification.

For the sake of concision, we show in this paper the main principles of the translation and we apply them to an example of a library management system. The complete algorithm and rules are presented in [18]. The paper is organized as follows. After a general introduction to EB³ in Sect. 2, Sect. 3 deals more specifically with EB³ attribute definitions. Then, Sect. 4 shows, after a short introduction to B, how to synthesize B specifications from EB³ attribute definitions. Section 5 is a discussion about the verification of static data integrity constraints. Finally, Sect. 6 concludes this paper by giving some perspectives.

2   Specifying Information Systems with the EB³ Method

The core of EB³ [14] includes a process and a formal notation to describe a complete and precise specification of the input-output behaviour of an IS. An EB³ specification consists of the following elements:

1. a user requirements class diagram which includes entities, associations, and their respective actions and attributes. These diagrams are based on the entity-relationship model concepts [8].
2. a process expression, denoted by main, which defines the valid input traces;
3. recursive functions, defined on the valid input traces of main, that assign values to entity and association attributes;
4. input-output rules, which assign an output to each valid input trace.

EB³ differs from the other process algebraic languages by the following characteristics. First of all, EB³ has been specially created for IS specification. Hence, the specification of the inputs and of the outputs of the system is divided in two parts. The semantics of EB³ is a trace-based semantics. Process expressions represent the valid input traces of the IS, while outputs are computed from valid EB³ traces. The syntax of process expressions has been simplified and adapted to IS with respect to other process algebra languages like CSP [20]. In particular, EB³ process expressions are close to regular expressions, with the use of the sequence operator and the Kleene closure (see Sect. 2.2).

The denotational semantics of an EB³ specification is given by a relation R defined on $\mathcal{T}(\text{main}) \times O$, where $\mathcal{T}(\text{main})$ denotes the finite traces accepted by main and O is the set of output events. Let trace denote the system trace, which is a list comprised of *valid* input events accepted so far in the execution of the system. Let $t::\sigma$ denote the right append of an input event σ to trace t, and let [] denote the empty trace. The operational behaviour is defined as follows.

```
trace := [];
forever do
    receive input event σ;
    if main can accept trace::σ then
        trace := trace::σ;
        send output event o such that (trace, o) ∈ R;
    else
        send error message;
```

2.1   Example: A Library Management System

We illustrate the main aspects of this paper by using a simple library management system. The system has to manage book loans to members. A book is acquired by the library. It can be discarded, but only if it is not borrowed. A member must join the library in order to borrow a book. A member can transfer a loan to another member. A member can relinquish library membership only when all his loans are returned or transferred. Figure 1 shows the user require-

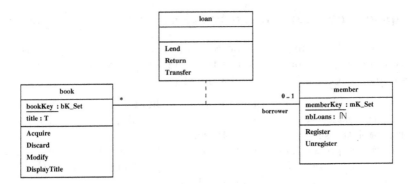

Fig. 1. EB³ specification: User requirements class diagram of the library

ments class diagram used to construct the specification. The signature of EB³ actions is the following.

```
Acquire(bId:bK_Set,bTitle:T):void
Discard(bId:bK_Set):void
Modify(bId:bK_Set,nTitle:T):void
DisplayTitle(bId:bK_Set):(title:T)
Register(mId:mK_Set):void
Unregister(mId:mK_Set):void
Lend(bId:bk_Set,mId:mK_Set):void
Return(bId:bK_Set):void
Transfer(bId:bK_Set,mId:mK_Set):void
```

The special type void is used to denote an action with no input-output rule; the output of such an action is always ok.

2.2   Process Expressions

An input event σ is an instantiation of (the input parameters of) an action. The signature of an action a is given by a declaration

$$a(q_1 : T_1, \ldots, q_n : T_n) : (q_{n+1} : T_{n+1}, \ldots, q_m : T_m)$$

where $q_1, \ldots, q_n$ are input parameters of types $T_1, \ldots, T_n$ and $q_{n+1}, \ldots, q_m$ are output parameters of types $T_{n+1}, \ldots, T_m$. An instantiated action $\mathsf{a}(t_1, \ldots, t_n)$ also constitutes an elementary process expression. The special symbol "_" may be used as an actual parameter of an action, to denote an arbitrary value of the corresponding type. Complex EB³ process expressions can be constructed from elementary process expressions (instantiated actions) using the following operators: sequence (.), choice (|), Kleene closure (^*), interleaving (|||), parallel composition (|| , *i.e.,* CSP's synchronisation on shared actions), guard (==>), process call, and quantification of choice (|x:T: ...) and interleaving (|||x:T: ...). The EB³ notation for process expressions is similar to Hoare's CSP [20]. The complete syntax and semantics of EB³ can be found in [14].

For instance, the EB³ process expression for entity type *book* is of the following form:

```
book(bId : bK_Set) =
Acquire(bId,_).
(
    ( | mId : mK_Set : loan(mId,bId) )^*
  |||
    Modify(bId,_)^*
  |||
    DisplayTitle(bId)^*
).
Discard(bId)
```

where `loan` is the process expression for association *loan*; the definition of `loan` has been omitted for the sake of concision. Firstly, book entity `bId` is produced by action `Acquire`. Then, it can be borrowed by only one member entity `mId` at once (quantified choice " | mId : mK_Set : ..."). Indeed, process expression `book` calls process expression `loan`, that involves actions `Lend`, `Return` and `Transfer`. The Kleene closure on `loan` means that an arbitrary number of loans can be made on book entity `bId`. At any moment, actions `Modify` and `DisplayTitle` can be interleaved with the actions of `loan`. Action `Modify` is used to change the title of the book, while action `DisplayTitle` outputs the title of the book. Finally, book entity `bId` is consumed by action `Discard`. The complete process expressions for the example are given in [18].

2.3   Input-Output Rules

The system trace is usually accessed through recursive functions that extract relevant information from it. Relation R is defined using input-output rules and recursive functions on the system trace. Input-output rules are of the following form:

> RULE *Name*
> Input *ActionLabel*
> Output *RecursiveFunction*
> END;

For instance, the following input-output rule is defined for action `DisplayTitle`:

```
RULE R
Input DisplayTitle(bId)
Output title(trace,bId)
END;
```

When action `DisplayTitle` is a valid input event, then the recursive function `title` is called to compute the value of attribute *title*. Such recursive functions defining attributes are presented in Sect. 3.

3   EB³ Attribute Definitions

In IS, attributes of associations and entities are the main elements, because they represent the knowledge contained in the IS that can be read to answer requests from users or updated to reflect evolutions of the IS. In EB³, the definition of an attribute is a recursive function on the traces accepted by process expression `main`. This function computes the attribute value. There are two kinds of attributes in a requirements class diagram: key attributes and non-key attributes.

3.1   Defining Key and Non-key Attributes in EB³

In the following definitions, we distinguish functional terms from conditional terms. A *functional term* is a term composed of constants, variables and functions of other functional terms. To make the translation into B easier, we consider only in these terms operators that are defined in the B language. The data types in which constants and variables are defined can be abstract or enumerated sets, useful basic types like $\mathbb{N}, \mathbb{Z}, \ldots$, Cartesian product of data types and finite powerset of data types. A *conditional term* is of the form **if** *pred* **then** w_1 **else** w_2 **end**, where *pred* is a predicate without quantifiers and w_i is either a conditional term or a functional term. Hence, a conditional term can include nested **if** statements, whereas a functional term cannot contain an **if** statement.

Key Definitions. A key is used in IS to identify entities of entity types or associations: each key value corresponds to a distinct entity of the entity type. The key of an association is formed with the keys of its corresponding entity types. Let e be an entity type with a key composed of attributes $k_1, \ldots, k_m$. In EB³, the key of e is defined by a *single* attribute definition for the set $\{k_1, \ldots, k_m\}$; it is a total function $eKey$ of the following form:

$$eKey\ (s : \mathcal{T}(\text{main})) : \mathbb{F}(T_1 \times \cdots \times T_m) \ \triangleq$$
$$\textbf{match } last(s) \textbf{ with}$$
$$\bot \qquad : u_0,$$
$$a_1(\overrightarrow{p_1}) : u_1,$$
$$\ldots$$
$$a_n(\overrightarrow{p_n}) : u_n,$$
$$\_ \qquad : eKey(front(s));$$

where $T_1, \ldots, T_m$ denote the types of key attributes $k_1, \ldots, k_m$ and expression $\mathbb{F}(S)$ denotes the set of finite subsets of set S. A key function typically returns the set of key values of the active (created) entities of the entity type. A recursive function definition is always given in this CAML-like style (CAML is a functional language [7]). Standard list operators are used, such as *last* and *front* which respectively return the last element and all but the last element of the list; they return the special value $\perp$ when the list is empty.

Expressions $\perp : u_0$, $a_1(\overrightarrow{p_1}) : u_1$, ..., $a_n(\overrightarrow{p_n}) : u_n$ and $\_ : eKey(front(s))$ are called *input clauses*. In an input clause, expression $a_i(\overrightarrow{p_i})$ denotes a *pattern matching* expression, where a_i denotes an action label and $\overrightarrow{p_i}$ denotes a list whose elements are either variables, or the special symbol '$\_$' which stands for a wildcard, or ground functional terms. Special symbol '$\perp$' in input clause $\perp : u_0$ pattern matches with the empty trace, while symbol '$\_$' in $\_ : eKey(front(s))$ is used to pattern match with any list element. Expressions $u_0, \ldots, u_n$ denote functional terms. Let $var(e)$ denote the free variables of e. For each input clause, we have $var(u_i) \subseteq var(\overrightarrow{p_i})$. The syntax of key definitions is given in [19].

For example, the key of entity type book is defined by:

$$bookKey(s : \mathcal{T}(\text{main})) : \mathbb{F}(bK\_Set) \triangleq$$
$$\textbf{match } last(s) \textbf{ with}$$
$$\perp \qquad\qquad : \emptyset,$$
$$\textsf{Acquire}(bId, \_) : bookKey(front(s)) \cup \{bId\},$$
$$\textsf{Discard}(bId) \quad : bookKey(front(s)) - \{bId\},$$
$$\_ \qquad\qquad : bookKey(front(s));$$

Non-key Attributes. The definition of a non-key attribute is quite similar. A non-key attribute depends on the key of the entity type or of the association. In EB^3, each non-key attribute b_i is defined as follows.

$$b_i\ (s : \mathcal{T}(\text{main}), \overrightarrow{k} : T_1 \times \cdots \times T_m) : T_i \triangleq$$
$$\textbf{match } last(s) \textbf{ with}$$
$$\perp \qquad : u_0,$$
$$a_1(\overrightarrow{p_1}) : u_1,$$
$$\ldots$$
$$a_n(\overrightarrow{p_n}) : u_n,$$
$$\_ \qquad : b_i(front(s), \overrightarrow{k});$$

Parameter $\overrightarrow{k} = (k_1, \ldots, k_m)$ denotes the list of key attributes, and $T_1, \ldots, T_m$ are the types of $k_1, \ldots, k_m$. The codomain T_i is the type of non-key attribute b_i. It always includes $\perp$ to represent undefinedness; hence, EB^3 recursive functions are always total. Moreover, all the functions and operators are strict, *i.e.*, $\perp$ is mapped to $\perp$.

In non-key attribute definitions, expressions $u_0, \ldots, u_n$ denote either functional or conditional terms. For each input clause, we have $var(u_j) \subseteq var(\overrightarrow{p_j}) \cup var(\overrightarrow{k})$. Any reference to a key $eKey$ or to an attribute b_j (j can be equal to i)

in an input clause is always of the form $eKey(front(s))$ or $b_j(front(s), ...)$. The syntax of non-key attributes is provided by [19].

For example, the definitions of attributes *title* and *nbLoans* are the following ones.

$$title(s : \mathcal{T}(main), bId : bK\_Set) : T \; \triangleq$$

$\quad$ **match** $last(s)$ **with**

$\bot$	$: \bot,$	(I1)
$\mathsf{Acquire}(bId, bTitle)$	$: bTitle,$	(I2)
$\mathsf{Discard}(bId)$	$: \bot,$	(I3)
$\mathsf{Modify}(bId, nTitle)$	$: nTitle,$	(I4)
$-$	$: title(front(s), bId);$	(I5)

$$nbLoans(s : \mathcal{T}(main), mId : mK\_Set) : \mathbb{N} \; \triangleq$$

$\quad$ **match** $last(s)$ **with**

$\quad \bot \qquad\qquad\qquad\quad : \bot,$

$\quad \mathsf{Register}(mId) \qquad\; : 0,$

$\quad \mathsf{Lend}(\_, mId) \qquad\quad : 1 \; + \; nbLoans(front(s), mId),$

$\quad \mathsf{Return}(bId) \qquad\qquad : \textbf{if } mId = borrower(front(s), bId)$

$\qquad\qquad\qquad\qquad\qquad \textbf{then } nbLoans(mId) \; - \; 1 \textbf{ end},$

$\quad \mathsf{Transfer}(bId, mId') : \textbf{if } mId = mId'$

$\qquad\qquad\qquad\qquad\qquad \textbf{then } nbLoans(front(s), mId) \; + \; 1$

$\qquad\qquad\qquad\qquad\qquad \textbf{else if } mId = borrower(front(s), bId)$

$\qquad\qquad\qquad\qquad\qquad\qquad \textbf{then } nbLoans(front(s), mId) \; - \; 1 \textbf{ end}$

$\qquad\qquad\qquad\qquad \textbf{end},$

$\quad \mathsf{Unregister}(mId) \qquad : \bot,$

$\quad - \qquad\qquad\qquad\qquad : nbLoans(front(s), mId);$

Since any reference to a key $eKey$ or to an attribute b in an input clause is always of the form $eKey(front(s))$ or $b(front(s), k_1, ..., k_m)$, expression $front(s)$ is now omitted in the next references to recursive functions in the paper, *e.g.*, $eKey$ and $b(k_1, ..., k_m)$.

3.2   Computation of Attribute Values and Properties

When the function associated to attribute b is evaluated with valid trace s as input parameter, then all the input clauses of the attribute definition are analysed. Let $b(s, v_1, ..., v_n)$ be the attribute to evaluate and ρ be the substitution $\overrightarrow{k} := v_1, ..., v_n$. Each input clause $a_i(\overrightarrow{p_i}) : u_i$ generates a pattern condition of the form

$$\exists \, (var(\overrightarrow{p_i}) - \overrightarrow{k}) \bullet last(s) = a_i(\overrightarrow{p_i}) \, \rho \; .$$

where the right-hand side of the equation denotes the application of substitution ρ on input clause $a_i(\overrightarrow{p_i})$. Such a pattern condition holds if the parameters of the last action of trace s match the values of variables $\overrightarrow{k}$ in $\overrightarrow{p_i}$. The first pattern condition that holds in the attribute definition is the one evaluated. Hence, the ordering of these input clauses is important.

When a pattern condition $a(\overrightarrow{p}) : u$ evaluates to true, an assignment of a value for each variable in $var(\overrightarrow{p})$ has been determined. Functional terms are directly used to compute the attribute value. Predicates of conditional terms determine the remaining free variables of u in function of the key values and/or the values of $last(s)$.

For instance, we have the following values for $title$ (see Sect. 3.1):

$$title([\,], b_1) \overset{(I1)}{=} \bot$$
$$title([\mathsf{Register}(m_1)], b_1) \overset{(I5)}{=} title([\,], b_1) \overset{(I1)}{=} \bot$$
$$title([\mathsf{Register}(m_1), \mathsf{Acquire}(b_1, t_1)], b_1) \overset{(I2)}{=} t_1$$

In the first example, the value is obtained from input clause (I1), since $last([\,]) = \bot$. In the second example, we first applied the wild card clause (I5), since no input clause matches Register, and then (I1). In the third example, the value is obtained immediately from (I2).

Since the size of a valid trace is finite and decreases at each recursive call and since the input clause for an empty trace is always defined, then the computation of attribute values terminates. We suppose that EB³ attribute definitions satisfy the following consistency condition: when a non-key attribute b returns a value other than $\bot$ for a key value, then the key function should contain that key. In other words, the entities that are concerned by the computation of the new value of attribute b exist.

4   Generating B Specifications for EB³ Attribute Definitions

4.1   An Overview of B

B is a formal method [1] that supports a large segment of the software development life cycle: specification, refinement and implementation. In B, specifications are organized into abstract machines (similar to classes or modules). Through refinement steps and proofs, the code can be proven to satisfy its specification. The B method is supported by several tools, like Atelier B [6], Click'n Prove [2] and the B-Toolkit [4].

Let us now focus on the B specification language for the purposes of this paper. Each abstract machine encapsulates state variables (introduced by keyword **VARIABLES**), an invariant constraining the state variables (**INVARIANT**), an initialization of all the state variables (**INITIALISATION**), and operations on the state variables (**OPERATIONS**). The invariant is a first-order predicate in a simplified version of the ZF-set theory, enriched by many relational operators. Abstract sets or enumerated sets (**SETS**) are used for typing the state variables.

In B, state variables are modified only by means of substitutions. The initialization and the operations are specified in a generalization of Dijkstra's guarded command notation, called the Generalized Substitution Language (GSL), that allows the definition of non-deterministic and preconditioned substitutions. An operation in an abstract machine is generally a preconditioned substitution. It is then of the form **PRE** P **THEN** S **END**, where P, called the precondition, is a first-order predicate, and S is a substitution. The state transition specified by a preconditioned substitution is guaranteed only when the precondition is satisfied.

4.2   The Example Translated into B

The following B specification is generated from the EB[3] specification of the library management system described in Sect. 2.1 with the algorithm presented in the next subsection Sect 4.3.

The first part of the specification, that contains the state variables and the invariant properties, is called the *static* part.

> MACHINE $B\_Library$
> SETS mK_Set; bK_Set; T
> VARIABLES $memberKey$, $nbLoans$, $bookKey$, $title$, $loan$
> INVARIANT $memberKey \subseteq mK\_Set$ $\wedge$ $nbLoans \in memberKey \rightarrow NAT$ $\wedge$
> $bookKey \subseteq bK\_Set$ $\wedge$ $title \in bookKey \rightarrow T$ $\wedge$
> $loan \in bookKey \nrightarrow memberKey$
> DEFINITIONS $borrower(x) \triangleq loan(x)$

In the invariant, symbol $\rightarrow$ denotes a particular kind of relation, that is a total function, while $\nrightarrow$ is a partial function. NAT is a predefined type of the B language that represents the natural numbers. The clause **DEFINITIONS** introduces the abbreviations used in predicates, expressions and substitutions.

The initialization and the operations compose the *dynamic* part of a B machine.

> INITIALISATION
> $memberKey, nbLoans, bookKey, title, loan := \emptyset, \emptyset, \emptyset, \emptyset, \emptyset$

Symbol $:=$ denotes the assignment substitution. The initialization is here a multiple substitution that initializes each state variable in the left-hand side to $\emptyset$.

> OPERATIONS
>   **Acquire**$(bId, bTitle) \triangleq$
>   PRE $bId \in bK\_Set$ $\wedge$ $bTitle \in T$
>   THEN
> $bookKey := bookKey \cup \{bId\}$ $||$ $title := title \cup \{bId \mapsto bTitle\}$
>   END;

Symbol $||$ denotes the parallel composition of substitutions. This means that substitutions $bookKey := bookKey \cup \{bId\}$ and $title := title \cup \{bId \mapsto bTitle\}$ are simultaneously executed. Notation $a \mapsto b$ denotes an element of a relation. For instance, $bId \mapsto bTitle$ is added to $title$ by operation **Acquire**. In the following operations, the *dom* operator, applied to a relation, gives its domain. Symbol $\vartriangleleft$ denotes the domain anti-restriction operator while $\vartriangleleft\!\!\!-$ is the override operator.

Let r be a relation and A be a set, these three operators are defined as follows: $dom(r) = \{a \mid (a,b) \in r\}$, $A \lhd r = \{(a,b) \mid (a,b) \in r \ \wedge \ a \notin A\}$ and $r \lhd\!\!\!- A = (dom(A) \lhd r) \cup A$.

> **Discard**$(bId) \triangleq$
> PRE $bId \in bK\_Set \ \wedge \ bId \notin dom(loan)$
> THEN
> $bookKey := bookKey - \{bId\} \ \| \ title := \{bId\} \lhd title$
> END;
> **Modify**$(bId, nTitle) \triangleq$
> PRE $bId \in bK\_Set \ \wedge \ nTitle \in T$
> THEN
> $title := title \lhd\!\!\!- \{bId \mapsto nTitle\}$
> END;
> **Transfer**$(bId, mId) \triangleq$
> PRE $bId \in bK\_Set \ \wedge \ bId \in bookKey \ \wedge \ bId \in dom(loan) \ \wedge$
> $nbLoans(borrower(bId)) \geq 1 \ \wedge \ mId \in mK\_Set \ \wedge$
> $mId \in memberKey \ \wedge \ mId \neq borrower(bId)$
> THEN
> $loan := loan - \{(bId, borrower(bId))\} \cup \{(bId, mId)\} \ \|$
> $nbLoans := nbLoans \lhd\!\!\!- \{(mId \mapsto nbLoans(mId) + 1),$
> $(borrower(bId) \mapsto nbLoans(borrower(bId)) - 1)\}$
> END

For the sake of concision, the other operations have been omitted.

4.3   From EB^3 Attribute Definitions to B Substitutions

The main difference between EB^3 and B is that EB^3 is an event-based language, while B is a state-based language. The consequences on the attribute definitions are the following ones. In EB^3, the values of an attribute are defined from a recursive function on the valid traces of the system. For each attribute, its associated recursive function specifies what is the effect of each action of the system on the attribute values when this action is accepted and effectively executed by the system. In B, the specification is radically orthogonal. Attributes are defined as state variables of the system. Each B operation, that corresponds to an EB^3 action, specifies what are the substitutions on the state variables of the system, when this operation is executed.

The algorithm for synthesizing B specifications from EB^3 attribute definitions consists of four steps:

1. generate the static part and the signature of operations of the B machine from the user requirements class diagram, the signature of EB^3 attribute definitions and the signature of actions in EB^3,
2. generate the substitutions for the initialization,
3. generate the substitutions for the operations,
4. complete the operation specifications by generating the weakest preconditions.

The main principles of step 1 are presented in Sect. 4.4. We generate from EB^3 attribute definitions the substitutions for the initialization (step 2) and the operations (step 3) of the B specification of the system. This is the topic of Sect. 4.5. The B specification obtained after step 3 is not sufficient to discharge the proof obligations linked to the preservation of the invariant properties. In Sect 5, we show how to use the tool Atelier B [6] to compute the weakest precondition for each operation such that the invariant obtained from step 1 is preserved (step 4).

4.4 Static Part and Signature of Operations

In practice, B specifications are synthesized with the same identifiers as in EB^3. To syntactically distinguish identifiers of the EB^3 specification from those of the B specification, we denote by id_B the B identifier corresponding to identifier id_F in EB^3.

The static part of B specifications is automatically obtained by translation from the requirements class diagram. Each recursive function k_F defining a key in the EB^3 specification corresponds to a state variable k_B in B. The invariant for k_B is an inclusion of the form $k_B \subseteq T_B$, where T_B represents the set of all the possible values of k_F. Each non-key attribute b_F of the class diagram corresponds to a state variable b_B. The invariant is of the form $b_B \in k_B \rightarrow T_B$ or $b_B \in k_B \nrightarrow T_B$ (depending on whether b_F admits null values), where k_B is the state variable that corresponds to the key of the entity type or the association in which b_F is defined and T_B represents the set of all the possible values of b_F. The signature of attribute definitions provides the types that are not shown on the requirements class diagram. We consider only binary associations, because n-ary associations can always be decomposed into $n-1$ binary associations with additional constraints. Each association asc_F corresponds to a state variable asc_B that is a relation between the key state variables of the two entity types that compose the association. According to the multiplicity of asc_F, asc_B, or its inverse, is defined by a partial function, an injection, etc. The translation rules for the static part are presented in [10, 23]. For the sake of concision, we generate a single B machine that contains all the operations. This has no influence on the algorithms described in the paper.

For each action defined in EB^3, an operation is created in B. The signature of B operations comes from the signature of actions in the EB^3 specification. Thus, EB^3 action $\mathbf{a}_F(q_{1_F} : T_{1_F}, \ldots, q_{n_F} : T_{n_F}) : (q_{n+1_F} : T_{n+1_F}, \ldots, q_{m_F} : T_{m_F})$ is translated into a B operation of the following signature:

$$q_{n+1_B}, \ldots, q_{m_B} \longleftarrow \mathbf{a}_B(q_{1_B}, \ldots, q_{n_B}) \triangleq$$
$$\text{PRE } q_{1_B} \in T_{1_B} \wedge \ldots \wedge q_{n_B} \in T_{n_B}$$
$$\text{THEN } \ldots$$
$$\text{END};$$

When the output parameter type of action $\mathbf{a}_F$ is void, then the operation has no output in B. Typing constraints in the precondition also come from the signature of actions.

4.5   General Process for Synthesizing Substitutions

Because step 2 is similar, and even simpler than step 3, we just summarize in this paper the synthesis of substitutions for the **INITIALISATION** clause. For each attribute definition b_F, there exists an input clause of the form $\perp : u$. It denotes the initial value of the attribute and therefore corresponds to the initialization substitution of the state variable that represents this attribute. The most common value for u is $\emptyset$ (for a key) or $\perp$ (for a non-key attribute), which corresponds in B to a substitution of the form $b_B := \emptyset$.

To generate the operation substitutions of the B machine, we must analyse the input clauses of EB^3 attribute definitions to determine which attributes are affected by the execution of action a_F and what is the effect of a_F on these attributes. Because of the pattern matching analysis described in Sect. 3.2, an attribute b_F may be affected by action a_F if there exists at least one input clause of the form $a_F(\overrightarrow{p_I}) : u$ in the definition of b_F. The set of such attributes is $B(a_F)$. To avoid confusion with the formal parameters of action a_F, each actual parameter p of an input clause is now denoted by p_I. For each attribute b_F of $B(a_F)$, there may be several input clauses $a_F(\overrightarrow{p_{j_I}}) : u_j$ with the same label a_F. The list of these input clauses is denoted by $IC(b_F, a_F)$. Since the first input clause that evaluates to true is the one to be executed, analysis of input clauses of $IC(b_F, a_F)$ is done in their declaration order.

When expression u_j in an input clause is a functional term, its translation into B is quite straightforward. On the contrary, when expression u_j is a conditional term, then we must analyse the different conditions in the **if** predicates. The crux of the analysis is to determine which key values are affected by the reception of an input event a_F. That is, when event a_F is received, what are the key values $\{\overrightarrow{v}\}$ such that $b_F(t :: a_F, \overrightarrow{v}) \neq b_F(t, \overrightarrow{v})$. The variables in $\overrightarrow{k} \cap var(\overrightarrow{p})$ are determined by the pattern of an input clause $a_F(\overrightarrow{p_I})$. The variables in $\overrightarrow{k} - var(\overrightarrow{p_I})$ are determined by the conditions in the conditional term u_j. Moreover, the functional terms in the **then** parts of u_j can be valid only for some conditions on the parameters $\overrightarrow{p}$ described in the **if** predicates. We use a binary tree called *decision tree* to analyse the **if** predicates. For instance, the conditional term associated to input clause $\mathsf{Transfer}_F(bId_I, mId'_I)$ in attribute definition $nbLoans_F$ contains two nested **if then else end** expressions. With the pattern matching condition itself, one cannot determine the key variable mId of this input clause. The **if** conditions then allow us to bind mId to the formal parameters of $\mathsf{Transfer}_F$. In the first **then** expression, the functional term is applied to a key entity $mId = mId'_I$, while, in the second one, it corresponds to a key value $mId = borrower_F(bId_I)$. Our general algorithm is provided in Fig. 2.

Once all the substitutions S_b have been generated for each attribute b_F of $B(a_F)$, then operation a_F is translated into B. If $B(a_F) = \{b_1, \ldots, b_m\}$, then the substitution for a_B is: $S_{b_1} \parallel \ldots \parallel S_{b_m}$. We now focus on the construction of decision trees and on the synthesis of substitutions. The other points are detailed in [18].

For each action a_F of the EB^3 specification
 determine attributes $B(a_F)$ that are affected by the reception of a_F
 for each attribute b_F of $B(a_F)$
  determine input clauses $IC(b_F, a_F)$ of the form $a_F(\overrightarrow{p_I}) : u$
  for each input clause $a_F(\overrightarrow{p_I}) : u$ of $IC(b_F, a_F)$
   determine the pattern matching condition
   identify the free variables of u with the formal parameters $\overrightarrow{q_I}$
   identify the hypotheses under which u is valid
  generate a decision tree for b_F
  generate a substitution formula S_b for b_B
 generate the substitutions for operation a_B

Fig. 2. The general synthesis algorithm

4.5.1 Decision Tree

A decision tree, whose leaves are all functional terms, is built for each attribute b_F in order to determine, for each input clause $a_F(\overrightarrow{p_{ji}}) : u_j$ of $IC(b_F, a_F)$,

- the mapping θ_{u_j} that binds the free variables of input clause $a_F(\overrightarrow{p_{ji}})$ to the formal parameters of action $a_F(\overrightarrow{q_F})$,
- and, if u_j is a conditional term, the functional terms $u_{j,i}$ derived from the **then** parts of u_j and the associated conditions $\varPhi_{u_{j,i}}$ in the **if** parts of u_j,

where $u_{j,i}$ is the functional term of the i-th leaf of the subtree corresponding to the j-th input clause of $IC(b_F, a_F)$ of attribute b_F and $\varPhi_{u_{j,i}}$ is the conjunction of conditions ϕ labelling the path's edges leading to functional term $u_{j,i}$.

 Mapping θ_{u_j} is determined from the pattern matching condition of input clause $a_F(\overrightarrow{p_{ji}})$ with EB^3 action $a_F(\overrightarrow{q_F})$. For instance, the pattern matching condition for input clause Transfer$_F(bId_I, mId'_I)$ in attribute definition $nbLoans_F$ is $bId_I = bId_F \wedge mId'_I = mId_F$. In practice, θ_{u_j} is identified to an extended mapping that binds the free variables of the input clause to the B counterparts of the EB^3 formal parameters. Thus, $\theta_{u_j} = \{bId_I \leftarrow bId_B, mId'_I \leftarrow mId_B\}$.

 The decision tree associated to attribute b_F is built as follows. The root is b_F. The leaves correspond to the different input clauses $a_F(\overrightarrow{p_{ji}}) : u_j$ of $IC(b_F, a_F)$. Each leaf is of the form u_j, whose edge is labelled by a condition ϕ on parameters $\overrightarrow{k}$ to pattern match input clause $a_F(\overrightarrow{p_{ji}}) : u_j$. The rightmost leaf is always $b_F(front(s), \overrightarrow{k})$, that correspond to the recursive call of attribute definition b_F when any input clause matches with the last input of trace s. When an expression u_j is a conditional term, then the corresponding leaf is replaced by a decision subtree whose leaves are all functional terms. The conditions c in the **if** parts of u_j are then analysed to generate new nodes such that the children of a node are its **then** and **else** subterms, whose respective edges are labelled by c and $\neg c$.

 For instance, the decision tree of input clause Transfer$_F$ in attribute definition $nbLoans_F$ is represented in Fig. 3. There is only one input clause for action Transfer$_F$ in attribute definition $nbLoans_F$. A first leaf is the functional term associated to condition $mId = mId'_I$. The second leaf corresponds to predicate

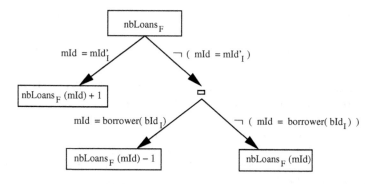

Fig. 3. The decision tree of input clause $\mathsf{Transfer}_F$ in $nbLoans_F$

$mId \neq mId'_I \wedge mId = borrower(bId_I)$. The last leaf is a recursive call of $nbLoans_F$.

4.5.2   B Substitutions

In the following formulas, θ_{u_j} not only binds the free variables of the input clause to the B formal parameters, but also transforms each occurrence of an attribute call $b_F(front(s), \overrightarrow{p_F})$ into a B expression of the form $b_B(\overrightarrow{p_B})$. The enumeration of these substitution elements is omitted from the description of θ_{u_j} in the sequel, for the sake of concision.

Let b_F be a key of $B(a_F)$, then expressions u_j in the input clauses of $IC(b_F, a_F)$ are all functional terms. Substitution b_B for a_B is directly defined by:

$$b_B := u_j \theta_{u_j}$$

For instance, the substitution formula for input clause $\mathsf{Acquire}_F(bId_I, bTitle_I)$ in the key definition $bookKey_F$ of entity type book is:

$$bookKey_B := (bookKey_F \cup \{bId_I\})\theta_u$$

where $\theta_u = \{bId_I \leftarrow bId_B, bTitle_I \leftarrow bTitle_B\}$. Then, by applying θ_u, we directly obtain the B substitution of operation **Acquire**$_B$ for state variable $bookKey_B$.

If b_F is a non-key attribute, then its decision tree is analysed to generate a *substitution formula* that defines the whole set of substitutions for b_B. The relevant paths are those that start from the root and lead to a leaf which is distinct from a recursive call of b_F. Then, the substitution formula for b_B is:

$$b_B := (A \triangleleft b_B) \triangleleft R \qquad (1)$$

where A is the following set defined for every $u_{j,i} = \bot$:

$$A = \{c \mid \exists \overrightarrow{k} \cdot \bigvee_j \left(c = (\overrightarrow{k})\theta_{u_j} \wedge \bigvee_i \Phi_{u_{j,i}} \theta_{u_j} \right)\}$$

and R is defined for every $u_{j,i} \neq \perp$ by:

$$R = \{(c,d) \mid \exists \vec{k} \cdot \bigvee_j \left(c = (\vec{k})\theta_{u_j} \; \wedge \; \bigvee_i (\Phi_{u_{j,i}} \wedge d = u_{j,i}) \theta_{u_j} \right) \}$$

Let us now explain what sets A and R represent. The disjunction on j represents the different input clauses with the same label in attribute b_F. So each branch j in A and R corresponds to one input clause. When $u_{j,i}$ is $\perp$, then attribute b_F becomes undefined at the corresponding key value determined by θ_{u_j} and $\Phi_{u_{j,i}}$. Each branch i of the disjunction in set A represents such a key value. For instance, action $\mathsf{Discard}_F(bId_F)$ sets the value of attribute $title_F$ to $\perp$ for book entity bId. From (1), we deduce: $title_B := A \lhd title_B$, where A is defined as follows.

$$A = \{c \mid \exists bId_I \cdot (c = bId_I) \, \theta_u \wedge true \, \theta_u\}$$

Let us note that bId_I is directly bound by the pattern matching condition, and θ_u is simply $\{bId_I \leftarrow bId_B\}$. Consequently, $A = \{bId_B\}$ and the corresponding substitution in operation $\mathsf{Discard}_B$ is then: $title_B := \{bId_B\} \lhd title_B$.

R is the set of maplets that assign new values to b_B. The first disjunction on j represents the different input clauses with the same label in attribute b_F. Let us now focus on the j-th input clause. If u_j is a functional term, then the corresponding maplet is (c,d), where c is the key value determined by θ_{u_j} and d is the attribute value $u_j\theta_{u_j}$. If u_j is a conditional term, then several key values are concerned; they are determined by θ_{u_j} and $\Phi_{u_{j,i}}$. Each branch i represents a key value and its associated attribute value $u_{j,i}\theta_{u_j}$. For instance, the conditional term for input clause $\mathsf{Transfer}_F$ in attribute definition $nbLoans_F$ involves two entities of attribute key mId: mId'_I and $borrower_F(bId_I)$. The generated substitution formula is the following: $nbLoans_B := nbLoans_B \lhd R$, where R is defined by:

$$R = \{(c,d) \mid \exists mId \cdot (c = mId) \, \theta_u \wedge$$
$$((mId = mId'_I \wedge d = nbLoans_F(mId) + 1) \, \theta_u) \vee$$
$$((mId \neq mId'_I \wedge mId = borrower_F(bId_I) \wedge d = nbLoans_F(mId) - 1) \, \theta_u)\}$$

Let us note that mId remains a free variable after taking the pattern matching condition into account: $\theta_u = \{bId_I \leftarrow bId_B, mId'_I \leftarrow mId_B\}$.

The general form (1) of substitutions generates a syntactically correct B substitution but it is not the most suitable format to easily prove invariant preservation. Hence, we have defined in [18] simplification rules that transform this substitution into a more suitable format. In particular, some rules are defined to generate **IF THEN ELSE** substitutions. For instance, let us consider the above-mentioned set R obtained for attribute $borrower_B$. To simplify the substitution, we can apply θ_u and then remove the existential quantification by using candidate c for mId (i.e., apply the so-called one-point rule of predicate calculus):

$$R = \{(c,d) \mid (c = mId_B \wedge d = nbLoans_B(c) + 1) \vee$$
$$(c \neq mId_B \wedge c = borrower_B(bId_B) \wedge d = nbLoans_B(c) - 1)\}$$

Set R is not equal to the simpler set used in operation **Transfer** in Sect. 4.2:

$$\{(mId \mapsto nbLoans(mId)+1), (borrower(bId) \mapsto nbLoans(borrower(bId))-1)\}$$

To have an equality, one must consider the condition $mId_B \neq borrower_B(bId_B)$ as an hypothesis. This condition cannot be generated from the recursive functions defining the attributes. However, it occurs as a guard of action Transfer in the EB^3 process expression, since a member cannot transfer a loan to himself. Hence, if we take these EB^3 action guards as hypotheses in the generation algorithm, we can propagate the equalities on c and simplify R into an enumerated set and obtain the B substitution of operation **Transfer** in Sect. 4.2; moreover, we must add this condition to the precondition of operation **Transfer**. This is a general pattern that often occurs in EB^3 specifications.

5   Proving Static Data Integrity Constraints

An operation precondition can generally be divided in three parts:

1. the typing constraints for input parameters,
2. the weakest precondition required to preserve the invariant of the machine,
3. and the condition required to impose ordering constraints on operations.

The first part can be generated from EB^3 action signature, as already shown. The second part is required to preserve static data integrity constraints. Recall that the first three steps of our approach allows one to systematically generate the invariant I coming from the constraints of the class diagram and the substitutions S of each operation of the system. The last one is more difficult to address and usually requires creativity, except for EB^3 action guards which can be automatically included in the operation precondition.

The second part can be generated as follows. The semantics of B substitutions [1] is defined by their weakest precondition. Let S be a substitution and R a predicate, expression $[S]R$ denotes the weakest precondition such that substitution S is guaranteed to establish predicate R. As a proof obligation, each operation of a B abstract machine must satisfy the following property: $INV \wedge P \Rightarrow [S]INV$, where INV is the invariant of the abstract machine, P is the operation precondition and S is the operation substitution. To discharge the proof obligation, we must add at least $[S]INV$ to the precondition. Hence, the operation preserves the invariant properties generated from the class diagram.

By using Atelier B [6], we have been able to determine the weakest preconditions of the operations from the B machine described in Sect. 4. It consists in trying to automatically discharge the proof obligations and to deduce from the unproved subgoals the weakest preconditions. This approach is quite similar to the identification of preconditions in Z with the tool Z/EVES described in [21]. For instance, operation **Discard** (see Sect. 4.2) is defined as follows.

Discard$(bId) \triangleq$
PRE $bId \in bK\_Set \; \wedge \; bId \notin dom(loan)$

THEN
$$bookKey := bookKey - \{bId\} \quad || \quad title := \{bId\} \lhd title$$
END;

Predicate $bId \notin dom(loan)$ has been generated to preserve the invariant property $loan \in bookKey \nrightarrow memberKey$. The precondition of this operation still requires its third part, which is the ordering constraint that a book must have been created before it can be deleted (*i.e.*, $bId \in bookKey$). However, our algorithm cannot generate it.

The generation of the weakest precondition takes its relevance in the context of proving the refinement of an EB³ specification by a B specification [13]. This proof ensures that the behaviour of the EB³ specification is equivalent to the behaviour of the B specification. By generating the weakest precondition in B, we ensure that the EB³ specification satisfies the static data integrity constraints.

Since it is not easy in EB³ to prove static data integrity constraints, we take advantage of our translation algorithm to use B to state and prove additional static data integrity constraints, which are fundamental elements of an IS specification. Static constraints also include safety properties, which cannot be derived from the static structure described by the requirements class diagram. For instance, the number of loans of each member could be limited to five books. We can state this property in the B invariant as follows: $\forall mId \in memberKey \bullet nbLoans(mId) \leq 5$. By proving refinement between B and EB³, we show that the EB³ specification satisfies this property. When refinement cannot be proved, the refinement proof obligations highlight missing guards in the EB³ specification or improper scenarios defined by the process expressions and the attributes.

Missing guards can also be identified by automatically adding to the precondition the hypothesis required to simplify R obtained from (1) into an enumerated set. This is a heuristic which has allowed us to identify errors in earlier versions of our EB³ specification.

6   Conclusion and Perspectives

Several approaches deal with the integration of state-based and event-based specifications, such as csp2B [5], CSP || B [9], CSP-OZ [11] or Circus [24]. The main characteristics of IS lead us to choose B and EB³ for specifying them [12,15]. In particular, EB³ and B are complementary to take the main properties of IS into account: EB³ provides a formal, quite intuitive, way to specify the life cycles of the system entities and B is a state-based formal language that allows us to specify and verify the invariant properties of the system. We aim at defining an integrated approach called EB⁴ [15] that consists in using EB³ to specify the functional behaviour of IS, and then to use B invariants to specify and prove safety properties about this specification.

EB⁴ distinguishes itself from the aforementioned approaches as follows. CSP-OZ and Circus integrate two specification paradigms (state-based and process expressions) into a single language with a unified semantical framework that covers both paradigms. CSP || B and csp2B split the specification in two parts: control is expressed by a process expression; data is described by a B specification. In EB^4, the EB^3 specification is complete in itself; the B specification is partly generated from the EB^3 specification; it is used to state static data integrity constraints. Moreover, both csp2B and CSP || B do not support arbitrary process expressions, in order to simplify either the translation process (csp2B) or the proof process. In addition, CSP || B verifies the consistency between B and CSP through model checking instead of theorem proving. EB^4 is closer to the csp2B approach, where the CSP specification is translated into B. However, the syntax of CSP is not convenient for specifying IS (prefixing, no Kleene closure, cumbersome sequential composition). Moreover, csp2B allows CSP processes to control B machines by identifying CSP events to B operations, while EB^4 does not provide such mechanisms.

In EB^4, the EB^3 specification is translated into an equivalent B specification. In [13], Frappier and Laleau have used the B refinement relation to prove that the ordering properties specified in EB^3 are satisfied by the B counterpart. In this paper, we have shown how to generate the minimal consistent B specification that corresponds to EB^3 attribute definitions. The generation of explicit B substitutions is detailed in [18]. The only part that is now missing for a complete translation is the generation of control preconditions that represent ordering constraints.

From the B specification, one can use B refinement techniques described in [22] to implement the system with SQL. In [16, 17], we show how to synthesize relational database transactions from EB^3 attribute definitions. We plan to implement tools to support these translations from EB^3 to B and from EB^3 to relational databases. A more general work is the translation into B of EB^3 process expressions.

References

1. Abrial, J.R.: *The B-Book: Assigning programs to meanings*, Cambridge University Press, 1996.
2. Abrial, J.R., Cansell, D.: Click'n Prove: Interactive proofs within set theory. In *TPHOLs 2003, Rome, Italy*, LNCS 2758, Springer-Verlag, September 2003.
3. Abrial, J.R., Mussat, L.: Introducing dynamic constraints in B. In *2nd Conf. on the B Method*, LNCS 1393, Springer-Verlag, 1998.
4. B-Core (UK) Ltd.: B-Toolkit, `http://www.b-core.com/btoolkit.html`
5. Butler, M.: csp2B: a practical approach to combining CSP and B. *Formal Aspects of Computing*, **12**(4), 2000, pp 182–198.
6. Clearsy: Atelier B, `http://www.atelierb-societe.com`
7. Cousineau, G., Mauny, M.: *The functional approach to programming*, Cambridge University Press, 1998.
8. Elmasri, R., Navathe, S.B.: *Fundamentals of Database Systems*, 4th edition, Addison-Wesley, 2004.
9. Evans, N., Treharne, H., Laleau, R., Frappier, M.: How to verify dynamic properties of information systems. In *2nd IEEE Intern. Conf. SEFM, Beijing, China*, IEEE Computer Society Press, September 2004.

10. Facon, P., Laleau, R., Nguyen, H.P.: Mapping object diagrams into B specifications. In *Method Integration Workshop, Leeds, UK*, Series EWICS, Springer-Verlag, 1996.
11. Fischer, C.: *Combination and implementation of processes and data: from CSP-OZ to Java*. Ph.D. Thesis, University of Oldenburg, 2000.
12. Fraikin, B., Frappier, M., Laleau, R.: State-Based versus Event-Based Specifications for Information Systems: a Comparison of B and EB^3, *Software and System Modeling*, **4**(3), July 2005, pp 236–257.
13. Frappier, M., Laleau, R.: Proving event ordering properties for information systems. In *Proc. ZB 2003, Turku, Finland*, LNCS 2651, Springer-Verlag, June 2003.
14. Frappier, M., St-Denis, R.: EB^3: an Entity-Based Black-Box Specification Method for Information Systems. *Software and System Modeling*, **2**(2), July 2003, pp 134–149.
15. Gervais, F.: EB^4 : *Vers une méthode combinée de spécification formelle des systèmes d'information*. Dissertation for the general examination, GRIL, Université de Sherbrooke, Québec, June 2004.
16. Gervais, F., Frappier, M., Laleau, R.: Generating relational database transactions from recursive functions defined on EB^3 traces. In *Proc. SEFM 2005, Koblenz, Germany*, IEEE Computer Society Press, September 2005.
17. Gervais, F., Frappier, M., Laleau, R.: How to synthesize relational database transactions from EB^3 attribute definitions? In *Proc. MSVVEIS 2005, Miami, USA*, INSTICC Press, May 2005.
18. Gervais, F., Frappier, M., Laleau, R.: Synthesizing B substitutions for EB^3 attribute definitions. Technical Report **683**, CEDRIC, Paris, France, November 2004.
19. Gervais, F., Frappier, M., Laleau, R., Batanado, P.: EB^3 attribute definitions: Formal language and application. Technical Report **700**, CEDRIC, Paris, France, February 2005.
20. Hoare, C. A. R.: *Communicating Sequential Processes*. Prentice Hall, Englewood Cliffs, 1985.
21. Ledru, Y.: Identifying pre-conditions with the Z/EVES theorem prover. In *Proc. 13th International Conf. on Automated Software Engineering*, IEEE Computer Society Press, 1998.
22. Mammar, A., Laleau, R.: Design of an automatic prover dedicated to the refinement of database applications In *Proc. FM'2003, Pisa, Italy*, LNCS 2805, Springer-Verlag, pp 834-854, September 2003.
23. Nguyen, H.P.: *Dérivation de spécifications formelles B à partir de spécifications semi-formelles*. Ph.D. Thesis, CEDRIC, CNAM, Évry, December 1998.
24. Woodcock, J.C.P., Cavalcanti, A.L.C.: The semantics of Circus. In *Proc. ZB 2002, Grenoble, France*, LNCS 2272, Springer-Verlag, 2002.

CZT Support for Z Extensions

Tim Miller[1], Leo Freitas[2], Petra Malik[3], and Mark Utting[3]

[1] University of Liverpool, UK
tim@csc.liv.ac.uk
[2] University of York, UK
leo@cs.york.ac.uk
[3] University of Waikato, New Zealand
{petra, marku}@cs.waikato.ac.nz

Abstract. Community Z Tools (CZT) is an integrated framework for the Z formal specification language. In this paper, we show how it is also designed to support extensions of Z, in a way that minimises the work required to build a new Z extension. The goals of the framework are to maximise extensibility and reuse, and minimise code duplication and maintenance effort. To achieve these goals, CZT uses a variety of different reuse mechanisms, including generation of Java code from a hierarchy of XML schemas, XML templates for shared code, and several design patterns for maximising reuse of Java code. The CZT framework is being used to implement several integrated formal methods, which add object-orientation, real-time features and process algebra extensions to Z. The effort required to implement such extensions of Z has been dramatically reduced by using the CZT framework.

Keywords: Standard Z, Object-Z, TCOZ, *Circus*, parsing, typechecking, animation, design patterns, framework, AST.

1 Introduction

The Z language [1] is a formal specification notation that can be used to precisely specify the behaviour of systems, and analyse them via proof, animation, test generation, and so on. Z was approved as an ISO standard in 2002, but currently there are few tools that conform to the standard.[1] The Community Z Tools (CZT) project [2] is an open-source Java framework for building formal methods tools for standard Z and Z extensions.

CZT[2] provides the basic tools expected in a Z environment, such as conversion between LaTeX, Unicode and XML formats for Z, and parsing, unparsing, typechecking and animation tools, with a WYSIWYG Z editing environment integrated within the jEdit[3] editor. There are also several more experimental

---

[1] CADiZ (http://www-users.cs.york.ac.uk/~ian/cadiz) is the only Z tool that conforms closely to the Z standard. It is freely available, but is not open-source and does not aim at supporting Z extensions.

[2] See http://czt.sourceforge.net.

[3] See http://www.jedit.org.

J. Romijn, G. Smith, and J. van de Pol (Eds.): IFM 2005, LNCS 3771, pp. 227–245, 2005.

tools under development, such as a Z-to-B translator and a semi-automated GUI-builder for Z specifications. However, the main design goal of CZT is to provide a framework which makes it easy to develop new Z tools. This paper describes how the framework also makes it easy to develop tools for extensions of Z.

In recent years, there has been an increasing interest in combining different programming paradigms within a uniform formal notation, where Z plays a central role. This has given rise to many Z extensions, which add features such as process algebras [3, 4, 5], object orientation [6, 7], time [8, 9], mobility [10], and so forth.

Among these extensions, CZT supports Object-Z [6], a specification language that extends Z with modularity and reuse constructs that resemble the object-oriented programming paradigm. Such constructs include classes, inheritance, and polymorphism. CZT supports Object-Z in the form of parsing, typechecking, and other facilities. CZT is also being used to develop extensions for Timed Communicating Object-Z (TCOZ) [8], which is a blend of Object-Z and Timed-CSP [11], as well as extensions for *Circus* [5], a unified refinement language that combines Z, CSP [12], and the refinement calculus [13], with Hoare and He's *Unifying Theories of Programming* (UTP) as the semantic background [14][4].

This paper describes the engineering techniques used in the CZT framework to maximise extensibility and reuse. Most of these techniques could also be applied to frameworks for other integrated formal methods, especially when the framework must support several different extensions of a common base language (like the role of Z in CZT).

In Section 2, we present a method for specifying an XML interchange format that maximises extensibility. Section 3 describes the automatic generation and design of the *Annotated Syntax Tree* (AST) classes. Section 4 presents a method for generating parsers, scanners, and other related tools for the different Z extensions, and Section 5 presents the design of the CZT typecheckers, which are tailored for extendibility and reuse. Section 6 briefly presents the CZT animator, ZLive, and discusses the possibility of using this to animate extensions to Z. Section 7 presents the design of the *specification manager*, an integral component of CZT that caches information about specifications to improve the efficiency of the tools. Section 8 gives an overview of related work. Finally, Section 9 concludes the paper and discusses the future of the CZT project.

2   XML Schemas

The first step in designing the CZT tools and libraries was the development of an XML schema that describes an XML markup for Z specifications (ZML) [15]. This is an interchange format that can be used to exchange parsed Z specifications between sessions and tools written in different languages.

Standard Z allows specifications to be exchanged using Unicode, LATEX or email markup. However, implementing a parser for such specifications is a nontrivial task that can take several months. ZML, in contrast, can be parsed im-

---

[4] See http://www.cs.york.ac.uk/circus/

mediately since virtually all programming languages provide XML reading and writing libraries.

The idea of using XML for Z has also been explored in the Z/EVES theorem prover [16]. It allows one to create a customised theorem prover with additional tactics tailored for a particular specification by modifying the XML representation of the Z specification in Z/EVES [17]. The main problem however, is the lack of a common standard.

The XML schema for ZML was carefully designed, via consensus between several groups of interested people, by selecting the best features of the abstract syntaxes of CADiZ, Zeta and the Z standard. ZML supports several kinds of extensibility:

Extensible Annotations: Each Z construct can be *annotated* with arbitrary information, such as type information, comments, anticipated usage, and source-file location.

Extensible ASTs: This allows Z extensions to add new kinds of expressions, predicates, paragraphs, *etc.*

Extensible Schemas: The standard XML schema features, such as namespaces and importing, mean that Z extensions can be defined without modifying the original ZML schema.

The following strategies have been used to achieve these kinds of extensibility.

The *"any"* element can be used in an XML schema to enable instance XML documents to contain additional elements not specified by the schema. This concept has been used to define annotations. That is, an annotation to a term can either be one of the annotations defined in the XML schema for Z, or any other kind of data. New kinds of annotations can be added without changing the ZML schema. This allows a tool builder to decide what data makes sense for a particular tool. Tools that do not use a particular kind of annotation simply ignore those annotations.

A typical style of defining XML schemas or DTDs is to explicitly list the possible alternatives for expressions, predicates, *etc.* This makes it difficult to extend the syntax of ASTs to allow new kinds of expressions or predicates. In contrast, ZML uses *inheritance* (*substitution groups* in XML schema terminology) extensively throughout the XML schema. Abstract elements are used to provide placeholders for their derived elements. For example, the abstract element `Para` is the parent of all concrete Z paragraphs, such as axiomatic paragraphs (element `AxPara`), and free types paragraph (element `FreePara`). Other elements that contain paragraphs, like Z section (element `ZSect`), are defined to contain a *reference* to the abstract `Para` element. This allows any subtype of `Para` to be used instead. This has the same extensibility advantages as subtyping in object-oriented languages.

A Z extension can add new kinds of paragraphs, expressions and predicates, simply by extending these ZML inheritance hierarchies. It is important to note that this can be done without modifying the ZML schema file. Instead, the Z extension creates a new XML schema which *imports* the original ZML schema file, then defines the additional constructs using a new namespace. This means that several separate extensions of Z can easily coexist. For example, the XML schema for Object-Z imports the ZML schema file, and defines a new paragraph for classes (element `ClassPara`) that is derived from element `Para` defined in the ZML schema. Instance documents of the Object-Z schema can now contain class paragraphs in addition to the standard Z paragraphs wherever an element `Para` is expected. Thus, an Object-Z specification in XML format can contain a mixture of Z and Object-Z constructs, such as:

```
<Z:ZSect>
  <OZ:ClassPara> ...  <Z:True/> ... </OZ:ClassPara>
</Z:ZSect>
```

This process of extending the XML schema can be done multiple times, so that even a Z extension can be extended. For example, the additional elements provided by the Object-Z XML schema are further extended by the TCOZ XML schema. Again, the definitions of the elements for TCOZ are encapsulated into a TCOZ XML schema file, and the ZML and Object-Z XML schemas do not need to be modified. Similarly, the *Circus* extension for CZT is encapsulated into a *Circus* XML schema file that extends the main standard Z schema. This approach of extension via inclusion is explored throughout the different layers of CZT tools. The resulting net effect is that once one package is finished, it can be directly extended through inheritance, hence simplifying the task of extending standard Z to a great extent.

The use of XML in CZT has proved to be an efficient and extensible solution for representing a Z specification and its extensions. The XML approach helps to clarify design decisions in a straightforward fashion. This representation is the key for the integrated development and exchange of information among different Z tools.

3   Java AST Classes

To manipulate Z *Annotated Syntax Trees* (AST) within Java (or any other programming language), we must convert ZML files into Java objects. This could easily be done using one of the Java XML reader/writer libraries, such as DOM, but this would result in a very generic interface to the Java objects — to the programmer they would appear to be an N-ary tree of `Element` and `Text` objects. This does not accurately reflect Z syntax or semantics, is not elegant, and is error-prone to use.

Instead, we provide a customised Java interface for each Z construct, with appropriately named *get* and *set* methods for each subcomponent. This makes programs more readable, and provides much stronger typechecking. However, there are some situations where the generic N-ary tree view is more convenient (for example, writing a deep copy procedure), so our Java interfaces also provide a low-level generic view of each node, via the following two methods:

```
Object[] getChildren();  // return all children of this node
Term create(Object[] args); // create a new version of this node,
                            // with the given children.
```

Having these two alternative views of each node of the AST gives the best of both worlds — one can write generic tree traversal algorithms using the above two methods, as well as readable and type-safe Z-specific syntax manipulations using the node-specific get and set methods.

In fact, these CZT Java AST interfaces and their implementation classes are automatically generated from the XML schemas described in the previous section using our code generator *GnAST* (GeNerator for AST). The generated code looks similar to the code produced by Java data binding tools like JAXB[5] or Castor[6]. While the main purpose of a Java binding tool is to provide the ability to convert from XML format to Java objects and vice versa, the main purpose of GnAST is to generate well-designed AST classes. For example, the AST classes generated by GnAST support an extensible variant of the visitor design pattern [18, 19].

The automatic AST generation from the XML schemas dramatically reduces the time required to develop a new Z extension, ensures a common style of interface, and improves maintainability. For instance, the complete AST folder representing standard Z contains around 420 Java files. GnAST has also been used to generate AST interfaces and classes for Object-Z, TCOZ, and *Circus*. In total, from the four XML schema files for standard Z and its extensions, GnAST automatically generates around 2300 Java files. This provides a very convenient and consistent way to obtain AST interfaces and classes for Z extensions that fit well into the AST for standard Z.

The visitor design pattern [18, 19] makes it very easy to write tools like type-checkers and printers, which need to traverse an AST. It allows new traversal operations to be defined without modifying the AST classes. To define a new operation, all one needs to do is to implement a new visitor class.

The visitor design pattern used in CZT has been described in detail in [2]. It is a variant of the *acyclic visitor* [20] pattern and the *default visitor* [21] pattern. Its additional advantages over the standard visitor pattern are that it allows the AST interfaces and classes to be extended without affecting existing visitors, and that it allows a visitor to take advantage of the AST inheritance relationships. For example, a copy visitor that copies an AST can provide a default behaviour for `Term`, the base of the AST inheritance hierarchy. Since AST classes for extensions also derive from `Term`, this copy visitor works for any extension. On the other hand, if the default copy behaviour is not wanted for a particular extension class, say `XYZ`, one can simply add a `visitXYZ` method to the copy visitor, and that method will be used instead of the default `visitTerm` method.

This has a big impact on the applicability of visitors for extensions like Object-Z, TCOZ, and *Circus*. Firstly, it ensures that the Z AST classes can be extended without having to modify existing Z visitors like typechecker, printer, *etc.* Secondly, it makes it easy to extend existing visitors to handle Z extensions — one can simply define a new visitor class which inherits behaviour from an

---

[5] See `http://java.sun.com/xml/jaxb/`

[6] See `http://www.castor.org/`

existing Z visitor and adds a few methods for the new or changed language constructs. Finally, by defining default behaviours for abstract classes such as `Expr` or `Decl`, it is possible to implement tools that are applicable to all Z extensions.

In conclusion, the CZT AST classes provide:

A Choice of Coding Style: One for **generic low-level** algorithms and the other for **node-specific high-level** algorithms.

Automation: the AST classes are generated automatically by **GnAST**.

Reuse of Algorithms: The CZT **visitor pattern** allows AST traversal algorithms to be reused and extended in flexible ways.

Extensibility: the standard Z AST can easily be extended by defining new **XML schemas**.

4   Parsers, Scanners, and Related Tools

CZT includes a suite of important tools for operations such as parsing, typechecking, and markup conversion. In addition to a parser and typechecker for Z, an Object-Z parser is provided, and *Circus* and TCOZ parsers, as well as an Object-Z typechecker, are under development. The Object-Z, TCOZ, and *Circus* tools extend the Z tools by adding support for the additional constructs these languages provide. As each language is an extension of Z, it is tempting to just keep adding to the tools for each extension, and use the largest superset of all extensions. For example, use the TCOZ tools to parse and typecheck Z. However, this has two distinct problems. Firstly, one aim of the CZT project is to create tools that strongly conform to the Z standard. However, allowing extra constructs to be parsed and using different type-rules will break the strong conformance. Secondly, the extensions of Z are not linear. For example, Object-Z extends Z with class paragraphs, and TCOZ extends Object-Z with concurrency operators, but *Circus* extends neither of these — only Z. Therefore, CZT requires an approach that produces separate tools for each Z extension, maximises the commonality between the parsers, and minimises versioning and maintenance problems via reuse.

4.1   Parsers and Scanners

CZT includes parsers for standard Z specifications given either in Unicode or LaTeX markup. Support for email markup is planned. Java Cup[7] is used to generate the CZT parsers from an LALR grammar, and JFlex[8] is used to generate the scanners.

Unfortunately, it is quite difficult to reuse code from an automatically generated scanner or parser, and neither Java Cup nor JFlex explicitly supports inheritance for parser or scanners respectively. To avoid duplicated code, XML templates that contain the different parser and scanner variants are used. From this, the different source files for each Z extension are generated using XSLT[9],

---

[7] See http://www.cs.princeton.edu/~appel/modern/java/CUP/

[8] See http://jflex.de/

[9] See http://www.w3.org/TR/xslt

a language for transforming XML documents. This maximises the commonality between the parsers and minimises versioning and maintenance problems.

All parser and scanner variants are maintained in master XML files. Each master file contains several XML tags that are used for substituting text for each Z extension. For example, the `<package/>` tag is placed wherever one would normally write the Java package name, so that each parser and scanner can be contained in their own package. The tags `<add: extension>` and `</add: extension>` are used to wrap around code that are specific to particular Z extensions. Thus, to add a new type of expression to the Object-Z parser, one would add a new production to the appropriate grammar rule in the master file, and place it between the `<add:oz>` and `</add:oz>` tags. In other programming languages, conditional compilation could be used to achieve the same result. However, as Java does not support conditional compilation, we use the XML template translation approach.

To generate the individual Java Cup files for each extension of Z, XSLT is used to include the necessary code, and to substitute in values for tags. For example, to generate the Object-Z parser, XSLT is applied to the master file, and supplied with the three arguments below:

1. `"class"` substituted with `"Parser"`.
2. `"package"` substituted with `"net.sourceforge.czt.parser.oz"`.
3. code in `"oz"` tags to be included.

Similar rules are specified for each parser and scanner variants. The result is a series of Java Cup and JFlex files, one for each language, which can then be used to generate the parser and scanner code.

The use of XML templates enables parsing code to be reused and easily maintained. Extending the parser and scanner for a new language can be done by just adding the respective grammar and lexer rules together with few modifications such as those parameters above. For example, we are experimenting the incorporation of the available *Circus* parser [22] rules within the flexible CZT framework. The obvious advantages are the widely tested and supported standard Z classes, LaTeX markup and Unicode, visiting and other facilities.

4.2 Multiple Markups

CZT supports multiple markups for each Z extension. The different markup languages suit different communities. For example, LaTeX is preferred by researchers, while Unicode WYSIWYG editing might be more attractive for students or industrial users. At present, Unicode, LaTeX, and the XML format are supported. Adding additional markups is straightforward, as this section will present. XML markup is not considered any further because it can be parsed immediately using existing XML parsers. CZT uses JAXB[10] to unmarshal an XML document into a tree of Java objects, and then uses the visitor design pattern to convert this tree into an AST.

---

[10] See http://java.sun.com/xml/jaxb/

In order to avoid having to provide a parser for each markup language, all specifications are first translated into Unicode and subsequently parsed by a Unicode parser[11]. This also makes sure that names in the AST are markup independent: they are represented in Unicode independently on the actual markup used in the source document. This is a necessary precondition of allowing different sections of a specification to be written in different markups. If a parser for a new markup is required, only a translator to Unicode needs to be implemented.

A consequence of this architecture is that extensions of Z need to support at least Unicode. CZT provides a Z Unicode scanner, which performs lexical analysis on a Unicode stream and breaks it into the necessary tokens. A scanner for a Z extension can be derived by adding additional scanner rules to the CZT scanner template as described above. In order to support LaTeX markup, it is convenient to provide a LaTeX toolkit section for a given extension that defines new operators for that language. In addition to defining new operators, these LaTeX markup documents contain LaTeX markup directives [1, 2] used to specify how certain LaTeX commands are to be converted into Unicode. The LaTeX to Unicode translator parses these definitions and converts each LaTeX command into the corresponding Unicode sequence. However, LaTeX \begin{xxx} and \end{xxx} environments cannot be defined using LaTeX markup directives. If a Z extension needs to provide new LaTeX environments, the LaTeX to Unicode converter needs to be adapted directly. Again, this is possible by adding new rules to the converter template file.

An additional benefit of this approach is that it reduces the number of converters needed between languages. That is, CZT currently implements LaTeX to Unicode and Unicode to LaTeX converters. In the future, we plan to implement an email to Unicode converter to allow parsing of specifications written in email. Using this and the Unicode to LaTeX converter, we could convert email to LaTeX. So, using an intermediate format reduces the number of converter tools that need to be implemented from $M * (M - 1)$ to $2 * (M - 1)$, in which M is the number of markup languages supported.

In conclusion, CZT supports extensions to parser and scanners using:

XML Templates for Code Sharing: XML templates are used to maximise code reuse for the parser and scanner scripts.

Unicode as an Intermediate Format: Unicode is used as an intermediate format to simplify the process of writing scanners and reduce the number of converters needed between markups.

5   Typecheckers

Typecheckers in CZT are written in a different way from the parsers and scanners. Each Z extension has its own typechecker, and while reuse is of high importance, using XML templates is unnecessary because unlike the parsers, Java interfaces and inheritance can be used to extend the typecheckers.

---

[11] See [2] for a more detailed description of the parser architecture.

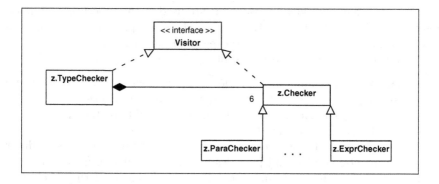

Fig. 1. UML class diagram for Z Typechecker

The Z typechecker is the base implementation. When a Z specification AST is passed to this typechecker, it applies all the typechecking rules and, if the specification is type-correct, it returns TRUE and annotates the original AST with type information as defined in the ISO standard [1–Section 10]. If the specification contains type errors, the result is FALSE, the AST is unchanged and a list of error messages describing the type errors (including their line and column position) is made available.

Most of the typechecker is written using visitors, which can be extended as discussed in Section 3. While it is tempting to write the typechecker as one large visitor, this would create maintenance problems as this visitor would be quite large and monolithic. So we use a more sophisticated and extensible design, shown in Fig. 1.

This breaks up the overall task of typechecking into several (currently six) smaller `Checker` visitors — each subclass of `Checker` typechecks a different kind of syntactic construct such as paragraphs, predicates, expressions, *etc.* The `Checker` class itself defines some shared resources, such as typing environments and the type unification facilities, as well as common "helper" methods used throughout the implementation such as error reporting. In addition, each checker subclass object has a reference back to the top-level `TypeChecker` object, which has links to all the checkers — this allows one checker to call another via the `TypeChecker` object.

For example, for typechecking a schema text of an `AxPara`, the `ParaChecker` class, which typechecks Z paragraphs, needs to typecheck both the declarations and the predicate parts of the schema text. Although visiting through the given AST is the general solution, the typechecking of the declarations part is delegated to the `DeclChecker` class, whereas the typechecking of the predicate part is delegated to the `PredChecker` class. The `DeclChecker` in turn uses the `ExprChecker` to ensure that expressions defining the declaring variables type are well-formed. Because each of these visitors share the same `TypeChecker` reference, and hence the same references to type environments, the declarations added to the type environment by the `DeclChecker` will be accessible by the other checkers.

There are a few additional classes that are used in the typechecker, but not shown in Fig. 1, such as the `UnificationEnv` class that performs the unification of two types for type inference and for checking type consistency.

The advantages of this typechecker design include:

- Methods that are common to all the `Checker` subclasses can be put in the `Checker` superclass. Data that is shared between the checkers can be managed by the `Typechecker` class and made accessible to the checkers in a controlled way via access methods.
- Splitting the overall typechecking task into several parts increases modularity and maintainability, and provides better encapsulation for the different checkers. This aids debugging and allows development of the checkers to be somewhat independent (for example, assigned to different teams or to different iterations of an agile lifecycle).
- Each `Checker` subclass is typechecking similar kinds of nodes (*e.g.*, all expressions), so can have a uniform visiting protocol, which increases regularity and helps to reduce errors. For example, all the visitor methods of the `ParaChecker` class, which typechecks Z paragraphs, return a `Signature` of the name and type pairs declared in that `Para`. In contrast, the `ExprChecker` class typechecks expression nodes and all its visitor methods return a `Type` with resolved reference parameters in which type unification has already been performed.
- By defining several `Checker` subclasses over the same kinds of AST nodes, it becomes easy to have multiple algorithms over the same syntax nodes. For example, post-checking for unresolved set and reference expressions, which may introduce an unresolved type, is implemented as a second kind of `ExprChecker`. This post-typechecking pass ensures that all implicit parameters such as generics actuals have been completely determined. This would not be possible with a single monolithic visitor design, because one could not have two `visitRefExpr` methods in the same visitor.

Fig. 2 shows how this design is extended to define a typechecker for a Z extension — Object-Z in this case. A new package (oz) is created for the Object-Z typechecker. In this package, a new `oz.Checker` class is implemented, which inherits the base `z.Checker` class. In this new class, any common methods that are to be used by the Object-Z typechecker are implemented, and existing methods are overridden or overloaded if additional functionality is needed. Then, new `Checker` subclasses are created, one for each kind of language entity that requires Object-Z-specific typechecking. Each of these checkers (the `oz.XXXXChecker` subclasses in Fig. 2) implement the visitor methods only for Object-Z constructs and for any Z constructs that require additional Object-Z-specific checking. The remaining standard Z constructs are handled by delegation to the original `z.XXXXChecker` object.

It is interesting to see how this delegation is achieved, given that Java does not support multiple inheritance. We rely on the general visiting protocol described in Section 3 and in [2]. For example, the `oz.ExprChecker` class catches all Object-Z-specific expressions. It also implements an additional `visitExpr`

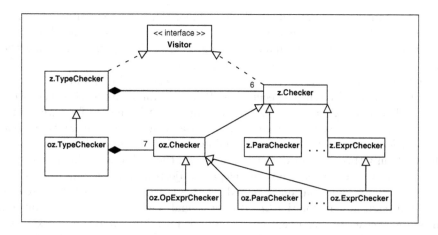

Fig. 2. UML class diagram for Object-Z Typechecker

method which "catches" all remaining `Expr` AST nodes and uses the visitor from `z.ExprChecker` to check those nodes.

```
private z.ExprChecker zExprChecker_;
...
public Object visitExpr(Expr expr) {
  return expr.accept(zExprChecker_);
}
```

The Z typechecker has a reference to a `z.ExprChecker` object, but in the Object-Z typechecker, this points to an `oz.ExprChecker` instead. When an Object-Z expression is typechecked, it is handled directly by the `oz.ExprChecker` instance. When a standard Z expression is typechecked, the above `visitExpr` method is called, delegating the typechecking to an instance of `z.ExprChecker`. Any subexpressions of the Z expression are passed back to the top-level typechecker, which uses the `oz.ExprChecker` instance, to ensure that Object-Z subexpressions are checked correctly.

This also allows type-rules to be overridden. For example, a selection expression, $a.b$, in standard Z requires that a is a schema binding, whereas in Object-Z, a can also be an object. The `ExprChecker` in the Object-Z implements the visit method for such expressions, and this method first checks if a is an object, and if not, delegates the call to the Z typechecker.

Although this is an unusual design, it has proven to provide good and elegant support for extension. An alternative approach that we considered was for the Object-Z checkers to directly subclass the Z checker subclasses (*e.g.*, `oz.ParaChecker` to inherit `z.ParaChecker`). However, this would have meant that the common code implemented in the current `oz.Checker` class would have had to have been implemented in the base `Checker` class, which would have resulted in an undesirable strong coupling between all of the typecheckers.

Other components are extended using inheritance. For example, the class UnificationEnv, which is responsible for type unification, is extended by overriding its unify method to handle the new Object-Z types, while using the superclass's unify method for standard Z types.

Our experience is that the above extensible typechecker design makes it much easier to build multi-lingual typecheckers. That is, a family of typechecker objects for Z and various extensions of Z. For example, a static checker for Circus that checks some context-sensitive rules such as variable and action declaration scope has been developed following the guidelines for Z and Object-Z typecheckers. This took only three to four days to develop and the task was made significantly easier because of the code reuse and elegant object-oriented design of the CZT typechecker. The information collected by this static checker is being used as an initial environment for the *Circus* operational semantics [23]. In the future, this static checker can also be used as the basis for a full *Circus* typechecker; the type-rules for *Circus* are under development in [24]. An obvious advantage of reusing the base Z typechecker is that the *Circus* typechecker will already enforce standard Z typechecking conformance. Therefore, one can concentrate on the implementation of new type-rules for *Circus* in this available skeleton for a *Circus* typechecker.

In conclusion, CZT supports extendibility in its typecheckers by:

Using Multiple Visitors: A separate visitor is used for each group of type-rules; this provides a straightforward way to implement type-rules for new constructs (by adding new visitors), or override existing type-rules (by subclassing existing visitors).

Sharing Common Code via Inheritance and Delegation: Methods used throughout the typechecker are shared in several abstract super classes that are reused via both inheritance and delegation.

Sharing Resources: The TypeChecker class is used by visitors to provide access to common resources and to other visitors.

6   Animation

Further to parsing and typechecking standard Z and its extensions, CZT also provides animation facilities with its ZLive tool. Z animation is particularly useful for testing, rapid prototyping, and experimenting with specifications. In addition, given suitable restrictions to finite state models, an animator can be used for finite theorem proving (or theorem testing), and model checking. An extensive discussion and comparison of Z animation tools available is given in [25].

6.1   Extending ZLive

ZLive is an animator capable of evaluating predicates and expressions using mode analysis [26]. Mode analysis consists of including additional (type and formulae ordering) information not present in specifications, which enable evaluation and animation. The architecture of ZLive is an evolution of a previous Z animator implemented in Haskell[12].

The ZLive architecture is divided into six tasks. Firstly, a target expression is given. Secondly, the definitions are unfolded so that schema inclusions are grounded to base terms. Next, the unfolded definitions are flattened into a normal form of atomic predicates. After that, possible evaluation modes are calculated for each flatten predicate. These moded-predicates are then reordered according to the cheapest solution order in terms of number of solutions. Finally, all solutions are lazily enumerated as requested.

ZLive currently supports basic logic and arithmetic operators (*e.g.*, $\forall$, $\exists$, $\neg$, $\wedge$, $-$, $+$, $*$, $\leq$, $<$, div, mod, succ), set representations (comprehension, ranges, and displays), unfolding of simple definitions, tuples, and schema bindings. For efficient execution, the main issue is to find a good reordering of atomic predicates which minimises the expected enumeration time. Currently ZLive uses a naive algorithm for this, but in the future we expect to implement a best-first or A^* path-finding algorithm.

It is desirable to provide animation facilities for Z extensions as well as for standard Z. To extend ZLive to animate a new Z extension, there are three possible approaches:

Explicit Inclusion: Animation support for each new language construct, including any new evaluation algorithms, is directly added to ZLive by adding new Java classes and methods. This would use interfaces, inheritance and visitors to achieve an extensible architecture, similar to the CZT typechecker.

Transformation to Standard Z: If each new construct of the Z extension can be transformed back into standard Z using rewriting rules, then ZLive can be used directly on the result of that translation. This approach is being used to develop an Object-Z animator, with Object-Z objects being transformed into Z bindings, *etc.* This approach of rewriting specifications is similar to the Z refinement calculus [27, 13].

Meta-Level Animation: If the operational semantics of the new language can be given in standard Z, one can use ZLive directly to animate the new Z extension by animating its operational semantics. Although this is a meta-level approach to execution, which usually results in very slow performance, the performance impact should be less in this case, because any standard Z constructs within the Z extension can animated efficiently and directly by ZLive. That is, only the new constructs have to be animated by the slower, meta-level approach. This approach is taken for animating the operational semantics of *Circus* [23].

Depending on the new language constructs to be animated, these possibilities can be combined.

---

[12] See http://www.cs.waikato.ac.nz/~marku/jaza/

6.2   Extension Example: Animating *Circus*

We are currently experimenting using ZLive within the development of a model checker for *Circus* [28]. Among other aspects, we are particularly interested in integration of model checking and theorem proving facilities for *Circus*. In this direction, animation plays an important part in the evaluation of Z terms used to describe state aspects of dependable and distributed systems.

The *Circus* model checker architecture is divided into four main tasks as shown in Fig. 3. The first two involve parsing a *Circus* specification in LaTeX to produce an CZT AST, and typechecking to produce an annotated AST$_+$. They use the CZT parser and typechecker described in earlier sections. The last two stages involve compilation and refinement search. From the annotated AST$_+$ the compiler builds a *Predicate Transition System* (PTS) that finitely represent (possibly infinite specifications) base on the operational semantics of *Circus* [23]. Both the PTS and the AST$_+$ are given to the model checker engine that integrates refinement model checking algorithms [29, 30] together with theorem proving and debugging functionalities[13]. The result is a (possibly empty) set of witnesses representing failed refinement conditions. More details of this architecture can be found in [28].

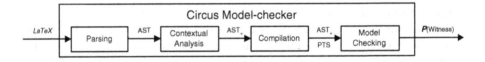

Fig. 3. *Circus* Model Checking Stages

In this architecture, ZLive is used from two different perspectives: (i) to animate the Z part of *Circus* specifications, and (ii) to evaluate the operational semantics of *Circus* given in Z, while performing the model checking search.

To implement the first perspective, we are extending ZLive via *direct inclusion* of several Z constructs (like θ and some schema operators) that are frequently used in *Circus* specifications but not yet implemented by ZLive. To implement the second perspective, we are using the *meta-level animation* approach to animate the operational semantics of the CSP parts of *Circus*.

The *transformation to standard Z* approach could also be used to animate the CSP parts of *Circus*. To have confidence in the correctness of this approach, it would be desirable to have correctness proofs for the rewriting laws. As *Circus* is heavily based on the notion of stepwise refinement, this transformation approach would fit nicely with the philosophy of *Circus*. Work in this direction of a refinement calculus for *Circus* is under development [31]. It also includes the basis for a *Circus* theorem prover [32].

The theorem proving module in the *Circus* model checker (which is used both in the compiler and refinement engine), dispatches requests for evaluation

---

[13] See http://www.cs.york.ac.uk/circus/model-checker

of Z expressions and predicates. These are either verification conditions over the state operations defined in Z, or possible enabling paths available for investigation from the behavioural actions given using CSP. They are both given as standard Z statements from the operational semantics of *Circus*. At this point, theorem proving is usually necessary to discharge proof obligations, and transform expressions or predicates. Nevertheless, for specifications with simple state operations, animation is also a good idea that could improve the automation levels of the model checking process.

The role ZLive plays in this scenario is to tackle the requests to evaluate Z expressions and predicates from the theorem proving module within the compiler and refinement engine. As the operational semantics of *Circus* is given in Z itself, we can use ZLive as a meta-level animator for simple specifications, hence enabling automatic model checking of state-rich *Circus* specifications.

With a few improvements and extensions to the current implementation of the schema calculus in ZLive, it should be possible to automatically model check simple-state *Circus* specifications within ZLive. Furthermore, as the theorem proving integration architecture of the *Circus* model checker allows pluggable solutions suitable for individual contexts, if ZLive cannot handle some complex *Circus* specifications, we can still resort to some alternative solution such as SAT solvers, and general-purpose theorem provers.

These *Circus* tools, some of which are currently under development, give some good examples of how to integrate different CZT tools across different notations and tool boundaries, from standard Z parsing through to extended typechecking and animation for *Circus*.

7   Specification Manager

One of the core components of the CZT framework is the *specification manager*, which is an extensible repository for formal methods objects. Most of the tools mentioned in the previous sections use the specification manager to enquire about specific aspects of a specification. For example, to be able to parse a Z section, the Z parser needs the operator definitions of the parent sections. In order to typecheck a Z section, the section must be parsed and the parents of that section typechecked. To print a Z section in LaTeX markup, the operator definitions and LaTeX markup directives of the parent sections are needed.

While it would be possible to hard-code these dependencies and let, for example, the LaTeX markup printer call the parser for the parent sections directly, it is more convenient, extensible, and efficient to have a central repository that is responsible for this task. The CZT specification manager caches information about all the specifications and Z sections that are being processed and automatically runs tools such as markup converters, parsers and typecheckers when necessary. The caching of the parsed form of commonly used objects, such as standard toolkit sections, avoids repeated parsing and analysis of these objects and can give significant performance improvements.

Abstractly, the cache is a mapping from a key to the actual data. The key is a (String, Class) pair, where the String is usually the name of the section, and the Class is the Java class of the type of data associated with this key. This allows several different kinds of objects to be associated with one section, and provides some dynamic type security. For example, the Z parser adds the AST of a specification it has parsed to the specification manager. The type of a Z section in Java is ZSect.class. Thus the AST for a section called foo is cached under the key (''foo'', ZSect.class).

The CZT specification manager supports two important kinds of extensibility:

Type Extensibility: Z extensions can easily use the specification manager to store new types of information, since the flexible (String, Class) key system allows arbitrary Java objects to be stored and retrieved. That is, the kinds of objects managed by the specification manager are open-ended, rather than being a fixed set of Z-related objects.

Command Extensibility: A Z extension can easily add or override the *default commands* of the specification manager. The default commands of the specification manager are responsible for automatically computing requested objects; they are implemented using the command design pattern [18]. For example, if the AST for section foo (*i.e.*, data of type ZSect.class) is required and has not already been cached, the Z parser is called by the specification manager in order to parse the specification file containing section foo. Here, the Z parser is the default command to compute data of type ZSect.class. A Z extension that needs to use a different parser can simply override the default command associated with the type ZSect.class. For example, the specification manager can be configured to always use the Object-Z parser.

A major advantage of this default command approach is that it simplifies tool development and makes tools more flexible, because a particular tool does not have to know which other tools to use in order to find information about a section — it simply requests the key that it wants and the specification manager will locate the information if it is able. This gives a more flexible, *plugin* style of tool development.

8   Related Work

Integrated formal methods frameworks have been investigated in the past. Anderson *et al.* [33] discuss a framework for integrating different formal methods tools. However, their aim is to specify generic interfaces to support integration of formal methods tools. Three types of interfaces are used: between the engineer and the tools; between cooperating tools; and between the tools and the project environment. They achieve this by using an *Encapsulation Toolkit* to allow a formal methods tool to communicate with other components in an intermediate format, and an *Active Document Toolkit* to allow communication between tools and their human users. The goals of this project are different to CZT, which aims to provide components for Z tools that can be extended and integrated into the project or other tools.

Brillant[14] is an open-source project with similar aims to CZT, but for the B method. It aims to integrate several existing projects (BCaml, jBTools and ABTools), which all contain parsers and typecheckers for various dialects of B. Brillant is an approach to integrating these tools in a loosely-coupled style, with tools being written in several different languages (OCaml, Java and XSLT) and communicating via a common XML format for B machines. Brillant includes a translator from UML to B, plus some experimental B extensions (Event B and a real-time extension of B based on the duration calculus), but the extensions seem to be designed on an individual basis, rather than being tightly integrated extensions of a core architecture like in CZT. The extensible architecture of CZT, and of course, the consistent use of Java for writing the tools, enables a higher degree of reuse.

Other formal methods toolkits exist, such as the RODIN project[15] for the B specification language, and the Overture toolset[16] for VDM, but they focus on providing specific tool support for their respective languages, whereas CZT aims to provide extensible components that can also be used by other tools.

Projects such as Eclipse[17] and UQ*[18] are projects aimed at providing generic language-based environments for software development. However, these projects are not tailored towards formal methods, and provide support for generic languages, leaving the development of parsers, typecheckers, and other language-specific tools up to users who want such support. CZT is exactly the opposite of this, in that it focuses only Z and various Z extensions, allowing specific components, such as parsers and typecheckers, to be included within the framework. Therefore, CZT could be integrated into the Eclipse or UQ* environments.

9   Conclusions and Future Work

In this paper, we have presented a variety of reuse and extensibility mechanisms that makes the CZT framework an ideal starting point to develop new integrated formal methods tools for Z and its extensions. We have shown how the XML schemas for Z, and for extensions of Z, support reuse and extension of the Z language. They also enable automatic generation of Java AST classes with two levels of interface, and a consistent implementation of the CZT visitor pattern.

Using examples from Object-Z, TCOZ, and *Circus*, we have discussed several practical strategies and techniques that allow the CZT tools like parsers, typecheckers, and animators developed for standard Z to be reused within these Z extensions in a way that minimises code duplication and maintenance. The

---

[14] See https://gna.org/projects/brillant.

[15] See http://rodin-b-sharp.sourceforge.net/.

[16] See http://www.overturetool.org/.

[17] See http://www.eclipse.org/.

[18] See http://www.itee.uq.edu.au/~uqstar/.

strategies and techniques presented can also help developers of integrated formal methods tools not based on Z to make their framework as extensible as possible.

We plan to develop additional tools for Z and its extensions, as well as extending the CZT framework itself. For instance, extensions of ZLive providing Object-Z constructs, schema unfolding, predicate reordering, rewriting rules, and a tactic language in the spirit of ANGEL [34] are on our agenda. These improvements would enable a basis for an extensible theorem prover for standard Z and its extensions that is open-source and cross-platform.

Z parsing and typechecking is neither a novel idea, nor a unavailable resource. Nevertheless, flexible and integrated open-source support for ISO standard Z heavily focused on strong conformance and extensibility has not previously been available. The **philosophy CZT advocates is simple: provide an open-source framework with a set of tools for editing, parsing, typechecking and animating formal specifications written in Z, with support for Z extensions**. As new extensions are included and the framework matures, we expect it to become the common base for a growing number of strongly conforming tools for Z and its extensions.

References

1. ISO/IEC 13568: Information Technology—Z Formal Specification Notation—Syntax, Type System and Semantics. First edn. ISO/IEC (2002)
2. Malik, P., Utting, M.: CZT: A Framework for Z Tools. In Treharne, H., King, S., Henson, M., Schneider, S., eds.: ZB 2005: Formal Specification and Development in Z and B: 4th International Conference of B and Z Users, Guildford, UK, April 13-15, 2005. Proceedings, Springer-Verlag (2005)
3. Fischer, C.: How to combine Z with process algebras. Technical report, University of Oldenburg (1998)
4. Fischer, C.: Combination and Implementation of Process and Data: from CSP-OZ to Java. PhD thesis, University of Oldenburg (2000)
5. Woodcock, J., Cavalcanti, A.: A Concurrent Language for Refinement. 5th Irish Workshop on Formal Methods (2001)
6. Smith, G.: The Object-Z Specification Language. Advances in Formal Methods. Kluwer Academic Publishers (2000)
7. Cavalcanti, A.L.C., Sampaio, A., Woodcock, J.C.P.: Unifying Classes and Processes. Journal on Software and Systems Modelling (2005) To appear.
8. Mahony, B., Dong, J.S.: Timed Communicating Object-Z. IEEE Transactions on Software Engineering **26** (2000) 150–177
9. Sherif, A., He, J.: Toward a Time Model for *Circus*. In George, C., Miao, H., eds.: ICFEM 2002. Volume 2495 of LNCS., Springer-Verlag (2002) 613–624
10. Tang, X., Woodcock, J.: Towards Mobile Processes in Unifying Theories. In Cuellar, J., Liu, Z., eds.: SEFM2004: the 2nd IEEE International Conference on Software Engineering and Formal Methods. (2004) 44–53
11. Schneider, S., Davies, J.: A Brief History of Timed CSP. Theoretical Computer Science **138** (1995) 243–271
12. Roscoe, A.W.: The Theory and Practice of Concurrency. 1st edn. International Series in Computer Science. Prentice-Hall (1997)
13. Morgan, C.: Programming from Specifications. Second edn. Prentice-Hall (1994)

14. Hoare, C., Jifeng, H.: Unifying Theories of Programming. First edn. International Series in Computer Science. Prentice-Hall (1998)
15. Utting, M., Toyn, I., Sun, J., Martin, A., Dong, J.S., Daley, N., Currie, D.: ZML: XML Support for Standard Z. In: ZB 2003: Formal Specification and Development in Z and B: Third International Conference of B and Z Users, Turku, Finland, June 4-6, 2003. Proceedings, Springer-Verlag (2003) 437–456
16. Meisels, I., Saaltink, M.: Z/Eves 1.5 Reference Manual. ORA Canada. (1997) TR-97-5493-03d.
17. Saaltink, M., Meisels, I.: The Core Z/Eves API (DRAFT). Technical Report TR-99-5540-xx, ORA Canada (2003)
18. Gamma, E., Helm, R., Johnson, R., Vlissides, J.: Design Patterns: Elements of Reusable Object-Oriented Software. Addison Wesley, USA (1995)
19. Mai, Y., de Champlain, M.: A Pattern Language To Visitors. In: The 8th Annual Conference of Pattern Languages of Programs (PLoP 2001), Monticello, Illinois, USA. (2001)
20. Martin, A.C.: Acyclic visitor. In Martin, R.C., Riehle, D., Buschmann, F., eds.: Pattern Languages of Program Design 3, Addison-Wesley Longman Publishing Co., Inc. (1997)
21. Nordberg III, M.E.: Default and Extrinsic Visitor. In Martin, R.C., Riehle, D., Buschmann, F., eds.: Pattern Languages of Program Design 3, Addison-Wesley Longman Publishing Co., Inc. (1997)
22. Barbosa, A.: A Parser for *Circus*. Graduation Research Project (2002)
23. Woodcock, J., Cavalcanti, A., Freitas, L.: *Circus* Operational Semantics. In: Proceedings of Formal Methods Europe. (2005)
24. Xavier, M.: *Circus* Type-checker. Master's thesis, Universidade Federal de Pernambuco, Brazil (2006) In preparation.
25. Utting, M.: Data Structures for Z Testing Tools. Technical report, University of Waikato, Hamilton, New Zeland (1999)
26. Winikoff, M.: Analysing modes and subtypes in Z specifications. Technical Report 98/2, University of Melbourne, Department of Computer Science, Parkville, Victoria 3052, Australia (1998)
27. Cavalcanti, A.: A Refinement Calculus for Z. PhD thesis, Oxford University (1997) Also published as a PRG Technical Monograph at web.comlab.ox.ac.uk/oucl/publications/monos/prg-123.html.
28. Freitas, L.: Model Checking *Circus*. PhD thesis, Univeristy of York (2005) To appear in October 2005.
29. A. W. Roscoe: Model checking CSP. In book: A Classical Mind: Essays in Honour of C. A. R. Hoare (1994) 353–378
30. Cleaveland, R., Hennessy, M.: Testing Equivalence as a Bisimulation Equivalence. Formal Aspects of Computing 5 (1993) 1–20
31. Oliveira, M.: A Refinement Calculus for *Circus*. PhD thesis, University of York (2005) To appear in December 2005.
32. Oliveira, M., Cavalcanti, A., Woodcock, J.: Unifying Theories in ProofPowerZ. draft, Univeristy of York (2005)
33. Anderson, P., Goldsmith, M., Scattergood, B., Teitelbaum, T.: An Environment for Integrating Formal Methods Tools. In: User Interfaces for Theorem Provers. (1997)
34. Martin, A.P., Gardiner, P.H.B., Woodcock, J.C.P.: A Tactic Calculus. Formal Aspects of Computing 8 (1996) 244–285

Embedding the Stable Failures
Model of CSP in PVS

Kun Wei and James Heather

Department of Computing, University of Surrey, Guildford, Surrey GU2 7XH, UK
{k.wei, j.heather}@surrey.ac.uk

Abstract. We present an embedding of the stable failures model of CSP in the PVS theorem prover. Our work, extending a previous embedding of the traces model of CSP in [6], provides a platform for the formal verification not only of safety specifications, but also of liveness specifications of concurrent systems in theorem provers. Such a platform is particularly good at analyzing infinite-state systems with an arbitrary number of components. We demonstrate the power of this embedding by using it to construct formal proofs that the asymmetric dining philosophers problem with an arbitrary number of philosophers is deterministic and deadlock-free, and that an industrial-scale example, a 'virtual network' [21], with any number of dimensions, is deadlock-free. We have established some generic proof tactics for verification of properties of networks with many components. In addition, our technique of integrating FDR and PVS in our demonstration allows for handling of systems that would be difficult or impossible to analyze using either tool on its own.

Keywords: CSP, theorem prover, liveness, deadlock, determinism.

1 Introduction

Concurrent systems are often complex because they consist of many components that can run independently and simultaneously. Proving properties of these systems is also often a difficult task. CSP provides a rich notation for modelling these kinds of system, and the many laws of CSP can be used to verify specifications of such systems, thus enabling designers to check whether the systems meet desired properties or not. However, constructing proofs of correctness by hand is arduous and error-prone.

One highly successful solution to this problem is FDR [9], which is a powerful model-checking tool providing automated analysis and verification of CSP process descriptions. In conjunction with many advanced techniques including data independence [11] and hierarchical compression [15], FDR can in many cases deal efficiently with processes with vast or even infinite state spaces. However, most classes of infinite-state processes are out of reach of model-checking with current techniques. Data independence allows model-checking of systems that have an infinite state space on account of an infinite datatype, but not of systems with an arbitrary number of concurrent processes. The alternative is to take a theorem-proving approach, which allows us to reason about arbitrary processes.

J. Romijn, G. Smith, and J. van de Pol (Eds.): IFM 2005, LNCS 3771, pp. 246–265, 2005.

PVS [4, 5], the *Prototype Verification System*, is an interactive theorem prover based on a form of higher-order logic. It provides an environment for constructing precise specifications, and for efficient mechanized verification. Although it is similar in many ways to other theorem provers such as Isabelle/HOL [13] and IMPS [8], it supports a richer type system, and checks semantic consistency for a PVS specification. PVS is also a natural choice for this work because of previous work in [6, 19, 7] where the authors represent the denotational semantics of the traces model of CSP in PVS and then apply their proof strategy to model and verify various safety properties of security protocols. Since the stable failures model records both traces and failures information, we choose to take Dutertre and Schneider's PVS traces embedding and augment it with stable failures.

The extension from Dutertre and Schneider's encoding of the traces model to our embedding of the stable failures model is not at all trivial. They do not consider various important operators of CSP, such as successful termination and sequential composition; our embedding, however, does include these operators, along with various laws about their behaviour. In addition, in order to verify deadlock freedom and determinism, we have formally proved many crucial rules, including the unique fixed point theorem, deterministic induction and various deadlock rules. These rules have previously been proved only by hand; we here give rigorous machine-verified proofs.

Dutertre and Schneider's embedding could prove only safety properties; our platform can verify liveness properties (for example, deadlock freedom and determinism), which cannot be analyzed in the traces model. We will show in this paper how to prove determinism and deadlock freedom of the asymmetric dining philosophers network with an arbitrary number of philosophers, using mathematical induction. In the case of deadlock freedom, the work in PVS essentially reduces the problem to a very small model-checking verification exercise involving under 100 states. Although the proof could be completed entirely in PVS, it would be extremely tedious and time-consuming to perform this model-checking manually in a theorem prover; the more natural approach, and the one adopted here, is to use FDR to complete the finite-state model-checking part of the verification. The main idea of the proof comes from [15], which uses a hierarchical compression technique in FDR to prove the case with very large numbers of philosophers.

Moreover, we have formally proved some of the deadlock rules described in [14], which can be used to construct deadlock-free networks. These formal proofs provide rigorous verification of the rules. The significance of these rules is that FDR can then verify deadlock freedom of complex networks by analysis of individual components of the network. Here we show how to construct the formal proof of these rules, and then use the rules to prove deadlock freedom of a case study in PVS.

In contrast to model-checking, embedding the semantics of CSP into higher-order logics provides mechanical support for verifying the correctness of properties in a system. In the early stage, Camilleri [2] has shown how a theorem prover based on higher-order logic can provide a natural framework for mechanizing CSP. However, his mechanization was slightly restricted since both the semantics of CSP and theorem-proving tools have been improved over the past decade.

Tej and Wolff [20] provide a basic platform of encoding the denotational semantics of the CSP failures/divergences model in Isabelle/HOL, along with verifying the consistency of theories and a number of algebraic laws. Our experience suggests, however, that simply providing an embedding is far from sufficient to allow one to verify properties of systems in practice. We therefore have built up a large number of theorems and lemmas to support the verification of particular properties of practical systems. Isobe and Roggenbach [10] propose a new tool called CSP-Prover which provides an encoding of the CSP stable failures model. It appears that this encoding, based on the theorem prover Isabelle/HOL, is essentially an extension of Tej and Wolff's work; their formalization supports the theory of complete metric spaces as well as the theory of complete partial orders, allowing it to deal with a much wider class of properties of recursion. We have taken a similar approach in our model; furthermore, we have established a class of generic proof tactics, and shown how to combine the use of FDR and a theorem prover so that we are able to model and verify properties of many different types of system.

Brooke [1] uses Timed CSP and PVS and FDR to construct tool-supported proofs to verify properties of systems on an industrial scale. Another successful case is the programming language *Circus* [3, 16], which combines CSP and Z to specify, validate and develop real-time programs. All *Circus* refinement laws are proved using the theorem prover ProofPower-Z.

The remainder of the paper is organized as follows. We will give a brief introduction to the notation of CSP and the denotational semantics of the stable failures model; we then show how to embed this model in PVS; we present some generic proof tactics and our case study, proving using our formalization that the asymmetric dining philosophers with an arbitrary number of philosophers is deadlock-free and deterministic, and that a 'virtual network' [21] with any number of dimensions is deadlock-free as a consequence of various deadlock rules; finally, we give conclusions and discuss future work.

2   CSP Notation

CSP is an event-orientated language for describing concurrent systems and their interactions. A system can be considered as a process that might be hierarchically composed of many smaller processes. An individual process can be combined with events or other processes by operators such as prefixing, choice, parallel composition, and so on. There are four semantic models available—traces, stable failures, failures/divergences, and failures/divergences/infinite traces—and which one is chosen depends on what properties of the system one is trying to analyze. In this paper, we choose the CSP stable failures model since this provides a rich enough framework for analysis of deadlock freedom and determinism (for processes known to be non-divergent).

The traces model is the simplest model, in which processes are described according to sequences of events they engage in. The stable failures model, described in detail in [14, 18], records stable failures as well as traces.

Traces tell us exactly what a process can do, but nothing about what it can refuse to do. A refusal set is a set of events from which a process can fail to accept anything no matter how long it is offered; a failure is then defined as a pair (t, X), where $t \in traces(P)$ and X is a refusal of the process P after it has performed the trace t. If the trace t can make no internal progress, this failure is called a *stable failure*.

The basic syntax of CSP we use is described by the following grammar:

$$P ::= Div \mid Stop \mid Skip \mid a \rightarrow P \mid P_1 \;\Box\; P_2 \mid P_1 \sqcap P_2 \mid$$
$$P_1 \underset{A}{\parallel} P_2 \mid P \setminus A \mid f(P) \mid P_1;\; P_2$$

where we assume Σ is a universal set including all possible events for processes under consideration, a is an element of Σ, and A is a subset of Σ.

Div is a process which does nothing except diverge. *Stop* is a stable deadlocked process that never performs any events. *Skip* is used to denote successfully termination, and it expresses this by means of the termination event $\checkmark$, which is not a member of Σ. The process $a \rightarrow P$ behaves like P after performing the event a.

The external choice $P_1 \;\Box\; P_2$ may behave either like P_1 or like P_2, depending on what events its environment initially offers. The traces of internal choice $P_1 \sqcap P_2$ are the same as those of $P_1 \;\Box\; P_2$, but the choice in this case is nondeterministic.

The interface parallel $P_1 \underset{A}{\parallel} P_2$ is the process where all events in the interface A must be synchronized, and other events can be performed independently. The interleaving and alphabetized parallel operators can be defined in terms of interface parallel.

The hiding process $P \setminus A$ will pass through the same events as P, but events in the set A become be invisible. The renamed process $f(P)$ means that, for example, an event a in such a process is completely replaced by $f(a)$ where f is a mapping function. The sequential composition $P_1;\; P_2$ passes control to P_2 when P_1 terminates successfully.

Note that recording only stable failures is not enough because it is not guaranteed that every process has one. For instance, after a process diverges—that is, after it reaches a state from which it can perform an infinite sequence of internal events—it may never reach a stable state, and hence has no more stable failures. Therefore, it is necessary to record traces separately in the stable failures model; each process is represented as the pair $(traces(P), failures(P))$.

The stable failures model consists of all those pairs (T, F) with $T \subseteq \Sigma^{*\checkmark}$ and $F \subseteq \Sigma^{*\checkmark} \times \mathbb{P}(\Sigma^{\checkmark})$ [1] that satisfy the following conditions:

---

[1] Σ^* is the set of all finite sequences over Σ and $\mathbb{P}(\Sigma)$ is a powerset; $\Sigma^{*\checkmark} = \Sigma^* \cup \{t^\frown \langle\checkmark\rangle \mid t \in \Sigma^*\}$ and $\Sigma^{\checkmark} = \Sigma \cup \{\checkmark\}$.

$$T \text{ is non-empty and prefix closed} \tag{SF1}$$

$$(t, X) \in F \Rightarrow t \in T \tag{SF2}$$

$$(t, X) \in F \wedge Y \subseteq X \Rightarrow (t, Y) \in F \tag{SF3}$$

$$(t, X) \in F \wedge (\forall a \in Y)(t \frown \langle a \rangle \notin T \Rightarrow (t, X \cup Y) \in F) \tag{SF4}$$

$$t \frown \langle \checkmark \rangle \in T \Rightarrow (t, \Sigma) \in F \tag{SF5}$$

$$t \frown \langle \checkmark \rangle \in T \Rightarrow (t \frown \langle \checkmark \rangle, X) \in F \tag{SF6}$$

The stable failures model deliberately ignores divergence; in situations in which divergence is not an issue, this brings considerable convenience in the form of reduced complexity of the model. For instance, if we know in advance that a process is divergence-free, using the stable failures model can greatly reduce the complexity of the refinement (regardless of whether we are doing theorem-proving or model-checking).

Divergence is not considered as deadlock in the stable failures model, though it is considered as deadlock in failures/divergences. This is precisely what we need here: we shall make considerable use of the fact that hiding of events makes no difference to deadlock freedom. Our formalization follows the denotational semantics of CSP. Detailed semantics of the stable failures model can be found in [14].

3   Embedding CSP Semantics in PVS

As a first step, we need to formalize the CSP notation in PVS. Dutertre and Schneider's embedding of the traces model in PVS [6] already defines most of the notation that we need; we extend it to the stable failures model, introducing along the way the new operators and laws of CSP that we will require.

The stable failures model is represented by pairs (T, F) in which T is a set of traces that forms the semantics of a process in the traces model. The classic formalization of traces is to simply consider traces as lists of events.

The special event $\checkmark$ is not a member of Σ and can never be performed by a process unless this is the last event that it engages in. To represent the extended alphabet $\Sigma^{\checkmark}$, we define a datatype as follows:

```
E [T:TYPE]: DATATYPE WITH SUBTYPES TE, NTE
  BEGIN
    tick:tick?:TE
    ES(a:T):non_tick?:NTE
  END E
```

where we also define two subtypes TE and NTE. Here, NTE is used to represent Σ.

PVS provides a predefined abstract datatype list. Thus, the type trace defined as follows is simply a subtype of list.

```
trace: TYPE ={ l:list[E] | tick_free?(front(l)) }
```

where the function `front` returns the entire list except for the final element, and `tick_free?` is a predicate that determines whether or not the list includes the event $\checkmark$. The expression above therefore ensures that $\checkmark$ cannot appear except at the end of a trace.

3.1   Processes

Processes in the stable failures model consist of pairs (T, F) that satisfy the six conditions mentioned in Section 2. Our definition of processes relies on PVS subtyping: `process` is a subtype of `SF` defined as follows:

```
SF: VAR [set[trace[T]], set[[trace[T],set[E]]]]
process:TYPE= {SF | SF1(SF) and SF2(SF) and SF3(SF) and
               SF4(SF) and SF5(SF) and SF6(SF) }
```

where SF1–SF6 are the six predicate type functions derived from the stable failures model's conditions (SF1)–(SF6) from Section 2. Note that T is a type parameter which denotes the type of elements of a trace, and `trace[T]` will automatically add in the special event $\checkmark$.

Table 1. CSP syntax

Operation	CSP	CSP$_M$	PVS
Stop	*Stop*	STOP	Stop
Skip	*Skip*	SKIP	Skip
Prefix	$a \rightarrow P$	a -> P	a >> P
External choice	$P_1 \square P_2$	P1 [] P2	P1 \/ P2
Internal choice	$P_1 \sqcap P_2$	P1 |~| P2	P1 /\ P2
Interface parallel	$P_1 \underset{A}{\\|} P_2$	P1 [|A|] P2	Par(A)(P1,P2)
Alphabetized parallel	$P_1 {}_A\\|_B P_2$	P1 [A||B] P2	Par(A,B)(P1,P2)
Interleave	$P_1 \\|\\|\\| P_2$	P1 ||| P2	P1 // P2
Hiding	$P \setminus A$	P\A	P/A
Renaming	$f(P)$	P[a<->b]	Re(P, f)
Sequential composition	$P_1;\ P_2$	P1;P2	Seq(P1,P2)

All of CSP's main operators are listed in Table 1, with the standard CSP syntax, the CSP$_M$ syntax (as used in FDR), and PVS's syntax. Note that in this paper, we consider only injective renaming since it leaves the behaviour of a process unchanged except for the names of the actions, and it thus has a rich set of laws. Even so, injectivity is not sufficient for some laws in the stable failures model: sometimes we need the renaming function to be bijective. (This is clearly an issue only when Σ is infinite.)

We also define *indexed* versions of the choice and parallel operators, which are often used in analyzing a large network. In particular, we use `Echoice(P)` and `Par(A)(P)` to denote $\square_{i \in I} P_i$ and $\parallel_{i=1}^{n} (P_i, A_i)$ respectively, where P is a parametric process and A is a parametric set.

FDR's main function is to determine whether one process refines another. In the stable failures model, this equates to checking whether the traces and failures of one process are subsets of the traces and failures of the other:

$$ P \sqsubseteq_F Q \equiv traces(P) \supseteq traces(Q) \wedge failures(P) \supseteq failures(Q) $$

The idea of refinement is still kept in verifying properties of processes in PVS. For example, for proving a process Q deadlock-free, we often explicitly construct a deadlock-free specification P, then check whether Q refines P or whether Q is a subset of P. Obviously, if Q refines P and P is deadlock-free, then Q is deadlock-free as well.

We use the relation '<=' to denote refinement of processes in PVS: `Q <= P`, representing $P \sqsubseteq Q$ in CSP, corresponds to $Q \subseteq P$. Since '<=' and `subset?` have been predefined in the prelude library of PVS, we rewrite them so that they can compare a pair of sets. So `<=` is defined as the following:

```
<=(Q, P) : bool = subset?(Q, P)
```

3.2 Fixed Points and Recursive Processes

Some processes, called recursive processes, may run indefinitely, instead of executing for a finite number of steps and then stopping; Unfortunately, we cannot define such processes directly in PVS since a theorem prover will not allow us to get away with any kind of recursive definition unless we can demonstrate that it is well-defined.

The formalization used in [6] to deal with recursive processes is the 'μ-calculus' theory, which uses a μ operator ('mu' in PVS) to compute the least fixed point of a monotonic function[2]. We have extended this to the stable failures model since all CSP operators are monotonic over the stable failures model with respect to the refinement order and the subset order. We also have proved a general fixed point induction theorem, which is crucial in analyzing refinement of recursive processes:

```
induction: PROPOSITION
   (FORALL X : X<=H IMPLIES  F(X)<=H) IMPLIES mu(F)<=H
```

We also have extended the least-fixed-point theory to represent mutually recursive processes. The general case of a mutual recursion is concerned with a family or *vector* of processes $\underline{X}$, and the recursive definition then takes the

---

[2] A monotonic function in this context is a function F such that if $Q \leq P$ then $F(Q) \leq F(P)$.

form $\underline{X} = \underline{F}(\underline{X})$ where $\underline{F}$ is a function from a vector of processes to a vector of processes. It is still appropriate to use the least fixed point of the function $\underline{F}$ to represent a mutual recursion. In addition, we have proved that all lemmas and induction theorems of the least fixed point still hold in mutual recursions.

In order for fixed points to be useful, we will usually want to show that a function has a unique fixed point. Roscoe [14] shows how to apply a restriction operator and a constructive function to demonstrate the existence of a unique fixed point. We first formally define the restriction operator

```
chop(P, n):process[T]=( {t| P'1(t) and length(t) <= n},
                        {(t,A)| P'2(t,A) and length(t) < n})
```

where the purpose of '*chop*' is to restrict the process P so that it can never perform any traces of greater than length $n \in \mathbb{N}$. Note that we here use '<' for stable failures in the definition because we want to make such a definition consistent with a fact that *Div* is the least element in the subset order.

We then say that F is *constructive* if

```
constructive?(F):bool= FORALL P,Q,n: chop(P,n)=chop(Q,n)
                       IMPLIES chop(F(P),n+1)=chop(F(Q),n+1)
```

For a function F, we have that whenever $F(X) = X$ and $F(Y) = Y$ then $X = Y$, then we say that F has a unique fixed point. The mathematical background of the unique fixed point theorem is not covered in this paper; Roscoe [14] gives a detailed explanation in terms of partial orders and of metric spaces.

In addition, we have proven a number of algebraic laws which are essential in the verification of properties of processes, whereas these laws can help us to verify the consistency of the CSP semantics.

4   Generic Proof Tactics

Our aim in embedding the denotational semantics of the stable failures model of CSP into PVS is not only to verify the consistency of theories and algebraic laws of CSP, but also to build up some strategies so that we can check properties of various infinite-state systems. The focus is especially on liveness properties, which cannot be analyzed in the traces model. Our first step in this direction is the verification of some general properties such as determinism and deadlock freedom.

4.1   Determinism

A deterministic process always behaves in the same way when offered exactly the same inputs. The most obvious practical benefit is that this kind of process is testable because its behaviour does not vary unless the external inputs are changed.

Of course, only processes known to be divergence-free can be verified in the stable failures model, because this model cannot detect divergence. In Figure 1,

```
determinism  [T:TYPE ] : THEORY
  BEGIN
  IMPORTING fixed_points[T]

  t: VAR trace[E]
  a: VAR E
  n: VAR nat
  A,B: VAR set[E]
  P,Q,X: VAR process[E]
  F: VAR [process[E]->process[E]]

  DET?(P):bool= FORALL t,a: P'1(add(t,a))
                     IMPLIES NOT P'2((t,singleton(a)))

  det_stop: LEMMA    DET?(Stop[E])
  det_prefix: LEMMA  DET?(P)  IMPLIES DET?(a>>P)
  det_par: LEMMA DET?(P) AND DET?(Q) IMPLIES DET?(Par(A,B)(P,Q))

  det_seq: LEMMA DET?(P) AND DET?(Q) IMPLIES DET?(Seq(P,Q))
  det_chop: LEMMA DET?(P) IFF (FORALL n: DET?(chop(P,n)))
  det_subset: LEMMA (DET?(P) AND Q <= P ) IMPLIES DET?(Q)

  det_induction: LEMMA ( constructive?(F) AND (EXISTS X: DET?(X))
          AND (FORALL X: DET?(X) IMPLIES DET?(F(X))) )
                     IMPLIES  DET?(mu(F))

END determinism
```

Fig. 1. Examples of deterministic rules

the definition DET? states that a deterministic process can not accept an event a as well as being able to refuse this event; here, add(t,a) adds the event a onto the end of the trace t. Note that E has been previously defined as a datatype including the special event $\checkmark$.

Some CSP operators preserve determinism: if P and Q are deterministic then so are *Stop*, $a \rightarrow P$, $P \ _A\|_B \ Q$ and sequential composition $P;Q$. Such laws and some useful lemmas are also listed in Figure 1. Furthermore, if $initials(P)$ and $initials(Q)$ are disjoint then $P \ \Box \ Q$ is also deterministic. Here, $initials(P)$ is the set of all of P's initial events; for example, it can be defined as follows:

$$initials(P) = \{a \in \Sigma^{\checkmark} \mid \langle a \rangle \in traces(P)\}$$

Proving determinism of non-recursive processes is often not difficult but it can be time consuming. For recursive processes, one has to apply an induction rule such as det_induction in Figure 1 to make any progress; this rule states that if F is constructive and determinism-preserving then the least fixed point of F is also deterministic.

Note that the induction rule here does not imply that every recursive deterministic process is the least fixed point of a constructive determinism-preserving function. In addition, it is also possible in some cases to infer the determinism of $mu(F)$ directly. Usually, however, the easiest way to prove that a recursive process is deterministic is by means of this theorem. For this reason, the determinism induction theorem proved here will be extremely useful in many applications.

4.2   Deadlock Freedom

One of the most important concepts concerning concurrent systems is deadlock, which arises when no further progress can be made. Deadlock is a kind of liveness property, so we cannot detect or reason about it using traces alone. The stable failures model, however, is quite suitable for describing deadlock freedom. The definition of deadlock freedom as well as some laws are given in Figure 2.

Divergence is considered deadlock-free in the stable failures model, while it is not deadlock-free in the failures/divergences model. The usual way to prove deadlock freedom of a recursive process is to define a deadlock-free specification explicitly, and prove that the process is a refinement of the specification; then obviously the refining process is deadlock-free as well.

```
deadlock_free [T: TYPE] : THEORY
  BEGIN
  ....
  a: VAR E
  t: VAR trace[E]
  P,Q: VAR process[E]
  A: VAR set[E]
  f: VAR [set[E]->set[E]]

  DLF?(P):bool = FORALL t:  P'1(t) IMPLIES NOT P'2((t,fullset))

  dlf_prefix: LEMMA  DLF?(P) IMPLIES DLF?(a>>P)
  dlf_echoice: LEMMA DLF?(P) AND DLF?(Q) IMPLIES DLF?(P\/Q)
  dlf_hide: LEMMA DLF?(P) IFF DLF?( P/ A )
  dlf_rename: LEMMA injective?(f)
                      IMPLIES (DLF?(P) IFF DLF?(Re(P,f)))
  dlf_subset: LEMMA subset?(P,Q) AND DLF?(Q) IMPLIES DLF?(P)
  ....

END deadlock_free
```

Fig. 2. Generic deadlock-free rules

Figure 2 also shows two important laws, `dlf_hide` and `dlf_rename`, that are extremely useful in the analysis of deadlock freedom in the stable failures model. These two facts underpin the definition of deadlock freedom: deadlock means reaching a state where no further progress is possible regardless of whether the actions are renamed or hidden.

Deadlock freedom is a global property; in other words, we cannot guarantee that if all components of a network are individually deadlock-free then the whole network will also be deadlock-free. Often, the complexity and the work of verification of a particular property can be greatly reduced by decomposing a global property of a network into local properties of the network's components; this is not easy to do, however, with deadlock freedom.

There are, however, some deadlock rules that can be used to analyze a large network locally rather than considering the whole network all the time. Roscoe [14] gives various deadlock rules, and shows how to apply these rules to prove deadlock freedom of some large networks. We have proved some of these deadlock rules at a formal level, in order to be able to construct formal proofs of deadlock freedom of various networks.

The terminology introduced here is taken from [14]. We consider a network $V = \left\|_{i=1}^{n} (P_i, A_i)\right.$, which is a parallel composition of a finite sequence of processes $\langle P_1, \ldots, P_n \rangle$ and their alphabets. We shall suppose that V is triple-disjoint[3], and that no component process ever terminates or deadlocks. In such a network, a state is defined as the pair $(s, \langle X_1, ..., X_n \rangle)$ in a network V where $s \in (\bigcup_{i=1}^{n} A_i)^*$, $(s \upharpoonright A_i, X_i) \in failures(P_i)$, and $X_i \supseteq \Sigma \setminus initials(P_i/(s \upharpoonright A_i))$. Here, $\upharpoonright$ is the projection operator and $\setminus$ is to calculate difference of two sets. Therefore, a state is in deadlock if the union of all refusal sets X_i is equal to the Σ.

The concepts that we shall need, such as *ungranted request*, *conflict* and so on are now straightforward to define formally in Figure 3. Note that we here completely ignore the event $\checkmark$ since the assumption is that no P_i can terminate. In a state $(s, \langle X_P, X_Q \rangle)$, we say there is an *ungranted request* from P to Q in the composition $P \,_A\|_B\, Q$ if P can communicate in B but they can not agree on any communication in $A \cap B$. Obviously, ungranted requests are the underlying factors that result in deadlock. We here use a predicate `ung_request?(A,B)(P,Q)(t,X1,X2)` in Figure 3 to define such an ungranted request.

There is a *conflict* between P and Q if there is an ungranted request in both directions. The formal definition may be expressed as `CF?(A,B)(P,Q)` in Figure 3. Additionally, a *strong conflict* is a conflict in which one of the two processes has its only ungranted request to the other. Finally, a network V is *conflict-free* if no pair of its nodes is in conflict. We here use `CFF?(X)(S)` to describe this property in Figure 3.

The following fundamental result quoted from [14] underlies all of the deadlock rules.

---

[3] If P_i, P_j and P_k are three distinct nodes of V, then $A_i \cap A_j \cap A_k = \emptyset$.

```
conflict[T:TYPE]: THEORY
  BEGIN
  ....
  A,B,X1,X2:VAR set[T]
  P,Q: VAR process[T]
  t: VAT trace[T]
  ....
  ung_request?(A,B)(P,Q)(t,X1,X2):bool = P'2(proj(t,A),X1) AND
          Q'2(proj(t,B),X2) AND subset?(sigma(t),union(A,B)) AND
          subset?(complement(initials(P,proj(t,A))),X1) AND
          subset?(complement(initials(Q,proj(t,B))),X2) AND
  subset?(union(complement(X1),complement(X2)), intersection(A,B))
          AND intersection(B,complement(X1)) /= emptyset AND
          subset?(intersection(B,complement(X1)),X2)

  CF?(A,B)(P,Q):bool=EXISTS t,X1,X2: ung_request?(A,B)(P,Q)(t,X1,X2)
                                AND ung_request?(B,A)(Q,P)(t,X2,X1)

  SCF?(A,B)(P,Q):bool=EXISTS t,X1,X2: ung_request?(A,B)(P,Q)(t,X1,X2)
                                AND ung_request?(B,A)(Q,P)(t,X2,X1)
     AND ( subset?(complement(X1), B) OR subset?(complement(X2), A) )
  ....
  CFF?(X)(S):bool= FORALL i,j: i/=j IMPLIES
                                NOT CF?(X(i),X(j))(S(i),S(j))
  SCFF?(X)(S):bool= FORALL i,j: i/=j IMPLIES
                                NOT SCF?(X(i),X(j))(S(i),S(j))
  ....
END conflict
```

Fig. 3. The definitions of ungranted request and conflict

Fundamental Principle of Deadlock. *If V is a network which satisfies our basic assumptions and which is free of strong conflict, then any deadlock state of V contains a proper cycle of ungranted requests.*

To prove this law, we have to define a finite network, as in Figure 4, which guarantees the existence of a proper cycle of ungranted requests. One of the most important laws with regard to ungranted requests is dl_ung_request which shows that in a deadlock state, for any node, there always exist two other distinct nodes such that the three nodes together form a sequence of ungranted requests. The proof of this fundamental law comes as a fairly straightforward consequence of the lemma dl_ung_request, because any ungranted request from any process S_i to another process S_j will then guarantee an ungranted request from S_j to some S_k, and so on; this sequence must repeat since the network is finite. In the formal definition listed in Figure 4, we use a predicate DL?(V'2)(V'3)

```
deadlock_rules[T:TYPE]: THEORY
  BEGIN
  ....
  NET:TYPE=[size,[below[size]->set[E]],[below[size]->process[T]]]
  V: VAR NET

  dl_ung_request: LEMMA (Assump?(X)(S) AND SCFF?(X)(S) AND DL?(X)(S))
                               IMPLIES
    FORALL i:EXISTS j,k: (S(i)/=S(j) AND S(j)/=S(k) AND S(i)/=S(k))
    AND (EXISTS t,X1,X2:ung_request?(X(i),X(j))(S(i),S(j)(t,X1,X2)))
    AND (EXISTS t,X1,X2:ung_request?(X(j),X(k))(S(j),S(k)(t,X1,X2)))


  ....
  fundamental_princple: LEMMA (ASSUMP?(V'2)(V'3) AND CFF?(V'2)(V'3)
                  AND DL?(V'2)(V'3)) IMPLIES  cycle?(V)

  pre_rule2?(V):bool =  ASSUMP?(V'2)(V'3) AND CFF?(V'2)(V'3) AND
         ( (EXISTS t,X1,X2: V'3(j)<=V'3(i) AND
               ung_request?(V'2(i),V'2(j))(V'3(i),V'3(j))(t,X1,x2))
           IMPLIES ( FORALL (k:{x:nat|V'3(x)<=V'3(i) AND
                          intersection(V'2(x),V'2(i))/=emptyset}):
                          EXISTS t,X1,X2:
               ung_request?(V'2(k),V'2(i))(V'3(k),V'3(i))(t,X1,X2)) )

  deadlock_rule2: LEMMA  pre_rule2?(V) IMPLIES (NOT DL?(V'2)(V'3))
  ....
  END deadlock_rules
```

Fig. 4. The deadlock rules

to denote deadlock of the network, and use a predicate `cycle?(V)` to show that there exists at least one cycle of ungranted requests in the network.

By making use of this fundamental principle, we have proved Deadlock Rule 2 quoted from [14] as well:

Deadlock Rule 2. *Suppose V is conflict-free and has a node ordering $<$ such that whenever node P_i has a request to any P_j with $P_j < P_i$, then it has a request to all its neighbours P_k such that $P_k < P_i$. Then V is deadlock free.*

The formal proof just translates the one given in [14] into PVS. If V can deadlock, then there is a cycle of ungranted requests which must contain one maximal P_i; necessarily P_i has an ungranted request to P_{i+1} less than itself, then it also has a request to P_{i-1}; and this violates the assumption of conflict freedom. Such a rule is formally expressed in Figure 4 where `<=` denotes a partial order, and we also find out any process's neighbours by only comparing their algebras.

5   Case Study

We show the power of the formalization of CSP semantics by two examples: the dining philosophers problem and the 'virtual network' [21].

5.1   The Dining Philosophers Problem

The dining philosophers problem was first described by Edsger W. Dijkstra in 1965. It is a classic multi-process synchronization problem. The problem consists of n philosophers sitting at a table with a bowl of spaghetti in the middle. Between each pair of adjacent philosophers, there is a single fork; and to eat, a philosopher must be holding both of the forks that are beside him. We assume all philosophers pick forks up in the same order—right hand first—and do not put down any fork they have picked up until they have grabbed both. Figure 5 shows the dining philosophers network's structure, composed of philosopher/fork pairs.

It is quite straightforward to prove determinism of the n dining philosophers problem in combination with the det_induction rule in Figure 1 and the properties of various CSP operators. In Figure 6, H(i,j)(X) and F(i,j)(X) are used to express the behaviour of an individual philosopher and fork respectively where i denotes the total number of philosophers; pick(j,j) denotes that the jth philosopher picks up the jth fork, and so does putdown(j,j); inc(i,j) denotes addition modulo i. Note that each philosopher and fork process is parameterized not only by its index but also by the total number of philosophers, since this affects the modular calculation. Moreover both the philosopher and the fork are recursive processes, and we use the least fixed points of the functions H and F to represent them in PVS. Here PandF(i,j) is used to represent the combination of

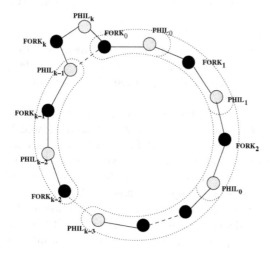

Fig. 5. Inductive structure of dining philosophers

```
philosopher_det: THEORY
  BEGIN
  ....
  H(i,j)(X): process[events] = pickup(j,j)>>(pickup(j,inc(i,j))>>
                 (putdown(j,inc(i,j))>>(putdown(j,j)>>X)))
  F(i,j)(X): process[events] =( (pickup(j,j)>>(putdown(j,j)>>X))
               \/ (pickup(dec(i,j),j)>>(putdown(dec(i,j),j)>>X)))

  PHIL(i,j): process[events] = mu(H(i,j))
  FORK(i,j): process[events] = mu(F(i,j))
  PandF(i,j):process[events] =
                    Par(AP(i,j),AF(i,j))(PHIL(i,j),FORK(i,j))
  ....

  P(n)(m):process[events] = PandF(n,m)
  APF(n)(m):set[events] = union(AP(n,m),AF(n,m))
  COLLEGE(n): process[events] = Par(APF(n))(P(n))

  fork_det: LEMMA DET?(FORK(i,j))
  phil_det: LEMMA DET?(PHIL(i,j))
  pair_det: LEMMA DET?(PandF(i,j))
  college_det: LEMMA DET?(COLLEGE(n))
  ....
END philosopher_det
```

Fig. 6. proving determinism of the dining philosophers problem

a philosopher and his right-hand fork where AP(i,j) and AF(i,j) denote their alphabets.

For constructing the proof, we need only to prove that the processes PHIL(i,j) and FORK(i,j) are deterministic; then the alphabetized parallel combination PandF(i,j) is deterministic by means of the **det_par** rule in Figure 1; the entire system COLLEGE(n) is then also deterministic since it consists of PandF(n,m) for $m < n$.

Deadlock freedom is a more tricky issue. Obviously for the dining philosophers problem, the one and only one situation causing deadlock is that in which all philosophers hold their right-hand forks simultaneously and wait for their neighbours to put down their forks. There are many modifications one can make to avoid deadlock, one of which results in the asymmetric dining philosophers problem: one philosopher picks up a left-hand fork first.

The basic strategy we adopt is similar to an induction used in [15], where the authors use a hierarchical compression technique in FDR to prove the case with huge numbers of philosophers. The key idea is that by hiding their internal events and carefully renaming their interface events, we can prove that any number $(n > 1)$ of right-handed pairs of philosophers and forks are equivalent. The

```
philosopher_dlf:THEORY
  BEGIN


  ....
  H(i,j)(X): process[events] =
        IF j=0 THEN pickup(j,inc(i,j))>>(pickup(j,j)>>
                (putdown(j,j)>>(putdown(j,inc(i,j))>>X)))
        ELSE pickup(j,j)>>(pickup(j,inc(i,j))>>
                (putdown(j,inc(i,j))>>(putdown(j,j)>>X)))
        ENDIF
  ....


  PL(n:{x:int|x>2})(m:{x:int|m>0 and m<n})
                            :process[events]= PandF(n,m)
  C(n):process[events] = Par(APF(n))(PL(n))
  COLLEGE(n):process[events] = Par(I(n))(PandF(n,0),C(n))
  ....


  phil3_dlf: LEMMA DLF?(COLLEGE(3))
  phil_key: ASSUMPTION
     (Par(APF2(k))(PL2(k))/IE(k)
        =Re((Par(APF3(k+1))(PL3(k+1))/IE(k+1)), f)

  phil_dlf_hr: LEMMA C(n)/IE(n) = Re(C(n+1)/IE(n+1),f)
  phil_dlf: LEMMA DLF?(COLLEGE(n))
  ....
  END philosopher_dlf
```

Fig. 7. Proving the asymmetric dining philosophers problem deadlock-free

proof starts from the case with $n = 3$ philosophers; then, for the inductive step, we assume that the case of $n = k$ philosophers is deadlock-free, and show that the system remains deadlock-free when the number of philosophers is $n = k + 1$.

Figure 7 roughly shows the inductive steps of proving that the asymmetric dining philosophers network is deadlock-free. First of all, the definition of the philosophers has been changed since we force the zeroth philosopher to pick up his left-hand fork first. Figure 5 also shows how we deduce deadlock freedom of $k + 1$ philosophers from the case of k philosophers. The key to achieving this step is to prove the equivalence of two processes: k philosophers and $k + 1$ philosophers. Such an idea is proved in the lemma phil_dlf_hr in Figure 7 where C(n) is restricted to be the parallel combination of pairs of philosophers and forks without involving the pair of the zeroth philosopher and his right-hand fork.

Certainly, it is unnecessary to compare all pairs, and we need to concentrate only on the last two pairs in the circle of Figure 5. The key to the induction is that if we hide the internal events of the parallel combination of PandF(k,k-2) and PandF(k,k-1), it is equivalent to the parallel combination of PandF(k+1,k-2), PandF(k+1,k-1) and PandF(k+1,k) with their internal events hidden and pickup(k,0) and putdown(k,0) renamed as pickup(k-1,0) and putdown(k-1,0) respectively. Therefore, it is transformed into the lemma phil_key in Figure 7 in which IE(k) and IE(k+1) denote the sets of internal events and f is a bijective function which performs the renaming operation. To get the final result that the case of $k + 1$ philosophers is deadlock-free, we have to combine two laws, dlf_hide and dlf_rename, which are mentioned in the above section. Consequently, the proof is completely established in the lemma phil_dlf in Figure 7.

Note that although it would be possible to prove the lemma phil_key in PVS, it would be in one sense perverse to do so, since it is essentially a very small model-checking exercise. It would take a long time to trace through the states of each side one by one checking for correspondence; FDR, on the other hand, can verify the equation in a fraction of a second. The approach we take, therefore, is to build this equation into the PVS theory as an assumption, and then prove it in FDR. In this way, we harness the power of the theorem prover for establishing results about an infinite-state system, whilst retaining the speed and automation of a model-checker for certain small parts of the proof. Using PVS in combination with FDR, then, we have successfully proven the asymmetric dining philosophers network with an arbitrary number of philosophers to be deadlock-free. This strategy of using a theorem prover and a model checker in concert is extremely powerful: the different types of tool complement each other very well. By using both together, we can analyze systems that would be out of reach of either individually.

5.2   The Virtual Network

We now demonstrate the use of Deadlock Rule 2 by means of a routing algorithm example called the 'virtual network', quoted in [14] and originally given in [21]. Suppose we want to send a package from any one of the nodes $N_{i,j}$ to any other in a rectangular grid. It seems that the above rule can not directly applied to this system. Roscoe however wisely divides each node $N_{i,j}$ in the system into two parallel processes $I_{i,j}$ and $O_{i,j}$, and defines a partial order such that $I_{i,j} \leq I_{i',j'}$ iff $i \leq i' \wedge j \leq j'$, $O_{i,j} \leq O_{i',j'}$ iff $i \geq i' \wedge j \geq j'$, and $I_{i,j} \leq O_{i',j'}$ for all i,j,i',j', to satisfy the assumptions of this rule.

This partial order implies that a package is transmitted through $I_{i,j}$ in increasing index order, whereas through $O_{i,j}$ it is in decreasing index order. For example, if a package is sent from $N_{1,3}$ to $N_{2,2}$, then the path is $\langle I_{1,3}, I_{2,3}, O_{2,3}, O_{2,2} \rangle$. The CSP code used to represent such a system using mutual recursion can be found in [14], and we here transform it into PVS in Figure 8 where IN(i,j) and OUT(i,j) are used to represent the two synchronized processes, and VN denotes the entire system. Obviously, this system transparently satisfies the requirements of Rule 2.

```
virtual_network:THEORY
....
F(i,j)(X)(0):process[events] =
   in(x,y,m)>>X(1)\/(I_up(x,y,m)>>X(1) \/ I_left(x,y,m)>>X(1))
F(i,j)(X)(1):process[events] =
               IF i<x THEN I_right(x,y,m) >> X(0)
                 ELSIF j<y THEN I_down(x,y,m) >> X(0)
                     ELSE over(x,y,m) >> X(0) ENDIF

H(i,j)(Y)(0):process[events]=
   over(x,y,m)>>Y(1)\/(O_down(x,y,m)>>Y(1)\/O_right(x,y,m)>>Y(1))
H(i,j)(Y)(1):process[events]=
               IF i>x THEN O_left(x,y,m) >> Y(0)
                 ELSIF j>y THEN O_up(x,y,m) >> Y(0)
                   ELSE out(x,y,m) >> Y(0) ENDIF

IN(i,j):process[events] = mu(F(i,j))
OUT(i,j):process[events] = mu(H(i,j))
....
deadlock_check: LEMMA pre_rule2?(VN)

END virtual_network
```

Fig. 8. The virtual network

By making use of Deadlock Rule 2, we have additionally formally proved that a network with any number of dimensions is deadlock-free. In the definition of such a rule, we use an interpreted type size to denote the size of the network; in other words, the number of dimensions of the network can be anything drawn from the type of size.

Proving the new network to be deadlock-free needs careful work, because there are a number of issues involved—for instance, checking whether the network meets freedom of conflict, one of the assumptions of Rule 2, and proving that two mutually recursive processes are conflict-free. Along the way, we have constructed various theorems such as the *conflict free induction* theorem to cope with recursive processes. The final result is a proof of correctness that cannot be easily established in a model checker.

6   Conclusion and Future Work

In this paper, we have presented an embedding of the stable failures model of CSP into PVS that preserves the algebraic properties of CSP, and then used this formalism to prove determinism and deadlock freedom of the asymmetric dining philosophers problem with an arbitrary number of philosophers, and an example of layered routing. Theorem proving is a good complement of model-checking tools such as FDR, which can efficiently verify finite-state systems, but which cannot verify infinite-state systems without outside help.

One of the biggest advantages of a theorem prover is that it is possible to reason about systems with massive or infinite state spaces, admittedly at the cost of sacrificing automatic proof. Verifying a system like our example requires considerable work. However, PVS is a deductive system in which all completed proofs can be used in later proofs. In the course of constructing this proof, we have amassed many lemmas and theorems that will make proving properties of other systems substantially less time-consuming, both for us and for others.

The stable failures model, as well as allowing one to verify properties relating to deadlock freedom, contains sufficient detail to specify many other liveness properties. We are in the process of building up a general platform that provides mechanical assistance for formal analysis of liveness properties of systems. We believe that our model can be used in many different application areas, such as verification of security protocols and general communication protocols. For example, Schneider [17] has modelled and analyzed some properties of a non-repudiation protocol using the traces model of CSP, but some of the other (alleged) properties of the protocol can be formulated only in terms of liveness, and treatment of them requires consideration of failures as well as traces. In addition, we have analyzed and verified the fairness property of the timed Zhou-Gollmann non-repudiation protocol using FDR, and work is in progress on extending this analysis in PVS to cover an infinite network of communicating agents. Denial of service is also naturally specified as a liveness property [12], and one that we expect to be able to use our work to analyze.

We aim in future work to apply our model to other types of network and investigate possible ways to analyze liveness properties of other systems. In our long-term plan, we hope to extend our model to the failures/divergences model; we would like then to extend it further to include infinite traces, which is an area that currently has no tool support at all.

References

1. P. Brooke. *A Timed Semantics for a Hierarchical Design Notation*. PhD thesis, University of York, 1999.
2. A. J. Camilleri. Higher order logic mechanization of the CSP failure-divergence semantics. Technical report, HP Lab Bristol, 1990.
3. A. L. C. Cavalcanti, A. C. A. Sampaio, and J. C. P. Woodcock. A Refinement Strategy for Circus. *Formal Aspects of Computing*, 15(2-3):146–181, unknown 2003.
4. J. Crow, S. Owre, J. Rushby, and N. Shankar. A tutorial introduction to PVS. In *Workshop on Industrial-Strength Formal Specification Techniques*, Boca Raton, Florida, Apr. 1995.
5. J. Crow, S. Owre, J. Rushby, and N. Shankar. *PVS Prover Guide, PVS Language Reference, PVS System Guide*. SRI International, 2001.

6. B. Dutertre and S. A. Schneider. Embedding CSP in PVS: an application to authentication protocols. In E. Gunter and A. Felty, editors, *Theorem Proving in Higher-Order Logics: 10th International Conference, TPHOLs '97*, volume 1275 of *Lecture Notes in Computer Science*. Springer-Verlag, 1997.

7. N. Evans and S. A. Schneider. Analysing Time Dependent Security Properties in CSP using PVS. In *ESORICS 2000*, volume 1895 of *Lecture Notes in Computer Science*. Springer-Verlag, 2000.

8. W. M. Farmer, J. D. Guttman, and J. F. Thayer. IMPS: An Interactive Mathmetical Proof System. *Journal of Automated Reasoning*, 11:213–218, 1993.

9. Formal Systems (Europe) Ltd. Failures-Divergence Refinement—FDR 2 user manual, 1997. Available from Formal Systems' web site at `http://www.formal.demon.co.uk/FDR2.html`.

10. Y. Isobe and M. Roggenbach. A generic theorem prover of CSP refinement. *TACAS 2005*, LNCS 3440, 2005.

11. R. Lazić. *A semantic study of data-independence with application to the mechanical verification of concurrent systems*. PhD thesis, Oxford University, 1999.

12. C. A. Meadows. Open issues in formal methods for cryptographic protocol analysis. In V. I. Gorodetski, V. A. Skormin, and L. J. Popyack, editors, *MMM-ACMS*, volume 2052 of *Lecture Notes in Computer Science*, pages 237–250. Springer, 2001.

13. L. C. Paulson. A formulation of the simple theory of types (for isabelle). In P. Martin-Löf and G. Mints, editors, *Conference on Computer Logic*, volume 417 of *Lecture Notes in Computer Science*, pages 246–274. Springer, 1988.

14. A. W. Roscoe. *The Theory and Practice of Concurrency*. Prentice-Hall International, 1998.

15. A. W. Roscoe, P. H. B. Gardiner, M. Goldsmith, J. R. Hulance, D. M. Jackson, and J. B. Scattergood. Hierarchical compression for model-checking csp or how to check 10^{20} dining philosophers for deadlock. In E. Brinksma, R. Cleaveland, K. G. Larsen, T. Margaria, and B. Steffen, editors, *TACAS*, volume 1019 of *Lecture Notes in Computer Science*, pages 133–152. Springer, 1995.

16. A. Sampaio, J. Woodcock, and A. Cavalcanti. Refinement in Circus. In L. Eriksson and P. Lindsay, editors, *FME 2002: Formal Methods - Getting IT Right*, volume 2391 of *Lecture Notes in Computer Science*, pages 451–470. Springer-Verlag, unknown 2002.

17. S. A. Schneider. Formal analysis of a non-repudiation protocol. In *Proceedings of the 11th IEEE Computer Security Foundations Workshop*, 1998.

18. S. A. Schneider. *Concurrent and real-time systems: the CSP approach*. John Wiley & Sons, 1999.

19. S. A. Schneider and J. Bryans. CSP, PVS and a Recursive Authentication Protocol. In *DIMACS Workshop on Formal Verification of Security Protocols*, Sept. 1997.

20. H. Tej and B. Wolff. A corrected failure-divergence model for CSP in Isabelle/HOL. In J. S. Fitzgerald, C. B. Jones, and P. Lucas, editors, *FME*, volume 1313 of *Lecture Notes in Computer Science*. Springer, 1997.

21. J. Yantchev and C. Jesshope. Adaptive, low latency, deadlock-free packet routing for networks of processors. In *IEE Pro E*, May 1989.

Model-Based Prototyping of an Interoperability Protocol for Mobile Ad-Hoc Networks

Lars M. Kristensen[1,*], Michael Westergaard[1], and Peder Christian Nørgaard[2]

[1] Department of Computer Science, University of Aarhus,
IT-parken, Aabogade 34, DK-8200 Aarhus N, Denmark
{kris, mw}@daimi.au.dk
[2] Ericsson Danmark A/S, Telebit,
Skanderborgvej 222, DK-8260 Viby J, Denmark
Peder.Chr.Norgaard@ericsson.com

Abstract. We present an industrial project conducted at Ericsson Danmark A/S, Telebit where formal methods in the form of Coloured Petri Nets (CP-nets or CPNs) have been used for the specification of an interoperability protocol for routing packets between fixed core networks and mobile ad-hoc networks. The interoperability protocol ensures that a packet flow between a host in a core network and a mobile node in an ad-hoc network is always relayed via one of the closest gateways connecting the core network and the mobile ad-hoc network. This paper shows how integrated use of CP-nets and application-specific visualisation have been applied to build a model-based prototype of the interoperability protocol. The prototype consists of two parts: a CPN model that formally specifies the protocol mechanisms and a graphical user interface for experimenting with the protocol. The project demonstrates that the use of formal modelling combined with the use of application-specific visualisation can be an effective approach to rapidly construct an executable prototype of a communication protocol.

Keywords: Model-driven prototyping; animation; Coloured Petri Nets; mobile ad-hoc network.

1   Introduction

The specification and development of communication protocols is a complex task. One of the reasons is that protocols consist of a number of independent concurrent protocol entities that may proceed in many different ways depending on when, e.g., packets are lost, timers expire, and processes are scheduled. The complex behaviour makes the design of protocols a challenging task. Protocols operating in networks with mobile nodes and wireless communication present an additional set of challenges in protocol engineering since the orchestration of realistic scenarios with many mobile nodes is impractical, and the physical characteristics of wireless communication makes reproduction of errors and scenarios almost impossible.

---

* Supported by the Danish Natural Science Research Council.

J. Romijn, G. Smith, and J. van de Pol (Eds.): IFM 2005, LNCS 3771, pp. 266–286, 2005.

We present a case study from a joint research project [15] between the Coloured Petri Nets Group [6] at University of Aarhus and Ericsson Danmark A/S, Telebit [7]. The research project applies formal methods in the form of Coloured Petri Nets (CP-nets or CPNs) [13,16] and the supporting CPN Tools [5] in the development of Internet Protocol Version 6 (IPv6) [12] based protocols for ad-hoc networking [24]. An ad-hoc network is a collection of mobile nodes, such as laptops, personal digital assistants, and mobile phones, capable of establishing a communication infrastructure for their common use. Ad-hoc networking differs from conventional networks in that the nodes in the ad-hoc network operate in a fully self-configuring and distributed manner, without any preexisting communication infrastructure such as base stations and routers.

CP-nets is a graphical discrete-event modelling language applicable for concurrent and distributed systems. CP-nets are based on Petri nets [27] and the programming language Standard ML (SML) [30]. Petri nets provide the foundation of the graphical notation and the basic primitives for modelling concurrency, communication, and synchronisation. The SML programming language provides the primitives for the definition of data types, modelling data manipulation, and for creating compact and parameterisable models. CPN models are executable and describe the states of a system and the events (transitions) between the states. CP-nets includes a module concept that makes it possible to organise large models into a hierarchically related set of modules. The CPN modelling language is supported by CPN Tools and have previously been applied in a number of projects for modelling and validation of protocols (see, e.g., [17,8,9,23]).

The use of formal modelling languages such as CP-nets for specification and validation of protocols is attractive for several reasons. One advantage of formal models is that they are based on the construction of executable models that make it possible to observe and experiment with the behaviour of the protocol prior to implementation using, e.g., simulation. This typically leads to more complete specifications since the model will not be fully operational until all parts of the protocol have been at least abstractly specified. A model also makes it possible to explore larger scenarios than is practically possible with a physical setup. Another advantage of formal modelling is the support for abstraction, making it possible to specify protocols while ignoring many implementation details.

From a practical protocol engineering viewpoint, the use of formal modelling also have some shortcomings. Even if the modelling language supports abstraction and a module concept there is in most cases an overwhelming amount of detail in the constructed model. This is a disadvantage, in particular when presenting and discussing the design with colleagues unfamiliar with the applied modelling language. This means that a formal specification in many cases is accompanied by informal drawings being developed in parallel. The level of detail can also be a disadvantage when exploring the protocol design via, e.g., simulation. Furthermore, even if a model is executable, it still lacks the application- and domain-specific appeal of a conventional prototype.

The contribution of this paper is to present a model-based prototyping approach where formal modelling is integrated with the use of an animation GUI for visualising system behaviour to address the shortcomings of formal modelling discussed above. The approach has been applied to an interoperability protocol for routing packets between nodes in a mobile ad-hoc network and hosts in a fixed core network. Formal modelling is used for the specification of the protocol mechanisms and an application- and domain-specific GUI [28] is added on top of the CPN model. The result is a *model-based prototype* in which the animation GUI makes it possible to observe the behaviour of the system and provide stimuli to the protocol. The use of an underlying formal model is fully transparent when experimenting with the prototype. The animation GUI has been used in the project both internally during protocol design and externally when presenting the designed protocol to management and protocol engineers not familiar with CPN modelling.

The rest of the paper is organised as follows. Section 2 gives a brief introduction to the network architecture and the interoperability protocol, and Sect. 3 presents the model-based prototyping approach. Section 4 presents selected parts of the CPN model specifying the interoperability protocol. Section 5 presents the graphical animation user interface and package applied in the project. Finally, Sect. 6 sums up the conclusions and presents related work.

2   The Interoperability Protocol

Figure 1 shows the hybrid network architecture captured by the model-based prototype. The network architecture consists of two parts: an IPv6 core network (left) and a mobile ad-hoc network (right). The core network consists of a Domain Name System (DNS) Server and Host 1. The mobile ad-hoc network contains three mobile nodes (Ad-hoc Node 3-5). The core network and the mobile ad-hoc network are connected by Gateway 1 and Gateway 2. A routing protocol for conventional IP networks (such as OSPF [18]) is deployed in the core network and a routing protocol for ad-hoc networks (such as OLSR [4]) is used in the mobile ad-hoc network. The purpose of the interoperability protocol is to ensure that packets are routed between hosts in the core network and nodes in the mobile ad-hoc network via the closest gateway.

The gateways periodically announce their presence to nodes in the mobile ad-hoc network by sending *gateway advertisements* containing an IPv6 *address prefix*. The address prefixes announced by the gateways are assumed to be unique, and the advertisement can be distributed to the ad-hoc nodes using, e.g., flooding. The interoperability protocol does not rely on a specific dissemination mechanism for the gateway advertisements. The interoperability protocol generalises to an arbitrary number of gateways and mobile nodes. Figure 1 shows the concrete setup represented in the model-based prototype.

IPv6 addresses [11] are 128-bit and by convention written in hexadecimal notation in groups of 16 bits separated by colon (:). Leading zeros are skipped within each group and a double colon (::) is a shorthand for a sequence of zeros. Addresses consists of an *address prefix* and an *interface identifier*. Address prefixes are written on the form x/y where x is an IPv6 address and y is the

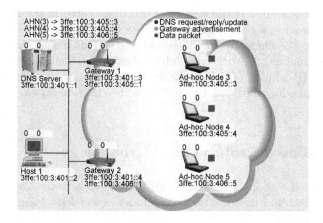

Fig. 1. The hybrid network architecture

length of the prefix. The mobile nodes in the ad-hoc network configure IPv6 addresses based on the received gateway advertisements. In the network architecture depicted in Fig. 1, Gateway 1 is announcing the 64-bit address prefix 3ffe:100:3:405::/64 and Gateway 2 is announcing the prefix 3ffe:100:4:406::/64. It can be seen from the labels below the mobile nodes that Ad-hoc Node 3 and Ad-hoc Node 4 have configured IP addresses based on the prefix announced by Gateway 1, whereas Ad-Hoc Node 5 has configured an IP address based on the prefix announced by Gateway 2. For an example, Ad-hoc Node 3 has configured the address 3ffe:100:3:405::3.

Each of the gateways has configured an address on the interface to the ad-hoc network based on the prefix they are announcing to the ad-hoc network. Gateway 1 has configured the address 3ffe:100:3:405::1 and Gateway 2 has configured the address 3ffe:100:3:406::1. The gateways have also configured addresses on the interface to the core network based on the 3ffe:100:3:401::/64 prefix of the core network. Host 1 in the core network has configured the address 3ffe:100:3:401::2 and the DNS server has configured the address 3ffe:100:3:401::1. The ad-hoc nodes may receive advertisements from both gateways and configure an IPv6 address based on each of the prefixes. The reachability of the address prefixes announced by the gateways in the ad-hoc network are announced in the core network via the routing protocol executed in the core network.

The basic idea in the interoperability protocol is that the mobile nodes register the IPv6 address in the DNS database which corresponds to the preferred (closest) gateway. Updates to the DNS database relies on the Dynamic Domain Name System Protocol [31]. The entries in the DNS database related to the mobile nodes are shown to the upper left in Fig. 1. For an example, it can be seen that the entry for Ad-hoc Node 3 (AHN(3)) is mapped to the address 3ffe:100:3:405::3. When a mobile ad-hoc node discovers that another gateway is closer, it will send an update to the DNS server causing its DNS entry to be changed to the IPv6 address based on the prefix announced by the new gateway. It is assumed that the routing protocol executed in the mobile ad-hoc network will provide the information required for a mobile node to determine its distances to the currently reachable gateways. This means that when Host 1 wants to communicate, with e.g., Ad-hoc Node 3 and makes a DNS request to resolve the IP address of Ad-hoc Node 3, the DNS server will return the IP address corresponding to the prefix announced by the gateway closest to Ad-hoc Node 3.

3   Model-Based Prototyping Methodology

Figure 2 shows the approach taken to use CPN models to develop a prototype of the interoperability protocol. A CPN model (lower left of Fig. 2) has been developed by modelling the natural language protocol specification [22] (lower right) of the interoperability protocol. The modelling activity transforms the natural language specification into a formal executable specification represented by the CPN model. The CPN model captures the network architecture depicted in Fig. 1 and the protocol mechanisms of the interoperability protocol, e.g., the periodic transmission of advertisements, the dynamic updates of the DNS database, and traffic flows between hosts in the core network and nodes in the ad-hoc network. The resulting model can already be viewed as an early prototype since it is possible to execute and experiment with the protocol at the level of the CPN model. Since CP-nets is a graphical modelling language, it is possible to observe the execution of the model directly on the CPN model.

The CPN model provides a very detailed view on the execution of the system and it can be an advantage to provide a high-level way of interacting and experimenting with the prototype. Furthermore, when presenting the protocol design to people not familiar with CP-nets, it can be an advantage to be able

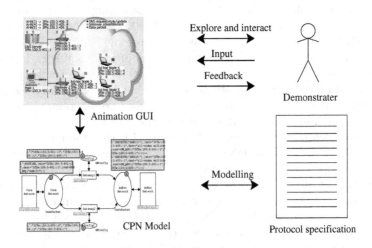

Fig. 2. Model-based prototyping approach

to demonstrate the prototype without directly relying on the CPN model but more application and domain specific means. To support this, an *animation GUI* (top left of Fig. 2) has been added on top of the CPN model. This graphics visualises the execution of the prototype using the graphical representation of the network architecture previously shown in Fig. 1. The graphics is updated by the underlying CPN model according to the execution of the protocol.

In addition to observe feedback on the execution of the system in the animation GUI, it is also possible to provide input to the system directly via the animation GUI. In the prototype, it is possible for the demonstrator (e.g., a protocol engineer) to move the nodes in the ad-hoc network and to define traffic flows from the host in the core network to the nodes in the mobile ad-hoc network. The animation GUI has been implemented using a general visualisation package and framework [28] developed in the course of the project (see Sect. 4).

Altogether the approach makes it possible to explore and demonstrate the prototype of the interoperability protocol based on the CPN model that formally captures the design, but doing it in such a way that the use an underlying formal model is transparent for the observer and the demonstrator.

4   The CPN Model

This section presents the CPN model specifying the interoperability protocol. The complete CPN model is hierarchically structured into 18 modules. As the CPN model is too large to be presented in full in this paper, we present only selected parts of the CPN model. The aim is to show how the key aspects of the interoperability protocol have been modelled. The key concepts of CP-nets will be briefly introduced as we proceed with the presentation. The reader is referred to [16] for a comprehensive introduction to CP-nets.

4.1   Model Overview

The module concept of CP-nets is based on the notion of *substitution transitions* which have associated *submodules* describing the compound behaviour represented by the substitution transition. A submodule of a substitution transition may again contain substitution transitions with associated submodules. Figure 3 shows the top level module of the CPN model which is composed of three main parts represented by the rectangular substitution transitions CoreNetwork (left), Gateway1 and Gateway2 (middle), and AdHocNetwork (right). The substitution transition CoreNetwork and its submodules model the core network, the substitution transition AdHocNetwork and its submodules model the mobile ad-hoc network, and the submodules of the two Gateway substitution transitions model the operation of the gateways connecting the core network and the mobile ad-hoc network. The text in the small rectangular box attached to each substitution transition gives the name of the associated submodule.

The state of a CPN model is represented through *places* (drawn as ellipses). There are four places in Fig. 3. The places CoreNetwork and AdHocNetwork are

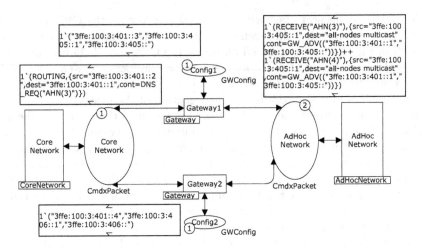

Fig. 3. System module – top-level module of the CPN model.

used for model modelling the packets in transit on the core network and ad-hoc network, respectively. The state of a CPN model is a distribution of tokens on the places of the CPN model. Figure 3 depicts a state where there is one token on place CoreNetwork and two tokens on place AdHocNetwork. The number of tokens on a place is written in the small circle attached to the place. The *data values* (colours) of the tokens are given in the filled box positioned next to the small circle. As an example, place CoreNetwork contains one token with the colours:

```
(ROUTING, {src="3ffe:100:3:401::2", dest="3ffe:100:3:401::1",
          cont=DNSREQ("AHN(3)")})
```

representing a DNS request in transit from Host 1 to the DNS server. Place Ad-HocNetwork contains two tokens representing gateway advertisements in transit to nodes in the ad-hoc network. The two Config places each contains a token representing the configuration of the corresponding gateway. It consists of the IP address of the interface connected to the core network, the IP address of the interface connected to the ad-hoc network, and the prefix announced.

The data values (colours) of tokens that can reside on a place are determined by the *colour set* of the place which by convention is written below the place. Colour sets are similar to types known from conventional programming languages. Figure 4 lists the definitions of the colour sets (types) used in the System module. IP addresses, prefixes, and symbolic IP addresses are represented by colour sets IPAdr, Prefix, and Symname all defined as the set of strings. The colour set PacketCont and Packet are used for modelling the IP packets. The five different kinds of packets used in the interoperability protocol are modelled by PacketCont:

DNS_REQ modelling a DNS request packet. It contains the symbolic IP address to be resolved.

DNS_REP modelling a DNS reply. It contains the symbolic IP address and the resolved IP address.

```
(* --- Addressing --- *)
colset Prefix = string;   (* address prefixes *)
colset IPAdr = string;    (* IP addresses     *)
colset SymName = string;  (* symbolic names   *)

colset SymNamexIPAdr = product SymName * IPAdr;
colset IPAdrxPrefix = product IPAdr * Prefix;

(* --- packets --- *)
colset PacketCont = union DNS_REQ : SymName +         (* DNS Request     *)
                          DNS_REP : SymNamexIPAdr + (* DNS Reply       *)
                          DNS_UPD : SymNamexIPAdr + (* DNS Update      *)
                          GW_ADV  : IPAdrxPrefix +  (* Advertisments   *)
                          PACKET;                   (* Generic payload *)

colset Packet = record src  : IPAdr *
                       dest : IPAdr *
                       cont : PacketCont;

colset Cmd = union ROUTING +
                   RECEIVE      : IPAdr +
                   FLOODING     : IPAdr +
                   GWAHNROUTING : IPAdr +
                   AHNGWROUTING : IPAdr;

colset CmdxPacket = product Cmd * Packet;

(* --- Gateways configuration --- *)
colset GWConfig = product IPAdr * IPAdr * Prefix;
```

Fig. 4. Colour set definitions used in the System module.

DNS_UPD modelling a DNS update. It contains the symbolic IP address to be updated and the new IP address to be bound to the symbolic address.

GW_ADV modelling the advertisements disseminated from the gateways. An advertisement contains the IP address of the gateway and the announced prefix.

PACKET modelling generic payload packets transmitted between hosts and the mobile nodes.

The colour set Packet models the packets as a record containing the source, destination, and the content. The actual payload (content) and layout of packets are indifferent for modelling the interoperability protocol and has therefore been abstracted away. The colour set Cmd is used to control the operation of the various modules in the CPN model. The colour set GWConfig models the configuration information of the gateway.

4.2   Modelling the Core Network

Figure 5 shows the CoreNetwork module modelling the core network. This module is the immediate submodule of the substitution transition CoreNetwork of the System module shown in Fig. 3. The *port place* CoreNetwork is assigned to the CoreNetwork *socket place* in the System module (see Fig. 3). Port places are indicated by the In , Out , or I/O tags associated with them. The assignment of a port place to a socket place means that the two places are linked together and will always have identical tokens. By adding and removing tokens from port places, it is possible for a submodule to exchange tokens with its environment. The substitution transition Routing represents the routing mechanism in the core network. The substitution transition Host represents the host on the core network, and the substitution transition DNS Server represents the DNS server.

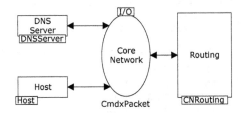

Fig. 5. Core Network module – modelling the core network

Hosts. Figure 6 depicts the Host module modelling the host on the core network. The port place CoreNetwork (bottom) is assigned to the CoreNetwork socket place in the CoreNetwork module (see Fig. 5). The module models the transmission of packets from the host to one of the mobile ad-hoc nodes. The substitution transition Flows (top) is used for interfacing with the animation GUI. We will return to this issue in Sect. 5.

The remaining places and transitions are used for modelling the behaviour of the host. The rectangles in Fig. 6 are ordinary transitions (i.e., not substitution transitions) which means that they can become *enabled* and *occur*. The dynamics of a CPN model consists of occurrences of enabled transitions that change the distribution of tokens on the places. An occurrence of a transition removes tokens from places connected to incoming arcs of the transition and adds tokens to places connected to outgoing arcs of the transition. The colours of the tokens removed from input places and added to output places are determined by *evaluating* the *arc expressions* on the arcs surrounding the transition. The arc expressions are written in the SML programming language. Data values must be bound to the *variables* appearing in the surrounding arc expressions before the arc expressions can be evaluated. This is done by creating a *binding element* which is a pair (t, b) consisting of a transition t and a *binding* b assigning data values to the variables of the transition. A binding element (t, b) is enabled iff the multi-set of tokens obtained by evaluating each input arc expression is a subset of the tokens present on the corresponding input place.

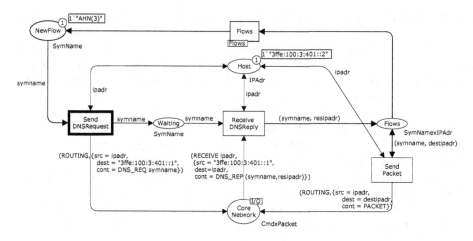

Fig. 6. Host module – modelling the host

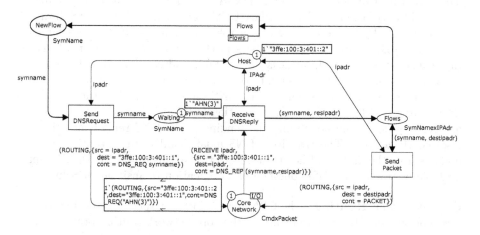

Fig. 7. Host module – after occurrence of SendDNSRequest transition.

When the user defines a flow in the animation GUI, a token will appear in place NewFlow with a colour corresponding to the symbolic name of the mobile ad-hoc node which is the destination of the packet flow. An example is given in Fig. 6, where the NewFlow place contains a token corresponding to the user having defined a flow to Ad-hoc Node 3. This enables the SendDNSRequest transition in a binding where the value "AHN(3)" is bound to the variable symname of type SymName and the variable ipadr is bound to the value of the token on place Host specifying the IP address of the host.

When the SendDNSRequest transition occurs in the binding described above, it will remove tokens from places NewFlow and Host, and add tokens to the output places Host, Waiting, and CoreNetwork. Tokens are added to the Host place since SendDNSRequest and Host are connected by a double arcs which is a short-hand for an arc in each direction having identical arc expressions. The colour of the tokens added are determined by evaluating the expressions on the output arcs. The resulting state is shown in Fig. 7. A token representing the IP address of the host is put back on place Host, a token representing the symbolic name to be resolved is put on place Waiting, and a token representing a DNS request has been put on place CoreNetwork.

The reception of the DNS reply from the DNS server is modelled by the transition ReceiveDNSReply which causes the token on place Waiting to be removed and a token to be added on place Flows. This corresponds to the host entering a state in which packets can be transmitted to the mobile ad-hoc node. The sending of packets is modelled by the transition SendPacket. The user may then decide (via the animation GUI) to terminate the packet flow which will cause the token on place Flows to be removed, and transmission of packets will cease. A host can have concurrent flows to different mobile ad-hoc nodes.

Domain Name Server and Database. Figure 8 shows the DNSServer module modelling the DNS Server. The place DNSAdr contains a token corresponding to the IP address of the DNS Server. Place DNSDatabase models the DNS database entries on the DNS Server. There is a token on place DNSDatabase for each entry in the DNS database. The entries in the DNS database are modelled as tuples where the first component is the symbolic address (name) and the second component is the IP address bound to the symbolic name in the first component.

There are two possible events in the DNS server modelled by the transitions DNSRequest and DNSUpdate. The transition DNSRequest models the reception of DNS requests (from hosts) and the sending of the DNS reply containing the resolved IP address. The transition DNSUpdate models the reception of DNS updates from the mobile ad-hoc nodes. Both transitions access the DNSDatabase for lookup (transition DNSRequest) and modification (transition DNSUpdate).

Core Network Routing. The CPN model does not specify a specific routing protocol but only the requirements to the core network routing protocol. This

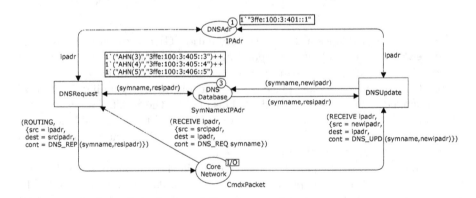

Fig. 8. DNSServer module – modelling the DNS Server

Fig. 9. CNRouting module – Routing in the core network

means that any routing protocol that meets these requirements can be used to implement the interoperability protocol. The routing mechanism in the core network is abstractly modelled by the CNRouting module shown in Fig. 9. The place RoutingInformation models the routing information computed by the specific routing protocol in operation. This place contains a token that makes it possible given a prefix, to find the IP address of the corresponding gateway on the core network. This specifies the requirement that the gateways are required to participate in the routing protocol of the core network and announce a route to the prefix that they are advertising in the mobile ad-hoc network. This enables packets for nodes in the mobile ad-hoc network to be routed via the gateway advertising the prefix that matches the destination IP address of the packet. The transition Route models the routing of the packet on the core network. It uses the routing information on place RoutingInformation to direct the packet to the proper gateway. The function FindNextHop in the *guard expression* of the transition computes the IP address of the next hop gateway using the routing information and destination IP address of the packet.

4.3   Modelling the Gateways

The role of the gateway is to relay packets between the core network and the mobile ad-hoc network, and to periodically send advertisements to the mobile ad-hoc network. Figure 10 shows the Gateway module modelling the operation of the gateways. This module is the submodule of the two substitution transitions Gateway1 and Gateway2 on the System module. This means that there will be two *instances* of the Gateway module - one for each of the substitution transitions. Figure 10 shows the instance corresponding to Gateway1. The port place CoreNetwork is assigned to the socket place CoreNetwork and the port place AdHocNetwork is assigned to the socket place AdHocNetwork on the System module. The place Config contains a token giving the configuration of the gateway.

The relay of packets from the core network to the mobile ad-hoc network is modelled by the transition AHN_CoreTransmit and the relay of packets from the mobile ad-hoc network to the core network is modelled by the transition Core_AHNTransmit. Packets to be transmitted from the core network to the ad-hoc network are represented by tokens in the place CoreNetwork. When the transition Core_AHNTransmit occurs corresponding to the relay of a packet from the core network to the ad-hoc network, this token will be removed from the CoreNetwork place and a new token representing the packet added to the place

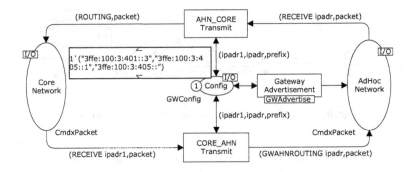

Fig. 10. Gateway module – modelling the operation of the gateways

AdHocNetwork. The relay of packets from the AdHocNetwork to the CoreNetwork is modelled in a similar manner by the transition AHN_CoreTransmit. The periodic transmission of advertisements on the mobile ad-hoc network is modelled by the substitution transition GatewayAdvertisement. The presentation of the submodule associated with this substitution transition has been omitted.

4.4 Modelling the Mobile Ad-Hoc Network

Figure 11 depicts the AdHocNetwork module which is the top level module of the part of the CPN model modelling the mobile ad-hoc network. The place Nodes is used to represent the nodes in the mobile ad-hoc network. The place RoutingInformation is used to represent the routing information in the ad-hoc network which is assumed to be available via the routing protocol executed in the ad-hoc network. This routing information enables among other things the nodes to determine the distance to the reachable gateways. Detailed information about the colour of the token on place RoutingInformation has been omitted.

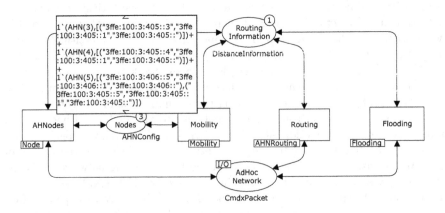

Fig. 11. AdHocNetwork module – modelling the ad-hoc network

```
  (* --- ad-hoc nodes --- *)
  colset AHId = int with 1..5;
  colset AHNode = union AHN : AHId;

5 (* --- distance information --- *)
  colset Distance = union REACH : Dist + NOTREACH;
  colset DistanceEntry = product AHNode * IPAdr * IPAdr * Distance;
  colset DistanceInformation = list DistanceEntry;

10 (* --- configuration information for ad-hoc nodes --- *)
  colset AHNIPConfig = product IPAdr * IPAdr * Prefix;
  colset AHNIPConfigs = list AHNIPConfig;
  colset AHNConfig = product AHNode * AHNIPConfigs;
```

Fig. 12. Colour definitions used in the AdHocNetwork module

Figure 12 lists the definition of the colour sets used in the AdHocNetwork module. The topology of the mobile ad-hoc network is abstractly represented by only representing the distance from each of the ad-hoc nodes to the two gateways. The reason is that it is only the relative distance to the two gateways which are of relevance to the operability protocol – not the complete topology. The colour set DistanceInformation is used to keep track of the reachability between the nodes in the ad-hoc network and the gateways. The distance information is a list with an entry for each pair of ad-hoc node and gateway. Each entry is again list consisting of a four-tuple (colour set DistanceEntry). Each entry consists of the symbolic name of the mobile ad-hoc node, its IP address (if configured), the IP address of the gateway (if configured), and the distance to the gateway. The gateway may also be unreachable in which case the distance is set to NOTREACH.

The colour set AHNConfig is used to model the configuration information for the mobile ad-hoc nodes. Each ad-hoc node is represented by a token on place Nodes and the colour of the tokens specifies the name of the node and a list of configured IP addresses. Each configuration of an IP address specifies the IP address configured, and the IP address and prefix of the corresponding gateway. It is possible for a mobile ad-hoc node to configure an IP address for multiple gateways. The node will ensure that the DNS database always contains the IP address corresponding to the *preferred gateway*.

There are four substitution transitions in the AdHocNetwork module corresponding to the components of the ad-hoc network represented:

AHNodes represents the behaviour of the nodes in the mobile ad-hoc network. This will be presented in more detail below.

Mobility represents the mobility of nodes in the ad-hoc network, i.e., that the nodes may move closer or further away from the gateways. We will return to the modelling of mobility in Sect. 5.

Routing represents the routing protocol executed in the ad-hoc network. The purpose of the routing protocol in the context of the interoperability protocol is to provide the nodes with information about distances to the gateways.

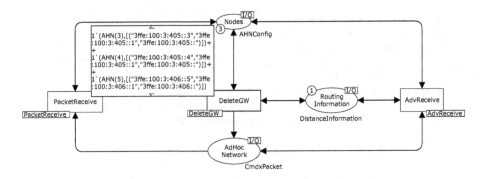

Fig. 13. Node module – modelling an ad-hoc node

The routing is abstractly modelled in a similar way as the routing mechanism in the core network and will not be discussed further in this paper.

Flooding models the dissemination of advertisements from the gateways. A detailed presentation of this part of the model has been omitted.

Figure 13 depicts the Node module specifying the operation of the ad-hoc nodes. The module has three substitution transitions. PacketReceive represents the reception of packets from hosts in the core network. The submodule PacketReceive of this substitution transition is shown in Fig. 14. The transition PacketReceive models the reception of a packet and consumes the token on place AdHocNetwork corresponding to the packet being received. AdvReceive represents the reception of advertisements from the gateways. A node changes its preferred IP address if the received advertisement is from a gateway which is closer than the gateway corresponding to the currently preferred gateway (if any). If the node configures a new preferred IP address based on the received advertisement, then it will send an update to the DNS server containing the new preferred IP address. DeleteGW represents the case where the gateway corresponding to a configured IP address becomes unreachable. The assumption is that this will be detected via the routing protocol executed in the ad-hoc network or if advertisement has not been received for a specified amount of time. The submodules of the AdvReceive and DeleteGW are similar in complexity as the submodule of the PacketReceive substitution transition in Fig. 14 and has been omitted.

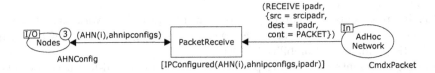

Fig. 14. PacketReceive module – modelling reception of payload packets

5   The Animation Graphical User Interface

The animation GUI has been implemented based on a general animation package [28] developed in the course of the project. The animation package provides a general framework for adding various diagram types on top of executable models. The animation package is not designed specifically for CPN models, but is applicable also to other modelling formalisms.

The architecture of the model-based prototype developed in the project is depicted in Fig. 15 and consists of three main parts: The CPN Tools GUI (left), the CPN simulator (middle), and the animation GUI (right). The CPN Tools GUI and the CPN simulator constitute the CPN computer tools used in the project. CPN models are constructed using the CPN Tools GUI and the CPN simulator implements the formal semantics of CP-nets for execution of CPN models. The simulator communicates via the XML-RPC [32] infrastructure with the animation GUI to display the execution of the CPN model using the domain-specific graphics and for receiving stimuli/input from the demonstrator. The specific visualisation means are determined by the set of animation plug-ins used in the animation GUI. One animation plug-in was used to obtain *interaction graphics* in the form shown in Fig. 16. A second animation plug-in was used to obtain feedback in the form of message sequence charts (MSCs).

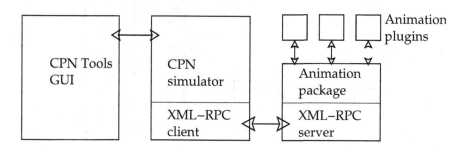

Fig. 15. Architecture of the model-based prototype

Fig. 16 shows a representative snapshot of the application-specific during the execution of the CPN model. The IP addresses configured by the individual nodes are shown as labels below the nodes. For an example, Ad-hoc Node 3 has configured two IP addresses: 3ffe:100:3:405:3 and 3ffe:100:3:406:3. The convention is that the preferred IP address is the topmost address in the list below the node. The entries in the DNS database are shown in the upper left corner. It shows the entries for each of the three ad-hoc nodes. The two numbers written at the top of each node are counters that provide information about the number of packets on the incoming (left) and outgoing (right) interfaces of the nodes. Transmissions of advertisements from the gateways are visualised by green dots. Transmission of payload packets are visualised using read dots, and DNS packets are visualised using blue dots. Fig. 16 shows an example where Host 1 is transmitting a payload packet to Ad-hoc Node 3.

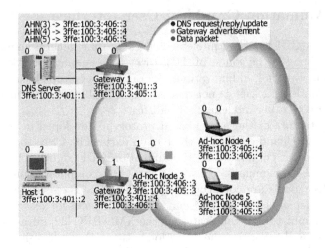

Fig. 16. Snapshot of the interaction graphics

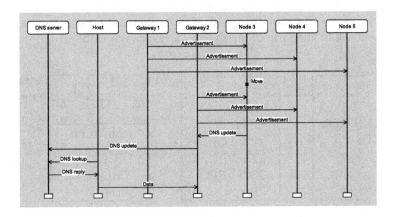

Fig. 17. Message sequence chart generated by the animation GUI

The user can move the nodes in the ad-hoc network thereby changing the distances to the two gateways. It is also possible to define a flow from the host in the core network to one of the nodes in the mobile ad-hoc network by clicking on the read square positioned next to each of the ad-hoc nodes. The square will change its colour to green once the CPN model has registered the flow. The flow can be stopped again by clicking on the (now green) square next to the mobile ad-hoc node. Finally, it is possible to force the transmission of an advertisement from a gateway by clicking on the gateway.

Figure 17 shows an example of a MSC creating based on a simulation of the CPN model. The MSC shows a scenario where Ad-hoc Node 3 makes a Move and discovers that Gateway 2 is now the closest gateway. This causes it to send a DNS update to the DNS server. The last part of the MSC shows the host initiating a packet flow to Ad-hoc Node 3.

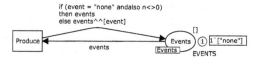

Fig. 18. Poll module – Polling the animation GUI for events

Graphical feedback from the execution of the CPN model is achieved by attaching *code segments* to the transitions in the CPN model. These code segments are executed whenever the corresponding transition occurs in the simulation/execution of the CPN model. As an example, the transition Route (see Fig. 9) has an attached code segment which invokes the primitives required for animating the transmission of packets in the core network.

The CPN model receives input from the animation GUI by polling the animation GUI for events. The Poll module shown in Fig. 18 polls the animation GUI for events at regular intervals during the execution of the CPN model and puts events into a list on the place Events, thereby implementing an event queue between the animation GUI and the CPN model. Parts of the CPN model that is to react on events from the animation GUI are linked to the Event place and are able to consume events from the event queue. The transition Produce polls the animation GUI for events.

6   Conclusions

We have presented our model-based prototype approach and demonstrated its use on an interoperability protocol. In addition to providing a detailed specification of the interoperability protocol via the constructed CPN model, the work has also highlighted the following characteristics and aspects of a model-based (virtual) prototyping approach:

Representation. The use of an animation GUI on top of the CPN model has the advantage that the behaviour observed by the user is as defined by the underlying model that formally specifies the design. The alternative would have been to implement a separate visualisation package in, e.g., JAVA, totally detached from the CPN model. We would then have obtained a model closer to the actual implementation. The disadvantage of this approach would have been a double representation of the dynamics of the interoperability protocol.

Transparency. The use of a domain specific graphical user interface (the animation GUI) has the advantage that the design can be experimented with and explored without having knowledge of the CPN modelling language. This has been shown in practise at a demonstration to management with no CPN knowledge.

Controllability. A model-based prototype is easier to control compared to a physical prototype, in particular in the case of mobile nodes and wireless communication where scenarios can be very difficult to control and reproduce.

Abstraction. Implementation details can be abstracted away and only the key part of the design have to be specified in detail. As an example, in the CPN model of the interoperability protocol we have abstracted away the routing mechanisms in the core and ad-hoc networks, and the mechanism used for distribution of advertisements. Instead, we have modelled the service provided by these components. The possibility of making abstraction means that it is possible to obtain an executable prototype without implementing all components.

Feasibility. The use of a model means that there is no need to invest in physical equipment and there is no need to setup the actual physical equipment. This also makes it possible to investigate larger scenarios, e.g., scenarios that may not be feasible to investigate with the available physical equipment.

Related Work. Integrated use of visualisation and formal modelling has also been considered for CP-nets in earlier work in the area of embedded systems [26], telecommunication protocols [3], pervasive electronic patient records [2], and software for mobile phones [19]. The case studies in [26, 3, 2, 19] all applied the Mimic/CPN [25] package, an internal part of the Design/CPN [1] tool. The approach presented in this paper relies on an external application handling the visualisation, which we find is a more flexible approach as it allows us to use existing software libraries supporting different diagram types. In Mimic/CPN, input from the user is only possible by showing a modal dialog, meaning the simulation of the model is stopped while the user is expected to input information. The animation package presented in this paper avoids this by using an asynchronous event queue polled by a transition in the model. As part of future work, we plan to eliminate polling by allowing external applications to directly produce and consume tokens on special *external places*.

Visualisation is also available in other tool sets. ExSpect [29] allows the user to view the model state by associating widgets with the state of the model and asynchronously interact with the model using simple widgets. In this way, one creates simple user interfaces for displaying information and simple interaction. LTSA [20] allows users to animate models using an animation library called SceneBeans [21]. In LTSA animations are tied to the models by associating each animation activity with a clock; resetting a clock corresponds to starting an animation sequence, and events in the animation corresponds to progress of the clock. PNVis [14] associates objects of a 3D world with tokens, and is suitable for modelling physical systems, but not immediately applicable for network protocols. The Play-Engine [10] supports the developer in implementing a prototype by inputting scenarios (play-in) via an application-specific GUI, and then execute the resulting program (play-out). Compared to our approach this makes the model implicit as the model is created indirectly via the input scenarios. We view an explicitly created model as an advantage when the prototype is to serve as a basis for an actual implementation of the system. The reason is that an implicitly created model is difficult to interpret as it is automatically generated.

In conclusion, the work presented in this paper has demonstrated that using CP-nets and the supporting computer tools for building a model-based prototype can be a viable and useful alternative to building a physical prototype. Furthermore, the CPN model can also serve as a basis for further development of the interoperability protocol, e.g., by refining the modelling of the routing and dissemination mechanisms to the concrete protocols that would be required to implement the solution. There is still a gap from the CPN model to the actual implementation of the interoperability protocol, but the CPN modelling has yielded an executable prototype that can be used to explore the solution and serve as a basis for the later implementation.

Acknowledgements. The authors gratefully acknowledge the support of their colleagues in BAE SYSTEMS plc, Ericsson Microwave Systems AB and Ericsson Danmark A/S, Telebit, and support from the UK, Swedish and Danish MoDs under the EUCLID/Eurofinder programme, Project RTP6.22 (B2NCW). The authors would also like to acknowledge Rolf Christensen for his contributions.

References

1. Design/CPN. Online www.daimi.au.dk/designCPN.
2. C. Bossen and J.B. Jørgensen. Context-descriptive prototypes and their application to medicine administration. In *DIS '04: Proc. of the 2004 conference on Designing interactive systems*, pages 297–306, New York, NY, USA, 2004. ACM Press.
3. C. Capellmann, S. Christensen, and U. Herzog. Visualising the Behaviour of Intelligent Networks. In *Services and Visualisation, Towards User-Friendly Design*, volume 1385 of *LNCS*, pages 174–189. Springer-Verlag, 1998.
4. T. Clausen and P. Jacquet. Optimised Link State Routing Protocol (OLSR). RFC 3626, October 2003.
5. CPN Tools. www.daimi.au.dk/CPNTools.
6. The CPN Group at University of Aarhus. www.daimi.au.dk/CPnets.
7. Ericsson Danmark A/S, Telebit. www.tbit.dk.
8. S. Gordon, L.M. Kristensen, and J. Billington. Verification of a Revised WAP Wireless Transaction Protocol. In *Proc. of ICATPN'02*, volume 2360 of *LNCS*, pages 182–202. Springer-Verlag, 2002.
9. B. Han and J. Billington. Formalising the TCP Symmetrical Connection Management Service. In *Proc. of Design, Analysis, and Simulation of Distributed Systems*, pages 178–184. SCS, 2003.
10. D. Harel and R. Marelly. *Come, Let's Play.* Springer-Verlag, 2003.
11. R. Hinden and S. Deering. Internet Protocol Version 6 (IPv6) Addressing Architecture. RFC 3513, April 2003.
12. C. Huitema. *IPv6: The New Internet Protocol.* Prentice-Hall, 1998.
13. K. Jensen. *Coloured Petri Nets - Basic Concepts, Analysis Methods and Practical Use. Vol. 1-3.* Springer-Verlag, 1992-1997.
14. E. Kindler and C. Páles. 3D-Visualization of Petri Net Models: Concept and Realization. In *Proc. of ICATPN 2004*, volume 3099 of *LNCS*, pages 464–473. Springer-Verlag, 2003.
15. L.M. Kristensen. Ad-hoc Networking and IPv6: Modelling and Validation. www.pervasive.dk/projects/IPv6/IPv6_summary.
16. L.M. Kristensen, S. Christensen, and K. Jensen. The Practitioner's Guide to Coloured Petri Nets. *Journal on Software Tools for Technology Transfer*, 2(2):98–132, 1998.

17. L.M. Kristensen and K. Jensen. Specification and Validation of an Edge Router Discovery Protocol for Mobile Ad-hoc Networks. In *Integration of Software Specification Techniques for Application in Engineering*, volume 3147 of *LNCS*, pages 248–269. Springer-Verlag, 2004.

18. A. Lindem. OSPF for IPv6. Internet-draft, March 2005.

19. L. Lorentsen, A-P Tuovinen, and J. Xu. Modelling Features and Feature Interactions of Nokia Mobile Phones Using Coloured Petri Nets. In *Proc. of ICATPN 2002*, volume 2360 of *LNCS*, pages 294–313, 2002.

20. J. Magee and J. Kramer. *Concurrency – State Models and Java Programs*. John Wiley & Sons, 1999.

21. J. Magee, N. Pryce, D. Giannakopoulou, and J. Kramer. Graphical Animation of Behavior Models. In *Proc. of 22nd International Conference on Software Engineering*, pages 499–508. ACM Press, 2000.

22. P.C. Nørgaard. NCW Routing in Tactical Networks. Ericsson Danmark A/S, Telebit. Technical Report.

23. C. Ouyang and J. Billington. On Verifying the Internet Open Trading Protocol. In *Proc. of 4th International Conference on Electronic Commerce and Web Technologies*, volume 2738 of *LNCS*, pages 292–302. Springer-Verlag, 2003.

24. C.E. Perkins. *Ad Hoc Networking*. Addison-Wesley, 2001.

25. J. L. Rasmussen and M. Singh. *Mimic/CPN. A Graphical Simulation Utility for Design/CPN. User's Manual.* www.daimi.au.dk/designCPN.

26. J.L. Rasmussen and M. Singh. Designing a Security System by Means of Coloured Petri Nets. In *Proc. ICATPN 1996*, volume 1091 of *LNCS*, pages 400–419. Springer-Verlag, 1996.

27. W. Reisig. *Petri Nets*, volume 4 of *EATCS Monographs on Theoretical Computer Science*. Springer-Verlag, 1985.

28. TIN-CPN. wiki.daimi.au.dk/tincpn.

29. The ExSpect tool. www.exspect.com.

30. J.D. Ullman. *Elements of ML Programming*. Prentice-Hall, 1998.

31. P. Vixie. Dynamic Updates in the Domain Name System. RFC 2136, April 1997.

32. D. Winer. XML-RPC Specification. www.xmlrpc.org/spec.

Translating Hardware Process Algebras into Standard Process Algebras: Illustration with CHP and LOTOS

Gwen Salaün and Wendelin Serwe

INRIA Rhône-Alpes / VASY, 655, avenue de l'Europe,
F-38330 Montbonnot St Martin, France
{Gwen.Salaun, Wendelin.Serwe}@inria.fr

Abstract. A natural approach for the description of asynchronous hardware designs are hardware process algebras, such as Martin's CHP (*Communicating Hardware Processes*), TANGRAM, or BALSA, which are extensions of standard process algebras with particular operators exploiting the implementation of synchronisation using handshake protocols.

In this paper, we give a structural operational semantics for value-passing CHP. Compared to existing semantics of CHP defined by translation into Petri nets, our semantics handles value-passing CHP with communication channels open to the environment and is independent of any particular (2- or 4-phase) handshake protocol used for circuit implementation.

In a second step, we describe the translation of CHP into the standard process algebra LOTOS, in order to allow the application of the CADP verification toolbox to asynchronous hardware designs. A prototype translator from CHP to LOTOS has been successfully used for the compositional verification of the control part of an asynchronous circuit implementing the DES (*Data Encryption Standard*).

1 Introduction

In the currently predominating synchronous approach to hardware design, a global clock is used to synchronise all parts of the designed circuit. This method has the drawback that the global clock requires significant chip space and power. Asynchronous design methodologies [12] abandon the notion of global clock: the different parts of an asynchronous circuit evolve concurrently at different speeds, with no constraints on communication delays. The advantages of asynchronous design include reduced power consumption, enhanced modularity, and increased performance. However, asynchronous design raises problems that do not exist in the synchronous approach, e.g. proving the absence of deadlocks in a circuit. Furthermore, an established asynchronous design methodology with industrial tool support is still lacking.

Adequate description languages are necessary to master the design of asynchronous circuits. Several process algebras dedicated to the description of asynchronous hardware have been proposed, as for instance CHP (*Communicating*

J. Romijn, G. Smith, and J. van de Pol (Eds.): IFM 2005, LNCS 3771, pp. 287–306, 2005.

Hardware Processes) [17], TANGRAM [14], or BALSA [6], which allow the description of concurrent processes communicating via handshake synchronisations. In these languages, there is no global clock, but each process may have its own local clock as in GALS (*Globally Asynchronous, Locally Synchronous*) architectures. The global control flow results from processes waiting for their partner to engage in a handshake communication. These *hardware* process algebras are based on similar principles as *standard* process algebras [2, 7] (such as ACP, CCS, CSP, LOTOS, μCRL, etc.). Especially, they provide operators such as nondeterministic choice, sequential and parallel composition. However, compared to standard process algebras, they offer extensions that capture the low-level aspects of hardware communications. In particular, communication in CHP, TANGRAM, or BALSA is not necessarily atomic (as it is in standard process algebras), and may combine message-passing with shared memory communication. For instance, the *probe* operator [16] of CHP allows to check if the communication partner is ready for a communication, but without performing the communication actually.

CHP, TANGRAM, and BALSA are supported by synthesis tools that can generate the implementation of a circuit from its process algebraic description. For instance, the TAST tool [19] can generate netlists from CHP descriptions and is being used to design complex circuits, e.g. by STMicroelectronics, France Telecom R&D, and the asynchronous hardware group of the CEA/Leti laboratory [1]. Our goal is to enable the verification of asynchronous hardware designs with CADP [9], a toolbox for verifying LOTOS [13] specifications.

In this paper, we give an SOS (*Structural Operational Semantics*) [2, chapter 3] semantics for value-passing CHP. Compared to the most recent semantics [20] for CHP, which is defined by translation into Petri nets, our semantics handles value-passing CHP with communication channels open to the environment and is independent of any particular (2- or 4-phase) handshake protocol (cf. Section 2.2) used for circuit implementation. We present in a second step the principles of a translation from CHP into LOTOS. A prototype translator has been implemented and successfully used for the compositional verification of an asynchronous implementation of the DES (*Data Encryption Standard*) [18].

As regards related work, we notice that the semantics of hardware process algebras is usually not given in terms of SOS rules (as it is the case for standard process algebras), but rather by means of a translation into another formalism, as for instance handshake circuits for TANGRAM [22], Petri nets for CHP [20], and CSP for BALSA [23]; in that respect, we believe that our SOS semantics is an original contribution. As regards verification of asynchronous circuits described using process algebra, there is very little related work. [4] proposes a translation of CHP into networks of communicating automata. Contrary to our approach, [4] can only handle CHP processes with intertwined sequential and parallel compositions by flattening parallel processes, which is less efficient than the compositional approach presented in this paper. [23] sketches, but does not detail, a translation of BALSA into CSP. A major difference between [23] and our approach is that [23] cannot translate a BALSA process B independently of the

BALSA processes communicating with B, whereas our approach is generic in the sense that each CHP process is translated into LOTOS regardless of its context.

The remainder of the paper is organised as follows. Section 2 presents CHP and highlights its probe operator. An SOS semantics for CHP is given in Section 3, and compared to the Petri net based semantics given for CHP in [20]. Section 4 presents translation rules from CHP into LOTOS, and reports on an experiment with a prototype translator. Finally, Section 5 gives some concluding remarks.

2   Main Principles of CHP

In this section, we focus on the behavioural part of CHP and omit additional structures such as modules or component libraries present in the full CHP [19].

2.1   Syntax

A CHP *description* is a tuple $\langle \mathcal{C}, \mathcal{X}, \hat{B}_1 \parallel \cdots \parallel \hat{B}_n \rangle$ consisting of a finite set of *channels* $\mathcal{C} = \{c_1, \ldots, c_n\}$ for handshake communication, a finite set of *variables* $\mathcal{X} = \{x_1, \ldots, x_n\}$ and a finite set of concurrent *processes* $\hat{B}_i$ communicating by the channels. Without loss of generality, we suppose that all identifiers (channels and variables) are distinct — this can be achieved by using a suitable renaming.

A channel c is either binary (between two processes) or unary (between a process and the environment); in the latter case, c is also called a *port*; the predicate $port(c)$ holds iff c is a port. Channels are unidirectional, i.e. a process can use a channel either for *emissions* or for *receptions*. Also, a process is either *active* or *passive* for a given channel. We write $active(i, c)$ (respectively $passive(i, c)$) if process $\hat{B}_i$ is active (respectively passive) for channel c. This distinction between active and passive is also present in other hardware process algebras such as TANGRAM and BALSA. Note that $passive(i, c)$ is not the negation of $active(i, c)$, since for a process $\hat{B}_i$ not using c both $active(i, c)$ and $passive(i, c)$ do not hold. Binary channels can only connect matching processes, i.e. for each binary channel, there is one emitter and one receiver, as well as an active and a passive process, both notions being orthogonal. Let $\mathcal{C}_i$ be the set of channels used by $\hat{B}_i$.

Each variable is local to a single process, i.e. the set $\mathcal{X}$ is the disjoint union of n sets $\mathcal{X}_1, \ldots, \mathcal{X}_n$, each $\mathcal{X}_i$ containing the local variables of process $\hat{B}_i$. There are no shared variables between processes. We suppose the existence of a set of predefined data types (natural numbers, Booleans and bit vectors) with side-effect-free *operations*, written $f_1, \ldots, f_n$. Variables and channels are typed; the type of a variable x (respectively a channel c) is written as $type(x)$ (respectively $type(c)$).

The behaviour of a process B[1] is described using assignments, communication actions, collateral and sequential compositions, and nondeterministic guarded commands, according to the following grammar:

$B ::= \texttt{nil}$ *deadlock*[2]

---

[1] B stands for any process, whereas $\hat{B}_i$ is one of the n processes of the CHP description.

	skip	*null action*
	$x\!:=\!V$	*assignment*
	$c!V$	*emission on channel c*
	$c?x$	*reception on channel c*
	$B_1 ; B_2$	*sequential composition*
	B_1 , B_2	*collateral composition*
	$@[G_1 \Rightarrow B_1; T_1 \ \ldots \ G_n \Rightarrow B_n; T_n]$	*guarded commands*
$G ::=$	V	*Boolean value expression*
	$c \# V \ \mid \ c \#$	*probe on passive channel*
$T ::=$	break $\mid$ loop	*terminations*
$V ::=$	$x \ \mid \ f(V_1, \ldots, V_n)$	*value expression*

Collateral composition has higher priority than sequential composition, but brackets can be used to express the desired behaviour, e.g. "B_1, $(B_2 ; B_3)$".

The collateral composition "," and the parallel composition of processes "$\|$" correspond to two different notions of concurrency. The parallel composition "$\|$" specifies concurrent execution with handshake communications between processes, whereas collateral composition "," specifies concurrent execution without any communication, neither by handshakes nor by variables. The following constraints hold for a process "B_1 , B_2": if B_1 modifies a variable x, B_2 must neither access the value of x nor modify x, and the sets of channels used by B_1 and B_2 must be disjoint (which also prohibits two interleaved emissions or receptions on a same channel).

As regards guarded commands, the guards are either Boolean value expressions or probes on channels for which the process is passive. The keyword break indicates that the execution of the guarded command terminates, whereas loop indicates that $@[G_1 \Rightarrow B_1; T_1 \ \ldots \ G_n \Rightarrow B_n; T_n]$ must be executed once more, thus allowing loops to be specified in CHP. The version of CHP implemented in TAST [19] also allows deterministic guarded commands which are a particular case of nondeterministic guarded commands with mutually exclusive guards. Therefore we consider only nondeterministic guarded commands in this paper.

2.2 Informal Semantics of Handshake Communication in CHP

Communication between concurrent processes in CHP is implemented by means of hardware handshake protocols. There exists different protocols, as for instance the 2-phase protocol (based on transition signalling) and the 4-phase protocol (based on level signalling) [20]. Each CHP channel c is translated into a set of wires x_c needed to carry data transmitted on c and two control wires c_{req} and c_{gr} implementing an access protocol to x_c. The 2-phase protocol for communication between two processes B_1 (active) and B_2 (passive) on a channel c consists of the following phases:

---

[2] The deadlocking process nil is not present in the version of CHP implemented in TAST [19], but is required for the definition of the SOS semantics.

1. *Initiation.* B_1 sends a *request* to B_2 by performing an electronic transition ("zero-to-one" or "one-to-zero") on c_{req}.
2. *Completion.* B_2 sends an acknowledgement (or *grant*) to B_1 by performing an electronic transition on c_{gr} and the emitted value is assigned to the variable of the receiver, using the wires x_c.

In a 4-phase protocol, sending a request (respectively acknowledgement) is implemented by a value of 1 on wire c_{req} (respectively c_{gr}). After two phases similar to a 2-phase protocol, two additional phases implement the *return-to-zero*, first of c_{req}, then of c_{gr}. Common to both protocols is that a communication on a channel c is initiated by the process active for c, which is blocked as long as the communication has not been completed by the passive process.

The probe operation of CHP was introduced in [16] and has been found to be useful in the design of asynchronous hardware. The notation "$c\#$" allows a passive process (either emitter or receiver) to check if its active partner has already initiated a communication on c. The notation "$c\#V$", which can only be used by a receiver, checks if the sender has initiated the emission of the particular value V. Contrary to classical process algebra operators, the probe allows a process to obtain information about the current internal state (communication initiated or not) of a concurrent process without performing the communication actually. Typically, probes are used for multiple reads, executing "$c\#V$" several times, which avoids the introduction of an additional variable to store V.

Similar operators are also present in other hardware process algebras. For instance, BALSA provides a particular form of reception, called *input enclosure* [6], that allows the receiver to perform several commands before acknowledging the reception, whereas the sender witnesses an atomic communication.

2.3 Running Example: An Asynchronous Arbiter

Throughout this paper we consider the example of an asynchronous arbiter presented in [20], which we generalise in two ways: we use value-passing communications instead of pure synchronisations and we model an arbiter open to its environment by keeping the shared resource outside of the arbiter example itself.

Arbiters are commonplace in digital systems, wherever a restricted number of resources (such as memories, ports, buses, etc.) have to be allocated to different client processes. We consider the situation where two clients compete for accessing a common resource. Each client transmits a request for the resource to the arbiter via an individual channel (c_1 or c_2). A third channel allows the arbiter to send the number of the selected client (1 or 2) to the environment, i.e. the resource. The arbiter chooses nondeterministically between the clients with pending requests. The corresponding CHP description is $\langle \{c, c_1, c_2\}, \{x\}, \text{client-1} \parallel \text{client-2} \parallel \text{arbiter} \rangle$, where all three channels have an active emitter and a passive receiver, where variable x — taking values in the set $\{1, 2\}$ — is local to the arbiter, and where the three processes are described as follows:

client-1: $@[true \Rightarrow c_1!1; \texttt{loop}]$
client-2: $@[true \Rightarrow c_2!2; \texttt{loop}]$
arbiter: $@[c_1 \,\#1 \Rightarrow (c!1, c_1?x); \texttt{loop} \quad c_2 \,\#2 \Rightarrow (c!2, c_2?x); \texttt{loop}]$

In this example, the arbiter uses the probe operator to check if a client has a pending request for the resource.

3   A Structural Operational Semantics for CHP

In this section, we give an SOS semantics for CHP with value-passing communications. Contrary to the existing semantics for CHP [17, 20], we define the semantics of CHP without expanding communications according to a particular handshake protocol. Thus, our approach is general in the sense that it gives to any CHP description $\langle \mathcal{C}, \mathcal{X}, \hat{B}_1 \parallel \cdots \parallel \hat{B}_n \rangle$ a unique behavioural semantics by means of an LTS (*Labelled Transition System*). In this LTS, a state contains two parts (data and behaviour); a transition corresponds either to an observable action (communication on a channel)[3] or an internal action, written τ, of a process. Following [20], internal actions are generated whenever a process assigns one of its local variables. Our definitions adopt the usual interleaving semantics of process algebras, i.e. at every instant, at most one observable or internal action can take place.

We first present the notion of environment describing the data part of our semantics. Then, we define the behavioural part in two steps, starting with the semantics of a single process evolving independently, followed by the semantics of a set of communicating processes $\hat{B}_1 \parallel \cdots \parallel \hat{B}_n$. Finally, we compare our semantics with the two semantics of [20] for 2- and 4-phase handshake protocols.

3.1   Environments

The main semantic difficulty in CHP is the handling of the probe, since this operator exploits the fact that communication is not atomic at the lower level of implementation. Inspired by the actual hardware implementation of CHP, we associate to each channel c a variable noted x_c that is modified only by the process active for c, but might be read by the process passive for c. For a channel c with an active emitter, the type of x_c is $type(c)$; the active emitter assigns the emitted value to x_c when initiating the communication, and resets x_c (to the undefined value, written $\bot$) when completing the communication. A variable x_c is equal to $\bot$ iff all initiated communications on c have been completed. For a channel with an active receiver, the type of x_c is the singleton $\{ready\}$ representing that the active receiver has initiated the communication. Formally, we define the extended set of variables as $\mathcal{X}^* = \mathcal{X} \cup \{x_c \mid c \in \mathcal{C}\}$, and define $\mathcal{X}_i^*$ as the set of the local variables of $\hat{B}_i$ and all the variables x_c such that channel c is used by $\hat{B}_i$. Notice that the additional variables x_c allow to ensure that a

---

[3] CHP has no hiding or restriction operator; thus all inputs and outputs are observable.

value sent by the active process on channel c can be read — or probed — as often as desired by the passive process before completion of the communication.

We define an environment E on $\mathcal{X}^*$ as a partial mapping from $\mathcal{X}^*$ to ground values (i.e. constants), and write environments as sets of associations $x \mapsto v$ of a ground value v to a variable x. Environment updates are described by the operator $\oslash$, which is defined as follows:

$$(\forall x \in \mathcal{X}^*)\ (E_1 \oslash E_2)(x) = \begin{cases} E_1(x) & \text{if } E_2(x) = \bot \\ E_2(x) & \text{otherwise} \end{cases}$$

The environment obtained by resetting a variable x to $\bot$ in an environment E is described by the function $reset(E, x)$.

The semantics of a value expression V is defined by the usual evaluation function $eval(E, V)$ extended for the probe operator:

$$\begin{aligned} eval(E, x) &= E(x) \\ eval\big(E, f(V_1, \ldots, V_n)\big) &= f\big(eval(E, V_1), \ldots, eval(E, V_n)\big) \\ eval(E, C\,\texttt{\#}) = true &\iff E(x_c) = ready \\ eval(E, C\,\texttt{\#}V) = true &\iff E(x_c) = eval(E, V) \end{aligned}$$

3.2 Behavioural Semantics for a Single Process

Our semantics associates to each process $\hat{B}_i$ an LTS $\langle \mathcal{S}_i, \mathcal{L}_i, \rightarrow_i, \langle E_i, \hat{B}_i \rangle \rangle$, where

- The set of states $\mathcal{S}_i$ contains pairs $\langle E, B \rangle$ of a process B and an environment E on $\mathcal{X}_i^*$.
- The set of labels $\mathcal{L}_i$ contains emissions, receptions, τ (representing assignments to local variables), and a particular label $\sqrt{}$ representing successful termination.
- The transition relation "$\rightarrow_i$" is defined below by SOS rules similar to those used for BPA$_\varepsilon$ (*Basic Process Algebra with ε*) in [2, chapter 3]; as for BPA$_\varepsilon$, we write $\langle E, B \rangle \sqrt{}$ to mean $\langle E, B \rangle \xrightarrow{\sqrt{}}_i \langle E, \texttt{nil} \rangle$.
- The initial state is $\langle E_i, \hat{B}_i \rangle$, where the initial environment E_i assigns the undefined value $\bot$ to all variables of $\mathcal{X}_i^*$.

Rules for nil and skip. There are no rules for **nil**. The process **skip** always terminates successfully.

$$\overline{\langle E, \texttt{skip} \rangle \sqrt{}}$$

Rules for Assignments. An assignment can always be executed and modifies the environment by updating the value associated to the assigned variable:

$$\overline{\langle E,\ x\texttt{:=}V \rangle \xrightarrow{\tau}_i \langle E \oslash \{x \mapsto eval(E, V)\},\ \texttt{skip} \rangle}$$

Rules for Emissions. A passive emission is always possible. An active emission on a channel c involves two transitions: the first one assigns a value to x_c and the second one completes the communication by resetting x_c.

$$\frac{passive(i,c)}{\langle E,\ c!V\rangle \xrightarrow{c!\,eval(E,V)}_i \langle E,\ \texttt{skip}\rangle}$$

$$\frac{active(i,c) \qquad eval(E,x_c)=\bot}{\langle E,\ c!V\rangle \xrightarrow{\tau}_i \langle E\oslash\{x_c\mapsto eval(E,V)\},\ c!V\rangle}$$

$$\frac{active(i,c) \qquad eval(E,x_c)\neq\bot}{\langle E,\ c!V\rangle \xrightarrow{c!\,eval(E,V)}_i \langle reset(E,x_c),\ \texttt{skip}\rangle}$$

Rules for Receptions. These rules are dual of those for emissions.

$$\frac{passive(i,c)}{\langle E,\ c?x\rangle \xrightarrow{c?\,eval(E,x_c)}_i \langle E\oslash\{x\mapsto eval(E,x_c)\},\ \texttt{skip}\rangle} \qquad (\mathsf{Recv_p})$$

$$\frac{active(i,c) \qquad eval(E,x_c)=\bot}{\langle E,\ c?x\rangle \xrightarrow{\tau}_i \langle E\oslash\{x_c\mapsto ready\},\ c?x\rangle}$$

$$\frac{active(i,c) \qquad eval(E,x_c)\neq\bot \qquad V\in type(c)}{\langle E,\ c?x\rangle \xrightarrow{c?V}_i \langle reset(E,x_c)\oslash\{x\mapsto V\},\ \texttt{skip}\rangle} \qquad (\mathsf{Recv_a})$$

Contrary to rule $(\mathsf{Recv_p})$, which uses the value of x_c as the received value, rule $(\mathsf{Recv_a})$ enumerates all possible values that might be received on channel c.

Rules for Sequential Composition. These rules are as usual.

$$\frac{\langle E,\ B_1\rangle \xrightarrow{L}_i \langle E',\ B_1'\rangle}{\langle E,\ B_1;B_2\rangle \xrightarrow{L}_i \langle E',\ B_1';B_2\rangle} \qquad \frac{\langle E,B_1\rangle\surd \qquad \langle E,B_2\rangle \xrightarrow{L}_i \langle E',B_2'\rangle}{\langle E,\ B_1;B_2\rangle \xrightarrow{L}_i \langle E',B_2'\rangle}$$

Rules for Collateral Composition. These rules are as usual.

$$\frac{\langle E,\ B_1\rangle \xrightarrow{L}_i \langle E',\ B_1'\rangle}{\langle E,\ B_1,B_2\rangle \xrightarrow{L}_i \langle E',\ B_1',B_2\rangle} \qquad \frac{\langle E,\ B_2\rangle \xrightarrow{L}_i \langle E',\ B_2'\rangle}{\langle E,\ B_1,B_2\rangle \xrightarrow{L}_i \langle E',\ B_1,B_2'\rangle}$$

$$\frac{\langle E,B_1\rangle\surd \qquad \langle E,B_2\rangle\surd}{\langle E,\ B_1,B_2\rangle\surd}$$

Rules for Guarded Commands. The rules for guarded commands express that a branch whose guard is true can be selected. If the chosen branch ends with `break`, the guarded command terminates when the branch terminates; if it ends with `loop` the guarded command will be executed once more after executing the branch.

$$\frac{(\exists i) \qquad eval(E,G_i)=true \qquad T_i=\texttt{break} \qquad \langle E,B_i\rangle \xrightarrow{L}_i \langle E',B_i'\rangle}{\langle E,\ \texttt{@}[G_1\Rightarrow B_1;\ T_1\ \ldots\ G_n\Rightarrow B_n;\ T_n]\rangle \xrightarrow{L}_i \langle E',\ B_i'\rangle}$$

$$\frac{(\exists i) \qquad eval(E, G_i) = true \qquad T_i = \texttt{loop} \qquad \langle E, B_i \rangle \overset{L}{\longrightarrow}_i \langle E', B'_i \rangle}{\langle E, \, \texttt{@[}G_1 \Rightarrow B_1; T_1 \; \ldots \; G_n \Rightarrow B_n; T_n \texttt{]} \rangle \overset{L}{\longrightarrow}_i \langle E', \, B'_i; \, \texttt{@[}G_1 \Rightarrow B_1; T_1 \; \ldots \; G_n \Rightarrow B_n; T_n \texttt{]} \rangle}$$

3.3   Semantics for Communicating Processes

The semantics of a CHP description $\langle \mathcal{C}, \; \mathcal{X}, \; \hat{B}_1 \parallel \cdots \parallel \hat{B}_n \rangle$ is defined by the parallel composition of the LTSs $\langle \mathcal{S}_i, \mathcal{L}_i, \to_i, \langle E_i, \hat{B}_i \rangle \rangle$ produced for the individual processes $\hat{B}_i$ as defined in Section 3.2. This yields a new LTS $\langle \mathcal{S}, \mathcal{L}, \to, \langle E, \hat{B}_1, \ldots, \hat{B}_n \rangle \rangle$, where:

– The set of states $\mathcal{S}$ contains tuples $\langle E, B_1, \ldots, B_n \rangle$ of n processes $B_1, \ldots, B_n$ and a global environment E on $\mathcal{X}^* = \bigcup_{i=1}^{n} \mathcal{X}_i^*$. E is the union of the local environments E_i on $\mathcal{X}_i^*$ of the processes $\hat{B}_i$. The sets $\mathcal{X}_i^*$ are disjoint for the sets $\mathcal{X}_i$ (local variables of $\hat{B}_i$), but for each binary channel c, the variable x_c occurs in $\mathcal{X}_i^*$ and $\mathcal{X}_j^*$ ($i \neq j$); this is not a problem, since x_c is only modified by the process active for c.
– The set of labels $\mathcal{L}$ is the union of the sets of labels $\mathcal{L}_i$ minus labels corresponding to receptions on binary channels. We represent synchronised communications (i.e. an emission and a reception) using the same symbol "!" as for emissions (following the convention used in CADP).
– The transition relation "$\to$" is defined by the three SOS rules below.
– The initial state is $\langle E, \hat{B}_1, \ldots, \hat{B}_n \rangle$, with an empty initial environment E.

Let $internal(i, L)$ be the predicate that holds iff L is internal or a communication on a port (i.e. a unary channel open to the environment):

$$(\forall i, L) \; internal(i, L) \Longleftrightarrow L = \tau \; \vee \; \big((\exists c, V) \, (L = c!V \; \vee \; L = c?V) \wedge \; port(i, c) \big)$$

The first SOS rule describes the local — or internal — evolution of the i-th process B_i independently of the others. It models either an assignment to a variable, or the communication on a port c which is open to the environment and does not need to be synchronised with another process B_j ($i \neq j$).

$$\frac{(\exists i) \qquad \langle E, B_i \rangle \overset{L}{\longrightarrow}_i \langle E', B'_i \rangle \qquad internal(i, L)}{\langle E, B_1, \ldots, B_i, \ldots, B_n \rangle \overset{L}{\longrightarrow} \langle E', B_1, \ldots, B'_i, \ldots, B_n \rangle}$$

The next rule describes the synchronisation between processes B_i and B_j communicating on channel c, B_i being the emitter and B_j the receiver.

$$\frac{(\exists i) \; \langle E, B_i \rangle \overset{c!V}{\longrightarrow}_i \langle E', B'_i \rangle \qquad (\exists j) \; \langle E, B_j \rangle \overset{c?V}{\longrightarrow}_i \langle E'', B'_j \rangle}{\langle E, B_1, \ldots, B_i, \ldots, B_j, \ldots, B_n \rangle \overset{c!V}{\longrightarrow} \langle reset(E'', x_c), B_1, \ldots, B'_i, \ldots, B'_j, \ldots, B_n \rangle} \quad \text{(Com)}$$

Note that i and j in rule (Com) are different and uniquely defined, since the communication model is binary (one sender, one receiver for a given channel).

Note also that, if E' and E differ in rule (Com), then the only possible modification (resetting x_c) is applied to E'' in the right hand side of the conclusion of rule (Com).

The rules presented so far are sufficient to define the semantics of (closed) systems without passive ports, i.e. unary channels for which no process $\hat{B}_i$ is active. The following rule completes the semantics by modelling the environment as an active process that communicates with each passive port c.

$$\frac{(\exists i)\ passive(i,c) \quad (\forall j)\ \neg active(j,c) \quad eval(E, x_c) = \bot \quad V \in type(x_c)}{\langle E, B_1, \ldots, B_n \rangle \xrightarrow{\tau} \langle E \oslash \{x_c \mapsto V\}, B_1, \ldots, B_n \rangle} \text{ (Env)}$$

This rule is similar to those employed in the definition of semantics for asynchronous processes communicating via shared memory, as for instance concurrent constraint programming [5] or concurrent declarative programming [21, Table 5.3, page 142].

Example 1. This example shows the necessity of rule (Env). Consider the following two processes $B_1 = @[c_1 \#1 \Rightarrow (c!1, c_1?x); \text{loop}]$ and $B_2 = @[c_2 \#2 \Rightarrow (c!2, c_2?x); \text{loop}]$ corresponding to the two branches of the arbiter of Section 2.3. Here, c_1 and c_2 are passive ports open to the environment. Without rule (Env), both B_1 and B_2 would be equivalent to the deadlock process nil. However, while "$B_1 \parallel$ client-2" is equivalent to nil, "$B_2 \parallel$ client-2" is not (the corresponding LTS has 8 states and 12 transitions). Rule (Env) solves this issue by giving a different semantics to B_1 and B_2.

Example 2. Figure 1 gives the LTS generated for the arbiter of Section 2.3. To keep the size of Figure 1 as small as possible, we minimised the LTS with respect to strong bisimulation (merging states that differ only in the value of variable x when x is no longer used). This is similar to the state reduction approach for process algebra described in [10].

3.4   Comparison with the Existing Petri Net Translation

In this section, we compare our SOS semantics with the "implicit" semantics proposed for CHP in [20] by a translation of CHP into Petri nets. [20] only handles a subset of CHP that, compared to full CHP presented in Section 2, is restricted in two ways: it allows only pure synchronisations (instead of value-passing communications) and forbids ports open to the environment. By handling full CHP, our semantics allows to describe circuits with inputs and outputs properly.

Translation of CHP to Petri Nets. Similar to our SOS semantics, [20] defines the translation of a CHP description $\langle \mathcal{C}, \mathcal{X}, \hat{B}_1 \parallel \cdots \parallel \hat{B}_n \rangle$ into Petri nets in two successive steps:

– In a first step the Petri nets corresponding to the processes $\hat{B}_i$ are constructed separately following the patterns sketched in [20]. Petri net places

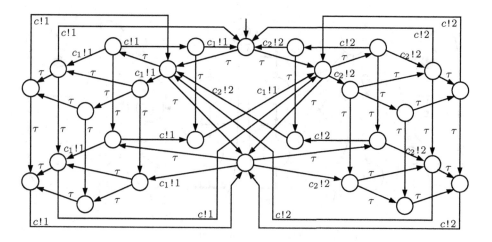

Fig. 1. LTS for the arbiter example

may be labelled with assignments, emissions, and receptions. Petri net transitions may be labelled with the guards of CHP guarded commands. To fire a transition, its input places must contain a token and the guard (if any) must be true.

- In a second step, the separate Petri nets are merged into one global Petri net. To model synchronisation on channels, [20] gives two different translations, depending on the handshake protocol (2- or 4-phase) used for the implementation. In both cases, channels are modelled by additional places and transitions that encode the chosen handshake protocol. Notice that for each channel c the places labelled "$c!$" and "$c?$" are kept separate, i.e. there is no transition merging as in [11].

The generated Petri net is one-safe, i.e. in every reachable marking, each place contains at most one token.

Example 3. Consider the CHP description $\langle \{c_1, c_2\}, \{x\}, $ client-1 $\parallel$ client-2 $\parallel$ arbiter$\rangle$, where channels c_1 and c_2 have an active emitter and a passive receiver, where variable x is local to the arbiter, and where the three processes are defined as follows:

client-1: $@[true \Rightarrow c_1!; \text{loop}]$
client-2: $@[true \Rightarrow c_2!; \text{loop}]$
arbiter: $@[c_1 \#1 \Rightarrow x:=1; c_1?; \text{loop} \quad c_2 \#2 \Rightarrow x:=2; c_2?; \text{loop}]$

This example is an adaptation of the arbiter of Section 2.3 in order to meet the restrictions of [20]. The corresponding Petri net for a 4-phase protocol is (adapted from [20, Figure 11]) shown in Figure 2. Places are represented by circles, and transitions by thick lines. Whenever a place is both an input and an output place of some transition, we use a double-headed arrow (as for places labelled c_{1req}, c_{1gr}, c_{2req}, and c_{2gr}). The Petri nets corresponding to the three

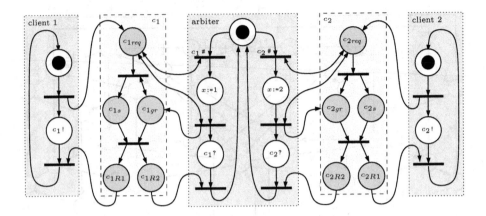

Fig. 2. Petri net for the arbiter example

Fig. 3. Duplication of Petri net places

processes are framed in dotted boxes. The places modelling the channels c_1 and c_2 are framed in dashed boxes.

Relation Between SOS and Petri Net Semantics. In order to relate the Petri nets proposed in [20] with the LTSs produced by our semantics, one needs to generate the LTSs corresponding to the Petri nets. This is not immediate, since the Petri nets of [20] have a different behaviour than ordinary Petri nets. For instance, if two places with action (e.g. "c_1!" and "c_2!" in Figure 2) have a token, then interleaved transitions have to be created for these actions. From [20] and following discussions with the first author of [20], we conjecture that these LTSs can be obtained by the following two steps.

– First, the Petri net model of [20] with actions attached to places needs to be transformed into a more standard model where actions are attached to transitions. As shown in Figure 3, each Petri net place q labelled with an action a (i.e. emission, reception, or assignment) is replaced by two places q_1 and q_2 and a new Petri net transition labelled with action a. Place q is replaced by q_1 (respectively q_2) in the sets of output (respectively input) places of all transitions. In the case a transition t has q both as an input and an output place (i.e. t corresponds to a double-headed arrow), q is replaced by q_2 in the sets of input and output places of t.

– Then, we compute the LTS for the modified Petri net by applying the standard marking graph construction algorithm. We label the transitions of the generated LTS with emissions and receptions labelling Petri net transitions. If a Petri net transition is not labelled with an emission or a reception, the corresponding LTS transition is labelled with τ.

We can now compare the LTS_{SOS} obtained by our SOS semantics and LTS_{PN} obtained after translation of CHP into Petri nets, transformation, and marking graph construction. Given that [20] does not deal with value-passing communications and open systems, this is only possible for closed systems with pure synchronisations.

A first remark is that the places and transitions added to the Petri nets for the communication channels introduce τ transitions in LTS_{PN} that might not have a counterpart in LTS_{SOS}. Thus, LTS_{SOS} and LTS_{PN} are not strongly equivalent. A second remark is that the sets of labels of LTS_{SOS} and LTS_{PN} might be different. On the one hand, LTS_{PN} might contain both, "$c!$" and "$c?$" as labels, since the places labelled "$c!$" and "$c?$" are kept separate in the Petri nets of [20]. On the other hand, for closed systems LTS_{SOS} does not contain labels of the form "$c?$". Establishing an equivalence relation between LTS_{SOS} and LTS_{PN} would probably require to rename into τ all labels of LTS_{PN} corresponding to communications by active processes and to replace all remaining "$?$" by "$!$"; we conjecture that after these transformations, LTS_{SOS} and LTS_{PN} are equivalent with respect to branching equivalence, but this remains to be proved.

4   Principles of a Translation from CHP to LOTOS

In order to check the correctness of asynchronous circuit designs (e.g. absence of deadlocks), our approach is to translate CHP into LOTOS so that existing tools (namely, the CADP verification toolbox [9]) can be applied. A tutorial of the ISO standard LOTOS [13] can be found in [3]. We highlight first the main features of the translation of CHP into LOTOS:

– CHP types (natural numbers, Booleans, bit vectors, etc.) are translated into LOTOS sorts (i.e. algebraic data types).
– CHP functions are translated into LOTOS operations, the semantics of which is defined using algebraic equations.
– A CHP channel c is translated into a LOTOS gate with the same name c.
– A CHP variable x is translated into one or more LOTOS variables (i.e. *value identifiers* in the LOTOS standard terminology) with the same name and the same type as x. Several LOTOS variables might be required since LOTOS variables are single-assignment, whereas CHP variables are multiple-assignment.
– Sequential composition "$;$" in CHP is symmetric, whereas LOTOS has two different operators for sequential composition: an asymmetric action prefix "$;$" and a symmetric sequential composition "$>>$". Variables assigned on the left hand side of a CHP "$;$" can be used on the right hand side, whereas variables assigned on the left hand side of a LOTOS "$>>$" must be explicitly

listed (in an `accept` clause) to be used in the right hand side. Furthermore, ">>" creates an internal τ transition, contrary to the ";" operator of both CHP and LOTOS. There are two options when translating CHP to LOTOS. A simple approach is to use only ">>". A better approach is to use the LOTOS ";" whenever possible, and ">>" only when needed. In this paper, we adopt the second approach which generates better LOTOS code at the expense of a more involved translation.

- CHP has a neutral element (`skip`) for its sequential composition, whereas LOTOS lacks neutral elements both for ";" (which is asymmetric) and for ">>" (which creates a τ transition).
- CHP has a loop operator, whereas LOTOS does not; CHP loops have to be translated into recursive processes in LOTOS.
- CHP guards are either Boolean expressions or probes, whereas LOTOS guards are Boolean expressions only.

4.1   Principles of Translating a Single Process

The translation of a CHP process $\hat{B}_i$ is described by the recursive function $c2l_i(B, D, U, \Delta)$ with four parameters: B is a CHP process to translate and D, U, and Δ are alphabetically ordered sets of variables necessary to compute the variables to explicitly pass over LOTOS sequential compositions ">>". Intuitively, D is the set of variables that have a defined value before execution of B, U is the set of variables used after execution of B, and $\Delta \subseteq D$ is an auxiliary set of defined variables used to translate collateral compositions.

Data-flow Analysis. We introduce the following data-flow sets inspired from [10, Section 3]. Let $def(B)$ be the set of variables defined by process B:

$$def(\texttt{nil}) = def(\texttt{skip}) = def(c!V) = \emptyset \qquad def(x\texttt{:=}V) = def(c?x) = \{x\}$$
$$def(B_1; B_2) = def(B_1) \cup def(B_2) \qquad def(B_1, B_2) = def(B_1) \cup def(B_2)$$
$$def(\texttt{@[}G_1 \Rightarrow B_1; T_1 \ \ldots \ G_n \Rightarrow B_n; T_n\texttt{]}) = \textstyle\bigcup_{i=1}^{n} def(B_i)$$

Let $use_v(V)$ be the set of variables used by value expression V:

$$use_v(x) = \{x\} \qquad\qquad use_v\big(f(V_1, \ldots, V_n)\big) = \textstyle\bigcup_{i=1}^{n} use_v(V_i)$$

Let $use_g(G)$ be the set of variables used by guard G:

$$use_g(V) = use_v(V) \qquad use_g(c\texttt{#}) = \emptyset \qquad use_g(c\texttt{#}V) = use_v(V)$$

Let $use(B)$ be the set of variables used by process B before they are defined:

$$use(\texttt{nil}) = use(\texttt{skip}) = use(c?x) = \emptyset \qquad use(x\texttt{:=}V) = use(c!V) = use_v(V)$$
$$use(B_1; B_2) = use(B_1) \cup \big(use(B_2) \setminus def(B_1)\big)$$
$$use(B_1, B_2) = use(B_1) \cup use(B_2)$$
$$use(\texttt{@[}G_1 \Rightarrow B_1; T_1 \ \ldots \ G_n \Rightarrow B_n; T_n\texttt{]}) = \textstyle\bigcup_{i=1}^{n} \big(use_g(G_i) \cup use(B_i)\big)$$

Functionalities. The functionality of a CHP process B is given by the function $func(B, D, U)$, where D and U are two alphabetically ordered sets of variables with the same intuition as for $c2l_i$. A functionality is either `noexit` or `exit`(X), X being a possibly empty alphabetically ordered set of variables.

$func(\mathtt{nil}, D, U) = \mathtt{noexit}$ $func(\mathtt{skip}, D, U) = func(c!V, D, U) = \mathtt{exit}(D \cap U)$
$func(x\mathtt{:=}V, D, U) = func(c?x, D, U) = \mathtt{exit}((D \cup \{x\}) \cap U)$
$func(B_1; B_2, D, U) = func(B_1, B_2, D, U) =$
    if $func(B_1, D, U) = \mathtt{noexit} \lor func(B_2, D, U) = \mathtt{noexit}$
    then $\mathtt{noexit}$ else $\mathtt{exit}((D \cup def(B_1) \cup def(B_2)) \cap U)$
$func(@[G_1 \Rightarrow B_1; T_1 \ldots G_n \Rightarrow B_n; T_n], D, U) =$
    if $(\forall i)\, func(B_i, D, U) = \mathtt{noexit} \lor T_i = \mathtt{loop}$
    then $\mathtt{noexit}$ else $\mathtt{exit}(D \cup \bigcup_{i=1}^{n} def(B_i)) \cap U$

Using $func$, let $inf(B)$ be the predicate that holds iff $func(B, \emptyset, \emptyset) = \mathtt{noexit}$.

Preliminary Transformations. We first simplify the CHP processes by applying the following transformations successively:

- All occurrences of `skip` are removed wherever possible, based on the facts that (1) `skip` is neutral element for sequential and collateral composition, (2) any branch "$G \Rightarrow \mathtt{skip}; \mathtt{loop}$" of a guarded command can be removed, and (3) any $\hat{B}_i$ equal to `skip` can be removed from $\hat{B}_1 \parallel \cdots \parallel \hat{B}_n$. After these transformations, `skip` may occur only in branches "$G \Rightarrow \mathtt{skip}; \mathtt{break}$" of guarded commands.
- The abstract syntax tree of each CHP process is reorganised so as to be right bracketed (based on the associativity of CHP sequential composition). After transformation, each sequence "$B_1; B_2; B_3$" is bracketed as "$B_1; (B_2; B_3)$".
- If the rightmost process B_n of a maximal sequence "$B_1; \ldots; B_n$" ($n \geq 1$) is of the form "$x\mathtt{:=}V$", "$c!V$", or "$c?x$" (and not followed by `break` or `loop`), a final `skip` is added, leading to the sequence "$B_1; \ldots; B_n; \mathtt{skip}$".
- For each process of the form "$B_1; B_2$" such that $inf(B_1)$, B_2 will never be executed and can be removed. Similarly, in each process of the form "B_1, B_2" such that $inf(B_1)$ is the negation of $inf(B_2)$, we replace the process B_i ($i \in \{1, 2\}$) such that $inf(B_i)$ does not hold, by "$B_i; \mathtt{nil}$". Also, if $\neg inf(\hat{B}_i)$, then $\hat{B}_i$ is replaced by "$\hat{B}_i; \mathtt{nil}$". These transformations are needed to obey the static check of functionalities in LOTOS.

After these transformations, all assignments and all communications (emissions and receptions) are used in prefix-style, i.e. they occur only in processes of one of the forms "$x\mathtt{:=}V; B$", "$c!V; B$", and "$c?x; B$".

Translation of `nil` and `skip`. `nil` is translated into `stop`. After the preliminary transformations `skip` occurs only in a guarded command as a branch "$G \Rightarrow \mathtt{skip}; \mathtt{break}$" (this case is handled below with guarded commands) or at the end of a sequence; in this case: $c2l_i(\mathtt{skip}, D, U, \Delta) = \mathtt{exit}(\xi_1, \ldots, \xi_n)$, where the ξ_i are defined as follows. Let $\{x_1, \ldots, x_n\} = D \cap U$. Then $(\forall i)\ \xi_i = x_i$ if $x_i \in \Delta$ or $\xi_i =$ "any $type(x_i)$" otherwise.

Translation of "$x\!:=\!V;B$". An assignment to a variable x of type S is translated (generating an internal transition as in our SOS semantics and [20]) into:

$$c2l_i(\text{``}x\!:=\!V;B\text{''},D,U,\Delta) = \texttt{let } x\!:\!S = V \texttt{ in } \tau; \; c2l_i(B,D\cup\{x\},U,\Delta\cup\{x\})$$

Translation of Guards. Boolean expressions "$V \Rightarrow$" are directly translated into "$V \rightarrow$". To model the CHP probe operator for a channel c, we introduce an additional synchronisation on the corresponding LOTOS gate c. Probes are distinguished from actual communications by an additional offer "$!\,Probe$", where $Probe$ is a special constant belonging to an enumerated type with a single value. This translation is based on the value-matching feature of LOTOS synchronisation, which ensures that two offers "$!\,Probe$" will synchronise.

$$c2l_g(c\#) = c!\,Probe \qquad\qquad c2l_g(c\#V) = c!\,Probe!\,V,$$

Translation of "$c!V;B$" and "$c?x;B$". Translation of an emission or a reception on a channel c of type $S = type(c)$ depends whether process $\hat{B}_i$ is active or passive for c.

- The translation is straightforward if $passive(i,c)$ holds:
$$c2l_i(\text{``}c!V;B\text{''},D,U,\Delta) = c!V; \; c2l_i(B,D,U,\Delta)$$
$$c2l_i(\text{``}c?x;B\text{''},D,U,\Delta) = c?x\!:\!S; \; c2l_i(B,D\cup\{x\},U,\Delta\cup\{x\})$$

- If $active(i,c)$ holds, the translation is more involved because the active process $\hat{B}_i$ needs to allow its passive partner to probe channel c an arbitrary number of times. After a synchronisation labelled with "$!\,Probe$", $\hat{B}_i$ can only perform further synchronisations labelled with "$!\,Probe$", until the communication is completed. Therefore, for every occurrence of an active emission or an active reception on channel c in $\hat{B}_i$, we define an auxiliary LOTOS process $probed\_c$, the definition of which depends whether c is used for emission or reception.

  - An active emission "$c!V;B$" translates as follows:
    $$c2l_i(\text{``}c!V;B\text{''},D,U,\Delta) =$$
    $$\tau; \; probed\_c[c](V,x_1,\ldots,x_n) \gg \texttt{accept } x_1\!:\!S_1,\ldots,x_n\!:\!S_n \texttt{ in}$$
    $$c2l_i(B,D',U,\Delta\cap D')$$
    where $D' = D\cap(use(B)\cup U)$, $\{x_1,\ldots,x_n\} = D'$, and $(\forall i)$ $S_i = type(x_i)$. Process $probed\_c$ is defined by:
    ```
    process probed_c[c](x:S,x_1:S_1,...,x_n:S_n): exit(S_1,...,S_n) :=
        c!x; exit(x_1,...,x_n) [] c!Probe!x; probed_c[c](x,x_1,...,x_n)
    endproc
    ```

  - An active reception "$c?x;B$" translates as follows:
    $$c2l_i(\text{``}c?x;B\text{''},D,U,\Delta) =$$
    $$\tau; \; probed\_c[c](x_1,\ldots,x_n) \gg \texttt{accept } x_1\!:\!S_1,\ldots,x_n\!:\!S_n \texttt{ in}$$
    $$c2l_i(B,D',U,\Delta\cap D')$$
    where $D' = (D\cup\{x\})\cap(use(B)\cup U)$, $\{x_1,\ldots,x_n\} = D'$, and $(\forall i)$ $S_i = type(x_i)$. Process $probed\_c$ is defined by:
    ```
    process probed_c[c](x_1:S_1,...,x_n:S_n): exit(S_1,...,S_n) :=
        c?x:S; exit(x_1,...,x_n) [] c!Probe; probed_c[c](x_1,...,x_n)
    endproc
    ```

If $x \in \{x_1, \ldots, x_n\}$ and $x \notin D$, then x is removed from the parameters of process *probed_c*.

In both cases, the τ action preceding the call to *probed_c* is created by the assignment to x_c (cf. Section 3) and models the asymmetry of CHP communications, i.e. the fact that the active process chooses first. Notice that redundant process definitions can be avoided by defining *probed_c* only for all relevant subsets of $\{x_1, \ldots, x_n\}$; an approximation of these subsets can be computed by data-flow analysis.

Contrary to our approach, the translation from BALSA into CSP sketched in [23] uses pairs of actions with different names for representing (passive) input enclosures; the active process is translated accordingly. Our approach has the advantage that the translation of an active process is independent of the fact that the passive process probes or not.

Translation of "$B_1 ; B_2$". This translation rule applies only if B_1 is a collateral composition or a guarded command; all other cases have been handled before.

$$c2l_i(\text{"}B_1 ; B_2\text{"}, D, U, \Delta) =$$
$$c2l_i(B_1, \Delta', U', \Delta') \gg \text{accept } x_1 : S_1, \ldots, x_n : S_n \text{ in } c2l_i(B_2, D', U, \Delta')$$

where $U' = use(B_2) \cup (U \setminus def(B_2))$, $D' = (D \cup def(B_1)) \cap U'$, $\Delta' = (\Delta \cup def(B_1)) \cap U'$, and $\{x_1, \ldots, x_n\} = \Delta'$.

Translation of "B_1, B_2". A collateral composition is translated as follows:
$$c2l_i(\text{"}B_1, B_2\text{"}, D, U, \Delta) = c2l_i(B_1, D', U, \Delta_1) \ ||| \ c2l_i(B_2, D', U, \Delta_2)$$
where $D' = D \cup def(B_1) \cup def(B_2)$, $\Delta_1 = D' \setminus def(B_2)$, and $\Delta_2 = D' \setminus def(B_1)$.

Translation of Guarded Commands. Every guarded command $B = $ "$@[G_1 \Rightarrow B_1; T_1 \ \ldots \ G_n \Rightarrow B_n; T_n]$" is translated into a call to a process P_B

$$c2l_i(@[G_1 \Rightarrow B_1; T_1 \ \ldots \ G_n \Rightarrow B_n; T_n], D, U, \Delta) = P_B[\mathcal{C}_i](x_1, \ldots, x_n)$$

where $\{x_1, \ldots, x_n\} = D$. The auxiliary process P_B is defined by:

```
process P_B [C_i] (x_1 : S_1, ..., x_n : S_n): F
   c2l_g(G_1) c2l_i(B_1, D, U, Δ) >> c2l_t(T_1, B_1, D, U, Δ)   [] ··· []
   c2l_g(G_n) c2l_i(B_n, D, U, Δ) >> c2l_t(T_n, B_n, D, U, Δ)
endproc
```

$c2l_t(\text{loop}, B, D, U, \Delta) = \text{accept } x_1 : S_1, \ldots, x_n : S_n \text{ in } P_B[\mathcal{C}_i](x_1, \ldots, x_n)$
$c2l_t(\text{break}, B, D, U, \Delta) =$
   $\text{accept } x_1' : S_1, \ldots, x_m' : S_m \text{ in } c2l_i(\text{skip}, (D \cup def(B)) \cap U, U, \Delta)$

with $\{x_1', \ldots, x_m'\} = (D \cup def(B)) \cap U$. If $inf(B)$ then $F = \text{noexit}$; otherwise $func(B, D, U) = \text{exit}(\{x_1'', \ldots, x_k''\})$ and $F = \text{exit}(type(x_1''), \ldots, type(x_k''))$.

If a guarded command is the left hand side of a sequential composition "$@[\ldots]; B'$", we generate a second auxiliary process $P_{B'}$ (for B'); each **break** is translated into a call to $P_{B'}$ and the functionality F is computed with respect to B'. This avoids the introduction of a τ transition due to the **exit** (generated by the translation of **break**). For each B_i such that $inf(B_i)$, T_i is not translated at all.

4.2   Principles of Translating Several Concurrent Processes

The parallel composition "‖" of CHP is translated into the LOTOS operator
"|[···]|". In CHP, processes synchronise implicitly on channels with the same
name, whereas in LOTOS the set of gates for synchronisation has to be stated
explicitly. Our translation relies on the fact that the channels have pairwise
distinct names. The translation of $\langle \mathcal{C}, \mathcal{X}, \hat{B}_1 \parallel \cdots \parallel \hat{B}_n \rangle$ is defined recursively:

$$c2l(\text{``}\hat{B}_1 \parallel \cdots \parallel \hat{B}_n\text{''}, \mathcal{C}) = \text{if } n = 1 \text{ then } c2l_1(\hat{B}_1, \emptyset, \emptyset, \emptyset) \text{ else}$$
$$c2l_1(\hat{B}_1, \emptyset, \emptyset, \emptyset) \mid [chan(\hat{B}_1) \cap \mathcal{C}] \mid c2l(\text{``}\hat{B}_2 \parallel \cdots \parallel \hat{B}_n\text{''}, \mathcal{C} \setminus chan(\hat{B}_1))$$

where $chan(\hat{B})$ stands for the set of binary channels occurring in process $\hat{B}$.

4.3   Example of the Arbiter

The LOTOS behaviour obtained as translation of the arbiter described in Section 2.3 is defined by the following LOTOS code fragment:

```
client-1[c₁] |[c₁]| (client-2[c₂] |[c₂]| arbiter[c,c₁,c₂])
where (∀i ∈ {1,2})
  process client-i[cᵢ] : noexit :=
    τ; probed_cᵢ[cᵢ](i) >> client-i[cᵢ]
  endproc
  process arbiter[c,c₁,c₂] : noexit :=
    (c₁!Probe!1; (τ; probed_c[c](1) ||| c₁?x:S; exit) >> arbiter[c,c₁,c₂]) []
    (c₂!Probe!2; (τ; probed_c[c](2) ||| c₂?x:S; exit) >> arbiter[c,c₁,c₂])
  endproc
```

where the processes $probed\_c_{(j)}$ are defined as described in Section 4.1.

The LTS corresponding to this LOTOS specification has 82 states and 212
transitions. The LTS obtained after hiding all labels with "!Probe" offers was
found (by the BISIMULATOR tool of CADP) to be observationally (but not branching) equivalent to the one presented in Figure 1.

The reason why our translation does not preserve branching equivalence is
that a probe is translated into a τ transition that is not present in the SOS
semantics of Section 3. For instance, the LTS of Figure 1 contains a state (lower
middle of the graph) with two outgoing transitions labelled "$c_1!1$" and "$c_2!2$",
but no such state exists in the LTS obtained after our LOTOS translation, since
both branches of the "[]" choice in the arbiter start with a τ transition corresponding to a probe.

4.4   Application: An Asynchronous Implementation of the DES

We developed a prototype CHP to LOTOS translator, called chp2lotos, using the SYNTAX and LOTOS NT compiler construction technologies [8]. So far,
chp2lotos consists of about 2,000 lines of SYNTAX, 6,000 lines of LOTOS NT,
and 500 lines of C.

We have experimented `chp2lotos` on a case study tackled in [4], namely a
CHP description (1,600 lines) of an asynchronous implementation of the DES
(*Data Encryption Standard*) [18], from which `chp2lotos` produced about 1,600
lines of LOTOS. Since this case study contains many concurrent processes, direct
generation of the LTS failed due to lack of memory (after 70 minutes, the generated LTS had more than 17 million states and 139 million transitions). However,
using the compositional verification techniques (decomposing, minimising, and
recomposing processes) [15] of the CADP toolbox we generated an equivalent,
but smaller LTS (50,956 states and 228,136 transitions) in 8 minutes on a Sun-
Blade 100 (500 Mhz Ultra Sparc II processor, 1.5 GB of RAM). Compared to
[4][4], compositional techniques improves verification performance.

5   Concluding Remarks

In this paper, we gave an SOS semantics for the hardware process algebra CHP
with value-passing communication and ports open to the environment. Our semantics clarifies the definition of the probe operator. We investigated the relation
of our semantics with existing semantics based on a translation of CHP into Petri
nets. Based on our semantics, we outlined a translation of CHP into LOTOS, in
order to allow the reuse of existing formal verification tools, such as CADP, for
the analysis and validation of asynchronous hardware. Finally, we reported on a
first experiment with a prototype translator.

As regards future work, it would be interesting to characterise precisely the
weak equivalence preserved by our translation from CHP into LOTOS. We conjecture that observational equivalence is preserved, and that if the CHP description
does not contain any probe, branching equivalence is also preserved.

Acknowledgements. We are grateful to E. Beigné, F. Bertrand, D. Borrione,
M. Renaudin, and P. Vivet for interesting discussions on CHP and TAST, in
particular on the semantics of the probe operator. We thank the anonymous
referees for helpful comments on the preliminary version of this paper. We are
indebted to H. Garavel for his significant contributions to the final version.

References

1. E. Beigné, F. Clermidy, P. Vivet, A. Clouard, and M. Renaudin. An Asynchronous
   NOC Architecture Providing Low Latency Service and Its Multi-Level Design
   Framework. In *ASYNC'05*, pp. 54–63. IEEE Computer Society, Mar. 2005.
2. J. A. Bergstra, A. Ponse, and S. A. Smolka, editors. *Handbook of Process Algebra*.
   Elsevier, 2001.

---

[4] [4] managed to generate an LTS directly (5.3 million states, 30 million transitions) in
  65 minutes after replacing collateral compositions by sequential compositions in some
  well-chosen processes of the CHP description (according to the second author of [4]).
  When applying the same transformations on a LOTOS specification, we generated an
  equivalent LTS of the same size in 15 minutes.

3. T. Bolognesi and E. Brinksma. Introduction to the ISO Specification Language LOTOS. *Computer Networks and ISDN Systems*, 14(1):25–59, Jan. 1988.

4. D. Borrione, M. Boubekeur, L. Mounier, M. Renaudin, and A. Sirianni. Validation of Asynchronous Circuit Specifications using IF/CADP. In *VLSI-SoC 2003*, pp. 86–91, Dec. 2003.

5. F. S. de Boer and C. Palamidessi. A Fully Abstract Model for Concurrent Constraint Programming. In *CAAP'91*, *LNCS* 493, pp. 296–319. Springer, Apr. 1991.

6. D. Edwards and A. Bardsley. Balsa: An Asynchronous Hardware Synthesis Language. *The Computer Journal*, 45(1):12–18, 2002.

7. W. Fokkink. *Introduction to Process Algebra*. Texts in Theoretical Computer Science. Springer, 2000.

8. H. Garavel, F. Lang, and R. Mateescu. Compiler Construction using LOTOS NT. In *CC 2002*, *LNCS* 2304, pp. 9–13. Springer, Apr. 2002.

9. H. Garavel, F. Lang, and R. Mateescu. An Overview of CADP 2001. *EASST Newsletter*, 4:13–24, Aug. 2002.

10. H. Garavel and W. Serwe. State Space Reduction for Process Algebra Specifications. In *AMAST'2004*, *LNCS* 3116, pp. 164–180. Springer, July 2004.

11. H. Garavel and J. Sifakis. Compilation and Verification of LOTOS Specifications. In *International Symposium on Protocol Specification, Testing and Verification*, pages 379–394. IFIP, North-Holland, June 1990.

12. S. Hauck. Asynchronous Design Methodologies: An Overview. *Proceedings of the IEEE*, 83(1):69–93, Jan. 1995.

13. ISO/IEC. LOTOS — A Formal Description Technique Based on the Temporal Ordering of Observational Behaviour. International Standard 8807, Geneva, 1989.

14. J. L. W. Kessels and A. M. G. Peeters. The Tangram Framework (Embedded Tutorial): Asynchronous Circuits for Low Power. In *ASP-DAC 2001*, pp. 255–260. ACM, 2001.

15. F. Lang. Compositional Verification using SVL Scripts. In *TACAS'2002*, *LNCS* 2280, pp. 465–469. Springer, Apr. 2002.

16. A. J. Martin. The Probe: An Addition to Communication Primitives. *Information Processing Letters*, 20(3):125–130, Apr. 1985.

17. A. J. Martin. Compiling Communicating Processes into Delay-Insensitive VLSI Circuits. *Distributed Computing*, 1(4):226–234, 1986.

18. Data Encryption Standard (DES). Federal Information Processing Standards FIPS PUB 46-3, National Institute of Standards and Technology, Oct. 25 1999.

19. M. Renaudin. *TAST Compiler and TAST_CHP Language, Version 0.6*. TIMA Laboratory, CIS Group, 2005.

20. M. Renaudin and A. Yakovlev. From Hardware Processes to Asynchronous Circuits via Petri Nets: an Application to Arbiter Design. In *TOBACO'04*, June 2004.

21. W. Serwe. *On Concurrent Functional-Logic Programming*. Thèse de doctorat, Institut National Polytechnique de Grenoble, Mar. 2002.

22. K. van Berkel. *Handshake Circuits: An Asynchronous Architecture for VLSI Programming*. Cambridge University Press, 1993.

23. X. Wang, M. Kwiatkowska, G. Theodoropoulos, and Q. Zhang. Towards a Unifying CSP approach for Hierarchical Verification of Asynchronous Hardware. In *AVoCS'04*, *ENTCS* 128, pp. 231–246, 2004.

Formalising Interactive Voice Services with SDL

Kenneth J. Turner

Computing Science and Mathematics, University of Stirling, Stirling FK9 4LA, UK
kjt@cs.stir.ac.uk

Abstract. IVR (Interactive Voice Response) services are introduced with reference to VoiceXML (Voice eXtensible Markup Language). It is explained how IVR services can benefit from an underlying formalism and rigorous analysis. IVR services are modelled using CRESS (Chisel Representation Employing Systematic Specification) as a high-level graphical notation. Apart from being able to describe services, CRESS also introduces the notion of features. The translation of IVR descriptions into SDL is explored, along with how the generated SDL can be formally analysed.

Keywords: Feature, IVR (Interactive Voice Response), SDL (Specification and Description Language), Service, VoiceXML (Voice eXtensible Markup Language).

1 Introduction

1.1 Interactive Voice Response

The research reported here combines the power of two communications standards. IVR (Interactive Voice Response [17]) allows an automated enquiry system to deal with natural speech. SDL (Specification and Description Language [5]) is a standardised formal language for communications systems, although it has wider applicability. The primary goal has been to integrate a formal method into the currently informal practice used in industry. To enhance industrial attractiveness and usability, IVR services are described graphically. However, the graphical notation then needs a formal underpinning. This is achieved by denotational mapping that gives an SDL interpretation of each graphical construct. The work has introduced formal specification and rigorous analysis into the pragmatic and empirical development practices followed at present. It has thus been possible to integrate a formal method with informal and graphical techniques.

As an example of IVR, an airline might have an automated telephone system for booking flights or enquiring about arrivals. In comparison, touch-tone systems require the user to go through a series of menu selections. This style of system is much more inflexible and is often disliked by callers. It is therefore not surprising that IVR is a major growth area. IVR supports a high degree of automation that benefits the service provider through lower staff costs. IVR systems are also typically multi-lingual, supporting speech synthesis and speech recognition in multiple languages.

A number of approaches have been used for IVR, but among these VoiceXML (Voice eXtensible Markup Language [17]) has emerged as a major force. The existence of a standard increases compatibility among vendors. However the standard is not formalised, and leaves a number of areas open to interpretation. A formalisation of VoiceXML is helpful in making such aspects clear.

J. Romijn, G. Smith, and J. van de Pol (Eds.): IFM 2005, LNCS 3771, pp. 307–326, 2005.

IVR applications are usually developed with a specialised development environment. For some IDEs, the application can be debugged in this environment prior to deployment. For others, the application has to be debugged in the deployment environment. In either case, debugging is like program debugging: the code is run with sample inputs and the outputs are checked. There is little automated support for validation.

IVR languages tend to encourage complex control flow and spaghetti code – the kind of things that structured programming was developed to avoid. Even in a small IVR application there can be very many paths to test, so it is easy to miss some error cases. This paper uses the example of a hotel booking system. In just the basic application of figure 1, there are 266,304 paths that might be tested! Allowing for significant variations in the input data, the number of plausible test cases is very much larger. Formalising IVR descriptions gives access to rigorous analysis techniques. For example, an IVR application can be checked for general properties such as freedom from deadlock, livelock, unreachable code and unspecified receptions. More specialised properties can be investigated through the use of property checking or observer processes. Formal theories of test generation can be used to create useful test suites automatically.

IDEs for IVR development differ significantly even if they generate code for the same language. This means that the IVR source may then not be portable among different vendors. The IDEs also tend to be close to their target language, i.e. to be 'window dressing' on the underlying language. This means that the IVR application description is accessible only to specialists. There are usually many stakeholders in IVR development, including non-technical people such as managers, sales staff and customers. It would be useful if the description of an IVR application were meaningful to such individuals. Ideally, the description would be a graphical representation since this seems to find most favour in industry.

Although some IDEs can present an IVR application graphically, this is often structured in a way that closely reflects the supporting IVR language. This does not help to give a high-level overview of what is often a complex control structure. The IDEs focus on the details, hiding the 'big picture' of what is being described.

1.2 Developing Services with CRESS

CRESS (Chisel Representation Employing Systematic Specification) was developed for defining and formalising services of all types. The inspiration for CRESS was the Chisel notation developed by BellCore for telephony services. However, CRESS has grown considerably beyond Chisel in its capabilities and range of applications.

CRESS describes services graphically using a simple notation. BellCore's experience with Chisel was that this kind of notation can be understood by many stakeholders in service development. In fact, CRESS offers simplifications over Chisel that make it even more accessible. CRESS is relatively neutral with respect to the graphical notation. It merely requires directed graphs with three kinds of nodes: behaviour, comment and rule. As a result, any reasonable graph editor can be used. CRESS has its own editor called CHIVE (CRESS Hierarchical Interactive Visual Editor), but can also be used with the free graphical editors *Diagram!* and *yEd*.

CRESS is designed to be extensible for new application domains. The vocabulary and concepts used in each domain are defined by plug-in modules. CRESS has been used to define services from the IN (Intelligent Network [9]), Internet telephony [10, 12], IVR (Interactive Voice Response [12, 13, 14]) and Web Services [15]. These papers have focused on certain aspects such as the application domain or the target language. The contribution of the present paper is an explanation of how SDL is used to support CRESS descriptions of IVR services. The paper is complementary to [14], which discusses the same application domain from a LOTOS perspective. Since SDL is more widely used in industry than LOTOS, it is advantageous to underpin IVR services with SDL. From a technical perspective, SDL supports different kinds of formal analysis from LOTOS. In particular, analysis based on state space exploration is well supported by SDL tools.

CRESS diagrams are checked for syntactic and static semantic correctness. However to give the diagrams meaning, it is necessary to translate them into some target language. CRESS is neutral with respect to the choice of language; almost any constructive language should be suitable. It is, however, useful to classify the target languages as formal ones or implementation ones. Among formal languages, CRESS currently supports translation to SDL (Specification and Description Language [5]) and LOTOS (Language Of Temporal Ordering Specification [3]). The formal languages are used to give precise meaning to CRESS diagrams, and to support formally-based analysis and validation. Among implementation languages, CRESS currently supports translation to VoiceXML (for IVR) and BPEL (Business Process Execution Logic for web services).

1.3   Relationship to Other Work

There are many graphical notations in software engineering. However there are not so many graphical notations for services. Even fewer graphical notations have a formal interpretation. In data communications, SDL and MSCs (Message Sequence Charts [4]) are major examples. UCMs (Use Case Maps, e.g. [1]) have also been proven useful for describing services. However all the foregoing approaches are lacking in one or more of the following respects:

- they are too language-specific; a description reflects one language and cannot readily be translated to another form (e.g. for implementation or other formal analysis)
- they are too general; there is no support for particular application domains (which often require specialised functions and frameworks)
- they are too technical; descriptions can be understood only by those with specialised knowledge
- they are too informal; there may be no formal basis or only a limited one, and there is no support for rigorous analysis techniques.

CRESS aims to fill this void. It offers a graphical notation that is accessible to non-specialists, it provides a rigorous underpinning through formal languages, and it supports practical realisation through translation to implementation languages. It is important to realise that the *same* CRESS diagrams are used for all three purposes.

VoiceXML is one of many XML-based languages. Much work has, of course, been undertaken on formalising the data models and schemas implied by such languages. However, the semantics of XML-based documents if of course application-specific. The work of this paper can thus be seen as giving formal meaning to a particular class of XML documents (using VoiceXML).

Surprisingly, IVR has attracted almost no attention from the formal methods community. Apart from some general work on formally modelling multimodal systems [6], the author is not aware of any research comparable to the work reported here.

2   CRESS for IVR Services

2.1   IVR Services

The main behaviour of an IVR application (its service) is described by a CRESS root diagram. Suppose that the imaginary Happy Hotel wishes to allow automated telephone booking of rooms. Callers should be connected to an IVR application that takes their arrival date, length of stay and type of room. A sample dialogue might be as follows:

System: Happy Hotel Automated Reservation. Say Help or Exit at any time. Please book your room. What arrival date?
User: 12-25.
System: For how many nights?
User: 7
System: What kind of room?
User: Pardon?
System: Choose from Single, Double, Suite. What kind of room?
User: Single
System: You arrive 12-25 staying 7 nights in a Single. Do you wish to proceed?
User: Yes
System: Thank you for calling – goodbye.

The *Booking* diagram in figure 1 shows the core of the room booking application. A diagram often contains a rule box (rounded rectangle). In IVR applications, a **Uses** clause defines any variables used by the diagram. A rule box may also contain (parameterised) macro definitions, such as *Welcome* in this example. For other application domains, a rule box may define how diagrams depend on each other, and how input/output changes the state variables. Types apart from **Value** are possible in other domains.

A CRESS diagram contains behaviour nodes (ovals) that define actions, fields, inputs and outputs. Nodes are numbered for reference. The CRESS tools check the syntax and static semantics of diagrams, e.g. node numbers must not be repeated, and a node must not be immediately followed by both input and output behaviours. An empty behaviour node can be useful to connect other nodes (e.g. the one preceding nodes 4 and 9 in figure 1). The plug-in domain vocabulary defines what behaviour nodes may contain.

IVR applications usually collect information in forms. These contain fields that the user 'fills in' by speaking. Each field has an associated variable that holds the entered value. Fields are usually processed in sequence (though mixed-mode initiative forms allow flexibility as to order). An important characteristic of IVR is that once a field has been completed, then by default it plays no further part. (This may be overridden by design, e.g. a field variable can be cleared because a later choice invalidated it.) Two kinds of field are used in this example, though a **Menu** field is also possible for selection from a list of choices. The commonest kinds of field are:

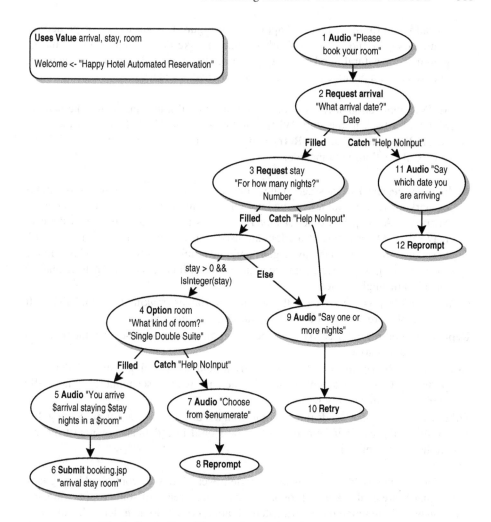

Fig. 1. CRESS Root Diagram for Hotel Room Booking Request

Option *variable prompt options [condition]* asks the user to speak input from a fixed set of options. The field variable and the user prompt message are given. Selection of the field may be made subject to an optional boolean condition. Figure 1 offers the Single, Double and Suite options for the choice of room (node 4).

Request *variable prompt grammar [condition]* resembles **Option**, but the speech input conforms to some grammar. In practice, IVR languages use many different types of grammar – often some BNF variant to define the syntax of what users may say. Speaker-independent speech recognition is very difficult, but IVR circumvents this by giving specific guidance to the speech recogniser as to what to expect. It is impracticable for CRESS to support the full variety of IVR grammar notations. Instead, CRESS supports the same predefined grammars as VoiceXML: booleans, currency amounts, dates, digit strings, numbers, phone numbers and times. These are sufficient for many practical applications. Figure 1 makes use of the predefined grammars *Date* (node 2) and *Number* (node 3). Like IVR, CRESS does not have a grammar for natural numbers. The length of stay collected in node 3 is therefore checked to be a positive integer (guard before nodes 4 and 9).

An IVR application such as figure 1 continues until a terminal node like node 6, where it cycles back to the start. What is not obvious in IVR is that many loops are implied. A **Reprompt** node or a **Retry** node implicitly loops back to the start as well.

In IVR, the actions may include:

Audio *message* speaks a message to the caller. The message may contain various kinds of markup. Variable values can be interpolated into the message using the notation *$variable*. As a special case, *$enumerate* means the current options that the user may select. Other forms of markup are used to give the pronunciation of a word, to say text in a particular way (e.g. as a phone number), or to give emphasis in the speech. Strings (e.g. messages) use double quotes. If necessary, a substring may be enclosed in single quotes.

Clear *[variables]* is used to clear the specified variables (making them undefined). If no variables are named, then all field variables are cleared.

Reprompt requires the user to repeat speech input, usually because what the user said was not understood.

Retry is like **Reprompt**, but clears the current field variable first. This action is supported by CRESS as a convenience for the case where user input is syntactically correct but semantically wrong.

Submit *URL variables* sends information from the user to a server for processing. For example, the user's information might be stored in a database or may trigger a further IVR application.

Behaviour nodes are linked by arcs whose traversal may be controlled by a guard. Event guards are enabled asynchronously by the occurrence of some event, while expression guards are immediately evaluated. Guard types are domain-defined, with event guards being distinguished by their names. Guards have the form:

expression is a boolean guard, with **Else** being used as the logical complement.

event [count] [condition] is an event guard. An optional prompt count and condition may determine when the event guard applies. The predefined events are **Cancel** (user cancellation), **Exit** (user termination), **Help** (user information request), **NoInput** (no user response), and **NoMatch** (invalid user response). In addition, a program-defined event may be thrown by the application. This may be a simple identifier such as *booking*, or may be a hierarchically constructed name such as *error.booking.room*. In IVR, events are caught and handled at four levels: platform (generic support), application, form and field. In fact, CRESS merges application and form level into one (i.e. all fields are collected into a single form).

Catch *events [count] [condition]* is a composite event guard for a list of events.

Filled is an event guard meaning the user has filled in a field with a valid response.

2.2   IVR Features

Features in General. CRESS allows the root diagram to be modified by additional diagrams. This follows telephony practice, where features are often used to extend the basic behaviour of a phone call. The use of IVR features is a new possibility created by CRESS. An approximate equivalent in VoiceXML is **SubDialog**, which behaves like a procedure call. However sub-dialogues execute in a separate context, limiting their applicability. They also have to be programmed explicitly into the application logic.

Experience from telephony shows that it is valuable to have additional features triggered implicitly by conditions that arise in a call. Similarly, it is useful to to have triggered features in IVR. Features encourage a more modular and reusable approach to IVR development.

Features in CRESS. The example of figure 1 is obviously incomplete as there is no way of identifying the caller. Although this could easily be included in the root diagram, this is likely to be a requirement of several applications. A separate *Contact* feature is therefore defined as shown in figure 2. The notation is very similar to that for a root diagram.

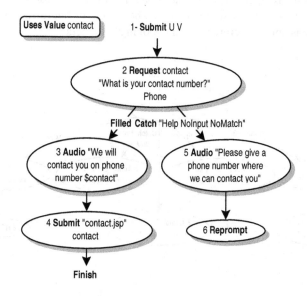

Fig. 2. CRESS Feature Diagram to obtain a Contact Phone Number

CRESS supports spliced (cut-and-paste) features and template (macro) features. Most features, like *Contact*, are of the template type. A template diagram resembles a root diagram, but begins with a trigger. In this case, the template matches any node that contains **Submit** with URL U and variables V. Parameters are pattern-matched to the triggering node; although not used in this template, their actual values may be used in the template definition.

The first template node also defines how it relates to the triggering node. Once a template instance has been created with actual parameters, it may be prefixed ('–') or appended ('+') to the triggering node. The effect of figure 2 is to instantiate the *Contact* feature and place it immediately before **Submit** in node 6 of figure 1.

A template may contain at most one **Finish** node where behaviour continues with the triggering diagram. The *Contact* feature captures the user phone number and stores it on the server. The idea is that hotel staff can then phone the user to confirm the reservation, and collect other information such as name and payment details.

Features and Event Handling. An IVR platform defines default handling for all the predefined events. However this is likely be too general for most applications. It is therefore normal to define appropriate event handlers for each application. Although only a room booking application is considered in this paper, the hotel is likely to require other IVR applications. These might, for example, give information about room availability, guest accounts and special events. It would be desirable if all these applications had a common 'feel', such as the way they respond to incorrect or missing user input.

Introduction in figure 3 is a template feature defined to introduce the hotel applications. If a graph is cyclic, its start node may be ambiguous. In such a case, an explicit **Start** node can be used. The designation 1+ **Start** as the trigger for *Introduction* means it is placed after the implicit start node at the beginning of figure 1. That is, the introduction feature is applied before the main booking behaviour.

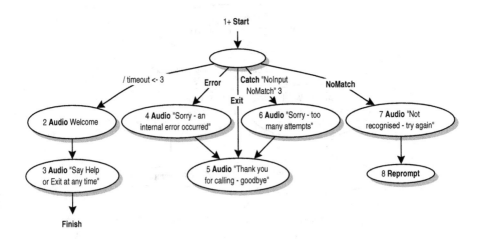

Fig. 3. CRESS Feature Diagram to introduce Happy Hotel Applications

Introduction may be used with the *Booking* application, but also with other hotel applications. In fact, it is sufficiently general that it could be used with a wide range of applications. For this reason, it uses the opening *Welcome* message defined as a macro by the root diagram (figure 1 in this case).

The *Introduction* feature includes several application-specific event handlers. Those for **Error, Exit** and **NoMatch** are likely to apply throughout the application. They are defined at form level, i.e. they apply to all fields. Each field will probably define its own handling of **Help** (which needs to be field-specific) and **NoInput** (which will probably be field-specific). Notice that **NoInput** is then handled at two levels (per field, and in the introduction), while **NoMatch** is handled in two places by the introduction.

It is undesirable to issue an indefinite number of prompts if the user repeatedly gives the wrong input. An event handler may be qualified by a prompt count and a condition. The first time a field prompt is issued, an internal prompt counter is set to 1; it is incremented on each subsequent reprompt. If the user does not respond correctly, the changed prompt count can select a different event handler. More explicit guidance might be issued, for example. In figure 3, the call is disconnected after three prompts.

The event model that CRESS inherits from IVR is comprehensive but complex. Suppose that some part of the booking system throws the event *error.booking.room*. It is first checked whether a handler for this event has been defined by the current field. If not, it is checked whether there is a handler for the more generic event *error.booking* (or failing that, just *error*). If a relevant field handler exists, the current prompt count is checked against that for the handler. If the handler has a condition, that too is evaluated. A handler is invoked only if matches the (hierarchic) name, prompt count and condition. If no matching field handler is found, the same procedure is repeated at form level. This allows forms to define generic event treatment on behalf of all their fields. If no form handler matches, then (in CRESS) the generic platform handlers are tried. If there is still no match, the application terminates with an error.

Apart from internal variables like the prompt count, an IVR environment defines platform variables. The most important of these are *bargein* (whether the user can interrupt a prompt or announcement) and *timeout* (which triggers a **NoInput** event). As part of the common properties for hotel applications, figure 3 sets *timeout* to three seconds.

Besides *Contact* and *Introduction*, other features may be useful for hotel bookings. The full hotel application suite is not discussed here. It includes features for collecting a guest's account number, asking for confirmation before proceeding, disallowing user barge-in, collecting a PIN for payment information, and disabling input timeout. These generic features are described for another IVR application in [14].

3   Translating IVR Diagrams to SDL

3.1   Specification Framework

CRESS diagrams for IVR can be translated into SDL for rigorous analysis and validation. The *same* diagrams are also translated into LOTOS for complementary analysis, and into VoiceXML for deployment. The generated SDL is embedded in a specification framework that provides general support for an IVR application. A framework is specific to a target language and an application domain, but is independent of any services or features that might be deployed. Developing a framework is thus a one-off activity.

Figure 4 shows the specification framework for IVR with SDL. For readers not familiar with SDL, [7] can be consulted as an introduction. SDL is based on communicating Extended Finite State Machines with Abstract Data Types. SDL has a graphical syntax, partly illustrated in figure 4: octagons are processes, arcs are signal routes, and signal lists are given in square brackets. SDL also has a mostly obvious textual syntax, used later in the paper. Each process **State** starts a transition with **Input** followed by other actions. These include **Output, Task** (typically assignments to variables), **Decision** (conditional branch) and **Join** (unconditional branch to a label for part of a transition). A transition usually ends with **NextState** (change to a new state) but may also **Stop** (process execution ceases). Free-standing code outside a transition may be prefixed by **Connection**.

SDL does not, of course, deal with speech so all input/output is in the form of text strings. The *User* channel is used for communication between the user and the IVR system. The *Serv* channel is used to receive submissions to the (web) server.

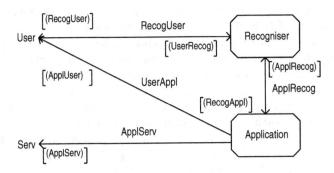

Fig. 4. CRESS Specification Framework for SDL Support of IVR

The system has one instance of the following processes that interact with the user:

Application. This is entirely generated from the CRESS diagrams to define the application logic. A clean separation is thus maintained between application-specific code and generic 'speech' recognition functions.

Recogniser. The 'speech' recogniser is fixed in the framework. When the application needs to fill in a field, it sends a request to the recogniser. This issues audio signals to the user as prompts. The recogniser parses user input according to the field grammar, responding with the filled-in field value or a failure response.

The signal routes between the processes are as follows:

UserAppl. From application to user: *Audio* ('spoken' messages).

RecogUser. From user to recogniser: *Voice* (what the users 'says'), *Tone* (touch-tone signals), *Event* (special requests such as for help). From recogniser to user: *Audio*.

ApplRecog. From application to recogniser: *Menu* (prompt for user selection from a menu), *Option* (prompt for user input from options), *Request* (prompt for user input conforming to some grammar). From recogniser to application: *Failed* (invalid user response), *Filled* (valid user response).

ApplServ. From application to server: *Submit* (web server submissions).

The specification framework defines a complex set of data types and associated operators (1,700 lines of SDL). The need for such elaborate data types is not so surprising, as the framework is broadly equivalent to an IVR platform. This has to parse user input according to many different kinds of grammars. It is not feasible for CRESS to support the entirety of JAVASCRIPT, which is part of VoiceXML. Instead, the SDL framework supports the main JAVASCRIPT functions for logical, arithmetic and string operations.

3.2 Variables and Expressions

Unlike SDL, VoiceXML variables are dynamically typed: the same variable may hold different kinds of values at different times. These values may be booleans, reals or strings. In addition, *null* (void) and *undefined* values are permitted. It is therefore necessary to translate VoiceXML variables into SDL variables with a variant type. Each SDL *Value* carries along its type as well as its actual value. All the usual SDL operators therefore have to be re-specified. For example, the '>' operator checks it is given values of type *Real*. The comparison is then performed on the actual values, and the result is converted to a value of type *Boolean*. Expressions in decisions and in operator calls also have to be converted into *Value* form.

Besides the application-defined variables, the translation includes the platform variables for barge-in and speech timeout. Internal variables are also defined for the current event, field number, options list and prompt count.

3.3 Behaviour

CRESS has generic support for translating signal inputs and outputs. As explained in [11], it can be extremely complex to translate CRESS inputs into SDL. Fortunately, the IVR use of inputs is straightforward. CRESS outputs are readily translated as SDL signal outputs. Each output is labelled with its diagram and node number so that another part of the diagram may branch to it. In IVR, the outputs are mainly **Audio** and **Submit**.

The translation of actions is domain-specific. In IVR, the actions predominate but have a simple translation. **Clear** gives variables undefined values. **Reprompt** branches to the first field. **Retry** is similar, but first assigns the current field variable an undefined value. It follows that the CRESS compiler must keep track of fields during translation.

A field first checks if its field variable has already been defined. If it is defined, the rules of IVR require the field to be ignored (i.e. to continue with the next field). If it is not defined, the prompt count is incremented and a *Menu*, *Option* or *Request* signal is sent to the recogniser. It is then necessary to wait for a *Filled* or *Failed* signal, as dictated by the user reaction. A *Filled* response conveys the input value for a field variable. A *Failed* response carries an error event (e.g. no input). In both cases, the response is sent to an event dispatcher generated for the application.

3.4 Guards

Guards in General. Expression guards simply map onto SDL decisions, with minor conversions to the operator and functions names used in SDL. The only small complication is that expression guards of type *Value* have to be converted into SDL booleans.

Event guards are, however, extremely difficult to translate. The behaviour following an event guard is translated as the start of an SDL connection (isolated piece of labelled code). If the corresponding event occurs, the event dispatcher branches to this label. This means the SDL is broken up into sections of code as dictated by the presence of event guards. Although the SDL control flow is then rather fragmented, it faithfully reflects the IVR logic.

The IVR event model was explained in section 2.2. A key problem is that IVR events are handled dynamically, whereas SDL requires a static definition of event handlers. The name of a program-defined event may in fact be constructed during execution. Fortunately the hierarchy of event handlers can be determined statically during translation. The CRESS compiler builds a table of the event handlers that apply at each level: platform, application/form and field. At each level, a handler is identified by its event name, prompt count (if any) and condition (if any).

An event may be explicitly thrown by the application, or may occur implicitly as a result of recognition. Event dispatcher code is generated by the CRESS compiler. The dispatcher uses the current field number (*field*), event name (*event*) and prompt count (*prompt*) to branch to the currently applicable handler.

The Event Dispatcher. As an example of the approach, figure 5 shows part of the SDL generated for the hotel booking system in section 2. The event dispatcher has *Event.0* as its entry point; the application branches to this label when an event occurs. Figure 5 deals with events in the scope of the *contact* field in figure 2 node 2. This field is numbered 5 within the full hotel application. The code has also been abbreviated by omitting uninteresting *False* branches and the ends of decisions. Comparison with figures 2 and 3 should show how the event dispatcher has been derived.

As it happens, all the events here are predefined ones. However program-defined event names (strings) are also possible. If an event matches a handler, the dispatcher branches to the given label. Platform event handlers are named *Event.1*, *Event.2*, etc. Form and field event handlers are labelled with the corresponding diagram name and node number. Since *Introduction* and *Contact* are defined by feature templates, they may have several instances. Their diagrams are therefore qualified by the instance number (*Introduction.1* and *Contact.1*).

To accommodate the event hierarchy, more specific handlers are checked first. Here, checks for prompt count 3 (or more) appear before other checks for the same event. If program-defined events were in use, the more specific ones would be checked first (e.g. *error.booking.room* before *error.booking*). If no handler matches, an error event is caused (translated as *Err* since **Error** is an SDL keyword).

The platform event handlers are generated by the translation. As examples, *Event.1* (**Cancel**) restarts from the first field, and *Event.2* (**Error**) terminates the application:

```
Connection Event.1:                          /* start platform handler for Cancel */
   Join BOOKING.2;                                /* restart from first field */

Connection Event.2:                          /* start platform handler for Error */
   Output Audio('There was an internal error');          /* Error audio */
   Stop;                                            /* end of behaviour */
```

```
Connection Event.0:                                    /* start event dispatcher */
  Decision field;                                                /* check field */
  ...                                                          /* fields 0 to 4 */
  (5):                                                      /* field Contact.2? */
    Decision Match(event,Cancel);                                   /* Cancel? */
    (True): Join Event.1;                                         /* to Event 1 */
    Decision Match(event,Err);                                       /* Error? */
    (True): Join Introduction.1.4;                        /* to Introduction.4 */
    Decision Match(event,Exit);                                       /* Exit? */
    (True): Join Introduction.1.5;                        /* to Introduction.5 */
    Decision Match(event,Filled);                                   /* Filled? */
    (True): Join Contact.1.3;                                  /* to Contact.3 */
    Decision Match(event,Help);                                       /* Help? */
    (True): Join Contact.1.5;                                  /* to Contact.5 */
    Decision Match(event,NoInput) And prompt >= 3;         /* NoInput prompt 3? */
    (True): Join Introduction.1.6;                        /* to Introduction.6 */
    Decision Match(event,NoInput);                                 /* NoInput? */
    (True): Join Contact.1.5;                                  /* to Contact.5 */
    Decision Match(event,NoMatch) And prompt >= 3;         /* NoMatch prompt 3? */
    (True): Join Introduction.1.6;                        /* to Introduction.6 */
    Decision Match(event,NoMatch);                                 /* NoMatch? */
    (True): Join Contact.1.5;                                  /* to Contact.5 */
    (False):                                               /* no event match */
      Task event := Err;                                     /* set error event */
      Join Event.0;                                          /* dispatch event */
```

Fig. 5. Extract of Event Dispatcher Code

3.5   Sample Translation to SDL

It was decided to translate CRESS diagrams into SDL 92 and not some later version. This is because tool support for SDL 96 onwards is often incomplete. By choosing SDL 92, CRESS can be used on the maximum number of systems.

The SDL specification equivalent to a CRESS description is substantially larger. For example, the complete hotel booking application consists of seven CRESS diagrams spanning three pages in total. These are automatically translated into 2,900 lines of SDL (including the 1,700 lines which are fixed in the specification framework). CRESS is thus a compact notation, as well as being reasonably comprehensible to non-specialists.

As a representative sample of the SDL generated from IVR diagrams, the following code shows how the *Contact* feature in figure 2 is translated. What follows is the literal output of the CRESS compiler. As will be seen, neatly laid out code is produced. Extensive comments are also generated to link the SDL back to the original diagrams. This is important since the code is analysed in SDL terms. If there are design errors, it must be easy to relate these to the original diagrams.

The **Request** field of figure 2 node 2 checks if the *contact* variable is defined. As this is template instance 1, its diagram is labelled *Contact.1* and its field variable is named *contact.1*. If the *contact* field has already been filled in, execution continues with the next field (i.e. the first instance of the *Confirm* feature). Otherwise the options list is emptied (this is not an **Option** field) and the prompt count is incremented. A *Request* signal is sent to the recogniser with the prompt string and the *Phone* grammar.

```
Contact.1.2:                                              /* Contact.1 request 2 */
   Decision contact.1 /= Undefined;                            /* check field */
   (True):                                                   /* ignore field? */
      Join Confirm.1.2;                                /* to Confirm.1 field 2 */
   (False):                                                    /* enter field */
      Task options := '', prompt := prompt + 1;        /* local variable update */
      Output Request('What is your contact number?',Phone);     /* request field */
      NextState Contact.1.2A;                          /* for recognition input */
   EndDecision;                                             /* end check field */
```

The feature now waits in state *Contact.1.2A* for the recogniser answer. A *Filled* response will set the field variable *contact.1*. The field number and event type are set prior to calling the event dispatcher; as shown in figure 5, this will branch to *Contact.1.3*. The prompt count is also reset, ready for the next field. If the recogniser gives a *Failed* response, this is also passed to the event dispatcher for action.

```
State Contact.1.2A;                                      /* Contact.1 field 2 */
   Input Filled(contact.1);                                  /* filled event */
      Task field := 5, event := Filled, prompt := 0;        /* set up event */
      Join Event.0;                                         /* dispatch event */
   Input Failed(event);                                      /* failed event */
      Task field := 5;                                       /* set up event */
      Join Event.0;                                         /* dispatch event */
```

A *Filled* response leads to audio confirmation for the user. The field variable *contact.1* is converted by the *String* operator and appended to the rest of the message. The contact phone number is also submitted to the server as a string. Since a list of variable values is sent, *MkString* converts the phone number to a one-item list. The application then continues with other parts of its logic.

```
Connection Contact.1.3:                                  /* Contact.1 output 3 */
   Output Audio('We will contact you on phone number ' // String(contact.1));
                                                         /* Contact.1 audio */

Contact.1.4:
   Output Submit('contact.jsp',MkString(String(contact.1)));  /* Contact.1 submit 4 */
```

If instead the recogniser gives a *Failed* response, the event dispatcher will analyse the event. As shown in figure 5, a **Help, NoInput** or **NoMatch** event will ordinarily cause a branch to *Contact.1.5*. Only after three prompts will the application/form handler for **NoInput** or **NoMatch** be invoked. For the initial attempts at input, the user is given an explanatory message and execution resumes from the first field. Since previous fields should have been defined by this point, the effect is to re-enter *Contact.1.2* and request a contact number again.

```
Connection Contact.1.5:                                  /* Contact.1 output 5 */
   Output Audio('Please give a phone number where we can contact you');
                                                         /* Contact.1 audio */

Contact.1.6:
   Join BOOKING.2;                                        /* Contact.1 reprompt 6 */
```

4   Validating the SDL Translation of IVR

4.1   Validation Cost

The translation of CRESS diagrams into SDL is fully automatic. The additional cost of validation is therefore defining what must be validated and performing this. As will be seen, desirable properties and use-case scenarios can be formulated compactly. Validation times are measured in seconds or minutes. The main cost of rigorous validation is thus identifying what must be checked. This, of course, requires human insight and effort, but is required anyway for any kind of testing. In fact, formalising desirable properties and behaviours is beneficial as it clarifies thinking about the system and what it must do. The scenarios used for validating CRESS also apply to testing the actual implementation. The costs of performing rigorous validation thus do not add much to the overall testing effort. And of course it is beneficial to find problems early before committing to an implementation.

Developers probably find operational thinking easier, so validation with use case scenarios is probably more natural. In fact, modern development practices often expect use case scenarios to be defined early on. It is reasonably straightforward to translate these into the form needed for validating SDL (see section 4.3). Defining abstract properties to be model-checked is more difficult, but nonetheless desirable in its own right.

The SDL validator used in this work supports several features to make validation practical. In particular, validation is viable even for large or infinite state spaces. For example, the validator can be instructed to treat certain classes of states as equivalent by coalescing certain values of state variables. Scenarios, being finite and concrete, can also be validated against specifications with infinite states.

4.2   Property-Based Validation

Validation in General. The benefit of translating IVR to SDL is that rigorous analysis can be performed. Simulation can, of course, be used to exercise the resulting specification. However as explained in section 1.1, the possible paths through an IVR application are usually too numerous for exhaustive evaluation. As a result, manual simulation is practical for only the main paths.

Automated validation is therefore desirable. However the sheer number of states makes this time-consuming or impracticable. In addition, the state variables usually take an infinite number of values. The validation should combine such variations into a number of equivalence classes. For example, the SDL validator can be told to treat as one any states where the prompt count exceeds 3. Another possible simplification is to omit certain state variables from the state if they are not significant. The current list of options, for example, might be unimportant. However if the options list is interpolated into user messages (with $enumerate), then this becomes significant.

The Telelogic TAU SDL tool suite [8] eases validation. Nonetheless, it requires an environment to supply suitable input values. A range of correct and incorrect user responses must be provided. For example in response to the prompt 'For how many nights?', the validator can be told to answer: 3, 1, 0, -1, 3.1, Cancel, Help or Exit.

The TAU validator also allows problems to be checked and reported using assertions. As this requires a descent into C, it is a less desirable approach and has not been used in the work reported here.

Rule Checking. SDL specifications of IVR are validated by checking the state space for certain properties. This is equivalent to model-checking. The TAU validator allows user-defined rules to be checked. Look again at the booking service in figure 1. Can this loop indefinitely? The most common cause of this in IVR is not setting a bound on the number of reprompts. The following user-defined rule can be validated:

exists R:Recogniser | R−>prompt > 3;

i.e. is there a state (**exists**) of the recogniser process R in which the internal prompt count (R−>*prompt*) exceeds 3? Running the validator with this rule shows that it can. The validator exhibits a trace with this property: the prompt for arrival date in figure 1 node 2 can be repeated indefinitely. This problem disappears when the *Introduction* feature of figure 3 is added to the base service. However the complex event model for IVR, especially its hierarchic nature, makes it difficult to be sure that no such 'holes' have been left in the specification. Formal validation confirms this.

The *Contact* feature of figure 2 should always announce a definite value for the contact phone number. However, an error in the application logic might fail to define this value. This is checked with the following validator rule:

siall S:Audio | S−>1 != 'We will contact you on phone number undefined';

i.e. do all signal instances (**siall**) for *Audio* avoid a first parameter ($S \rightarrow 1$) with an undefined phone number? As would be hoped, the validator confirms this cannot happen.

An IVR application should not cause any **Error** events (*Err* in SDL). The following validator rule checks for this:

siexists S:Failed | S−>1 = Err;

i.e. is there a signal instance (**siexists**) for signal *Failed* whose first parameter (S−>*1*) is *Err*? This should happen only if the application explicitly throws an **Error** event, e.g. due to some internal inconsistency that should not occur. Running the validator on the hotel booking example shows that this situation cannot arise.

Observer Processes. TAU also allows properties to be checked with observer processes. These allow very similar properties to be validated as user-defined rules. Slightly different checks are possible, e.g. for process termination. When it has finished handling one caller, an IVR application should cycle back to the beginning for the next caller. As an example of an observer process, the following monitors an IVR application to see if it ever stops:

```
Start;                                          /* start observer */
  Task A := GetPId('Application',1);            /* get process id for application instance 1 */
  NextState Ready;                              /* monitor system transitions */
  State Ready;                                  /* wait for next transition */
    Provided Terminated(A); Priority 1;         /* application has terminated? */
      Call Report('Application Died');          /* report termination */
      Stop;                                     /* finish observer */
    Provided True; Priority 2;                  /* otherwise */
      NextState −;                              /* continue */
```

If the TAU toolset is not being used, observer processes can still be defined explicitly to check system properties. However these cannot then benefit from the special support given by TAU. It is instead necessary to modify the system so that the observer processes can receive copies of the signals being sent and received. In fact, this approach allows monitoring of more complex situations than the isolated states and signals checked by the TAU validator. For example, section 2.2 mentions a confirmation feature for the hotel booking system. If the user decides not to proceed with a booking, the details should not be submitted to the server. An observer process can be defined to check the following situation: if the user does not agree to proceed, a *Submit* signal must not follow without an intervening request for new information.

4.3   Scenario-Based Validation

As an alternative to property checking, services/features can be characterised by use-case scenarios. These should capture the essential variations in how the service/feature ought to behave. Scenario-based testing can be performed using MSCs (Message Sequence Charts [4]). However it is convenient to have a language-neutral notation for defining scenarios. The approach described in this section is independent of the specification language (e.g. SDL) and the application domain (e.g. IVR). However, it dovetails neatly with the CRESS approach to service description.

This is the role of MUSTARD (Multiple-Use Scenario Test And Refusal Description) – the culinary complement to CRESS. As well as defining what scenarios *must* allow, MUSTARD allows also scenarios to define what *must not* be permitted. These refusal tests ensure that a specification is not too loose in what lets happen. For use with SDL, the MUSTARD scenarios are translated into MSCs. For space reasons, only a few short examples can be given here of MUSTARD. See [16] for an explanation of the approach. MUSTARD for validating LOTOS specifications is illustrated in [14].

The following scenario checks the booking service of figure 1. The environment may **send** signals to the IVR system or may **read** signals from it. These primitive actions are grouped by combinators into more complex scenarios. In the following, **succeeds** reports a pass verdict if the sequence of actions is respected by the system:

```
test(Booking,                                             % booking scenario
   succeed(                                                % successful booking
      read(Audio,Happy Hotel Reservations),               % get welcome message
      read(Audio,Say Help or Exit at any time),           % get help message
      read(Audio,Please book your room),                  % get booking message
      read(Audio,What arrival date?),                     % get date prompt
      send(Voice,20041031),                               % select 31st Oct 2004
      read(Audio,For how many nights?),                   % get nights prompt
      send(Voice,14),                                     % select 14 nights
      read(Audio,What kind of room?),                     % get room prompt
      send(Voice,Double),                                 % select double room
      read(Audio,You arrive 20041031 staying 14 nights in a Double)))   % get confirm
```

The *Booking* scenario defines a complete trace of the system behaviour. However, it is often desirable to focus on just the key behaviour. With initial capitals, the **Send** and **Read** actions absorb (i.e. allow but ignore) intervening system output.

As an example of a refusal test, the following checks that booking details are not sent to the server if the user decides not to confirm the booking. A refusal test is defined with **refuses**. This defines the initial behaviour steps in the scenario. The last behaviour step (which may be composite) must not occur. In the following example, the user books a room and then declines to proceed. The final step (recording the booking on the server) must not occur. If it does, the system is incorrect and the scenario fails. If the booking is not sent to the server, the system is correct and the scenario passes.

```
test(Confirm,                                    % confirmation scenario
  refuse(                                         % refusal sequence
    Send(Voice,0521),                             % select 21st May
    Send(Voice,1),                                % select 1 night
    Send(Voice,Suite),                            % select a suite
    Read(Audio,Do you wish to proceed?),          % get confirm prompt
    Send(Voice,No),                               % disagree
    Read(Server,booking.jsp,0521,1,Suite)))   % get server request (must not happen)
```

MUSTARD has other capabilities for defining flexible scenarios, e.g. alternative or parallel behaviour. Scenarios may also depend on the presence or absence of certain features. MUSTARD scenarios are automatically validated against IVR specifications generated by CRESS. In fact, a double benefit is obtained from the scenarios. When the implementation is deployed, the *same* scenarios can be used to validate the actual system.

Although MUSTARD is used to validate scenarios in isolation, it is particularly useful for investigating interactions where a combination of independently designed features interfere with each other. Feature interaction is a well-studied topic in telephony [2]. An insight is given by [14] into how feature interactions can arise in IVR.

When MUSTARD validates a specification, it should yield pass verdicts for all features. If a scenario fails, MUSTARD exhibits traces leading up to the failure point. This allows the specifier to investigate the problem, e.g. using simulation. The failure traces are re-presented in MUSTARD form, irrespective of the validation language or tool. This is essential since the aim of CRESS and MUSTARD is to hide the underlying formalism from the tool user; a user of CRESS need not be familiar with formal methods.

5   Conclusion

An introduction and examples have been given to IVR services (Interactive Voice Response). Given the complex control flow and pragmatic nature of IVR, it has been argued that it is beneficial to have formal support using SDL (the standardised Specification and Description Language). It has been seen how IVR services can be described using CRESS (Chisel Representation Employing Systematic Specification). An overview has been presented of how these graphical descriptions are translated into SDL. For rigorous analysis of the generated specifications, validation of properties and scenarios has been discussed.

Using CRESS and SDL, it has been possible to support a significant portion of IVR services. The coverage is not complete, however, because IVR standards like Voice-XML are extremely large. For example, they include voice grammars, JAVASCRIPT and interfacing to web servers. Nonetheless, CRESS allows the key functionality of IVR applications to be captured. It has been argued that the graphical representation of IVR services is more accessible than VoiceXML. This opens up the description of IVR applications to a wider audience.

The major benefits of integrating SDL with IVR have been formalisation, rigorous analysis and validation of IVR services. In addition, insight has been gained into loosely specified aspects of the VoiceXML standard. In contrast, the pragmatic methods used currently in industry have to rely on expensive manual testing. The same CRESS diagrams are translated into SDL for formal analysis, and also into VoiceXML for real-life deployment. CRESS thus gains as both a specification aid and an implementation aid. The work has shown how to integrate an accessible notation with a formal underpinning into industrial practice.

[14] describes how IVR services were modelled and analysed using LOTOS (the standardised Language Of Temporal Ordering Specification). Superficially, LOTOS and SDL are similar in being constructive specification languages; however, they are very different in their details. LOTOS focuses on behaviour expressions that describe how a system evolves; SDL focuses on system states and transitions between these. LOTOS data operations are defined equationally, while SDL data operators are defined imperatively. In practice, the difference between these approaches is not so great. The same MUSTARD scenarios are used with both languages. CRESS generates LOTOS and SDL specifications of comparable size. The only significant difference between the approaches is in tool support. LOTOS tools are the result of research projects and are free; SDL tools are commercial. In practice, tools for both languages have been found to be suitable for rigorous analysis of different types.

CRESS has now been demonstrated in four application domains: Intelligent Networks, Internet Telephony, Interactive Voice Response and Web Services. It has shown itself to be adaptable and expressive for a variety of types of services. It has been possible to use CRESS on a wide range of features and to validate their behaviour in isolation and in combination.

Acknowledgements

Telelogic kindly provided an academic licence for the TAU toolset used in this work. The author also thanks Nuance Corporation for an academic licence to use Nuance V-Builder ^{TM} in the development of IVR applications.

References

1. D. Amyot, L. Charfi, N. Gorse, T. Gray, L. M. S. Logrippo, J. Sincennes, B. Stepien, and T. Ware. Feature description and feature interaction analysis with use case maps and LOTOS. In M. H. Calder and E. H. Magill, editors, *Proc. 6th. Feature Interactions in Telecommunications and Software Systems*, pages 274–289. IOS Press, Amsterdam, Netherlands, May 2000.

2. E. J. Cameron, N. D. Griffeth, Y.-J. Lin, M. E. Nilson, W. K. Schnure, and H. Velthuijsen. A feature-interaction benchmark for IN and beyond. *IEEE Communications Magazine*, pages 64–69, Mar. 1993.

3. ISO/IEC. *Information Processing Systems – Open Systems Interconnection – LOTOS – A Formal Description Technique based on the Temporal Ordering of Observational Behaviour.* ISO/IEC 8807. International Organization for Standardization, Geneva, Switzerland, 1989.

4. ITU. *Message Sequence Chart (MSC).* ITU-T Z.120. International Telecommunications Union, Geneva, Switzerland, 2000.

5. ITU. *Specification and Description Language.* ITU-T Z.100. International Telecommunications Union, Geneva, Switzerland, 2000.

6. J. A. Larson. Standard languages for developing multimodal applications. *http://www.larson-tech.com/Writings/multimodal.pdf*, Mar. 2005.

7. A. Sarma. Introduction to SDL-92. *Computer Networks*, 28(12):1603–1615, June 1996.

8. Telelogic. TAU 3.5 manuals, Aug. 2005.

9. K. J. Turner. Formalising the CHISEL feature notation. In M. H. Calder and E. H. Magill, editors, *Proc. 6th. Feature Interactions in Telecommunications and Software Systems*, pages 241–256. IOS Press, Amsterdam, Netherlands, May 2000.

10. K. J. Turner. Modelling SIP services using CRESS. In D. A. Peled and M. Y. Vardi, editors, *Proc. Formal Techniques for Networked and Distributed Systems (FORTE XV)*, number 2529 in Lecture Notes in Computer Science, pages 162–177. Springer, Berlin, Germany, Nov. 2002.

11. K. J. Turner. Formalising graphical service descriptions using SDL. In R. Reed and J. Reed, editors, *SDL 2003*, number 2708 in Lecture Notes in Computer Science, pages 183–202. Springer, Berlin, Germany, July 2003.

12. K. J. Turner. Representing new voice services and their features. In D. Amyot and L. Logrippo, editors, *Proc. 7th. Feature Interactions in Telecommunications and Software Systems*, pages 123–140. IOS Press, Amsterdam, Netherlands, June 2003.

13. K. J. Turner. Specifying and realising interactive voice services. In H. König, M. Heiner, and A. Wolisz, editors, *Proc. Formal Techniques for Networked and Distributed Systems (FORTE XVI)*, number 2767 in Lecture Notes in Computer Science, pages 15–30. Springer, Berlin, Germany, Sept. 2003.

14. K. J. Turner. Analysing interactive voice services. *Computer Networks*, 45(5):665–685, Aug. 2004.

15. K. J. Turner. Formalising web services. In F. Wang, editor, *Proc. Formal Techniques for Networked and Distributed Systems (FORTE XVIII)*. Springer, Berlin, Germany, June 2005. in press.

16. K. J. Turner. Validating feature-based specifications. *Software Practice and Experience*, May 2005. In press.

17. VoiceXML Forum. *Voice eXtensible Markup Language.* VoiceXML Version 2.0. VoiceXML Forum, Jan. 2003.

A Fixpoint Semantics of Event Systems With and Without Fairness Assumptions

Héctor Ruíz Barradas[1,2] and Didier Bert[2]

[1] Universidad Autónoma Metropolitana Azcapotzalco, México D. F., México
hrb@correo.azc.uam.mx, Hector.Ruiz@imag.fr
[2] Laboratoire Logiciels, Systèmes, Réseaux, LSR-IMAG, Grenoble, France
Didier.Bert@imag.fr

Abstract. We present a fixpoint semantics of event systems. The semantics is presented in a general framework without concerns of fairness. Soundness and completeness of rules for deriving *leads-to* properties are proved in this general framework. The general framework is instantiated to minimal progress and weak fairness assumptions and similar results are obtained. We show the power of these results by deriving sufficient conditions for *leads-to* under minimal progress proving soundness of proof obligations without reasoning over state-traces.

Keywords: Liveness properties, event systems, action systems, UNITY logic, fairness, weak fairness, minimal progress, set transformer, fixpoints.

1 Introduction

Action systems, or event systems, are useful abstractions to model discrete systems. Many formalisms have been proposed to model action systems. In these formalisms, the behavior of a system is specified by a collection of events (actions) executed atomically and it is described in terms of observations about the state of the system. As examples of action-based systems, we can cite Back's action system formalism [5], UNITY [8] and TLA [16]. Rigorous development of action systems has been tackled through stepwise refinement. Fairness is an important notion which helps to increase the abstraction level of a parallel or distributed system specification. In this context, fairness means that if a certain operation is possible, then the system must eventually execute it [16].

In this paper, we consider event systems where specification of events is given in a program-like notation, and we use temporal logic to specify liveness properties under two kinds of fairness assumptions: weak fairness and minimal progress. In our work, we consider modalities of type P *leads-to* Q, where P and Q are predicates on the state space of a system, with the informal meaning: "when the system arrives into a state satisfying P, eventually it *reaches* a state satisfying Q", and we demonstrate that the proof of this modality, under a weak fairness or minimal progress assumption, is equivalent to the proof of *termination* of iteration of events in the system.

Our study is founded on the fixpoint semantics of event systems, instead of sequences of states (computations), as it is traditionally done in the action-based

J. Romijn, G. Smith, and J. van de Pol (Eds.): IFM 2005, LNCS 3771, pp. 327–346, 2005.

systems cited above. Our approach is not a matter of predilection of habits, it allows us to make the notion of *reachability* under fairness assumptions equivalent to the one of *termination* of iteration of events. Moreover, it gives the foundations to our approach of stepwise refinement of event systems where preservation under refinement of liveness has a central role [24, 26].

This work has been originated in [23], where we proposed the integration of UNITY logic in the specification and proof of liveness properties in B event systems. In this manner, modalities correspond to liveness properties specified by the *leads-to* or *ensures* operators of UNITY logic. Our treatment of the equivalence between *reachability* and *termination* has been inspired from [14] where the results of soundness and completeness of rules to derive *leads-to* properties in UNITY logic are presented. As outcomes of our approach we give two examples of applications of these results: First we prove the sufficient conditions for liveness properties under minimal progress given in [2]. The second example is an original proof which gives sufficient conditions to derive a liveness property under minimal progress when the given property holds under weak fairness. This last result gives a deep insight into implementing fairness assumptions by abstract schedulers through stepwise refinement.

This paper is structured as follows. In Section 2, we recall the main works dealing with fairness in parallel programming and with the use of *weakest precondition semantics* in concurrent programs. We discuss about the new insights of our approach. In Section 3, we present a system as a set transformer and we give syntax and semantics of common set transformers used to model events in the system. In Section 4, we develop our semantics of event systems and we prove equality (soundness and completeness) between notions of termination and reachability. In Section 5, we give examples of sufficient conditions to derive liveness properties using the results of the previous section, as well as an example of application. Finally we give our conclusions and future work in Section 6.

2   Related Works

In this section we review some related works and we discuss about the positioning of our work and the contributions of this paper. The works presented have studied fairness in the context of program verification, program development, semantics or implementation of parallelism.

In [3, 4] an approach to program transformation is proposed, where weak or strong fair parallelism is reduced to ordinary parallelism. Apart from giving insight on fairness implementation, the transformation allows applying an extension of the proof system of Owicki-Gries [21] to the verification of programs. The transformation embeds a scheduler in the program, modeled by random assignment, which guarantees fair computations. Implementation of random assignment can provide concrete scheduling policies as round robin or queueing.

Fairness has been clearly defined in temporal logic, as well as different sorts of safety and liveness properties [18]. In [17] a proof system, founded in assertional reasoning, is proposed to verify reactive or concurrent programs. In the context of verification of temporal properties, model checking is a useful technique that can be applied in the case of finite-state systems. In [11] fairness assumptions are used to reduce the combinatorial explosion in the verification of abstract transition systems by model checking.

Computational models, for concurrent program development, can be represented by the do od construction of guarded commands. Different works can be distinguished according to the guards of the commands. The following paragraphs give a brief survey of formalisms where fairness plays a fundamental role.

The computational model of UNITY [8] can be modeled by a do od construction where the guard of the commands is always true. These statements are executed according to an "unconditional fairness" assumption, which indicates that in any computation any statement is infinitely often executed. Liveness properties are specified and proved by two relations on state predicates known as *ensures* and *leads-to*. *ensures* relation is defined by the Hoare triplets quantified over the statements of a program; the fairness assumption guarantees the execution of the helpful statement performing the basic progress specified by this relation. *leads-to* is defined as the transitive and disjunctive closure of *ensures*.

Following the computational model of UNITY, in [9] a calculus of predicate transformers is proposed to reason about safety and liveness properties. A program is a set of variables and a set of predicate transformers denoting the weakest precondition of non miraculous, always terminating and bounded nondeterministic statements. Progress properties are defined by a predicate transformer defined in [15] which is the strongest solution of a set of equations where the *ensures* relation forms the base case. In [19], the study of composition of *leads-to* properties is pursued. In this approach the predicate transformers defining *ensures* and *leads-to* properties proposed in [13] are used to develop a general theory of composition of *leads-to*. These predicate transformers are defined by the fixpoints of equations relating the weakest precondition of statements in a program.

More general computation models, where the guards of commands in the do od construction are state predicates, allow different definitions of fairness like weak or strong fairness. An early proposal of a predicate transformer, defined by fixpoint equations, characterizing the weakest precondition of do od constructions under weak fairness assumptions is presented in [22].

In [14], a methodology for designing proof systems for *leads-to* properties under various fairness assumptions is proposed. This work shows how the specification and proof of liveness properties in UNITY can be adapted to reason about different kinds of fairness. The methodology characterizes different kinds of fairness by CTL* formulae. These formulae are then characterized by fixpoint in the μ-calculus. Finally these fixpoint characterizations are used to propose various definitions of the *ensures* relation according to fairness assumptions.

Another approach to program development is given by TLA [16]. It is a temporal logic for specifying and reasoning, about concurrent and reactive systems. A specification is made up of formulae, expressing safety and fairness constraints on the execution of actions. Actions are modeled by the before-after relation between state variables. In this framework, refinement consists in providing more details in the specification of actions, and the correctness proof, becomes logical implication between specifications.

Actions systems [5] is an approach to program development, where actions are expressed in familiar sequential programming notations, and executed atomically. Refinement is verified by refinement relations defined among the abstract and concrete actions. In [6] the refinement of action systems is extended by considering fair action systems. Refinement relations under weak or strong fairness assumptions are defined. These definitions give sufficient conditions to guarantee total correctness of iteration of actions. Therefore, this approach of fairness is based on the basic techniques developed mainly for sequential programming.

Discussion

Our work is placed in the context of program development by stepwise refinement. It improves the original approach of modalities in B event systems proposed in [2]. We propose the use of UNITY logic in the specification and proof of liveness properties, under weak fairness or minimal progress assumptions. On another hand, it clarifies the close relation between reachability, as specified by *leads-to* properties, and termination of weak fair and unfair iteration of actions.

The original approach of modalities in [2] is very restricted. Specification of modalities requires definition of invariant predicates and variant functions. The reason of this restrictions is that the computational model, used to reason about modalities, is a do od construction without fairness assumptions. So, the proof of modalities becomes a proof of total correctness of a do od construction.

The computational model in our framework does not correspond to the model of UNITY, because the guards of events are not always enabled. Therefore, results of UNITY logic in [8, 9, 15, 19, 13], do not apply directly to our framework if the definition of the basic relation *ensures* is not changed. Our definition of *ensures* relation, in a more general computational model where the guards of actions are state predicates, is inspired from [14]. From this work, we get as well the idea of set transformers to denote *leads-to* properties.

Our set transformers for minimal progress (unfair) or weak fairness assumptions are defined in an original way. Our definition deepens and clarifies the idea of [2] and [6], about the relation between (unfair or weak fair) termination of iteration of events and reachability, as reflected by *leads-to* properties. Apart from set transformers denoting the actions of the system, our set transformers for *leads-to* are constructively built and use primitive set transformers such as iteration, unfair choice, fair choice, sequencing, guard and precondition, and it is not only a fixpoint equation, as the predicate transformers described above. We prove that our definitions fulfill the requirement of a sound and relative complete proof system for *leads-to* properties, as it was done in [14]. This is the first contribution of this paper.

The choice of definitions of *leads-to* properties, under minimal progress and weak fairness assumptions, is a result of our approach to program development by stepwise refinement. In fact, we expect that systems under weak fairness assumptions would be implemented, by refinements into concrete systems, where events are iterated under minimal progress assumptions. For this reason, we were interested in defining set transformers for *leads-to* properties in close relation with iteration of events. In this way, refining events gives insight in the sufficient conditions to guarantee the refinement of liveness properties [26]. Moreover, when a *leads-to* property holds in a refinement under weak fairness assumptions, and the refinement contains some mechanisms to ensure a fair interleaving of actions, we can guarantee, by conditions imposed to the events in the refinement, that the *leads-to* property yet holds under minimal progress assumptions. In this paper we state formally these facts by a proof rule which replace the ideas of program transformation to implement weak fairness, presented in [3], in the framework of refinement. This is the second contribution of this paper.

3   Set Transformers and UNITY Logic in Event Systems

In this section, we introduce the main considerations about event systems and the specification of liveness properties in UNITY logic. This section is divided in two parts. The first part presents an event system as a set transformer and introduces the notion of liberal set transformer, as well as the dovetail operator that is used to model a weak fairness assumption. In the second part, we recall the main ideas for the specification and proof of liveness properties under two fairness assumptions in UNITY logic.

3.1   Set Transformers

A set transformer is a total function of type $\mathbb{P}(\mathcal{U}) \to \mathbb{P}(\mathcal{U})$ for a certain set $\mathcal{U}$. An event system is made out of a family of events. Any event may be executed in any state where its *guard*, predicate on the state, holds. When the guard of an event holds, we say that the event is enabled. As in event-B systems, we considered a system with state variable x and invariant I. The state space u of the system are those states where I holds: $u = \{ z \mid I(z) \}$. Therefore events in the system are modeled by conjunctive set transformers E_i of type $\mathbb{P}(u) \to \mathbb{P}(u)$, where i belongs to certain finite index set L. Consequently, the system is modeled by a conjunctive set transformer S which is the bounded choice of events E_i: $S = \llbracket_{i \in L} E_i$. We denote by $\mathcal{S}$ the set of events in S: $\mathcal{S} = \{ E_i \mid i \in L \}$.

For any set transformer T of type $\mathbb{P}(u) \to \mathbb{P}(u)$ and subset r of u, $T(r)$ denotes the largest subset of states where execution of T must begin in order for T to terminate in a state belonging to r [1]. Primitive set transformers considered in this paper are similar to the primitive generalized substitutions in B: skip, bounded choice, sequence, guarded and conditioned set transformer. Following the work reported in [26], for any set transformer T, and subset r of u, we denote by $\mathcal{L}(T)(r)$ the *liberal set transformer* of T, which denotes the largest subset of states where the execution of S must begin in order for T to terminate in a state belonging to r or loop. Common set transformers and liberal set transformers are defined as follows:[1]

---

[1] For any set transformer T, $(\mathcal{L})(T)(r)$ denotes the definition, either for the set $T(r)$ or for the set $\mathcal{L}(T)(r)$.

$$(\mathcal{L})(skip)(r) = r \qquad\qquad (\mathcal{L})(F \mathbin{;} G)(r) = (\mathcal{L})(F)((\mathcal{L})(G)(r))$$
$$(\mathcal{L})(F \mathbin{[\!]} G)(r) = (\mathcal{L})(F)(r) \cap (\mathcal{L})(G)(r) \quad (\mathcal{L})(p \Longrightarrow F)(r) = \overline{p} \cup (\mathcal{L})(F)(r)$$

In the guarded event, $\overline{p}$ denotes $u - p$. For the preconditioned event we have $(p \mid F)(r) = p \cap F(r)$ and $\mathcal{L}(p \mid F)(r) = p \cap \mathcal{L}(F)(r)$ if $r \neq u$ and $\mathcal{L}(p \mid F)(r) = \mathcal{L}(F)(r)$ if $r = u$; this distinction is necessary to guarantee $\mathcal{L}(p \mid F)(u) = u$ as required. Definitions of liberal set transformers presented here are the set counterpart of definitions in [10].

The set transformers $F(r)$ and $\mathcal{L}(F)(r)$ for event F and postcondition r are related by the *pairing condition*: $F(r) = \mathcal{L}(F)(r) \cap \mathsf{pre}(F)$, where $\mathsf{pre}(F)$ is the termination set of F. So, we have $\mathsf{pre}(F) = F(u)$. From the pairing condition we conclude $F(u) = u \Rightarrow F(r) = \mathcal{L}(F)(r)$. We say that a set transformer F is *strict* when it respect the excluded miracle law: $F(\varnothing) = \varnothing$.

For any set transformer F, when $F(r)$ or $\mathcal{L}(F)(r)$ are recursively defined: $F(r) = \mathcal{F}(F(r))$ of $\mathcal{L}(F)(r) = \mathcal{G}(\mathcal{L}(F)(r))$, for monotonic functions $\mathcal{F}$ and $\mathcal{G}$, according to [12] we take $F(r)$ as the strongest solution of the equation $X = \mathcal{F}(X)$ and $\mathcal{L}(F)(r)$ as the weakest solution of the equation $X = \mathcal{G}(X)$. As these solutions are fixpoints, we take $F(r)$ as the least fixpoint of $\mathcal{F}$ (denoted $\mathsf{fix}(\mathcal{F})$) and $\mathcal{L}(F)(r)$ as the greatest fixpoint of $\mathcal{G}$ (denoted $\mathsf{FIX}(\mathcal{G})$).

The Dovetail Operator. To model a weak fairness assumption, we use the dovetail operator $\triangledown$ [7], which is a fair nondeterministic choice operator. The dovetail operator is used to model the notion of fair scheduling of two activities.

A motivating example of the use of the dovetail operator is given in [7]. In that example the recursive definition: $X = (n := 0 \mathbin{\triangledown} (X \mathbin{;} n := n + 1))$ which has as solution "set n to any natural number", is contrasted with the recursion $Y = (n := 0 \mathbin{[\!]} (Y \mathbin{;} n := n + 1))$ which has as solution "set n to any natural number or loop". The possibility of loop in X is excluded with the dovetail operator because the fair choice of statement $n := 0$ will certainly occur. In Y the execution of that statement is not ensured.

The semantic definition for dovetail operator in [7] is given by definition of its weakest liberal precondition predicate transformer (wlp) and its termination predicate hlt. We give an equivalent definition using the weakest liberal set transformer $\mathcal{L}$ and its termination set pre:

$$\mathcal{L}(F \mathbin{\triangledown} G)(r) = \mathcal{L}(F)(r) \cap \mathcal{L}(G)(r) \tag{1}$$
$$\mathsf{pre}(F \mathbin{\triangledown} G) = (F(u) \cup G(u)) \cap (\overline{F(\varnothing)} \cup G(u)) \cap (\overline{G(\varnothing)} \cup F(u)) \tag{2}$$

We recall that $\mathsf{grd}(F) = \overline{F(\varnothing)}$. From these definitions, in [26] we prove the guard of the dovetail: $\mathsf{grd}(A \mathbin{\triangledown} B) = \mathsf{grd}(A) \cup \mathsf{grd}(B)$.

3.2   Liveness Properties in Event Systems

In this section, we give a summary of some results in the specification and proof of liveness properties presented in [23], [24] and [26]. In these works, we propose the use of UNITY logic to specify and prove liveness properties in event-B systems.

Liveness properties are divided in two groups: basic and general liveness properties. Each one of these properties is specified by relations on the state of the system. In order to specify and prove these properties we consider a minimal progress or a weak fairness assumption.

Basic Properties Under Weak Fairness. A weak fairness assumption states that any continuously enabled event is infinitely often executed. For any event G in S we write $G \cdot P \gg_w Q$ (pronounced "by event G, P ensures Q") to specify that by the execution of event G in a state satisfying P the system goes to another state satisfying Q, under a weak fairness assumption. In [24] we proposed sufficient conditions WF0 and WF1, to guarantee the intended meaning of these properties. These conditions were stated in terms of state predicates P and Q, but we present them as set expression:

$$p \cap \overline{q} \subseteq S(p \cup q) \cap \mathsf{grd}(G) \cap G(q) \Rightarrow G \cdot x \in p \gg_w x \in q \qquad (3)$$

where x is the state variable of S, $p = \{z | z \in u \wedge P\}$ and $q = \{z | z \in u \wedge Q\}$.

Basic Properties Under Minimal Progress. In a minimal progress assumption, if two or more statements are enabled in a given state, the selection of the statement enabled for execution is nondeterministic. We write $P \gg_m Q$ (pronounced "P ensures Q") to specify that execution of any event of S, in a state satisfying P, terminates into a state establishing Q. In [23] we gave sufficient conditions MP0 and MP1 to prove basic properties under minimal progress. We present them as a set expression as follows, for sets p and q defined as above:

$$p \cap \overline{q} \subseteq S(q) \cap \mathsf{grd}(S) \Rightarrow x \in p \gg_m x \in q \qquad (4)$$

General Properties. General liveness properties are specified by the *leads-to* operator $\rightsquigarrow$. Depending on the fairness assumption considered, we have general liveness properties under minimal progress or weak fairness assumptions. However, the *leads-to* relation is defined, in the same way, as the closure relation, containing the base relation and it is both transitive and disjunctive. A property $P \rightsquigarrow Q$ holds in an event system, if it is derived by a finite number of applications of the rules defined by the UNITY theory:

	ANTECEDENT	CONSEQUENT
BRL	$P \gg Q$	$P \rightsquigarrow Q$
TRA	$P \rightsquigarrow R, R \rightsquigarrow Q$	$P \rightsquigarrow Q$
DSJ	$\forall m \cdot (m \in M \Rightarrow P(m) \rightsquigarrow Q)$	$\exists m \cdot (m \in M \wedge P(m)) \rightsquigarrow Q$

$P \gg Q$, in the BRL rule stands for the basic liveness property $G \cdot P \gg_w Q$ for some G in S in case where we consider a property under a weak fairness assumption or $P \gg_m Q$, in the case where we consider a minimal progress assumption.

4   Reachability and Termination

In this section, we prove soundness and (relative) completeness of rules BRL, TRA and DSJ for *leads-to* properties under minimal progress and weak fairness assumptions. The rules are sound if for any derived property $P \rightsquigarrow Q$, iteration of events, under minimal progress or weak fairness assumptions, starting in a state satisfying P, leads to a state where Q holds. Completeness of these rules is proved by showing that $P \rightsquigarrow Q$ can be derived from the fact that any iteration of events, starting in a state where P holds, terminates into a state satisfying Q.

We do not expect that any iteration of events in a system terminates into a certain state. However, an always terminating iteration can be modeled by supposing, just for the reasoning, that the events in the system are embedded in a certain guarded command. The iteration only proceeds when the guard of that event is enabled. *Termination* of the iteration will be in a state where the guard does not hold. In this way, if the guard of the iteration is $\neg Q$, and the iteration starts in a state where P holds, the system reaches a state where Q holds. *Reachability* from P to Q is then associated to termination of the iteration of events. In the following subsections, we formalize our claims in a general framework without concerns of fairness, and then we instantiate these results to minimal progress or weak fairness assumptions.

To simplify matters, the strongest invariant SI [27] is not considered here. Therefore, instead of implications in proof obligations (3) and (4), we consider it as equivalences. In [25] we restate the results given in this section to consider SI.

4.1   A General Framework

In this subsection, we define a set transformer to model iteration of events and we state its main characteristics. The set transformer is used to define the *termination* relation. Then, we give a representation of the *leads to* relation of UNITY as a relation between subsets of u and we use it to define the *reachability* relation. Finally we prove equality between *termination* and the *reachability* relations.

4.1.1   Termination

We consider a set transformer W which models a *step* of the iteration of events in a system S. At this time we only state that W must be *monotonic* and *strict*. When we instantiate the iteration under a fairness assumption, the meaning of W will be given in terms of S. For any r in $\mathbb{P}(u)$, $W(r)$ denotes the largest subset of states where the execution of W must begin in order for W to terminate in a state belonging to r.

To model the iteration of events until the system reaches a state in a certain set r in $\mathbb{P}(u)$, we define a guarded event $\mathcal{F}(r)$:

$$\mathcal{F}(r) \,\widehat{=}\, (\overline{r} \Longrightarrow W) \tag{5}$$

for any $r \in \mathbb{P}(u)$, which allows iteration of W when the system stays in any state in $\overline{r}$. Iteration of $\mathcal{F}(r)$ is modeled by the $\widehat{}$ operator: $\mathcal{F}(r)\widehat{}$. As this operator has a recursive definition: $\mathcal{F}(r)\widehat{} = (\mathcal{F}(r) \,;\, \mathcal{F}(r)\widehat{}) \,[\!]\, skip$, the set where termination of $\mathcal{F}(r)\widehat{}$ is guaranteed ($\mathsf{pre}(\mathcal{F}(r)\widehat{})$) is given by $\mathsf{fix}(\mathcal{F}(r))$ [1].

As W may model an unbounded non deterministic set transformer, we use the *Generalized Limit Theorem* to formally justify that any iteration of $\mathcal{F}(r)$ starting in $\mathsf{pre}(\mathcal{F}(r)\hat{\,})$ terminates in some state of r. This theorem characterizes the least fixpoint of monotonic functions as an infinite join. We use the version presented in [20], instantiating the theorem to monotonic set transformers:

Theorem 1. (Generalized Limit Theorem) *Let f be a monotonic set transformer, and let f^α, for ordinal α, be defined inductively by*

$$f^\alpha = \bigcup \beta \cdot (\beta < \alpha \mid f(f^\beta)) \tag{6}$$

Then $\mathsf{fix}(f) = f^\alpha$ *for some ordinal* α.

As W is a monotonic function, $\mathcal{F}(r)$ is a monotonic set transformer, and theorem 1 can be applied to calculate the least fixpoint of $\mathcal{F}(r)$. According to the theorem, we conclude that $\mathcal{F}(r)^0 = \varnothing$ and $\mathcal{F}(r)^1 = r$ *because* W is strict. Moreover, for any ordinal α, $\mathcal{F}(r)^{\alpha+1} = \mathcal{F}(r)(\mathcal{F}(r)^\alpha)$ and $\mathcal{F}(r)^\alpha \subseteq \mathcal{F}(r)^{\alpha+1}$. This fact formally supports our claim that the termination set of $\mathcal{F}(r)\hat{\,}$ contains states where any iteration of $\mathcal{F}(r)$ terminates in a state into r. Now, we can define the *termination* relation $\mathcal{T}$ as follows:

Definition 1. (Termination Relation)

$$\mathcal{T} \mathrel{\hat{=}} \{\, a \mapsto b \mid a \subseteq u \wedge b \subseteq u \wedge a \subseteq \mathsf{fix}(\mathcal{F}(b)) \,\} \tag{7}$$

4.1.2   Reachability

As presented in section 3.2, *leads-to* relation of UNITY logic is defined as a relation between predicates on the state of programs. In this section we define an equivalent relation, $\mathcal{L}$, but instead of predicates, we define it as a relation between subsets of states in u ($\mathcal{L} \subseteq \mathbb{P}(u) \times \mathbb{P}(u)$). Any pair $a \mapsto b$ in $\mathcal{L}$ indicates that the system reaches a state in b, when its execution arrives at any state in a. For this reason, $\mathcal{L}$ is called the *reachability* relation.

Definition of $\mathcal{L}$ is given by induction. The base case needs definition of the basic relation $\mathcal{E}$ which is equivalent to the *ensures* relation. At this time $\mathcal{E}$ cannot be defined. As indicated in section 3.2, basic liveness properties depend on fairness assumptions. $\mathcal{E}$ will be defined in the following sections according to minimal progress or weak fairness assumptions. However, these definitions must satisfy two requirements. The first requirement is as follows: If $a \subseteq b$, for any a and b in $\mathbb{P}(u)$, then $a \mapsto b \in \mathcal{E}$ must hold. The second requirement relates $\mathcal{E}$ with the set transformer W: For any ordered pair $a \mapsto b \in \mathcal{E}$, the inclusion $a \cap \bar{b} \subseteq W(b)$ must hold. This inclusion indicates that any execution of W starting in $a \cap \bar{b}$, terminates into a state of b.

Definition 2. (Reachability Relation)
The reachability relation $\mathcal{L}$ is defined by the following induction scheme:
(SBR): $\mathcal{E} \subseteq \mathcal{L}$
(STR): $\mathcal{L} \,;\, \mathcal{L} \subseteq \mathcal{L}$
(SDR): $\forall (q, l) \cdot (q \in \mathbb{P}(u) \wedge l \subseteq \mathbb{P}(u) \Rightarrow (l \times \{q\} \subseteq \mathcal{L} \Rightarrow \bigcup(l) \mapsto q \in \mathcal{L}))$

Closure: $\forall l' \cdot (l' \in u \leftrightarrow u \wedge \mathcal{E} \subseteq l' \wedge l' \, ; \, l' \subseteq l' \wedge$
$\forall (q, l) \cdot (q \in \mathbb{P}(u) \wedge l \subseteq \mathbb{P}(u) \wedge l \times \{q\} \subseteq l' \Rightarrow \bigcup(l) \mapsto q \in l') \Rightarrow \mathcal{L} \subseteq l')$

$\bigcup(l)$ in the SDR rule and the closure clause, denotes the generalized union of subsets in l. Rules SBR, STR and SDR are the set counterpart of BRL, TRA and DSJ rules defined in section 3.2.

$\mathcal{L}$ is related to the *leads-to* relation by the following equivalence:

$$P(x) \rightsquigarrow Q(x) \equiv \mathsf{set}(P) \mapsto \mathsf{set}(Q) \in \mathcal{L} \tag{8}$$

where $\mathsf{set}(R)$, for any state predicate R, is the set $\{\, z \mid z \in u \wedge R(z) \,\}$. We note that property $P \rightsquigarrow Q$ in UNITY is equivalent to $P \wedge I \rightsquigarrow Q \wedge I$, considering I as an invariant of S, because the *leads-to* relation is defined in states reachable from the initial conditions [27]. The proof of this equivalence is given in [25].

4.1.3   Soundness and Completeness

We are now ready to state our main theorem, formally indicating that *termination* and *reachability* relations are equal:

Theorem 2. (Soundness and Completeness)
Let W be a monotonic and strict set transformer and $\mathcal{F}(r) = (\bar{r} \Longrightarrow W)$ for any r in $\mathbb{P}(u)$. Let relations $\mathcal{T}$ and $\mathcal{L}$ be defined as definitions 1 and 2 respectively. Considering (a) $a \mapsto b \in \mathcal{E} \Rightarrow a \cap \bar{b} \subseteq W(b)$, (b) $a \subseteq b \Rightarrow a \mapsto b \in \mathcal{E}$ and (c) $W(r) \mapsto r \in \mathcal{L}$, for any a, b and r in $\mathbb{P}(u)$, the equality $\mathcal{L} = \mathcal{T}$ holds.

Premises (a) and (b) were commented upon in the previous section. Premise (c) asserts that any set r is reached from the set $W(r)$ which is the largest subset of states where a step of the iteration terminates in r.

The proof of this theorem is given in two parts: first we prove the inclusion $\mathcal{L} \subseteq \mathcal{T}$ and then $\mathcal{T} \subseteq \mathcal{L}$.

Proof of $\mathcal{L} \subseteq \mathcal{T}$. The proof of this inclusion follows from the closure clause in definition 2, instantiating the quantified variable l' to relation $\mathcal{T}$. Then $\mathcal{L} \subseteq \mathcal{T}$ follows from $\mathcal{E} \subseteq \mathcal{T}$, $\mathcal{T};\mathcal{T} \subseteq \mathcal{T}$ and $l \times \{q\} \subseteq \mathcal{T} \Rightarrow \bigcup(l) \mapsto q \in \mathcal{T}$ for any l in $\mathbb{P}(\mathbb{P}(u))$ and q in $\mathbb{P}(u)$.

The proof of $\mathcal{E} \subseteq \mathcal{T}$ uses the following property for monotonic function f and iteration defined in (6):

$$\forall \alpha \cdot (f^\alpha \subseteq \mathsf{fix}(f)) \tag{9}$$

which is easily proved by transfinite induction. The proof of $\mathcal{E} \subseteq \mathcal{T}$ is given by the proof of $a \mapsto b \in \mathcal{E} \Rightarrow a \mapsto b \in \mathcal{T}$. From the premise and hypothesis (a) follows $a \cap \bar{b} \subseteq W(b)$. From this inclusion, (5), (6) and (9) follows $a \subseteq \mathsf{fix}(\mathcal{F}(b))$. Finally, from this inclusion and (7) the proof follows.

In order to prove the transitivity of $\mathcal{T}$, we need the following property:

$$a \mapsto b \in \mathcal{T} \Rightarrow \mathsf{fix}(\mathcal{F}(a)) \subseteq \mathsf{fix}(\mathcal{F}(b)) \tag{10}$$

for any a and b in $\mathbb{P}(u)$. Taking $a \mapsto b \in \mathcal{T}$ as a premise, and considering $\mathsf{fix}(\mathcal{F}(a))$ as the least fixpoint of $\mathcal{F}(a)$, in order to prove property (10) it suffices to prove $\mathcal{F}(a)(\text{fix}(\mathcal{F}(b))) \subseteq \text{fix}(\mathcal{F}(b))$, which follows directly from $a \mapsto b \in \mathcal{T}$ and $\mathcal{F}(b)(\text{fix}(\mathcal{F}(b))) = \text{fix}(\mathcal{F}(b))$. Now the proof of $\mathcal{T} ; \mathcal{T} \subseteq \mathcal{T}$ is equivalent to prove $a \mapsto b \in \mathcal{T} ; \mathcal{T} \Rightarrow a \mapsto b \in \mathcal{T}$ for any a and b in $\mathbb{P}(u)$. From the premise of the goal and (7) we derive $\exists c \cdot (a \subseteq \text{fix}(\mathcal{F}(c)) \wedge c \mapsto b \in \mathcal{T})$. Now, from this inclusion, (10) and transitivity of the inclusion, we obtain $a \subseteq \text{fix}(\mathcal{F}(b))$. Our goal follows from this last inclusion and (7).

Finally, the proof of $l \times \{q\} \subseteq \mathcal{T} \Rightarrow \bigcup(l) \mapsto q \in \mathcal{T}$ is as follows: From the premise and (7) we derive $\forall p \cdot (p \in l \Rightarrow p \subseteq \text{fix}(\mathcal{F}(q)))$. Our goal follows from (7) and $\bigcup(l) \subseteq \text{fix}(\mathcal{F}(q))$, which is derived from the last predicate. This last deduction concludes the proof of $\mathcal{L} \subseteq \mathcal{T}$.

Proof of $\mathcal{T} \subseteq \mathcal{L}$. The proof of this inclusion requires the following property:

$$\forall r \cdot (r \in \mathbb{P}(u) \Rightarrow \mathcal{F}(r)^\alpha \mapsto r \in \mathcal{L}) \quad \text{for any ordinal } \alpha \tag{11}$$

This property indicates that any iteration of $\mathcal{F}(r)$ eventually reaches r. The proof of (11) is done by transfinite induction; it is given in [25]. Using (11), we prove $\mathcal{L} \subseteq \mathcal{T}$ by the proof of $a \mapsto b \in \mathcal{T} \Rightarrow a \mapsto b \in \mathcal{L}$ for any a and b in $\mathbb{P}(u)$ as follows: From the premise and theorem 1 we derive $\exists \alpha \cdot (a \subseteq \mathcal{F}(b)^\alpha)$. From this derivation, hypothesis (b) of the theorem and SBR rule follows: $\exists \alpha \cdot (a \mapsto \mathcal{F}(b)^\alpha \in \mathcal{L})$. From this derivation and transitivity with (11) the goal follows. This deduction concludes the proof of theorem 2.

4.1.4   Link with Traces Semantics

At this point, the meaning of *leads-to* properties is given in terms of the least fixpoint of the set transformer $\mathcal{F}(b)$ for certain subset b of u. This set transformer denotes a step in the computations of the system if it is executed in a state where $\overline{b}$ holds. Therefore, $\text{fix}(\mathcal{F}(b))$ denotes the set of states where any computation can start and terminates in a state where b holds.

For any set transformer F, the associated before-after relation can be defined as in [2], for any subset p of u, by: $\text{rel}(F)^{-1}[p] = \overline{F(\overline{p})}$. Any pair $\sigma \mapsto \tau$ in this relation, indicates that execution of F in a state σ can reach the state τ. In the special case where $p = u$ in the above definition, we note that the guard of F corresponds to the domain of $\text{rel}(F)$, that is, to the set of states where F is enabled. Therefore $\text{rel}(F)^*$, the transitive and reflexive closure of $\text{rel}(F)$, contains all pairs $\sigma \mapsto \tau$, where τ can be reached from a repeated execution of F starting in σ. Moreover, from [1], the before-after relation of the iteration operator is given by: $\text{rel}(F^\smallfrown) = \overline{\text{pre}(F^\smallfrown)} \times u \cup \text{rel}(F)^*$, where $\text{pre}(F^\smallfrown)$, the set where termination of the iteration of F is guaranteed, is equal to $\text{fix}(F)$. From this equality, we can observe that the before-after relation of $F^\smallfrown$ contains the transitive and reflexive closure of $\text{rel}(F)$, as well as the Cartesian product $\{\delta\} \times u$, for any set δ where the iteration does not terminate. If for any different states σ and τ, such that $\sigma \mapsto \tau \in \text{rel}(F)^*$ holds, we can conclude that there is a sequence of states, or state traces, $\sigma_0, \sigma_1, \ldots, \sigma_n$ where $\sigma_0 = \sigma$, $\sigma_n = \tau$ and for any $i \geq 0$, $\sigma_i \mapsto \sigma_{i+1} \in \text{rel}(F)$ holds. Any state sequence starting in a state in $\overline{\text{pre}(F^\smallfrown)}$, is a divergent sequence. On the other hand, if the sequence starts in a state in $\text{pre}(F^\smallfrown)$, the sequence is finite and its last state is in $\overline{\text{dom}(\text{rel}(F))}$.

From the above discussion, in a way similar to [4], a semantic function in terms of state traces can be associated to $\mathcal{F}(b)$, for any σ in u, as follows:

$$\mathcal{M}[\![\mathcal{F}(b)]\!](\sigma) = \{\tau \mid \tau \in b \wedge \sigma \mapsto \tau \in \mathrm{rel}(\mathcal{F}(b))^*\} \cup \{\perp \mid \sigma \in \overline{\mathrm{fix}(\mathcal{F}(b))}\}$$

where the symbol $\perp$ is a special state denoting divergence. Now, if for any subset a of u, the inclusion $\mathcal{M}[\![\mathcal{F}(b)]\!](a) \subseteq b$ holds [2], that means that the iteration of events in the system leads to a state into b when its execution starts in a state in a. This interpretation of the inclusion allows us to define the truth value of a *leads-to* property: for any predicate P and Q, a liveness property $P \rightsquigarrow Q$ holds in a system ($\models P \rightsquigarrow Q$) if $\mathcal{M}[\![\mathcal{F}(b)]\!](\mathrm{set}(P)) \subseteq \mathrm{set}(Q)$ holds.

Considering the set of pairs $a \mapsto b$ satisfying $\mathcal{M}[\![\mathcal{F}(b)]\!](a) \subseteq b$, allow us to obtain an equivalent definition of the termination relation $\mathcal{T}$ presented in section 4.1.1. In this way, soundness of the rules BRL, TRA and DSJ, means that if $P \rightsquigarrow Q$ is derived from these rules ($\vdash \mathrm{set}(P) \mapsto \mathrm{set}(Q) \in \mathcal{L}$), then $\models P \rightsquigarrow Q$ holds. Relative completeness of these rules is proved by the implication $\models P \rightsquigarrow Q \Rightarrow \vdash \mathrm{set}(P) \mapsto \mathrm{set}(Q) \in \mathcal{L}$. These results are stated and proved in theorem 2 by the equality $\mathcal{L} = \mathcal{T}$.

Finally we note that the instantiation of $\mathcal{F}(b)$ to $\mathcal{F}_m(b)$ or $\mathcal{F}_w(b)$, as it will be done in the following sections, allows a rigorous definition of the semantic function under minimal progress or weak fairness assumptions respectively.

4.2   Minimal Progress

In this subsection, we define the *termination* and *reachability* relations under minimal progress and we prove that they satisfy the premises of theorem 2. Therefore we claim that relations $\mathcal{T}$ and $\mathcal{L}$ are equal in the case of minimal progress.

4.2.1   Termination Under MP

To model a step of the iteration of events of system S under minimal progress assumptions, we note that if we need to establish a certain postcondition when this step is achieved, any event in S must be able to establish the postcondition. Moreover, as we are interested in the execution of any event, we need to start the execution step in a state satisfying the guard of at least one event. Therefore, taking into account these considerations, we propose the following preconditioned set transformer:

$$W_m \triangleq \mathrm{grd}(S) \mid S \tag{12}$$

From the definition of preconditioned set transformer in section 3.1 we have $W_m(r) = \mathrm{grd}(S) \cap S(r)$. From monotonicity of S, we derive the monotonicity of W_m and $W_m(\varnothing) = (\mathrm{grd}(S) \cap S(\varnothing)) = \varnothing$ which proves the strictness of W_m.

The body of the iteration of events under minimal progress is the guarded event $\mathcal{F}_m(r)$ defined as follows:

$$\mathcal{F}_m(r) \triangleq \overline{r} \Longrightarrow W_m \tag{13}$$

---

[2] For any subset t of u, $\mathcal{M}[\![\mathcal{F}(b)]\!](t) = \bigcup_{\sigma \in t} \mathcal{M}[\![\mathcal{F}(b)]\!](\sigma)$.

Definition of the *termination* relation under minimal progress is given by all ordered pairs $a \mapsto b$ satisfying $a \subseteq \mathsf{pre}(\mathcal{F}_m(b)\hat{\ })$:

$$\mathcal{T}_m \mathrel{\widehat{=}} \{\, a \mapsto b \mid a \subseteq u \wedge b \subseteq u \wedge a \subseteq \mathsf{fix}(\mathcal{F}_m(b)) \,\} \tag{14}$$

4.2.2 Reachability Under MP

According to (4), the basic relation under minimal progress contains all ordered pairs $a \mapsto b$ from which we can derive a property $x \in a \gg_m x \in b$:

$$\mathcal{E}_m \mathrel{\widehat{=}} \{\, a \mapsto b \mid a \subseteq u \wedge b \subseteq u \wedge a \cap \overline{b} \subseteq S(b) \cap \mathsf{grd}(S) \,\} \tag{15}$$

From the definitions of $\mathcal{E}_m$ and W_m, the proof of premise (a) of theorem 2 for the case of minimal progress, $a \mapsto b \in \mathcal{E}_m \Rightarrow a \cap \overline{b} \subseteq W_m(b)$, follows immediately.

From the definition of $\mathcal{E}_m$, the implication $a \subseteq b \Rightarrow a \mapsto b \in \mathcal{E}_m$, premise (b) of theorem 2, follows immediately because $a \cap \overline{b} = \varnothing$.

Now, we use an induction scheme to define the *reachability* relation under minimal progress $\mathcal{L}_m$ similar to definition 2. Therefore $\mathcal{L}_m$ is the smallest relation containing the base relation $\mathcal{E}_m$ and it is both, transitive and disjunctive.

Finally we prove that the weakest precondition $W_m(r)$, for any $r \in \mathbb{P}(u)$ leads to r: $W_m(r) \mapsto r \in \mathcal{L}_m$. First, we note that $\mathsf{grd}(S) \cap S(r) \cap \overline{r} \subseteq \mathsf{grd}(S) \cap S(r)$ holds trivially. From this inclusion, (15) and (12), we derive $W_m(r) \mapsto r \in \mathcal{E}_m$. The goal follows from this derivation and rule SBR. It proves premise (c) of theorem 2 for the case of minimal progress.

At this time, monotonicity and strictness of W_m and premises (a), (b) and (c) of theorem 2 instantiated to the case of minimal progress have been proved. Therefore the equality between *termination* and *reachability* relations is stated:

$$\mathcal{T}_m = \mathcal{L}_m \tag{16}$$

4.3 Weak Fairness

In this subsection, we define the *termination* and *reachability* relations for weak fairness assumptions. We prove that premises of theorem 2, instantiated to the case of weak fairness assumptions, are satisfied with these definitions. Therefore we claim the equality between these relations.

4.3.1 Termination Under WF

We use the dovetail operator presented in section 3.1 to model a *fair loop* for a certain event G in $\mathcal{S}$:

$$Y(q)(G) \mathrel{\widehat{=}} \overline{q} \Longrightarrow ((S \mathbin{;} Y(q)(G)) \mathbin{\triangledown} (\mathsf{grd}(G) \mid G)) \tag{17}$$

The guard $\overline{q}$ of this loop prevents iteration of the fair choice in any state belonging to q. Informally, we expect that any execution of $Y(G)(q)$ in any state in $q \cup \mathsf{grd}(G)$ terminates. Execution of $Y(q)(G)$ in $\overline{q} \cap \mathsf{grd}(G)$ cannot loops forever because the dovetail operator prevents unlimited execution of the branch $S \mathbin{;} Y(q)(G)$. Moreover the set transformer $\mathsf{grd}(G) \mid G$ is always enabled

$(\mathsf{grd}(\mathsf{grd}(G) \mid G) = u)$ and therefore it will be eventually executed. All our claims are formally justified by the calculi of termination set and the liberal weakest precondition of $Y(q)(G)$, for any q and r, $r \neq u$ in $\mathbb{P}(u)$:

$$\mathsf{pre}(Y(q)(G)) = \mathsf{fix}(\overline{q} \cap G(\varnothing) \Longrightarrow \overline{S(q)} \mid S) \tag{18}$$

$$\mathcal{L}(Y(q)(G))(r) = \mathsf{FIX}(\overline{q} \Longrightarrow (\mathsf{grd}(G) \cap G(r) \mid S)) \tag{19}$$

The calculus of the termination set of $Y(q)(G)$ indicates that it contains chains of states related by the before-after relation associated with the set transformer $\overline{q} \cap G(\varnothing) \Longrightarrow \overline{S(q)} \mid S$, and terminating in $(\overline{q} \cap G(\varnothing) \Longrightarrow \overline{S(q)} \mid S)(\varnothing) = q \cup \overline{G(\varnothing)}$, which corresponds to the complement of the guard of the set transformer. The liberal set transformer of $Y(q)(G)$ to establish r corresponds to the union of subsets p of u, satisfying the condition $p \cap \overline{q} \subseteq \overline{G(\varnothing)} \cap G(r) \cap S(p)$. We remark that any state in $\mathcal{L}(Y(q)(G))(r)$ is in q or in the set where the helpful event G is enabled and able to establish r.

Properties (18) and (19) follow from the definitions of set transformers given in section 3.1 and the extreme solutions of the generated recursive equations. The proofs are in [25].

Using the pairing condition and $\mathcal{L}(Y(q)(G))(r) \subseteq \mathsf{pre}(Y(q)(G))$, for any q and r, the set transformer associated with the fair loop is:

$$Y(q)(G)(r) = \mathsf{FIX}(\overline{q} \Longrightarrow (\mathsf{grd}(G) \cap G(r) \mid S)) \tag{20}$$

From this definition follows the monotonicity of $Y(q)(G)$.

The fair loop $Y(q)(G)$ models a *fair G-step* in the iteration of events under weak fairness assumptions. We say that G is the helpful event in this G-step. A *fair step* in the iteration of events is modeled by the following set transformer:

$$W_w \triangleq \lambda r \cdot (r \subseteq u \mid \bigcup G \cdot (G \in \mathcal{S} \mid Y(r)(G)(r))) \tag{21}$$

From the guard of the dovetail operator defined in section 3.1 and (17), we conclude $\mathsf{grd}(Y(q)(G)) = \overline{q}$ for any G in $\mathcal{S}$ and $q \in \mathbb{P}(u)$; therefore strictness of W_w follows. In the other hand, from monotonicity of $Y(q)(G)$ follows the monotonicity of W_w.

The body of the iteration of events under weak fairness is the guarded event $\mathcal{F}_w(r)$ defined as follows:

$$\mathcal{F}_w(r) \triangleq \overline{r} \Longrightarrow W_w \tag{22}$$

Definition of the *termination* relation under weak fairness is:

$$\mathcal{T}_w \triangleq \{ a \mapsto b \mid a \subseteq u \wedge b \subseteq u \wedge a \subseteq \mathsf{fix}(\mathcal{F}_w(b)) \} \tag{23}$$

4.3.2   Reachability Under WF

We define the basic relation $\mathcal{E}(G)$ for a helpful event G, as the set of pairs $a \mapsto b$ from which we can derive a property $G \cdot x \in a \gg_w x \in b$ (3):

$$\mathcal{E}(G) \triangleq \{ a \mapsto b \mid a \subseteq u \wedge b \subseteq u \wedge a \cap \overline{b} \subseteq S(a \cup b) \cap \overline{G(\varnothing)} \cap G(b) \} \tag{24}$$

Now, the basic relation for weak fairness is:

$$\mathcal{E}_w \triangleq \bigcup G \cdot (G \in \mathcal{S} \mid \mathcal{E}(G)) \tag{25}$$

The proof of premise (a) of theorem 2 instantiated to weak fairness requires the following property:

$$\forall G \cdot (G \in \mathcal{S} \wedge a \mapsto b \in \mathcal{E}(G) \Rightarrow a \subseteq Y(b)(G)(b)) \tag{26}$$

In order to prove this property, we remark from (24) and premise of (26) that inclusion $a \cup b \subseteq (\bar{b} \Longrightarrow \mathsf{grd}(G) \cap G(b) \mid \mathcal{S})(a \cup b)$ holds. This inclusion proves that $a \cup b \subseteq \mathsf{FIX}(\bar{b} \Longrightarrow \mathsf{grd}(G) \cap G(b) \mid \mathcal{S})$ holds and from (20), $a \subseteq Y(b)(G)(b)$ follows. Then we give the proof of $a \mapsto b \in \mathcal{E}_w \Rightarrow a \cap \bar{b} \subseteq W_w(b)$: From (26) and (21) we derive $\exists G \cdot (G \in \mathcal{S} \wedge a \mapsto b \in \mathcal{E}(G)) \Rightarrow a \subseteq W_w(b)$. From this derivation and (25) we obtain $a \mapsto b \in \mathcal{E}_w \Rightarrow a \subseteq W_w(b)$. The goal follows from this last derivation and $b \subseteq W_w(b)$.

From (24) immediately follows $a \mapsto b \in \mathcal{E}(G)$, for any G in $\mathcal{S}$ if $a \subseteq b$ holds, and from (25) follows $a \subseteq b \Rightarrow a \mapsto b \in \mathcal{E}_w$. It proves premise (b) of theorem 2.

We use an induction scheme to define the *reachability* relation under weak fairness $\mathcal{L}_w$ similar to definition 2. Therefore $\mathcal{L}_w$ is the smallest relation containing the base relation $\mathcal{E}_w$ and it is both, transitive and disjunctive.

From (20) and (24) follows the property:

$$\forall (G, r) \cdot (G \in \mathcal{S} \wedge r \subseteq u \Rightarrow Y(r)(G)(r) \mapsto r \in \mathcal{E}(G)) \tag{27}$$

We use this property to prove the premise (c) of theorem 2: $W_w(r) \mapsto r \in \mathcal{L}_w$ as follows: From (27), (24) and SBR rule we derive $\forall G \cdot (G \in \mathcal{S} \Rightarrow Y(r)(G)(r) \mapsto r \in \mathcal{L}_w)$. From this predicate and the SDR rule we derive $\bigcup(\{ Y(r)(G)(r) \mid G \in \mathcal{S} \}) \mapsto r \in \mathcal{L}_w$. The goal follows from this derivation and (21).

At this time *termination* $(\mathcal{T}_w)$, basic relation $(\mathcal{E}_w)$ and *reachability* $(\mathcal{L}_w)$ relations for weak fairness assumptions have been defined. Monotonicity and strictness of the set transformer W_w, and premises (a), (b) and (c) of theorem 2 instantiated to the case of weak fairness have been proved. Therefore, the equality between *termination* and *reachability* relations under weak fairness is stated:

$$\mathcal{T}_w = \mathcal{L}_w \tag{28}$$

5   Deriving Liveness Properties

In this section, we present two examples where we show practical usefulness of equalities between *termination* and *reachability* relations under minimal progress and weak fairness assumptions. This section is divided in three parts. In the first part we state and prove the *Variant Theorem*, which allows us to prove termination of iterations over a set transformer if a variant decreases. In the second part we use this theorem to prove a sufficient condition allowing derivation of liveness properties under minimal progress. Finally, we give another sufficient condition to derive a liveness property under minimal progress when a similar property holds in weak fairness assumptions

5.1   The Variant Theorem

The variant theorem allows us to prove termination of iteration of conjunctive set transformers. This theorem considers a total function which maps each element of the state space to an element of a well founded order and a set which is invariant at each iteration of the set transformer. The theorem states that if any execution of the set transformer starting in a state in the invariant set and a certain value of the variant function, terminates in a state where the value of the variant is decremented, then the invariant set is contained in the termination set of the iteration of the set transformer. Formally, the theorem is stated as follows[3]:

Theorem 3. (Variant Theorem)
Let $V \in u \rightarrow \mathbb{N}$, $v = \lambda n \cdot (n \in \mathbb{N} \mid \{z \mid z \in u \wedge V(z) = n\})$ and $v' = \lambda n \cdot (n \in \mathbb{N} \mid \{z \mid z \in u \wedge V(z) < n\})$. For any conjunctive set transformer f in $\mathbb{P}(u) \rightarrow \mathbb{P}(u)$ and p in $\mathbb{P}(u)$, such that $v(n) \cap p \subseteq f(v'(n))$ and $p \subseteq f(p)$, for any n in $\mathbb{N}$, the inclusion $p \subseteq \text{fix}(f)$ holds.

The proof of this theorem uses the following property which holds under the premises of theorem 3:

$$\forall n \cdot (n \in \mathbb{N} \Rightarrow \bigcup i \cdot (i \in \mathbb{N} \wedge i \leq n \mid v(i)) \cap p \subseteq f^{n+1}) \tag{29}$$

This premise indicates that any state x of p, such that $V(x) = n$, for any value n of $\mathbb{N}$, is a state where the set transformer f can be iterated at most n times and terminate into a state where it is disabled. The proof of (29) proceeds by induction; it is presented in [25]. The proof of theorem 3 is as follows: From (29), (9), and definitions of v and v', we derive $\forall n \cdot (n \in \mathbb{N} \Rightarrow v'(n+1) \cap p \subseteq \text{fix}(f))$. From definitions of v and v' follows $\bigcup n \cdot (n \in \mathbb{N} \mid v'(n+1)) = \bigcup i \cdot (i \in \mathbb{N} \mid v(i))$. From the last two derivations we deduce $\bigcup i \cdot (i \in \mathbb{N} \mid v(i)) \cap p \subseteq \text{fix}(f)$. Finally, the goal follows from this inclusion and $\bigcup i \cdot (i \in \mathbb{N} \mid v(i)) = u$.

5.2   A Sufficient Condition for Minimal Progress

A system reaches a certain set from any set of starting states under minimal progress, if the set of depart is invariant in the system, it is contained in the guard of the system and each execution of the system decrements a variant. Formally, these conditions are stated as follows:

ANTECEDENT	CONSEQUENT
$\forall n \cdot (n \in \mathbb{N} \Rightarrow a \cap \bar{b} \cap v(n) \subseteq S(v'(n)))$ $a \cap \bar{b} \subseteq \text{grd}(S) \cap S(a)$	$a \mapsto b \in \mathcal{L}_m$

The proof of these conditions is as follows: From premises and (13) we derive $\forall n \cdot (n \in \mathbb{N} \Rightarrow a \cap v(n) \subseteq \mathcal{F}_m(b)(v'(n)))$. On the other hand, from premises

---

[3] In this theorem, the well-founded ordered set is taken to be $\mathbb{N}$, but we could take any other well-founded set.

and (13) follows: $a \subseteq \mathcal{F}_m(b)(a)$. From the last two derivations and theorem 3 we conclude $a \subseteq \text{fix}(\mathcal{F}_m(b))$. Finally, from this last derivation, (14) and equality (16), the goal follows.

The antecedent of this rule corresponds to the sufficient conditions in [2] to prove liveness properties and it is the only rule concerning the proof of liveness properties. Soundness of this rule is proved here in a more direct way.

Soundness of this rule is given without reasoning over state-traces, taking advantage of the fixpoint semantics approach.

5.3   From Weak Fairness to Minimal Progress

Using the variant theorem, we prove a sufficient condition to establish that a liveness property under minimal progress, follows from a corresponding property proved under weak fairness and from the decrement of a variant:

ANTECEDENT	CONSEQUENT
$\forall n \cdot (n \in \mathbb{N} \Rightarrow \overline{b} \cap v(n) \subseteq S(v'(n)))$	$a \mapsto b \in \mathcal{L}_m$
$a \mapsto b \in \mathcal{L}_w$	

As S is a conjunctive set transformer, from (12) and (13) we conclude that $\mathcal{F}_m(b)$ is conjunctive as well. Therefore the *Variant Theorem* can be used to prove this rule. However, in order to apply the theorem we need to identify an invariant set under $\mathcal{F}_m(b)$. The sets a and b cannot be proved as invariants, therefore we prove that the least fixpoint of $\mathcal{F}_w(b)$ is invariant under $\mathcal{F}_m(b)$, that is $\text{fix}(\mathcal{F}_w(b)) \subseteq \mathcal{F}_m(b)(\text{fix}(\mathcal{F}_w(b)))$. This proof requires the following lemma:

$$\forall \alpha \cdot (\mathcal{F}_w(b)^\alpha \subseteq b \cup (\text{grd}(S) \cap S(\text{fix}(\mathcal{F}_w(b))))) \tag{30}$$

The proof of (30) is done by transfinite induction; the proof is given in [25]. Using (30), the proof of sufficient conditions is as follows: From theorem 1, (30) and (13) we derive $\text{fix}(\mathcal{F}_w(b)) \subseteq \mathcal{F}_m(b)(\text{fix}(\mathcal{F}_w(b)))$. From this derivation, premise and (13) follows $\forall n \cdot (n \in \mathbb{N} \Rightarrow \text{fix}(\mathcal{F}_w(b)) \cap v(n) \subseteq \mathcal{F}_m(b)(v'(n)))$. From the last two conclusions, and theorem 3 we conclude $\text{fix}(\mathcal{F}_w(b)) \subseteq \text{fix}(\mathcal{F}_m(b))$. On the other hand, from premise, equality (28) and (23) follows $a \subseteq \text{fix}(\mathcal{F}_w(b))$. Finally, the goal follows from the last two conclusion, (14) and equality (16).

5.4   An Example of Application

In this section, we present an example where a *leads-to* property, proved in an abstraction under weak fairness assumption, is preserved in a refinement under minimal progress assumptions. By space considerations, we do not present any proof. All of them have been mechanically verified with the Click'n'Prove prover.

In figure 1 there is an abstract model of a producer-consumer system. It is made up of two events, which model the producer (*Prd*) and the consumer (*Cns*). The producer gets a data from a set *DATA* and puts it into a buffer *buf* (*buf* $\subseteq$ *DATA*). The consumer gets a data from the buffer and saves it in a store

str ($str \subseteq DATA$). We consider that event Cns is executed under a weak fairness assumption. We specify that the liveness property "any data in the buffer will be eventually consumed" must be satisfied by the system. Formally, it is stated as follows: $d \in buf \rightsquigarrow d \in str$, where d is universally quantified over $DATA$. As explained in [24], application of (3), allows us to claim that the basic property Cns if $x = d \cdot d \in buf \gg_w d \in str$, holds in the abstract model. That means that the helpful transition is performed by event Cns, when the chosen element is x, denoted by Cns if $x = d$. Then, by the BRL rule, the liveness property holds.

In figure 2 we show a refinement of the abstract system. The abstract buffer is refined by qu, an (injective) sequence of $DATA$, with gluing invariant $buf = \mathsf{ran}(qu)$. Two invariants are specified: $\mathsf{size}(qu) \leq mx$ (mx is the maximum size of qu) and $\mathsf{ran}(qu) \cap str = \varnothing$. As explained in [24, 26], two sufficient conditions (LIP and SAP) must be proved to guarantee the preservation of the *leads-to* property. The variant $qu^{-1}(d)$ was used in the proofs.

At this time, the property $d \in \mathsf{ran}(qu) \rightsquigarrow d \in str$ holds in the refined system, under weak fairness assumptions. However, we can proof that the variant $[\mathsf{card}(DATA - str), mx - \mathsf{size}(qu)]$ is decremented in a lexicographical order by events Prd and Cns when $d \notin str$ holds. Therefore, application of the rule of section 5.3, allows us to claim that $d \in \mathsf{ran}(qu) \rightsquigarrow d \in str$ holds in the refined system under a minimal progress assumption.

$Prd = $ ANY x WHERE $x \in DATA$ THEN $\quad buf := buf \cup \{x\}$ END; $Cns = $ ANY x WHERE $x \in buf$ THEN $\quad buf := buf - \{x\}$ $\|$ $\quad str := str \cup \{x\}$ END	$Prd = $ ANY x WHERE $x \in DATA \wedge x \notin str$ $\quad \wedge\, \mathsf{size}(qu) < mx \wedge x \notin \mathsf{ran}(qu)$ THEN $qu := qu \leftarrow x$ END; $Cns = $ SELECT $qu \neq []$ THEN $\quad qu := \mathsf{tail}(qu)$ $\|$ $\quad str := str \cup \{\mathsf{first}(qu)\}$ END

Fig. 1. Abstract producer-consumer   **Fig. 2.** Refined producer-consumer

6   Conclusions

We have presented a fixpoint semantics of event systems under minimal progress and weak fairness assumptions. Then we have proved soundness and completeness of rules for deriving *leads-to* properties under weak fairness and minimal progress assumptions. Finally we have proved sufficient conditions to prove a liveness property under minimal progress in two cases of hypothesis: every event decrements a variant under an invariant, or every event decrements a variant and the property holds under weak fairness.

The development of our semantics is structured. First we establish a general framework, without concerns of fairness, and we elaborate our notions of termination and reachability. Soundness and completeness of rules for *leads-to* are proved in this framework. The general framework is then instantiated to the cases of minimal progress and weak fairness assumptions and the corresponding results are proved. Each element in our models has a concrete representation as a set transformer. In particular, we stress how the weak fairness assumption is modeled by the dovetail operator.

We have stated a simple form of the variant theorem and given a simple proof of it. We remark the usefulness of this theorem in the proofs of liveness properties. Particularly we note the importance of conditions which guarantee the derivation of a certain liveness property $\mathcal{P}$ under minimal progress if $\mathcal{P}$ holds under weak fairness, and every element of the system decrements a variant. This is a new result which gives the possibility to *implement* fairness in a system.

Coming back to the various forms of description and semantics of action-based systems, we know that the program-like notation is very suitable for effective derivation of programs (e.g. action systems), while the logic-like notation is very suitable for the specification of properties and reasoning, when it is completed by a proof system (e.g. UNITY, TLA). The event-B formalism is in between, in the sense that the notation is program-like, but there is a way to express properties and to consider the system as predicate transformers, i.e. in the domain of logic reasoning. However, the semantics of action-based systems is either based on traces of states, or on properties of predicate transformers, without formal links between them. Here we represent both semantics in the framework of iteration of set transformers, and we prove that the reachability and the termination relations are equal under the conditions stated in the paper. We unify two fairness conditions (minimal progress and weak fairness) by considering them as various modalities to perform a fair progressing step in the system.

By using this formalization, we are able to justify the proof rules of the proof systems already presented in other frameworks, and also we can find out other theorems to justify new proof rules or new refinement rules, as it is done in the last section.

As a future work, we investigate how our approach can be extended to deal with composition of distributed event systems. Another line will be to consider how to instantiate the general framework for strong fairness and to investigate the links between strong fairness, weak fairness and minimal progress.

References

1. J.-R. Abrial. *The B-Book, Assigning Programs to Meanings.* Cambridge University Press, 1996.
2. J.-R. Abrial and L. Mussat. Introducing Dynamic Constraints in B. In *B'98: Recent Advances in the Development and Use of the B Method, LNCS 1393*, pages 83–128. Springer-Verlag, april 1998.
3. K. R. Apt and E.-R. Olderog. Fairness in parallel programs, the transformational approach. *ACM Transactions on Programming Languages and Systems*, 10(3):420–455, 1988.
4. K. R. Apt and E.-R. Olderog. *Verification of Sequential and Concurrent Programs.* Graduate texts in computer science. Springer-Verlag, second edition edition, 1997.
5. R.-J. Back and R. Kurki-Suonio. Decentralization of Process Nets with Centralized Control. In *2nd ACM SIGACT-SIGOPS Symp. on Principles of Distributed Computing*, pages 131–143, 1983.

6. R.-J. Back and Q. Xu. Refinement of Fair Action Systems. *Acta Informatica*, 35:131–165, 1998.
7. M. Broy and G. Nelson. Adding Fair Choice to Dijkstra's Calculus. *ACM Transactions on Programming Languages and Systems*, 16(3):924–938, May 1994.
8. K. M. Chandy and J. Misra. *Parallel Program Design. A Foundation*. Addison-Wesley, 1988.
9. K. M. Chandy and B. A. Sanders. Predicate transformers for reasoning about concurrent computation. *Science of Computer Programming*, 24:129–148, 1995.
10. S. Dune. Introducing Backward Refinement into B. In *ZB 2003: Formal Specification and Development in Z an B, LNCS 2651*, pages 178–196. Springer-Verlag, June 2003.
11. S. Chouali F. Bellegarde and J. Julliand. Verification of Dynamic Constraints for B Event Systems under Fairness Assumptions. In *ZB 2002 International Conference, LNCS 2272*, pages 481–500. Springer-Verlag, january 2002.
12. E.C.R. Hehner. do Considere od: A Contribution to the Programming Calculus. *Acta Informatica*, 11:287–304, 1979.
13. C. S. Jutla, E. Knapp, and J. R. Rao. A predicate transformer approach to the semantics of parallel programs. In *Proceedings of the Eight Annual ACM Symposium on the Principles of Distributed Computing*, pages 249–263, 1989.
14. C. S. Jutla and J. R. Rao. A Methodology for Designing Proof Rules for Fair Parallel Programs. *Formal Aspects of Computing*, 9:359–378, 1997.
15. E. Knapp. A predicate transformer for progress. *Information Processing Letters*, 33:323–330, 1989.
16. L. Lamport. The Temporal Logic of Actions. *ACM Trans. Program. Lang. Syst.*, 16(3):872–923, 1994.
17. Z. Manna and A. Pnueli. Completing the temporal picture. *Theoretical Computer Science*, 83(1):97–130, 1991.
18. Z. Manna and A. Pnueli. *The Temporal logic of reactive and concurrent systems : specification* . Springer, 1992.
19. D. Meier and B. A. Sanders. Composing leads-to properties. *Theoretical Computer Science*, 243:339–361, 2000.
20. G. Nelson. A Generalization of Dijkstra's Calculus. *ACM Transactions on Programming Languages and Systems*, 11(4):517–561, October 1989.
21. S. Owicki and D. Gries. An axiomatic proof technique for parallel programs. *Acta Informatica*, 6:319–340, 1976.
22. D. Park. A predicate transformer for weak fair iteration. In *Proceedings of the 6th IBM Symposium on Mathematical Foundations in Computer Science, Hakone, Japan*, pages 257–275. IBM, 1981.
23. H. Ruíz-Barradas and D. Bert. Specification and Proof of Liveness Properties under Fairness Assumptions in B Event Systems. In *Integrated Formal Methods, Third International Conference IFM 2002, LNCS 2335*, pages 360–379. Springer-Verlag, May 2002.
24. H. Ruíz-Barradas and D. Bert. Propriétés dynamiques avec hypothèses d'équité en B événementiel. In *AFADL'2004*, pages 299–313. LIFC, Besançon, France, 2004.
25. H. Ruíz-Barradas and D. Bert. A Fixpoint Semantics of Event Systems with and without Fairness Assumptions. Technical report, LSR-IMAG, Grenoble, 2005.
26. H. Ruíz-Barradas and D. Bert. Proof Obligations for Specification and Refinement of Liveness Properties under Weak Fairness. Technical Report 1071-I LSR 20, LSR-IMAG, Grenoble, 2005.
27. B. A. Sanders. Eliminating the Substitution Axiom from UNITY Logic. *Acta Informatica*, 3:189–205, 1991.

Consistency Checking of Sequence Diagrams and Statechart Diagrams Using the π-Calculus

Vitus S.W. Lam and Julian Padget

Department of Computer Science, University of Bath
{lsw, jap}@cs.bath.ac.uk

Abstract. UML 2.0, like UML 1.x, provides only a set of notations for specifying different aspects of a system. The problem of checking consistency between various types of models in software development is still not fully addressed. In this paper, we suggest the use of an algebraic approach for verifying whether consistency between sequence diagrams and statechart diagrams is preserved. First, statechart diagrams are encoded in the π-calculus. Then, each object in a sequence diagram is translated into its equivalent π-calculus definitions and verified against the corresponding statechart diagram represented in the π-calculus using the Mobility Workbench. The applicability of the proposed approach is illustrated with an agent-based payment protocol.

1 Introduction

In the Unified Modeling Language (UML) [15, 16], the dynamic behaviour of a model is represented using various types of diagrams including statechart diagrams and sequence diagrams. A statechart diagram specifies the complete lifecycle of an object, whereas a sequence diagram specifies the partial lifecycle of each object which takes part in an interaction. Due to the existence of two model views as well as different model versions, inconsistency between statechart diagrams and sequence diagrams occurs inevitably during the software development and software evolution processes. To ensure intra-model consistency (horizontal consistency [22]) is preserved in software development, this paper explores how the open bisimulation of the π-calculus [14, 12] is used for checking that a set of sequence diagrams is consistent with a corresponding set of statechart diagrams.

The remainder of the paper is organized as follows. Section 2 reviews related work. Section 3 gives a brief overview of sequence diagrams and statechart diagrams. Section 4 summarizes the major concepts of the π-calculus. The encoding of sequence diagrams and statechart diagrams in the π-calculus is described in Sections 5 and 6, respectively. Section 7 discusses the consistency checks between sequence diagrams and statechart diagrams. Concluding remarks are given in Section 8.

2 Related Work

There have been a number of attempts such as [6, 26, 25, 21, 4, 5, 3] on (i) generating a model from another type of model; and (ii) checking the consistency of dif-

J. Romijn, G. Smith, and J. van de Pol (Eds.): IFM 2005, LNCS 3771, pp. 347–365, 2005.

ferent types or versions of models. Approaches for generating statechart diagrams from a set of collaboration diagrams and synthesizing statechart diagrams from a collection of sequence diagrams are proposed in [6] and [26, 25], respectively.

Tsiolakis and Ehrig [21] use attributed graphs, graphical constraints and attributed graph grammars for checking consistency between class diagrams and sequence diagrams. Class diagrams are mapped to attributed graphs and graphical constraints and sequence diagrams are translated into attributed graph grammars. A class diagram is consistent with a sequence diagram if all the generated graphs of the attributed graph grammar coincide with the attributed graph and graphical constraints.

Engels et al. [4] propose an approach for checking consistency between (i) capsule statecharts and (ii) capsule statechart and protocol statechart. A capsule, which is regarded as a stereotyped active class [4], may have a number of ports linked up by connectors for communicating with other capsules. A capsule statechart associated with a capsule depicts how the capsule responds to various received signals, while a protocol statechart associated with a connector defines the sequence of signals exchanged through the connector between two capsules.

In [3], the evolution consistency between different versions of UML-RT models is analyzed using Communicating Sequential Processes (CSP). Likewise, Engels et al. in [5] determine the consistency between an old capsule statechart and a new capsule statechart of UML-RT models by verifying that the old capsule statechart is a refinement of the new capsule statechart. Unlike these previous studies [6, 26, 25, 21, 4, 5, 3], our work focuses on the verification of consistency between sequence diagrams and statechart diagrams using an algebraic approach.

Closely related work on the preservation of consistency between sequence diagrams and statechart diagrams includes [22, 2, 1]. Van Der Straeten et al. [22] transform class diagrams, sequence diagrams and statechart diagrams into description logic for checking consistency between different versions of these diagrams. Engels et al. [2] verify the consistency of sequence diagrams and statechart diagrams using dynamic meta modelling (DMM) rules. In contrast to [22, 2] which implement the consistency checks using description logic and testing, our approach is based on the open bisimulation of the π-calculus. In addition, our approach supports (i) incremental consistency checks by allowing a partial model i.e. an object of a sequence diagram to verify against its corresponding statechart diagram; and (ii) UML 2.0 instead of UML 1.x.

Dumond et al. [1] adopt the π-calculus as the underlying formalism for consistency checking. However, our work is significant different from their study as:

(i) our encoding of sequence and statechart diagrams is different;
(ii) we formally define the translation rules of sequence diagrams in terms of the π-calculus;
(iii) no translation rules of statechart diagrams are given in [1] and it is not clear how complete their transformation is;
(iv) an evaluation of our proposed approach by a case study is provided;
(v) only UML 1.x is considered in [1]; and
(vi) consistency between sequence and statechart diagrams is not formally specified in [1].

3 Behavioural Modelling in UML 2.0

Sequence diagrams and statechart diagrams, which are behavioural diagrams of UML, are graphical notations for modelling the dynamic aspects of a system. A sequence diagram shows in temporal order how interactions between a set of objects are represented as a sequence of messages exchanged. A statechart diagram specifies how an object responds to various events throughout its lifetime.

Figures 1–9 are sequence diagrams that model an extended SET/A protocol [10]. The SET/A protocol [19], which is an agent-based payment protocol based on Secure Electronic Transaction (SET) [11], provides a secure credit card payment in a mobile computing environment. The mobile agent travels from the cardholder's computer to the merchant's server, sends a purchase request to the merchant upon arriving at the merchant's server and waits for a response. On receipt of a response, the mobile agent departs the merchant's server and travels back to the cardholder's computer. To ensure that a transaction is resilient to the failure of the mobile agent, an extended SET/A which allows the cardholder to send an inquiry request directly to the merchant is proposed in [10].

Unlike UML 1.x [15], there is a rectangular frame around a sequence diagram in UML 2.0 [16]. The name of an interaction represented by the sequence diagram is in the upper left corner of the frame. It starts with a keyword *sd* as shown in Figures 1–9. An object is denoted as a rectangle. The objects, which take part in an interaction, are placed across the top of the sequence diagram. The dashed line connecting to an object represents the lifeline of the object. An asynchronous message visualized as an open arrow specifies a communication between two

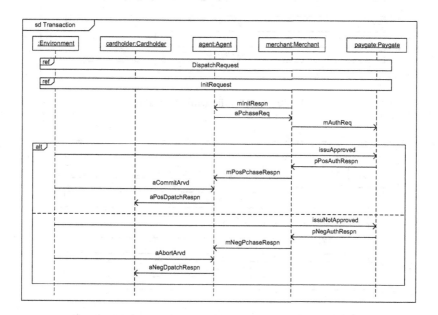

Fig. 1. A normal transaction of extended SET/A

objects. When compared with UML 1.x, UML 2.0 supports the reuse of an interaction through an interaction occurrence. The interaction operator *ref* of an interaction occurrence, like *sd*, is in the upper left corner of the frame. Similarly, the interaction operator *alt* introduced in UML 2.0 signifies a choice between a number of interaction fragments separated by dashed lines.

The sequence diagram *Transaction* in Figure 1 describes a normal transaction of the extended SET/A protocol. It consists of five objects that are instances of classes *Environment, Cardholder, Agent, Merchant* and *Paygate*. An interaction begins by referring to interaction occurrences *DispatchRequest* (Figure 4) and *InitRequest* (Figure 5). Asynchronous messages are sent from the object *merchant* to the object *agent*, the object *agent* to the object *merchant* and the object *merchant* to the object *paygate*, respectively. Two choices of behaviour, which represent positive and negative responses of the objects *paygate, merchant* and *agent*, are modelled as two interaction fragments using the interaction operator *alt*.

Figures 2 and 3 illustrate how the failures of the agent which are exceptional transactions of the extended SET/A protocol are specified as sequence diagrams. Figure 2, which refers to Figures 4, 6 and 7, depicts how the agent fails while

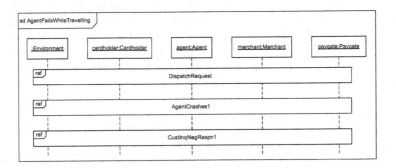

Fig. 2. Agent fails while travelling

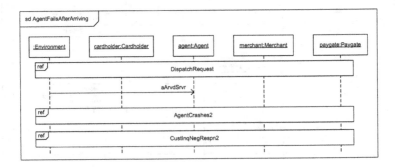

Fig. 3. Agent fails after arriving the merchant's server

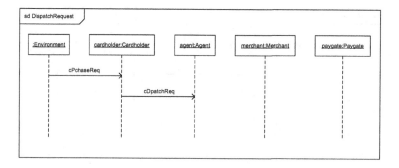

Fig. 4. A dispatch request

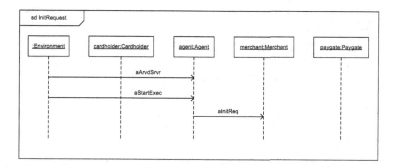

Fig. 5. An initialization request

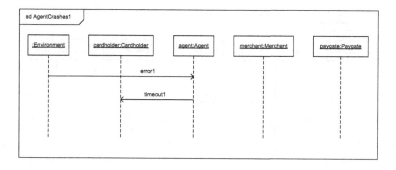

Fig. 6. An agent failure (while travelling)

travelling to the merchant's server. Figure 3, which refers to Figures 4, 8 and 9, shows how the agent fails after arriving the merchant's server.

Figures 10–13 show the statechart diagrams of the cardholder, agent, merchant and payment gateway. In statechart diagrams there are two basic entities: state and transition. *CBrowseCatalog* and *CWaitPchaseRespn* in Figure 10 are basic states. The arrow between the source state *CBrowseCatalog* and the tar-

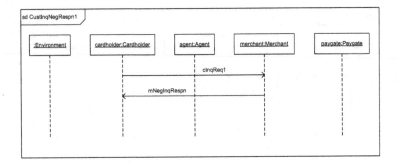

Fig. 7. A negative inquiry response (while travelling)

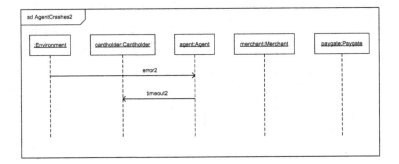

Fig. 8. An agent failure (after arriving)

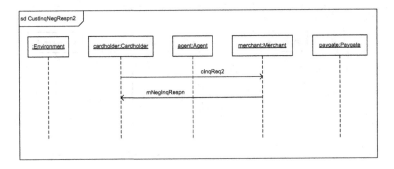

Fig. 9. A negative inquiry response (after arriving)

get state *CWaitPchaseRespn* is a notation for a transition. On receipt of an event *cPchaseReq*, the state *CBrowseCatalog* is exited, an event *cDpatchReq* is sent to the object *agent* and the state *CWaitPchaseRespn* is entered. The cardholder continues to wait in state *CWaitPchaseRespn* for a dispatch response or timeout event. Depending on whether a positive or negative dispatch response is received, the cardholder enters either a commit or an abort state and the

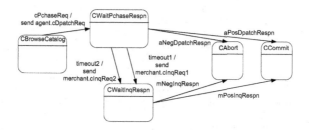

Fig. 10. Statechart diagram of the cardholder

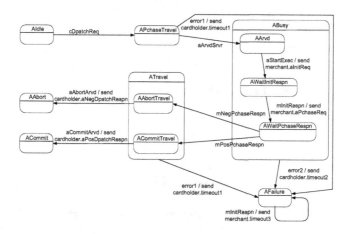

Fig. 11. Statechart diagram of the agent

transaction terminates. A *timeout1* event is generated if the agent fails while travelling to the merchant's server, a *timeout2* event is generated if the agent crashes after arriving at the merchant's server. An inquiry request is sent to the merchant whenever a timeout (*timeout1* or *timeout2*) occurs. Upon receiving an inquiry response from the merchant, the transaction terminates.

ATravel in Figure 11 is a non-concurrent composite state which only one of its direct substates is active at a time. The arrow which connects the source state *APchaseTravel* to the target state *AArvd* is an interlevel transition. It exits the state *APchaseTravel* and enters the substate *AArvd* by crossing the borders of the non-concurrent composite state *ABusy*.

The agent (Figure 11) travels from the cardholder's computer to the merchant's server across the network upon receipt of the dispatch request (*cDpatchReq*). After arriving at the merchant's server, the agent recommences execution, generates an initialization request (*aInitReq*), waits for an initialization response (*mInitRespn*) and returns a purchase request (*aPchaseReq*) to the merchant. On receiving a positive or negative purchase response, the agent departs the merchant's server, travels back to the cardholder's computer and returns a positive or negative dispatch response to the cardholder.

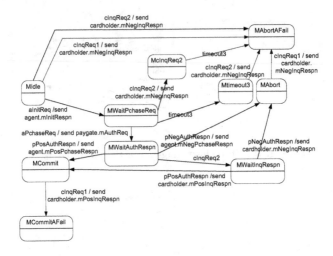

Fig. 12. Statechart diagram of the merchant

Fig. 13. Statechart diagram of the payment gateway

Upon receiving the initialization request (*aInitReq*), the merchant (Figure 12) generates an initialization response (*mInitRespn*), blocks until a purchase request (*aPchaseReq*) is received, sends an authorization request (*mAuthReq*) to the payment gateway and returns a purchase response to the agent when an authorization response is received from the payment gateway.

The payment gateway (Figure 13) returns either a positive or negative authorization response to the merchant according to the issuer's approval code.

4   The π-Calculus

The π-calculus is a process algebra for specifying concurrent systems in which the processes communicate over channels. As many variants of the π-calculus have been proposed, we briefly review the syntax and semantics of the π-calculus in this section. The reader is referred to [13, 17] for details.

We let $\mathcal{A}$ be a set of processes ranged over by P, Q, R, $\mathcal{N}$ be a set of channels (names) ranged over by x, y and $\mathfrak{F}$ be a set of process identifiers. A tuple of channels $x_1, x_2, \ldots, x_n$ is abbreviated to $\vec{x}$. The syntax and semantics of π-calculus process expressions are defined as follows:

$x(\vec{y}).P$: is an input prefix which receives channels along channel x and continues as process P with $y_1, y_2, \ldots, y_n$ replaced by the received channels. The input prefix $x().P$ is abbreviated as $x.P$.

$\overline{x}\langle\vec{y}\rangle.P$: is an output prefix which sends channels $y_1, y_2, \ldots, y_n$ along channel x and continues as process P. The output prefix $\overline{x}\langle\rangle.P$ is abbreviated as $\overline{x}.P$.

$P|Q$: represents concurrent processes P and Q are executing in parallel.

$P + Q$: represents a non-deterministic choice which either process P or Q proceeds. $\Sigma_{i=1}^{n} P_i$ abbreviates $P_1 + \ldots + P_n$.

$(\boldsymbol{\nu}\vec{x})P$: is a restriction which creates new channels $x_1, x_2, \ldots, x_n$ used for communication in process P.

$[x = y]P$: is a matching construct which proceeds as process P if channels x and y are identical; otherwise, behaves like a null process.

$\tau.P$: is an unobservable prefix which performs an internal action τ and continues as process P.

$A(x_1, x_2, \ldots, x_n) \overset{\text{def}}{=} P$: denotes a process identifier A which takes n parameters and behaves like process P. Process P may contain occurrences of A.

The input prefix $x(\vec{y}).P$ and restriction operator $(\boldsymbol{\nu}\vec{x})P$ bind $\vec{y}$ and $\vec{x}$ in P, respectively. Unlike the input prefix, the channels $\vec{y}$ in output prefix $\overline{x}\langle\vec{y}\rangle.P$ are free. The bound names and free names of P are defined as $bn(P)$ and $fn(P)$. The expression $fn(P) \cup fn(Q)$ is abbreviated as $fn(P, Q)$.

In the π-calculus, the notion of open bisimulation is used for determining whether two π-calculus processes are equivalent. Depending on the treatment of the internal actions, open bisimulation is classified into strong open bisimulation and weak open bisimulation. Weak open bisimulation is coarser as it does not differentiate between two π-calculus processes which differ from each other in sequences of internal actions.

5   Encoding Sequence Diagrams in the π-Calculus

In this section, we extend our previous work [9] by providing a theoretical foundation for the analysis and reasoning about the behaviour of sequence diagrams. An examination on how a subset of sequence diagrams are modelled in the π-calculus is given. The formalization is only limited to notational elements which are relevant to this paper. We do not consider synchronous messages, object creation and object destruction.

Rule 1. *Given an object o_1 is an instance of class C_1. The receipt of an asynchronous message e_1 as exemplified in Figure 14 is modelled in the π-calculus as:*

$$S_1(event_{o_1}, \vec{e}) \overset{\text{def}}{=}$$
$$event_{o_1}(x).$$
$$([x = e_1]S_2(event_{o_1}, \vec{e}) +$$
$$\Sigma_{i \neq 1}[x = e_i]S_1(event_{o_1}, \vec{e}))$$

Fig. 14. An incoming asynchronous message

The processes $S_1(event_{o_1}, \vec{e})$ and $S_2(event_{o_1}, \vec{e})$ represent, respectively, the states of the object o_1 before and after the message e_1 is received. The process $S_1(event_{o_1}, \vec{e})$ waits on channel $event_{o_1}(x)$ for an event. If an event e_1 is received, it evolves to process $S_2(event_{o_1}, \vec{e})$. Otherwise, it proceeds as itself.

Rule 2. *Given two objects o_1 and o_2 are instances of classes C_1 and C_2, respectively. The receipt of an asynchronous message e_1 by the object o_1 and the sending of an asynchronous message e_2 to the object o_2 as shown in Figure 15 are encoded in the π-calculus as:*

$$S_1(event_{o_1}, \vec{e}, event_{o_2}) \overset{def}{=}$$
$$event_{o_1}(x).$$
$$([x = e_1]\overline{event_{o_2}}\langle e_2\rangle.S_2(event_{o_1}, \vec{e}, event_{o_2}) +$$
$$\Sigma_{i \neq 1}[x = e_i]S_1(event_{o_1}, \vec{e}, event_{o_2}))$$

Upon receipt of an event e_1, the process $S_1(event_{o_1}, \vec{e}, event_{o_2})$ outputs an event e_2 on channel $event_{o_2}$ and continues as process $S_2(event_{o_1}, \vec{e}, event_{o_2})$.

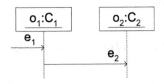

Fig. 15. Incoming and outgoing asynchronous messages

Rule 3. *Given an object o_1 of class C_1. The receipt of asynchronous messages e_1 and e_2 in an alternative combined fragment which corresponds to a choice between two alternatives as illustrated in Figure 16 is implemented in the π-calculus as:*

$$S_1(event_{o_1}, \vec{e}) \overset{def}{=}$$
$$event_{o_1}(x).$$
$$([x = e_1]S_2(event_{o_1}, \vec{e}) +$$
$$[x = e_2]S_3(event_{o_1}, \vec{e}) +$$
$$\Sigma_{i \notin \{1,2\}}[x = e_i]S_1(event_{o_1}, \vec{e}))$$

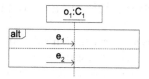

Fig. 16. An *alt* interaction operator

The interaction operator *alt* is represented in the π-calculus as a non-deterministic choice. Depending on whether event e_1 or e_2 is received, the process $S_1(event_{o_1}, \vec{e})$ proceeds as either process $S_2(event_{o_1}, \vec{e})$ or $S_3(event_{o_1}, \vec{e})$.

Example 1. We now illustrate how part of the sequence diagram *Transaction*, which is related to the object *cardholder*, is translated into the π-calculus. To make the π-calculus specifications easier to read, we define an abbreviation as follows:

$$\widetilde{e_{C_1}} = cPchaseReq, cDpatchReq, aPosDpatchRespn, aNegDpatchRespn$$

The sequence diagram *DispatchRequest* (Figure 4), which is referred by the sequence diagram *Transaction* (Figure 1), *AgentFailsWhileTravelling* (Figure 2) and *AgentFailsAfterArriving* (Figure 3), is described according to Rule 2 by the following π-calculus process:

$$C_1(event_C, \widetilde{e_{C_1}}, event_A) \stackrel{\text{def}}{=}$$
$$event_C(x).$$
$$([x = cPchaseReq]\overline{event_A}\langle cDpatchReq\rangle.C_2(event_C, \widetilde{e_{C_1}}, event_A) +$$
$$[x = aPosDpatchRespn]C_1(event_C, \widetilde{e_{C_1}}, event_A) +$$
$$[x = aNegDpatchRespn]C_1(event_C, \widetilde{e_{C_1}}, event_A))$$

The sequence diagram *Transaction* then refers to the sequence diagram *InitRequest*. As the object *cardholder* in the sequence diagram *InitRequest* does not have any incoming or outgoing message, we only need to consider how the alternative combined fragment is transformed into the π-calculus.

Based on Rule 3, the receipt of the messages *aPosDpatchRespn* and *aNegDpatchRespn* in the alternative combined fragment of the sequence diagram *Transaction* is expressed as a π-calculus process of the following form:

$$C_2(event_C, \widetilde{e_{C_1}}, event_A) \stackrel{\text{def}}{=}$$
$$event_C(x).$$
$$([x = aPosDpatchRespn]C_3(event_C, \widetilde{e_{C_1}}, event_A) +$$
$$[x = aNegDpatchRespn]C_4(event_C, \widetilde{e_{C_1}}, event_A) +$$
$$[x = cPchaseReq]C_2(event_C, \widetilde{e_{C_1}}, event_A))$$

Likewise, the objects *agent*, *merchant* and *paygate* in the sequence diagram *Transaction* are translated, respectively, into the π-calculus as 8, 5 and 4 process definitions.

6   Encoding Statechart Diagrams in the π-Calculus

This section presents a subset of translation rules and definitions proposed in [9, 7]. The formalizations of statechart diagrams in the π-calculus presented in [9,7] cover the essential notational elements including events, states, guard-conditions, actions, non-concurrent composite states, concurrent composite states and parameterized events. Unlike our previous work [9,7], this section focuses on the observable behaviour of statechart diagrams rather than on the execution semantics of statechart diagrams. For a formal treatment of execution semantics including run-to-completion step, event queue, conflicting transitions and firing priority scheme, we refer the reader to [9] for details.

We define $\mathcal{SC}$ as a set of statechart diagrams ranged over by F, G, H, $\mathcal{ST}$ as a set of states ranged over by S,T,V,W, $\mathcal{E}$ as a set of events ranged over by E, $\mathcal{E}_p$ as a set of parameterized events ranged over by $E(p_1, \ldots, p_n)$ and $\mathcal{TR}$ as a set of transitions ranged over by t. In addition, an infinite set of natural numbers $\mathbb{N}$ and infinite set of positive integers $\mathbb{Z}^+$ are assumed.

Rule 4. *The function $\phi_{event} : \mathcal{E} \to \mathcal{N}$ maps each event in a statechart diagram to a channel in the π-calculus.*

Rule 5. *The function $\phi_{state} : \mathcal{ST} \to \Im$ returns a unique process identifier for each state. Each process identifier $S_1(event, \vec{e}, \ldots) \in \Im$ is defined as*

$$event(x).([x = e_1] \ldots + \ldots + [x = e_n] \ldots)$$

where $\vec{e}$ stands for $e_1, \ldots, e_n$ and $\forall a \in \{\vec{e}\}.\phi_{event}^{-1}(a) \in \mathcal{E}$.

Rule 4 specifies that an event is modelled as a channel in the π-calculus. The inverse of ϕ_{event} denoted by ϕ_{event}^{-1} is a function from $\mathcal{N}$ to $\mathcal{E}$. Rule 5 stipulates that a state is encoded in the π-calculus as a process. The process determines what the event is by using a number of matching constructs.

We define $\mathcal{A}_{in} = \{x(\vec{y}) | x, \vec{y} \in \mathcal{N}\}$ to be a set of input actions and $\mathcal{A}_{out} = \{\overline{x}\langle\vec{y}\rangle | x, \vec{y} \in \mathcal{N}\}$ to be a set of output actions.

Definition 1. *The function arity: $(\mathcal{A}_{in} \cup \mathcal{A}_{out}) \to \mathbb{N}$ returns the number of channels which an input or output action takes as parameters.*

Rule 6. *A mapping between guard-conditions and output actions is defined as $\phi_{guard} : GCond \to \{\alpha | \alpha \in \mathcal{A}_{out} \wedge arity(\alpha) = 1\}$ where $GCond$ is a set of guard-conditions. The Boolean value of a guard-condition is tested by*

$$\overline{g}\langle x\rangle.x(y).([y = true] \cdots + [y = false] \cdots)$$

where $g, x, y, true, false \in \mathcal{N}$ and $\phi_{guard}^{-1}(\overline{g}\langle x\rangle) \in GCond$.

Rule 7. *Each action representing the invocation of an operation or the sending of a signal to an object is related to an output action in the π-calculus by $\phi_{action} : Act \to \mathcal{A}_{out}$ where Act is a set of actions.*

Rules 6 and 7 say that the guard-condition and action of a transition are both represented as an output action. Rule 6 defines how a guard-condition and its evaluation are formalized. The encoding uses two matching constructs to distinguish between the two truth values.

Rule 8. *The function* $\phi_{pevent} : \mathcal{E}_p \to \mathcal{N}$ *maps a parameterized event to a channel.*

Rule 9. *The receipt of a parameterized event* $E_1(p_1, \ldots, p_n) \in \mathcal{E}_p$ *is encoded as:*

$$event(x).([x = e_1]x(p_1, \ldots, p_n). \cdots + \cdots + [x = e_n] \cdots)$$

Rule 8 states that a parameterized event is translated into a channel. The parameters $p_1, \ldots, p_n$ of the parameterized event E_1 are received along the event channel e_1 as defined by Rule 9.

Definition 2. *The function* substates: $\mathcal{ST} \to 2^{\mathcal{ST}}$ *returns the direct substates that are directly contained in a composite state.*

Rule 10. *A non-concurrent composite state* S_1 *and its active direct substate* V_1 *are denoted as* $\phi_{state}(S_1) | \phi_{state}(V_1)$ *where* $V_1 \in substates(S_1)$ *and* $\phi_{state}(S_1)$ *and* $\phi_{state}(V_1)$ *are defined by:*

$$S_1(event_S, \vec{e}, event_V, pos, neg) \overset{\text{def}}{=}$$
$$event_S(x).(\boldsymbol{\nu}ack)$$
$$\overline{event_V}\langle x\ ack\rangle.ack(y).([y = pos] \cdots + [y = neg] \cdots)$$

$$V_1(event_V, \vec{e}, pos, neg) \overset{\text{def}}{=}$$
$$event_V(x\ ack).$$
$$([x = e_1]\overline{ack}\langle value_1\rangle. \cdots + \cdots + [x = e_n]\overline{ack}\langle value_n\rangle. \cdots)$$

where $value_i \in \{pos, neg\}$ *for* $i = 1, \ldots, n$.
Rules 10 specifies that a non-concurrent composite state and its active direct substates are denoted as processes which are running in parallel. The composite state broadcasts any received events to its substates. As the substates process the received event before the composite state, the lowest-first firing priority of UML semantics is preserved in our translation.

Example 2. The statechart diagrams for the cardholder, agent, merchant and payment gateway are given in Figures 10, 11, 12 and 13, respectively. As an illustration, we translate the states *CBrowseCatalog* and *CWaitPchaseRespn* in Figure 10 into the π-calculus. To improve the readability of the π-calculus specifications, an abbreviation is defined as follows:

$$\widetilde{e_{C_2}} = cPchaseReq, cDpatchReq, aNegDpatchRespn, aPosDpatchRespn,$$
$$timeout1, timeout2, cInqReq1, cInqReq2, mNegInqRespn, mPosInqRespn$$

According to Rules 4, 5 and 7, the state *CBrowseCatalog* is specified in the π-calculus as:

$$CBrowseCatalog(event_C, \widetilde{e_{C_2}}, event_A, event_M) \overset{\text{def}}{=}$$

$event_C(x).$

$([x = cPchaseReq]\overline{event_A}\langle cDpatchReq \rangle.CWaitPchaseRespn(event_C, \widetilde{e_{C_2}},$

$event_A, event_M) +$

$[x = aNegDpatchRespn]CBrowseCatalog(event_C, \widetilde{e_{C_2}}, event_A, event_M) +$

$[x = aPosDpatchRespn]CBrowseCatalog(event_C, \widetilde{e_{C_2}}, event_A, event_M) +$

$[x = timeout1]CBrowseCatalog(event_C, \widetilde{e_{C_2}}, event_A, event_M) +$

$[x = timeout2]CBrowseCatalog(event_C, \widetilde{e_{C_2}}, event_A, event_M) +$

$[x = mNegInqRespn]CBrowseCatalog(event_C, \widetilde{e_{C_2}}, event_A, event_M) +$

$[x = mPosInqRespn]CBrowseCatalog(event_C, \widetilde{e_{C_2}}, event_A, event_M))$

The process *CBrowseCatalog* inputs events on channel $event_C$. On receiving the event *cPchaseReq*, it sends the event *cDpatchReq* on the channel $event_A$ and continues as process *CWaitPchaseRespn*. Otherwise, it proceeds as itself.

In the π-calculus, the state *CWaitPchaseRespn* and the conflicting transitions are encoded as:

$$CWaitPchaseRespn(event_C, \widetilde{e_{C_2}}, event_A, event_M) \overset{\text{def}}{=}$$

$event_C(x).$

$([x = aNegDpatchRespn]CAbort(event_C, \widetilde{e_{C_2}}, event_A, event_M) +$

$[x = aPosDpatchRespn]CCommit(event_C, \widetilde{e_{C_2}}, event_A, event_M) +$

$[x = timeout1]\overline{event_M}\langle cInqReq1 \rangle.CWaitInqRespn(event_C, \widetilde{e_{C_2}}, event_A,$

$event_M) +$

$[x = timeout2]\overline{event_M}\langle cInqReq2 \rangle.CWaitInqRespn(event_C, \widetilde{e_{C_2}}, event_A,$

$event_M) +$

$[x = cPchaseReq]CWaitPchaseRespn(event_C, \widetilde{e_{C_2}}, event_A, event_M) +$

$[x = mNegInqRespn]CWaitPchaseRespn(event_C, \widetilde{e_{C_2}}, event_A, event_M) +$

$[x = mPosInqRespn]CWaitPchaseRespn(event_C, \widetilde{e_{C_2}}, event_A, event_M))$

The conflicting transitions are modelled as a non-deterministic choice which evolves to process *CAbort*, *CCommit* or *CWaitInqRespn* depending on whether the event *aNegDpatchRespn*, *aPosDpatchRespn*, *timeout1* or *timeout2* is received on the channel $event_C$. Similarly, we translate all other states into the π-calculus.

7   Verifying Intra-model Consistency

In UML, the behaviour of a system is modelled as collections of sequence diagrams and statechart diagrams. This section demonstrates the use of weak open bisimulation for verifying that a collection of sequence diagrams and a collection of statechart diagrams are consistent.

We let $\mathcal{SD}$ be a set of sequence diagrams. We define OBJ_{SD} as a set of objects of a sequence diagram $SD \in \mathcal{SD}$.

Definition 3. *The function $\phi : \mathcal{SC} \rightarrow 2^{\mathfrak{S}}$ translates a statechart diagram into the π-calculus as a set of process identifiers.*

Definition 4. *The function $\psi_{obj} : OBJ_{SD} \rightarrow 2^{\mathfrak{S}}$ transforms an object $o \in OBJ_{SD}$ of a sequence diagram $SD \in \mathcal{SD}$ into the π-calculus as a set of process identifiers.*

Definition 5. *The function $\psi_{SD} : \mathcal{SD} \rightarrow 2^{\mathfrak{S}}$, defined below, transforms a sequence diagram $SD \in \mathcal{SD}$ containing a set of objects OBJ_{SD} into the π-calculus as a set of process identifiers.*

$$\psi_{SD}(SD) = \bigcup_{o \in OBJ_{SD}} \psi_{obj}(o)$$

A statechart diagram and an object of a sequence diagram are both encoded in the π-calculus as a set of process identifiers. The transformation of a sequence diagram into the π-calculus is performed incrementally by converting each object of the sequence diagram to its equivalent π-calculus representation using the function ψ_{obj} defined in Definition 4.

Next, we introduce the name substitution function [14, 12, 17] and a number of labelled transitions [17, 24]. Then we recall the notion of weak open bisimulation [17, 23, 20, 18] in the π-calculus.

Definition 6. *The name substitution function $\sigma : \mathcal{N} \rightarrow \mathcal{N}$, written $\{\vec{x}/\vec{y}\}$, replaces each $y_i \in \mathcal{N}$ by $x_i \in \mathcal{N}$ for $1, \ldots, n$.*

The syntax and semantics of labelled transitions used in the definition of weak open bisimulation are given below:

$P \xrightarrow{\alpha} P'$: the execution of action α and process P becomes P'.

$P \Longrightarrow P'$: process P becomes P' after zero or more internal actions.

$P \stackrel{\alpha}{\Longrightarrow} P'$: is equivalent to $P \Longrightarrow \xrightarrow{\alpha} \Longrightarrow P'$.

$P \stackrel{\hat{\alpha}}{\Longrightarrow} P'$: $\begin{cases} P \stackrel{\alpha}{\Longrightarrow} P' \ if \ \alpha \neq \tau \\ P \Longrightarrow P' \ if \ \alpha = \tau \end{cases}$

Definition 7 (Weak Open Bisimulation [17]). *A symmetric binary relation $\mathcal{R}$ on processes is a weak open bisimulation if $(P, Q) \in \mathcal{R}$ implies $\forall \sigma$ whenever $P\sigma \xrightarrow{\alpha} P'$ where $bn(\alpha) \cap fn(P\sigma, Q\sigma) = \emptyset$ then, $\exists Q' : Q\sigma \stackrel{\hat{\alpha}}{\Longrightarrow} Q' \wedge (P', Q') \in \mathcal{R}$. P is weakly open bisimilar to Q, written $P \approx_o Q$, if they are related by a weak open bisimulation.*

We choose open bisimulation rather than early and late bisimulations as (i) the name instantiation of open bisimulation adopts a call-by-need approach which greatly reduces the number of substitutions and provides an efficient path for tool development; and (ii) the automated tool Mobility Workbench (MWB) [23, 24] supports only open bisimulation instead of early and late bisimulations.

Definition 8. *For a statechart diagram $F \in SC$ containing events $E_1, E_2, \ldots$, E_j and an object $o \in OBJ_{SD}$ of a sequence diagram SD consisting of messages $E_1, E_2, \ldots, E_k$ where $j, k \in \mathbb{Z}^+$ and $j \geq k$, the object o is consistent with the statechart diagram F, written $o \precsim_{obj} F$, iff $\psi_{obj}(o) \approx_o (\nu \phi_{event}(E_{k+1}) \phi_{event}(E_{k+2}) \ldots \phi_{event}(E_j)) \phi(F)$.*

We define the consistency between an object of a sequence diagram and a statechart diagram in terms of the weak open bisimulation [17, 23, 20, 18]. The consistency check is limited to the common behaviour of both diagrams through the use of a restriction.

Definition 9. *For a set of statechart diagrams $SC_{sys} \subseteq SC$ of a system sys which contains statechart diagrams F_i for $i = 1, \ldots, n$ and a sequence diagram SD which consists of objects o_i for $i = 1, \ldots, n$, the sequence diagram SD is consistent with the set of statechart diagram SC_{sys}, written $SD \precsim_{SD} SC_{sys}$, iff $\bigwedge_{i=1}^{n}(o_i \precsim_{obj} F_i)$.*

Definition 10. *Given a system sys consisting of a set of statechart diagrams $SC_{sys} \subseteq SC$ and a set of sequence diagrams $SD_{sys} \subseteq SD$ ranged over by SD_i for $i = 1, \ldots, n$, the set of sequence diagrams is consistent with the set of statechart diagrams, written as $SD_{sys} \precsim_{sys} SC_{sys}$, iff $\bigwedge_{i=1}^{n}(SD_i \precsim_{SD} SC_{sys})$.*

A sequence diagram and a set of statechart diagrams are consistent provided that each object of the sequence diagram is consistent with its corresponding statechart diagram in the set of statechart diagrams. Similarly, a set of sequence diagrams and a set of statechart diagrams are consistent if and only if each sequence diagram is consistent with the set of statechart diagrams.

Example 3. To verify the object *cardholder* of the sequence diagram *Transaction* (Figure 1) is consistent with the statechart diagram of the cardholder (Figure 10), we need to prove that the equivalence

$$C_1(event_C, \widetilde{e_{C_1}}, event_A) \approx_o$$
$$(\nu timeout1 \; timeout2 \; cInqReq1 \; cInqReq2 \; mNegInqRespn$$
$$mPosInqRespn \; event_M)$$
$$CBrowseCatalog(event_C, \widetilde{e_{C_2}}, event_A, event_M)$$

This statement of equivalence based on Definition 8 checks whether the corresponding π-calculus specifications of the object *cardholder* of the sequence diagram *Transaction* and statechart diagram of the cardholder are weakly open bisimilar or not.

Table 1. Performance of equivalence checking

	Statechart Diagrams			
	cardholder	agent	merchant	payment gateway
Sequence Diagrams				
Transaction				
cardholder	0.000	-	-	-
agent	-	0.859	-	-
merchant	-	-	0.078	-
paygate	-	-	-	0.000
AgentFailsWhileTravelling				
cardholder	0.016	-	-	-
agent	-	0.016	-	-
merchant	-	-	0.000	-
AgentFailsAfterArriving				
cardholder	0.016	-	-	-
agent	-	0.047	-	-
merchant	-	-	0.000	-

In order to prove the equivalence automatically, the π-calculus specifications are imported into the MWB. Table 1 shows the real time elapsed for the equivalence checking in seconds is 0.000. The value 0.000 means that an equivalence check finishes in a very short time which tends to zero. The test runs under Windows XP on a 2.4 GHz Pentium 4 PC with 512 MB of memory using MWB 3.122.

By a similar line of reasoning, we prove that the objects *agent, merchant* and *payment gateway* of the sequence diagram *Transaction* are weakly open bisimilar to the statechart diagrams of the agent, merchant and payment gateway, respectively. The results for the equivalence checks are given in Table 1. Applying Definition 9, we prove that the sequence diagram *Transaction* is consistent with the set of statechart diagrams of the extended SET/A protocol.

Likewise, we check that the sequence diagrams *AgentFailsWhileTravelling* and *AgentFailsAfterArriving* are consistent with the set of statechart diagrams of the extended SET/A protocol. Based on Definition 10, we conclude that the set of sequence diagrams and the set of statechart diagrams are consistent with respect to the extended SET/A protocol.

8   Conclusions

One of the challenges of UML is how to maintain intra-model consistency (horizontal consistency). In this paper, we have introduced three notions of consistency between (i) an object of a sequence diagram and a statechart diagram; (ii) a sequence diagram and a set of statechart diagrams; and (iii) a set of sequence diagrams and a set of statechart diagrams. The consistency checking problem between sequence diagrams and statechart diagrams is transformed into a problem of verifying whether the corresponding π-calculus specifications are weakly open bisimilar or not using the MWB. A running example, which is an agent-based payment protocol, has been given for illustrating that the proposed approach works in practice. Following the approach of SC2PiCal [8] which translates statechart diagrams into the π-calculus, we are currently developing a tool for transforming sequence diagrams into equivalent π-calculus representations.

References

1. Y. Dumond, D. Girardet, and F. Oquendo. A relationship between sequence and statechart diagrams. In *UML 2000*, 2000. http://www.disi.unige.it/person/ReggioG/UMLWORKSHOP/Girardet.pdf; accessed August 12, 2005.

2. G. Engels, J. Hausmann, R. Heckel, and S. Sauer. Testing the consistency of dynamic UML diagrams. In *IDPT 2002*, 2002. http://wwwcs.upb.de/cs/ag-engels/Papers/2002/EngelsHHS-IDPT02.pdf; accessed February 9, 2005.

3. G. Engels, R. Heckel, J.M. Küster, and L. Groenewegen. Consistency-preserving model evolution through transformations. In *UML 2002*, LNCS 2460, pages 212–227, 2002.

4. G. Engels, J.M. Küster, R. Heckel, and L. Groenewegen. A methodology for specifying and analyzing consistency of object-oriented behavioral models. In *ESEC/SIGSOFT FSE 2001*, pages 186–195. ACM Press, 2001.

5. G. Engels, J.M. Küster, R. Heckel, and L. Groenewegen. Towards consistency-preserving model evolution. In *Proceedings of the International Workshop on Principles of Software Evolution*, pages 129–132. ACM Press, 2002.

6. I. Khriss, M. Elkoutbi, and R. Keller. Automating the synthesis of UML statechart diagrams from multiple collaboration diagrams. In *UML 1998*, LNCS 1618, pages 132–147, 1999.

7. V.S.W. Lam and J. Padget. Consistency checking of statechart diagrams of a class hierarchy. To appear in Proceedings of 19th European Conference on Object-Oriented Programming.

8. V.S.W. Lam and J. Padget. An integrated environment for communicating UML statechart diagrams. To appear in Proceedings of 3rd ACS/IEEE International Conference on Computer Systems and Applications.

9. V.S.W. Lam and J. Padget. On execution semantics of UML statechart diagrams using the π-calculus. In *Proceedings of the International Conference on Software Engineering Research and Practice*, pages 877–882. CSREA Press, 2003.

10. V.S.W. Lam and J. Padget. Formal specification and verification of the SET/A protocol with an integrated approach. In *Proceedings of 2004 IEEE International Conference on E-Commerce Technology*, pages 229–235. IEEE Computer Society, 2004.

11. MasterCard and VISA. *SET Secure Electronic Transaction Books 1–3*, May 1997.

12. R. Milner. The polyadic π-calculus: A tutorial. In *Logic and Algebra of Specification, Proceedings of International NATO Summer School*, volume 94, pages 203–246. Springer-Verlag, 1993.

13. R. Milner. *Communicating and Mobile Systems: the π-Calculus*. Cambridge University Press, 1999.

14. R. Milner, J. Parrow, and D. Walker. A calculus of mobile process (Parts I and II). *Information and Computation*, 100:1–77, 1992.

15. OMG. OMG Unified Modeling Language specification version 1.5, March 2003. http://www.omg.org; accessed January 20, 2005.
16. OMG. UML 2.0 superstructure specification, August 2003. http://www.omg.org; accessed January 20, 2005.
17. J. Parrow. An introduction to the π-calculus. In A. Bergstra, J.A. Ponse and S.A. Smolka, editors, *Handbook of Process Algebra*, chapter 8, pages 479–543. Elsevier Science, 2001.
18. P. Quaglia. The π-calculus: Notes on labelled semantics. *Bulletin of the EATCS*, 68, June 1999.
19. A. Romão and M.M. da Silva. An agent-based secure internet payment system for mobile computing. In *Proceedings of TREC '98*, LNCS 1402, pages 80–93, 1998.
20. D. Sangiorgi. A theory of bisimulation for the π-calculus. In *CONCUR '93*, LNCS 715, pages 127–142, 1993.
21. A. Tsiolakis and H. Ehrig. Consistency analysis between UML class and sequence diagrams using attributed graph gammars. In *Proceedings of GraTra 2000 - Joint APPLIGRAPH and GETGRATS Workshop on Graph Transformation Systems*, pages 77–86, 2000.
22. R. Van Der Straeten, T. Mens, J. Simmonds, and V. Jonckers. Using description logic to maintain consistency between UML models. In *UML 2003*, LNCS 2863, pages 326–340, 2003.
23. B. Victor. *A Verification Tool for the Polyadic π-Calculus*. Department of Computer Systems, Uppsala University, 1994. Licentiate thesis.
24. B. Victor and F. Moller. The mobility workbench: A tool for the π-calculus. In *CAV '94*, LNCS 818, pages 428–440, 1994.
25. J. Whittle and J. Schumann. Generating statechart designs from scenarios. In *Proceedings of the 22nd International Conference on Software Engineering*, pages 314–323, 2000.
26. T. Ziadi, H. Hélouët, and Jean-Marc Jézéquel. Revisiting statechart synthesis with an algebraic approach. In *Proceedings of the 26th International Conference on Software Engineering*, pages 242–251, 2004.

An Integrated Framework for
Scenarios and State Machines

Bikram Sengupta[1] and Rance Cleaveland[2]

[1] IBM India Research Laboratory,
Block 1, Indian Institute of Technology,
Hauz Khas, New Delhi - 110016
bsengupt@in.ibm.com
[2] Department of Computer Science,
SUNY at Stony Brook, Stony Brook, NY 11794-4400, USA
rance@cs.sunysb.edu

Abstract. This paper develops a semantic framework for interpreting heterogeneous system specifications consisting of a mixture of scenario-based requirements and state-based design. Such specifications arise naturally in spiral- and refinement-based development methodologies in which parts of a system have detailed designs while others exist in more abstract form as a collection of requirements. More precisely, we consider the scenario-based notation of Triggered Message Sequence Charts (TMSCs) and the state-based notation of Communicating State Machines (CSMs), and show how they may be integrated in a semantic framework that is founded on the mathematical theory of acceptance trees. Our semantic theory is also equipped with a robust notion of refinement, which allows us to relate one heterogeneous specification with another. A case-study serves to illustrate the utility of our framework as a basis for the principled evolution of higher-level requirements to lower-level operational specifications.

Keywords: scenarios, state-machines, heterogeneous specifications, refinement orderings.

1 Introduction

Ample motivations exist for *heterogeneous specifications* that feature a mixture of high-level requirements and lower-level design artifacts . For example, in spiral system-development processes, requirements elicitation and system design often proceed hand in hand, with new requirements being added into specifications that contain significant design content. Again, intermediate stages of *refinement-based* strategies typically contain mixtures of designs and requirements, while the earliest phases of *component-based* software processes include both requirements for the eventual system to be implemented and detailed models of existing components to be used in the implementation. Finally, the Unified Modeling Language (UML) [13] supports notations for both requirements modeling (sequence diagrams) and operational design (state machines); for a truly "unified" framework, these notations should seamlessly integrate.

Any sort of precise reasoning about such heterogeneous specifications would require a formal semantic theory for uniformly interpreting and relating the constituent

J. Romijn, G. Smith, and J. van de Pol (Eds.): IFM 2005, LNCS 3771, pp. 366–385, 2005.
© Springer-Verlag Berlin Heidelberg 2005

notations. While there have been several efforts towards formalizing individual require-
ments/design languages (e.g. [2, 11]), research in the area of heterogeneous specifications has remained largely confined to the more theoretical domains of process algebra,
temporal logic and mu-calculus (e.g. [18, 5, 17, 20]). However, given the flexibility that
an integrated framework for requirements and design may bring to the development process, it is important to explore how the ideas from theoretical research may be adapted
to more accessible notations used in practice.

The goal of this paper is to propose such a framework for system specifications
consisting of a mixture of higher-level scenario-based requirements and lower-level
state-machine-based subsystem designs. More precisely, we consider the problem of in-
terweaving scenario-based requirements given as Triggered Message Sequence Charts
(TMSCs) [25] and subsystem designs given as Communicating State Machines (CSMs),
and show how they may be freely mixed in a semantic framework that is founded on
acceptance trees [14]. The rest of the paper is structured as follows. Section 2 reviews
relevant background information, while Section 3 details considerations for the formal
combination of TMSCs and CSMs. Section 4 presents a language for defining heterogeneous system specifications based on TMSCs and CSMs, and introduces our notion
of refinement. Section 5 uses a simple case study derived from an actual automated car-
diopulmonary resuscitation device to highlight the utility of our theory. Section 6 then
gives our acceptance-tree semantics for this language, while the remaining sections discuss related work, and offer our conclusions and directions for future research.

2   Background

In this section, we introduce the TMSC and CSM notations and the main ideas behind
the acceptance tree semantic model.

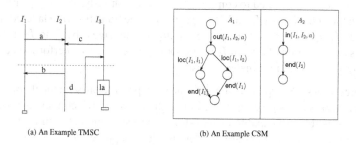

(a) An Example TMSC   (b) An Example CSM

Fig. 1. An Example TMSC and CSM

Triggered Message Sequence Charts: TMSCs have been proposed in [25] as a
scenario-based visual formalism for distributed systems. Like Message Sequence Charts
(MSCs) ([2],[21]), TMSCs describe system scenarios in terms of the sequence of atomic
events (message sends and receives, and local actions) that each parallel process (or *instance*) may engage in. The key novelty of TMSCs is that they enrich the MSC notation
with capabilities to express *conditional* and *partial* behavior.

Graphically, we represent TMSCs as in Fig. 1a. There are two new features in the visual syntax of TMSCs when compared to traditional MSCs. The first is the dashed horizontal line running through the instances, which partitions the sequence of events on an instance's axis into two subsequences: the first, located above the line, constitutes the instance's *trigger*, and the second, below the line, constitutes its *action*. This partition, in effect, forms the basis of a *conditional scenario*: for each instance, the execution of the action is conditional on the occurrence of the trigger. In other words, the behavior of the instance is constrained to its action *only* when it has executed its trigger; otherwise, there are no restrictions. The second new feature in a TMSC is the presence/absence of a small bar at the foot of each instance. The presence of such a bar (as in instance I_1 in Fig 1a) indicates that the instance cannot proceed beyond this point in the TMSC, while the absence (as in instance I_2) means that the behavior of this instance beyond the TMSC is left unspecified i.e. there are no constraints on its subsequent behavior. Such a scenario is thus *partial*, and may be extended in future.

The TMSC in Fig.1a may be read as follows: "If I_1 sends a to I_2, then it should receive b from I_2 and terminate; if I_2 receives a from I_1 and c from I_3, then it should send b to I_1 and d to I_3, and its subsequent behavior is left unspecified; if I_3 sends c to I_2 and receives d from I_2, then it should perform the local-action la and terminate".

Note that the instances are assumed to communicate asynchronously, and the trigger/action requirements are localized to each instance; also, a traditional MSC would correspond to an equivalent TMSC scenario where the trigger of each instance is empty, and all the instances terminate.

Communicating State Machines: In contrast to scenario-based notations that specify a system by depicting the interactions between the instances, state-based notations like Communicating State Machines (CSMs) [10] describe the behavior of the individual instances, with the parallel composition of these machines then describing the system behavior. An example CSM is shown in Fig. 1b. There are two instances in this CSM, I_1 and I_2, which are assumed to communicate asynchronously. A_1 and A_2 are automata describing the behaviors of I_1 and I_2 respectively. The transitions are labeled by events, where: out(I_1, I_2, a) corresponds to the sending of message a by I_1 to I_2; in(I_1, I_2, a) represents the reception of a from I_1 by I_2; loc(I_1, l) denotes the performance of a local action l by I_1; and end terminates an instance.

Acceptance Trees: Acceptance trees and the must preorder arise in the theory of testing of concurrent processes given in [14]. In this theory, tests, which may also be thought of as processes that are capable of reporting "success", interact with a process under test. When processes and tests are nondeterministic, a process may be capable both of passing and failing a test, depending on how nondeterministic choices are resolved. A process *must pass* a test if, regardless of how such choices are made, the process passes the test. One process refines another with respect to the must preorder if it must pass every test that the less refined process must. We now present some of the theory of this relation in a simplified setting in which there are no (1) unobservable actions and (2) divergent processes. We use an alternative characterization of the must preorder that is given in terms of the processes themselves, rather than tests. Specifically, the must preorder may be characterized in terms of *acceptance sets* when the processes are given as Labeled Transitions Systems (LTSs).

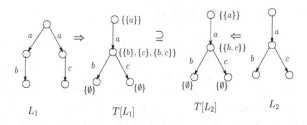

L_1 $T[L_1]$ $T[L_2]$ L_2

Fig. 2. The *must* preorder: $L_1 \sqsubseteq_{\text{must}} L_2$

Definition 1. *Let* $\mathcal{P} = \langle P, E, \longrightarrow, p_I \rangle$ *be a Labeled Transition System (LTS),where* P *is a set of states,* E *a set of events,* $\longrightarrow \subseteq P \times E \times P$ *the transition relation, and* $p_I \in P$ *the start state. Then, for* $p \in P$ *and* $w \in E^*$. *the following may be defined.*

$$L(\mathcal{P}) = \{w \in E^* \mid \exists p' \in P.p_I \xrightarrow{w} p'\} \text{ (Language)}$$
$$S_{\mathcal{P}}(p) = \{a \mid \exists p' \in P.p \xrightarrow{a} p'\} \text{ (Successors)}$$
$$Acc(\mathcal{P}, w) = \{S_{\mathcal{P}}(p') \mid p_I \xrightarrow{w} p'\} \text{ (Acceptance set)}$$

The language of a system contains its "execution sequences", while the successors of a state are the events enabled in the state. The acceptance set of a system after a sequence of events is a measure of nondeterminism: for each state reachable via w from the start state of $\mathcal{P}$, $Acc(\mathcal{P}, w)$ contains as an element, the events that are enabled in that state.

   We now define a *saturation operator*, *sat*, on acceptance sets. Let $\mathcal{A} \subseteq 2^E$; then $sat(\mathcal{A})$ is the least set satisfying:

1. $\mathcal{A} \subseteq sat(\mathcal{A})$.
2. If $A_1, A_2 \in sat(\mathcal{A})$ then $A_1 \cup A_2 \in sat(\mathcal{A})$.
3. If $A_1, A_2 \in sat(\mathcal{A})$ and $A_1 \subseteq A \subseteq A_2$, then $A \in sat(\mathcal{A})$.

The alternative characterization of $\sqsubseteq_{\text{must}}$ can now be given as follows [14].

Theorem 1. *Let* $\mathcal{P}_1 = \langle P_1, E_1, \longrightarrow_1, p_{I_1} \rangle$ *and* $\mathcal{P}_2 = \langle P_2, E_2, \longrightarrow_2, p_{I_2} \rangle$ *be two LTSs, and let* $E = E_1 \cup E_2$. *Then* $\mathcal{P}_1 \sqsubseteq_{\text{must}} \mathcal{P}_2$ *iff for all* $w \in E^*$, $sat(Acc(\mathcal{P}_1, w)) \supseteq sat(Acc(\mathcal{P}_2, w))$.

Intuitively, $\mathcal{P}_2$ refines $\mathcal{P}_1$ if it has "less nondeterminism." This alternative characterization forms the basis for representing processes as *acceptance trees* [14], which map sequences of events to acceptance sets.

Definition 2. *Let* $\mathcal{E}$ *be a finite set of events. Then an* acceptance tree *T is a function in* $\mathcal{E}^* \to 2^{2^{\mathcal{E}}}$ *satisfying:*

1. *For any* $w \in \mathcal{E}^*$, $sat(T(w)) = T(w)$.
2. *For any* $w, w' \in \mathcal{E}^*$, *if* $T(w) = \emptyset$ *then* $T(w \cdot w') = \emptyset$.
3. *For any* $w \in \mathcal{E}^*$, $e \in \mathcal{E}$, $T(w \cdot e) \neq \emptyset$ *iff there exists* $A \in T(w)$ *such that* $e \in A$.

We say that $T_1 \supseteq T_2$ *if for all* $w \in \mathcal{E}^*$, $T_1(w) \supseteq T_2(w)$.

For any LTS $\mathcal{P}$ there is an immediate way to construct an acceptance tree $T[\mathcal{P}]$: $T[\mathcal{P}](w) = sat(Acc(\mathcal{P}, w))$. It immediately follows that $\mathcal{P}_1 \sqsubseteq_{\text{must}} \mathcal{P}_2$ if and only if $T[\mathcal{P}_1] \supseteq T[\mathcal{P}_2]$. For example, in Fig. 2, $L_1 \sqsubseteq_{\text{must}} L_2$ because $T[L_1] \supseteq T[L_2]$.

3   Combining TMSCs and CSMs

As described in the introduction, our goal in this paper is to propose a framework that would allow TMSC and CSM specifications to interoperate. Our work is motivated by the fact that achieving a clean separation between requirements (where MSC-like scenarios are most often used) and design phases (where state-based notations are popular), as envisaged by the waterfall model of development, is frequently not feasible in practice. Firstly, requirements may change, or new requirements may emerge even as design proceeds, and these often have to be factored into the development process immediately. Secondly, a design prototype often provides an opportunity for detecting new/missed requirements, which may lead to a modification of the existing design. Then again, state machines are used as detailed requirements specification in many areas of practice e.g. aerospace industry, or they become de-facto requirements when non-functional requirements prescribe the re-use of existing state-based designs. For these reasons, scenarios and state machines frequently need to co-exist; while modeling languages like the UML include both notations, there is no underlying theory/framework that supports meaningful combination of scenarios and state machines. A truly unified approach to system development needs to address this missing link.

3.1   Semantic Considerations for a Common Framework

A natural question that arises is what are the requirements on an integrated framework for TMSCs and CSMs. Scenario-based approaches like TMSCs and state-machine descriptions like CSMs both specify system behavior in terms of sequences of events that may occur. However, the key difference is that a TMSC shows just one possible interaction between the instances; it is inherently incomplete in that no information is given about what else might happen. State-machine based descriptions like CSMs, on the other hand, are inherently more complete. The individual behavior of each instance is given, not in the context of a particular interaction, but generally over all of the interactions the instance takes part in; a behavior that is not explicitly shown, may thus be assumed to be *forbidden*.

Accordingly, any common account of TMSCs and CSMs should have the following features. (1) It should be able to express both underspecified behavior (e.g. TMSCs) as well as fully specified behavior (e.g. CSMs) in a uniform manner. (2) It should provide operators so that multiple scenarios may be woven together to provide more complete behavioral descriptions; it should allow networks of CSMs to be formed; it should also allow existing designs/requirements to be constrained by new requirements. (3) It should prescribe when one heterogeneous specification refines another; this relation should, among other things, define when a CSM correctly implements a TMSC specification.

We argue that a framework based on acceptance trees will have the right ingredients in these respects. Firstly, acceptance trees capture behavior that is execution-based, as is the case with TMSCs and CSMs. Secondly, acceptance sets can be used to represent behaviors at various levels of detail: informally, the less specified the behavior, the larger will be the acceptance set, whereas a singleton acceptance set will indicate fully specified (i.e. deterministic) behavior. Finally, the must pre-order is a robust refinement relation already defined on acceptance trees, that may be used to check the relationship between scenarios, state-machines, and a mixture of these notations, once they are interpreted as acceptance trees.

4   A Common Framework

We will now present a framework for integrating TMSCs and CSMs that is based on the ideas outlined above. The framework is an extension of the model we previously developed for TMSC-based requirements specifications [25] [23]. To support heterogeneity, we now advance that work in the following directions: (i) First, we incorporate facilities for describing state-based behavior of individual instances, and for composing these behaviors to generate CSMs. These are seamlessly integrated into our specification language to provide support for heterogeneous models. We also discuss practical considerations that arise from this integration (ii) In the next section, we illustrate through an extended case-study, how TMSC requirements and CSM designs may be interweaved using our integrated framework. The example is intended to give insight into the methodological aspects of the integration (iii) Finally, in Section 6, we present the formal semantics of the framework. The key additions are the acceptance tree semantics of individual state machines, their composition, and associated properties. Interestingly, this development helped us improve our previous formulation of the TMSC semantics, which we also outline.

We begin by presenting the syntactic details of the framework. The basic units of the framework are single TMSC scenarios (e.g. Fig. 1a) and single *instance state machines* (ISMs), e.g. A_1 in Fig. 1b. In addition, the framework offers a suite of composition operators, presented in the grammar below. The operators are driven by three considerations one may have for organizing system definitions. (i) *Structural:* A system might consist of parallel components, each with its individual requirements/design specification. The operators belonging to this category are $\bullet$ and $\|$. (ii) *Temporal:* A system might consist of several phases (e.g. initialization, operation, termination), occurring in a given order and specified independently. This is captured through the ; operator. Repetitive cycles may be captured through recursion (X). (iii) *Alternative:* Multiple specifications might be provided for a given behavior description, with the understanding that some or all of the specifications must be met. The $\mp$ and $\oplus$ operators support this consideration.

In addition, a requirements specification often contains a set of constraints "and"-ed together, which is captured through the $\wedge$ operator.

The specifications that may be built through the use of these operators are called "heterogeneous expressions", defined by the following grammar:

$$
\begin{array}{lll}
H ::= & M & \text{(single TMSC)} \\
\mid & S & \text{(single ISM)} \\
\mid & X & \text{(variable)} \\
\mid & H \bullet H & \text{(communicating parallel composition)} \\
\mid & H \parallel H & \text{(interleaving parallel composition)} \\
\mid & H \mp H & \text{(delayed choice)} \\
\mid & H \oplus H & \text{(internal choice)} \\
\mid & H ; H & \text{(sequential composition)} \\
\mid & H \wedge H & \text{(logical and)} \\
\mid & recX.H & \text{(recursive operator)}
\end{array}
$$

We now briefly explain the intended meaning of each operator. $\bullet$ is a communication operator between instances that are running concurrently. It is used to connect instance state-machines, and also instances within a single TMSC. $H_1 \parallel H_2$ denotes the "interleaving" parallel composition of expressions H_1 and H_2: it allows the interleaving of events from H_1 and H_2 while the expressions execute independently. $H_1 \mp H_2$ represents the "deterministic choice" between H_1 and H_2: a correct refinement must be able to behave like both H_1 and H_2 until their behaviors differ, at which point a choice is allowed. $H_1 \oplus H_2$ is the nondeterministic choice between H_1 and H_2; a successful refinement can choose either. In this respect $\oplus$ has overtones of logical disjunction. $H_1; H_2$ denotes the "instance-level" (asynchronous) sequential composition [3, 21]; an instance in H_1 is intended to execute to completion before being resumed in H_2, although an instance that terminates in H_1 may "continue" in H_2 even though other instances in H_1 have not finished. $H_1 \wedge H_2$ represents logical conjunction, and is primarily used in our framework to weave together individual constraints on system behavior and for refining initial design prototypes. Finally, the recursive operator $recX$ allows us to model infinite behavior of processes, where a new execution cycle starts whenever there is a reference to the variable used in the recursive definition (say X). Our framework may be extended further to include *scope* through the use of process algebraic constructs like *restriction* [22].

Practical Considerations. While our theory permits these operators to be used on any type of heterogeneous expressions, in practice, we anticipate that some operators may apply more readily to scenarios, and others to state-machines. For example, the operators $\mp$, $\oplus$ and $\parallel$ will probably be more useful in joining TMSC scenarios rather than instance state machines, since in the latter, choices are local and the notion of parallel execution is intrinsically linked to inter-instance communication (captured by $\bullet$). The same is the case with rec, since infinite behavior in state-machines may be easily expressed through loops. However, the sequential composition operator, ;, may be useful in connecting CSMs also, since it composes instance-by-instance i.e. it is based on the same level of granularity as CSMs. Finally $\wedge$ is a truly heterogeneous operator. It can be used to combine multiple TMSCs, each representing a different constraint, and also in combining an initial CSM design with a TMSC constraint to *refine* the former.

The formal semantics of heterogeneous expressions will be presented in Section 6. The basic idea is to interpret an expression H as an acceptance tree $T^\sigma[H]$, where σ is an environment mapping variables to acceptance trees, and is needed because heterogeneous expressions may contain variables. This will allow us to formulate a refinement relationship on heterogeneous expressions as follows:

Definition 3. *Let H_1 and H_2 be heterogeneous expressions. Then $H_1 \sqsubseteq_{must} H_2$ if and only if $T^\sigma[H_1] \supseteq T^\sigma[H_2]$, for any σ.*

Tool Support. Practical support for the above framework may be provided through the use of two tools, the Concurrency Workbench [6] and the Process Algebra Compiler [19]. These provide a platform where semantic rules may be encoded for constructing acceptance trees from heterogeneous expressions, which may also be checked for *refinement*. The TRIM tool [4] for TMSCs is based on this approach. Detailed discussion on this is however, beyond the scope of the current paper.

5 Case Study: Automated Resuscitation and Stabilization System

To illustrate the practical utility of our integrated framework, we will now present a case study in which TMSCs and CSMs will be effectively interweaved to support a step-wise evolution of system behavior from requirements to design. The system we consider is a medical device called Automated Resuscitation and Stabilization System (ARSS), which is a simplified version [24] of an automated resuscitation system developed by the Walter Reed Army Institute of Research [1]. The specification will be derived formally in a series of refinement steps, starting with high-level requirements expressed through TMSC scenarios, moving through intermediate heterogeneous descriptions consisting of a mixture of scenarios and state machines, and ultimately leading to precise per-instance state-based behavioral definitions.

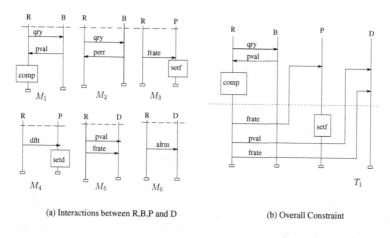

(a) Interactions between R,B,P and D   (b) Overall Constraint

Fig. 3. System Requirements

ARSS consists of a blood pressure measuring device (B), an infusion pump (P), a display and alarm unit (D), and a software component (R) that controls the resuscitation process. The goal is to automatically track a patient's blood pressure, and add fluids as necessary to stabilize the patient's condition. Each of B, P and D interacts only with R, and not with each other. Thus R and any one of the other physical units essentially form a *sub-system*, whose behavior may be independently modeled.

The requirements for ARSS are given by two types of scenarios: (i) there are MSC-like traditional scenarios depicting the possible interactions in each sub-system (Fig. 3a); these are grouped together using appropriate operators, to yield sub-system requirements specifications (ii) in addition, conditional scenarios based on TMSCs are used to convey requirements that span sub-systems (Fig. 3b).

Sub-system Requirements R and B. The possible interactions between R and B are depicted in TMSCs M_1 and M_2. R sends a query message (qry) to B and B responds by either sending the current blood-pressure *pval* to R (as in M_1), or sending an error message *perr* to R (as in M_2) in case there was an error in reading the pressure

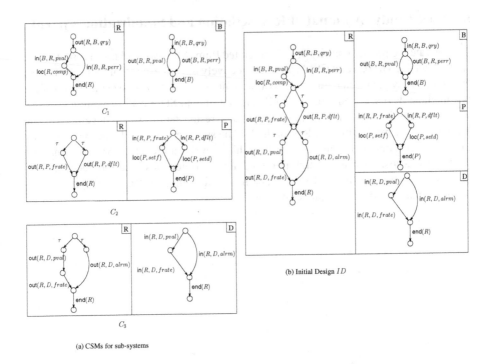

Fig. 4. Initial Design

(e.g. if the pressure source is lost for some reason). If R receives the correct value, it uses the current pressure to determine the rate at which fluids should be supplied to the patient; this is indicated by the local-action *comp*. The overall interaction between R and B is specified by the TMSC expression $RB = M_1 \mp M_2$. We use $\mp$ because the choice between M_1 and M_2 is *delayed* until B sends either *pval* or *perr* to R.

R and P. R may send two types of messages to P: (i) under normal operation, it sends the rate (*frate*) at which P should supply fluids to the patient (M_3) (ii) in case R is unable to compute the correct rate, it asks P to set the rate to a pre-determined safe default value (*dflt*) (M_4). In each case, P responds to these messages by performing appropriate local-actions to adjust the flow. The specification for this sub-system is given by $RP = M_3 \oplus M_4$. Here $\oplus$ is used because whether R can correctly compute the flow-rate depends on factors (in this case R's interaction with B) that are outside the purview of the interaction between R and P.

R and D. R may interact with D in the following ways: (i) R sends the current pressure value *pval* and flow-rate *frate* for display to D. This is depicted by the TMSC scenario M_5 (ii) if immediate attention of the care-giver is required, then R instructs D to sound an alarm (*alrm*), as shown in M_6. The interaction between R and D is expressed by $RD = M_5 \oplus M_6$. As before, $\oplus$ is used as the choice will be made internally by R depending on its interaction with the rest of the system.

Overall Constraints. These requirements constrain the way the sub-systems interact, and their role is to ensure that the desired functionality of the overall system is preserved. For ARSS, TMSC T_1 in Fig. 3b, is the initial global requirement that has to be satisfied. T_1 constrains the system behavior when the blood pressure has been read correctly, and ensures that the correct flow-rate is set and displayed when this happens.

Requirements Specification. We now glue together the "local" and "global" requirements to get the initial requirements specification. R begins each cycle by querying B about the current blood-pressure. It subsequently sends messages to P and D to control the flow-rate, and display appropriate messages or warn the care-giver. The base requirements BS is thus given by

$$BS = RB; RP; RD$$

These requirements are however, too coarse, and may lead to some undesirable execution sequences e.g. R sounding the alarm even when the pressure has been read correctly. Hence, the global constraint T_1 is used to refine BS. The initial requirements specification is thus given by

$$RS = BS \wedge T_1$$

Initial Design. The availability of sub-system level requirements means that instead of trying to design the whole system in a single attempt, we can first design each sub-system in isolation. A major benefit of this approach is that it promotes modular design and greatly aids subsequent system maintenance. Hence in the next step, we consider

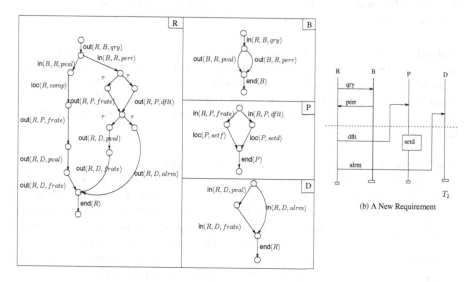

(a) Refined Design RD

(b) A New Requirement

Fig. 5. Refined Design

CSMs (Fig. 4a) for each scenario-based sub-system specification obtained above. It may be shown that $RB \sqsubseteq_{\text{must}} C_1$, $RP \sqsubseteq_{\text{must}} C_2$ and $RD \sqsubseteq_{\text{must}} C_3$. Note that R's τ transitions in C_2 and C_3 reflect the fact that it has to internally choose between M_3 and M_4 in RP and between M_5, M_6 in RD. Also, the $\bullet$ operator is implicit in each design e.g. C_1 is actually $A_R \bullet A_B$, where A_R and A_B denote the state-machines of R and B respectively, in C_1.

Replacing the sub-system specifications in BS by the corresponding refined CSMs, we obtain:

$$BS' = C_1; C_2; C_3$$

From the compositionality of our semantics (Section 6), it follows that $BS \sqsubseteq_{\text{must}} BS'$.

We now sequentially compose C_1, C_2 and C_3, to obtain our initial design ID, shown in Fig 4b. The state-machines for B, P and D in ID are the same as in BS'. The state-machine for R is obtained by "stitching" together its state machines in C_1, C_2 and C_3. Since R will terminate a cycle only after its interaction with D, this state machine is obtained by removing the $\text{end}(R)$ transition in C_1 (and C_2), and starting the execution of C_2 (and C_3) instead. We thus obtain the state-machine for R as shown in ID. It can again be proved that $BS' \sqsubseteq_{\text{must}} ID$. By transitivity of $\sqsubseteq_{\text{must}}$, we get the sequence $BS \sqsubseteq_{\text{must}} BS' \sqsubseteq_{\text{must}} ID$.

Intermediate Heterogeneous Design. Since $BS \sqsubseteq_{\text{must}} ID$, our initial design conforms to the base requirements. However, we now need to refine ID to ensure that it also satisfies the "global" constraint represented by T_1. Thus a "tighter" specification for the design is $ID \wedge T_1$. This heterogeneous expression enables us to precisely capture the current design state, where we have a coarse state-based design that must satisfy an additional scenario requirement T_1.

Refined Design. Since the constraint in T_1 is localized to each instance, and since we already have ISMs for these instances, refining ID is easy. We simply "walk through" each ISM in ID and remove execution traces that do not conform to the constraint on the instance as documented in T_1. This gives us the refined design RD (Fig. 5a). Note that in RD, unlike in ID, R always correctly sets the flow and displays messages on receiving $pval$.

New Requirement. In spiral/refinement-based development processes, new requirements are incrementally added to existing designs/prototypes. Now that we have a design RD that refines the requirements specification RS, let us assume that a new requirement T_2 (Fig. 5b) is added, which specifies how R should handle the erroneous condition when the pressure source is lost. Such a requirement may simply be part of the "scope" of the current iteration (e.g. requirements for normative (T_1) and erroneous (T_2) behavior may be handled in separate iterations of spiral development) or may have been discovered by analyzing the existing design (e.g. the CSM for R in RD indicates that R does not always sound the alarm when the pressure source is lost, i.e. when it receives $perr$); either way, the new requirement combined with the existing design is specified by the heterogeneous expression $RD \wedge T_2$.

Final Design. The behavior of R in RD is then refined to ensure that execution traces that violate T_2 are removed. Now that both normal and erroneous behaviors have been accounted for, the designers may choose CSM FD in Fig. 6 as the final design.

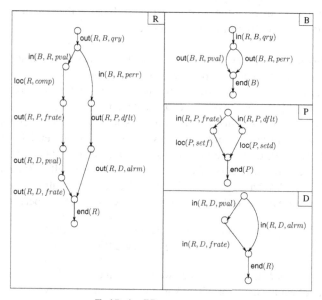

Final Design FD

Fig. 6. Final Design

It may be shown that $RD \wedge T_2 \sqsubseteq_{\text{must}} FD$. We thus have the sequence $RS \sqsubseteq_{\text{must}} BS'$ $\wedge T_1 \sqsubseteq_{\text{must}} ID \wedge T_1 \sqsubseteq_{\text{must}} RD \sqsubseteq_{\text{must}} RD \wedge T_2 \sqsubseteq_{\text{must}} FD$, as the specification evolved from scenario-based requirements (RS), to an imprecise CSM-based initial design (ID), that was refined using the requirement T_1 to get RD, which was again constrained using a new requirement T_2, to finally yield the correct design (FD).

Discussion. The above case study illustrates some general methodological advantages that our integrated framework offers. By providing a common platform for scenarios and state machines, the requirements and design phases are allowed to overlap. Thus we can have an initial design that implements base requirements, and then impose additional requirements on it. The final design may be built incrementally through several iterations, some involving scenarios, some state machines, and others a mix of both. Equally importantly, the framework brings technical rigor to bear on this process; while *compositionality* of the semantics supports uniform reasoning and promotes modular design, the precise notion of *refinement* provides a formal basis for assessing at each step, whether or not a more detailed specification is indeed faithful to the specification it is intended to elaborate on.

6   Semantics of Heterogeneous Expressions

We will now describe how heterogeneous expressions may be formally interpreted as acceptance trees. First, ISMs will be equipped with an acceptance tree semantics. Next we will define the • operator that may be used to weave ISMs into CSMs. We then describe how similar ideas may be used to derive acceptance trees of individual TM-SCs from acceptance trees of the TMSC instances. Finally, the semantics of the other operators, and also their properties are mentioned.

Events and Sequences. We fix finite sets $\mathbb{I}$, $\mathbb{M}$ and $\mathbb{A}$ as the set of all instances, message types and local action names, respectively. We write $\mathbb{R} = \{\mathsf{in}(I_i, I_j, m) \mid I_i, I_j \in \mathbb{I}, m \in \mathbb{M}\}$ for the set of all receive events, and similarly define $\mathbb{S} = \{\mathsf{out}(I_i, I_j, m) \mid I_i, I_j \in \mathbb{I}, m \in \mathbb{M}\}$ as the set of all send events, and $\mathbb{L} = \{\mathsf{loc}(I_i, \ell) \mid I_i \in \mathbb{I}, \ell \in \mathbb{A}\}$ as the set of all local actions. Our semantics also uses events of form $\mathsf{end}(I_i)$, where $I_i \in \mathbb{I}$, which instances emit when they terminate, and "potential events" of form $\mathsf{wait}(r)$, where $r \in \mathbb{R}$, to denote that an instance is capable of performing r once the corresponding send event occurs. $\mathbb{T}$ and $\mathbb{W}$ denote the set of all end events and wait events respectively. We write $\mathbb{E} = \mathbb{S} \cup \mathbb{R} \cup \mathbb{L} \cup \mathbb{T}$ as the set of all concrete events that may occur. For any event e, $\mathsf{active}(e)$ returns the instance that can perform e.

$$\mathsf{active}(e) = \begin{cases} I_i & \text{if } e = \mathsf{out}(I_i, I_j, m), \mathsf{loc}(I_i, \ell), \mathsf{end}(I_i) \\ I_j & \text{if } e = \mathsf{in}(I_i, I_j, m), \mathsf{wait}(\mathsf{in}(I_i, I_j, m)) \end{cases}$$

For any set of events E and instances $\mathcal{I}$, we then define $E_\mathcal{I} = \{e \mid e \in E, \mathsf{active}(e) \in \mathcal{I}\}$, i.e. the set of events in E for which some instance in $\mathcal{I}$ is active.

Definition 4. *Let* $w, w_1, w_2 \in \mathbb{E}^*$.

1. *$w_1 \preceq w_2$ holds if w_1 is a prefix of w_2. Also, $|w|_a$ denotes the number of occurrences of a in w.*
2. *The* projection, *$w \lfloor \mathcal{I}$, of w onto $\mathcal{I} \subseteq \mathbb{I}$ is the longest (not necessarily contiguous) subsequence of w containing only events in which instances in $\mathcal{I}$ are active:*

$$w \lfloor \mathcal{I} = \begin{cases} \epsilon & \text{if } w = \epsilon \\ e \cdot (w' \lfloor \mathcal{I}) & \text{if } w = e \cdot w', \mathsf{active}(e) \in \mathcal{I} \\ w' \lfloor \mathcal{I} & \text{if } w = e \cdot w', \mathsf{active}(e) \notin \mathcal{I} \end{cases}$$

3. *The receive event $\mathsf{in}(I_i, I_j, m)$ is called* enabled *by w if $|w|_{\mathsf{out}(I_i, I_j, m)} > |w|_{\mathsf{in}(I_i, I_j, m)}$. We use $e\mathcal{R}(w)$ to stand for all receive events enabled by w.*
4. *w is called* well-balanced *over an instance set $\mathcal{I}$ if for every $w' \preceq w$ such that $w' = w'' \cdot \mathsf{in}(I_i, I_j, m)$ and $I_i \in \mathcal{I}$, it is the case that $\mathsf{in}(I_i, I_j, m) \in e\mathcal{R}(w'')$.*

Acceptance Sets and Trees. If $\mathcal{A}_1$ and $\mathcal{A}_2$ are two acceptance sets, then we define

$$\mathcal{A}_1 \otimes \mathcal{A}_2 = sat\{A_1 \cup A_2 \mid A_1 \in \mathcal{A}_1, A_2 \in \mathcal{A}_2\}$$

$\otimes$ thus takes the saturated pairwise union of the operand acceptance sets. We use $\otimes_{k \in K}$ as the indexed version of $\otimes$.

By $T_{\mathcal{I}}$, we will denote an acceptance tree constructed over an universe of instances $\mathcal{I} \subseteq \mathbb{I}$. Acceptance trees will ultimately be defined over the set of all instances $\mathbb{I}$, and such acceptance trees are represented as $T_{\mathbb{I}}$, or simply T. However, as we will see, we may sometimes need to start with a reduced universe, say $\mathcal{I}$, and then "lift" it to a bigger universe, say $\mathcal{J} \supseteq \mathcal{I}$. This is done using a function $lift(\mathcal{J}, T_{\mathcal{I}}) = T_{\mathcal{J}}$, where,

$$T_{\mathcal{J}}(w) = \emptyset, \quad \text{if}$$

$$\quad \text{(i) } \exists e \in w.\mathsf{active}(e) \notin \mathcal{J}, \text{ or}$$

$$\quad \text{(ii) } \exists e \in w.\mathsf{active}(e) = I_p \in \mathcal{J} - \mathcal{I} \wedge e \neq \mathsf{end}(I_p), \text{ or}$$

$$\quad \text{(iii) } \exists I_p \in \mathcal{J}.|w|_{\mathsf{end}(I_p)} > 1$$

$$= \{S\} \otimes T_{\mathcal{I}}(w \lfloor \mathcal{I}) \quad \text{otherwise}$$

where, $S = \{\mathsf{end}(I_p) \mid I_p \in \mathcal{J} - \mathcal{I} \wedge \mathsf{end}(I_p) \notin w\}$. $lift$ "lifts" an acceptance tree defined using a restricted universe of instances $\mathcal{I}$, to the larger universe of instances $\mathcal{J}$, by adding in $\mathsf{end}(I_p)$ events $\forall I_p \in \mathcal{J} - \mathcal{I}$. Intuitively, when we have a specification S in which some instances are "missing", but we need to define an acceptance tree for S, we assume that all instances not explicitly mentioned in S are only capable of terminating. Towards that end, we define $Ins(S)$ to be the set of instances that are explicitly mentioned in S, where $Ins(M) = \mathcal{I}$, where M is a TMSC with instance set $\mathcal{I}$, $Ins(S_1 op S_2) = Ins(S_1) \cup Ins(S_2)$, where op is any of the heterogeneous binary operators, etc.

6.1 ISMs as Acceptance Trees

An Instance State Machine or ISM is a tuple $\langle I_p, A_p \rangle$, where I_p is the name of the instance, and $A_p = \langle Q_p, q_p^0, E_p, \delta_p \rangle$ represents the operational behavior of instance I_p, defined over a set of states Q_p, a start state q_p^0, a set of events E_p $(= \mathbb{E}_{\{I_p\}})$, and a transition relation $\delta_p \subseteq Q_p \times (E_p \cup \{\tau\}) \times Q_p$, where τ is a distinguished internal action used to represent internal nondeterministic choice behavior. Given any two states $q, q' \in Q_p$ we write $q \xrightarrow{e} q'$ in lieu of $(q, e, q') \in \delta_p$, and $q \xRightarrow{e} q'$, if there is a path from q to q' that contains event e, preceded or succeeded by some number of τ transitions. For a sequence of events w, $q \xRightarrow{w} q'$, if $q \xRightarrow{e_1} q_1 \xRightarrow{e_2} q_2 \ldots \xRightarrow{e_n} q'$, where $w = e_1 \ldots e_n$, and q_1, q_2 etc. are intermediate states. Note that although we handle τ transitions in an ISM (in the same manner as [14]), we do not permit divergence i.e. infinite τ transitions. We define $L(A_p)$, the language of A_p as the set of all its execution sequences: $L(A_p) = \{w \in E_p^* \mid \exists q' \in Q_p.q_p^0 \xRightarrow{w} q'\}$ Also, for $q \in Q_p$, let $Ev(q) = \{e \mid \exists q' \in Q_p.q \xrightarrow{e} q'\}$. $Ev(q)$ thus denotes the set of events labeling the outgoing transitions of state q in the automaton A_p. Finally, for a set of concrete (i.e. non-wait) events E, we define the enabled set $EN(E)$ as:

$$EN(E) = \{e \mid e \in E \wedge e \notin \mathbb{R}\} \cup \{\mathsf{wait}(r) \mid r \in \mathbb{R} \cap E\}$$

An out, loc and end is always enabled; an in event $r \in \mathbb{R}$ is not enabled unless the sender emits the corresponding out, and until then $\mathsf{wait}(r)$ is enabled.

Definition 5. *The acceptance tree* $T^\sigma_{\{I_p\}}[I]$ *of an ISM* $I = \langle I_p, A_p \rangle$, *after a sequence of events* $w \in E_p^*$ *and for an environment* σ *is defined as:*

$$T^\sigma_{\{I_p\}}[I](w) = \begin{cases} \emptyset & \\ \quad \text{if } w \notin L(A_p) & \\ sat\{EN(Ev(q')) \mid q_p^0 \overset{w}{\Longrightarrow} q', q' \not\longrightarrow\} & \\ \quad \text{otherwise} & \end{cases}$$

The acceptance tree $T^\sigma[I]$ is now defined as $T^\sigma[I] = lift(\mathbb{I}, T_{\{I_p\}})$.

6.2   CSMs: Network of ISMs

We will now describe the semantics of CSMs. Intuitively, CSMs consist of a "network" of ISMs connected via the $\bullet$ operator. Accordingly, the acceptance tree for a CSM C consisting of ISMs $\{IS_1, IS_2, \ldots IS_n\}$ will be derived by by first computing the acceptance trees of the individual ISMs in isolation, and then allowing them to communicate, so that a message sent by one instance may be received by another.

When we combine the acceptance sets of two ISMs that are communicating, the wait events have to be handled carefully. Firstly, some of the wait events may now become concrete in events; e.g. if I_p is waiting to receive m from I_q, then wait(in(I_q, I_p, m)) becomes in(I_q, I_p, m) when I_p and I_q are allowed to communicate and I_q sends m to I_p. Secondly, if I_p is capable of receiving a message m that I_q has sent, then our semantics disallows I_p from continuing to wait for any other message from I_q (though it can wait for messages from other instances). Accordingly, we define two functions, *convert-wait* to transform wait events into in events once the relevant messages have been sent, and *remove-wait* to disable wait events when another in event involving the same sender becomes enabled. These are defined below, where $\mathcal{A}$ is any acceptance set, and R any set of in events (that have become enabled).

$$convert\text{-}wait(\mathcal{A}, R) = \bigcup_{A \in \mathcal{A}} \{convert\text{-}wait\text{-}set(A, R)\}$$

$$convert\text{-}wait\text{-}set(A, R) = \bigcup_{e \in A} convert\text{-}wait\text{-}event(e, R)$$

$$convert\text{-}wait\text{-}event(e, R) = \begin{cases} \{e\} & \text{if } (e \in \mathbb{S} \cup \mathbb{R} \cup \mathbb{L} \cup \mathbb{T}) \\ & \vee(e = \text{wait}(r) \wedge r \notin R) \\ \{r\} & \text{if } e = \text{wait}(r) \wedge r \in R \end{cases}$$

In an analogous way, we can define *remove-wait*($\mathcal{A}$), which ultimately invokes

$$remove\text{-}wait\text{-}event(e, A) = \begin{cases} \emptyset & \text{if } e = \text{wait}(\text{in}(I_i, I_j, m)) \\ & \wedge \exists m'.\text{in}(I_i, I_j, m') \in A \\ \{e\} & \text{otherwise} \end{cases}$$

for each $A \in \mathcal{A}$. We now define a new function *handle-wait*, that takes an acceptance set $\mathcal{A}$ and an event sequence w, and suitably modifies the wait events in $\mathcal{A}$ based on the in events enabled by w: *handle-wait*($\mathcal{A}, w$) = $sat(remove\text{-}wait(convert\text{-}wait(\mathcal{A}, e\mathcal{R}(w))))$. We are now in a position to define the semantics of the $\bullet$ operator.

Definition 6. *Let H_1 and H_2 be two heterogeneous expressions where $Ins(H_1) = \mathcal{I}_1$, and $Ins(H_2) = \mathcal{I}_2$, and let $\mathcal{I} = \mathcal{I}_1 \cup \mathcal{I}_2$. Then, for $w \in \mathbb{E}_{\mathcal{I}}^*$, and an environment σ,*

$$T_{\mathcal{I}}^{\sigma}[H_1 \bullet H_2](w) = \emptyset, \quad \text{if}$$

$$\text{(i) } \mathcal{I}_1 \cap \mathcal{I}_2 \neq \emptyset, \text{ or}$$

$$\text{(ii) } w \text{ is not well-balanced over } \mathcal{I}$$

$$= \textit{handle-wait}((T_{\mathcal{I}_1}^{\sigma}[H_1](w_1) \otimes T_{\mathcal{I}_2}^{\sigma}[H_2](w_2)), w)$$

$$\text{o.w., where } w_1 = w \lfloor \mathcal{I}_1, w_2 = w \lfloor \mathcal{I}_2$$

We then have $T_{\mathcal{J}}^{\sigma}[H_1 \bullet H_2] = \textit{lift}(\mathcal{J}, T_{\mathcal{I}}^{\sigma}[H_1 \bullet H_2])$, and when $\mathcal{J} = \mathbb{I}$, we get $T^{\sigma}[H_1 \bullet H_2]$. Note that when H_1 and H_2 are ISMs, $H_1 \bullet H_2$ is a CSM, which may communicate with another ISM through $\bullet$. In fact the clause $\mathcal{I}_1 \cap \mathcal{I}_2 = \emptyset$ in the above definition is there primarily because we want to use $\bullet$ to compose state-machines of instances.

6.3   From TMSCs to Acceptance Trees

We now briefly sketch how single TMSCs may be interpreted as acceptance trees. The definition that we present here improves the one in [25], [23], where the acceptance tree of an instance in a TMSC was computed with respect to an environment that represented the set of enabled in events. Thus the acceptance tree function for an instance needed an additional parameter to model this environment. In contrast, here we first compute "pure" acceptance trees of instances, and then compose the trees in the same manner in which ISMs were composed using $\bullet$ to yield CSMs. This leads to a more intuitive semantics for TMSCs.

We first informally introduce the notion of a language $L_M(I_i)$, of an instance I_i in a TMSC M. The language records the possible sequences of events the instance might generate as it executes. Intuitively, if a sequence does not "satisfy" the trigger of I_i, then it is admitted as a sequence. Otherwise, it is constrained to satisfy the action of I_i. For a formal definition, the interested reader is referred to [25].

We also need the following operation on languages. Let E be a set of events, and let $L \subseteq E^*$. Then, for $w \in E^*$,

$$next(L, w) = \{e \mid \exists w' \in L.w \cdot e \preceq w' \wedge (e \in \mathbb{S} \cup \mathbb{L} \cup \mathbb{T}\}$$

$$\cup \{\mathsf{wait}(e) \mid \exists w' \in L.w \cdot e \preceq w' \wedge e \in \mathbb{R}\}$$

Definition 7. *Let $\mathcal{I}$ be the set of instances in a TMSC M, and $I_i \in \mathcal{I}$. Then, for $w \in \mathbb{E}_{\{I_i\}}^*$, the acceptance tree of I_i in M is defined as follows:*

$$T_{\{I_i\}}[I_i, M](w) =$$
$$\begin{cases} \emptyset \\ \qquad \text{if } w \notin L_M(I_i) \\ sat\{\{e\} \mid e \in next(L_M(I_i), w)\} \\ \qquad \text{o.w.} \end{cases}$$

The first clause handles the case when I_i is incapable of performing w, while the second one allows I_i to non-deterministically choose one of the possible "next" events (there may be more than one possible next event if, for example, the behavior of I_i in M is conditional or partial). We now define the acceptance tree of TMSC M.

Definition 8. *Let $\mathcal{I}$ be the set of instances in a TMSC M, and let $w \in \mathbb{E}_{\mathcal{I}}^*$. Then for any environment σ,*

$$T_{\mathcal{I}}^\sigma[M](w) = \emptyset$$

if w is not well-balanced over $\mathcal{I}$

$$= handle\text{-}wait((\otimes_{I_i \in \mathcal{I}} T_{\{I_i\}}[I_i, M](w\lfloor\{I_i\}), w)$$

otherwise

We now set $T^\sigma[M] = lift(\mathbb{I}, T_{\mathcal{I}}^\sigma[M])$.

6.4   Semantics of Expressions

As with •, the other operators are interpreted in terms of acceptance trees, and the construction of $T^\sigma[H]$ for an expression H, proceeds inductively on the structure of H. A full treatment of the other operators appear in [23] (an early version appeared in [25]). The definitions may be readily adapted in the heterogeneous context, and due to space constraints, we do not present the entire semantics here. As an example, however, here is the semantics of the $\oplus$ operator.

Internal Choice: $\oplus$ offers non-deterministic choice. Given two expressions H_1 and H_2, and a sequence of events w, $T^\sigma[H_1 \oplus H_2](w) = sat(T^\sigma[H_1](w) \cup T^\sigma[H_2](w))$.

6.5   The Must Pre-order and Properties of the Semantics

Our semantics for heterogeneous expressions may be shown to have the following properties:

Theorem 2. *The operators •, $\mp$, $\oplus$, $\wedge$ and $\|$ are commutative and associative, the operator ; is associative, and $\mp$, $\oplus$ and $\wedge$ are idempotent.*

The next result establishes that $\sqsubseteq_{must}$ is substitutive.

Theorem 3. *Let H_1, H_2 and H_3 be TMSC expressions such that $H_1 \sqsubseteq_{must} H_2$. Then the following hold:*

1. $H_1 \mp H_3 \sqsubseteq_{must} H_2 \mp H_3$
2. $H_1 \oplus H_3 \sqsubseteq_{must} H_2 \oplus H_3$
3. $H_1 \wedge H_3 \sqsubseteq_{must} H_2 \wedge H_3$
4. $H_1 \| H_3 \sqsubseteq_{must} H_2 \| H_3$
5. $H_1; H_3 \sqsubseteq_{must} H_2; H_3$ and $H_3; H_1 \sqsubseteq_{must} H_3; H_2$
6. *If $Ins(H_1) = Ins(H_2)$, then $H_1 \bullet H_3 \sqsubseteq_{must} H_2 \bullet H_3$.*
7. *If $Ins(H_1) = Ins(H_2)$, then $rec\, X.H_1 \sqsubseteq_{must} rec\, X.H_2$.*

This theorem establishes that our semantics is compositional in the following sense: a heterogeneous expression may be refined by refining its subexpressions in isolation.

7 Related Work

Several researchers have investigated scenario-based (e.g.[7],[9]) and state-based (e.g. [11],[10]) approaches to distributed system development. In the context of MSCs, a number of authors (e.g.[16],[15],[27]) have also investigated the translation of scenarios to state-based models. In particular, [26], [12] present methodologies that support an incremental elaboration of behavioral models, whereby intermediate state-based designs are analyzed and possible but unspecified scenarios are presented to the user, which may lead to a more comprehensive description of desired behavior. These are all useful approaches for automating, partially or completely, the extraction of design artifacts from scenarios, and for iterating between the requirements and design phases. In contrast to these approaches, however, the work presented in this paper is motivated by a different challenge: can we allow the requirements and design phases of distributed systems to truly *overlap*? If TMSC requirements and CSM designs are available, how do we integrate and analyze them? Accordingly, our contribution in this paper is not a translation scheme from TMSCs to CSMs but an integrated framework that (i) allows heterogeneous specifications involving TMSCs and CSMs to be formed and given a precise semantics (ii) relates one heterogeneous specification with another. Developers can use this framework to verify if an innovative design they have come up with indeed meets the original requirements, and at the same time, seamlessly "add-in" to this design, new requirements as they arise.

Another novel aspect of our framework is the use of the acceptance tree model as a common semantic basis for TMSCs and CSMs. Previous approaches have primarily explored trace equivalence relationships between scenarios and state machines. However, traces by themselves do not capture the level of detail in a specification, nor can they distinguish between behavior which is mandatory from that which is optional; this limits their usefulness as a semantic model in the early phases of the software life-cycle, where such issues naturally arise. We believe the acceptance tree model provides researchers with a far richer framework for analyzing evolving behavior, and is more suited as a common basis for scenarios and state machines. In fact its roots in the testing theory of processes also opens up possibilities of some interesting applications (e.g. automatic test case generation) in the software domain that we have begun to explore.

Previous work (e.g.[18],[5]) have also looked into the relation between temporal logic specifications and refinement-based ones. [20] presented a Logical Process Calculus (LPC) formalism for combining operational and declarative specifications; it combines the algebraic operators of Milner's *Calculus of Communicating Systems* (CCS) [22] with the logical operators of the *Alternation Free Linear Time μ Calculus* $LT\mu$ [8] along with a refinement preorder that conservatively extends both the must preorder as well as the $LT\mu$ satisfaction relation. While there are similarities between our work and [20] (e.g. the acceptance tree algebra presented here also includes both behavioral and logical operators), the specification notations we have considered here (scenarios and state-machines) are both execution-based.

8   Conclusions and Future Work

In this paper, we motivated the need for a common semantic platform that will allow requirements and design notations to inter-operate. We then proposed such a framework for requirements expressed in the TMSC language, and designs expressed as CSMs. The semantics is defined by translating heterogeneous expressions of TMSCs and CSMs to *acceptance trees*, which are equipped with a precise notion of refinement based on the *must* pre-order. A case-study illustrated the utility of our theory as a basis for the principled evolution of higher-level requirements to lower-level operational specifications.

One can visualize different specification formalisms to be placed on a continuum from "very partial" (e.g. temporal logic) to "very complete" (e.g. operational specifications), with scenarios placed somewhere in between. Thus a broader motivation for combining scenarios and state machines is to ultimately have a platform where system descriptions given in various levels of behavioral detail may be plugged in and allowed to interact. Hence, extending the framework presented here to cater to other notations, performing a detailed evaluation, and extending tool support [4], are directions we plan to investigate in future. Additionally, we intend to study the implementability of TMSC expressions, and how operational specifications may be synthesized from them.

References

1. Integrated medical systems inc.-lstat. *URL:http://www.lstat.com/lstat.html.*
2. Message sequence charts (MSC). *ITU-TS Recommendation Z.120*, 1996.
3. R. Alur and M. Yannakakis. Model checking of message sequence charts. *10th International Conference on Concurrency Theory*, LNCS 1664, Springer:82–97, 1999.
4. B.Sengupta and R.Cleaveland. TRIM: A tool for triggered message sequence charts. *Proceedings of 15th Computer Aided Verification Conference (CAV'03)*, pages 106–109, 2003.
5. B.Steffen and A.Ingólfsdóttir. Characteristic formulae for processes with divergence. *International Journal on Information and Computation*, 110(1):149–163, 1994.
6. R. Cleaveland, J. Parrow, and B. Steffen. The Concurrency Workbench: A semantics based tool for the verification of concurrent systems. *ACM Transactions on Programming Languages and Systems*, 15(1):36–72, 1993.
7. C.Rolland and C.Ben Achour et al. A proposal for a scenario classification framework. *Requirements Engineering journal*, 3, No. 1:23–47, 1998.
8. C.Stirling. Modal and temporal logics. *Handbook of Logic in Computer Science*, Vol.2:477–563, 1992.
9. W. Damm and D. Harel. LSCs: Breathing life into message sequence charts. *Formal Methods in System Design*, 19(1):45–80, 2001.
10. D.Brand and P.Zafiropulo. On communicating finite state machines. *Journal of the ACM*, 30(2):323–342, 1983.
11. J.P.Schmidt D.Harel, A.Pnueli and R.Sherman. On the formal semantics of statecharts. *Proceedings of 2nd IEEE Symposium on Logic in Computer Science*, pages 54–64, 1987.
12. E.Makinen and T.Systa. Mas - an interactive synthesizer to support behavioral modeling in uml. *23rd International Conference on Software Engineering*, pages 15–24, 2001.
13. G.Booch, I.Jacobson, and J.Rumbaugh. The unified modeling language user guide.
14. M. Hennessy. Algebraic theory of processes. *The MIT Press*, 1988.
15. J.Whittle and J.Schumann. Generating statechart designs from scenarios. *Internal Conference on Software Engineering*, pages 314–323, 2000.

16. I. Kruger, R. Grosu, P. Scholz, and M. Broy. From MSCs to statecharts. *International Workshop on Distributed and Parallel Embedded Systems*, pages 61–71, 1999.
17. L.Lamport. The temporal logic of actions. *TOPLAS*, 16(3):872–923, 1994.
18. M.C.B.Hennessy and R.Milner. Algebraic laws for nondeterminism and concurrency. *Journal of the ACM*, 32(1):137–161, 1985.
19. R.Cleaveland, E.Madelaine, and S.Sims. A front-end generator for verification tools. *Tools and Algorithms for the Construction and Analysis of Systems (TACAS), 1995*, LNCS volume 1019:153–173.
20. R.Cleaveland and G.Luettgen. A logical process calculus. *9th Int'l Workshop on Expressiveness in Concurrency*, Vol.68 of Electronic Notes in Theoretical Computer Science, 2002.
21. M. A. Reniers. Message sequence chart: Syntax and semantics. *PhD Thesis, Eindhoven University of Technology*, 1998.
22. R.Milner. Communication and concurrency. 1989.
23. B. Sengupta. Triggered message sequence charts. *Ph.D Thesis, SUNY Stony Brook*, 2003.
24. B. Sengupta and R. Cleaveland. Refinement-based requirements modeling using triggered message sequence charts. 11th IEEE Int'l Requirements Engineering Conference, 2003.
25. B. Sengupta and R. Cleaveland. Triggered message sequence charts. *ACM SIGSOFT 2002, 10th Int'l Symposium on the Foundations of Software Engineering (FSE-10)*, pages 167–176.
26. S.Uchitel, J.Kramer, and J.Magee. Behavior model elaboration using partial labelled transition systems. *Proceedings of ESEC/FSE*, pages 19–27, 2003.
27. S.Uchitel, J.Kramer, and J.Magee. Synthesis of behavioral models from scenarios. *IEEE Transactions on Software Engineering, Volume 29, Number 2*, 2003.

Consistency in UML and B Multi-view Specifications

Dieu Donné Okalas Ossami, Jean-Pierre Jacquot, and Jeanine Souquières

LORIA, Université Nancy 2, UHP Nancy 1,
Campus scientifique, BP 239,
54506 Vandœuvre-lès-Nancy Cedex, France
{okalas, jacquot, souquier}@loria.fr

Abstract. We present the notion of *consistency relation* in UML and B multi-view specifications. It is defined as a semantic relation between both views. It provides us with a sound basis to define the notion of *development operator.* An operator models a development step; it separates the design decisions from their expression in the specification formalisms. Operator correctness is defined as a property which guarantees that the application of an operator on a consistent specification state yields a consistent new state. An operator can be proven once and for all to be correct. A classical case-study, the Generalized Railroad Crossing (GRC), demonstrates how the different notions can be put in practice to provide specifiers with a realistic development model.

Keywords: consistency, verification, operator, multi-view, UML, B.

1 Motivations

It has been recognized for a long time that the development of quality software depends crucially on the quality of the initial specification. Currently, there are two mains streams of specification languages: graphical notations such as UML which are very effective for the discussion between users and developers but are poor for formal verifications, and mathematical notations such as B which are effective for verification but very poor for discussion. Our aim is to design a framework where both kinds of notations can be used together to fulfill the needs of all the people involved.

The approach aims to capitalize on existing languages rather than to define a new one. This allows us to reuse the efforts that have been made in the production of industrial tools such as Rational Rose[1] or ArgoUML[2] for the edition of UML diagrams, and such as *Atelier B* [24], *B−Toolkit* [3], or *B4Free* [4] for the formal verification of specifications.

Our approach builds on the works made on the transformation between UML and B. [7, 10, 11, 13, 14, 16, 22] have defined precise sets of transformation rules to generate a B specification from UML diagrams. These works allow specifiers to check UML specifications by using B-based theorem provers. On the other way, [5, 6, 25, 26] define rules to generate UML diagrams from a B specification. These works allow specifiers to present users with a "readable" specification in order to ease the discussion and agreement on what the planned software is supposed to do.

---

[1] http://www-306.ibm.com/software/rational/

[2] http://www.argouml.tigris.org

J. Romijn, G. Smith, and J. van de Pol (Eds.): IFM 2005, LNCS 3771, pp. 386–405, 2005.

Currently, case tools based on transformation rules, such as those proposed in [12, 23, 27], work with transformations in one direction. This is a consequence of the difficulty to integrate formalisms founded on different paradigms: object theory on the one hand and set theory on the other hand. This situation introduces a new problem: the specification development process is constrained in a highly unrealistic way. Let us suppose a specifier writes a first specification in UML; he then transforms it in B and checks it with the prover; likely, he will need to edit the B specification to discharge the proof. How can the changes be retrofitted in the UML design? The problem is the same in the other direction where the check will consist in a validation with users. Using a "reverse" set of transformation rules is not realistic since the result may lead to a specification very far from the original.

More generally, the transformation approach makes impossible opportunistic strategies where the specifier chooses at some time to focus his work on structural design with UML and at some other time to define formal properties with B, without any predefined order. Another approach consists in integrating formal definitions like data-types in UML state diagrams [2].

In our model, a specification is defined as a couple ⟨ $SpecUML$, $SpecB$ ⟩ where $SpecUML$ is a set of UML diagrams and $SpecB$ a set of B machines. Both parts are views of the *same* specification. The development of a multi-view specification is modeled as a sequence of applications of *operators* [18]. An operator models a development technique by separating the design decisions from their impact on the UML and B parts. In practice, application of an operator makes both views evolve simultaneously through the application of specific editing actions on each part while ensuring that both parts are kept consistent. The notion of consistency is then central to our model. It gives a precise meaning to the notion of multi-view specification. It provides us with the formal tool to define the correctness of operators.

The paper is organized as follows. Section 2 explicits the concept of operator and the consistency relation. Section 3 introduces the case study of the generalized railroad crossing (GRC). Section 4 presents an example of operator : *Refine–Data*. Section 5 presents the application of operators on the case study. Section 6 gives proofs on the preservation of the consistency relation with respect to the applied operators. Section 7 concludes the paper.

2   Operators and Multi-view Consistency

2.1   Framework for Operators

The development of a UML and B multi-view specification $Spec = \langle SpecUML,\ SpecB \rangle$ is done by the application of operators, making parallel couples of specifications ⟨$SpecUML$, $SpecB$⟩ evolve. An operator is composed of two parts: one working on $SpecUML$ and the second on $SpecB$. These parts constitute language specific operators, denoted by $\mathcal{O}_{UML}$ and $\mathcal{O}_B$.

An operator has application conditions, ensuring the preservation of a global property of the whole specification $Spec$. To make the couple of specifications ⟨$SpecUML$, $SpecB$⟩ evolve, we have to determine the kind of changes we want to achieve as well as their location. This corresponds to the selection of an operator. To guide the development, the *"Remain To Be Done"* clause provides information about which operators can be applied next in order to terminate a given development process. This means that operators must support the following combination features:

- *Recursion.* An operator can call itself.
- *Sequencing.* Operators can be sequenced to fire one after another.

2.2 Operator Template

The standard template for the definition of an operator is composed of various clauses. Each clause is optional except the first one. Each clause is described as follows:

1. **Parameters.** Determines parameters of the operator which are of two kinds, *In* and *Result*. They are both optional.
   - **In.** Designates elements needed to calculate the *Result* representations.
   - **Result.** Designates elements *created* by the operator. The *Result* parameters that are not included, default to the *In* parameters.

2. **Application conditions.** Defines the conditions which specify when the operator can be applied. Two kinds of conditions are identified : conditions related to UML (CONd_UML) and conditions related to B (COND_B).

Operator:*operator_Name*

Description. Natural language description of the purpose and effects of the operator.

Parameters.
- **In.**
  $\langle PARAM\_Name : TYPE\_PARAM \rangle *$
- **Result.**
  $\langle PARAM\_Name : TYPE\_PARAM \rangle *$

Application conditions.

- Related to *SpecB*
  $\langle COND\_B \rangle *$
- Related to *SpecUML*
  $\langle COND\_UML \rangle *$

Definition.

- **Context.** $\langle context \rangle$
- $\langle OPERATOR\_DEF \rangle$

Remains To Be Done. $\langle To\ Do\ Next \rangle$

Fig. 1. Operator template

3. **Definition.** Consists of:
   - **Context.** Determines the element(s) the operator is applied to.
   - $\langle OPERATOR\_DEF \rangle$. Determines the sequence of operators to be applied. $OPERATOR\_DEF$ is given by the following grammar:

$OPERATOR\_DEF ::= \langle \mathcal{O}_{UML}, \mathcal{O}_B \rangle$
   $| \ OPERATOR\_APP$
   $| \ OPERATOR\_DEF \ [; \ OPERATOR\_DEF]^*$
   $| \ \mathbf{IF} \ \langle \ COND \ \rangle \ \mathbf{THEN} \ OPERATOR\_DEF \ [; \ OPERATOR\_DEF]^*$

where:
   - $COND$ denotes a condition on the context or the parameters.
   - $OPERATOR\_APP$ denotes an operator's application consisting of the name of the operator and its parameters.

4. **Remains To Be Done.** Indicates which part of the specification has to be defined next.

2.3 Multi-view Consistency Relation

We consider the question of how the application of an operator has to be constrained so that its application on a current consistent specification state $\langle SpecUML, SpecB \rangle$, yields a consistent specification state $\langle SpecUML', SpecB' \rangle$. Let us denote $\mathcal{R}_{elc}$ the consistency relation between $SpecUML$ and $SpecB$.

Let $\mathbb{T}_{U \rightarrow B}$ be the set of UML to B transformation rules [9, 17] which associate each UML artifact with one or more B artifacts. These transformations are relative to UML 1.x [19]. $\mathcal{R}_{elc}$ is defined as a conjunction of four conditions:

1 *Syntactic conformance.* It states that both $SpecUML$ and $SpecB$ must be well-formed. It ensures that the specification conforms to abstract syntax specified by the meta-model, i.e. UML meta-model or B abstract syntax tree. Let $\mathcal{WF}(SpecUML)$ and $\mathcal{WF}(SpecB)$ be two predicates defining if a UML and a B specifications are well-formed.

2 *Local consistency.* It requires that both specifications must be internaly consistent. That means they do not contain contradictions, but they could be incompletely defined. We write it *consistent(SpecUML)* and *consistent(SpecB)*.

The global consistency is defined with respect to UML to B transformation rules designed by Meyer, Souquières and Ledang [9, 17].

3 *Elements traceability.* It states that for any elements of $ID(SpecUML)$, e_U, that can be transformed by a rule T, there exists in $ID(SpecB)$ a set of artifacts $\{e_B\}$ resulting from the application of T to e_U.

4 *Semantic preservation.* It states that any statement ϕ satisfying the semantics of $SpecUML$ must satisfy $SpecB$. The semantics of $SpecUML$ is defined as $\mathbb{T}_{U \rightarrow B}(SpecUML)$. This means that UML artifacts that have no B semantics defined in

$\mathbb{T}_{U \to B}$ are not concerned by the consistency relation $\mathcal{R}el_C$. This has important implications throughout the verification process. For example, it is well known that checking pairwise integration of a set of software specifications is only possible if one is able to transform them into a semantic domain supported by tools. B is our semantic domain and any UML statement that has no B formalization cannot be verified in our framework.

We use the B theorem prover to prove that a statement ϕ holds in *SpecB* (condition (2)) and due to *condition (3)*, we derive the consistency of *SpecUML*, and therefore the consistency of the multi-view specification *Spec*.

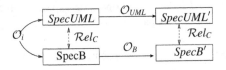

Fig. 2. UML and B consistency relation

Formally, the $\mathcal{R}el_C$ relation is defined as follows:

Definition 1 (Consistency relation)

SpecUML $\mathcal{R}el_C$ *SpecB* :

(1) $\mathcal{WF}(SpecUML) \land \mathcal{WF}(SpecB)$

(2) $consistent(SpecUML) \land consistent(SpecB)$

(3) $\forall\ e_U.(e_U \in ID(SpecUML_{|\mathbb{T}_{U \to B}})^a \Rightarrow$
$\exists\ \{e_B\}, T.(\{e_B\} \subseteq ID(SpecB) \land T \in \mathbb{T}_{U \to B} \land T(e_U) = \{e_B\}))$

(4) $\forall\ \phi.(\mathbb{T}_{U \to B}(SpecUML)^b \vDash \phi \Rightarrow SpecB \vDash \phi))$

---

^{a} $SpecUML_{|\mathbb{T}_{U \to B}}$ denotes the restriction of *SpecUML* to elements for which there is a transformation rule to B defined in $\mathbb{T}_{U \to B}$
^{b} $\mathbb{T}_{U \to B}(SpecUML)$ denotes the application of the set of UML to B transformation rules on *SpecUML*

3   A Case Study

The evolution of the specification and the verification of the consistency relation described in section 2.3 will be applied to the generalized railroad crossing example, called *GRC* in the sequel. We give a short description of the problem and an abstract specification on which the refinement can be introduced. Fig. 3 illustrates the structure of the *GRC* extracted from [21]. The system to be modeled consists of a gate, a controller and trains at a railroad crossing.

The railroad crossing lies in a region of interest *R*. Trains travel in one direction through *R*, and only one train per track is allowed to be in *R* at any moment. Sensors indicate when a train enters or exits the region *R*. For space and clarity reasons, we do not present in details the *GRC* problem, but only details which are relevant to illustrate our approach.

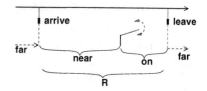

Fig. 3. The generalized railroad crossing

We will describe the development of the system step by step, starting with the UML specification which identifies some important entities. Note that we only focus on static aspects.

3.1 A First UML Specification

A *Train* may be in three states: *far*, *near* and *on*. The state of the train is determined by the information provided by sensors positioned on the track and by a clock. When a train leaves a region and enters another one, a signal is sent to the controller which reacts by sending appropriate signals to the gate. A train takes *2* to *5* time units to reach state *on* after it entered state *near*. It then leaves state *on* and therefore region *R* and reaches state *far* between *1* and *2* time units. Time information is stored in the variable *Ht*, which is initialized to *0* when a train enters state *near* and state *on*. The system must be safe: the gate must be down when trains reach state *on*. In order to have the gate closed when the fastest train reaches state *on*, the gate must be closed between *1* and *2* time units after trains entered region *R*.

The class *Train* is characterized by the following variables:

– *Ht*, which models the time taken by the train to reach each state,
– *pos*, which models the train states.

The class Train provides three methods, *arrive()*, *cross()* and *leave()*, for entering, crossing and leaving region *R*, respectively. The class diagram of the *GRC* and the behavior of the *Train* are presented in Fig. 4(a) and 4(b).

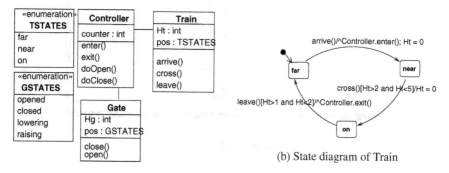

(a) Class diagram of the GRC

(b) State diagram of Train

Fig. 4. A first UML specification

3.2 The Corresponding B Specification

Figure 5 represents the abstract specification of the class *Train* obtained by an automatic translation of the UML specification (cf. Fig. 4). Each class with name *Class* is represented by an abstract machine with the same name, as discussed in [16]. For each class *Class*, a set *CLASS* is introduced to represent all possible instances of *Class*. A variable *class* ⊆ *CLASS* is used to identify current instances of *Class*. Attributes are modeled as functions from *class* to the attribute type as defined in the class. The type of functions reflects the participation and cardinality of the entity. Class operations are derived as B operations (e.g. *arrive, cross* and *leave* in the *Train* machine of Fig. 5) mirroring the syntactical structure of the associated state diagram. Operation parameters are typed and further constrained in the operation precondition. Operation bodies are automatically derived from transitions in the state diagram. In addition to machines representing classes, we introduce a special machine *Types*, which declares a number of shared sets or types. The others classes are derived in a similar way.

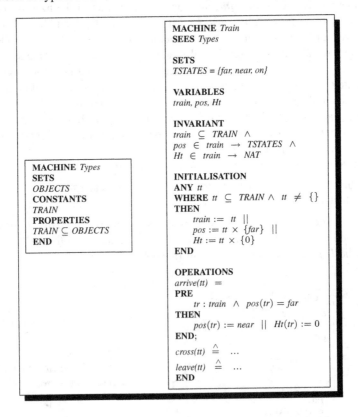

Fig. 5. Associated B Machines

3.3 Improving the Specification

Let's take the UML and B specification couple of Fig. 4(a) and 5 and consider that the user focuses his work on the B specification. He decides to observe more in details the behavior of the train in the state *near*, as described informally in Fig. 7 and graphically illustrated in Fig. 6.

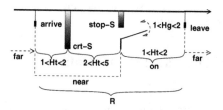

Fig. 6. Detailed GRC

If the train moves at great speed towards the crossing and arrives at point *crt-S* (critical state) in less than 2 time units, it must stop at *stop-S* (stop state). It then starts to move again, when the time variable *Ht* is greater than two time units. This is the time needed by the gate to be completely closed.

Fig. 7. Example of a critical property

The description of this property requires new variables, states, types, and constraints to be added to the initial specification of the train. This means that we have to improve the current couple of specifications so that it captures this new requirement. The refinement is an appropriate technique to express this critical property. For this purpose, we provide users with the *Refine-Data* operator, allowing to enrich the current specification in a stepwise manner. It also provides a way to strengthen invariants and to add details omitted in previous abstractions. The *Refine-Data* operator defined in this paper is used to replace some types and data in a specification by more concrete ones in order to increase efficiency or implementability. The replacement ends up in new entities, sets and constraints on the data space being introduced in the specification. Note that we do not attempt to provide a new definition of data refinement, rather we use the standard definition of refinement of state variables. From a practical perspective, we present the data refinement process as follows.

– First, concepts (e.g., refinement component, variables, types, classes, attributes, etc.) that form the basis for expressing properties are modeled. The *Refine-Data* operator is defined to act this role.
– Second, we consider concepts such as gluing invariants or additional constraints over data introduced previously to express logical links between concrete data and their abstract versions. This is achieved by using the *Model-Constraint* operator.

For naming UML and B model elements, we will consider the following notations:

– *ID* the set of all identifiers of the specification ($ID = ID(SpecB) \cup ID(SpecUML)$).
– $CMP(SpecB) \subseteq ID(SpecB)$ the finite set of B components (machine, refinement, implementation) names appearing in *SpecB*.

- *CLASS(SpecUML) $\subseteq$ ID(SpecUML)* the finite set of class names appearing in *SpecUML*.
- *ATT(C)* the finite set of attributes of a class $C \in$ *CLASS(SpecUML)*.
- *DATA(Ma)* the finite set of data, such as variables and constants, appearing in a B component *Ma $\in$ CMP(SpecB)*.

4   An Example of Operator: Refine-Data

Operator: Refine-Data
Description. This operator provides a scheme to refine data, replacing some types and data in a specification by more concrete ones in order to support the addition of functional details, to increase efficiency or implementability. Users must designate:

- a B component *Ma* to which the data to be refined belongs,
- a variable *v: S* the user wants to refine,
- a state s_i the user wants to precise, if the type S of v is a set of states $\{s_0, ..., s_i, ..., s_n\}$
- a set of concrete versions $\{s_{r_i}, ..., s_{r_j}\}$ the user wants to replace s_i with. If S is an abstract set, the user will give explicit values $\{s_{r_i}, ...s_{r_j}\}$ to it.

The following modifications are made to $\langle SpecUML, SpecB \rangle$:

In *SpecB*

1. If there is no already existing refinement Ma_r of Ma[3] (denoted by $Ma \sqsubseteq Ma_r$), a refinement Ma_r is automatically introduced. It models the following elements:

   (a) a *REFINES Ma* clause immediately after its header, identifying the single component *Ma* that it refines,

   (b) a set:
      i. $S_r = S \cup \{s_{r_i}, ..., s_{r_j}\}$ that refines the more abstract set S ($S \sqsubseteq S_r$) if S is an enumerated set. Note that S_r is composed of new state values, as well as of all values[4] in S or
      ii. $S_r = \{s_{r_i}, ...s_{r_j}\}$ if the to refined set S is abstract,

   (c) a set of state variables $\{v_{r_0}, ..., v_{r_i}, ..., v_{r_n}\}$ which take their values in S_r, if v must be refined by several variables,

   (d) a comment line $<$ *To do J(v, v_{r_i})* $>$ denoting the location to be replaced with the *gluing invariant* that relates the abstract state variable v and the concrete state variables $\{v_{r_0}, ..., v_{r_i}, ..., v_{r_n}\}$ and extra constraints (refinement conditions).

2. If there is already a refinement Ma_r of Ma, two cases can occur:

   (a) in the first case, additional local types, data and extra constraints may be added to Ma_r in a similar way than 1b and 1c,

---

[3] This is the case when the operator is applied for the first time on *Ma*.
[4] They are renamed in S_r in order to satisfy B naming conventions. For instance, s_i in S is renamed by s_iR in S_r.

(b) in the second case, Ma_r may be precised by means of a serie of refinements in a similar way than in the case 1. The refinement process will also iterate.

3. If the type of v is a predefined type, no new types are introduced.

In *SpecUML*

1. **In the class diagram**

   (a) a refinement component Ma_r corresponds to the class Ma_r,

   (b) a B variable v_r in Ma_r corresponds to an attribute v_r in the class that represents the refinement component Ma_r. The type and initial value of this attribute correspond to the type invariant and initialization substitution of the corresponding B variable,

   (c) a set S_r in B corresponds to an enumerated type in UML or in OCL,

   (d) the *REFINES* clause is modeled by an abstraction/refinement association with a <<*refines*>> stereotype,

   (e) the comment line $< To\ do\ J(v, v_{r_i}) >$ leads to the creation of a comment note in the class diagram, referencing the refinement link between the abstract and the refinement class.

2. **In the state diagram**

   (a) For a state s_{r_i} that refines a state s_i, a super-state s_i with sub-state s_{r_i} is drawn by nesting in the state diagram attached with the class Ma.

   (b) A set of state values $S_r = \{s_0R, ..., s_iR, s_{r_i}, ..., s_{r_j}, ..., s_nR\}$ refining an abstract set of state values S ($S \sqsubseteq S_r$) leads to the generation of a state diagram as shown below.

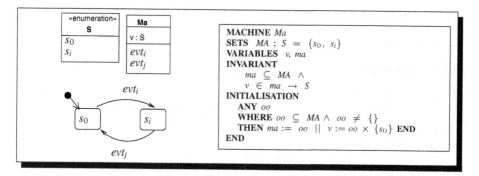

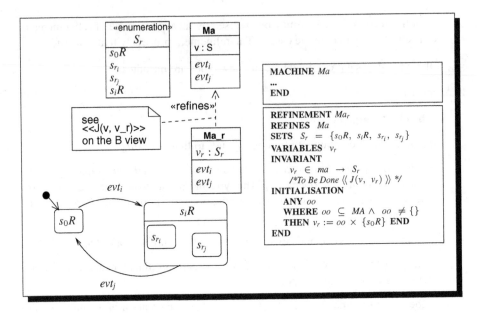

Result of the Refine-Data operator application

Parameters.

In

- Ma : identifier
- v : identifier
- $[s_i$: $State]^5$
- $[\{s_{r_i}, ..., s_{r_j}\}$: $States]$

Result.

- Ma_r : identifier
- v_r : identifier
- S_r : identifier

Application conditions.

1. Related to *SpecB*
   - $Ma \in CMP(SpecB) \wedge Ma ::= \text{MACHINE} \mid \text{REFINEMENT}$
   - $s_i \in S$
   - $v : S \wedge v \in DATA(Ma)$
   - $\forall s_k.(s_k \in \{s_{r_i}, ..., s_{r_j}\} \Rightarrow s_k \notin s_i)$

2. Related to *SpecUML*
   - $\exists C.(C \in CLASS(SpecUML) \wedge C \mapsto Ma)$
   - $\exists a.(a \in ATT(C) \wedge (a \mapsto v))$
   - $\exists T.(T \in TYPE(SpecUML) \wedge T \mapsto S)$

---

[5] $[x]$ denotes that x is optional.

Definition.

Context: *Ma*

IF (Ma ::= MACHINE ∨ Ma ::= REFINEMENT) ∧
  (v ∈ DATA(Ma) ∧ (S ::= AbstractSet ∨ S ::= EnumeratedSet))
THEN

$\mathcal{O}_{UML}$	$\mathcal{O}_B$	
$(AddClass(Ma_r) ; AddDependency(Ma, Ma_r, \text{«refines»}))$;	$AddRefinement(Ma, Ma_r)$	;
$AddType(S_r, \{s_{r_i}, ..., s_{r_j}\})^{*}$;	$AddSet(S_r, \{s_{r_i}, ..., s_{r_j}\})^{*}$;	
$AddAttribute(Ma_r, v_r)^{*}$	$AddVariable(Ma_r, v_r)^{*}$	

IF (Ma ::= MACHINE ∨ Ma ::= REFINEMENT) ∧
  (v ∈ DATA(Ma) ∧ S ::= PredefinedType)
THEN

$\mathcal{O}_{UML}$	$\mathcal{O}_B$	
$(AddClass(Ma_r) ; AddDependency(Ma, Ma_r, \text{«refines»}))$;	$AddRefinement(Ma, Ma_r)$	;
$AddAttribute(Ma_r, v_r)^{*}$	$AddVariable(Ma_r, v_r)^{*}$	

IF Ma ::= REFINEMENT ∧
  v ∈ DATA(Ma) ∧ (S ::= AbstractSet ∨ S ::= EnumeratedSet) ∧
  $\exists Ma_x.(Ma_x \in ID(Spec) \wedge Ma \sqsubseteq Ma_x)$
THEN

$\mathcal{O}_{UML}$	$\mathcal{O}_B$	
$AddType(S_r, \{s_{r_i}, ..., s_{r_j}\})^{*}$;	$AddSet(S_r, \{s_{r_i}, ..., s_{r_j}\})^{*}$;	;
$AddAttribute(Ma_x, v_r)^{*}$	$AddVariable(Ma_x, v_r)^{*}$	

IF Ma ::= REFINEMENT ∧
  v ∈ DATA(Ma) ∧ S ::= PredefinedType ∧
  $\exists Ma_x.(Ma_x \in ID(Spec) \wedge Ma \sqsubseteq Ma_x)$
THEN

$\mathcal{O}_{UML}$	$\mathcal{O}_B$
$AddAttribute(Ma_x, v_r)^{*}$	$AddVariable(Ma_x, v_r)^{*}$

Remains To Be Done. The introduced variable can be improved:
• Invariant and initialization comment lines have to be replaced by concrete constraints using for example the *Model-Constraint* operator.

5   Application to the Case Study

Let's take the couple of specifications of Fig. 4 and Fig. 5 and enrich it with new variables *posR* and *HtR* in order to model the property of Fig. 7. We decide to refine the *Train* machine, using the *Refine-Data* operator. The train machine and its related UML class and state diagram are interdependent representations. As one changes, the other one undergoes changes too. So, we instantiate twice the *Refine-Data* operator in order to introduce variables *posR* and *HtR*. The instantiation of this operator requires to set the actual parameters as shown in Fig. 8(a) and 8(b).

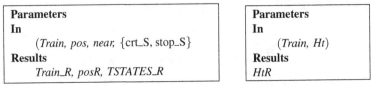

Parameters		Parameters
In		In
(Train, pos, near, {crt_S, stop_S}		(Train, Ht)
Results		Results
Train_R, posR, TSTATES_R		HtR

(a) First instantiation to introduce the variable *posR*

(b) Second instantiation to introduce the variable *HtR*

Fig. 8. Two instantiations of the *Refine−Data* operator

Fig.9 illustrates the result of the instantiation of the *Refine−Data* operator on the *Train* machine, where variables *posR* and *HtR* are introduced one after the other.

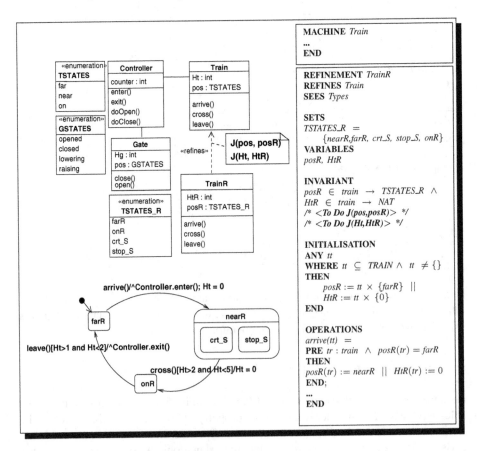

Fig. 9. Application of the *Refine−Data* operator on the train machine

One of the most important steps when refining specifications in B is formulating *gluing invariants* that relate concrete variables with their abstract versions. We assume that the data refinement process ends with formulating invariants over variables and types previously introduced by the *Refine-Data* operator in the first step. This is achieved by the *Model-Constraint* operator as indicated in the **Remains To Be Done** clause of the *Refine−Data* operator. Once the *Model-Constraint* operator has been applied, we can move on to deal with the consistency checking. For space and clarity reasons, we do not present the definition of the *Model-Constraint* operator in this paper.

For the *Model-Constraint* operator to work, users have to write the invariant *I* to be added, and to designate the component to which this constraint has to be introduced. The application ends with new constraints in B and OCL constraints or comment notes in UML. We give below one possible formulation of the gluing invariant (over variables *posR* and *HtR*, and their abstract versions *pos* and *Ht*) and constraints on the new functionality that can be given as parameter when instantiating the *Model-Constraint* operator.

Parameters
In

> *TrainR*

/* gluing invariants */
$\forall tr.(tr : train \Rightarrow$
$(posR(tr) = farR \Rightarrow pos(tr) = far) \wedge$
$((posR(tr) = crt\_S \ or \ posR(tr) = stop\_S) \Rightarrow pos(tr) = near) \wedge$
$(posR(tr) = onR \Rightarrow pos(tr) = on) \wedge$
$(HtR(tr) : 0..5 \Rightarrow HtR(tr) = Ht(tr)) \wedge$
/* constraints on the new functionality */
$(posR(tr) : \{ crt\_S, stop\_S, onR\} \Rightarrow HtR(tr) < 5) \wedge$
$(posR(tr) = crt\_S \ or \ posR(tr) = onR \Rightarrow HtR(tr) < 2))$

Fig. 10 shows the B specification of *TrainR* after the application of the *Constraint−Modeling* operator. Because existing OCL to B rules [11] are only defined for simple expressions, there is no creation of an OCL constraint for the introduced B invariant *I*.

6   Verification of the Operator's Correctness

In this section, we look at the correction aspect of the case-study. We show concretely how the definitions apply to the UML and B parts manipulated in the case-study. We also give some hints on how the correctness of the operators *Refine-Data* and *Model-Constraint* could be assessed.

6.1   Syntactic Well-Formedness

Both specifications must be checked for syntax and type correctness with their corresponding support tool. The B support tool we use for this case study, *atelierB*, confirms the well-formedness of the text shown in Fig. 10. The UML diagrams are also well-formed according to ArgoUML.

```
REFINEMENT TrainR
REFINES Train
SEES    Types
SETS TSTATES_R = {nearR, farR, crt_S, stop_S, onR}
VARIABLES posR, HtR
INVARIANT
posR ∈ train → TSTATES_R ∧
HtR ∈ train → NAT ∧
/* gluing invariants */
∀ tr.(tr : train ⇒
( posR(tr) = farR ⇒ pos(tr) = far ) ∧
( ( posR(tr) = crt_S or posR(tr) = stop_S ) ⇒ pos(tr) = near ) ∧
(posR(tr) = onR ⇒ pos(tr) = on ) ∧
( HtR(tr) : 0..5 ⇒ HtR(tr) = Ht(tr) ) ∧
/* constraints on the new functionality */
( posR(tr) : { crt_S, stop_S, onR} ⇒  HtR(tr) < 5 ) ∧
( posR(tr) = crt_S or posR(tr) = onR ⇒ HtR(tr) < 2 )
)
INITIALISATION
...
END
```

Fig. 10. B refinement of the class Train

6.2 Internal Consistency

The definition of operator correctness uses the strong hypothesis that each view in the initial state is internally consistent. While this condition is not much more than the well-formedness for the UML, it means full logical consistency for the B part.

```
Project status
+-----------+----+-----+-----+-----+-----+-----+
| COMPONENT | TC | POG | Obv | nPO | nUn | %Pr |
+-----------+----+-----+-----+-----+-----+-----+
| Train     | OK | OK  | 0   | 4   | 0   | 100 |
| TrainR    | OK | OK  | 3   | 10  | 0   | 100 |
| Types     | OK | -   |     |     |     |     |
+-----------+----+-----+-----+-----+-----+-----+
| TOTAL     | OK | -   | 3   | 14  | 0   | 100 |
+-----------+----+-----+-----+-----+-----+-----+
```

Fig. 11. Result of the verification of the B specification

The checking of *SpecB* follows the usual approach of the B method: to check initialization, to check pre and postconditions of operations with respect to the preservation of machine invariants, and to check inter-machine relations such as refinements. On the case-study, it is clear that the verification is done on two levels. The first level is the verification that the elements automatically introduced by the operator in *SpecB* are correct. The second level checks that the elements introduced by the user are consistent. In our case, the first level is mainly exemplified by the operator *Refine-Data*, while *Model-Constraint* is mostly about the second level.

SpecB has been submitted to the *atelierB*. All proof obligations generated by the REFINEMENT status of the TrainR have been discharged through the gluing invariant which was introduced by the application of the *Model-Constraint* operator. Figure 11 shows the summary of the verification printed by the tool.

6.3 Consistency Between Views

It is decomposed into the *elements traceability* and *semantics preservation* conditions. Let's consider:

- ⟨*SpecUML*, *SpecB*⟩ the specification couple of Fig. 4 and 5, respectively.
- ⟨*SpecUML'*, *SpecB'*⟩ the specification couple of Fig. 9 and 10, resulting from the application of the operators on ⟨*SpecUML*, *SpecB*⟩. Note that Fig. 10 includes the machine *Train* of Fig. 9.
- $\mathbb{T}_{U \rightarrow B}$ the set of UML to B transformation rules by Meyer [15] and Ledang [8].

```
MACHINE Train*                          MACHINE TrainR*
SEES Types                              SEES Types
SETS                                    SETS
TSTATES = {far, near, on}               TSTATES_R = {farR,nearR, crt_S, stop_S, onR}
VARIABLES                               VARIABLES
train, pos, Ht                          trainR, posR,HtR
INVARIANT                               INVARIANT
train ⊆ TRAIN ∧                         trainR ⊆ TRAINR ∧
pos ∈ train → TSTATES ∧                 posR ∈ trainR → TSTATES_R ∧
Ht ∈ train → NAT                        HtR ∈ trainR → NAT
INITIALISATION                          INITIALISATION
ANY                                     ANY
    tt                                      tt
WHERE                                   WHERE
    tt ⊆ TRAIN ∧ tt ≠ {}                    tt ⊆ TRAINR ∧ tt ≠ {}
THEN                                    THEN
    train := tt ||                          trainR := tt ||
    pos := tt × {far} ||                    posR := tt × {far} ||
    Ht := tt × {0}                          HtR := tt × {0}
END                                     END
OPERATIONS                              OPERATIONS
arrive(tt) =                            arrive(tt) =
PRE                                     PRE
    tr : train ∧ pos(tr) = far              tr : trainR ∧ posR(tr) = farR
THEN                                    THEN
    pos(tr) := near || Ht(tr) := 0          posR(tr) := nearR || HtR(tr) := 0
END;                                    END;

cross(tt) ≘ ...                         cross(tt) ≘ ...

leave(tt) ≘ ...                         leave(tt) ≘ ...
END                                     END
```

Fig. 12. B specification obtained by applying transformation rules

To check, we apply the transformation rules $\mathbb{T}_{U \to B}$ to *SpecUML'*. The interesting part of the B specification, the machines *Train** and *TrainR**, is given in Figure 12. It then proceeds by the verification of conditions 3 and 4 of $\mathcal{R}_{elc}$.

Condition 3 is proved by verifying that $ID(\mathbb{T}_{U \to B}(SpecUML')) = ID(SpecB')$. This is asserted in two steps:

- all new names introduced by the operators are present. This is easily seen,
- condition 3 holds for $\langle SpecUML, SpecB \rangle$. This is true by construction, cf. subsection 3.2.

The verification of condition 4 is more complex. When we look at Figure 12, we can see the following differences between *SpecB* and $\mathbb{T}_{U \to B}(SpecUML')$:

1. *TrainR** is a machine and is not related to *Train** by a refinement relation.
2. The machine *TrainR** introduces a new variable $trainR^6$ which is a subset of the set *TRAINR* representing possible instances of the class *TrainR*. *trainR* and *TRAINR* do not appear in *SpecB'*. As a consequence, variables *posR* and *HtR* in the machine *TrainR** which are modeled as functions from current instances set (*train*) to the corresponding type (*STATES_R* and *NAT* respectively), have now different domains.
3. the UML abstraction/refinement dependency is not modeled,
4. the added invariants in the machine *TrainR* of *SpecB'* do not appear since they have been represented as a comment note in *SpecUML'*.

So, to establish the property, we have to prove that the machine *TrainR** is a refinement of the machine *Train**. Concretely, we must find an abstraction function, ρ, defined as follows. Let us consider:

- S_{Ma_r} and S_{Ma} the sets of states of Ma_r and Ma respectively,
- Evt_{Ma_r} and Evt_{Ma} the sets of events of state machines of Ma_r and Ma respectively,
- $Trans_{Ma_r}$ and $Trans_{Ma}$ the sets of transitions of state machines of Ma_r and Ma respectively,

$\rho : Ma_r \to Ma$ is an abstraction relation which is a function from $S_{Ma_r} \cup Evt_{Ma_r} \cup Trans_{Ma_r}$ to $S_{Ma} \cup Evt_{Ma} \cup Trans_{Ma}$ and which maps

- Each state s_r of Ma_r to a state $\rho(s_r)$ of Ma,
- Each event e_r of Ma_r to an event $\rho(e_r)$ of Ma and
- Each transition t_r of Ma_r to a transition $\rho(t_r)$ of Ma.

Such that

- $\rho(s_{init_{Ma_r}}) = s_{init_{Ma}}$
- $Evt_{Ma}(\rho(t_r)) = \rho(Evt_{Ma_r}(t_r))$
- $source_{Ma}(\rho(t_r)) = \rho(source_{Ma_r}(t_r)) \wedge target_{Ma}(\rho(t_r)) = \rho(target_{Ma_r}(t_r))$

---

[6] For modeling effective instances of the class *TrainR*.

ρ is an abstraction function equivalent to a B refinement if the following properties hold:

1. $\forall\ s. \exists\ s_r.(s\ \in\ S_{Ma} \wedge s_r\ \in\ S_{Ma_r} \wedge \rho(s_r) = s)\ \wedge$
2. $\forall\ s. \exists\ t.(\ s\ \in\ S_{Ma} \wedge t\ \in\ Trans_{Ma} \wedge Evt_{Ma}(t)\ =\ e \wedge source_{Ma}(t)\ =\ s \Rightarrow$
$$(\forall\ s_r.(s_r\ \in\ S_{Ma_r} \wedge \rho(s_r)\ =\ s \Rightarrow \exists\ t_r.(t_r\ \in\ Trans_{Ma_r} \wedge$$
$$\rho(Evt_{Ma_r}(t_r))\ =\ e\ \wedge$$
$$\rho(t_r)\ =\ t\ \wedge$$
$$source_{Ma_r}(t_r)\ =\ s_r$$
$$)))$$
$$)$$

The first condition states that every state s of an abstraction Ma has some corresponding states of its refinement Ma_r. The second states that every event e which has an abstract transition from some state s has also a corresponding concrete transition from each corresponding state.

These conditions ensure that all properties expressed in Ma_r hold in the abstraction Ma and therefore the semantic preservation criteria is ensured. Actually, this condition is similar to the preservation of precondition requirement of B refinement.

The definition of ρ on our case study is as follows:

$\rho = \{farR \mapsto far, stop\_S \mapsto near, crt\_S \mapsto near, onR \mapsto on\}\ \cup$
$\quad \{arrive \mapsto arrive, cross \mapsto cross, leave \mapsto leave\}\ \cup$
$\quad \{(farR, arrive, nearR) \mapsto (far, arrive, near), (nearR, cross, onR) \mapsto (near, cross, on),$
$\quad (onR, leave, farR) \mapsto (on, leave, far)\}$

It is easily verified that the preceding properties holds by considering the gluing invariant.

7   Conclusion and Future Work

Combining UML notations and the B method is important for the use and the acceptance of formal methods as part of the development of high quality systems. We propose a framework allowing to define development operators making evolve UML and B multi-view specifications. The approach is not based on the application of transformation rules from UML to B or B to UML, but on the development of both specifications in an incremental way by applying operators. Operators enable the specifier to focus on methodological issues before addressing technical details related to each specification language.

We have proposed a definition of the consistency relation between both views of a specification expressed with UML and B, and two consecutive development states. The verification of the consistency is done once for all for each operator when defining them, relatively to a set of UML to B systematic transformation rules. It is partly automated and supported by the B prover.

As the case study shows, our approach does not pretend to automate the entire development of the specification. Technical and tedious syntactical details are taken care of by the operators but the design of important properties is still the specifier's responsibility.

An implementation of this framework with some operators is under development. It is an extension of the *ArgoUML+B* [12] platform, allowing to automatically transform some UML diagrams to B specifications (*ArgoUML+B* is based on the *ArgoUML*[7] project, dedicated to the edition and design of UML diagrams). This extension includes *SmartTools* [1, 20] to dynamically represent B specifications as instances of the B AST (abstract syntax tree), taking into account the multi-view specification.

We are looking at developing a library of useful operators. We have already identified and defined some restructuring operators such as modeling abstraction of generic classes from existing classes. We also need operators for the specification of system behaviours.

References

[1] I. Attali, C. Courbis, P. Degenne, A. Fau, J. Fillon, D. Parigot, C. Pasquier, and C. S. Coen. SmartTools: a development environment generator based on XML technologies. In *In XML Technologies and Software Engineering, Toronto, Canada. ICSE'01, ICSE workshop proceedings*, 2001.

[2] C. Attiogbé, P. Poizat, and G. Salaün. Integration of Formal Datatypes within State Diagrams. In *FASE'2003 - Fundamental Approaches to Software Engineering*, volume 2621 of *LNCS*, pages 341–355. Springer-Verlag, 2003.

[3] Oxford(UK) B-Core(UK) Ltd. *B-Toolkit User's Manual*. 1996.

[4] ClearSy. http://www.b4free.com/index.php.

[5] F. Houda and Stephan Merz. Transformation de spécifications B en diagrammes UML. In *Proceedings of AFADL'04, Besançon (Fr)*, 2004.

[6] A. Idani and Y. Ledru. Object Oriented Concepts Identification from Formal B Specifications. In *9th Int.Workshop on Formal Methods for Industrial Critical Systems (FMICS'04), Linz (AT)*, 2004.

[7] R. Laleau and F. Polack. A Rigorous Metamodel for UML Static Conceptual Modelling of Information Systems. In *Advanced Information Systems Engineering. 13th Int. Conf., CAiSE 2001, Proceedings*, volume 2068 of *LNCS*, pages 402–416. Springer, 2001.

[8] H. Ledang. *Traduction Systématique de Spécifications UML vers B*. PhD thesis, LORIA -Université Nancy2, novembre, 2002.

[9] H. Ledang and J. Souquières. Modeling class operations in B: application to UML behavioral diagrams. - *ASE2001: 16th IEEE International Conference on Automated Software Engineering, IEEE Computer Society, November*, 2001.

[10] H. Ledang and J. Souquières. Integrating Formalizing UML Behavioral Diagrams with B. *Workshop on Integration and Transformation of UML models, Malàga (S)*, 2002.

[11] H. Ledang and J. Souquières. Integration of UML and B Specification Techniques: Systematic Transformation from OCL Expressions into B. In *Proceedings of APSEC 2002 IEEE Computer Society*, 2002.

[12] H. Ledang, J. Souquières, and S. Charles. ArgoUML+B : Un outil de transformation systématique de spécifications UML vers B. In *Proceedings of AFADL'03, Rennes (Fr)*, 2003.

[13] R. Marcano and N. Levy. Transformation rules of OCL constraints into B formal expressions. In Jürjens, Cengarle, Fernandez, Rumpe, and Sandner, editors, *Critical Systems Development with UML – Proceedings of the UML'02 workshop*, pages 155–162, 2002.

---

[7] http://www.argouml.tigris.org

[14] R. Marcano and N. Levy. Using B formal specifications for analysis and verification of UML/OCL models. In L. Kuzniarz, G. Reggio, J. L. Sourrouille, and Z. Huzar, editors, *Workshop on Consistency Problems in UML-based Software Development. Workshop Materials*, pages 91–105, 2002.

[15] E. Meyer. *Développements formels par objets: utilisation conjointe de B et d'UML.* PhD thesis, LORIA -Université Nancy2, mars, 2001.

[16] E. Meyer and J. Souquières. A systematic approach to transform OMT diagrams to a B specification. *FM'99: World Congress on Formal Methods in the Development of Computing Systems, Toulouse (Fr)*, 1999.

[17] E. Meyer and J. Souquières. A systematic approach to transform OMT diagrams to a B specification. *FM'99: World Congress on Formal Methods in the Development of Computing Systems, Toulouse (Fr)*, 1999.

[18] D. Okalas Ossami, J. Souquières, and J.-P. Jacquot. Opérations de construction de spécifications multi-vues UML et B. In *Proceedings of AFADL'04, Besançon, France, June 16-18*. INRIA, 2004.

[19] OMG. Unified modeling language specification, version 1.5, March 2003. available from hhtp://www.omg.org.

[20] D. Parigot and C. Courbis. avaible at : http://www-sop.inria.fr/smartool/.

[21] P. Schnoebelen, B. Bérard, M. Bidoit, F. Laroussine, and A. Petit. *Vérification de logiciels -Techniques et outils du model-checking-.* Paris,Vuibert, 1999. ISBN 2- 7117-8646-3.

[22] C. Snook, M. Butler, and I. Oliver. Towards a UML profile for UML-B. Technical report, DSSE-TR-2003-3, Electronics and Computer Science, University of Southampton, 2003.

[23] C. Snook and M. Buttler. U2B: a tool for combining UML and B. Avaible at http://www.ecs.soton.ac.uk/ cfs/U2Bdownloads/.

[24] STERIA. *Manuel de référence du langage B.* -ClearSy-, novembre, 1998.

[25] B. Tatibouet, A. Hammad, and J.-C. Voisinet. From an abstract B specification to UML class diagrams. In *2nd IEEE International Symposium on Signal Processing and Information Technology (ISSPIT'2002)*, pages 5–10, 2002.

[26] B. Tatibouet and J.-C. Voisinet. Generating statecharts from B specifications. In *16th International Conference Software & Systems Engineering and their applications (IC-SSEA'2003)*, Paris (Fr), 2003.

[27] B. Tatibouet and J.C. Voisinet. jBtools and B2UML : a plateform and a tool to provide a UML class diagram since a B specification. In *ICSSEA : 14th International Conference on Software and Systems Engineering and Their Applications, Paris (Fr)*, volume 2, 2001.

Author Index

Lecture Notes in Computer Science

For information about Vols. 1–3698

please contact your bookseller or Springer

Vol. 3750: J.S. Duncan, G. Gerig (Eds.), Medical Image Computing and Computer-Assisted Intervention – MICCAI 2005, Part II. XL, 1018 pages. 2005.

Vol. 3749: J.S. Duncan, G. Gerig (Eds.), Medical Image Computing and Computer-Assisted Intervention – MICCAI 2005, Part I. XXXIX, 942 pages. 2005.

Vol. 3748: A. Hartman, D. Kreische (Eds.), Model Driven Architecture – Foundations and Applications. IX, 349 pages. 2005.

Vol. 3747: C.A. Maziero, J.G. Silva, A.M.S. Andrade, F.M.d. Assis Silva (Eds.), Dependable Computing. XV, 267 pages. 2005.

Vol. 3746: P. Bozanis, E.N. Houstis (Eds.), Advances in Informatics. XIX, 879 pages. 2005.

Vol. 3745: J.L. Oliveira, V. Maojo, F. Martín-Sánchez, A.S. Pereira (Eds.), Biological and Medical Data Analysis. XII, 422 pages. 2005. (Subseries LNBI).

Vol. 3744: T. Magedanz, A. Karmouch, S. Pierre, I. Venieris (Eds.), Mobility Aware Technologies and Applications. XIV, 418 pages. 2005.

Vol. 3740: T. Srikanthan, J. Xue, C.-H. Chang (Eds.), Advances in Computer Systems Architecture. XVII, 833 pages. 2005.

Vol. 3739: W. Fan, Z.-h. Wu, J. Yang (Eds.), Advances in Web-Age Information Management. XXIV, 930 pages. 2005.

Vol. 3738: V.R. Syrotiuk, E. Chávez (Eds.), Ad-Hoc, Mobile, and Wireless Networks. XI, 360 pages. 2005.

Vol. 3735: A. Hoffmann, H. Motoda, T. Scheffer (Eds.), Discovery Science. XVI, 400 pages. 2005. (Subseries LNAI).

Vol. 3734: S. Jain, H.U. Simon, E. Tomita (Eds.), Algorithmic Learning Theory. XII, 490 pages. 2005. (Subseries LNAI).

Vol. 3733: P. Yolum, T. Güngör, F. Gürgen, C. Özturan (Eds.), Computer and Information Sciences - ISCIS 2005. XXI, 973 pages. 2005.

Vol. 3731: F. Wang (Ed.), Formal Techniques for Networked and Distributed Systems - FORTE 2005. XII, 558 pages. 2005.

Vol. 3729: Y. Gil, E. Motta, V. R. Benjamins, M.A. Musen (Eds.), The Semantic Web – ISWC 2005. XXIII, 1073 pages. 2005.

Vol. 3728: V. Paliouras, J. Vounckx, D. Verkest (Eds.), Integrated Circuit and System Design. XV, 753 pages. 2005.

Vol. 3726: L.T. Yang, O.F. Rana, B. Di Martino, J. Dongarra (Eds.), High Performance Computing and Communications. XXVI, 1116 pages. 2005.

Vol. 3725: D. Borrione, W. Paul (Eds.), Correct Hardware Design and Verification Methods. XII, 412 pages. 2005.

Vol. 3724: P. Fraigniaud (Ed.), Distributed Computing. XIV, 520 pages. 2005.

Vol. 3723: W. Zhao, S. Gong, X. Tang (Eds.), Analysis and Modelling of Faces and Gestures. XI, 4234 pages. 2005.

Vol. 3722: D. Van Hung, M. Wirsing (Eds.), Theoretical Aspects of Computing – ICTAC 2005. XIV, 614 pages. 2005.

Vol. 3721: A. Jorge, L. Torgo, P.B. Brazdil, R. Camacho, J. Gama (Eds.), Knowledge Discovery in Databases: PKDD 2005. XXIII, 719 pages. 2005. (Subseries LNAI).

Vol. 3720: J. Gama, R. Camacho, P.B. Brazdil, A. Jorge, L. Torgo (Eds.), Machine Learning: ECML 2005. XXIII, 769 pages. 2005. (Subseries LNAI).

Vol. 3719: M. Hobbs, A.M. Goscinski, W. Zhou (Eds.), Distributed and Parallel Computing. XI, 448 pages. 2005.

Vol. 3718: V.G. Ganzha, E.W. Mayr, E.V. Vorozhtsov (Eds.), Computer Algebra in Scientific Computing. XII, 502 pages. 2005.

Vol. 3717: B. Gramlich (Ed.), Frontiers of Combining Systems. X, 321 pages. 2005. (Subseries LNAI).

Vol. 3716: L. Delcambre, C. Kop, H.C. Mayr, J. Mylopoulos, Ó. Pastor (Eds.), Conceptual Modeling – ER 2005. XVI, 498 pages. 2005.

Vol. 3715: E. Dawson, S. Vaudenay (Eds.), Progress in Cryptology – Mycrypt 2005. XI, 329 pages. 2005.

Vol. 3714: H. Obbink, K. Pohl (Eds.), Software Product Lines. XIII, 235 pages. 2005.

Vol. 3713: L.C. Briand, C. Williams (Eds.), Model Driven Engineering Languages and Systems. XV, 722 pages. 2005.

Vol. 3712: R. Reussner, J. Mayer, J.A. Stafford, S. Overhage, S. Becker, P.J. Schroeder (Eds.), Quality of Software Architectures and Software Quality. XIII, 289 pages. 2005.

Vol. 3711: F. Kishino, Y. Kitamura, H. Kato, N. Nagata (Eds.), Entertainment Computing - ICEC 2005. XXIV, 540 pages. 2005.

Vol. 3710: M. Barni, I. Cox, T. Kalker, H.J. Kim (Eds.), Digital Watermarking. XII, 485 pages. 2005.

Vol. 3709: P. van Beek (Ed.), Principles and Practice of Constraint Programming - CP 2005. XX, 887 pages. 2005.

Vol. 3708: J. Blanc-Talon, W. Philips, D.C. Popescu, P. Scheunders (Eds.), Advanced Concepts for Intelligent Vision Systems. XXII, 725 pages. 2005.

Vol. 3707: D.A. Peled, Y.-K. Tsay (Eds.), Automated Technology for Verification and Analysis. XII, 506 pages. 2005.

Vol. 3706: H. Fukś, S. Lukosch, A.C. Salgado (Eds.), Groupware: Design, Implementation, and Use. XII, 378 pages. 2005.

Vol. 3704: M. De Gregorio, V. Di Maio, M. Frucci, C. Musio (Eds.), Brain, Vision, and Artificial Intelligence. XV, 556 pages. 2005.

Vol. 3703: F. Fages, S. Soliman (Eds.), Principles and Practice of Semantic Web Reasoning. VIII, 163 pages. 2005.

Vol. 3702: B. Beckert (Ed.), Automated Reasoning with Analytic Tableaux and Related Methods. XIII, 343 pages. 2005. (Subseries LNAI).

Vol. 3701: M. Coppo, E. Lodi, G. M. Pinna (Eds.), Theoretical Computer Science. XI, 411 pages. 2005.

Vol. 3700: J.F. Peters, A. Skowron (Eds.), Transactions on Rough Sets IV. X, 375 pages. 2005.

Vol. 3699: C.S. Calude, M.J. Dinneen, G. Păun, M. J. Pérez-Jiménez, G. Rozenberg (Eds.), Unconventional Computation. XI, 267 pages. 2005.